The Lincoln Way, the Truth, and Your Life

Reflections on Leadership and Faith

Jim Pingel

LifeRich
PUBLISHING

LifeRich Publishing books may be ordered through booksellers or by contacting:

LifeRich Publishing
1663 Liberty Drive
Bloomington, IN 47403
www.liferichpublishing.com
844-686-9607

ISBN: 978-1-4897-3004-6 (sc)
ISBN: 978-1-4897-3003-9 (hc)
ISBN: 978-1-4897-3005-3 (e)

Library of Congress Control Number: 2020913459

Print information available on the last page.

LifeRich Publishing rev. date: 01/08/2021

To my father for his unconditional support in
everything and ability to dream big.

To my mother, whose love and service to family knows no bounds.

To my wife for her patience and love despite my many flaws.

To my son Josh, whose kindness is contagious
and who never seems to have a bad day.

To my daughter for her fearlessness, determination, and laugh.

To my Savior, Jesus Christ, for making all things possible.

Contents

Religion and Relationships

Vision

The Calling

Preface

On Good Friday, April 14, 1865, Abraham Lincoln wakes up around seven o'clock in the morning and reads a few pages of the Bible. He has breakfast with his wife, Mary, and his oldest son, Robert—who shares his experience of standing on the porch of Wilmer McLean's house when General Robert E. Lee surrendered to Union forces, unofficially ending the war. After giving his father a portrait of Lee, Robert discusses his postwar plans. Father lets it be known that he wishes to see his son go back to Harvard to finish law school.

After completing some correspondence and paperwork, Lincoln visits the War Department for any updates before his cabinet meeting at 11:00 a.m. During the meeting, cabinet members collectively ponder Confederate General Joseph E. Johnston's next moves in North Carolina. Lee has already resigned his commission, but Johnston has not.

Lincoln shares a dream he had the previous night—the usual dream that comes before almost every successful battle. He sees himself on board a vessel that moves very quickly to an unknown destination on an indefinite shore. He wonders what it means.

They then talk about reconstruction plans and the challenges of providing amnesty for Confederate officers. Some hope these Confederate officers simply move to another country.[1]

Lincoln has never looked better to his cabinet. Secretary of War Edwin Stanton notes the president's cheerfulness and hopefulness. Frederick Seward, subbing for his father, Secretary of State William Seward, insists that Lincoln looks visibly relieved and content. Acknowledging the obvious—that the brutal war has ended and lifted a burden that tormented the commander in chief for more

[1] Johnson, *The Last Weeks*, 255–86.

than four years—Treasury Secretary Hugh McCulloch comments that he has never seen the president look so joyous, bright, and happy. To James Harlan, Secretary of the Interior-designate, Lincoln seems "transfigured," for his customary expression of melancholy and sadness has been replaced with serenity and joy. He looks fulfilled and content.[2]

Around three o'clock, Lincoln breaks away from his executive duties to take an open carriage ride with his wife, Mary. They go to the Navy Yard, a place Lincoln visits often to relieve stress. He converses with several sailors aboard the *Montauk*—a Union ironclad that was hit forty-seven times during the assault on Charleston harbor. Despite enduring the leadership hardships of a brutal civil war for the past four years, Lincoln remains, according to his wife, "cheerful—almost joyous."[3] Responding to her surprise at his cheerfulness, Lincoln notes that the war has come to a successful close, and this realization is reason enough to be joyous. Lincoln adds that they must both be more cheerful in the future. The war and the loss of their beloved son Willie has taken its toll on both of them. They need to turn the page, leave the carnage and suffering behind, and look forward to a more joyous chapter in their twilight years.

On their carriage ride, Lincoln also tells Mary that he cannot wait for his second term to end so that they can travel in Europe. He wants to visit the Holy Land too. After returning from overseas, perhaps they will trek over the Rocky Mountains to California. He is not sure if he wants to settle down in Springfield or travel throughout the country.[4]

When they return, they visit with guests before eating supper and preparing to depart for Ford's Theatre. Mary soon develops a headache, however, and wants to stay home. Since their attendance

---

[2] Burlingame, *Lincoln*, 806.

[3] Donald, *Lincoln,* 593.

[4] Donald, *Lincoln*, 570; Caravan, *Lincoln's Final Hours*, 45.

has been publicly disclosed in local newspapers and is expected, the president does not want to disappoint the audience. He insists that they keep their commitment. Besides, he tells Mary, guests will continue to stop by the Executive Mansion to give their well-wishes and congratulations on the war effort, so they will get no reprieve from the public eye anyway.

While Mary prepares for the evening, Lincoln and one of his bodyguards, William Crook, make a quick trip to the War Department to see if there is any news from the front in North Carolina. On their walk over, Lincoln frightens Crook with a statement. "I believe there are men who want to take my life," he asserts. "And I have no doubt they will do it." [5]

"Why do you think so, Mr. President?" Crook nervously inquires.

"Other men have been assassinated," Lincoln responds.

"I hope you are mistaken, Mr. President."

On their return to the Executive Mansion, Crook begs Lincoln not to attend the theater. Lincoln assures him that everything will be fine, even telling Crook that he does not need to stay on as an extra guard. "It has been advertised that we will be there," the president explains, "and I cannot disappoint the people. Otherwise I would not go. I do not want to go." Crook is surprised by this acknowledgment because he knows how much Lincoln loves the theater. Crook says good night to the president as he always has before departing. Lincoln usually responds in the same manner, but not on this evening. Instead of saying good night, Lincoln says, "Good-*bye,* Crook." Lincoln's subtle but significant word change troubles Crook.

Ward Hill Lemon, the head of Lincoln's security detail, also advises the president not to venture about town, especially to the theater. Earlier in the day, Secretary of War Stanton warned Lincoln

---

[5] This quotation and the following excerpts from the conversation with William Crook are taken from Oates, *With Malice Toward None,* 429; O'Reilly, *Killing Lincoln,* 180; Johnson, *The Last Weeks,* 273-274.

of assassination rumors. Washington, DC, is the Union capital, but its character as a Southern town persists in April 1865. Confederate sympathies and anger over the war and the freeing of slaves remain high, keeping the city on edge. Stanton advised both Lincoln and Grant not to go to the theater. Lincoln insisted, and Stanton counseled him to take a bodyguard. Stanton was worried, however, knowing that in the past, Lincoln eluded the soldiers provided to escort him on his nightly walks and trips home. The war secretary could never understand why the president did not seem to want protection. The only reason Lincoln eventually allowed soldiers or bodyguards to protect him was that he knew they would be disciplined if they did not execute Stanton's orders. Lincoln never wants to see soldiers court-martialed—or even shot.[6]

The Lincolns have invited several other couples to join them for the evening, to no avail. Mrs. Ellen Stanton and Mrs. Julia Grant cannot stand to be around Mary after experiencing her petty jealousies and wrath.[7] They have declined the invitation to join the Lincolns for the production of *Our American Cousin*. Others simply do not want to be entertained or to attend a theater on Good Friday. Ultimately, Major Henry Rathbone and his fiancée, Miss Clara Harris, agree to accompany the Lincolns to the play.[8]

---

6 Oates, *With Malice Toward None*, 417; O'Reilly, *Killing Lincoln*, 156, 177–78.

7 Johnson, *The Last Weeks*, 255–86. The afternoon of the assassination, Julia Grant received an invitation via messenger that may or may not have been sent by Mary Lincoln. Reflecting back after the assassination, Julia Grant thought the invitation seemed more like a command than a request. She also said that the messenger did not dress like someone sent by the First Lady—he appeared in casual and sloppy attire. The man would not leave for a while, insisting that the newspaper said the Grants would be at the theater. "I have thought since that this man was one of the band of conspirators in that night's tragedy," Julia Grant wrote many years after the episode. The Grants would be followed throughout the night.

8 Donald, *Lincoln*, 593–94.

After visiting with more guests, the Lincolns finally leave the Executive Mansion later than they desire. Lincoln's bodyguard on duty, John Parker, is a man who has an appalling record of drunkenness, insubordination, and inefficiency. He has just recently been hired, and he has already gone ahead to Ford's Theatre. Soon he will leave his post to go drink at a tavern across the street during the play.

As the Lincolns arrive and settle into the president's box in Ford's Theatre, the audience and actors stop and give the president a standing ovation. The orchestra breaks out "Hail to the Chief." Onstage, Harry Hawk, the male lead, ad-libs a line used often and made famous by the storytelling chief executive: "This reminds me of a story, as Mr. Lincoln would say." The audience roars and claps, and Lincoln smiles. The hysteria and pent-up celebration last for almost five minutes.[9]

Meanwhile, John Wilkes Booth,[10] a talented actor and radical supporter of the Confederacy, enters Ford's Theatre and quickly

---

[9] Oates, *With Malice Toward None*, 430; Canavan, *Lincoln's Final Hours*, 73; Sandburg, *Lincoln*, 706–7.

[10] Steers, "The Assassination," 171; Johnson, *The Last Weeks*, 241. Well-liked by most who knew him, John Wilkes Booth had become one of America's greatest actors by 1864—extremely handsome, personable, generous, and outgoing. A New York newspaper called him "a rare specimen of manly beauty," and Henry Ford dubbed him "the handsomest man in America." He had inky black hair, glowing black eyes, bright white teeth, and a silky black mustache. He stood five feet eight inches tall. Women found him irresistible and "crowded around him like doves at a grain basket" (Canavan, *Lincoln's Final Hours*, 26–29, 35). Waitresses often neglected their other tables and offered him free steaks. Hotel maids went out of their way to take special care of his room. He received hundreds of love letters a year. Booth made twenty thousand dollars a year as an actor (just five thousand less than the president), performing in Chicago, St. Louis, and Washington. Always fashionably dressed, he had polished manners and graceful moves. He could move like a cat onstage; he once jumped ten or more feet during a performance of *Macbeth*. Indeed, he became known as one of the best gymnasts in the country and leaped over scenery five feet tall to wild applause. He might have let the cheering go to his head, however, as he never felt the need to take

ascends toward the president. He shows a calling card to Charles Forbes, Lincoln's footman, and enters the box. Booth, who knows

---

voice lessons or acting instructions. He exhibited an arrogance beyond his considerable skill and talent level.

Booth had come to hate the president. Born in a slaveholding state, Maryland, the twenty-six-year-old "thought of himself as a Northerner who understood the South." The youngest son of an alcoholic and mentally unstable father, and his mother's "darling in her brood of ten children," he attended several private schools with mixed results (Donald, *Lincoln*, 585, 588). He grew up with the conviction that he belonged to the lifestyle of the Southern gentry. From the age of seventeen, he appeared constantly on stage. He came from a family of actors and theatrical producers. Holding conventional Southern views about slavery, Booth deemed the peculiar institution a blessing from God—for white Southerners and for the slaves themselves. He firmly believed the United States existed for white men. Moreover, he hated Republicans and what he determined was treasonous legislation pushed by radical Republicans. He personally witnessed the execution of John Brown after the Harper's Ferry uprising. While he did not immediately enlist in the Confederate Army, claiming he did not want to upset or worry his mother, his contempt for Lincoln remained palpable and public. He mocked Lincoln's physical appearance, pedigree, anecdotes, and public demeanor, as well as the president's attempts to eradicate slavery.

After Lincoln was reelected in 1864, Booth made plans to kidnap the president. Booth's chronic hoarseness might have compelled him to consider another career—worried, perhaps, that his future aspiration as an actor might be in jeopardy. His investment failures in Pennsylvania oil schemes also contributed to his general unhappiness and discontent. Soon he began confiding in Confederate secret service agents about how he might kidnap the president in exchange for thousands of captured Confederate soldiers who were languishing in Northern prisons.

Obsessed with abducting Lincoln, he acted on his own, especially with the demise of the Confederacy. As his drinking got out of control, he increasingly came to think of himself as the Brutus who would take down the despotic Caesar of the Union. On April 11, after listening to Lincoln speak about giving suffrage to blacks who were educated or had served in the Union armies, Booth vowed that it would be the last speech Lincoln would ever make. He plotted to move forward with an assassination rather than an abduction attempt against the president.

the production by heart, waits for Harry Hawk to deliver the one line that always brings the house down with thundering laughter. When the moment occurs, he takes his single-shot derringer and pulls the trigger behind the president's head.

The ball enters Lincoln's brain and lodges behind his left eye. He slumps forward in his chair, motionless. Some audience members leap from their seats at the sound of the gunshot, only to sit down when others cry out, "Down in front!" assuming the gunfire is part of the play. The musicians in the orchestra pit, however, know better and are stunned.[11] Attempting to impede Booth's escape, Major Rathbone is cut and badly wounded by Booth.[12]

Suddenly, Booth leaps almost twelve feet from the box to the stage, catching his right foot on the box decorations as he drops. Between the shot and the leap, only thirty seconds elapse. Gathering himself on stage, Booth turns to the audience and hollers, "Sic semper tyrannis"—"This always to tyrants." Suddenly, a spine-chilling scream is heard from the box above.[13]

Eventually, Lincoln is transported across the street to the house of William Petersen, a merchant-tailor. Due to Lincoln's height, they lay him diagonally on the bed where he will remain for the next nine hours as he struggles to breathe. Throughout the deathwatch, numerous people walk in and out of the house, not knowing what to do. Artists come and go, imbibing the somber scene. Government officials wander about, grappling with the magnitude of what has happened on this "Night of Horrors." They learn that other

---

11 Canavan, *Lincoln's Final Hours*, 76–77.

12 Hodes, *Mourning Lincoln*, 49. Rathbone would never fully recover from the mental anguish of his encounter with Booth. Years later, he would murder his wife and end his life in an asylum.

13 Canavan, *Lincoln's Final Hours*, 147. Booth would be killed twelve days after murdering Lincoln at a farm just south of the Rappahannock River. His last words are disputed. Some said he said nothing. Others said he whispered, "Tell Mother I died for my country." Others claimed he asked to have his hands held up before him and said, "Useless, Useless."

government members, like William Seward, survive assassination attempts.

Mary, after picking up papers that have fallen out of Lincoln's hat, walks back and forth from the death room throughout the morning. One time she sinks onto the bed and cries, "Kill me. Kill me. Kill me. Shoot me too!"[14] By four o'clock in the morning, her grief is so great that she pulls her hair out by the handful. Those who observe her actions are horrified but do nothing. They are relieved when her oldest son, Robert, persuades his mother to stop the self-abuse.

When Lincoln's breathing grows unnaturally loud, like a snore, Mary lets out a yelp that enrages Stanton. He orders the First Lady be removed from the room. Even after Mary's ejection, more than twenty visitors remain at Lincoln's bedside in a room that is eighteen feet by twenty feet.

At 7:22 a.m., the death rattle comes and the breathing stops. The sixteenth president of the United States has died in a humble room only slightly smaller than the log cabin he was born into fifty-six years earlier.[15]

The family minister, Dr. Phineas T. Gurley, pastor of New York Avenue Presbyterian Church, has been at the Petersen home during the last few hours. He leads a prayer amid sobs in the background. Then Stanton, who once called Lincoln an "ape" and "fool" but has grown close to him during the last few years, says of his friend and president, "Now he belongs to the ages."[16] Mary, who sits in

---

[14] The quotation and the following excerpts were taken from Caravan, *Lincoln's Final Hours,* 109.

[15] Caravan, *Lincoln's Final Hours*, 89, 109, 112–13, 116.

[16] Caravan, *Lincoln's Final Hours,* 118. Caravan notes that another witness remembered Stanton saying, "That's the last of him." According to another historian, we do not know for sure if Stanton said "Now he belongs to the ages" (Fox, *Lincoln's Body*, 45, 322). No one reported having heard Stanton say this in 1865. The statement was first reported twenty-three years later in the ten-volume 1890 biography of Lincoln written by his secretaries John Hay and John Nicolay. Perhaps Americans wanted some memorable last words from

the parlor of the Petersen home after her husband passes, notes that her husband's "dream was prophetic" about not lasting through the war.[17] She begs God to take her life too.

Across the way at Grover's Theatre, Lincoln's young son Tad and his tutor are watching *Aladdin and the Wonderful Lamp* when the theater manager comes forward, "pale as a ghost," and with a look of "mortal agony" on his face.[18] He announces to a shocked audience that the president has been shot at Ford's Theatre. In the midst of the uproar that follows, Tad darts away "like a young dear, shrieking in agony." He screams repeatedly, "They have killed Papa dead. They've killed Papa dead!"[19] Most of the audience, thrown into confusion and beginning to leave the premises, calms down and remains at Grover's Theatre for a while after one convinces the gathered audience that pickpocket artists conceived the whole disturbance.[20]

Union General Ulysses S. Grant, while eating supper, receives a telegram announcing Lincoln's death. After hanging his head for a few moments in silence, he tells his wife to prepare for the most painful and horrible news he could share. In addition to his grief, the general immediately worries about the future of the Union and particularly the Confederate states. Lincoln's "tenderness and magnanimity" will be sorely missed in healing and binding the nation together again.[21]

A one-time presidential rival of Lincoln, Secretary of State William Seward, bedridden after a previous near-fatal carriage

---

Lincoln's deathbed scene. In Steven Spielberg's epic movie *Lincoln*, religious sentiment is depicted at the deathbed scene as a bright white light shines down on Lincoln from above. Some believe Stanton said, "Now he belongs to the angels" (Hodes, *Mourning Lincoln*, 5).

[17] Oates, *With Malice Toward None,* 433.

[18] Goodwin, *Team of Rivals,* 741.

[19] Goodwin, *Team of Rivals,* 742.

[20] Canavan, *Lincoln's Final Hours*, 2.

[21] Goodwin, *Team of Rivals,* 742.

accident and the attempt on his life, does not hear of Lincoln's death immediately. His caretakers withhold the information, fearing he will not be able to sustain the shock. On Easter Sunday, however, as he looks out his home window, he notices the War Department's flag flying at half-mast. He tells his attendant that the president is dead. When the attendant tries to deny it, Seward responds soberly with tears running down his cheeks, "If he had been alive he would have been the first to call on me."[22]

Only hours after Lincoln's death, Stanton orders embalmers to keep the purple bruises under Lincoln's eyes. While the embalmers want make the president look natural, Stanton insists that the purple splotches remain as historical evidence for all those who will view his body lying in state. Fighting for what he believed to be just and right, Lincoln has made the ultimate sacrifice. He should be remembered for his courage and martyrdom.[23]

On Easter Sunday morning, Tad stops a gentleman who has called upon his mother. "Do you think my father has gone to heaven?" he asks the man.

"I have not a doubt about it," the man replies.

"Then," Tad exclaims, choking up, "I am glad he has gone there, for he never was happy after he came here. This was not a good place for him!"[24]

For the next few months after the "Night of Madness," twelve-year old Tad tries to comfort his mother. "Don't cry so, Mamma," he implores her more than once. "I cannot sleep if you cry! Papa was good, and he has gone to heaven. He is happy there. He is with God and brother Willie. Don't cry, Mamma, or I will cry too."[25]

Indeed, Abraham Lincoln resides in heaven. Or does he?

---

[22] Goodwin, *Team of Rivals*, 744–45.

[23] Fox, *Lincoln's Body*, 103. For days after Lincoln's death, Stanton's grief would be almost uncontrollable. At the mere mention of Lincoln's name, he would break down and weep bitterly. Goodwin, *Team of Rivals*, 743.

[24] Carpenter, *Six Months at the White House*, 310.

[25] Packard, *Lincolns in the White House*, 249.

Introduction

The Lincoln We Need to Know

For inquire, please, of bygone ages,
and consider what the fathers have searched out.
For we are but of yesterday and know nothing,
for our days on earth are a shadow.
Will they not teach you and tell you
and utter words out of their understanding?
—Job 8:8–10

Why another book on Abraham Lincoln?

In 1936 one historian wondered if the Lincoln theme had been exhausted.[1] Yet the works about the nation's sixteenth president keep coming. As the "the quintessential American icon," and "our most cherished historical possession," according to one notable biographer, Lincoln remains the most written about American by a significant margin.[2]

Almost anything associated with Lincoln sells. A running joke in the publishing business is that the title of a surefire bestseller would be *Lincoln's Doctor's Dog* because of the combination of favorite subjects.[3] He is fascinating and irresistible. Not only have thousands of books been written about him, but more than a dozen major motion pictures (including one depicting him as a vampire hunter) have been released, with more to surely come. In fact, more books, poems, anecdotes, and quotations have been written about Lincoln than all the other United States presidents combined, and

---

[1] Manning, *Father Lincoln*, 186.

[2] McPherson, "We Cannot Escape History," 1.

[3] Peterson, *Lincoln in American Memory*, 195.

that is not even counting the vast number of other quotations that are attributed to him. Only Jesus Christ surpasses Lincoln in the number of works written about a particular individual.[4]

When Lincoln died in the spring of 1865, he became an instant American icon. Everyone wanted a piece of him, figuratively and literally. Indeed, as soon his body had been wrapped in blankets and placed in a quickly assembled pine box, residents began taking and hoarding whatever treasures they could find. Albert Daggett, a nineteen-year-old State Department clerk, told his mother that he took numerous relics from the assassination event—torn-off pieces of Lincoln's collar, sheets, and a blood-stained pillow case. William Clark claimed to have found "a lock of Lincoln's hair" and squirreled away "a piece of linen with a portion of his brain."[5] Since Lincoln had died on Clark's bed, Clark told his sister that he had kept the pillow case from the moment of death. Five days after the assassination, he still slept on the deathbed, using "the same coverlid"[6] that shielded Lincoln while he lay unconscious and dying. Other doctors and surgeons kept pieces of the president's hair. One cut off the blood-soaked cuffs from his shirt and placed them in an envelope for safekeeping. Dr. Curtis kept pieces of bone from the

---

[4] Mukunda, *Indispensable*, 63, 82; Wheeler, *Faith and Courage*, x; Holzer et al., *Exploring Lincoln*, 2; Szasz and Szasz, *Lincoln and Religion*, 73. Szasz and Szasz indicate that approximately sixteen thousand books have been written on Lincoln. Miller, *Lincoln's Virtues*, 19–20, 33. There have been some strange books published on Lincoln, which include *Lincoln on the Coming of the Caterpillar Tractor*; *Abraham Lincoln as a Potential Lion* (which started out as a talk to the Lions Club of Millersburg, Pennsylvania); *Lincoln the Comforter Together with a Story of Lincoln's First Pet*; *Lincoln the Athlete and Other Stories*; *Abe's First Fish* (a play); *Little Sermons on Socialism by Abraham Lincoln*; *Abraham Lincoln, the New Dealer of His Day*; *The Man Who Married Lincoln's Parents*; *The Mystic Number Seven in the Life of Abraham 7 Lincoln 7*; *Lincoln Never Smoked a Cigarette*; and *Abe & Fido: Lincoln's Love of Animals and the Touching Story of His Favorite Canine Companion.*

[5] Fox, *Lincoln's Body*, 62.

[6] Fox, *Lincoln's Body*, 62.

president's head. He and his mother later donated these pieces to a museum.[7]

Lincoln remains the consummate representative of everything idyllic in the American dream. His name was proposed for the states of Wyoming and one of the Dakotas. He is held up as the standard in civic education. One Ohio Supreme Court judge insisted that Lincoln should be "a staple of American education," and that every American high school should teach the life of Lincoln for at least one whole year in the curriculum.[8]

Lincoln's image has never been more popular than it is today. Insurance companies, anti-foot odor products (where his nose on the penny is turned up in disgust), pharmaceutical companies, and many other organizations and businesses use his image in advertisements, marketing campaigns, and branding. Lincoln is malleable, likable, and comforting. He has become the everyman of our democracy and the grandfather of the American family. Lincoln seemingly could do it all during his lifetime, and it seems that Americans and American companies are still making him, or his image, do it all for them too.[9]

Lincoln was a striver and moralist; many consider him the greatest self-made man in American history.[10] A decade after Lincoln passed, General William Tecumseh Sherman said, "Of all the men I ever met, he seemed to possess more of the elements of greatness, combined with goodness, than any other."[11] General Ulysses Grant

---

[7] Fox, *Lincoln's Body*, 63–64.

[8] Peterson, *Lincoln in American Memory*, 142, 197; Goodwin, *Leadership*, 19. Lincoln himself would have found great humor and irony in this statement, since he did not receive much formal education in his life. He did believe, however, that education must be a priority for every citizen. Americans should read about and study the history of their country and "appreciate the value of our free institutions." Lincoln argued that the story of America's birth should "be read of, and recounted, so long as the bible shall be read." His generation, and everyone after it, must preserve the "proud fabric of freedom."

[9] Blight, "The Theft of Lincoln in Scholarship," 269–70, 272.

[10] Guelzo, *Man of Ideas*, 11; Lehrman, *Lincoln "by littles,"* iv.

[11] Goodwin, *Team of Rivals,* 713.

stated that Lincoln "was incontestably the greatest man I ever knew."[12] Poet and journalist Walt Whitman fancied that at future commemorations, ancient soldiers would be approached by young men who would have "eager questions" about Lincoln. "What! Have you seen Abraham Lincoln—and heard him speak—and touch'd his hand?" Whitman spoke for his generation: "Abraham Lincoln seems to me the grandest figure yet, on all the crowded canvas of the Nineteenth Century."[13]

Many contemporaries declared Lincoln a superior president to George Washington. Both were great men and leaders, but Lincoln's mind and oratorical abilities were far superior to those of the Master of Mount Vernon. The formal and statuesque Washington earned the people's respect, but Lincoln won their hearts. Washington certainly remained the father of the country, but Lincoln became the savior of the nation. While some noted that Washington brought freedom to three million colonists over his career, Lincoln, in one proclamation, freed four million slaves *and* saved the Union. Lincoln the Liberator trumped Washington the Patriot.[14]

Today Lincoln is generally regarded as America's greatest president, followed closely by Washington and Franklin Delano Roosevelt. While Washington is appropriately seen as a gentleman and a stoic aristocrat, Lincoln is viewed as earthy—a more relatable, alluring, everyday man. This character contrast has moved Lincoln past Washington as the American first in the hearts of his countrymen.[15]

In addition to his common man appeal, Lincoln's accomplishments and achievements, like those of Washington, were significant and ushered in magnificent turning points in history. According to historian Henry Adams, who compared "Leaders of

---

[12] Goodwin, *Team of Rivals,* 747.

[13] Goodwin, *Team of Rivals*, 747.

[14] Burlingame, *Lincoln*, 2:831.

[15] Duetsch and Fornieri, *Lincoln's American Dream*, 142; Kautz, "Democratic Statesmanship of Lincoln," 150; Fox, *Lincoln's Body*, xi.

Destiny" to ship commanders, leaders must have "a course to steer" and "a port to seek." [16] More than any other president, Lincoln had left behind a redeveloped and transformed nation.

In the many key areas in which American presidents are judged—character, vision, competence, economic policy, preserving and extending liberty, defense, national security, foreign policy—Lincoln rates a five on five star scale. He ended slavery, saved the Union, gave a new birth of freedom, and wrote eloquent addresses and speeches that etched his noble and timeless convictions into the heart of the American character. Moreover, he literally sacrificed his life in service to his country, dying as a martyr.[17] In honor of his service as president of the United States, three national holidays—Presidents' Day, Memorial Day, and Thanksgiving—are directly connected to him. Even in this time of historical revisionism and social upheaval, Lincoln remains a universally beloved American. Business and marketing leaders insist that no matter the product, if you tie it to Lincoln, it is guaranteed to sell.[18]

It is not only his presidential achievements, however. People remain fascinated by the character and biography of the man. If, as Heraclitus, a Greek philosopher, declared two millennia ago that "a man's character is his fate," then it is no wonder that Lincoln accomplished so much.[19] One biographer states that Lincoln became an exemplary leader and successful president because of a "psychological maturity" unmatched in the history of American public service.[20] Overcoming the economic and emotional poverty of his upbringing, Lincoln developed an extraordinary consciousness and resilient character worthy of imitation today.

The five great themes of Lincoln's biography—savior of Union, Great Emancipator, man of the people, First American, and self-made

---

[16] Merry, *Where They Stand*, 165, 179.

[17] Winik, "Lincoln," 81.

[18] Wheeler, *Faith and Courage*, x.

[19] Felzenberg, *The Leaders We Deserved*, 11.

[20] Burlingame, *Lincoln*, 1:xii.

man—all emanate from his rectitude and character. Lincoln's image is certainly represented in his support for nationality, humanity, democracy, Americanism, and individual opportunity.[21] A fervent nationalist at a time when most were aggressive localists, Lincoln took his role seriously as the "warrior of the American dream."[22]

Lincoln's specialness comes not only from what he believed, but how his life story shaped his worldview on these issues and how he communicated them with such clarity and certitude. Put another way, the Lincoln message resonates because of the life story of the messenger and his ability to connect with people.

Lincoln is an accessible and beloved figure of Americans today, just as he was in his time, because of his common-man presentation and appeal. Outside the House of Commons, the British have a statue of Lincoln, "the man who came from nowhere."[23] He did not act like an over-the-top Founding Father or some marble man. One day Lincoln told his personal secretary, John Hay, about a dream he had after a guest said of him, "He is a very common-looking man." In his dream, Lincoln relished his own reply: "The Lord prefers common-looking people … that is the reason he makes so many of them."[24] To most Americans, Lincoln thought, acted, and talked like their next-door neighbors.

Brilliant as were the intellect and vocabulary that he possessed, Lincoln never talked down to the American people or acted like a condescending aristocrat. "We don't feel at all out of place when we wake up and ask Lincoln just what he would do, without having to take on the lacy complexities of Washington's resignation letter or his farewell orders to the Continental Army," writes one biographer. "We can still laugh at Lincoln's jokes; we do not know whether Washington ever told any jokes."[25] Every generation looks to Lincoln

---

[21] Peterson, *Lincoln in American Memory*, 27.

[22] Oates, *Lincoln*, 59, 126.

[23] Wood, "Tragic Sensibility," 233.

[24] Goodwin, *Team of Rivals*, 593.

[25] Guelzo, *Man of Ideas*, 4.

for strength, wisdom, and inspiration. Many want to be more like him.[26]

Lincoln truly possessed a common touch. Accessible to everyone, he gave no one preferential treatment. Kind to all, he did not let anyone speak for him. Like a farmer on the rugged frontier, Lincoln spoke his own thoughts and convictions. He demonstrated courage and held himself accountable. To many Americans in his day, he became a new kind of hero—a democratic hero. The rise of Lincoln did not fit the mold of leaders in his time or any previous time. He ascended to the world stage not because of corruption, wealth, power, or heredity, but due to hard work, persistence, skill development, a focus on continuous improvement, and his uniqueness. There were other presidents who claimed that they came from log cabins and the common man, but none felt, looked, or sounded as authentic as Lincoln.

Horace Greeley, editor of *New York Tribune*, said, "The masses thought of him as one with whom they had been splitting rails on a pleasant spring day or making a prosperous voyage down the Mississippi on an Illinois flat-boat, and found him a downright good fellow."[27]

Joseph Gillespie, a legal and political friend of Lincoln for three decades, recalled that Lincoln possessed "no super human qualities (which we call genius) but he had those which belong to mankind generally in an astonished degree" and "in larger measure than any man of modern times."[28] Lincoln's popularity came because he had succeeded under the most excruciating circumstances while looking every bit the part of the common man. The masses loved "seeing one of their own class elevated" and exhibiting competence and success "by doing things in their way."[29] Born "a common person," Lincoln, through hard work, became an "uncommon" Machiavellian

---

[26] McGovern, *Lincoln*, 2.

[27] Peterson, *Lincoln in American Memory*, 31.

[28] Wilson, *Herndon's Informants*, 184.

[29] Wilson, *Herndon's Informants*, 184.

politician who became a statesman. His leadership style remains one of America's greatest gifts to democracy.[30]

The nicknames of Lincoln, even before he became the Great Emancipator—Old Abe, Honest Abe, Father Abraham, Rail-splitter—reveal an affection for a common man who confronted and overcame the everyday tests and temptations of character that they faced. One of their own, Lincoln made the hometown and common folk proud.

That Lincoln freed the slaves should not be underestimated as a factor in his popularity in today's pluralistic and multicultural society. In a nation full of discourse on diversity, equity, and social justice issues, Lincoln freed those held in bondage for over two centuries. While Washington remains the founder and father of the nation, Lincoln is the restorer and redeemer of it.

The Christian overtones of Lincoln's redeemer image remain powerful and poignant today despite the shift to a postmodern, post-Christian culture. Some argue that Lincoln lived the greatest life "since Jesus Christ."[31] Leo Tolstoy, a Russian regarded as one of the greatest writers of all time, called him "a Christ in miniature."[32] Like Moses, the Republican deliverer led his people through the wilderness during the horrific years of the peculiar institution, and died before entering the Promised Land. Struck down on Good Friday, Lincoln, like Jesus, endured a martyr's death for the people, even those enslaved. Like Jesus, Lincoln came to set people free. A few days before his assassination, the president entered Richmond much like Christ did on Palm Sunday in Jerusalem. Like Jesus, the president died on a Friday, as a sacrifice for the people.

He became the redeemer president, redeeming the country from its so-called original sin of slavery.[33] When Lincoln died, orators, editors, ministers, and statesmen across the land called him the

---

30 Williams, "Lincoln—Our Ever Present Contemporary," 155.

31 Owen, *The Man and His Faith*, viii.

32 Jones, *Lincoln and the Preachers*, 164.

33 Guelzo, *Lincoln*, 440.

"savior of his country." Clergymen evoked Isaiah's image of the Suffering Servant. Christ died so that people could enjoy heaven. Lincoln died so that they could enjoy a better life on earth. Jesus died for the world; Lincoln died for his country.

Ohio Congressman, Union general, and future president James A. Garfield declared that Lincoln's death paralleled "that of the Son of God who cried out, 'Father, forgive them for they know not what they do.'" [34] So beloved and revered was Lincoln by the people that many interpreted his assassination as God's way of thwarting idolatry.[35]

Of course, black citizens and freed slaves held a special regard for Lincoln, their "modern Moses."[36] Lincoln had been crucified for them. God had chosen him for the ultimate act of selflessness. Lincoln did more than free the slaves; he died for them. "I confess," Booker T. Washington said in 1909, "that the more I learn of Lincoln's life the more I am disposed to look at him … not merely as a statesman, but as one to whom I can certainly turn for help and inspiration—as a great moral leader, in whose patience, tolerance, and broad human sympathy there is salvation for my race, and for all those who are down, but struggling to rise."[37] One former slave, interviewed in the 1930s, maintained that he thought often about Lincoln and how hard it must have been to "give up his life for de United States. But Christ died to save de world an Lincoln died to save de United States. And Lincoln died more Christlike dan any other man dat ever lived."[38] Lincoln's actions and fortitude in freeing the slaves assured his fame.

In a moving eulogy on his friend, ex-slave and abolitionist Frederick Douglass labeled Lincoln the "black man's President."[39]

---

34 Smith, *Faith and the Presidency*, 121–22.

35 Burlingame, *Lincoln*, 2:832.

36 Fox, *Lincoln's Body*, 75.

37 Peterson, *Lincoln in American Memory*, 173.

38 Fox, *Lincoln's Body*, 168.

39 Guelzo, *Lincoln*, 350.

Having been the first president to demonstrate a respect for the rights of blacks, to rise above the prejudices of the time, and to easily and comfortable converse with black people without condescension or disdain, Lincoln earned Douglass's praise and gratitude.

On two different occasions, the governor of Connecticut had to wait to meet with the president because Lincoln and Douglass were conversing. In one of those meetings, the two men talked for over an hour while the governor lingered. Douglass took immense pride in this event and later speculated that it probably marked the first time in American history when a governor had to bide his time while the president conversed with a black man in the Executive Mansion.[40]

While many contemporaries lauded the president's achievements, many hated him—more than any other leader in modern history according to one contemporary *New York Times* writer. During the 1860 campaign, critics called Lincoln a "nutmeg dealer," a "horse-swapper," and a "nightman."[41] Historians often rank Lincoln as America's greatest president, but many contemporaries did not share this opinion. He was scorned by members of both political parties. A majority of Republicans believed him unsuited for the presidency and doubted he had the ability to win the war as late as the summer of 1864.[42] There is a strong historical case for labeling Lincoln the most despised and reviled president in American history. Having received more than eighty death threats during his presidency, he kept of packet of them in a desk drawer, which he labeled "Assassination."[43] Many more might have sent him death threats, if they only knew how to write.

Lincoln critics exist today as they did in his time. Detractors point to his slowness in freeing the slaves, some questionable statements he made in regard to race, his failure to advocate or initiate policy to eradicate the institution of slavery while running

---

40 Burlingame, *Lincoln*, 2:830.

41 Smith, *Faith and the Presidency,* 123.

42 Gienapp, "Lincoln and Presidential Leadership," 65.

43 O'Reilly, *Killing Lincoln*, 99.

for president in 1860, his expansion of executive power, his alleged civil liberty abuses during the war (including censoring of the press), and his reticence to share his innermost thoughts.

There is no question that Lincoln had shortcomings and a sinful nature. Yet even Lincoln's sins and mistakes have helped to raise his historical profile, because he learned from them. Moreover, Lincoln worked in earnest to fulfill a moral vision he had for the nation, despite his personal fallibility and failures. He made momentous moral decisions that affected the course of history. Along the way, Lincoln learned to overcome deficiencies, self-doubts, and adversity (both internal and external).[44] Students of Lincoln, especially of his early life, identify with his rise and the hardships he had to overcome. Emotionally vulnerable, he struggled with mental problems and melancholy, even depression. The story of Lincoln does not belie the legend, but simply reveals the human behind the hero.[45] "I love him," W. E. B. DuBois wrote in 1922, "not because he was perfect, but because he was not yet triumphed."[46]

Leo Tolstoy, the greatest writer of his age, noted that Lincoln "really was not a great general like Napoleon or Washington; he was not such a skillful statesman as Gladstone or Frederick the Great." Lincoln's "supremacy expresses itself altogether in his peculiar moral power and in the greatness of his character. Washington was a typical American. Napoleon was a typical Frenchman, but Lincoln was a humanitarian as broad as the world." The Russian writer claimed that Lincoln "was bigger than his country—bigger than all the Presidents together. We are still too near his greatness," but after a few centuries more, "our posterity will find him considerably bigger than we do. His genius is still too strong and too powerful for the common understanding, just as the sun is too hot when its

---

44 Oates, *Lincoln*, 57, 146.

45 Wilson, "Herndon's Lincoln," 29.

46 Blight, "The Theft of Lincoln in Scholarship," 273.

light beams directly on us."[47] Tolstoy's words have turned out to be as prescient as they were profound at the time.

Americans have almost always favored and admired the underdog, and the Lincoln story certainly fits that narrative. Constantly ridiculed and underrated in his own time as "a simple Susan, a baboon, an aimless punster, a smutty joker," Lincoln would get the last laugh as he ascended to the most powerful office in the land.[48] He confounded people, particularly the Northern intelligentsia, who constantly underestimated him. They could never wrap their brains around the notion that such a man—one with little formal education, scant familiarity with polite society, limited military experience, limited practice in the ways of Washington, no experience living or traveling abroad, no powerful mentors, and a peculiar way of expressing himself—could be so unorthodox, so effective, and ultimately so successful.[49]

Before Lincoln took the oath of office, Harriet Beecher Stowe compared the nation to a ship on a perilous passage with Lincoln at its helm. Could this plain backwoodsman—"with no more culture, instruction, or education than any such working man may obtain," and with "the eyes of the princes, nobles, aristocrats, of dukes, earls, scholars, statesmen warriors" all looking on—"really get that ship through?"[50]

That Lincoln, a common backwoodsman, not only got the nation through the brutal Civil War but led with skill, tenacity, determination, and moral conviction, soothed and inspired the people. He played big during the national crisis. A gentle man with a generous heart, Lincoln demonstrated his iron will and grit to see a difficult mission to fruition.[51] Yet even as he displayed persistence, purpose, and resolve to win the war and eradicate slavery from the

---

[47] Goodwin, *Team of Rivals*, 748.

[48] Donald, *Lincoln Reconsidered*, 3.

[49] Wilson, *Lincoln's Sword*, 281; Winik, "Lincoln," 82.

[50] Shenk, *Lincoln's Melancholy*, 172.

[51] Miroff, *Icons of Democracy*, 85.

country, Lincoln never lost himself, his amiable personality, or his compassion. He remained the same man whether he was in a bar or in a cabinet meeting, in private or in public.

P.B. Day, a Protestant preacher in Hollis, New Hampshire, gave a eulogy after Lincoln's death, noting that "love is a rare attribute in the chief magistrate of a great people." While most people "have so long regarded an iron will … as the first requisite for a ruler … MR. LINCOLN has changed our views." The American people "loved him because he first loved them."[52]

Great leaders are often known by single words and phrases. While Lincoln became known as the Great Emancipator, most common folk were more familiar with and preferred the monikers of Rail-splitter and Honest Abe. Contemporary critic and poet Richard H. Stoddard said of Lincoln:

> A laboring man, with horny hands,
> Who swung the axe, who tilled the lands—
> One of the people, born to be
> Their conscious epitome.[53]

After Lincoln's assassination, Minister Theodore L. Cuyler grieved so deeply that he could not write a sermon. As he told his New York congregation, Father Abraham, or Uncle Abe, had been family to almost everyone.[54]

Lincoln's personality and character, as much as his intelligence and will, helped the North win the Civil War. In 1866, the president's personal secretary, John Hay, said that despite his boss's foibles, Lincoln possessed a character only surpassed by Jesus Christ. A psychologically mature and honest man, the president gallantly suppressed his own ego as he focused on winning the Civil War. A less conscientious man would have fallen prey to pettiness, envy,

---

[52] Fox, *Lincoln's Body*, 116; Winik, "Lincoln," 83–87.

[53] Peterson, *Lincoln in American Memory*, 30.

[54] Burlingame, *Lincoln*, 2:829.

jealousy, self-righteousness, false pride, vanity, and other egotistical temptations, and would not have been able maintain the resolve required to lead the Union to victory.

Lincoln's personality and character, coupled with his exceptionally eloquent speeches and letters, inspired profound confidence and trust among the American people. Few leaders in American history possessed these combined qualities the way Lincoln did.[55]

One historian described the life of Lincoln as the supreme metanarrative of the American experience.[56] He personifies the ideal republican life course: self-improvement in youth, public service in adulthood, and sacrifice for the people at the peak of his powers and influence. For a common backwoodsman, who at one time assessed that he had "done nothing to make any human being remember that he had lived," Lincoln left quite a legacy—one that continues to inspire everyday folk today.[57]

All frontier families embraced the notion of sacrifice. Parents had to sacrifice niceties and leisure in order to put food on the table for their children. Children often sacrificed their own dreams to help make ends meet on the family farm. Family members sacrificed their lives to protect one another from wild animals, Indian attacks, and the ravages of disease. Union and Confederate soldiers sacrificed their lives for cause and country in the Civil War. These sacrificial realities of the time were personified in the life of Lincoln. He not only understood but lived a life of sacrifice as the people had. Furthermore, when he died by an assassin's bullet, Lincoln provided the ultimate sacrifice—his own life—for sake of the Union.[58]

A 1952 advertisement for John Hancock Mutual Life Insurance Company asked, "Why do we love this man, dead long before our time, yet dear to us as a father?" It answered, "Abe Lincoln always did what most people would have done, said what most people

---

[55] Burlingame, *Lincoln*, 2:833–34.

[56] Krannawitter, *Vindicating Lincoln*, 140.

[57] Fox, *Lincoln's Body*, 327.

[58] Fox, *Lincoln's Body*, xiv, 132.

wanted said, thought what most people thought when they stopped to think of it. He was everybody grown a little taller—the warm and living proof of our American faith that greatness comes out of everywhere when it is free to come."[59]

On March 4, 1861, Lincoln gathered himself as he prepared to step up to the podium to give his first inaugural address. He quickly realized that he needed to take off his hat and put it somewhere. Since there was no room on the lectern, he turned to his defeated Democratic rival, Stephen Douglas, who graciously rose to take the hat. Sitting down, Douglas turned to the man sitting next to him and said, "If I can't be President, I can at least hold his hat."[60]

The Lincoln Memorial, located on the Mall in Washington, DC, tries to capture Americans' fascination and appreciation for Lincoln's humanity and leadership legacy. Over thirty feet tall, the monument is surrounded by tablets upon which are engraved two of his great speeches—the Emancipation Proclamation and the second inaugural address.[61]

Had Lincoln gone down in defeat in the presidential election of 1864, history would have categorized him primarily as a failure—an ineffective president who could not win the war or unify the government. Indeed, perhaps one final lesson of the Lincoln legacy is that hardship and setbacks often must unfold before a major accomplishment or breakthrough can be achieved. Great leaders may not be viewed as "great" until the very end of their lives, or even after their earthly lives have passed.

Biographers and historians love Lincoln because they can study his past, see the obstacles he faced and overcame, and evaluate the

---

59 Landis and Milkis, *Presidential Greatness*, 200, 237.

60 Lehrman, *Lincoln "by littles,"* 173.

61 Shenk, *Lincoln's Melancholy*, 8. Lincoln's melancholy, or depression, is a story for our time. Depression affects well over 100 million people a year and is the world's leading cause of disability. In 2000, over a million people killed themselves—about equal to the number of deaths from war and homicide that year put together. Fox, *Lincoln's Body*, 218–19.

power of his words. Lincoln's gift for language, often poetic, made his words soar like a "comet streaking across the humdrum political sky" then and still "shine brightly and illuminate our lives" now.[62]

There are difficulties a biographer will experience in researching and writing about Lincoln. A plethora of trivial facts and sentimental stories are told about the man, and some are even authentic. There is a formidable body of scholarship on the many different aspects of his life, leadership, and legacy. Furthermore, one must contend with Lincoln's inner elusiveness, especially when it comes to matters of faith. He shared very little about his feelings, even with his closest friends and his wife.[63]

There are many high-quality Lincoln biographies—some that are rather short in length and others that are multivolume tomes filled with biographical and historical detail. Lincoln's life, after all, is enjoyable and intellectually stimulating to read about. His story also happens to sell again and again. Who would you rather take the time to read about, Franklin Pierce or Abraham Lincoln?

This Lincoln biography is distinct in two specific ways. First, the reader will explore the life of Lincoln under four major themes or categories: family values, the making of a leader, religion and relationships, and vision.

Second, this work divides each topic into three parts: "The Lincoln Way," "The Truth," and "Your Life." In each chapter, the reader will discover "The Lincoln Way"—how he lived his life, what he valued, how he made decisions, and what the outcomes of his actions were. The intent is to show the reader how Lincoln did it, wrote it, thought about it, or changed it.

"The Truth" section analyzes the particular theme or themes of the chapter from a biblical perspective. This is what God's Word tells us about this particular topic.

---

62 Gienapp, "Lincoln and Presidential Leadership," 81–84.

63 Miroff, *Icons of Democracy*, 83–84; Oates, *With Malice Toward None*, 99.

The final section of each chapter, "Your Life," provides questions related to the topic. The intent is to give the reader an opportunity to reflect on his or her own life and ask the question, "How can I apply the lessons learned from Lincoln's life and God's Word to my own life and faith walk?"

Since this book is written in a thematic format, readers can jump from chapter to chapter if they like or read the chapters chronologically. While the work covers Lincoln's life extensively, it does not cover his life comprehensively. Those looking for detailed analyses of his view of the slavery issue, his legal decisions, or how he handled his many Civil War generals, to name a few examples, will be disappointed. There are plenty of Lincoln biographies that delve deeply into these focal points and more.

The Triune God is a God of history. He tells us "things that we have heard and known" or that "our fathers have told us" should be shared with our children. The Psalm continues that Christian leaders are called to "tell to the coming generation the glorious deeds of the Lord, and his might, and the wonders that he has done."[64] We are to "remember the days of old; consider the years of many generations" and listen to our fathers, mothers, and elders in what they have to share with us, especially regarding the Christian faith.[65] We can learn much—for today and eternity—from the many wonderful, illuminating, historical accounts in Scripture. "Now these things happened to them as an example," the Bible explains, "but they were written down for our instruction, on whom the end of the ages has come."[66]

While this work combines three of my loves—history, leadership, and God's Word—the target audience are those who simply want to become, by God's grace, more effective and compelling Christian leaders. This book is for anyone who wants to grow as a leader,

---

[64] Ps. 78:3–4.

[65] Deut. 32:7.

[66] 1 Cor. 10:11.

reflect on what the Bible says about leadership, or pursue an interest in Abraham Lincoln's life story. If you are not a Christian, take a chance and get out of your comfort zone. Read it and treat yourself to a new cultural learning experience. There is much wisdom to draw from by reading all sections of this book.

In August 1863, during the excruciatingly grisly days of the Civil War, Lincoln's personal secretary, John Hay, wrote this about his boss in his journal: "The Tycoon is in fine whack. I have rarely seen him more serene and busy … The most important things he decides and there is no cavil. I am growing more and more firmly convinced that the good of the country absolutely demands that he be kept where he is until this thing is over. There is no man in the country, so wise, so gentle, and so firm. I believe the hand of God placed him where he is."[67]

Wherever you are right now in your life, God has placed you there for a reason. He has also placed this book in your hands for this time. My hope and prayer is that you will gain much wisdom, confidence, and inspiration that will be applicable and beneficial to your life in this world and the next.

---

[67] Leidner, *Lincoln's Gift*, 189.

FAMILY VALUES

1

Father Figuring

What father among you, if his son asks for a fish,
will instead of a fish give him a serpent; or if he
asks for an egg, will give him a scorpion?
—Luke 11:11–12

The Lincoln Way

Fathers leave paths for their sons—sometimes one to follow, and sometimes one to shun.

One of the most heartbreaking aspects of Abraham Lincoln's life was the relationship he had with his father. Born on Sunday, February 12, 1809, at Sinking Spring Farm, near Hodgenville, Kentucky, Abe entered the world as the son of Thomas Lincoln, a man who had overcome much hardship in his life. When Thomas was only eight years old, he witnessed his father's death from an attack by Native Americans while clearing a field. In addition to the obvious psychological trauma of losing his father so early in life, Thomas suffered materially too—living with his uncles during his adolescent years in Tennessee and Kentucky. With his father's passing, Thomas lost the chance of inheriting land on the frontier. He became a wanderer, living in many temporary shelters before the age of twenty-one, and six more dwellings as adult. A life of continuous migration was a legacy he would pass on to his son.[1]

[1] Freehling, *Becoming Lincoln*, 2; Winkle, *Young Eagle*, 10.

Abe Lincoln perhaps never fully comprehended how hard his father had to work and how much he had to overcome.[2] Although their Sinking Spring home measured approximately sixteen by eighteen feet, the Lincolns were far from destitute. Thomas owned three modest farms simultaneously during most of Abe's boyhood years. Moreover, his skills as a carpenter provided furniture for their home and income from sales to other families. Like many settlers, the Lincolns planted corn, beans, squash, pumpkins, and whatever else could be grown to provide for the family.

After a little more than two years in possession of the property, a lawsuit by a New York land speculator over legitimate custody of the Sinking Spring Farm compelled Thomas to move his family to Knob Creek Valley in the spring of 1811. Similar to their first cabin, their home on Knob Creek consisted of a single room with a door, a window, and a sleeping loft. Since their abode sat near a major road, the family encountered travelers from all regions of the young republic—a very intellectually and socially stimulating environment for someone with Abe's curiosity and precociousness.

Thomas would continue to uproot his family frequently during the formative years of Abe's life.[3] In 1816, the Lincolns left Kentucky because of continuing land claim disputes and the likelihood that they would lose the Knob Creek Farm as they had the Sinking Spring Farm. They eventually arrived in Indiana, where the federal government sold each acre of land for two dollars and, more importantly, secured all land titles for buyers.[4] During the last

---

2 Donald, *Lincoln*, 22.

3 Winkle, *Young Eagle*, 11; Brue, "Through the Cumberland Gap," 18, 23.

4 Winkle, *Young Eagle*, 11; Wheeler, *Faith and Courage*, 42; Bartelt, *Lincoln's Indiana Youth*, 12–13. Land claims were often "shingled," or overlapped like shingles on a cabin roof, in Kentucky. The antiquated system of using metes and bounds (verbal land description) was especially challenging when natural features changed over time. Almost 50 percent of Kentucky's pioneers lost their land through faulty land titles and primitive record keeping. Thomas lost two of his first farms in this manner. Daniel Boone likewise lost almost

leg of their daunting journey through Kentucky's wooded frontier, Thomas and Abe literally cut through unbroken forest and hacked their way to their home site in present-day Spencer County. Along the way, they lost much of their cargo when their flatboat, filled with family possessions and whiskey—the cash of the frontier—capsized.

Thomas marked his land claim with a brush pile in each corner. Unfortunately, he made a poor choice of location, since the homestead was over a mile from Pigeon Creek, the nearest water source. For years thereafter, young Abe spent countless hours walking several miles each day, hauling precious fresh water for the entire family.

Thomas also postponed building a log cabin for over a year, choosing instead to construct a "half-faced camp"—a shed of poles enclosed on three sides, but wide open on the fourth. Since the back of the crude shelter slanted down to its foundational log, not even Abe's short sister, Sarah, could stand up there. The Lincoln family could never let the fire go out for fear of wild animals attacking them at night.[5] Abe spent the next fourteen, formative years of his life at what would become known as his boyhood home.

Many Lincoln biographers present Lincoln's father as a lazy, shiftless man, but this is not an accurate depiction. At age nineteen Thomas served with the Kentucky militia, and at the age of twenty-four he worked as a constable in Cumberland County. After the family moved to Hardin County, a sheriff entrusted the twenty-five-year-old Thomas with guarding prisoners and seizing suspicious white characters and slaves traveling without permits. Storekeepers in Elizabethtown later hired him to take flatboats down the Ohio and Mississippi rivers to sell cargo in New Orleans.[6] Since farming did not meet all of his household's financial and economic needs,

---

everything he owned in Kentucky. This reality may have partially inspired Abe to become a surveyor as a young man.

[5] Freehling, *Becoming Lincoln*, 15; Bartelt, *Lincoln's Indiana Youth*, 11, 16; Wheeler, *Faith and Courage*, 43.

[6] Sandburg, *Lincoln*, 4.

Thomas spent much of his time as a carpenter, building cabinets, doors, window frames, crafted furniture, and coffins. He erected several cabins, stores, and churches in the Elizabethtown area and earned a reputation as an honest, reliable craftsman.[7]

Nevertheless, as Thomas aged, endured the hardships of frontier life, lost his land titles in Kentucky, and failed to find prosperity in Indiana, he did lose some of his drive at the exact time his son entered adulthood.[8] As young Abe grew in confidence and independence, he may have lamented what appeared to be a shrinking father who lacked the grit, persistence, and will to make a better life for himself and his family.

On the move during his early childhood years, isolated in an unbroken wilderness setting, and later struck by economic hardship, young Abe never had a chance to accumulate a tight knit group or social circle, which may have contributed to his awkwardness and reticence in social settings.[9]

The family moved yet again in 1830, settling near Decatur, Illinois.[10] There Lincoln helped his father break the prairie, raise crops, split rails, and build the family log cabin. Soon after the Lincolns established themselves, they endured a bout of "Illinois shakes"—malaria—which severely afflicted several family members. To make matters worse, a once-in-a-generation blizzard, later known as the Winter of the Deep Snow, killed most of their livestock.

---

[7] Kigel, *Becoming Lincoln*, 25.

[8] Neely, "Early Years," 5.

[9] Lehrman, *Lincoln "by littles,"* 10.

[10] Bartelt, *Lincoln's Indiana Youth*, 40. There is evidence the Lincoln family had a comfortable lifestyle established in Spencer County, Indiana, at the time of their move to Illinois. They were building a new house. Dennis Hanks, a cousin of Lincoln's mother, had lost cows to milk sickness and wanted to move to Illinois because there were no milk plants there. Abraham might have found his father's acquiescence to Dennis Hanks another example of weakness, ineptitude, or rootlessness. Kiger, *Becoming Lincoln*, 124. Thomas sold Little Pigeon Creek farm for a loss. He had bought the eighty acres at two dollars an acre and tended the land for fourteen years. He sold it for $125.

In the spring of 1831, after the winter thaw, Thomas decided to move his family back to Indiana, where life had been relatively more prosperous. Indiana, however, would not become the land of Lincoln. Tired of a crude life of subsistence farming and what he called "parental tyranny" that accompanied his father's indolence and acceptance of a hopeless status quo, the twenty-two year-old Lincoln chose to remain in Illinois.[11] His family headed to Coles County. They would never get to Indiana, occupying three more Coles County homes in six years before an exasperated Sarah ceased all further uprooting. Abe gathered his meager belongings, wrapped them in a bandanna, and tied it to the end of a stick. He left for New Salem.[12]

Father and son certainly had some things in common. At five feet ten inches tall, Thomas was shorter, stockier, and much more muscular than his beanpole son. But both Thomas and Abe demonstrated impressive physical strength—a quality of importance out on the frontier—and were known to be powerful wrestlers. Both had black hair.

Beyond the physical comparisons, Thomas had a reputation for being a raconteur and a conversationalist who enjoyed good company and dialogue with common folk. He loved eliciting laughter and applause.[13] The 228-acre Knob Creek Farm, which stood along the old Cumberland Trail stretching from Louisville to Nashville, provided a perfect location for farmers, peddlers, and preachers to tell their tales. Night after night, Abe watched his father swap stories with visitors and neighbors alike. Thomas's quick wit, talent for

---

[11] Burlingame, *Lincoln,* 1:51.

[12] Kiger, *Becoming Lincoln*, 142.

[13] Burlingame, *Lincoln*, 1:5. Thomas once told the story of his second wife asking him whether he liked his first wife or her best. To make his point, he shared an anecdote about a Kentuckian, John Hardin, who had two good-looking horses. When a neighbor asked Hardin which horse he liked best, he said that since one horse kicked and the other bit, he did not know which horse was worse.

mimicry, and uncanny memory became one of the greatest legacies he imparted to his son.[14]

In many ways, Thomas showed himself to be an upstanding American citizen. By almost all accounts, "Uncle Tommy" loved to entertain and showed good hospitality and generosity. He possessed common sense and never seemed to lose his cool or take offense. Thomas was sober, paid taxes, sat on juries, and served on the county slave patrol. He did not chase gold, use profane or vulgar language, indulge in card games, or fight—though he did not refrain from taking on bullies. The most frequently used adjective to describe the Abe's father was "honest." Despite his lack of formal education, Thomas appeared to be well respected in the community.[15] His son Abe would demonstrate and become renowned for many of these same traits.

As far as character flaws, Thomas could often be aloof and glum. Occasionally, he succumbed to bouts of depression and withdrew from people, sometimes wandering in his fields for hours.[16] Many Lincoln family members suffered from depression and melancholy over the years, including its most famous member.[17]

As much as father and son seemed to have in common, they were also profoundly different, particularly their mindsets and aspirations (or lack thereof). Sadly, these differences seemed to crowd out the

---

14 Goodwin, *Team of Rivals*, 50.

15 Keneally, *Lincoln*, 2, 6; Oates, *With Malice Toward None*, 5–6; Winkle, *Young Eagle*, 140, 143–44; Clinton, "Family," 25; White, *Lincoln*, 13; Kigel, *Becoming Lincoln*, 17.

16 Burlingame, *Lincoln*, 1:5–6. Thomas's moments of depression are certainly understandable. In addition to the hardships enumerated above, he endured the deaths of his second son in 1813, his wife in 1818, and his daughter in 1828. He often stated that everything he touched either died or was lost.

17 Shenk, *Lincoln's Melancholy*, 11–12. Depression ran in the Lincoln family. Both his parents had melancholy. Lincoln's mother is particularly described as sad by many contemporaries. Lincoln's great-uncle had a "deranged mind," and his uncle Mordecai had broad mood swings. A first cousin had a daughter committed to an insane asylum in Illinois.

commonalities and contributed to an irremediable chasm in their relationship—a sad and discouraging case study in what could have been. Having lost his own father at a young age, Thomas *could* have showered love unconditionally upon his son and affirmed Abe's eventual successes in life, but he did not do so. Imagine the tales old Thomas could have told about his son's triumphs as a lawyer, state senator, and congressman. Sadly, these opportunities never came to fruition.

On the other side of the coin, Abe *could* have shown his father more love and respect, knowing all that his father had overcome. Abe *could* have honored his father later in life by staying in regular contact and visiting him more often. Lincoln *could* have written glowingly about his father, expressing appreciation for all that his father had taught him, in the personal biography he published when running for president. He did not.

Indeed, the relationship *could* have blossomed into a loving, lifelong one of mutual respect and admiration, but that did not happen. Instead, the historical record is clear that they never grew close or showed affection for one another.

One main difference between father and son is that one settled for being while the other focused on becoming. Thomas labored to survive, while Abe lived to rise. Indeed, Thomas did not possess certain attributes his son would become famous for—intellectual power, ambition, idealism, eloquence, spirituality, political wisdom, judgment, and leadership. Plodding, average, plain, illiterate (he could not write anything other than his signature), Thomas gave the appearance of an intellectually inferior man with little ambition. Nothing Thomas did turned out well other than his jokes. As a farmer, he chose poor land to till on the Sinking Spring Farm during Abe's first two years of life. After abandoning that farm in 1811, he chose a poor location again on Knob Creek. In 1816, he selected 160 acres of heavily timbered land in Indiana and built a cabin one mile away from a reliable freshwater source. He made other poor farming decisions in Illinois during the 1830s and 1840s. Many neighbors and associates indicated that his carpentry skills were rudimentary and "tolerable."[18] Some complained about his work.

Unlike his son's drive, Thomas' lack of ambition and management grew more pronounced as he aged. He grew more shiftless and less effective in managing even the basic necessities of farm maintenance. Shanty remained dilapidated and the soil uncultivated. Thomas did not bother to farm three-quarters of his 160 acres. Neighbors saw him frequently hunting and roaming around like a "piddler" but not making necessary repairs or improving his farmland. Living in perpetual poverty did not seem to bother him. He had no stable, no outhouse, no shrubbery, and barely any trees on his property.[19] He did not seem to be bothered in the least by these realities.

Thomas managed his family's limited assets poorly and exhibited ignorance and extreme gullibility. He once took pigs down the Ohio River on a flatboat and made a deal with some quick-witted bargainers, who took his cargo and promised to meet him in New Orleans to pay him. Arriving in New Orleans, he waited for days and never received compensation. A "classic Southern backcountry cracker," as one biographer notes, Thomas lost money buying and selling farms and lost out on potential income by loafing, fishing, and hunting instead of farming.[20] Thomas's indolence, lack of ambition, and denigration of formal education put him at odds with his intelligent and enterprising son.

The fact that young Abe loved to read provided a significant bone of contention and worldview clash between son and father. Out on the frontier, children were a vital part of the family economic unit and were expected to do their part for the survival of the family.[21] Thomas thought books were a luxury and a distraction for Abe. He often found his bookish son reading or telling tales to the neighbors

---

[18] Burlingame, *Lincoln*, 1:6, 8.

[19] Burlingame, *Lincoln* 1:8.

[20] Burlingame, *Lincoln,* 1:9–10. Crackers were famously easygoing, imprudent, lazy, and restless.

[21] Clinton, "Family," 253; Manning, *Father Lincoln*, 7.

when he should have been felling trees, digging up stumps, splitting rails, plowing, weeding, or planting. Thomas would throw clods of dirt at his son when he spotted Abe conversing with strangers. Abe did not help matters when he corrected his father's diction or language. Thomas sometimes took a strap and whipped his son for laziness, a parenting practice that was not uncommon at the time. One time Abe endured a beating for freeing a bear cub caught in his father's trap. Occasionally, Thomas even destroyed Abe's books, expensive and scarce as they were on the frontier.[22] Five years after Lincoln left his father's home, Thomas scoffed at his son's desire for an education, even making the argument that Abe would be better off without it—like father, like son.[23]

Instead of appreciating and cherishing the best in each other, they focused on perceived shortcomings. Lincoln saw his father's inadequacies and worked hard to make sure his life did not turn out that way. Thomas saw his son's interest in reading and learning as an unwelcome disruption of the rugged work ethic required for any success as a subsistence farmer. The father liked working with his hands, while the son enjoyed to working with his head.[24]

Thomas would never learn to respect an erudite man like his son, and Abe would never become interested in subsistence farming like his dad.[25] Hunting in particular was a subsistence skill that Abe found abhorrent. When Abe shot and killed a turkey just before his

---

[22] Holzer and Garfinkle, *A Just and Generous Nation*, 16; Goodwin, *Team of Rivals*, 53; Burlingame, *Lincoln*, 1:11; Freehling, *Becoming Lincoln*, 17. Reading at night was a difficult endeavor in small quarters and using hazardous oil lamps. Most of young Lincoln's reading had to take place during the daylight hours, precious work time for a farmer.

[23] Burlingame, *Lincoln*, 1:11.

[24] Manning, *Father Lincoln*, 1, 3.

[25] Burlingame, *Lincoln*, 1:221. Lincoln's Springfield neighbors observed that the Lincoln home and yard almost always appeared to be in disarray. A visitor in 1860 noted broken panes of glass by the front door and broken blinds on the side of the house.

ninth birthday, he regretted the carnage so much that he never shot a large game animal again. His aversion to hunting shocked and disappointed his father, who truly enjoyed a good kill and thrived with a rifle in his hand. Since frontier families depended on game for food, Thomas wondered how his son would ever learn to provide for himself or his future family.[26]

Bitterness eventually crept into the father-son relationship. One night Abe sneaked out of the cabin to join friends in a raccoon hunt. When Thomas's dog, Joe, barked incessantly, Abe and his friends allowed Joe to tag along. As soon as his friends killed the coon, however, they sewed its skin around Joe and sent the dog home. On the way, larger canines attacked and killed Joe. Joe's death shocked and incensed Thomas. Abe expressed joy that Joe would never go on another coon hunt. Perhaps he still resented his father for making the decision to kill his pet pig.[27]

After he left his father's home, Lincoln learned to admire articulate, educated, professional men who were *not* like his dad. When he moved to New Salem in the 1830s, for example, Lincoln developed a strong affection for a gentleman named Bowling Green. A rotund, easygoing, jovial man who loved to read, Green also served as learned man of society—a justice of the peace, canal commissioner, doorkeeper of the Illinois House of Representatives, judge of elections, county commissioner, sheriff, and candidate for state senate. Lincoln boarded at Green's home, and Green became a second father to him—a loving, respectable father. Green looked on Lincoln with pride and pleasure, insisting that Abe was a man after his own heart. Green fed Lincoln's voracious appetite for reading and learning, stimulated his interest in law, and encouraged him to pursue politics.

After Green died of a stroke in 1842, his widow, Nancy, asked Abe to speak at the memorial service. Sobbing with emotion,

---

26 Manning, *Father Lincoln*, 8.

27 Burlingame, *Lincoln*, 1:33.

Lincoln could barely offer a few choked words.[28] He never expressed anything close to that kind of sentiment for his own father.

There is no doubt that Abe did not fit the typical profile of a frontier boy. In a society of hunters and riflemen, he detested hunting and did not care for guns. In a country full of fisherman, he did not like to fish. While many boys toyed with animals and treated them cruelly, Lincoln protected and rescued critters of all kinds. In a countryside of farmers, Lincoln preferred to read and eventually eschewed the farmer's life. On the frontier where many were indifferent to education, Lincoln cared about it so intensely, he taught himself.[29]

While father and son also disagreed on politics—Thomas was a Democrat and Jackson man, while Abe supported the Whig Party and Jackson's hated rival, Henry Clay—perhaps the most peculiar and instructive difference between the two emanated from their divergent allegiance to organized religion. Lincoln's parents were "Hard Shell Baptists"—sometimes also called "Primitive," "Anti-Mission," or "Separate Baptists"—who believed nothing could be added to the pristine gospel of Christ and the church He founded, including creeds, missionary work, Sunday school, musical instruments, or even paid and educated clergy. As conservative Calvinists who had an unshakable devotion to the doctrine of predestination, Hard Shell Baptists did not evangelize because God had already determined who would be saved or not.[30]

While Thomas was a devoted member of Baptist churches in Kentucky, Indiana, and Illinois throughout his life, Abe never officially joined any church. Thomas must have been disappointed in his son's refusal, and this tension may explain why Lincoln never pushed religion on his own sons.[31] Furthermore, the Calvinist

---

[28] Burlingame, 1:86–87.

[29] Miller, *Lincoln's Virtues*, 43–44.

[30] Leidner, *Lincoln's Gift*, 10; Mansfield, *Lincoln's Battle with God*, 23; Guelzo, *Man of Ideas*, 33–34.

[31] Manning, *Father Lincoln*, 11.

belief in predestination disturbed Lincoln. He tried to reconcile it throughout his life. Among other sentiments, Lincoln doubted the notion that God would choose someone like him for salvation.

While Lincoln disdained the uneducated element of his parents' church and wrestled intellectually with the doctrine of predestination, he admired and embraced his father's church's position on slavery. Thomas and Nancy Lincoln actually left South Fork Baptist Church in 1807 over a dispute about slavery. In the slave state of Kentucky, they helped found the Little Mount Baptist Church, located three miles from Sinking Spring Farm, on antislavery tenets. As he grew up, young Abe almost certainly heard many conversations on the topic of slavery.[32] The irony for biographers who discourage any consideration of a Christian Lincoln is that the Great Emancipator was nurtured by the teachings and doctrines of an ultraconservative church held sacred by his uneducated father.

Sadly, the relationship between father and son had no poignant comeback, no touching reconciliation, not even a tender moment of genuine affection. Hollywood will never do a story on the relationship between Thomas and Abraham Lincoln because no one would want to see the ending. Abe became a "non-Tom Lincoln"—a non-hunter, non-fisherman, non-illiterate, non-farmer, non-carpenter, non-manual laborer, non-husband of an uneducated, penniless bride, non-demanding parent, non-Democrat, non-church member, and especially a non-wanderer.[33]

---

[32] White, *Lincoln*, 18; Keneally, *Lincoln*, 3. Thomas' antislavery sentiment remained both a moral issue and an economic one. The presence of slavery in Kentucky affected free laborers such as Thomas. Workers had to compete with slaves who were "hired out" by owners to do farm work. As a result, wages stayed low for free laborers. A state without slavery offered a higher economic ceiling for men who needed to supplement their farm income. Bartelt, *Lincoln's Indiana Youth*, 12.

[33] Freehling, *Becoming Lincoln*, 26.

Taken one year before he passed away in 1851, this photo of Thomas Lincoln reveals a hardened man and some of the facial features he would pass on to his son Abe. (Library of Congress, LC-DIG-ppmsca-19418)

After Lincoln broke away from his father's grip at the age of twenty-two, they rarely corresponded or saw each other. For twenty-four years, including the entire time he lived in Salem and Springfield, Lincoln never invited his parents to visit him or his family, though it is doubtful they would have come anyway. Lincoln's parents never met their daughter-in-law or grandchildren.

Traditionally, Lincoln's ancestors named their eldest sons after the paternal grandfather. Thomas had honored his father by naming his first son Abraham. Abraham and Mary, however, named their first son, Robert, after Mary's father. Only after Thomas passed away did Abe name his fourth son after his father, and even then preferred to call the boy by the nickname Tad.[34]

---

[34] Winkle, *Young Eagle*, 132, 220.

There were occasional visits from a duty-bound son when Lincoln rode the Illinois circuit near his father's home in Coles County. Even during these visits, however, Lincoln stayed with his friend Dennis Hanks rather than his dad.[35] In the 1840s, when Thomas got into deeper financial difficulties—probably due to poor investment in a saw and gristmill, encouraged by his lazy and irresponsible stepson, John Johnston—Lincoln paid his father two hundred dollars for the east forty acres of his Illinois farm. The payment, or gift, allowed Lincoln's parents to have "use and entire control" of the land during their lifetimes.[36] In other words, Lincoln purchased the house and land and deeded it back to his parents.

When Lincoln was serving in Congress, Thomas begged for a loan of twenty dollars to prevent his farm from being sold to satisfy a long-forgotten debt. Abe sent the money immediately but suspected tomfoolery from his stepbrother John.[37]

The relationship between father and son was never filled with hatred. It was only devoid of affection. Lincoln was a dutiful son to the extent his time and interests permitted.

In January 1851, Lincoln received word that Thomas was dying, but he did not go to visit his ailing father. Two years earlier, when his father likewise appeared to be on his deathbed, Lincoln had suspended a campaign to secure a federal appointment in the General Land Office. By the time he arrived in Coles County, his father's health had improved considerably. The suspension of his campaign cost Lincoln the appointment he so ardently desired. The next winter, Lincoln ignored letters from his stepbrother describing Thomas's declining health. Lincoln felt Johnston was crying wolf. Even after a friend verified his father's sickness, Lincoln still did not undertake the three-day buggy ride to see his father. Instead, he maintained his everyday schedule. Perhaps Lincoln did not want

---

[35] Burlingame, *Lincoln*, 1:10.

[36] Donald, *Lincoln*, 152.

[37] Basler, Lincoln to Thomas Lincoln and John D. Johnston, December 24, 1848, *CW*, 2:15.

to leave his wife, who had just given birth to their third son, Willie, and was still mourning the death of their second son, Eddie, who passed on February 1, 1850.[38]

In a letter to his stepbrother, Lincoln explained that he did not want his father or mother to lack any comfort if their health deteriorated or if they suffered. If Johnston needed to use the Lincoln name to secure a doctor or any other medical attention for his father during his present illness, Lincoln advised him to do so. Nevertheless, due to Mary's condition, he would not be traveling to see his dad. "I sincerely hope Father may yet recover his health," he wrote, "but at all events tell him to remember to call upon, and confide in, our great, and good, and merciful Maker who will not turn away from him in any extremity." Demonstrating his familiarity of Scripture, Lincoln added that God "notes the fall of a sparrow, and numbers the hairs of our heads," and therefore would "not forget the dying man, who puts his trust in Him." Then he closed the letter with a very revealing statement on his relationship with his dad: "Say to him that if we could meet now, it is doubtful whether it would not be more painful than pleasant." If his father were to die, "he will soon have a joyous meeting with many loved ones gone before; and where the rest of us, through the help of God, hope ere-long to join them."[39]

A few days after Lincoln wrote this letter, Thomas died. His most famous son did not attend his funeral or purchase a gravestone for him.

Lincoln's autobiography, written in 1860 for the purpose of a presidential election campaign, certainly did not portray a devoted son's love for his father. Speaking through the editor, Lincoln explained that Thomas, "even in childhood was a wandering laboring boy, and grew up literally without education." His father

---

[38] Donald, *Lincoln*, 152–53; Leidner, *Lincoln's Gift*, 63; Manning, *Father Lincoln*, 59. It is revealing that Lincoln did not even inform his parents of his son Eddie's death.

[39] Basler, Lincoln to John Johnston, January 12, 1851, *CW*, 2:96–97.

"never did more in the way of writing than to bunglingly sign his own name."[40] Lincoln added no more about his father.

A decade after Thomas passed, Lincoln was on his way to the White House as president-elect. He stopped to see his father's grave. With a penknife, he cut out the initials T. L. on an oak board and placed it at the head of the grave. A souvenir hunter would soon steal the board. Three years after Lincoln's assassination, Mary wrote to Lincoln's stepmother, claiming that her husband had fully intended to visit his father's grave, in the summer of 1865, and install a headstone and footstone exhibiting his father's name and age. While Mary promised Sarah Bush Lincoln that she would carry out her late husband's wish, she never did. Thomas's grave remained unmarked until Robert Lincoln paid for a permanent tombstone sometime after 1880.[41]

A few months after Lincoln's death, Dennis Hanks, his friend and cousin of Lincoln's mother, was asked about Lincoln's relationship with his father. "I never could tell whether Abe loved his father very well or not," he reported. "I don't think he did."[42]

The relationship between Thomas and Abe truly disappoints and saddens all who hope to read about a loving relationship between father and son. Nevertheless, Thomas did have a significant impact on the destiny of his son, if not in a romanticized manner. For the *absence* of a father's affection spurred the son to rise beyond Thomas in many vocations—as father, husband, community leader, lawyer, and politician. The allure and benefits of political power and fame often appeal to those who have damaged self-esteem or who have been traumatized in their upbringing. Perhaps embarrassed by his family, particularly his father, Lincoln wanted to show that a real man could triumph over a meager education and humble beginnings. Early in his political career, the leading citizens of Logan

---

[40] Basler, Lincoln's Autobiography Written by John L. Scripps, June, 1860, *CW*, 4:61.

[41] Manning, *Father Lincoln*, 74.

[42] Wilson, *Herndon's Informants*, 176.

County, Illinois, proposed to name their county seat after him. Lincoln demurred, asserting that anything named Lincoln did not amount to much.[43] And yet, stirring beneath the surface of the former penniless, backwoods boy was an ambition to make a name for himself—all the way to the highest office in the land.

In the late summer of 1864, President Lincoln told the 166th Ohio Regiment that he temporarily occupied "this big White House," and that he was "a living witness that any of one of your children may look to come here as my father's child has." He added that they all had "an open field and fair chance" and "equal privileges in the race of life, with all its desirable human aspirations." This ability to rise and to make something special of one's life was America's "inestimable jewel."[44] If Lincoln could be better than his father and rise to prominence, so could anyone.

One cannot help but wonder if Lincoln's lifelong melancholy and frequent silence emanated from a broken relationship with his father. Lincoln loved to laugh, joke, listen to good stories, and tell tall tales just like his dad. He also loved to reflect on the ways of God, talk about the big philosophic and religious questions of the day, and share his dreams with many associates in his life. Yet, as best we can tell from the historical record, he and his father rarely, if ever, shared special conversations.

Lincoln loved to fix and improve things. He wanted to build a more prosperous life for himself and the country. Progress and fulfillment fueled him. Alas, for all of his impressive accomplishments, Lincoln failed to build a more meaningful relationship with his father. A joy-filled, prosperous, deepening, life-affirming father-son relationship remained elusive to the end.

The legacy of Thomas and Abe Lincoln is truly one of what *could have been.* Fathers and sons can take note of the life lessons

---

[43] Burlingame, *Lincoln*, 1:172–73.

[44] Basler, Lincoln's Speech to One Hundred Sixty-Sixth Ohio Regiment, August 22, 1864, *CW*, 7:512.

in their relationship, especially the missed opportunities. The way things *are* and the way things *ought to be* do not have to be two very different things.

The Truth

Scripture is filled with accounts of selfless, Christ-centered fathers and derelict, negligent ones. The influence of a father often has an eternal impact on his children, particularly in their faith walk. Moreover, the Bible gives much insight into how a father should raise his children. As children of God, we are not to scorn the Lord's discipline or "be weary of his reproof" but understand and appreciate that "the Lord reproves him whom he loves, as a father the son in whom he delights."[45] In the same manner, loving fathers are not to spare the rod, but properly discipline their children.[46] Yet they are also to show compassion to their children, just as "the Lord shows compassion to those who fear him."[47] They are not to provoke their offspring so that they become discouraged[48] or grow angry, "but bring them up in the discipline and instruction of the Lord."[49]

God loves being the Heavenly Father and having a Son with whom He was well pleased.[50] This is why His plan of salvation—to send His one and only Son in the flesh, to save humanity from our sins—remains such an incredible act of mercy, grace, and love.

Our Heavenly Father has high expectations for earthly fathers. "I have no greater joy," Scripture tells us, "than to hear that my children are walking in the truth."[51] Fathers and mothers are to "train up a

---

[45] Prov. 3:11–12.

[46] Prov. 13:24.

[47] Ps. 103:13.

[48] Col. 3:21.

[49] Eph. 6:4.

[50] Matt. 3:17.

[51] 3 John 1:4.

child in the way he should go" so that "even when he is old he will not depart from it."[52] As the spiritual heads of households,[53] fathers are particularly charged with laying the foundation of Christ in their children's lives.[54] Fathers should be diligent in sharing God's Word with their children. They should "talk of them when you sit in your house, and when you walk by the way, and when you lie down, and when you rise."[55] God's Word should be "a sign on your hand" and written "on the doorposts of your house and on your gates."[56] A successful father, in God's eyes, is one whose children are righteous and wise in the ways of the Lord.[57]

Unfortunately, in today's world, too many children are growing up with dysfunctional, absent, or abusive fathers. Many never even know their fathers. We should not be surprised that these children grow up to be skeptical, even belligerent, at the notion of a merciful and loving Heavenly Father. These folks especially need to hear that they do indeed "have one Father, who is in heaven,"[58] and that we all are children of a Heavenly Father, whether we want to claim the truth or not.[59]

Your Heavenly Father, of course, will never abandon or forsake you. He will never harm or abuse you. He loves you so much that He "sent his Son to be the Savior of the world."[60] And your Heavenly Dad has big plans for you. For you are His clay. He is your Potter, and you are all the work of His hand.[61] Happy and blessed Heavenly Father's Day—always!

---

[52] Prov. 22:6.

[53] 1 Cor. 11:3; Eph. 5:22-33.

[54] 1 Cor. 3:11.

[55] Deut. 6:6-7.

[56] Deut. 6:8-9.

[57] Prov. 23:24.

[58] Matt. 23:9.

[59] 1 John 3:1.

[60] 1 John 4:14.

[61] Isa 64:8.

Your Life

There is a delicate balance between disciplining and encouraging a child. While Thomas disciplined his son plenty, Abe never really felt nurturing and encouraging love from his father. How do the Bible passages you just read demonstrate this balance in disciplining your child while also lifting him or her up with encouragement and support?

After reading about the relationship between Abraham and Thomas Lincoln, how does it make you want to be a better father/mother or better son/daughter?

One challenge we face in contemporary times is that too many sons and daughters have dysfunctional relationships or no relationships with their fathers. How might a poor or nonexistent relationship with one's earthly father impact one's relationship with one's Heavenly Father?

What gives you the greatest comfort in knowing you have a Heavenly Father?

2

Mothers Know Best

I am reminded of your sincere faith, a faith that dwelt first in your grandmother Lois and your mother Eunice and now, I am sure, dwells in you as well.
—2 Timothy 1:5

The Lincoln Way

As leadership is influence, mothers are among the most impactful leaders in human history.

Lincoln was blessed with two mothers in his lifetime. Both not only recognized the specialness and precociousness of their son but also encouraged the development of his mind and worldview. The world is forever indebted to their indelible, behind-the-scenes legacy.

Nancy Hanks, Lincoln's first and biological mother, married at the age of twenty-three, was seven years younger than her husband Thomas. She was as tall as he was, delicate, bony, and sinewy. Nancy had dark hair and hazel eyes and was known more for her inward beauty than her outward beauty. Abe once compared her to a woman he courted, who was missing teeth and had a weather-beaten appearance overall. Nancy may have suffered from consumption during Abe's upbringing, exhibiting signs such as frequent coughing and raspy breathing. Contemporaries often commented that she looked melancholy, gloomy, sad, and depressed. Neighborhood ladies stopped visiting her because she did not return their social calls. Perhaps she suffered from some chemical imbalance. She continually displayed her grief over the loss of an infant son, Thomas. She may have heard the rumors about her illegitimacy and her mother's chastity—as well as her own.

Despite her melancholy and homely appearance, many contemporaries noted her kindness, tenderness, affection, charitableness, and wrestling skill (not a rarity for women on the frontier during those times). Many characterized her as a brilliant or intellectual person who could read but did not know how to write. Abe later described her as "intellectual" and a "woman of genius."[1] Many neighbors and associates of the Lincolns claimed that Nancy far surpassed Thomas in almost every way.[2]

Besides being a source of gossip in the community, her illegitimate birth had an impact on her son. Near the end of his life, Lincoln told a friend that his maternal grandfather was an aristocratic Virginia farmer or planter, without providing the name. Tales of his mom's seedy reputation provoked scorn from neighbors and made Abe ashamed of her and her family. Nevertheless, Lincoln asserted, late in his life and with some pride, that illegitimate children often exceed others in matters of intellect and shrewdness.[3] Perhaps the contempt his family endured because of his mother's illegitimacy taught Lincoln how *not* to treat people. Instead, he would be charitable, kind, and forgiving to others—key traits that he exhibited throughout his life.[4]

In addition to passing on height, physical strength, wrestling prowess, and melancholy, Nancy nurtured her son's love for reading and learning. She was known to have a fine singing voice and a gift for memorization. She frequently recounted Bible stories and recited bits of poetry for her children. She could deliver speeches from Shakespeare, tales from *Aesop's Fables,* and haunting accounts

---

[1] Burlingame, *Lincoln,* 1:12.

[2] Clinton, "Family," 250; Keneally, *Lincoln*, 1; Oates, *With Malice Toward None*, 5; Donald, *Lincoln*, 23; Mansfield, *Lincoln's Battle with God*, 3.

[3] Burlingame, *Lincoln*, 1:13–14.

[4] Clinton, "Family," 253.

of burning Protestants from John Foxe's *Book of Martyrs.* She also mastered and taught large portions of the Declaration of Independence and the Constitution. Nancy was more Mary than Martha; her housekeeping took a backseat to her children's education. Abe and his sister Sarah learned how to read and write because of Nancy's daily direction. Like most mothers, she wanted to create a better quality of life for her children. Not only did she ignite Abe's literary sense; she demonstrated skill in articulating the world to her son in an inspiring manner. Under her tutelage and care, Lincoln fell in love with learning.[5]

Of all the things she passed on to her children, Nancy believed God's Word was the most important thing one could learn. Indeed, Nancy and Thomas Lincoln were religious folk. They met at a religious camp meeting in South Fork Creek in Kentucky. They each routinely made extensive trips to attend such meetings. Nancy taught her kids how to read the Bible, made them memorize Bible passages, and recited prayers daily with them.[6]

Tragically, at the age of thirty-four, Nancy died rather suddenly from a milk-sickness disease that swept through southwest Indiana in 1818.[7] There were no doctors around to help. As a nine-year old, Abe watched his mother suffer the symptoms—dizziness, nausea, stomach pains, constant vomiting, cold hands, cold feet, a ghoulish white coating to the tongue and mouth, and the trembles—in the confines of a small, overcrowded cabin.[8] On her deathbed, Nancy urged Sarah and Abe to be kind to one another, their father, and the world. She wanted them to "live as they had been taught by her to love men" and to revere "and worship God."[9] Abe helped make her

---

[5] Mansfield, *Lincoln's Battle with God*, 4–5; Clinton, "Family," 253.

[6] Oates, *With Malice Toward None*, 5.

[7] Burlingame, *Lincoln*, 1:25. Humans contracted milk-sickness by consuming the milk of cows that had eaten weeds or white snakeroot containing the toxic substance tremotol. Keneally, *Lincoln*, 5.

[8] Kigel, *Becoming Lincoln*, 47.

[9] Wilson, *Herndon's Informants*, 40.

coffin "but never got over the mizable way his mother died," said Nancy's cousin and Abe's close companion, Dennis Hanks.[10]

The winter months after his mother passed were some of the gloomiest and loneliest of Lincoln's life. In his vulnerable state, Abe found no support from his unsympathetic father, who failed to provide even the most rudimentary physical, spiritual, emotional, or psychological care after Nancy's death. Instead of tending his children, Thomas went to Kentucky to sell pork and find a new spouse. Abe, age ten, and Sarah, age twelve, had to fend for themselves on the Indiana farm for most of 1819. Neighbors noticed their near-nudity and leathery stomachs. Moreover, with no communication, Sarah and Abe may have thought their father too had died. The trauma and adverse childhood experience added to Lincoln's already fragile psychological makeup and may have contributed to his lifelong struggle with depression.[11]

Abe never forgot his "angel" mother and the impact she had on his life. "I remember her prayers and they have always followed me," he once recalled. "They have clung to me all my life."[12] He remembered her voice and how she taught him and his sister to study the Bible every day. One neighbor recalled how Lincoln said "the

---

[10] Bartelt, *Lincoln's Indiana Youth*, 22.

[11] Burlingame, *Lincoln*, 1:26–27. One positive aspect of the ordeal of losing their mother is that Abe became very close to his sister, Sarah, who had more time for him than his father did and seems to have embraced his unorthodox ways without reservation (Lehrman, *Lincoln "by littles,"* 8). Strong and independent like her mother, Sarah cooked for and took care of Abe and her mother's cousin, Dennis Hanks, while Thomas Lincoln looked for a new wife in Kentucky. Sarah was much like her brother, a "quick minded woman" with a "good humored laugh" who could put anyone at ease. When she died young after giving birth, a relative reported that Lincoln "sat down on a log and hid his face in his hands while tears rolled down though his long bony fingers. Those present turned away in pity and left him to his grief." He had lost the two women he loved. "From then on," said a neighbor, "he was alone in the world you might say" (Goodwin, *Team of Rivals*, 48–49).

[12] Clinton, "Family," 2008, p. 252.

Bible she read and had taught him to read was the greatest comfort he and his sister had after their mother was gone."[13] Abe "was often & much moved by the stories" of Scripture, Dennis Hanks said.[14] To another neighbor, Lincoln said that "the Fundamental truths reported in the four gospels as from the lips of Jesus Christ that I first heard from the lips of my mother are settled and fixed moral precepts with me."[15]

Another friend recollected Lincoln explaining that his mother's instruction "in letters and morals, and especially the Bible stories, and the interest and love he acquired in reading the Bible through this teaching of his mother, had been the strongest and most influential experience of his life." Whenever he read certain Bible passages, "which he had in early boyhood committed to memory by hearing her repeat them as she went about her household tasks, the tones of his mother's voice would come to him and he would seem to hear her speak those verses again."[16]

Unfortunately, Lincoln never got around to marking his mother's grave with a stone. He planned to do so in the spring of 1865, but his assassination left his desire unfulfilled. While Nancy only had nine short years to shape her son, she succeeded splendidly.[17] "All that I am or hope ever to be I get from my mother," Lincoln once told his law partner, William Herndon. "God bless her."[18]

God blessed Lincoln again with a second mother. Having abandoned his children to look for a new wife, Thomas Lincoln achieved his goal and married Sarah Bush Johnston on December 2,

---

[13] Kigel, *Becoming Lincoln*, 52.

[14] Wilson, *Herndon's Informants*, 37.

[15] Kigel, *Becoming Lincoln*, 31.

[16] Mansfield, *Lincoln's Battle with God*, 15.

[17] Winkle, *Young Eagle*, 14. Until the twentieth century, mothers rarely lived to see all of their children reach adulthood, usually leaving at least one minor child behind. In fact, during Lincoln's time, 25 percent of all children lost a parent before the age of fifteen.

[18] Mansfield, *Lincoln's Battle with God*, 2.

1819, after Thomas paid off her debts in Elizabethtown, Kentucky. The thirty-year old widow of a Hardin County jailer, Sarah (Thomas called her Sally) had three children between the ages of five and nine. Attractive, tall, sprightly, talkative, proud, kind, and charitable, she impressed everyone who met her with her industriousness, strength, vigor, intelligence, and gentleness. A good housekeeper with good manners and a gift for managing children, she earned an exemplary reputation.

Thomas may have courted her before he wed Nancy. He heard that Sarah had lost her husband in the summer of 1816. As she needed a husband and he needed a wife, their match made economic and social sense. After the marriage, they moved her belongings to Indiana, where Abe and his sister first met their new mother.[19]

When Sarah entered the reeling Lincoln household, she immediately provided the loving attention the Lincoln children needed. She literally scrubbed them clean, took the lice out of Abe's hair, mended their clothes, and made them look more human. Sarah brought refinement and a woman's touch to the frontier home—comfortable bedding, a walnut dresser, a table, chairs, a spinning wheel, and utensils. A vigorous taskmaster, she had Thomas install a floor, a window, a sleeping loft, a new roof, and a door in their overcrowded cabin. Most importantly, she brought the gift of unconditional love and showed no favoritism among her biological children—Elizabeth, John, and Matilda—and her stepchildren—Sarah and Abe. She and her children brought life and excitement to the dour Lincoln family. By the spring of 1820, the Lincoln family had been reborn.[20]

---

[19] Burlingame, *Lincoln*, 1:27; Donald, *Lincoln*, 27. Bartelt, *Lincoln's Indiana Youth*, 24.

[20] Burlingame, *Lincoln*, 1:27; Donald, *Lincoln*, 28; Bartelt, *Lincoln's Indiana Youth*, 24; Keneally, *Lincoln*, 5; Clinton, "Family," 256; Wilson, *Herndon's Informants*, 41; Kigel, *Becoming Lincoln*, 55–56.

Lincoln's stepmother, Sarah Bush Johnston, in her later years (permission granted by the Lincoln Financial Foundation Collection).

Much like Nancy did, Sarah recognized Abe's singularity and special talents. She brought three books from Kentucky to Indiana—*Webster's Speller*, *Robinson Crusoe*, and *The Arabian Nights*—and immediately gave them to her bright and inquisitive stepson. He devoured them.[21] She also protected Abe from Thomas's scorn.[22] Though she remained illiterate, Sarah enrolled Abe in a class taught by a local schoolmaster a mile from the Lincoln cabin. When this school closed, Abe and his sister were sent to another school even farther away.[23]

One historian has called Sarah Lincoln the greatest stepmother of all time.[24] Considering all the hardship young Abe endured, Sarah gave her stepson the chance of a promising future when it looked

---

21 Winkle, *Young Eagle*, 18. Legend holds that Dennis Hanks chided Lincoln for reading *The Arabian Nights*, calling the book "a pack of lies." Lincoln's response: "Mighty fine lies."

22 Burlingame, *Lincoln*, 1:28.

23 Clinton, "Family," 256.

24 Donald, "Those Around Him," 35.

like he had none.[25] Most importantly, she truly loved the precocious lad she had gained through her second marriage. "He was the best boy I ever saw … I can say what scarcely one woman, a mother, can say in a thousand and it is this," she reflected after his assassination, "Abe never gave me a cross word or look and never refused in fact, or Even in appearance, to do any thing I requested him. I never gave him a cross word in all my life. He was Kind to Every body and to Every thing and always accommodate others if he could—would do so willingly if he could."[26]

Abe never forgot his stepmother's intervention in his family's crisis, nor her kind, nurturing, encouraging manner throughout his upbringing. Many years later he told a friend that his stepmom "had been his best Friend in this world & that no Son could love a Mother more than he loved her."[27] He remained grateful and indebted to her for the rest of his life.[28]

On his way to Washington as president-elect in 1861, he made a stop in Coles County, Illinois, to visit his seventy-three-year-old stepmother for what turned out to be an emotional encounter. "The parting between him & his Mother was very affectionate," said an eyewitness. After she embraced him, Sarah expressed concern that "she would never be permitted to see him again" because "she felt that his enemies would assassinate" him. A dutiful stepson, Lincoln reassured his worried stepmother that "they will not do that" and that she should "trust in the Lord and all will be well." He promised that they would see each other again.[29] History, unfortunately, would prove Sarah right.

---

25 Wheeler, *Faith and Courage*, 52.

26 Wilson, *Herndon's Informants,* 106–9.

27 Wilson, *Herndon's Informants,* 136.

28 Burlingame, *Lincoln,* 1:28. Curiously, he seldom visited his stepmother even after his father, Thomas, died. Perhaps he did not want to return to the cabin and setting which would remind him of his sad state of affairs and dysfunctional relationship with his father while growing up in Indiana.

29 Wilson, *Herndon's Informants,* 137.

Nancy and Sarah made up one of the greatest two-for-ones in American history—two wonderful mothers for one special son. One brought Lincoln into the world and the other saved him from it. Both passed on habits and dispositions that would serve Lincoln well in various vocations and endeavors throughout his life. Both lived, modeled, and passed on the teachings of the Christian faith. What Lincoln lacked in material possessions, formal education, and paternal relationship was amply compensated for in the love and support of his two mothers. The love they showed and the faith they passed down became a legacy that still inspires today.

The Truth

Other than Jesus's agape and sacrificial love on the cross, there is nothing more special than a mother's love for her child. The fact that God chose and designed mothers to carry children in their wombs for nine months provides an intimacy with their children that men can never quite understand. We know that "children are a heritage from the Lord, the fruit of the womb a reward."[30]

Carrying their children to term and giving birth are just two of the many ways mothers make an incredible impact on their children. As mentally strong as Abraham Lincoln became, he would not have turned out to be the man he was without the love, comfort, and direction his two mothers provided for him. Lincoln, like all children, needed nurturing.

The love a mother has for her child is a wonderful way of illuminating God's love for His children. The Bible says, "As one whom his mother comforts, so I will comfort you; you shall be comforted in Jerusalem."[31]

Beyond providing comfort and all the basic survival needs for a child, a mother's greatest calling is passing on faith to her children. A

---

[30] Prov. 127:3.

[31] Isa. 66:13.

loving mother wants what is best for her child in this world and the next. Just like a father, a mother is to "train up a child in the way he should go; even when he is old he will not depart from it."[32] Children are to honor their father and mother. God requires you to "keep your father's commandment, and forsake not your mother's teaching."[33]

In the book of Proverbs, God reveals the desirable attributes of a Christian woman: "Strength and dignity are her clothing, and she laughs at the time to come. She opens her mouth with wisdom, and the teaching of kindness is on her tongue. She looks well to the ways of her household and does not eat the bread of idleness. Her children rise up and call her blessed; her husband also, and he praises her: 'Many women have done excellently, but you surpass them all.' Charm is deceitful, and beauty is vain, but a woman who fears the LORD is to be praised."[34]

There is a lot of pressure on mothers today. Too many are raising their children alone, with no help from absentee fathers. All women work long hours while raising a family and trying to meet the ever-growing cultural demand to be the All-American everywomen.

Despite these societal pressures, most mothers rise to the occasion when it comes to their children. Most work hard to make earthly homes that are safe and comforting for their children. In addition, Christian mothers want to inculcate in their children a desire to one day reach their heavenly home. Mothers know that what is best for their children is a growing and active faith in Jesus Christ. A mother's love can set her child on a path to the way, the truth, and the ultimate life.

---

[32] Prov. 22:6.

[33] Prov. 6:20.

[34] Prov. 31:25–30.

Your Life

In all the ways that Lincoln's two mothers blessed his life, what specifically did you find most special or touching about Nancy or Sarah?

Nancy and Sarah were strong Christians who not only talked about the faith but lived it. Moreover, they made it their mission to pass on the faith to their children. Both especially encouraged Lincoln's Bible reading. What faith legacy or legacies did your mother leave you?

In the Proverbs 31 passage, what does the Bible say in terms of encouraging wives or mothers how to live at all times?

3

Dating Game

But the Lord said to Samuel, "Do not look on his appearance or on the height of his stature, because I have rejected him. For the Lord sees not as man sees: man looks on the outward appearance, but the Lord looks on the heart."
—1 Samuel 16:7

The Lincoln Way

Relationships often offer opportunities for growth and learning—about others, the world, and one's self.

For all of Lincoln's renown, no one ever accused him of being a ladies' man. In fact, Lincoln acted awkwardly around young women, and they made fun of him for it. He once went to a party and shouted, "Oh boys, how clean these girls look."[1] On a different occasion, he called on a young woman named Anna Rodney and angered a family member of hers when he asked, "Is Miss Rodney handy?"[2]

His physical appearance and dress did not help his cause. He often came to social events wearing buckskin clothing and rough Conestoga boots, or trousers that were too short and exposed his shins. In an age when most men grew to be five feet six or seven, Lincoln reached six feet four and weighed over two hundred pounds by the age of seventeen. While he excelled at frontier games, or

[1] Donald, *Lincoln*, 84.

[2] Keneally, *Lincoln*, 33.

"trials" as they were called—jumping, running, hopping, pitching quoits, swimming, and shooting—these physical feats could not overshadow his singularly odd physical appearance. In addition to "tall" and "long," the most common words used to describe Lincoln were "ungainly," "stooped," "lanky," "long-armed," "gawky," "raw," and "bony"[3]—and these words came from people who liked him. Others routinely called him "homely," "grotesque," and, later in life, "baboon" and "gorilla." One witness claimed that Lincoln had longer arms than any human being he had ever seen. In truth, when his arms were at his sides, his fingers could touch a point lower on his legs (by nearly three inches) than that of a normal person.[4] The backwoods boy simply looked backwards and freakish to most young ladies.

Despite his inelegant appearance, the young Lincoln was interested in women. In his early twenties, while living in New Salem, Illinois, rumors circulated about his sexual adventures. He reportedly sired children with several different women, though at least one of these stories seems to have been a joke. Occasionally, Lincoln demonstrated a voyeuristic streak. He asked a New Salem farmer to notify him every time a mare and his stud horse were about to breed. The farmer did so, and Lincoln always attended. As a storyteller, Lincoln loved to share sexual jokes.[5] Giving a formal lecture on discoveries and interventions, he speculated on

---

[3] Miller, *Lincoln's Virtues,* 4.

[4] Goodwin, *Team of Rivals,* 50; Fox, *Lincoln's Body,* 7; Keneally, *Lincoln,* 23; Winkle, *Young Eagle,* 64; Wheeler, *Faith and Courage,* 56–57. Lincoln's legendary strength gave him confidence and notoriety on the frontier. He could take two axes by the ends of their handles and raise them, elbows locked, straight over his head. He could also lift and carry a six-hundred-pound chicken house. Lincoln's strength helped him become an outstanding wrestler. His successful wrestling match with Jack Armstrong, a leader of the Clary Grove Boys in New Salem, allowed him to become a respected member of that community.

[5] Burlingame, *Lincoln,* 1:199-200.

the first invention—the fig-leaf apron. Eve took the leading role, he explained, while Adam did nothing more than stand by and "thread the needle."[6]

The historical record is unclear, but he may have patronized prostitutes, as other militiamen did, at a brothel in Galena, Illinois, during his service in the Black Hawk War. His future law partner, William Herndon, however, later reported that Lincoln remained chaste until his first and only love, Ann Rutledge, died in 1835. In his misery after her passing, Herndon alleges that Lincoln and his best friend, Joshua Speed—a real ladies' man—became "quite *familiar*" with women.[7] According to Herndon, Lincoln also told him that he had acceded to a "devilish passion" for a girl in Beardstown, Illinois, and had contracted syphilis—something that some historians have speculated about in explaining why Lincoln would call off his engagement to Mary Todd.[8]

According to Speed, Lincoln visited a prostitute in Springfield but refused to go through with the act when he came up two dollars short of the required fee. When the prostitute indicated that she trusted him to pay the two dollars at a future date, Lincoln declined, insisting that he did not wish to act on credit in case he could not eventually pay. He also did not want to cheat the prostitute of her dues. When Lincoln offered her three dollars for her time, the woman declined and reportedly called Lincoln the most conscientious man she had ever known.[9]

Shortly after he arrived in New Salem in 1831, Lincoln boarded at the tavern of James Rutledge, who happened to be one of the founders of New Salem. There Lincoln met Rutledge's daughter Ann—an eighteen-year-old beauty who had blue eyes, light auburn hair, a rosy complexion, and cherry-red lips. She was an intelligent

---

6 Basler, Lincoln's Second Lecture on Discoveries and Inventions, February 11, 1859, *CW,* 3:360.

7 Burlingame, *Lincoln,* 1:198-199.

8 Burlingame, *Lincoln*, 1:198; Keneally, *Lincoln*, 19.

9 Wilson, *Herndon's Informants*, 719.

lady of exquisite beauty, renowned by many as the prettiest girl in New Salem. Ann dressed in simple but perfect taste, loved to sew and quilt, maintained a superb household, and demonstrated kindness and angelic sweetness to everyone she met.[10] Like many other men, Abe immediately took a liking to the vivacious tavern owner's daughter.

Unfortunately for Abe, Ann Rutledge was already engaged to another gentlemen, John McNamar, twelve years older than she. When Abe returned from the Black Hawk War in the summer of 1832, McNamar had already left for New York. McNamar soon found that his family's finances were in shambles. He did not return as promised and stopped sending letters home.

Lincoln felt sorry for Ann as the months of her fiancé's departure turned into years—but not too sorry. Soon he began escorting her on long evening walks. He did daily chores for her. They went to cornhuskings and quilting bees, and took horse rides together. They read and studied, sang from old hymn books, and conversed about the world. Eventually, they fell in love with one another—two intelligent, witty souls who enjoyed each other's company.

Most New Salem residents claimed they got engaged in 1835, but planned to delay their marriage for one year so Ann could honorably break her engagement to McNamar and Lincoln could finish the bar.[11] Ann Rutledge, recalled one neighbor, "was a woman of Exquisite beauty, but her intellect was quick, Sharp, deep & philosophic as well as brilliant ... She was beloved by everybody and everybody respected and loved her—so sweet & angelic she was." He added, "She was a woman worthy of Lincoln's love & she was most worthy of his."[12]

A storybook marriage, however, would never come to fruition. Ann Rutledge died on August 25, 1835, after contracting and

---

[10] White, *Lincoln*, 100; Wheeler, *Faith and Courage*, 78; Winkle, *Young Eagle*, 150.

[11] Burlingame, *Lincoln*, 1:99; Wheeler, *Faith and Courage*, 79.

[12] Wilson, *Herndon's Informants*, 21.

enduring typhoid fever for a few miserable weeks. While New Salem withstood one of the hottest and worst years of typhoid fever in its history, the strain of being engaged to two men certainly weakened her physical condition. In the months before she contracted the fever, Ann found herself unable to eat or sleep. Since McNamar failed to write or return to New Salem, she could not get a resolution to her guilt-ridden dilemma.[13]

When she was on her deathbed, Ann's persistent requests finally persuaded her physician to allow Lincoln to see her. No one knows what the two said to each other behind the closed door, but they both knew her life would end very soon.[14]

After Ann's life came to a tragic end, Lincoln seemed quite changed to local residents. He appeared lost, indifferent to the world around him, wrapped in profound thought, and with little to say.[15] He would take a gun and wander off into the woods by himself. Neighbors worried that he had lost his mind, and mobilized to keep him safe. Everybody "who knew & saw him pronounced him *crazy*," said one New Salem resident.[16] Soon Lincoln went into a severe depression and thought about committing suicide for months. He "told me that he felt like Committing Suicide often," remembered Mentor Graham.[17] Friends took turns watching over him. Another villager said, "Lincoln was locked up by his friends … to prevent derangement or suicide."[18] One reported that "we watched during

---

[13] Goodwin, *Team of Rivals*, 55. Several of Lincoln's friends perished in the epidemic of 1835. Wheeler, *Faith and Courage*, 80, 83. Soon after Ann Rutledge's death, John McNamar—with his mother, brothers, sisters, and an abundance of family possessions—returned to New Salem. He intended to finally reclaim his fiancée. Lincoln commiserated with him but let on nothing of what Ann had meant to him. McNamar decided to stay in New Salem and later married another.

[14] Kigel, *Becoming Lincoln*, 211,

[15] Shenk, *Lincoln's Melancholy*, 19.

[16] Wilson, *Herndon's Informants*, 397.

[17] Wilson, *Herndon's Informants*, 243.

[18] Wilson, *Herndon's Informants*, 13.

storms, fogs, damp gloomy weather ... for fear of an accident."[19] In a sane moment, Lincoln confided to a friend that he did not carry a knife because he worried about what he might do to himself when alone.[20] He told another that he could not bear the idea of the rain pelting Ann's grave.[21]

Lincoln had lost loved ones before—his brother Thomas, his sister Sarah, and his mother Nancy. By almost all accounts, however, Ann had been the love of his life. Lincoln thought he had found the one woman who, far from ridiculing him, made him feel special. His bouts with depression and melancholy, already present, increased significantly after Ann's passing. Some observers said he never regained the joy that Ann Rutledge brought out in him.[22]

Historians lament the fact that no correspondence between Ann and Abe remains in existence. While there are many testimonials from New Salem neighbors, no one truly knows the devastation he suffered with her passing. Many decades later, someone asked Lincoln about his dark days after her death. "I loved the woman dearly & sacredly," he said. "She was a handsome girl and would have made a good loving wife ... I did honestly & truly love this girl & think often of her now."[23]

As Lincoln slowly gathered himself from his heartbreak and depression, he threw himself into the study of law to distract from his misery. He also found a new girlfriend about a year after Ann died. Older, plumper, and better educated than Ann Rutledge, thanks to her wealthy Kentucky family, Mary Owens had black hair, dark eyes, fair skin, and magnificent white teeth. She impressed many with her sharp intellect, quick wit, conversation, and lively disposition. When Mary came to New Salem to visit her sister, Betsy Abell, in 1833, Lincoln enjoyed their conversations on politics

---

[19] Wilson, *Herndon's Informants,* 21.
[20] Wilson, *Herndon's Informants,* 205.
[21] Wilson, *Herndon's Informants,* 557.
[22] Shenk, *Lincoln's Melancholy,* 13–14.
[23] Wilson, *Herndon's Informants,* 440.

and found her affable.[24] After Ann died, Betsy suggested that Mary return to New Salem in 1836 to wed Abe.

Perhaps Abe was missing the intimate female companionship he had enjoyed with Ann. Whatever his motivation, he agreed to Betsey's proposal.[25]

Lincoln found Mary more rotund and less attractive than he remembered, however, when she arrived in 1836. Lincoln later told a friend that the "old maid" reminded him of his mother, "not from withered features, for her skin was too full of fat … but from her teeth, weather-beaten appearance in general, and … her present bulk in less than thirty five or forty years." In short, Lincoln "was not all pleased with her." Nevertheless, trying to persuade himself that Mary's inner qualities were noble and that he "had told her sister that I would take her for better or for worse," Lincoln wanted to stick to his word, especially since he believed "no other man on earth would have her."[26]

After they spent time together for several months, the courtship unraveled because the two simply had no chemistry together, and they knew it. Mary found Lincoln insensitive and devoid of chivalry. On one occasion, they were riding horses with other couples and came upon a creek. The other men gallantly helped their female companions cross, but not Mary's fiancé. Mary chided him for his lack of courtliness, and Lincoln laughed. He responded that he knew she could take care of herself.[27]

On another occasion, Abe and Mary accompanied Nancy Green, who felt compelled to carry her misbehaving forty-pound youngster up a steep hill. Mary badgered Lincoln for not offering to carry the child. When she told him that he would not make a good husband, Lincoln laughed off this incident too.[28]

---

24 Burlingame, *Lincoln,* 1:169-170.

25 Donald, *Lincoln*, 67.

26 Basler, Lincoln to Mrs. Orville Browning, April 1, 1838, *CW*, 1:117–19.

27 Burlingame, *Lincoln*, 1:170–71.

28 Wilson, *Herndon's Informants*, 262.

A year after Lincoln died, Mary reflected that Lincoln had a good heart but "was deficient in those little links which make up the great chain of a woman's happiness." She admitted that her "feelings were not sufficiently enlisted to have the matter consummated."[29]

Lincoln attempted to talk Mary out of their engagement in the spring of 1837. He insisted that she "would not be satisfied" with him, especially since she would have to be "poor without the means of hiding your poverty." Lincoln wondered if she "could bear" being poor. "My opinion is that you had better not do it," since the hardship would exceed what she had been accustomed to living in Kentucky.[30] Nonetheless, with a deep sense of duty and to fulfill his pledge, he asked for Mary's hand in marriage.

Then came a stunner: Mary Owens rejected this proposal and several follow-up proposals. Lincoln found himself "mortified almost beyond endurance." His "vanity was deeply wounded by the reflection." Humiliated that someone would reject "me with all my fancied greatness," Lincoln admitted that he had "made a fool of myself." He concluded that he would never marry and would "never be satisfied with any one who would be block-head enough to have me."[31] Eventually, Lincoln believed that Mary and her family rejected him because of his inferior social class, appearance, pedigree, and education. He battled this inferiority complex most of his adult life.[32]

While embarrassing at the time, the rejection may have been opportune; Mary Owens apparently did not measure up to the high bar that Ann Rutledge had set in Lincoln's life. Mary filled a void. To use the modern vernacular, she provided a rebound relationship. His courtship of Mary lacked the romance and passion he had felt for Ann. Both relationships ended suddenly, shockingly, and in hurtful ways.

---

[29] Wilson, *Herndon's Informants,* 256.

[30] Basler, Lincoln to Mary Owens, May 7, 1837, *CW,* 1:78.

[31] Basler, Lincoln to Mrs. Orville Browning, April 1, 1838, *CW,* 1:117–19.

[32] Burlingame, *Lincoln*, 1:171–72.

Lincoln learned a lot about himself and life during his courtship days. While there had been joys in his dating life, there had also been profound heartbreak. Love brought both joy and sorrow. Moreover, as mentally tough and disciplined as he remained, he learned that he could break down emotionally and psychologically. Melancholy was a thorn in his side for the rest of his life. Debilitating depression resurfaced periodically. Yet he proved—with the help of friends, doctors, and an inner core of persistence and grit—that he could recover.

If he were ever to marry in the future, perhaps he would find someone who could meet his expectations and love him and his peculiarities without undue drama. Perhaps.

The Truth

Abraham Lincoln, like the rest of us, sinned and made mistakes. While the historical record is not conclusive on his sex life before marriage, we know that many struggle to "flee youthful passions"[33] and "flee sexual immorality."[34] The Bible teaches that "marriage be held in honor among all," and that "the marriage bed be undefiled, for God will judge the sexually immoral and adulterous."[35]

Before we judge Lincoln or others too harshly, however, we as Christians must remember that Jesus said anyone "who looks at a woman with lustful intent has already committed adultery with her in his heart."[36] To be sure, one would be hard pressed to find anyone who has not committed adultery in his heart. Of course, there is the other side of the coin, where people have no problem with fornication or sexual hookups. They want to be their own gods

[33] 2 Tim. 2:22.

[34] 1 Cor. 6:18.

[35] Heb. 13:4.

[36] Matt. 5:28.

and live lives without guilty consciences. They want to do what is right in their own eyes.[37]

Sometimes in our fallen state, we try to do what is right but cannot, due to our weak and sinful flesh. As the Bible explains, even though we know what is right and wrong, we still choose the wrong. We have "the desire to do what is right, but not the ability to carry it out." We do not want to do wrong, but we do it anyway because of "the sin that dwells within" us.[38]

What about melancholy and depression? Before the fall of Adam and Eve, these medical conditions did not exist. God created a perfect world and everything He touched was "very good."[39] After the Fall, sin entered the world and brought melancholy and depression.

No one chooses to be melancholy or depressed. Yet many suffer from these conditions, as did Lincoln. Depression, for example, is one of the leading causes of death today and is a growing problem, particularly for young people. Some forms of melancholy and depression need to be dealt with by professionals. Almost all of us, however, endure bouts of despondency, sadness, anxiety, and worry in our lives.

The Bible does not promise that good and faithful Christians will be immune to these challenges in their lives. Instead, the Bible says that "when the righteous cry for help, the Lord hears and delivers them out of all their troubles. The Lord is near to the brokenhearted and saves the crushed in spirit."[40] Jesus exhorts, "Come to me, all who labor and are heavy laden, and I will give you rest."[41] Scripture clearly and frequently asserts that God will always be with us, but especially in gloomy and despondent times. "Fear not, for I am with you," God reminds us. "Be not dismayed, for I am your God; I will strengthen you, I will help you, I will uphold you with my righteous

---

[37] Josh. 17:6.

[38] Rom. 7:15–20.

[39] Gen. 1:31.

[40] Ps. 34:17–18.

[41] Matt. 11:18.

right hand."[42] The challenge is for us to remember to call on our Lord and Savior, and to listen to His voice and caring guidance.

Of course we often want our pain to leave immediately. "Answer me quickly, O Lord! My spirit fails! Hide not your face from me, lest I be like those who go down to the pit." The Psalmist, however, continues by encouraging us to turn to our loving and caring God: "Let me hear in the morning of your steadfast love, for in you I trust. Make me know the way I should go, for to you I lift up my soul."[43] Indeed, God's timing and thoughts are different and higher than ours.[44]

While we may not always see or fully understand the reasons for our suffering beyond the fact that we live in a sinful, fallen world, one positive outcome of trying experiences can be a closer relationship with God. Jesus promises that He will always be with us in good times and bad. David knew this comfort: "Even though I walk through the valley of the shadow of death, I will fear no evil, for you are with me; your rod and your staff, they comfort me."[45] Jesus came into the world so that "you may have peace," even though He acknowledges that "in the world you will have tribulation. But take heart; I have overcome the world."[46] Indeed, our Lord "heals the brokenhearted and binds up their wounds."[47] We can find joy, peace, and contentment knowing that Jesus is a lamp that lightens our darkness.[48] As the Bible says, "Blessed be the God and Father of our Lord Jesus Christ, the Father of mercies and God of all comfort, who comforts us in all our affliction, so that we may be able to comfort

---

[42] Isa. 41:10.
[43] Ps. 143:7–8.
[44] Isa. 55:8–9.
[45] Ps. 23:4.
[46] John 16:33.
[47] Psalm 147:3.
[48] 2 Sam. 22:29.

those who are in any affliction, with the comfort with which we ourselves are comforted by God."[49]

Your Life

Both male and female contemporaries mocked Lincoln for his physical appearance and awkwardness. Have you ever been ridiculed for your physical appearance? How did this teasing have an impact on you?

How does dating help prepare a Christian for what to look for in a potential spouse? How can dating experiences cause anxiety, hurt, despondency, and even depression?

Melancholy and depression hit Lincoln hard after Ann Rutledge's death and would remain psychological obstacles for the rest of his life. Melancholy and depression are serious issues for many people today and can often only be overcome with professional help and the grace of God. What encouragement does the Bible provide for you when you might be depressed?

---

[49] 2 Cor. 1:3–4.

4

Something about Mary

He who finds a wife finds a good thing
and obtains favor from the Lord.
—Proverbs 18:22

The Lincoln Way

Leaders must be committed.

On November 4, 1842, Abraham Lincoln married Mary Todd in front of a fireplace in her sister's home in Springfield, Illinois. Lincoln was ten years older than Mary. He wrote to a friend a few days later, "Nothing new here, except my marrying"—which, to Lincoln, remained a "matter of profound wonder."[1]

The real wonder is that the marriage came to fruition at all, considering their uneven and unconventional courtship as well as divergent backgrounds. Mary was the daughter of Robert Todd, a prosperous merchant, mill owner, banker, state senator, and slave owner in Lexington, Kentucky. She had grown up with privilege and the finer things in life. She attended the best of private schools, studying grammar, geography, arithmetic, penmanship, singing, poetry, and literature. She also learned to speak and write French. Having mastered the dances and social etiquette of a Southern belle, she completed her education at the age of seventeen and was considered fully prepared for marriage.

---

[1] Basler, Lincoln to Samuel Marshall, November 11, 1842, *CW*, 1:305.

Soon she moved to the new state capital in Springfield, Illinois—a place where prosperous, eligible bachelors roamed and young, single women came to meet them. She lived with her sister Elizabeth Edwards and Elizabeth's husband, Ninian, as well as three cousins.[2]

Moving to Springfield meant that Mary could finally escape an overcrowded home and what she referred to as a "desolate" childhood.[3] Having lost her mother, Eliza Todd, when Mary was just six, Mary watched her beloved father remarry seventeen months later—much too soon for her liking. His new wife, the former Elizabeth Humphreys, produced nine children in the next fifteen years, adding to the six living children from Robert Todd's first marriage.

Eliza Todd's children resented their inhospitable stepmother, who conspicuously favored her own children while treating her stepchildren with cold indifference. Perhaps what hurt Mary and her siblings the most was that their father gave his new wife almost all his attention. Mary's mother may have been the one who physically passed away, but she felt that her father had disappeared too. Moreover, as a high-strung, oversensitive individual from the beginning, Mary did not receive the training she needed in useful virtues such as patience and self-control. As one historian asserts, she always demonstrated an "orphan's questing edginess and insecurity."[4]

Interestingly, Eliza Todd's children grew critical of slavery as they matured, while their stepfamily increasingly rose to the peculiar institution's defense.[5] The divide over slavery only added to the discord, and would also cause problems for Mary later as the nation's First Lady.

---

[2] Donald, *Lincoln*, 84; Oates, *With Malice Toward None*, 54.

[3] Turner and Turner, Mary Lincoln to Eliza Stuart Steele, May 23, 1871, *Mary Todd Lincoln*, 588–89.

[4] Keneally, *Lincoln*, 35; Turner and Turner, *Mary Todd Lincoln*, 4–5.

[5] Winkle, *Young Eagle*, 160–61; Packard, *Lincolns in the White House*, 16; Oates, *With Malice Toward None*, 53–54.

Ninian and Elizabeth Edwards were two of the leading Whigs and socialites in Springfield, and their hilltop mansion served as a scenic place for young couples to mingle and picnic.[6] The Edwards home was where Abe and Mary first met, late in 1839.

Mary Todd certainly stood out. At twenty-one years of age, she was pert, intense, lively, and bright-eyed. She was buxom, with a glowing complexion, abundant auburn hair, and shapely arms and shoulders (which she displayed liberally for the time). Ninian Edwards once said Mary "could make a bishop forget his prayers."[7] Politically astute and a terrific flirt, she had plenty of male suitors—including Stephen Douglas, the man whom her future husband would famously debate in the 1858 Illinois Senate race.[8]

The relationship started on the dance floor. Their striking physical differences—he was tall, lanky, haggard, and plain, while she was short, buxom, perky, and pretty—made for an odd-looking couple. Their differing pedigrees were also evident—a "Bluegrass daughter" of a well-to-do Southern family paired with the "bottomland" son of Thomas and Nancy Hanks.[9] Apparently, their first dance did not go well. "Miss Todd, I want to dance with you in the worst way," Lincoln offered that first night. While she

---

6 Oates, *With Malice Toward None*, 52.

7 Keneally, *Lincoln*, 35; Donald, *Lincoln Reconsidered*, 81.

8 Shenk, *Lincoln's Melancholy*, 47. The 5' 4" Stephen Douglas and 5' 2" Mary Todd had a lot going for each other besides their relative heights. Douglas proposed to Mary, and the couple almost got engaged. Political differences may have been the only obstacle keeping them from marriage. As a staunch Whig, Mary could not bring herself to wed a resolute Democrat. Ironically, after being rejected, Douglas allegedly told Mary that she had "thrown away" her best chance to "rule in the White House" (Leidner, *Lincoln's Gift*, 37). Later, when Mary became the First Lady in the White House, she revealed to a confidante that she had turned Douglas's proposal down with these prophetic words: "I can't consent to be your wife. I shall become Mrs. President, or I am the victim of false prophets, but it will not be as Mrs. Douglas" (Baker, *Mary Todd Lincoln*, 84–85).

9 Baker, *Mary Todd Lincoln*, 84.

accepted, Mary later playfully recounted the dance to her cousin Elizabeth, saying that he "certainly" danced in the worst way.[10]

Despite their obvious differences, the couple had much in common besides their Kentucky roots. Both had lost their mothers at an early age. One reason Abraham might have been attracted to Mary is that she possessed protective, maternal instincts. Both liked poetry and Shakespeare and would often read stories to each other. Both were intellectually curious and believed in the value of education and self-improvement. Both loved politics and the Whig Party. In fact, Mary loved talking politics more than was socially acceptable for ladies in those days. She enjoyed attending parades, listening to speeches, and talking about the 1840 presidential election with her future husband. Both wanted to reside in the Executive Mansion someday.[11]

By the late summer of 1840, Mary and Abe were "a-courtin'," and they got engaged in December. Then, rather suddenly to the Springfield community, Abe terminated the engagement. For a compilation of reasons, Lincoln had concluded that he and Mary were simply not compatible for marriage. For starters, while the Edwards family probably had no problem with Abe and Mary's interaction as long as they were in groups, they did not approve of a more serious relationship. They refused to endorse a match. Eventually, they forbade Abe from appearing at their home.

The Edwards and Todd families were probably at first bewildered, then deeply disturbed at the impending matrimony. They had hoped that Mary would come to see the incongruity of each partner's long-term prospects. The hostility the Edwardses directed toward Lincoln, especially Mary's sister Elizabeth, caused Lincoln great personal anguish and embarrassment and only added to his insecurity about women and marriage. Abe may have understandably grown bitter

---

[10] White, *Lincoln*, 110.

[11] Manning, *Father Lincoln*, 22; White, *Lincoln*, 110; Baker, *Mary Todd Lincoln*, 85–86; O'Reilly, *Killing Lincoln*, 155–56.

toward Mary's family for how they treated him. Only one "d" existed in the word "God," Lincoln remarked, but two "d's" were required to spell "Todd."[12]

In addition, Mary's constant teasing, which veered into verbal abuse, over his social inadequacies certainly made a psychological impact on Lincoln and may have reopened old wounds. Perhaps he really came to fear that he could not make a suitable income or provide a home for his future well-to-do spouse. If Mary harangued him for his appearance, behavior, and social status now, she would not react well later, when they lived beneath the standard of her upbringing. As young attorney and legislator, Lincoln knew that his income would fluctuate and had no guarantees.

There were many other pressures building on Lincoln at this time. He knew his law partnership with John Stuart, who had been in Washington for two years and had been reelected to serve in Congress for two more, would soon be dissolved. His best friend, Joshua Speed, was moving to Kentucky with his new bride. Lincoln still owed money on his personal "national debt" from failed business ventures in New Salem.[13] Furthermore, ever since the Panic of 1837, the internal improvements program to which he had dedicated his political life and reputation had all but bankrupted the state of Illinois. By 1839, with mounting debt and corruption among private builders, projects were being shut down.

In national politics, William Henry Harrison, the Whig candidate for whom Lincoln had campaigned so rigorously, won the presidency but lost the state of Illinois. Having politicked in front of hostile crowds and neglected his law practice, Lincoln returned to Springfield physically exhausted, emotionally spent, and financially diminished. Yet he got no relief. He had to take on a heavy caseload to make up for the time he'd missed. Due to the crushing state

---

[12] Oates, *With Malice Toward None*, 55–56; Baker, *Mary Todd Lincoln*, 89; Turner and Turner, *Mary Todd Lincoln*, 24.

[13] Donald, *Lincoln*, 87; Wheeler, *Faith and Courage*, 96.

debt, the Illinois legislature was preparing a vote to eliminate the state bank, a pillar of the Whig program. It was necessary to prevent a quorum of legislators to stymie the vote. Lincoln literally had to jump out of a window to make this happen. A local newspaper joked that Lincoln was not hurt "as it was noticed that his legs reached nearly from the window to the ground!"[14]

In addition to political, economic, and class considerations, Lincoln may have contracted a venereal disease. He would not have wanted to infect Mary or father defective children, as manuals at the time stated definitively would happen.[15]

The bottom line is that Lincoln was confronting many traumatic, potentially life-altering situations at the same time as his engagement and with a marriage date in clear sight.

For their part, Elizabeth and Ninian Edwards claimed that the engagement ended because of Mary's "flirtations" with Senator Douglas and their own assertions that the couple "were raised differently and had no congruity, no feelings" and were not "alike." When Mary "flirted with Douglas in order to spur Lincoln to a greater love," Lincoln "was undemonstrative" and "somewhat

---

[14] Shenk, *Lincoln's Melancholy*, 45–46.

[15] Baker, *Mary Todd Lincoln*, 87–88; Keneally, *Lincoln*, 37–38; Fox, *Lincoln's Body*, 287. More than 50 percent of nineteenth-century men contracted a venereal disease. Historians still debate whether Lincoln had syphilis. William Herndon is the only one to provide any evidence on this topic. Lincoln allegedly took mercury pills three times a day—the preferred treatment for syphilis since the sixteenth century. Lincoln confided to Herndon that he had contracted the disease in 1836 when he went to Beardstown where he had a "devilish passion" and caught the disease from a prostitute. Often the first symptoms of syphilis—the venereal sores—and lesions of primary syphilis eventually vanish but may return years later in the form of a rash, lesions on hands and feet, and on one's back. Either Lincoln caught the disease or thought he did. He even wrote to Dr. Daniel Drake of Cincinnati, "the Benjamin Franklin of the West," to seek treatment of whatever ailed him (Epstein, *Portrait of a Marriage*, 19).

cold."[16] Lincoln may have thought that Mary wanted to be released from their engagement, since she continued flirting with other men, including a Whig widower named Edwin Webb and Lincoln's good friend Joseph Gillespie. Everyone in Springfield knew that Mary Todd had a great many beaus.[17]

The tipping point for Lincoln's dissolution of the engagement, however, most likely occurred because of a pretty new arrival in November 1840. Despite the fact that he was almost twice her age, Lincoln fell in love with eighteen-year old Matilda Edwards, cousin of Ninian Edwards. Matilda came to Springfield for the winter, accompanied by her father, a member of the general assembly. A tall, graceful, self-assured, curly-haired blonde who had a gentle temperament, Matilda would receive marriage proposals from twenty-two men before eventually marrying. Even Mary admitted that she had never seen a more beautiful girl than Matilda Edwards. She also noticed that Matilda had drawn an entourage of interested suitors—including Lincoln.

Some of Lincoln's friends observed that he would not leave Matilda's side. They criticized him for giving her so much attention while engaged to Mary. Perhaps Lincoln's decision to end his engagement with Mary revolved around a guilty conscience.[18] Lincoln's best friend, Joshua Speed, later stated that "Lincoln did love Miss Edwards" and "Mary saw it." She knew this to be "the reason of his change of mind."[19] Many years later, Elizabeth and Ninian

---

[16] Wilson, *Herndon's Informants*, 623.

[17] Shenk, *Lincoln's Melancholy*, 49. Mary may have been flirting to tease out Lincoln's interest. Maybe she had not decided yet and wanted an open field. Or perhaps she strayed, as Lincoln would with Matilda Edwards. In 1865, Mary wrote an interesting letter in which she admitted that she had "doubtless trespassed, many times & oft, upon his great tenderness & amiability of character" two years before they eventually wed.

[18] Shenk, *Lincoln's Melancholy*, 48; Burlingame, *Lincoln*, 1:183; Goodwin, *Team of Rivals*, 97.

[19] Wilson, *Herndon's Informants*, 475.

Edwards claimed that Mary released Abe from their engagement due to his interest in Matilda Edwards. Mary let Lincoln go "to set herself right and to free Mr Lincoln's mind." Yet Mary let it be known that she "had not Changed her mind, but felt as always."[20]

Whatever the reasons, Lincoln eventually drafted a breakup letter and asked Joshua Speed to deliver it for him. Speed refused. Abe finally went to Mary and told her that he did not love her. When Mary began to weep, however, he lost his nerve. He found himself in tears and then embraced and kissed her. The engagement stayed intact, but just for a few more days. Lincoln met Mary a second time on January 1, 1841—a date that Lincoln would later refer to as the "Fatal First."[21] They quarreled and ended the engagement. Mary sent a letter releasing him while acknowledging that she still loved him the way she always had.[22]

The breakup forced a major breakdown. Lincoln could not sleep. Rarely absent from the Illinois legislature, he now missed many sessions and votes, including an unheard-of six consecutive days of

---

20 Wilson, *Herndon's Informants,* 444.

21 Shenk, *Lincoln's Melancholy*, 55. The "Fatal First" of November 1841 was also the day Speed's partnership in the store officially dissolved, ending his business ties to Springfield and allowing him to head for Kentucky. Lincoln, who had lived with Speed above the store, had to move out. January 1, 1841, marked the deadline for the state of Illinois to pay its debt, largely accrued because of the internal improvements program Lincoln had championed. If the state did not make its debt payment, it would go into receivership. Furthermore, Shenk suggests that Lincoln learned on this day that Speed had proposed to Matilda Edwards the previous night. In Lincoln's time, New Year's Eve had a prominent place on the social calendar—traditionally a time when male suitors declared their intentions. It is also interesting to note that Ninian Edwards later told William Herndon that he wanted Lincoln's best friend, Joshua Speed, to marry Matilda and Abe to wed Mary for political reasons. Yet Matilda refused to marry Speed as she had Stephan Douglas (Wilson, *Herndon's Informants,* 133).

22 Goodwin, *Team of Rivals*, 98; Donald, *Lincoln*, 87; Baker, *Mary Todd Lincoln*, 90–91.

the January session. When he did come, he appeared hollow-eyed, unshaven, and emaciated. He could not speak above a whisper.[23] He became the talk of the town, and the local newspaper poked fun at his "indisposition." [24] Lincoln was confined to bed and required medical attention. When not at the legislature, he spent many hours in the presence of Dr. Anson Henry, who diagnosed him with "hypochondriaism."[25] Lincoln fell into a deep depression.

Ninian Edwards told Herndon that Lincoln became "crazy as a loon" after the breakup.[26] His depression grew so dark, friends had to remove all razors, knives, and pistols[27]—anything that could be used to inflict self-harm—from his room so "that he might not commit suicide."[28] Another friend said Lincoln "came within an inch of being a perfect lunatic for life."[29] Even Lincoln declared himself the "most miserable man living ... To remain as I am is impossible; I must die or be better it appears to me."[30]

In nineteenth-century America, a matrimonial pledge was considered a legally binding contract, much like any commercial agreement. The rejected had the right to seek damages via litigation. As an attorney who had represented a plaintiff in such a "breach of promise" suit, Lincoln knew this better than almost anyone.

Even more than legalities, however, Lincoln treasured his integrity. He had extended himself and pledged his allegiance to Mary, and then pulled back. His conscience troubled him immensely, and he fell apart, knowing the thing he cared about most—his reputation—had been severely damaged.[31]

---

[23] Epstein, *Portrait of a Marriage*, 26.

[24] Shenk, *Lincoln's Melancholy*, 57.

[25] Basler, Lincoln to John Stuart, January 20, 1841, *CW*, 1:228.

[26] Wilson, *Herndon's Informants*, 133.

[27] Wilson, *Herndon's Informants*, 475.

[28] Hertz, *The Hidden Lincoln*, 37.

[29] Baker, *Mary Todd Lincoln*, 90-91.

[30] Baker, *Mary Todd Lincoln*, 90–91.

[31] Shenk, *Lincoln's Melancholy*, 48.

Lincoln tried to rise out of his severe melancholy. In August 1841, Lincoln visited Joshua Speed at his Farmington, Kentucky, plantation. His good friend lifted his spirits. Speed's mother gave Lincoln a Bible and urged him to read it and embrace its precepts and promises.[32] "Tell your mother that I have not got her 'present' with me," Lincoln wrote while on the circuit a few weeks later, "but that I intend to read it regularly when I return home." He did not doubt that Scripture was "the best cure for the 'Blues' could one but take it according to the truth."[33]

Meanwhile Mary did her best to deal with their breakup, even as they both resided in Springfield. She was a tormented soul, but not as much as Lincoln. She hoped he would get over his melancholy. To her credit, though her friends belittled Lincoln's bumpkin-like qualities and suitors continued to pursue her, Mary saw enormous potential in the man.[34] "Lincoln deems me unworthy of notice," she wrote a friend, "as I have not met him in the gay world for months." She maintained that "others were seldom gladdened by his presence" as much as her. She wished "that 'Richard' should be himself again." Her reference to Shakespeare's tortured Richard II—a deposed English king who talked of "graves, worms, and epitaphs"—not only revealed the common fondness she and Abe shared for the Bard but also her keen recognition of the specialness of Lincoln.[35]

As the weeks of 1841 and early 1842 passed, Lincoln poured himself into his law work. His partnership with Stuart dissolved, but he formed a new one with Stephen T. Long, an active leader in the Whig Party.[36] He also briefly dated and proposed to a sixteen year-old girl named Sarah Rickard, the sister of Mrs. William Butler, at whose home Lincoln boarded. Showing his normal good humor,

---

[32] Donald, *Lincoln*, 88–89.

[33] Basler, Lincoln to Mary Speed, September 27, 1841, *CW*, 1:261.

[34] Keneally, *Lincoln*, 38-39.

[35] Baker, *Mary Todd Lincoln*, 91.

[36] Oates, *With Malice Toward None*, 58–59.

Lincoln insisted that a Sarah should marry an Abraham. She rejected his offer, however, explaining that he felt too much like an older brother rather than a potential marriage partner.[37]

Still, Lincoln could not completely shake his despondency or be happy knowing how badly he had hurt Mary. "That still kills my soul," he told Speed.[38]

Joshua Speed played a crucial role in Lincoln's comeback and eventual reconciliation with Mary. After Speed took a bride, Lincoln asked him repeatedly about his happiness, or lack thereof, in marriage. Joyously content, Speed surprised Lincoln with his strong endorsement of married life. Speed later said that "if I had not been married & happy, far more happy than I ever expected to be," Lincoln "would not have married."[39]

To Speed, Lincoln confided his regret at not being able to keep his word to Mary. "Before I resolve to do the one thing or the other," he wrote his friend in the summer of 1842, "I must regain my confidence in my own ability to keep my resolves when they are made"—something Lincoln once "prided myself as the only, or at least the chief, gem of my character." Until he regained this character gem, he could not trust himself "in any matter of much importance." He went on to say that he had always been "superstitious," and that "God made me one of the instruments of bringing your Fanny and you together," a union Lincoln had "no doubt He had fore-ordained." He concluded by quoting Scripture: "What he designs, he will do for *me* yet. 'Stand *still* and see the salvation of the Lord' is my text just now."[40]

As would be the case in many different vocations of his life, Lincoln made a comeback. Sometime in 1842, more than a year after Mary and Abe broke their engagement, Eliza Francis, wife of local newspaper editor Simeon Francis, invited each to her home,

---

37 Burlingame, '*Lincoln*, 1:187; Shenk, *Lincoln's Melancholy*, 56.

38 Basler, Lincoln to Joshua Speed, March 27, 1842, *CW*, 1:282.

39 Wilson, *Herndon's Informants*, 431.

40 Basler, Lincoln to Joshua Speed, July 4, 1842, *CW*, 1:289–90.

unbeknownst to the other. Once both of them were sitting in her parlor, she encouraged them to be friends again.

Soon they began meeting discreetly at the Francis home and at the home of Lincoln's physician and Whig friend, Dr. Anson Henry. Dr. Henry probably encouraged the reunification in the belief that marriage would be good medicine for Abe.[41]

Partisan politics also helped bring Mary and Abe back together. The State Bank of Illinois, which Lincoln had often defended in the state legislature, had been forced to close. Its notes became worthless. As commerce slowed in the state, James Shields, the Democratic state auditor, declared that the bank's notes would not be accepted as payment for taxes. Only gold and silver coin would be accepted. Seeing a growing threat to the Illinois economy, Lincoln satirized Shields in the *Sangamo Journal*, in a series of letters supposedly written by a rough, uneducated, but shrewd widow named Rebecca. Mary and a friend who shared the same political passion took over the writing of the series.[42]

Sometime in the summer of 1842, the conflict got personal when Shields found himself at a dinner at a friend's house along with Mary and Abe. Shields was aggressively courting Mary's best friend, Julia Jayne, at the time. He gave Julia relentless uninvited attention, pressing up next to her at dinner parties and seeking her hand beneath tables. In antebellum America, eligible ladies often kept a pin or two tucked at the waistband as a defense against gentlemen who crossed the line of decency. When Shields made one too many unwanted moves against Julia, she pinned him. Thanks to Mary, Lincoln knew the backdrop of the situation and laughed when Shields expressed pain, amazement, and anger.

Later that week, the *Sangamo Journal* published a particularly pointed attack on Shields that included a reference to the pinning incident. Thoroughly embarrassed, Shields demanded a formal

---

41 White, *Lincoln*, 113; Donald, *Lincoln*, 90; Shenk, *Lincoln's Melancholy*, 94.

42 Donald, *Lincoln*, 90–92; Keneally, *Lincoln*, 41–42.

apology and satisfaction from the unidentified writer, who by this time was Mary, her friend, or both.[43]

Wanting to protect Mary and her friend, Lincoln stepped forward and identified himself as the author of the Rebecca letters. Shields then proposed a duel, and Lincoln accepted. After crossing over the river into Missouri, where dueling was legal, the seconds and friends of Lincoln and Shields talked them out of the duel.

The Shields episode revealed much about the reconciliation and growing relationship between Mary and Abe. They bonded over their attacks on the state's Democratic auditor. The entire affair provided much-needed amusement and an emotional reset for both. Impressed with Abe's chivalric defense, Mary sensed his deeper commitment to her. Six weeks after the duel with Shields ended peacefully, Abe and Mary finally married.[44]

For Lincoln, the Shields incident was one of the most important turning points in his life. Lincoln prided himself on being a peacemaker, one who settled quarrels rather than started them. He realized he had a deeper problem. Two years earlier, he had savagely ridiculed Jessie Thomas in a campaign speech. While the crowd rolled with laughter and loved the wicked mimicry, Lincoln saw the absolute misery on Thomas's face. His own boorish behavior bothered him so much that he sought out Thomas the next day and apologized. However, the damage had already been done, and the incident long remained known as "the skinning of Thomas."

Two years later, Lincoln repeated the same kind of cruelty and stupidity with Shields, and it embarrassed him. He wanted to do better and be kinder. Lincoln never wrote another anonymous letter, and he instructed Mary very clearly never to mention the event again. When an army officer brought up the duel to Lincoln during

---

43 Epstein, *Portrait of a Marriage,* 39–41.

44 Baker, *Mary Todd Lincoln*, 95–97.

the Civil War, Lincoln admonished the man that if he wanted to remain friends with Lincoln, he should never do so again.[45]

Ignoring the taboo of marrying on a Friday, Mary and Abe exchanged vows in front of approximately thirty people on November 4, 1842, in the home of Ninian and Elizabeth Edwards, with Reverend Charles Dresser, an Episcopal minister, presiding.[46] Lincoln gave Mary a wedding ring with the inscription "Love is Eternal." Later that night, he drove their carriage through a heavy rain to the Globe Tavern, where Lincoln had rented a single room as their home.[47]

Though Mary and Abe's reconciliation had been on display for months, many were still surprised at the hastily arranged nuptial. Some described the marriage as a political union or policy match all around—he got social prestige and closer access to the movers and shakers in the Whig Party, while she got public prominence and a direct connection to a rising political star. Others insisted that he married for honor, duty, and the integrity of his word.[48]

Elizabeth Todd Edwards, Mary's sister, who had been so critical of their engagement a year before, offered an interesting perspective later. Lincoln had always been charmed with Mary's wit, wisdom, and conversation, she noted. When Mary spoke, he "would listen and gaze upon her as if drawn by some superior power, irresistibly so" and "never scarcely say a word."[49] Edwards admitted that she

---

[45] Wheeler, *Faith and Courage*, 94–94; Donald, *Lincoln*, 90–92.

[46] Oates, *With Malice Toward None*, 63. Sadly, not one member of Lincoln's family received an invitation or attended his wedding. Thomas and Sarah Lincoln knew nothing about the wedding until he dropped by weeks later, on business in Coles County, and told them.

[47] Epstein, *Portrait of a Marriage*, 51; Oates, *With Malice Toward None*, 63.

[48] Owen, *The Man and His Faith*, 52; Keneally, *Lincoln*, 42; Burlingame, *Lincoln*, 1:196–97.

[49] Wilson, *Herndon's Informants*, 443–45. The quotes in the remainder paragraph are all attributed to the same interview Elizabeth Todd Edwards gave to William Herndon.

did not think Mary and Abe were "suitable to each other & said so to Mary." Nevertheless, Mary "was an extremely ambitious woman," and believed that she "was destined to be the wife of some future President. Said it in my presence in Springfield and said it in earnest." Mary chose Lincoln over Douglas because she thought Lincoln had a better chance of being president. Even though Elizabeth Edwards frowned upon Mary and Abraham's relationship during the first go-around because "their natures, mind, education, raising etc. were so different" and "they could not live happy as husband and wife," she eventually said favorable things about Lincoln—conveniently after his assassination: "I respect & love Mr Lincoln, think he was a great man, a good man & an honest one."

The historical record shows that there was indeed something special about Mary Todd Lincoln. Out of all of Robert Todd's children, Mary was the only one who ventured outside of a traditional aristocratic track and showed some audacity in marrying a man like Lincoln. The fact that she saw greatness in a freakish-looking, self-taught, penniless lawyer born in the backwoods is a credit to her intuition. Any successes he might have would only add luster to her decision and persistence.[50]

On their wedding day, one of the groomsmen said that "Lincoln looked and acted like as if he was going to the Slaughter."[51] Lincoln admitted that he felt pressured into the marriage. While he was dressing for the ceremony, someone asked him where he was headed. Lincoln replied, "To hell I suppose."[52]

Over the next twenty-three years, the Lincoln marriage endured many trials, but had its share of heavenly moments too. Mary relentlessly pushed her husband toward greatness while also causing him innumerable hardships. Lincoln provided Mary support and life purpose while also failing to completely understand her sacrifices.

---

50 Turner and Turner, *Mary Todd Lincoln*, 4.

51 Wilson, *Herndon's Informants*, 251.

52 Donald, *Lincoln*, 1:93.

The story of the Lincoln courtship is filled with timeless themes and everyday, real-world experiences—a clash of two socioeconomic statuses; separation and reconciliation; sickness and recovery; honor and integrity; patience and persistence; ambition and love; mercy and grace. We all can learn from it.

The Truth

One of Lincoln's self-acknowledged low points in his life was when he publicly mocked James Shields. Most of us have probably hurt someone with our sarcasm, whether intentionally or unintentionally, or had our own feelings hurt by words from someone else.

The Bible says, "Let no corrupting talk come out of your mouths, but only such as is good for building up, as fits the occasion, that it may give grace to those who hear."[53] According to Scripture, "A fool gives full vent to his spirit, but a wise man quietly holds it back."[54] Moreover, God's Word encourages Christians to remember our identity and the witness we give to others, even in the spoken or written word. God is "our Father; we are the clay, and you are our potter; we are all the work of your hand."[55]

People judge Christians based on what we do and what we say. Made in the image of God and redeemed by His Son on the cross, we are to remember that Jesus died for every soul on this earth. Jesus did not go up on a cross so that we could take people down with harsh and unkind words. The Bible is filled with passages that exhort us to "keep your tongue from evil and your lips from speaking deceit."[56] Therefore our prayer and Christ-centered standard should always

---

53 Eph. 4:29.

54 Prov. 29:11.

55 Isa. 64:8.

56 Ps. 34:13.

be to "let the words of my mouth and the meditation of my heart be acceptable in your sight, O Lord, my rock and my redeemer."[57]

The words we speak at weddings are significant. God's Word tells us, "It is not good that the man should be alone; I will make him a helper fit for him … Therefore a man shall leave his father and his mother and hold fast to his wife, and they shall become one flesh."[58]

Jesus reiterated the magnitude of marriage when He said, "Have you not read that he who created them from the beginning made them male and female, and said, 'Therefore a man shall leave his father and his mother and hold fast to his wife, and the two shall become one flesh'? So they are no longer two but one flesh. What therefore God has joined together, let not man separate."[59]

Designed by God, marriage is meant to be a wonderful blessing to both the man and woman. As special as marriage is, however, it should not be entered into lightly or without Christian discernment. A wise pastor once said that when you are dating, you should look at your potential spouse with eyes wide open. Once you marry, then you should look at your partner with eyes half shut.

Marrying someone who shares the same Christian faith is essential for one's faith walk and growth here on earth. Together, husband and wife are either moving toward God or away from Him. The Bible warns that we should "not be unequally yoked with unbelievers. For what partnership has righteousness with lawlessness? Or what fellowship has light with darkness?"[60]

Moreover, God gives clear directives on how a Christian marriage should look and be lived out daily. He tells wives to "submit to your own husbands, as to the Lord. For the husband is the head of the wife even as Christ is the head of the church, his body, and is himself

---

[57] Ps. 19:14.

[58] Gen.2:18, 24.

[59] Matt. 19:4–6.

[60] 2 Cor. 6:14.

its Savior. Now as the church submits to Christ, so also wives should submit in everything to their husbands."[61]

"Submission" is a word which, unfortunately, is not always appreciated today. Yet to God, submission is a beautiful thing. After all, Jesus submitted to the Father and His plan of salvation when Jesus went to the cross to pay the price for our sins. If Jesus can submit, so can wives.

But God's directions for marriage are not just for the wives. God's Word says that husbands should love their wives "as Christ loved the church and gave himself up for her, that he might sanctify her, having cleansed her by the washing of water with the word, so that he might present the church to himself in splendor, without spot or wrinkle or any such thing, that she might be holy and without blemish. In the same way husbands should love their wives as their own bodies. He who loves his wife loves himself."[62]

If "submission" is not a word always valued today, "sacrifice" is certainly a word that is not lived on a daily basis either. Husbands are to sacrifice themselves, to give themselves up for their wives.

There is no question that prosperous and loving marriages are difficult to maintain in our world today. In fact, the institution of marriage—between one man and one woman—continues to be assaulted by Satan and secular forces. Satan knows what he is doing. He knows that marriage is an immense blessing instituted by God. He will not relent in his attacks on marriage. Moreover, since no one is perfect, both wives and husbands sin, act selfishly, and hurt one another.

Thank goodness Jesus wants to be the center of any relationship, and especially the relationship between husband and wife. Both husband and wife need to remember that Jesus died and paid the price for one's spouse. The Bible encourages married couples and all

---

[61] Eph. 5:22–24.

[62] Eph. 5:22–28.

of us to remember these words: "Above all, keep loving one another earnestly, since love covers a multitude of sins."[63]

Marriage is also a gift from God—a blessing of profound wonder, joy, and contentment. Husband and wife are blessed to share "conjugal rights"[64] with one another, be "fruitful and multiply,"[65] and to know the intimacy and partnership of being of one flesh—spiritually, emotionally, physically, and psychologically. "For as woman was made from man, so man is now born of woman. And all things are from God."[66]

Man and woman were not meant to be alone. God designed man and woman to be together in holy matrimony, even using marriage as an image of His love for the church here on earth. When a man and woman say, "I do," they are entering into a covenant created by God and designed for one another's earthly and eternal good.

Your Life

Many of Mary and Abraham's contemporaries did not feel they should marry, due to their incompatibility, different upbringings, unequal class status, dissimilar temperaments, and many more reasons. Did anyone ever tell you that you should jettison your dating or marriage partner because you could do better? Did anyone ever tell you that you did not deserve to be with someone because *you* did not measure up? How did it make you feel? How did you respond?

From a historical distance, it is easy to criticize Mary and Abraham's friends and relatives who did not think the couple should date or

63 1 Pet. 4:8.

64 1 Cor. 7:3.

65 Gen. 1:27–28.

66 1 Cor. 11:12.

marry. What would you do or say, however, if a loved one dated someone far below your standards, or who you thought might be harmful to your loved one's well-being and future happiness?

How does our culture today chip away at or denigrate the institution of marriage? What can you do about it?

What's the most beautiful thing about a Christian marriage?

5

Reality Marriage

It is better to live in a desert land than with
a quarrelsome and fretful woman.
—Proverbs 21:19

The Lincoln Way

Partners have the potential to lift one another up or bring each other down—or both at the same time.

Often overlooked in the Lincoln legacy are the lessons to be learned from the Lincoln marriage. The rawness and realness of the marriage—the sin, grace, joys, sorrows, triumphs, hardships, and complexity—make the Lincoln union difficult to denigrate or enshrine. As husband and wife, both Abe and Mary reveal significant character flaws, selfishness, and dysfunctions, but also perseverance, resilience, and grit. Like most married couples, they had bad days and good days. They were real people with real shortcomings and real blessings. Like most couples, they had to work at and nurture their marriage.

Abe had an easier time adjusting to married life than Mary did. He had endured economic hardship and frugality for much of his life, while Mary had been used to material luxury and other aristocratic benefits. She had never had to face economic hardship or rise out of poverty. As a husband and soon-to-be father, Abe found that married life provided immense satisfaction, security, and public esteem, perhaps for the first time. Mary had to confront new challenges such as housekeeping, cooking, budgeting, producing babies, caring for children, washing clothes, nursing, and enduring the reality of a working and moody husband. While marriage augmented Abe's continuing ascendance into the middle class, Mary's class status waned.[1]

After their wedding, the newlyweds took up residence in the Globe Tavern, a simple, two-story wooden structure with thirty rooms. Their bed occupied most of their eight-by-fourteen room on the second floor. The most comfortable place Abe had ever resided, the hotel represented a big step down for Mary compared to her father's spacious home in Lexington and the Edwardses' luxurious mansion. For the first time in her life, Mary had no personal servants or slaves, no storage for her possessions, and no private room where she could entertain guests. Moreover, the stingy owner of the tavern provided little food and few candles. Mary's sisters, who had attempted to dissuade her from marrying Lincoln in the first place, did not want to be seen near the tavern and soon dropped her from their social circle.[2]

Mary gave birth to the couple's first child, Robert, less than nine months after they were married. Some have speculated that Mary seduced Abraham the night before the wedding so that he would feel obligated to marry her. As her time in the White House would eventually show, Mary had no problem justifying unethical behavior to get what she wanted. Moreover, at the age of twenty-three, she was four years older than the average age at which women got married in Sangamon County at that time. Mary may have worried that her prime years were passing her by. The most voluptuous woman Herndon ever knew, Mary certainly lived with passion and knew how to make herself desirable to young gentlemen,

---

[1] Oates, *With Malice Toward None*, 64; Winkle, *Young Eagle*, 229.

[2] Donald, *Lincoln*, 94–95; Winkle, *Young Eagle*, 223–25.

especially one with as much passion as Abe. Mary's niece labeled her an "incorrigible flirt."[3]

The birth of Robert motivated the Lincolns to find bigger living quarters. They rented and eventually purchased a three-room house in the fall of 1843 from the Reverend Charles Dresser, the Episcopal minister who married them. Mary's well-to-do father helped the young couple with the purchase of the home and also financed the hiring of a maid.[4]

The Lincolns lived a typical middle-class Victorian marriage. Abe operated in the public domain of work and politics. Mary ruled the home and family.[5] Mary addressed her husband as "Mr. Lincoln," while he addressed her as "Mary" publicly and "Puss," "little woman," or "child-wife" in private.[6] After the birth of their first son, Abe almost always addressed her as "Mother." While no early feminist, Mary never fully embraced the expected and traditional roles of a homemaker and wife in her day. She never seemed afraid to share her thoughts, about politics or anything else.[7]

Husband and wife quickly adjusted to each other's foibles and became more intimately aware of each other's engrained personality traits. Abe frequently woke up with night terrors, trembling and speaking gibberish. He could sink into melancholy moments after telling jokes with great enthusiasm and laughter. He could become silent and stare off into space—so unreachable that Mary once threw coffee in his face at a dinner table full of guests to get his attention.[8]

On the other hand, Abe saw the depth of Mary's emotions and experienced her outbursts, which she often later expressed great remorse over, begging for forgiveness. She loved and hated intensely. Her temper could be ugly and devastating. She possessed a childlike

---

3 Burlingame, *Lincoln*, 1:197–98.

4 Epstein, *Portrait of a Marriage*, 82.

5 Winkle, *Young Eagle*, 214.

6 Donald, *Lincoln*, 95.

7 Packard, *Lincolns in the White House*, 15.

8 Epstein, *Portrait of a Marriage*, 57–59.

fear of thunder and lightning, mice, and burglars. When their son Robert wandered off, she would become hysterical and order her husband home from the office immediately. Almost every time, Abe patiently tended to her every need, and she basked in his kind attention and care.

When Abe left on his many circuit trips, Mary would ask neighbors to stay at their home. Once, after discovering that Robert had swallowed some lime near the outhouse, Mary lost complete control—repeatedly screaming that her son would die, until a neighbor came and washed Robert's mouth out.[9]

This picture, taken by Nicholas Shepherd in 1846, shows the vivacious and spirited Mary Lincoln before the deaths of her sons robbed her of much of her vitality. (Library of Congress, LC-USZ6-2094)

[9] Oates, *With Malice Toward None*, 65; Manning, *Father Lincoln*, 36.

Mary and Abe balanced each other well. Noting their height differential, Abe often jested that he was the long and she the short of it. On their bad days, he could become depressed and melancholy while she became excited and hot-tempered. He exuded kindness and had many friendly associates. She demonstrated snobbishness and found herself socially isolated. He depended on solitude and his inner resources. She fed off of interaction and the attention and admiration of others. Scruffy, humble, and self-confident, Abe offset Mary's fashion fetishes, egotism, and self-doubt. While he brought home news of the outside world and updates on the politics of the day, she gentrified her husband and provided social training in middle-class etiquette. Indifferent to what people thought of his appearance, he did not bother to sit up if he happened to be sprawled out on the floor when visitors came. She, having grown up in an aristocratic home, felt embarrassed when he answered the doorbell in his shirtsleeves.[10]

Both bucked conventional wisdom when it came to domestic life. Mary did not do house chores. Slaves had done the cooking and cleaning during her upbringing. Those duties were beneath her. Abe, however, had no problem dressing their kids, doing chores, or even cooking, especially before they hired a maid. Often after he returned from his law office, he put on a large blue apron and did whatever needed to be done in the kitchen. Yet he did not enjoy yardwork of any kind. He planted a few rose bushes in front of their Springfield home, but not much else. Some of his neighbors, pitying the sorry state of his yard, planted flowers and grasses to make the property more attractive.[11]

Historians and biographers have been far kinder to Abe than to Mary, perhaps because this portrayal enhances the apparent greatness of America's most original president. Many have rendered

---

[10] Baker, *Mary Todd Lincoln*, 131–32; Donald, *Lincoln*, 107.

[11] Burlingame, *Lincoln*, 1:219; Epstein, *Portrait of a Marriage*, 208; Manning, *Father Lincoln*, 29.

her, as one historian notes, "the most detested public woman in American history."[12] Indeed, the litany against Mary is deep and wide: she had provincial social skills; only married Lincoln to satisfy her ambition; embarrassed him with spoiled fits of rage, hysteria, and even madness; offended his friends; tried to isolate him from women and social life in general; drove him out of their home with her constant hectoring; and physically assaulted him. Herndon said she made Lincoln's life at home dismal and miserable. As First Lady, according to one historian, she reigned as a woman who was impossible to please and "whose shrieks made the White House tremble."[13]

Mary did indeed have flaws and demons. Often unable to control her emotions, she suffered from manic depression and may have been bipolar.[14] Herndon thought that Mary changed after she got married. Before marriage, she could be pleasant, polite, intelligent, witty, and charming. As soon as she got married, however, Mary became "material, avaricious, insolent, mean, insulting, imperious"—a "she wolf."[15] Others referred to her as a "tigress" and a "female wildcat." Later, when she became First Lady, Lincoln's personal secretaries referred to her as "Her Satanic Majesty." The White House physician thought Mary the "perfect devil," and another in the Executive Mansion referred to her as a hyena.

Wherever she went, everyone knew Mary by her wild temper. Her tantrums caused great difficulties with housemaids, icemen, storekeepers, delivery boys, hired help, and, of course, her husband. Witnesses saw her berate and physically assault him with regularity.

---

[12] Baker, *Mary Todd Lincoln*, xiii.

[13] Conroy, *Lincoln's White House*, 50; Oates, *Lincoln*, 177.

[14] Epstein, *Portrait of a Marriage*, 45; McPherson, *Lincoln*, 11. Someone said that Mary "was either in the garret or the cellar"—a revealing historical glimpse of what we might now call a manic-depressive diagnosis (Packard, *Lincolns in the White House*, 16–17).

[15] Burlingame, *Lincoln*, 1:201. The ensuing quotes in the remainder of the paragraph come from this same source.

When Lincoln wanted to buy an apple from a local farmer, Mary thrashed Lincoln with such violence that some feared for his safety.

One morning at the Globe Tavern, Mary came late for breakfast, which inconvenienced other guests, since boardinghouse etiquette dictated that no one ate until all guest were seated at the table. Lincoln gently reproached her as she entered the room. Mary instantly sprang up, threw a cup of coffee at him, and fled the scene in hysterics. Without saying a word, the humiliated Lincoln sat as others cleaned him up.

During dinner one night in 1860, Lincoln cracked a joke that Mary did not find humorous. She flung a cup of hot tea across the table at Lincoln's head and left the room in a fury. Another evening, Lincoln was fully absorbed in the newspaper. Mary asked him several times to add wood to the dying fire in the parlor. Ignored, she clubbed him in the face with a piece of wood, ensuring he would hear her next request. After going to the drugstore to purchase gelatin, the hardening ingredient for a plaster bandage, Lincoln appeared the next day in court with a bandage on his nose.

Routinely in private and in public, Mary assaulted her husband. She hit him in the face when he brought home the wrong meat. She attacked him with vegetables. She threw a bucketful of water on him from their upstairs window. Neighbors witnessed her chasing him from the house with a broom and, one time, with a knife. Books, papers, and small pieces of furniture were hurled out of the house.

No wonder Lincoln never wanted to invite guests to his home. He even purchased a couch to sleep on in his law office during nights of domestic trouble. Mary's tantrums and abuse may have inadvertently helped him professionally in the long term, since he never pursued domesticity. Instead, he focused his energies on politics and law—vocations in which he was nurtured and affirmed. Painful and embarrassing as these many difficult moments were, without Mary and her temper, the country may never have had a President Lincoln.[16]

Mary ruined any potential sympathy she may have garnered in her struggle with depression because of her prodigious vanity and sharp tongue. A propensity for cutting and sarcastic remarks compelled many to eschew her socially. Neighbors almost always invited the Lincoln children over to their homes to play, not wanting their own kids to endure the wrath of Mary at the Lincoln residence. While Lincoln's striking emotional intelligence, self-control, and ability to read people marked him out among his peers, Mary did not comprehend how others viewed her outbursts—or perhaps she did not care.[17]

For his part, Abe put up with Mary's outbursts with surprising calm, impressing even his in-laws. Dealing with Mary's temper required daily awareness and patience. He often stopped in the kitchen, for example, to inquire about his wife's mood before entering the main house. Perhaps he had sympathy for her, knowing her family's history of depression and how she had given up a life of leisure to marry him.

Mary's unceasing worry over their poor economic standing and her dread of poverty bothered her immensely throughout their marriage. Obsession with their finances spurred her into fits of alternating binge purchasing (especially of clothes and furnishings) and fanatical miserliness.

Abe believed that many of her outbursts occurred while she endured debilitating migraine headaches, something she would complain about for years. He may have felt guilty about his busy work and social schedule, which took him away from her for months at a time. Every spring, as well as during the months Lincoln rode his circuit, Mary's severe headaches returned. She was home alone for

---

[16] Burlingame, *Lincoln*, 1:202–4, 212; Donald, *Lincoln Reconsidered*, 86; Winkle, *Young Eagle*, 227; Epstein, *Portrait of a Marriage*, 191–93.

[17] Burlingame, *Lincoln*, 1:174, 220; Winkle, *Young Eagle*, 229.

months, in charge of their children and of a heavy workload for the house. When Abe came home after a busy day in court or working with clients, he often sat by the fireplace to read up on court cases or politics, his mind deeply engaged elsewhere rather than focused on Mary. He frequently failed to consider how Mary had been cooped up all day with infants, craving adult conversation.[18]

Years later, a Springfield neighbor remembered that "Lincoln and his wife got along tolerably well, unless Mrs. L got the devil in her." When that happened, "Lincoln paid no attention, would pick up one of his Children & walked off, would laugh at her, pay no Earthly attention to her when in that wild furious Condition." The neighbor added, "I don't think Mrs. Lincoln was as bad a woman as She is represented … She always said if her husband had Staid at home as he ought to, that She could love him better."[19]

Lincoln's long absences from home remained a constant challenge and source of stress in the Lincoln marriage. From 1846 to 1860, he was absent from home almost half the time. His duties as a traveling lawyer on the Illinois eighth circuit covered almost 830 miles. Traveling by horse and carriage, since there were no railroads to shorten his travel time, Lincoln had ample opportunity to mingle with folks for political purposes and build name recognition. He truly enjoyed interacting with the locals. Meanwhile, without a nurse, husband, or a grandparent nearby to provide support, Mary struggled to raise their boys and maintain the household largely on her own.[20]

In the spring of 1856, while her husband worked the circuit, Mary decided to have their Springfield home remodeled and expanded now that they had three sons and a live-in maid. She wanted to

---

[18] Burlingame, *Lincoln*, 1:210; Keneally, *Lincoln*, 44; Donald, *Lincoln Reconsidered*, 86, 107–8.

[19] Wilson, *Herndon's Informants*, 453.

[20] Epstein, *Portrait of a Marriage*, 230; Baker, *Mary Todd Lincoln*, 108, 120, 153. During the Lincoln-Douglas debates in the summer of 1858, Mary hardly saw her husband at all.

upgrade the house to befit a prominent public man. So Mary had a second floor added. When Abe returned, he saw a beautifully finished two-story Greek Revival home, painted chocolate brown with dark green shutters. Stunned, he could not help but joke to a neighbor that he wondered where the Lincoln family currently lived. He complained about the cost to Mary, which only made her determined to be more covert about her future spending.[21]

Some argue that one reason Lincoln stayed on the court circuit for such long periods of time, including the weekends, was that he had no desire to go home. Even though he endured mud in winter and dust in summer, dirty and greasy dining rooms, and tavern bedrooms overrun with mosquitos, fleas, and bedbugs,[22] being away from home was his Heaven, William Herndon explained, because staying home was his Hell.[23] Herndon labelled Lincoln's home an "ice cave" with "no soul, fire, cheer, or fun in it."[24]

Lincoln's long absences from home were one reason Mary insisted on coming to Washington upon his election to Congress in the fall of 1846. Of course, Mary also sincerely desired to aid her husband's political aspirations as well as her own ambitions. Unfortunately, things did not go as Mary hoped. She soon became not only a burden to her husband but despondent at her own situation. The entire Lincoln family resided in a small, smoky room with two beds, a chamber pot, and a pile of wood with bugs in it. Few other wives of congressmen were in Washington. Her husband wanted to go bowling and to dine with his colleagues for leisure and networking purposes. Mary did not make a single friend and spent many winter nights alone. Disenchanted with the licentious behavior

---

[21] Donald, *Lincoln*, 197.

[22] Donald, *Lincoln,* 147.

[23] Burlingame, *Lincoln*, 1:328.

[24] Guelzo, *Lincoln*, 113.

of congressmen and disappointed in her aspirations, after three long months she took their boys to Kentucky and stayed with her family.[25]

Even as Lincoln networked and became a social highlight at the bowling alley by his clumsiness, zest, and humor, he missed his wife and boys.[26] He aptly captured the dilemma of being married to Mary: "In this troublesome world, we are never quite satisfied," he wrote her in the spring of 1848. "When you were here, I thought you hindered me in attending to business, but now, having nothing but business … it has grown exceedingly tasteless to me … Don't let the blessed fellows forget father."[27]

One of those fellows, Eddie, fell ill on December 11, 1849. Mary and Abe hovered over their son as chills, severe coughing, and fevers came and went. Unfortunately, Eddie had contracted acute pulmonary tuberculosis. During fifty-two harrowing days, Abe observed the depth of his wife's obsessiveness and anxiety. Deep in thought and misery, Mary developed a bizarre habit of pulling out her hair, strand by strand.

The Lincolns were frequent drugstore shoppers, and they administered a variety of medicines and remedies to Eddie, to no avail. Mary's brother-in-law, a doctor, prescribed medication for diphtheria, but diphtheria usually passed after three weeks and Eddie did not improve. Based on her brother's advice, Mary even applied cough-suppressing opium to Eddie's chest, but it did not stop his decline.

Their precious son eventually died on February 1, 1850, thirty-seven days before his fourth birthday. In the span of six months, Mary had lost her father and maternal grandmother to a cholera outbreak and her son to diphtheria.[28]

---

25 Epstein, *Portrait of a Marriage*, 122–23; Oates, *With Malice Toward None*, 79.

26 Goodwin, *Team of Rivals*, 120.

27 Basler, Lincoln to Mary Todd Lincoln, April 16, 1848, *CW*, 1:465–66.

28 Manning, *Father Lincoln*, 57; Turner and Turner, *Mary Todd Lincoln*, 40; Epstein, *Portrait of a Marriage*, 159–60. Modern historians believe Eddie died

Eddie's funeral took place in the parlor of the Lincoln family home on the day after he died. Dr. James Smith, pastor of the First Presbyterian Church in Springfield, led the service and read the traditional burial reading from the *Book of Common Prayer*. After Eddie's body had been lowered into the ground, Lincoln returned home and noticed the last prescription card written by the doctor for Eddie. He picked it up, looked at it, and threw it. Then he burst into tears as he left the room. Lincoln later told an attorney friend that if he "had twenty children he would never cease to sorrow" for the one he lost.[29] As Lincoln wrote his step-brother, Eddie "was not our first, but our second child. We miss him very much."[30]

A week after Eddie died, a poem entitled "Little Eddie" appeared in the *Illinois State Journal*. Describing a "pure little bud in kindness given, in mercy taken to bloom in heaven," the poem reveals the acute pain of a father losing a son as well as the assurance and relief that his son now rested "at the Savior's feet." The "Angel Boy" had gone home, for "such is the Kingdom of Heaven."[31] On Eddie's tombstone were inscribed the words, "Edward B. Son of A. & M. Lincoln died Feb. 1, 1850. Age 3 years 10 months 18 days. Of such is the kingdom of Heaven."[32]

Dr. James Smith frequently visited the grieving parents. He gave them a copy of his 676-page book, *The Christian's Defence*, which helped catapult Lincoln onto a path of spiritual growth. Mary noted that her husband became more religious after Eddie's death. Soon after the funeral, the Lincolns rented a pew at the First Presbyterian Church.[33]

Lincoln had to grieve apart from Mary, for Eddie's death stunned and permanently damaged her already fragile psyche. According to a

---

from pulmonary tuberculosis.

29 Manning, *Father Lincoln*, 60.

30 Basler, Lincoln to John D. Johnston, February 23, 1850, *CW*, 2:76-77.

31 Burlingame, *Lincoln*, 1:359.

32 Manning, *Father Lincoln*, 65.

33 Burlingame, *Lincoln*, 1:359.

neighbor, she lay prostrate, refused to eat, and could not cope with the tragic loss.[34]

Due to high infant mortality rates, parents in Lincoln's time were often encouraged to refrain from forming strong emotional attachments to their children, as a defense mechanism, but the Lincolns did not adhere to this particular societal teaching.[35] Mary also did not accept the notion that the loss of a child was part of God's plan. She wanted to "get the better of destiny," and "raged against Eddie's desertion" for years.[36] In the aftermath of their son's passing, Abe provided much more care and loving support to Mary than she afforded him. He had to be the strong one. In this regard, he remained the giver and she the taker in the relationship. Tragically, this would not be the last child the Lincolns would lose before their own deaths.

For all of the considerable hardship, embarrassment, and exhausting drama she brought to their marriage, Mary did provide several special benefits to her husband. Her kindness and generosity, though too infrequent, could light up their home. Shortly after the birth of their son Tad in 1853, Mary breastfed her son alongside the baby of a sick neighbor who could not nurse. Neighbors and townspeople noticed how Mary often met her husband at the front gate. The two would walk together to their door, swinging their clasped hands and joking like little children.

When Mary lost her temper, she often quickly asked forgiveness. While both Mary and Abe were too indulgent with regard to their children's behavior, Mary successfully raised three of their four sons

---

34 Epstein, *Portrait of a Marriage*, 159–60.

35 Keneally, *Lincoln*, 56. Child deaths were common enough for books of etiquette, like *The Mother's Assistant*, to advise Christian mothers how to behave when they lost their children.

36 Manning, *Father Lincoln*, 54; Baker, *Mary Todd Lincoln*, 127–28.

through the stage of high infant mortality, before healthy sanitation became the norm.[37]

Many contemporaries wondered why Lincoln would stay with such a volatile, abusive wife, but the evidence suggests he loved her nonetheless. Dr. James Smith knew the couple for almost a decade in Springfield. Twice a month he visited the Lincolns and spent the evening in their home. Abe gave Mary "a heart overflowing with love and affection" and remained "a most faithful, loving and Affectionate husband." Smith further testified that during his frequent stays, he "never saw a frown upon" Lincoln's "brow or heard him utter a harsh or unkind word to his Lady or any of her Children, but seemed overflowing with geniality, good humour and Kindness, Clear proofs of his love and Affection" for his wife.[38]

Though Lincoln worried that Mary's volatile temper might erupt at a moment's notice, her refined taste and experience with large social events did provide a pleasing ambience at political gatherings in their Springfield home. Mary loved to attend strawberry parties, for example, and the Lincolns did their part in graciously hosting such gatherings too. When in the right mood, the pleasure of Mary's wit and charm could exceed even the joy people felt in celebrating the ripe red berry.[39]

Lincoln's ultimate rise to the presidency would most likely never have happened without Mary and her courage to buck the conventional role of a nineteenth-century housewife. He needed her and her drive to attain political success. She had, of course, great family connections, which aided Lincoln's rise. She helped her husband keep the pulse of local, state, and national politics by reading newspapers and books, and frequently interacting with and charming local politicians. She taught her husband the social

---

37 Donald, *Lincoln*, 158; Epstein, *Portrait of a Marriage*, 91, 176–77; Baker, *Mary Todd Lincoln*, 120; Donald, *Lincoln Reconsidered*, 85.

38 Wilson, *Herndon's Informants*, 549.

39 Epstein, *Portrait of a Marriage*, 208, 225.

etiquette expected of men of influence. And she dutifully represented the married couple in church and other social settings.[40]

During their courtship—two decades before Lincoln became the nation's sixteenth president—Mary often told others that Abe would be elected president and she would become First Lady someday. She did not marry Abe for his looks, after all, but because she knew he had it in him to ascend to the highest office in the land.[41] Lincoln's onetime law partner and mentor, John Stuart, confirmed Mary's significance in Abe's rise to the presidency. "His wife made him Presdt," he noted after Lincoln's death. Mary "had the fire, will and ambition," along with Lincoln's own talents, to make it happen. "If Mr. Lincoln had married another woman," he said, Lincoln "would have been a devoted husband and a very, *very* domestic man." Lincoln's "dormancy" and "vegetable constitution," Stuart asserted, "needed driving" and he "got that" in large part from his wife.[42]

Mary deserves enormous credit for being one of the few, perhaps only, individuals who saw greatness in the gangly backwoods attorney. Throughout his fluctuating career and episodes of depression, she never let him quit the pursuit of a high-profile career in politics. Of course, Mary understood that to achieve her own fame in the public realm, she needed her husband to rise. Both had set their sights on the presidency, and both needed to do their parts. After his failed bid to become the vice-presidential candidate with John Fremont on the 1856 Republican ticket, she never lost faith in him or his abilities. "Nobody knows me," Lincoln lamented after his political setback. Fierce Mary stayed resolute and responded, "They soon will."[43]

In late May 1860, after Lincoln received confirmation that he had been selected the Republican nominee for president, he teased his friends that they had better shake his hand now before he became

---

[40] Donald, *Lincoln Reconsidered*, 84.

[41] Burlingame, *Lincoln*, 1:211.

[42] Wilson, *Herndon's Informants*, 63–64. Stuart indicated in the same letter that "the marriage of Lincoln to Miss Todd was a policy Match all around."

[43] Keneally, *Lincoln*, 63; Baker, *Mary Todd Lincoln*, 144, 148.

president. Then he prepared to head home explaining that "there is a little woman at our house who is probably more interested in this dispatch than I am."[44] A few months later, Lincoln would be elected the sixteenth president of the United States.

For almost two decades, Abe and Mary dreamed about becoming president and First Lady respectively. They had endured and overcome much together, including the loss of their beloved Eddie, and learned much about each other as husband and wife. Nothing they would face in the White House, it seemed, could overwhelm them or test their marriage beyond the breaking point.

The Lincoln marriage is a case study of a reality marriage. Abe and Mary were each blessed with wonderful gifts and talents, and human frailties and flaws too. They endured sorrows and hardships and experienced joys and successes. Through all of the ups and downs, their marriage persevered. Lincoln biographers rarely list Lincoln's marriage as one of his greatest accomplishments. More than an achievement, however, perhaps this imperfect marriage should be praised, appreciated, and studied for the blessing that it brought and how God used it for His purposes.

The Truth

Nowhere in the Bible does it say that marriage is easy. However, the Bible is full of references to the sacrificial love that is required of all marriages. Of course, the love between one man and one woman in holy matrimony is inspired by the love of Christ Himself. For even while we were still despicable sinners, "Christ died for us."[45] Moreover, Jesus tells us that "this is my commandment, that you love one another as I have loved you."[46]

---

[44] Donald, *Lincoln*, 241.

[45] Rom. 5:8

[46] John 15:12.

Scripture is filled with admonitions and exhortations on marriage. "A hot-tempered man stirs up strife," for example, "but he who is slow to anger quiets contention."[47] Wives should be prudent and not quarrelsome.[48] Every husband should "love his wife as himself"; every wife should respect her husband.[49] Husbands and wives should remember to be patient and not proud, nor quick "to become angry, for anger lodges in the bosom of fools."[50]

In the book of Colossians, God shares how Christians should treat each other in general, but the words certainly apply to husband and wife. "As God's chosen ones," Christians should live with "compassionate hearts, kindness, humility, meekness, and patience, bearing with one another and, if one has a complaint against another, forgiving each other; as the Lord has forgiven you, so you also must forgive." Of course, "above all these put on love, which binds everything together in perfect harmony." Husband and wife, as well as all Christians, should "let the peace of Christ rule in your hearts," "be thankful," and "let the word of Christ dwell in you richly, teaching and admonishing one another in all wisdom, singing psalms and hymns and spiritual songs, with thankfulness in your hearts to God." As a husband, wife, or single person, God tells you that "whatever you do, in word or deed, do everything in the name of the Lord Jesus, giving thanks to God the Father through him. Wives, submit to your husbands, as is fitting in the Lord. Husbands, love your wives, and do not be harsh with them."[51]

Manifestation of the fruits of the Spirit is a good sign that a marriage is centered on Christ. The relationship between husband and wife should exhibit "love, joy, peace, patience, kindness, goodness, faithfulness, gentleness, self-control."[52]

---

47 Prov. 15:18.

48 Prov. 19:14, 21:9.

49 Eph. 5:33.

50 Eccles. 7:9.

51 Col. 3:12–19.

52 Gal. 5:22–23.

There is a reason that the great "love chapter of the Bible" as it is known, 1 Corinthians 13, is often used at weddings. Perhaps more than any other relationship, a Christian marriage should display sacrificial love—love that is patient and kind, does not envy or boast, and is not arrogant or rude. Love, especially in a marriage, "does not insist on its own way; it is not irritable or resentful; it does not rejoice at wrongdoing, but rejoices with the truth. Love bears all things, believes all things, hopes all things, endures all things."[53]

Your Life

Too many people today think love and marriage are about emotion. When they read about Mary and Abraham's idiosyncrasies, shortcomings, and selfish acts, some people might defend the case for the breakup of that marriage. Reflecting on the words of Scripture, however, how would you explain the love that should exist between husband and wife, despite the selfishness and sinfulness of each?

Abe's long absences from home was one of Mary's greatest burdens. Having a spouse away from home for months at a time can be harsh even if the absence is not intended that way. On the other hand, Mary's temper tantrums were a long-standing embarrassment and mental anguish for him. How should a Christian spouse deal with either one of these situations? What would you do if burdened with one of these marriage realities?

How might the death of a child, as the Lincolns endured with their young son Eddie, strengthen a marriage or weaken a marriage?

---

[53] 1 Cor. 13:4–7.

6

Spotlight Marriage

In the same way, let your light shine before others,
so that they may see your good works and give
glory to your Father who is in heaven.
—Matthew 5:16

The Lincoln Way

If true character is revealed in private, then perseverance is surely exhibited in public.

No matter how prepared they think they might be, no married couple can adequately ready themselves for the spotlight that comes with the presidency. Nevertheless, the Lincolns eagerly anticipated their new life in Washington, DC. They had dreamed of serving in the nation's capital for decades. Their time had finally arrived.

The Lincolns traveled over nineteen hundred miles from Springfield to Washington in the winter of 1861. They made several whistle-stop speeches from the back of a train car as they passed through small towns and big cities throughout Illinois, Indiana, Ohio, Pennsylvania, New York, and Maryland. During these stops, the president-elect tried to calm an agitated nation deeply divided over issues like the expansion of slavery, the tariff, fugitive slaves, and other sectarian issues. He would soon find out his words had little impact in averting the secession of several Southern states.

This 1861 photo by Matthew Brady captures Mary Lincoln in all her glory as her dream of getting to the White House comes true. (Library of Congress, LC-DIG-ppmsca-19221)

Mary had more immediate and personal concerns. Rumors of a plot to assassinate her husband forced a physical split; the president-elect left his wife and kids behind to covertly pass through Baltimore at night to arrive in Washington. While Lincoln's clandestine action elicited charges of cowardice from critics, Mary realized that in many ways, the presidency now superseded their marriage. Having pledged his devotion to Mary in holy matrimony, Lincoln would soon take an oath to serve the American people. Mary's interests and the people's interests were bound to differ. The reality marriage had met a new fork in the road.[1]

---

1 Epstein, *Portrait of a Marriage*, 297.

The Lincoln family brought something new to the Executive Mansion (not in those days called the White House, a nickname that caught on during Teddy Roosevelt's first administration)—namely, young children. The First Lady and the president allowed their boys to race up and down stairs from the attic to the cellar of the old mansion, taking possession of every closet, nook, and cranny, as only rambunctious and curious children can do. Ten and eight years old respectively when they came to Washington, Willie and Tad brought youthful exuberance, distraction, and much-needed joy to an Executive Mansion soon to be engulfed by the deadly Civil War.

The Lincolns soon discovered that the Executive Mansion functioned like a hotel lobby: anyone could and did enter, loiter, and carry on as if the building were some kind of café. Not only did the Lincolns lose their privacy, but threats of assassination came regularly. After the whole family got sick one night, the couple suspected that someone had sneaked into the kitchen and poisoned their food. Another time they feared that someone had slipped into the stables and tried to poison Mary's long-tailed black carriage horses with flour of sulfur.[2] The Lincolns clearly were not in Springfield anymore.

Right from the beginning of their presidential tenure, Abe and Mary endured wrath and hatred from different regions of the populace. The president received a stream of death threats and was reviled in much of the South for his campaign pledge to limit slavery. Southerners loathed the First Lady for being a traitor to her upbringing and class. Northerners suspected her of retaining a secret loyalty to her native South, a slight that gained momentum when four of her brothers and three of her brothers-in-law enlisted in the Confederate army. Easterners in general regarded Mary as an uncouth woman and often depicted her as a Native American woman

---

[2] Wheeler, *Faith and Courage*, 168; Epstein, *Portrait of a Marriage*, 318, 320, 324.

smoking a corncob pipe.[3] The Washington press, uncomfortable with her palpable ambition and unconventional courage for a woman of the time, derisively referred to her as Madame President. No First Lady entered the White House with so much scorn and disdain.

Mary did not improve the contemptuous image many had of her when she decided to embark upon a clothes-shopping bender in New York before the inauguration. She justified her exorbitant purchases as befitting a president's wife, and privately wanted to erase the press's crude frontier portrayal of her. Mary not only spent more than the Lincolns could afford, but she set herself up for blackmail and other unethical financial entanglements before her husband had taken the oath of office.[4]

In the months after the inauguration, as her husband dealt with the tumultuous events of secession and the start of the Civil War, Mary took control of a dilapidated and unattractive Executive Mansion in desperate need of attention.[5] She had the mansion scrubbed, painted (two coats on the exterior), and plastered. She also

---

[3] Packard, *Lincolns in the White House*, 85; Donald, *Lincoln at Home*, 22.

[4] Packard, *Lincolns in the White House*, 52–53. William Wood, for example, the administration's new acting commissioner of public buildings and the government officer responsible for paying the doorkeepers and groundsmen, steered Mrs. Lincoln to merchants so that he could receive kickbacks (his salary was a meager $2,000). Keneally, *Lincoln*, 106. In June 1861, Lincoln received an anonymous letter implying that Mary and Wood were having an adulterous relationship.

[5] Donald, *Lincoln at Home*, 23. In addition to the broken furniture, peeling wallpaper, worn carpet, and torn draperies, eleven basement rooms were rat-infested. Conway, *Lincoln's White House*, 33. Even the elegant parlors were frayed around the edges. Family quarters were tainted by dingy carpets, greasy wallpaper, and ancient grime. Packard, *Lincolns in the White House*, 50–51. Since the Executive Mansion had been treated as an unguarded tourist attraction, the damage it endured from visitors continued to be significant and relentless. Tourists seemed compelled to take anything not nailed down—ornaments, bric-a-brac, curtains, etc. Conway, *Lincoln's White House*, 243. After Lincoln's death, the plundering of the Executive Mansion would commence anew. In addition to dozens of unguarded mementos and

had the residence refurbished in almost every way, from chandeliers to throw rugs. New gas pipes were run through the walls, and a new furnace ensured that fireplaces would no longer be the only source of heat in the winter. Potomac River water was piped in. Mary overlooked nothing and made the interior much more attractive, clean, and livable.[6]

Unfortunately, she spent the entire congressional allocation ($20,000 for furnishings and $6,000 for repairs) for the presidential term in the first few months of the Lincolns' occupancy, an embarrassing secret she tried to keep from her husband. In desperation, she let John Watt, the White House gardener, show her ways to cover the deficit by fraudulent means. Throughout the first term, Mary padded bills for household expenditures and presented vouchers for nonexistent purchases. Eventually, Congress would be forced to quietly pass two deficiency appropriations to cover Mary's reckless expenditures, much to her husband's embarrassment.[7] Critics blamed the president for "Her Royal Majesty's" spending on rich dresses, jewelry, luxurious living, and adornment of the Executive Mansion while soldiers died and families suffered.

Regardless of what others thought or how much she embarrassed her husband, Mary continued to spend money. She took additional expensive shopping excursions to the upscale Ladies' Mile, as it was known, in New York City throughout the couple's presidential years.

---

knickknacks which would disappear, carpets and upholstery would also be sliced and taken.

[6] Conway, *Lincoln's White House*, 92–93; Packard, *Lincolns in the White House*, 87.

[7] Donald, *Lincoln*, 312–313; Epstein, *Portrait of a Marriage*, 341. Watt billed the Treasury for flowers, food, wine, pots, manure, and even the labor of workers and horses that had rendered small services for the Executive Mansion. Once the press got wind of this scheme, they dubbed the fraud "the Manure Fund." Keneally, *Lincoln*, 115. Mary once had Watt cook the books to indicate a purchase of one thousand dollars' worth of seeds. They split the funding of the fictional expenditure.

Not only did she like to shop, but the "fiercely fashionable"[8] Mary purchased the most expensive and finest quality things.

Sometimes her purchases were for the Executive Mansion and sometimes they were for herself. In her first trip to New York after the inauguration, she ordered a $2,500 carpet for the East Room of the White House. That sum exceeded most Americans' wages for an entire year. The Executive Mansion doorkeepers only made $600 per year. No matter. From wallpaper and draperies to lace shawls and low-cut gowns, Mary's purchasing power knew no bounds.[9]

Mary was easy to spot on her epic shopping trips. Reporters followed her around and wrote about her exorbitant purchases. She had become a shopaholic and seemingly could not accumulate enough stuff. When the Lincolns moved to the Soldiers' Home in the summer of 1863, observers were stunned that the First Lady required a train of nineteen wagons to haul out her supplies and clothing, just for a few weeks of summer living.[10] One senator noted that she had "degenerated from the industrious and unpretentious woman that she was in the days when she used to cook old Abe's dinner and milk the cows with her own hands. Now her only ambition seems to be to exhibit her own milking apparatus to the public gaze."[11]

Mary's obnoxious spending habits embarrassed and infuriated her husband in the midst of a costly and deadly civil war. Once he discovered Mary's pathetic financial predicament, he told her that he would "pay for it out of my pocket first" since "it would stink the nostrils of the American people to have it said the President of the United States had approved a bill over-running an appropriation of $20,000 for *flub dubs,*" for the Executive Mansion, "when soldiers cannot have blankets."[12] The president's stern words stirred Mary's

---

[8] Oates, *With Malice Toward None*, 273.

[9] Packard, *Lincolns in the White House*, 53–54; Conway, *Lincoln's White House*, 92; Epstein, *Portrait of a Marriage*, 331.

[10] Donald, *Lincoln at Home*, 48.

[11] Canavan, *Lincoln's Final Hours*, 171–72.

[12] Oates, *With Malice Toward None*, 275.

impulsivity and anger, helped incite sudden surges of frugality, and compelled her to more carefully hide her expenditures. She had manure sold from the White House stables in order to bring in extra income. Instead of milk from the Executive Mansion dairy being sent to area hospitals, as had been the presidential tradition, Mary had it sold from the back door to pay off her debts.[13]

As her husband's reelection loomed in the fall of 1864, Mary rightly worried that her $27,000 debt and her spending habits would be exposed and exploited by Democrats and Lincoln critics, as well as by merchants to whom she owed money. While she had decreased her compulsive spending on decorating the Executive Mansion, she continued to purchase expensive clothing and jewelry from New York and Philadelphia merchants—including a $2,000 shawl, a pear-and-diamond ear ring, two diamond-and-pearl bracelets, and a rumor that she bought 300 pairs of kid gloves. "I must dress in costly materials," she insisted to her dressmaker, Elizabeth Keckley. "The people scrutinize every article that I wear with critical curiosity." She continued her justification: "The very fact of having grown up in the West, subject me to more searching observation." She knew that if her husband were reelected, she could "keep him in ignorance of my affairs; but if he is defeated, then the bills will be sent in, and he will know all."[14] After Lincoln's win in 1864, Mary almost immediately spent two thousand dollars on a new inaugural gown and nearly three thousand dollars on pearl, amethyst, and diamond jewelry. She also sent used Executive Mansion furniture to Springfield rather than putting it up for auction as the law required.[15] Mary's spending remained out of control.

Mary embarrassed and pained her husband in many ways and never fully understood why everything she said or did in Washington

---

[13] Conway, *Lincoln's White House*, 97.

[14] Keneally, *Lincoln*, 155; Donald, *Lincoln*, 540; Packard, *Lincolns in the White House*, 177. Mary's debts were the equivalent of well over a quarter of a million dollars in today's money.

[15] Packard, *Lincolns in the White House*, 209–10; Burlingame, *Lincoln*, 2:701.

would be scrutinized. She expected deference from the very people she insulted. She meddled and threw fits regarding patronage and cabinet issues, used vulgar language in front of prominent guests, produced public temper tantrums, and accused cabinet members of stabbing her husband in the back. She often ordered a row of the best seats at Grove's Theatre or Ford's Theatre but did not leave a gratuity. Mary expected private boxes to be given to her gratis. She disrespected dry good cleaners, bullied department store clerks, and often left stores without paying her bills. Rumors spread of her unfaithfulness to her husband, especially when she spent time with William Wood on shopping sprees to New York. She leaked her husband's 1861 State of the Union speech to a newspaper editor—some claimed in return for a substantial monetary gift. She wore dresses which were long in the train but short at the top with plunging and daring necklines.[16]

Almost any time anyone gave her husband attention, particularly women, Mary seethed and aggressively intervened. Early in the war, a tall, beautiful woman came to visit Lincoln. She fell on her knees, wrapped her arms around Lincoln's knees, and pleaded her case. "Out of the room, you baggage," Mary blurted.[17] Lincoln learned very early in his marriage that he had to ask whom he could and could not talk to. This presented a great challenge, since Mary had no friends inside and few outside the White House.

Ms. Kate Chase, the stunning and accomplished daughter of Treasury Secretary Salmon Chase, did not make Mary's safe-to-see list. Since Chase wanted to be president, his dutiful daughter and her husband established a saloon in town that continually offered entertainment for high society folk. Since most people in Washington considered Kate Chase the most vivacious woman around, these events were well attended, much to the extreme irritation and

---

[16] Burlingame, *Lincoln*, 2:263–75, 701; Donald, *Lincoln*, 324.

[17] Burlingame, *Lincoln*, 2:783.

jealousy of Mary Lincoln. Therefore, when the White House had a social function, Mary refused to invite Ms. Chase.

When Lincoln attended Kate's wedding in November 1863, Mary chastised her husband for kowtowing to the enemy. When he put Mr. and Mrs. Chase on a guest list for a January 1864 state dinner, Mary lost control and went on a rampage that truly shocked the staff in the Executive Mansion. Jealousy had gotten the best of her.[18]

Any woman of grace, beauty, and allure in close proximity to the president threatened and disturbed Mary. One day in the spring of 1865, Mary exploded at Julia Grant for sitting down at the dinner table without her permission. She treated Edwin Stanton's wife in the same manner. Both learned very quickly that they wanted nothing to do with the First Lady. Indeed, whenever someone captured the president's attention, Mary's irrepressible jealousy burst to the surface. Abe often told associates that his wife did not feel well and that he needed to take her on a walk.[19]

One day late in the war, while Lincoln was visiting Grant's army at City Point, the beautiful and vivacious wife of General Ord rode past the First Lady's carriage on a highly spirited horse. The president was on a horse next to her. Worried that others might mistake Mrs. Ord for her, Mary spewed rage and jealousy.[20] When

---

[18] Epstein, *Portrait of a Marriage*, 414–15. While getting ready for a reception, Lincoln once asked Mary which women he could speak to and proposed some nominees. She rejected many of the names. "Well, mother, I must talk with someone. Is there anyone that you do not object to? If you will not tell me who I may talk with, please tell me who I may *not* talk with." She gave him three names including Kate Chase, "the prettiest Kate in Christendom" (Conway, *Lincoln's White House*, 101).

[19] Burlingame, *Lincoln*, 2:779; Epstein, *Portrait of a Marriage*, 484–85.

[20] Johnson, *Last Weeks of Lincoln*, 105. Mary Ord is described as a "remarkably handsome woman and a most accomplished equestrienne," who handled her horse expertly and with "extreme grace." Before Mary Lincoln even saw Mary Ord that fateful day, the First Lady had experienced a rough ride to the front. While their ambulance carriage had additional springs installed to

Julia Grant tried to settle her down, Mary turned on Mrs. Grant and insulted her. After catching up to the riders, the First Lady disembarked from the carriage and went right at Mrs. Ord, calling her vile names in front of officers. Mary's tongue-lashing brought Mrs. Ord to tears. She innocently asked what she had done wrong. Observers were stunned at Mary's pugnacious behavior.

Yet she would not let up. At dinner that night, Mary urged her husband to remove General Ord from command. For the next few days, officers and soldiers pitied their commander in chief as Mary harangued him in front of public officials for giving Mrs. Ord too much attention. Lincoln was calm and stoic during the First Lady's unending rants, but observers could see the suffering on the president's face. When Lincoln tried to calm Mary, she exploded at him. With all the worries of war on his mind, Lincoln found no public support in the company of a very jealous First Lady.[21]

Mary often berated her husband for other reasons too. The Lincolns attended a fair to benefit the Christian Commission in late February 1864. The leaders of the organization asked Lincoln to say a few words. Since he had been promised that he would not have to speak at the event, Lincoln was unprepared and his remarks were less than memorable—except to Mary, who desperately wanted him reelected later that fall. Afterward, the First Lady scolded him for giving the worst speech she had ever heard. Elizabeth Keckley reported that Mary often hurt the tenderhearted Lincoln deeply in

---

make their ride more comfortable, they actually made it worse. When one of the wheels struck an obstacle or ran over a tree trunk, the new springs bounced passengers out of their seats with more force than before the springs were fitted. Mary hit her head on the ambulance roof with great force, which triggered a severe headache (possibly a migraine). Her irritable and impatient dispositions already heightened because of the head injury, Mary Lincoln had already berated horses, the driver, aides, and Julia Grant before she even encountered Mary Ord riding with her husband.

[21] Burlingame, *Lincoln*, 2:781–82.

"unguarded moments."[22] In addition, many people witnessed the "she devil" physically assault her husband too.[23]

While many of Mary's character flaws were visible to the public, most contemporaries were unable to see the challenges the First Lady endured behind the scenes. Some physicians have variously attributed her bizarre and inconsistent behavior to bipolar disorder, syphilis, diabetes, chronic fatigue disorder, or Lyme disease. One cardiologist wrote that Mary Lincoln may have suffered from "pernicious anemia," which is caused by vitamin B_{12} deficiency. Other historians believe Mary suffered from mental illness of some sort, as she was committed to a mental institution in 1875.[24]

While many certainly saw her tantrums and abuse, many failed to recognize the better angels of Mary's nature and the blessings she brought to the Lincoln marriage. Few noticed the time she took to visit hospital wards and offer flowers and consolation to wounded Union soldiers. Few knew of her compassion for Southern blacks, or contrabands, and how hard she worked to find employment for them as they streamed into the capital throughout the war. Few understood how lonely and unfulfilled Mary was while her husband dealt with his numerous obligations during the war. Few realized how male rogues, sycophants, and deceitful newspaper reporters tried to take advantage of her loneliness by flattering her in order to acquire inside information about war strategy and the president. Few praised her faithfulness to her husband. Few saw how the First Couple treasured their daily four o'clock carriage ride around Washington, evenings at local theaters, or visits to the Soldiers' Home a few miles outside of the capital. Immensely proud of her husband, Mary frequently told people his heart was as big as his arms were long. Abe and Mary remained faithful and devoted despite the

---

[22] Burlingame, *Lincoln*, 2:784–85.

[23] Guelzo, *Lincoln,* 112.

[24] Johnson, *Last Weeks of Lincoln*, 109.

leadership demands of a violent civil war and the spotlight of the presidency.[25]

Contemporaries who could not understand why Abe stayed with Mary overlooked or underestimated the many blessings he enjoyed and appreciated about his wife. The two shared a love for politics and political heroes like Henry Clay. During their time in Springfield, Abe frequently consulted with Mary on political decisions. When they arrived at the pinnacle of the political world, he treasured Mary's confidence and edification. Unlike most politicians or media members, Mary had recognized her husband's brilliance from the very beginning of his political ascent. She predicted that he would become president for over two decades. Once in the Executive Mansion, she remained fiercely loyal to him—no small thing, considering the cruel and frequent criticism he received from Republicans and Democrats alike.

Mary's loyalty to her husband cannot be underestimated. Lincoln understood that her ties to the South, to her family, to the Union, and to him were under constant scrutiny. Mary's loyalty was suspect from the earliest days of the presidency because she had one full brother, three half brothers, and three brothers-in-law in the Confederate army. She could not afford to publicly mourn the loss of loved ones in battle, and her three half brothers—Sam, David, and Aleck Todd—were all killed. Even as she privately mourned, she acknowledged that these loved ones had been enemies of her

---

[25] Clinton, "Mourning in America," 82; Oates, *With Malice Toward None*, 274; Keneally, *Lincoln*, 108; Donald, *Lincoln*, 108; Oates, *Lincoln*, 179; Donald, *Lincoln at Home*, 47; Epstein, *Portrait of a Marriage*, 419; Goodwin, *Team of Rivals*, 609. One owner estimated that Lincoln saw over one hundred plays at his theater in the four years he was president. Lincoln went mostly with Seward, but Nicolay, Hay, and Stoddard (his three young assistants) also went often with him, as did Noah Brooks, Mary, and Tad. Lincoln also came by himself and enjoyed slipping in the back right of the audience as the show began.

nation and her husband. She told her a friend that they would "kill my husband if they could and destroy our government."[26]

Mary's half sister, Emilie Todd Helm, also lost her husband during the conflict. Before the beginning of the war, Lincoln had offered Ben Helm a safe federal army post because he genuinely loved his brother-in-law and wanted Mary's sister close at hand. When Lincoln heard of Ben's death, he said he felt "as David did of old when he was told of the death of Absalom."[27]

None of the Lincolns' love and mourning, however, mattered to Emilie Todd Helm. When she came to visit Mary in December 1863, Lincoln had to grant her a special pass to travel in Union states. Even after this kind gesture, Helm still refused to take an oath to the Union or acknowledge Lincoln as the real president (her president remained Jefferson Davis).

Despite Helm's intransigence, Lincoln let her stay in the Executive Mansion with a military escort, in an effort to provide comfort to Mary and to honor her family. Newspapers once again accused Mary of being a Confederate spy, and senators, congressmen, and military officers like General Sickles—who lost a leg at the Battle of Gettysburg—criticized the president for allowing a traitor to reside in the White House.

Unfortunately, Helm did not reciprocate Lincoln's generosity and kindness. The next summer she asked him for a license to sell six hundred bales of cotton, something the president could grant only if she took an oath of allegiance to the Union. When she refused, he felt duty bound to deny her request. Emilie wrote a scathing letter blaming the deaths of her husband and other Confederate Todds squarely on the Lincolns. Emilie's line "I also remind you that your minié bullets have made us what we are" hurt and angered Mary.[28]

---

[26] Goodwin, *Team of Rivals*, 359; Packard, *Lincolns in the White House*, 163–64.

[27] Packard, *Lincolns in the White House*, 163.

[28] Keneally, *Lincoln*, 153–54.

Due to her feeling of betrayal, and also out of loyalty to her husband and the Union cause, Mary never spoke to her sister again.

Just as the Civil War wreaked havoc on families and the psyche of the nation, so too did the war dramatically impact the Lincoln marriage. Mary's migraine headaches grew more frequent and painful during their days in the Executive Mansion. Lincoln was always a gangly specimen, but the stress and unending duties of the conflict interfered with his eating habits and made him look perilously thin. Mary tried to get her husband to eat more, to no avail.[29]

As he entered his second term, many associates noticed that Lincoln had become a very different man. He remained "the same kindly, genial, and cordial spirit he had been at first," said John Hay, "but the boisterous laughter became less frequent year by year; the eye grew veiled by constant meditation on momentous subjects; the air of reserve and detachment from his surroundings increased."[30]

The couples' communication and intimacy suffered during the last few years of the war. Abe often stayed late at the Executive Mansion or the telegraph office, working on war details or waiting for updates on troop movements. Too weary to talk much when he did come home late, he felt he could not confide in Mary anyway because she had demonstrated that she could not keep government affairs to herself. When she tried to inquire about such matters, he gave her evasive and generalized answers that did not quench her political and intellectual curiosity. On the other hand, Mary did not want to converse about "forbidden subjects" like her financial debt or shopping trips. A mutual reticence or unease existed at home, and neither knew quite how to handle the new norm.[31] While no sacrifice equaled that of soldiers dying for the cause or families losing loved ones to disease, the war required the Lincolns to sacrifice much of

---

[29] Oates, *Lincoln*, 179.

[30] Goodwin, *Team of Rivals*, 702.

[31] Oates, *With Malice Toward None*, 408–9.

their marriage for the cause too. Every day each of them carried the burdens of the war in their own unique ways.

There is no norm for a wartime marriage in the public eye. The fact that no portrait exists of the First Family, or even of Lincoln with his wife, is revealing and illustrative. Uncomfortable with the contrast of her short and squat frame beside that of her tall and thin husband, Mary did not ever want to be seen in an unflattering light. Yet such family portraits might have helped garner sympathy for her and her many plights as First Lady.[32] As was the case with many of her contemporaries, historians and biographers primarily portray Mary as a dark and gloomy reality Lincoln had to overcome while working to save the Union. His legacy shines overwhelmingly in the annals of history.

The truth is that their marriage was in the spotlight for the entirety of the war and his presidency. A spotlight reveals everything—the ups and downs, the strengths and weaknesses, the good and bad of the main performers. On the positive side of the ledger, there is Abe's patience and gentle understanding of his wife as well as Mary's tenacious public support for her husband. On the negative side, there is his aloofness as well as her abuse, deceit, and addictions. To be sure, there is much one can learn from a marriage that stuck together despite all the hardship and scrutiny.

The Truth

Mary Lincoln's jealousy of the attention her husband received from others, particularly women, developed into a real trial in the Lincoln marriage. Jealousy certainly can grow out of control and ruin a relationship. Scripture says that "a tranquil heart gives life to the flesh, but envy makes the bones rot."[33] The Bible also teaches

---

[32] Packard, *Lincolns in the White House*, 207.

[33] Prov. 14:30.

jealousy is one of "works of the flesh," and those who are jealous "will not inherit the kingdom of God."[34]

On the other hand, our great and good God, according to Scripture, is a "jealous God" because He wants our hearts and minds centered on Him.[35] One blessing of Christian marriage is that each partner can remind the other to stay focused on their relationship with God. Together they can grow closer to God and truly understand that He is all they need to flourish and live a life of peace, joy, and contentment.

Unfortunately, too many people in this world look to other things—sex, drugs, material goods, popularity, identity politics, fame—to fill their spiritual cups and make themselves feel worthy or happy. Later, sometimes too late, they realize that these worldly things may make them feel better about themselves for a moment, but do not last. They fill their souls with worldly things like a sugar high, then come crashing down after the buzz wears off, feeling more empty and vulnerable than before.

For too many people today, just like Mary Lincoln, the insatiable desire to acquire material possessions is one of those addictions that can lead to discontent, dissolution, bitterness, and emptiness. Of course, people justify the pursuit of worldly things for many selfish reasons. They may truly believe that wealth will fill a hole in their lives and give them satisfaction, meaning, and power.

The Bible warns how wealth can twist the human heart and cause people "to be haughty" and "set their hopes on the uncertainty of riches" instead of God, "who richly provides us with everything to enjoy."[36] Instead, those who focus on God and His Word "are to do good, to be rich in good works, to be generous and ready to share, thus storing up treasure for themselves as a good foundation for the future, so that they may take hold of that which is truly life."[37]

---

[34] Gal. 5:19-20, 21.

[35] Deut. 4:24.

[36] 1 Tim. 6:17

[37] 1 Tim. 6:18–19.

Indeed, everything "that is in the world—the desires of the flesh and the desires of the eyes and pride in possessions—is not from the Father but is from the world."[38]

Scripture explains that "those who desire to be rich fall into temptation, into a snare, into many senseless and harmful desires that plunge people into ruin and destruction. For the love of money is a root of all kinds of evils. It is through this craving that some have wandered away from the faith and pierced themselves with many pangs."[39] Money itself is not the evil, but the *love* of money. If you make a lot of money, good for you! Use it for God-pleasing things. If you love money and material things with your whole heart and mind, however, then you are crowding out the love and attention that should be going to God, family, and other loved ones.

There is no doubt that money and material goods have powerful allure for the frail human heart and mind. Jesus, who talked about money more than any topic other than the kingdom of heaven, warns about the temptation of wealth: "It is easier for a camel to go through the eye of a needle than for a rich person to enter the kingdom of God."[40] He also asserts that you should "be on your guard against all covetousness, for one's life does not consist in the abundance of his possessions."[41] The Bible exhorts you to "keep your life free from love of money, and be content with what you have, for he has said, 'I will never leave you nor forsake you.'"[42] Wealth can be fleeting. Today you can have it; tomorrow it can be gone. And as the saying goes, you cannot take it with you after you pass from earth.

Jesus encourages Christians to recognize true riches in life. "Do not lay up for yourselves treasures on earth, where moth and rust destroy and where thieves break in and steal, but lay up for yourselves treasures in heaven, where neither moth nor rust destroys and where

---

[38] 1 John 2:16.

[39] 1 Tim. 6:9-10.

[40] Matt. 19:24.

[41] Luke 12:15.

[42] Heb. 13:5.

thieves do not break in and steal. For where your treasure is, there your heart will be also."[43] Notice that He *does not* say that where your heart is, there your treasure will be also. In this sense, Jesus is data-driven. He knows where your heart and mind are focused, even if you say differently. Human talk can often be cheap. Moreover, the human heart can be fooled, can change, and can be distracted.

Jesus is the real treasure in your life. He never changes and will never abandon you. He walked the talk. He took action. He died and rose for you. He loves you. He is your everlasting treasure.

Your Life

Often we look at celebrities, politicians, entertainers, or other famous people and think about the material benefits that their social status brings. How did the pressures and challenges Mary and Abe endured as First Lady and president impact their relationship as husband and wife? Why should we be careful to judge other marriages or people who have very public profiles?

Mary's jealousy of anyone giving attention to her husband was quite profound. Have you been jealous of attention given to your spouse? Or have you been given special attention by others and noticed that it bothered your spouse? What should you do in either case?

What are some of the lessons God's Word teaches about the desire for material possessions or the love of money?

Jesus says, "By this all people will know that you are my disciples, if you have love for one another" (John 13:35). Specifically about

[43] Matt. 6:19–21.

marriage, He says, "So they are no longer two but one flesh. What therefore God has joined together, let not man separate" (Matt. 19:6). How does the Lincoln marriage measure up in your opinion? What lessons can we learn from analyzing their marriage and reflecting on God's Word? What more would you want to know about their marriage?

7

Prince of Rails

He was still speaking when, behold, a bright cloud overshadowed them, and a voice from the cloud said, "This is my beloved Son, with whom I am well pleased; listen to him."
—Matthew 17:5

The Lincoln Way

To follow in the footsteps of an effective leader is difficult, particularly if that leader is one's father.

Life would not be easy for any Lincoln child. Born on August 1, 1843, Robert Lincoln entered the world at a time when his father's circuit court duties and political ambitions kept him on the road and away from home for much of Robert's upbringing.

While father and son may not have been able to spend as much time together as either would have liked, they did have a loving and respectful relationship. Unlike his own father, Abe encouraged Robert to attend to his studies throughout his childhood. The Lincolns provided the best private education they could by enrolling Robert at Springfield Academy, where he studied for three years. During the next four years, Robert studied at Illinois State University prep school, where he earned an unimpressive B average.

Dreaming of a Harvard law degree, Bob traveled to Cambridge, Massachusetts, in August 1859, only to fail the entrance exams. After Robert was denied admittance to Harvard, the Lincolns registered their sixteen year-old at a boarding school, Phillips Exeter Academy, in New Hampshire. There, he excelled. Visiting Robert for several days after his Cooper Union Speech in late February 1860, Lincoln delighted in his son's brilliance and growing confidence. These were the "charmed" days between father and son, which had not materialized earlier in their relationship.

Robert eventually gained admittance to Harvard. He wanted to become a lawyer, which became a source of pride for his father.[1] Before classes began, Robert stumped for his father in northeastern states during the 1860 presidential campaign. Once at Harvard, Robert endured ridicule and criticism because of his father. Most Easterners only knew the cruel frontier caricatures exploited by Lincoln's political enemies during the campaign. They piled on the insults, sensing Robert's unwillingness to respond. He admitted that his father was "the queerest old cuss you ever saw" to some upperclassmen trying to humiliate him.[2] Robert may have been embarrassed by some of the things his father had said and done, or he may have simply wanted to blend in with the student body by downplaying his father's political preeminence.

To make matters worse, after Robert accompanied his mother on her pre-inaugural shopping trip to New York City, the press dubbed him the "Prince of Rails"—a reference to his father's rail-splitting reputation and to the Prince of Wales, heir to the British throne, who had famously visited the White House during President Buchanan's final months.[3]

Once Lincoln had been elected president of the United States, Robert rode with his father on the train from Springfield to Washington, DC. In Washington, Lincoln panicked when he realized Robert had rather nonchalantly misplaced the draft of the

---

1 Freehling, *Becoming Lincoln*, 239–40; Manning, *Father Lincoln*, 108–10, 114, 186. That Robert chose to follow in his father's footsteps with a career in law and public service suggests that Lincoln succeeded as a dad whereas his own father, Thomas, had failed.

2 Packard, *Lincolns in the White House,* 69.

3 Packard, *Lincolns in the White House*, 70.

inaugural address. However, by the early hours of Inauguration Day, Lincoln was able to read over the relocated address several times and then ask Robert to read it aloud so that he could hear how it sounded.[4] Together father and son embraced a special moment during no ordinary time in American history.

Unfortunately, the heavy wartime duties required of a commander in chief, and Robert's studies in Cambridge, prohibited the two from spending much time together during the Lincoln administration. Robert later explained that "any great intimacy between us became impossible. I scarcely even had ten minutes quiet talk with him during his Presidency, on account of his constant devotion to business."[5] Knowing the relentless demand on the president's time, Robert visited the Executive Mansion only a few times.

With the Union position at one of its tenuous low points, and with a reelection campaign in full swing, Lincoln did not make it to Robert's commencement ceremony at Harvard in the spring of 1864. Enrolled at Harvard Law School, Robert received criticism for not serving in the Union army. In addition to being called a coward, he endured a law professor's harangue of his father for abusing the Constitution, especially the attempt to suspend the writ of habeas corpus. Few people realized that Mary Lincoln adamantly opposed Robert serving in the Union army, fearing the loss of yet another son. Eventually, Robert got his way, much to his mother's objections and devastation, and enlisted in the army. He became "exceedingly popular," according to one fellow officer, because of his geniality, hard work, and refusal to receive any special treatment.[6]

On the morning of Lincoln's assassination, father and son shared a special moment, though neither realized it would be their last breakfast together. Glad that his eldest son had returned safely from the war front, Lincoln celebrated and relished his son's company.

---

[4] Burlingame, *Lincoln*, 2:7; Manning, *Father Lincoln*, 114, 117.

[5] Goodwin, *Team of Rivals*, 541.

[6] Lachman, *The Last Lincolns*, 15; Manning, *Father Lincoln*, 177.

Lincoln expressed joy that Robert planned to return to Harvard Law School and become a lawyer. Mary invited their son to join them at Ford's Theatre for an evening performance of *Our American Cousin,* but Robert politely declined. He wanted to spend a quiet evening with his close friend and his father's personal secretary, John Hay—a decision that would fill him with guilt for the rest of his life.[7]

This Matthew Brady photo of Robert Lincoln was taken in 1865, the year that Robert's father was assassinated. (Library of Congress, LC-DIG-ppmsca-19229)

Robert received universal praise for how he took care of his mother and younger brother, Tad, after his father's horrid death. "His manly bearing," said one presidential assistant, "made me feel that he was a worthy son of a worthy father."[8] Shortly after his father's passing, he resigned his army captain's commission and personally inspected the president's box at Ford's Theatre. He noticed a chair

[7] Manning, *Father Lincoln*, 178; Peterson, *Lincoln in American Memory*.

[8] Lachman, *The Last Lincolns*, 58–59.

at the rear of the box, close to the door where the assassin Booth had entered. Perhaps if he had been sitting in it that night, he could have stopped Booth. Over the years, Robert would return several times to Ford's Theatre, always wondering what he might have been able to do if he had only accepted his parent's invitation to attend the show.

Robert would become Lincoln's only son to survive into adulthood. In addition to dealing with the guilt of his father's assassination, he would experience a different kind of heartache in taking care of his highly volatile and erratic mother for decades. He would eventually be compelled to commit his mother to an insane asylum and endure her wrath and disownment.

Professionally, Robert would go on to become an immensely successful and prominent Chicago lawyer. He served as secretary of war in the James Garfield and Chester Arthur administrations. Upon observing President Garfield's assassination and passing in his bed, Robert, unfortunately, became the first man to witness two presidential deathwatches. After his tenure as war secretary, friends encouraged him to run for the highest political office in the land, but he refused. Instead President Benjamin Harrison appointed him minister to Great Britain in 1889.

Less than a decade later, Pullman Car Company named him president pro tempore of the company following the death of its founder, George Pullman. The company made Robert the permanent president four years later. During his tenure at Pullman, the company experienced significant growth, and Robert became a very wealthy man. In addition to his financial success, the son of the Great Emancipator made his own reputation for benevolence toward African Americans as the Pullman Company became the nation's largest employer of Negroes.[9] While he did not have to rise from poverty as his father did, Robert made a mark in the world and displayed charity to all people. His father would have been proud.

---

[9] Lachman, *The Last Lincolns*, 268; Manning, *Father Lincoln*, 182; Peterson, *Lincoln in American Memory*, 258.

Robert Lincoln's last major public appearance came in the nation's capital at the Lincoln Memorial dedication service on May 30, 1922. The statue of Abraham Lincoln was nineteen feet tall and made of Georgia marble; Robert saw his father memorialized in stone. In the wall behind the statue are the words, "In this temple as in the hearts of the people for whom he saved the union the memory of Abraham Lincoln is enshrined forever." On the southern wall is an inscription of Lincoln's Gettysburg Address, and on the northern wall is his second inaugural address. A mural depicting the Angel of Truth freeing a slave is also present at the site. Robert received the greatest ovation of the day from the many distinguished guests who attended the event. He returned often to the memorial.[10]

Robert spent the last years of his life living at his spectacular estate, Hildene, located in Manchester, Vermont, near the location where his mother had occasionally visited to escape the trials of wartime Washington. He died in his bed on July 26, 1926, at the age of eighty-two. His wife had him buried at Arlington National Cemetery against his wishes. His son, Abraham Lincoln II, had passed in 1890 at the age of sixteen. Robert had placed the boy's casket in the family tomb in Springfield. Robert's wife moved their son's remains to Arlington too after Robert died. Present in the aftermath of the assassination of Presidents Lincoln, Garfield, and McKinley, Robert lies not far from the burial site of President John F. Kennedy, the fourth chief executive to be struck down by an assassin's bullet. Not always able to be close to his busy father when he lived, Robert's remains came in close proximity to all four of America's assassinated presidents.[11]

Some historians and biographers contend that Robert's words demonstrate a strained and distant relationship between father and son. A closer examination of the historical record, however, reveals

---

[10] Lachman, *The Last Lincolns*, 363; Packard, *Lincolns in the White House*, 263–65.

[11] Packard, *Lincolns in the White House*, 263–65; Manning, *Father Lincoln*, 183.

that Robert did not want to indulge biographers and historians with the more sensational aspects of his father's personal life, especially while his mother remained alive and in torment about the loss of her husband. Robert spoke sparingly about his father and did not divulge much about anything. He minimized his relationship with his dad in order to keep the press away and retain some measure of family privacy.

Robert knew full well, for example, that biographers were seeking information about Lincoln's relationship with Ann Rutledge and attempting to dig up dirt in order to portray his mother in a negative light. "While it is true," Robert wrote shortly after his father's death, "that the details of the private life of a public man have always a great interest in the minds of some—it is after all his works which make him live—& the rest is but secondary."[12] Having failed to safeguard his father from an assassin's bullet, Robert played the protector of his mother and father's legacy.

Robert deserves immense credit for growing up and facing the scrutiny that inevitably came as the eldest child of the Great Emancipator. Not only did he accomplish great things in his personal and professional lives; he also became his own man. Robert witnessed his father's rise as a national figure, public service as president, and inspiration to the American experience. The Prince of Rails could have fallen off the tracks at any time in his life, and most people would have excused his behavior if he had. Instead, he thrived and traveled his own path, just as his father had before him.

The Truth

It's not easy being a parent, especially a Christian one. To be sure, Christian parents are to help their children grow into the unique men and women God created them to be. More importantly, they are to share God's Word and teach the Christian faith. As the

[12] Manning, *Father Lincoln,* xiii, 99.

Psalmist writes, parents, "even to old age and gray hairs," are to proclaim God's "might to another generation" and to all who can hear.[13] Moms and dads are not to deny or hide God's Word "from their children, but tell to the coming generation the glorious deeds of the Lord, and his might, and the wonders that he has done."[14] Each generation must commend God's works to another, and declare His mighty acts.[15]

If parents truly love their children, they will want to give them the very best thing for their lives on earth and for eternity. God explains:

> Hear, my son, and accept my words, that the years of your life may be many. I have taught you the way of wisdom; I have led you in the paths of uprightness. When you walk, your step will not be hampered, and if you run, you will not stumble. Keep hold of instruction; do not let go; guard her, for she is your life … My son, be attentive to my words; incline your ear to my sayings. Let them not escape from your sight; keep them within your heart. For they are life to those who find them, and healing to all their-flesh. Keep your heart with all vigilance, for from it flow the springs of life.[16]

Robert Lincoln loved his parents, and wanted the best for them too. Robert, as a dutiful son, worked hard to protect his father's legacy. He did not want biographers, historians, or the general public to know everything about his father and mother, probably because he did not want his mother to be hurt or his father's legacy to be tarnished in any way.

---

13 Ps. 71:18.

14 Ps. 78:4.

15 Ps. 145:4.

16 Prov. 4:10–13, 20–23.

As Christians, however, we know that God sees us in every moment. Indeed, He is right beside us and inside us, thanks to the Holy Spirit. God hears us and knows our every thought, word, and deed. The old saying that true character is revealed when no one is looking may encourage ethical behavior and integrity in one way. On the other hand, the realization that sinful character is revealed to God in private and public moments is also frightening. "Nothing is covered up that will not be revealed, or hidden that will not be known," Jesus said. "Therefore whatever you have said in the dark shall be heard in the light, and what you have whispered in private rooms shall be proclaimed on the housetops."[17] "'Can a man hide himself in secret places so that I cannot see him?' declares the Lord. 'Do I not fill heaven and earth?' declares the Lord."[18]

God sees you—all of you. "And no creature is hidden from his sight, but all are naked and exposed to the eyes of him to whom we must give account."[19] While there is, perhaps, a comfort knowing that the general public may not know about your specific sins or sinful behavior, God will still know.

The good news is that God had a plan of salvation arranged since the beginning of time to rescue you (and all of humankind) from depravity. The Bible says, "He has delivered us from the domain of darkness and transferred us to the kingdom of his beloved Son."[20] Or as the gospel of John puts it so eloquently, "God so loved the world, that he gave his only Son, that whoever believes in him should not perish but have eternal life."[21] Because of Jesus, when God sees you, He sees His Son interceding for you, covering over you, and protecting you. You do not have to hide anything. You are seen by God. You are loved by Him. You are His son or daughter.

---

[17] Luke 12:2–3.

[18] Jer. 23:24.

[19] Heb. 4:12–13.

[20] Col. 1:13.

[21] John 3:16.

Your Life

How are you like your mom and dad but different from them? What do you attribute your similarities and differences to?

As a parent, how can you pass on values and faith to your children while giving them the space and time to grow into their own people?

Knowing that God is an all-seeing and all-hearing God, how does that truth make you feel, think, and act in private and public?

Knowing that God is a God of grace and mercy, how does that truth make you feel, think, and act in private or public?

8

Parenting Paradigm

Behold, children are a heritage from the Lord,
the fruit of the womb a reward.
—Psalm 127:3

The Lincoln Way

Parenting is the toughest and most rewarding vocation on earth.

Too often history uncovers esteemed public figures who were despised by their children in private. Lincoln does not fit that mold. Lincoln's kids loved him dearly. Determined that they would have a very different relationship with him than he did with his father, Lincoln did everything in his power to make sure his kids experienced a happy, joy-filled upbringing. He struggled nevertheless—the same way many modern day fathers do—in balancing a successful career with the crucial vocation of fatherhood. Like most dads, sometimes he succeeded and sometimes he failed.[1]

Lincoln had a special relationship with each of his four sons. Robert, his firstborn, knew his father as a rising country lawyer and politician. He would campaign for his dad in the 1860 presidential election and visit the White House. Eddie tragically died of consumption just before the age of four, in 1850. Afterward, Lincoln grew closer to several pastors and ministers who would have a profound influence on his life. The most revealing portraits

[1] Manning, *Father Lincoln*, xii, 186.

of Lincoln the father, however, encompass the relationships he had with his two youngest sons, William (Willie) and Thomas (Tad).

Born ten months after the death of Eddie, Willie reminded most contemporaries of his father, except he was considered more handsome. Studious, intelligent, methodical, thoughtful, imaginative, curious, articulate, frank, precocious, and lovable were all terms commonly used to describe him. Willie exhibited great intellect and promise. He excelled in grammar, writing, and poetry. In his leisure time, he loved drawing up railway timetables and managing imaginary train routes. An energetic lad, Willie certainly acted like any mischievous boy and drove his tutors wild with good-natured disobedience from time to time. Like his father, Willie demonstrated a comfort with solitude. He often secluded himself in his mother's bedroom while reading a book or writing poetry. Possessing a keen sense of history, Willie kept newspaper clippings about his father's inauguration, the Civil War, and deaths of important politicians.[2]

Willie was a good example for his younger brother Tad. He took religious instruction seriously. Both boys went to the Taft residence on Saturday mornings to study Sunday school lessons, and Willie embraced biblical instruction earnestly and with a childlike faith. After he learned about keeping the Sabbath day holy, for example, he no longer went on carriage rides with his brother or parents on Sunday afternoons—though he had no problem playing with his friend Bud on Sundays. Instead of creating a distraction in the pews, he sat in church and paid great attention to the pastors' messages. When Tad received a scolding for creating a disturbance during a church service, he blurted out in front of the entire congregation, "Just keep your eyes on Willie, sitting there good as pie."[3]

With Eddie having passed, Robert being a bit distant, and Tad being afflicted with learning disabilities, Mary and Abe not only

---

[2] Conway, *Lincoln's White House*, 38; Oates, *With Malice Toward None*, 288; Manning, *Father Lincoln*, 129.

[3] Manning, *Father Lincoln*, 127.

had great expectations for Willie but probably anticipated that he would be their prime caretaker later in life. Almost everyone who knew the Lincolns considered Willie the favorite of both parents. Good-looking, cheerful, polite, and mature for his age, Willie was liked by almost everyone who met him, despite his occasional rambunctiousness. One cabinet member wrote in his diary that the Lincolns "idolized" Willie.[4] Mary referred to him as "my comfort."[5] Since he received so much praise for looking, talking, and acting like his father, most assumed Willie was Abe's favorite child too.[6]

Born in April 1853, with an unusually large head and a skinny body, Thomas was named after Lincoln's recently deceased father and soon acquired the nickname Tad after Lincoln called him a little tadpole. The name would stick for the rest of his life. The only Lincoln child ever baptized, Tad struggled throughout his life with a speech impediment—a lisp—due to a cleft palate.[7] While Willie had the mind and disposition of his father, Tad inherited his father's long limbs, dark hair, and murky complexion as well as his mother's propensity for fits of rage.[8]

Lincoln wanted to be closer to Willie and Tad than he had been to his eldest son. With improvements in transportation—the spread of railroads in particular—Lincoln could travel home more often for weekends. Springfield residents called him "hen pecked" since he spent so much time with the boys and often took over for Mary. Lincoln loved carting his boys around town in a wagon, reading from a book that he held in one hand. When they got older, he would hold their hands as they walked the neighborhoods. When one got tired, he set that boy up on his shoulders for a ride home.[9] He wrestled constantly with the boys, even in front of guests, and

4 Sandburg, *Lincoln,* 290.

5 Wheeler, *Faith and Courage*, 169.

6 Clinton, "Family," 164; Lachman, *The Last Lincolns*, 37.

7 Donald, *Lincoln*, 154; White, *Lincoln*, 181–82.

8 Lachman, *The Last Lincolns*, 27.

9 Donald, *Lincoln*, 159.

always stopped working on his tasks whenever the boys demanded his attention. Even Mary, who also let the boys run free, thought her husband's indulgence went too far. "It is my pleasure that my children are free—happy and unrestrained by parental tyranny," Lincoln said to Mary, drawing a contrast with his own childhood. "Love is the chain whereby to lock a child to his parent."[10]

The parenting paradigm the Lincolns established allowed their two youngest boys to wreak havoc everywhere they went.[11] In Lincoln and Herndon's law office, Willie and Tad took down books, emptied trash cans, dumped coal ashes, and danced on the pile. To Herndon's dismay, Lincoln did nothing. "Had they s—t in Lincoln's hat and rubbed it on his books, he would have laughed and thought it was smart," he asserted. "I wanted to wring their little necks and yet out of respect for Lincoln I kept my mouth shut."[12] Lincoln adored his children, liked and disliked what they liked and disliked.

---

[10] Manning, *Father Lincoln*, 81.

[11] Mary and Abe's laissez-faire parenting started with Robert and Eddie. One great illustration of this occurred in the fall of 1847, when the Lincolns went to Kentucky to visit Mary's family. Joseph Humphreys, a nephew of Mary's stepmother Elizabeth Todd, happened to be on the same train as the Lincoln family. Having never met before, the Lincolns and Humphreys made the entire trip without realizing the family connection. When Humphreys, who had no luggage and was traveling alone, arrived before the Lincolns, he told Mrs. Todd about his journey. "Aunt Betsey, I was never so glad to get off a train in my life. There were two lively youngsters on board who kept the whole train in turmoil, and their long-legged father, instead of spanking the brats, looked pleased as Punch and aided and abetted the older one in mischief." As the Lincolns approached the Todd house, Humphreys looked out the window and, realizing who they were, exclaimed, "Good Lord, there they are now!" He quickly left the house and never returned during the Lincolns' visit (Manning, Father Lincoln, 39). Donald, *Lincoln*, 109. Lincoln used to make fun of his wife for the whippings she tried to give Robert. After Eddie's birth, both parents gave up disciplining their offspring.

[12] Donald, *Lincoln*, 160.

While Herndon referred to them as "little devils," he acknowledged how Lincoln loved them with a full and tender heart.[13]

Both boys had their mischievous sides and moments. Tad often acted up in church. One time Lincoln took the misbehaving Tad home "slung over his father's arm like a pair of saddlebags." Other times when Tad let loose with a temper tantrum, Lincoln used his oversize arms to keep Tad at arm's length, laughing as the boy tried in vain to kick him in the face. Willie once ran naked down the street when Mary turned her back on him to prepare a bath. Lincoln watched in amusement as Mary became hysterical. Lincoln eventually chased Willie down and hoisted him up on his shoulders for the return home.[14]

Contemporaries were astonished at the lack of discipline Lincoln administered. One day while he played chess in his office with Judge Samuel Treat, Tad or Willie delivered repeated calls to come home for dinner. Engrossed in the chess match, Lincoln lost track of time and continued to play. Exasperated, the boy kicked the chess board, causing the pieces to fly all over the office. The stunning thing, according to Judge Treat, was that Lincoln did not lose his cool or scold his son. Instead Lincoln told the judge they would have to resume their game some other time, took his boy by the hand, and left. Another version of the story had Judge Treat reprimanding Lincoln for not punishing his son. "Considering the position of your pieces, Judge, at the time of the upheaval," Lincoln allegedly responded, "I think you had not reason to complain."[15]

The two boys loved their pranks and brought an incredible amount of youthful energy to the Executive Mansion. On the train trip from Springfield to Washington, as Lincoln prepared to assume the presidency, Willie and Tad asked visitors who came aboard, "Do

---

13 Packard, *Lincolns in the White House*, 75; Burlingame, *Lincoln*, 1:254.

14 Manning, *Father Lincoln*, 83–84.

15 Manning, *Father Lincoln*, 81, 214.

you want to see Old Abe?" They would then point out someone beside their father.

Once they took up residence, the roof of the Executive Mansion became a playground and a military fort for the boys. They painted small logs to look like cannons and fired away at unseen Confederates across the Potomac River. They also tried a doll named Jack, found him guilty of desertion, shot him to death, and buried him in the White House lawn. When the gardener dug Jack up for a rose bed, Tad and Willie went to their father to grant Jack a pardon. Lincoln, on executive stationery, wrote "The Doll Jack is pardoned by order of the President" and signed it "A. Lincoln."[16]

Willie and Tad often broke into their father's office in the middle of meetings. They ran and yelled throughout the corridors of the Executive Mansion in front of annoyed politicians. Tad liked to stand in front of the grand staircase and collect a nickel "entrance fee" from callers on the way to visit the president. They collected animals too; ponies, kittens, white rabbits, a turkey, a goat that slept in Tad's bed, and a dog named Jip that curled up in Lincoln's lap at meals. After discovering how the White House bell system worked, with cords running down to various rooms below for Lincoln or the staff to pull when they wanted something, the two boys rang all the bells at once, setting the mansion into pandemonium. Tad also once ate all the strawberries prepared for a state dinner. Since children were something new at the Executive Mansion, the boys received lots of new gifts including a pony for Willie, which he allowed Tad to ride, and two small and beloved goats, Nanko and Nanny—which proceeded to tear up the Executive Mansion garden. Occasionally Tad harnessed Nanko up to a chair, which served as a cart, and once drove through the East Room during a reception. The hysterical scene had dignified matrons lifting up their hoop skirts to avoid a

[16] Oates, *With Malice Toward None,* 287-288.

collision with Nanko and a boisterous Tad before the two exited the room.[17] The Lincoln boys constantly rocked the president's house.

While Willie could calm down and quietly entertain himself, Tad's personality kept his parents on the move. Only eight years old when they entered the People's House, Tad could not read or dress himself. Yet he did manage to terrorize the Executive Mansion by breaking into cabinet meetings and running up to his father "like a small thunderbolt," said one observer.[18] He constantly demanded that his father hug him or hold him on his lap and read him a story. During one meeting, Tad marched into the room, beating a drum. His father told him to make less noise. Tad continued to beat the drum throughout the meeting without any follow-up from Lincoln. On another occasion, Tad kicked a ball and broke a mirror. When a senator chastised the boy for his mishap, he replied: "I don't believe Paw will care."[19]

Though a bright lad, Tad struggled with reading. Lincoln, who loved to read, tried to lessen Mary's concern about Tad's learning disabilities. Their son had plenty of time to learn how to read, write, and "get poky."[20] While Tad often got frustrated that others could not understand him, Lincoln could always decipher Tad's words and desires. For this reason and so many others, Tad adored his father. He often hung out with Lincoln in his office until he fell asleep. Lincoln would eventually carry him off to bed.

A few days before the 1864 presidential election, when Pennsylvania soldiers quartered at the White House were casting their absentee ballots, Tad watched the voting from his father's office with great interest. Teasingly, Lincoln asked his son if his pet turkey intended to vote too (the turkey was following soldiers as they walked to the polling location). "Oh, no," Tad replied. "He is

---

[17] Donald, *Lincoln,* 275, 309; Oates, *With Malice Toward None,* 287-288.

[18] Wheeler, *Faith and Courage,* 169.

[19] Conway, *Lincoln's White House,* 40.

[20] Donald, *Lincoln*, 428.

not of age." Lincoln delighted in retelling the exchange for weeks.[21] Tad's learning and speech struggles, when added to his tender heart, genuine happiness, and zest for life, made him an endearing and lovable son.[22]

After Willie's tragic death in February 1862, Abe grew even closer to Tad. He planned to give Tad everything he could no longer give his departed Willie.[23] Even in the midst of his executive busyness and civil war, Lincoln found time to take Tad to Stuntz's toy shop frequently. "I want to give him all the toys I did not have and all the toys that I would have given the boy who went away," he explained.[24] Tad certainly took advantage of his father's indulgence, demanding and obtaining even more favors from his father. Lincoln issued "official requests" on Tad's behalf to the secretary of navy for a sword, the secretary of war for some flags, and to an army captain to locate "a little gun he cannot hurt himself with."[25] In February, 1864, when a fire burned down the Executive Mansion stables, Lincoln tried to save the steeds to no avail. Concerned for their President's safety, guards pulled him back from the blaze. Abe and Tad wept for the loss, especially because Willie's pony was among the animals killed.

---

21 Goodwin, *Team of Rivals*, 665; Manning, *Father Lincoln*, 159.

22 Donald, *Lincoln*, 428; Wheeler, *Faith and Courage*, 169.

23 Burlingame, *Lincoln*, 2:301–2.

24 Clinton, "Family," 265.

25 Clinton, "Family," 265.

This Alexander Gardner photo of Lincoln and Tad is believed to have been taken in early February 1865. After Willie's passing in 1862, Lincoln and Tad grew even closer as father and son. (Library of Congress, LC-USZ62-7990)

With the loss of Willie, Mary's incapacitating grief, and the daily trials of leading the Union, Lincoln and Tad needed each other more than ever during the last two years of the Lincoln presidency. In Tad, Abe had a companion, a source of amusement, and a welcome distraction from challenging duties.[26] While heading to Fortress Monroe one day, Lincoln tried to converse with government officials about administrative business, but Tad kept interrupting. "Tad, if you will be a good boy," said an exasperated Lincoln, "and not disturb me any more till we get to Fortress Monroe, I will give you a dollar." The proposal worked only for a few short minutes. Tad soon forgot his promise and continued on as noisy and disruptive as

[26] Manning, *Father Lincoln*, 163.

ever. When the traveling party reached their destination, however, Tad had no conscience about demanding the dollar. Lincoln looked at his son and asked, "Tad, do you think you have earned it?" Tad replied in the affirmative. Lincoln gave him the dollar. "Well, my son, at any rate, I will keep *my* part of the bargain."[27]

In the final days of the war, Tad held his father's hand as they toured the dusty, rubble-strewn streets of Union-occupied Richmond, Virginia. The touching scene—showing father and son physically and emotionally close—might also have been the first time young Tad understood the magnitude of his father's work. Tad witnessed freed slaves running up and thanking his father for their liberty. He also observed his father's humility in telling the freedmen to give God the praise and glory, not him. That his father did not gloat about the Union conquest of Richmond, but demonstrated graciousness and class, also made an impression on his son.[28]

Shortly after Lincoln's assassination, Dr. Phineas Gurley, the pastor who had delivered the eulogy at Willie's funeral, approached the surviving son. "Where is my Pa? Where is my Pa?" Tad repeatedly cried. "Taddy, your Pa is dead," Gurley said somberly. Tad immediately became inconsolable. "O what shall I do? What shall I do?" he wailed. "My brother is dead. My father is dead. O what shall I do?" Even amidst his grief, Tad knew what he had lost in the death of his father. "What will become of me? Oh what shall I do? O mother you will not die will you? O don't you die ma. You won't die will you mother? If you die I shall be all alone." Even Gurley could not contain his tears upon witnessing Tad's meltdown.[29]

After Tad and his mother moved out of the Executive Mansion a few weeks later, workmen found Tad's vast collection of toy soldiers. These hand-carved figurines were his favorite playthings—and they had been purchased by his father. Tad had left the beautiful toy

---

27 Carpenter, *Six Months in the White House*, 116.

28 Manning, *Father Lincoln,* 175.

29 Manning, *Father Lincoln,* 180.

soldiers behind because he could no longer bear to see them without thinking about his loving dad.[30]

In the aftermath of his father's death, Tad showed his father's compassion and tenderness by rarely leaving his disconsolate mother's side. When they returned from Europe in the spring of 1871, they ran into John Hay, formerly one of Lincoln's personal secretaries, in New York City. Hay noted Tad's stunning physical and emotional growth since he had last seen the obnoxious, lawless, "absolute tyrant" six years earlier. Sobered and "fixed" by his father's assassination, Tad had grown up to become a fine, gracious man who was benevolent, tender, and compassionate to his mother. Hay thoroughly enjoyed his visit and found Tad to be a "cordial, frank, warm-hearted boy" and "greatly improved" by his time abroad.[31]

When Mary and Tad returned to Chicago in May 1871, Tad developed a chest cold. As a teenager he had endured several bronchial infections, but this time his condition became more severe. Every breath felt like a knife plunging into his chest. Diagnosed with dropsy, Tad had in fact contracted pleurisy, a viral infection that in that era often accompanied tuberculosis. After being cared for by Tad for years after her husband's death, Mary now tried to care for Tad—to no avail. This would be the fourth deathbed vigil Mary would have to observe with her immediate family. After a few weeks, Tad's lungs became so full of mucus and fluid that he could not breathe if he lay down. He had to be propped up day and night. His heart, compressed by bodily fluids, stopped beating on July 15, 1871. The boy who had once lit up the White House with energy, vitality, and noise had passed at the age of eighteen.

Tad's coffin arrived at Oak Ridge Cemetery in Springfield a few weeks later. His remains were placed in the same tomb as his beloved

---

[30] Lachman, *The Last Lincolns*, 46.

[31] Lachman, *The Last Lincolns*, 159.

brother, Willie, and the brother he had never met, Eddie. Tad's body rested next to his father once again.[32]

While Eddie, Willie, and Tad had all died much too young, they did have the privilege of experiencing a wonderful, loving relationship with their father. For Willie and Tad especially, the fact that their father had risen to the highest office in the land mattered much less than being able to read a book or wrestle with their dad in his office. Lincoln left important legacies in many public and private ways.

The Truth

One of the reasons parenting is a tough job is because it often requires tough love. In a world that craves instant gratification, too many parents are not willing to administer proper discipline for fear of not being liked by their children. Yet what children often need more than anything is discipline and tough love. Like a tree that needs to be pruned for years before it fills out and forms a beautiful canopy, a child needs to be constantly disciplined so that they can grow deep roots and strong, fruitful branches.

Yet there is a proper balance to be established between a parent's discipline on the one hand and a loving kindness on the other. Abraham Lincoln's life displays the two extremes. His father only gave him discipline, never compassion or gentleness. When Abe became a father, he rarely administered any kind of discipline to his children.

The Bible teaches moderation in parenting. "Do not withhold discipline from a child," Scripture says, "if you strike him with a rod, he will not die."[33] At the same time, the Bible teaches that "as a father

---

[32] Lachman, *The Last Lincolns*, 161-167.

[33] Prov. 23:13.

shows compassion to his children, so the Lord shows compassion to those who fear him."[34]

Children are to listen to and never forsake their parents' instruction, for it is like "a graceful garland for your head and pendants for your neck."[35] So too are we, as God's children, to embrace the tough love and discipline our Heavenly Father gives to us. As the Bible teaches:

> It is for discipline that you have to endure. God is treating you as sons. For what son is there whom his father does not discipline? If you are left without discipline, in which all have participated, then you are illegitimate children and not sons. Besides this, we have had earthly fathers who disciplined us and we respected them. Shall we not much more be subject to the Father of spirits and live? For they disciplined us for a short time as it seemed best to them, but he disciplines us for our good, that we may share his holiness. For the moment all discipline seems painful rather than pleasant, but later it yields the peaceful fruit of righteousness to those who have been trained by it.[36]

The most important thing parents can do for their children, however, is to teach them God's Word and the love of Jesus Christ. When the disciples refused to allow children to come to Jesus "that he might lay his hands on them and pray," Jesus showed His displeasure and said, "Let the little children come to me and do not hinder them, for to such belongs the kingdom of heaven." Then "he laid his hands on them and went away."[37] Indeed, the Bible asserts

---

[34] Ps. 103:13.

[35] Prov. 1:8–9.

[36] Heb. 12:7–11.

[37] Matt. 19:13–15.

that "all your children shall be taught by the Lord, and great shall be the peace of your children."[38]

God commands you to "train up a child in the way he should go; even when he is old he will not depart from it."[39] Christian parents can especially appreciate the scriptural admonition to continue in what "you have learned and have firmly believed, knowing from whom you learned it and how from childhood you have been acquainted with the sacred writings, which are able to make you wise for salvation through faith in Christ Jesus."[40]

Children grow up fast, and there is nothing guaranteed here on this earth, including the number of days one will live. As a parent, guardian, grandparent, or caring individual, do not wait to teach children what is most important. Jesus paid the price for their sins. They are forgiven.

This life will pass away in the blink of an eye, but eternity is forever. If you love or care for someone, make sure this individual is raised in the nurture and admonition of the Lord. Even with adults who do not know the Lord, go ahead and share God's Word with them. We are all children of a Heavenly Father. Share the life-changing and life-saving grace of Jesus Christ. Keep Jesus and the good news "on your heart," and teach God's Word "diligently to your children," in your home, "and when you walk by the way, and when you lie down, and when you rise."[41] Make your home a house of the Lord.

Your Life

Sometimes you learn what to do by watching others. Sometimes you learn what *not to do* by watching others. In regard to child-rearing,

---

[38] Isa. 54:13.

[39] Prov. 22:6.

[40] 2 Tim. 3:14–15.

[41] Deut. 6:6–9.

some say that you will parent your children in the same manner that your parents parented you. Lincoln proved otherwise. How was the way you raised your children similar to the manner in which your parents raised you? How was it different?

According to Scripture, what is emphasized in regard to parental discipline? What is the most important thing parents can teach their children?

What do you want your children to remember about you?

9

Party and a Funeral

So it is not the will of my Father who is in heaven
that one of these little ones should perish.
—Matthew 18:14

The Lincoln Way

Effective leaders must learn how to handle and embrace mountaintop experiences as well as valley moments.

No parent wants to bury a child before the parent's own earthly passing. Unfortunately, the Lincolns saw two of their sons suffer and die agonizing deaths at very young ages. Mary later witnessed a third son's death from an excruciating disease at the early age of eighteen. While Mary and Abe endured and managed their grief differently, Lincoln in particular did not feel comfortable exhibiting sorrow in public. He was conscious that many other families had lost loved ones in a brutal civil war, which ultimately claimed the lives of over six hundred thousand Americans. Many households were losing sons, but the country had only one president.

Early in their marriage, in February 1850, the Lincolns lost their beloved three-year old son Eddie. Like many who lose a child, the Lincolns displayed remarkable perseverance and resilience as they moved on with their lives—though neither was ever quite the same.[1]

---

[1] Winkle, *Young Eagle*, 284. The Lincolns overindulged and overprotected Tad and Willie after Eddie's death from consumption. Mary, for example, developed a paranoia about the world outdoors, in particular fretting about

After assuming the office of the presidency, the Lincolns, being savvy politicians, were the first residents of the Executive Mansion to see the potential of making their home a national stage. As has become standard operating procedure for presidential administrations today, the Lincolns brought in artists and performers as part of their official political outreach.[2] They also continued an existing tradition of Tuesday evening levees, which were open to the public.

Mary, however, had even bigger plans. Early in her husband's first term, she scheduled a grand party and sent out five hundred invitations. In previous administrations, social events at the Executive Mansion had been primarily state dinners. This gathering would be different. Mary intended to build an aura about the Lincoln presidency as well as show off the refurbished mansion. Not liking the exclusivity of the event, or the optics of hosting a ball while soldiers suffered, Lincoln tried to talk Mary out of the gala.[3] He gave in to his wife's wishes after a spirited argument. Many in Washington felt snubbed when they did not receive an invitation to "the Greatest Show on earth," as one Lincoln aide dubbed the event.[4] After some political reconsideration, an additional three hundred invitations were sent out.

The evening of the gala finally came on February 5, 1862. Newspaper reporters would later praise Mary's "social innovation" as resounding success and a one-of-a-kind event.[5] Carriages

---

intruders, dogs, and fires that continually plagued the city. She would scream and call for neighbors help when stove or grease fires occurred or little dogs entered the yard. Abe overreacted too taking Robert, after he had received a dog bite, all the way to Terre Haute, Indiana, to a doctor who supposedly had magic healing powers to prevent rabies. In fairness, intruders, fires, dogs, and infectious diseases did take their toll in everyday life, even in Springfield, Illinois.

[2] Clinton, "Mourning in America," 75.

[3] Epstein, *Portrait of a Marriage*, 354–55.

[4] Conway, *Lincoln's White House*, 144.

[5] White, *Lincoln*, 476.

started arriving around nine o'clock, filled with sword-wearing, decked-out diplomats, generals, cabinet members, Supreme Court justices, senators, and representatives. Fresh flowers adorned tables, chandeliers, and vases everywhere. Wearing a new black swallowtail coat, the president greeted guests in the East Room with Mary, who wore a white silk dress decorated with hundreds of small black flowers and a remarkably low neckline.[6] Throughout the evening, the marine band played, including a new song titled "Mary Lincoln Polka." The high point came at 11:30 p.m., when servants unveiled a beautiful table full of food and pastries. It had taken five days, under Mary's micromanaging supervision, for the finest New York caterers to prepare the repast. Sugary models of a Union warship, Fort Sumter, and Fort Pickens were surrounded by mounds of turkey, duck, ham, terrapin, and pheasant. A ten-gallon bowl containing a punch made of champagne, arrack, and rum also dazzled the guests. Dinner was served until three, and many guests stayed until daybreak.[7]

Though Lincoln did receive criticism for holding "The Lady President's Ball" during wartime, most considered the gala a triumph.[8] One newspaper called the party "the most superb affair of its kind ever seen."[9] "Those who were here," Lincoln's personal secretary John Nicolay told his fiancée, "will be forever happy in the recollection of the favor enjoyed, because their vanity has been tickled with the thought that they have attained something which

---

6 Packard, *Lincolns in the White House*, 113–14, 117. Mary's low cut dress drew double takes and snide criticism. One senator insisted that Mrs. Lincoln had put her "bosom on public display." Even Mary's husband told her earlier in the evening that she should take some of the dress's long train and use some of it to cover her chest. "Whew! Our cat has a long tail to-night," Lincoln told his wife.

7 Donald, *Lincoln*, 335–36; Epstein, *Portrait of a Marriage*, 359–61. The Lincolns spent a thousand dollars of their own money on the gala.

8 Conway, *Lincoln's White House*, 149.

9 Keneally, *Lincoln*, 118.

others have not."[10] Mary, dubbed "our fair 'Republican Queen,'" had pulled off the smash social event of a generation.[11]

While the party sizzled with splendor on the main floor, upstairs the Lincolns' son burned with a deadly fever. A few days before the gala, Willie had come down with a slight chill. On the night of the party, the illness—believed to "bilious fever" or typhoid—became acute. The Lincolns contemplated canceling the reception, but the family doctor assured them that Willie faced no immediate danger.

So the Lincolns played good hosts and faked a celebratory gaiety, all while worrying about their son's deteriorating health. Both left the reception several times to run upstairs and check on Willie's condition.[12] What should have been Mary's triumphant moment became a nightmare from which she would never fully recover.

The swampy, low-lying location of the Executive Mansion was probably to blame for Willie's fatal disease. Infested with rats, mildew, and wretched odors, the cellar presented a continuing health hazard. Since window screens had not yet been invented, bugs invaded the building and tormented everyone. Flies were so prevalent, they almost completely blackened tablecloths and flew into people's mouths at dinner. To close windows meant enduring sweltering heat and humidity. Foul-smelling people who had not bathed in weeks came from everywhere to visit the president. They wore woolen clothes that reeked, since deodorants, antiperspirants, and dry cleaning was not yet prevalent. Men spit tobacco everywhere. Since animal and human feces clogged the streets of Washington, especially from soldiers and their horses, visitors inevitably stepped in excrement and ground it into the mansion's flooring. No wonder that Mary worked so hard to turn the residence into a cleaner and more pleasant home for her family.[13]

---

[10] Goodwin, *Team of Rivals*, 417.

[11] Goodwin, *Team of Rivals*, 417.

[12] Turner and Turner, *Mary Todd Lincoln*, 121; Donald, *Lincoln*, 336.

[13] Packard, *Lincolns in the White House*, 62, 64–66; Conway, *Lincoln's White House*, 105; Burlingame, *Lincoln*, 2:297–98, 301.

Immediately behind the Executive Mansion lay the reeking Washington Canal, which flowed along what would one day become the Mall. The abandoned commercial canal—filled by overflow from the Potomac River and numerous polluted tributaries—was a filthy, dark home to innumerable mosquitos and gave off the foulest smells. Full of garbage, rotted produce, discarded fish, animal feces from numerous horse stables and corrals, human excrement, floating animal carcasses, and even an occasional human corpse, the "God-forsaken hole" was a breeding ground for malaria, tuberculosis, cholera, typhoid, dysentery, and smallpox.[14] When Willie and Tad played war games on top of the Executive Mansion and got thirsty, servants sent water up to them—liquid that came from newly installed taps that connected to the filthy canal and the Potomac River.[15]

Despite the doctor's initial assurance, Willie's condition worsened in the weeks after the grand event. Burning with high temperatures, he drenched his bedsheets daily in sweat. In addition, Willie endured vomiting, diarrhea, and gastric pain.[16] Newspapers began to report on the lad's worsening condition as Lincoln canceled cabinet meetings and Mary skipped her regular White House levee. All through the ordeal, the First Lady faithfully sat by Willie's bedside and held her son's hand as she and Abe watched their son's labored breathing. Willie's best friend, Bud Taft, visited hoping to inspire a recovery.

---

[14] Conway, *Lincoln's White House*, 106; Canavan, *Lincoln's Final Hours*, 10; Packard, *Lincolns in the White House*, 7.

[15] Epstein, *Portrait of a Marriage*, 356–57.

[16] Lachman, *The Last Lincolns*, 40. Dr. Stone misdiagnosed Willie's disease as malaria and gave him calomel—a toxic, mercury-based chemical used as a diuretic at the time. Willie's bouts of diarrhea and vomiting were not typically symptoms of typhoid fever. The bizarre and ineffective treatment—administering beef tea, blackberry cordial, and bland pudding—hastened Willie's demise.

One particular cruelty of bilious fever is that it comes and goes over a period of days, often giving false hope of recovery. So when Willie seemed better on February 10, spirits ascended momentarily. The typhoid came back, however, with a slow and steady vengeance, eroding his intestinal wall from the inside. In time, it perforated the bowel, spilling bacteria into his abdominal cavity and bloodstream. He lapsed into a coma on February 18. His lungs filled with fluid the next day and he acquired pneumonia. On February 20, fifteen days after the grand gala event, Willie died.

"Well, Nicolay," Lincoln said to his personal secretary as he stepped into his office, "my boy is gone—he is actually gone!" The president then burst into tears and left to give what comfort he could to Tad, who had contracted the same illness.[17]

With Mary inconsolable and with Tad still suffering, Lincoln had little opportunity to grieve. Tad had overheard the screaming, sobbing, and wailing coming from his brother's room. Sad and frightened at his brother's passing, he surely worried that death would come for him too. According to Elizabeth Keckley, Mary's confidante and dressmaker, the president looked like a weak child when he climbed into bed to comfort his littlest boy. Tad, perhaps, consoled his father as much as Abe did his son.[18]

A few days later, as Keckley washed and dressed Willie's body, Lincoln confessed, "My poor boy, he was too good for this earth. God called him home. I know that he is much better off in heaven, but then we loved him so. It is hard, hard to have him die."[19] Repeatedly he lamented on the toughest ordeal of his life. His body

---

[17] Manning, *Father Lincoln*, 139; Donald, *Lincoln*, 336; Epstein, *Portrait of a Marriage*, 364, 366; Lachman, *The Last Lincolns*, 41; Clinton, "Mourning in America," 77; Packard, *Lincolns in the White House*, 115, 119. Both Willie and Tad had suffered measles some eleven months earlier. In addition, Willie had had scarlet fever the previous winter, though Tad did not. These two diseases, in all likelihood, had considerably weakened Willie's immune system.

[18] Epstein, *Portrait of a Marriage*, 367.

[19] Clinton, "Mourning in America," 77.

shook with emotion as he sobbed and buried his face in his hands. For weeks afterward, as Willie had died on a Thursday, Lincoln would take time away from work on Thursdays to mourn.[20]

On February 24, Dr. Phineas Gurley, pastor of Mary's New York Avenue Presbyterian Church, conducted Willie's funeral in the East Room of the White House. Mary could not bring herself to attend, but even so, she cruelly asked Mrs. Taft to keep her children, Bud and Holly—Willie and Tad's favorite playmates—away from the funeral, because it made Mary "feel worse to see them."[21] Sadly, Bud and Holly Taft would never see Tad or his parents again.

A violent thunderstorm took place in Washington the day of Willie's funeral. Nevertheless, members of Congress, the cabinet, generals, and diplomats came to pay their respects. Gurley eulogized Willie for a half hour, praising the boy's precociousness, sweet disposition, and promise. He told those gathered that an entire nation mourned and prayed for the president, and that God's grace would be sufficient even in the midst of such pain and tragedy.[22]

In the last paragraph in his funeral sermon, Gurley said:

> Only let us bow in His presence with an humble and teachable spirit; only let us be still and know that He is God; only let us acknowledge His hand, and hear his voice, and inquire after His will, and seek his holy spirit as our counselor and guide, and all, in the end, will be well. In His light shall we see light; by His grace our sorrows will be sanctified—they will be made a blessing to our souls—and by and by we shall have occasion to say, with blended gratitude and rejoicing, "It is good for us that we have been afflicted."[23]

---

20 Burlingame, *Lincoln*, 2:298.

21 Manning, *Father Lincoln*, 142.

22 Epstein, *Portrait of a Marriage*, 369–70.

23 Mansfield, *Lincoln's Battle with God*, 141.

Moved by the sermon, Lincoln asked Gurley for a copy and sent him a gold-headed cane to express the Lincolns' sincere appreciation. He and Mary would reread and share the sermon with grief-stricken friends for months afterward.

After the sermon, Willie's Sunday school class followed the casket to the hearse. Almost everyone present, including Lincoln's future adversary General George McClellan, could not hold back their tears.[24] Placed in Georgetown's Oak Hill Cemetery, Willie's body would eventually be moved to Springfield. In the first days after the entombment, Lincoln twice visited the cemetery alone. Each time he lifted up the coffin's lid to look at his son's dead body.[25]

The Lincoln family tragedy had not quite made a turn yet; Tad still suffered from his sickness, and Mary's grieving turned to grave despair. The president asked Mary Jane Welles, the wife of Gideon Wells, secretary of the navy, for help in the immediate term. Having lost five children herself, Wells found comfort in her Christian faith and the belief that she would see her children again in heaven.

Lincoln then asked Dorothea Dix, a nurse and activist for the insane, who had called to express her condolences, to recommend a good woman to take care of his wife and son for a longer duration. Dix sent a nurse, Rebecca Pomroy, a deeply religious woman who had lost her husband and two sons during the war. She was a godsend to Lincoln and a bright light in a very dark time. She understood what the Lincolns were enduring. She told the president that thousands of Northerners were praying for him and Tad every day. Lincoln covered his face and wept after hearing her words of comfort.

A few days later, while looking at a bedridden Tad, Lincoln asked Pomroy to pray that his son's life might be spared, as well as for Lincoln himself. Pomroy not only affirmed that she would pray for them both, but reassured Lincoln that her Christian faith had sustained her through loss. In the days that followed, they

---

24 Mansfield, *Lincoln's Battle with God*, 141.

25 Packard, *Lincolns in the White House*, 122.

talked freely about their faith and the Bible. Lincoln told her that the Psalms were some of his favorite Bible passages because they possessed wisdom and inspiration for each day of the week.[26]

Lincoln appreciated Pomroy's candor and revelation that it had taken her time to come to peace with her husband and two sons' deaths. He asked her several times to recite the ways God provided care, comfort, and eventually peace to her soul. Pomroy gladly shared her faith walk through her dark valley. When Lincoln asked how she had achieved this peace, she responded that God "does all things well" and that Lincoln simply needed to trust in God and His plans. The president responded, "I wish I had that childlike faith you speak of, and I trust He will give it to me. I had a good Christian mother, and her prayers have followed me thus far through life." When Pomroy eventually left the Executive Mansion to resume her previous duties, a grateful president told her, "When you get to be an old lady, Mrs. Pomroy, tell your grandchildren how indebted the nation was to you in holding up my hands in time of trouble."[27]

While Pomroy's words and presence made an impact on the president, she had less success with Mary. After Willie's death, the First Lady stayed in bed for three weeks and failed to look after Tad. The mere mention of Willie's name elicited fits of weeping and incapacity. In the weeks after Willie's death, she cried so much that she suffered permanent eye damage. In addition to sending all of Willie's toys and clothes away, never again would she enter the bedroom where Willie had passed, nor the Green Room, where his body had been embalmed. When she eventually emerged from her room, she covered herself in layers of black veils and crepe.

---

[26] Epstein, *Portrait of a Marriage*, 372–73; Burlingame, *Lincoln*, 2:299; Leidner, *Lincoln's Gift*, 147–48; Goodwin, *Team of Rivals*, 421.

[27] "Employees and Staff: Rebecca R. Pomroy (1817-1884)," Mr. Lincoln's White House (website), The Lehrman Institute, accessed May 4, 2020, http://www.mrlincolnswhitehouse.org/residents-visitors/employees-and-staff/employees-staff-rebecca-r-pomroy-1817-1884/.

A few weeks after Willie's death, Mary's younger half brother, Sam, died fighting for the Confederacy at the Battle of Shiloh. Already grieving, she could not show public expression of mourning the death of a Confederate.

For a year, all social activities at the Executive Mansion were suspended. The First Lady forbade the marine band's weekly concert on the grounds, and quickly lost the sympathy of a public that had grown used to ubiquitous wartime casualties. As the weeks went by, she could sleep only under the influence of laudanum. She lashed out at friends and family alike.

Not understanding why her son perished while the Taft children survived, she never allowed Willie and Tad's childhood friends to enter the White House again. Whatever joy Mary had found in being in the Executive Mansion permanently disappeared after Willie's death. She eventually viewed her son's passing as punishment for her vanity, the decision to launch such an opulent party, and living as an exalted First Family.[28] "Our home is very beautiful," she wrote a friend three months after Willie's death, "the world still smiles & pays homage, yet the charm is dispelled—everything appears a mockery, the idolised one, is not with us."[29] Mary later reflected that "I had become, so wrapped up in the world, so devoted to my own political advancement that I thought of little else." God had "forsaken" her in taking away "so lovely a child."[30]

For Mary, the pain and guilt would not go away. She would forever be "an altered woman," as her caretaker Keckley described her.[31] When Julia Taft made a surprise visit to the Executive Mansion in the winter of 1864, Mary tried to make nice initially—perhaps feeling guilty for banning the Taft children from the Executive Mansion. Then Tad walked in the room. Seeing Julia, he threw

---

[28] Packard, *Lincolns in the White House*, 123; Donald, *Lincoln*, 337–38; Epstein, *Portrait of a Marriage*, 370–71; Lachman, *The Last Lincolns*, 48.

[29] Goodwin, *Team of Rivals*, 421.

[30] Goodwin, *Team of Rivals*, 421–22.

[31] Goodwin, *Team of Rivals*, 422–23.

himself on the floor, kicking and screaming. After servants removed Tad from the room, Mary explained, "You must excuse him Julia. You know what he remembers." Julia Taft never saw Mary or Tad again.[32]

The president patiently and persistently tried everything to rally the First Lady, to little avail. Her grief was so profound, he once led her to a window and pointed out the insane asylum in the distance, warning that he would send her there if she did not control her despair.[33] Mary would end up being placed in an insane asylum in the not too distant future.

Lincoln expressed his own grief over a long period of time. He put a picture Willie had painted of an Illinois landscape on the mantel in his Executive Mansion office. He showed it to almost every visitor.[34] For months on each Thursday, the day of Willie's death, Lincoln secluded himself in the Prince of Wales Room for an hour to grieve alone. Observers would see Lincoln emerge from the room with red eyes from weeping. At night, he lay down in bed with Tad, who received no care from his incapacitated mother.

In early February 1864, the Executive Mansion stables were set on fire by an arsonist. Lincoln raced to the scene in an attempt to rescue the horses, but government officials restrained him, noting that the blaze had become uncontrollable. Six horses burned to death. When an associate found Lincoln in tears, Tad explained that one of the ponies had belonged to his brother Willie.[35] The memories would not fade.

Lincoln tried to alleviate his grief by spending more time with Tad. Still heartbroken himself, Tad rarely let his father out of his sight. "The bond that had always been uncommonly close between them," reported Lincoln's secretary John Nicolay, "grew stronger after

---

32 Lachman, *The Last Lincolns*, 48.

33 Burlingame, *Lincoln*, 2:300–301.

34 Conway, *Lincoln's White House*, 150.

35 Epstein, *Portrait of a Marriage*, 371; Goodwin, *Team of Rivals*, 603.

Willie's death."[36] Having already lost two of his sons prematurely, Lincoln made sure to prioritize time with his youngest.

As the Lincolns continued to grieve, they relied on their religious faith in different ways. No matter what pastors like Washington clergyman Francis Vinton, or Phineas Gurley, at New York Avenue Presbyterian Church, said to comfort her, Mary struggled to accept the precept that the "Lord giveth and the Lord taketh away."[37] Five months after Willie's death, she questioned why God would forsake her and take their son away. A faithful churchgoer, Mary did not want to become a blasphemer and admitted that her current feelings could lead her down that path. Nevertheless Mary came to believe that every time her family made a political advancement, God responded by punishing them. In addition, Mary continued to internalize the guilt she felt over her decision not to cancel the ball.[38]

Not wanting to accept God's plans and timing, Mary turning to spiritualists for solace. Some six million Americans subscribed to spiritualist beliefs in the 1860s, many of them grieving mothers and fathers who had lost children in the Civil War.[39] Several of Mary's friends were spiritualists, as were many of her contacts in New York City—one reason she loved to visit there so often. Her personal assistant, Lizzie Keckley, had sought out spiritualists after her only son was killed in the war. Denied a deathbed interview with her son, Keckley told Mary about having conversations with her son's

---

36 Manning, *Father Lincoln*, 147. One of the truly sad scenes after Willie's death occurred when Tad gave away his train set to his aunt Elizabeth, requesting that she send it to her grandson Lewis. Tad simply could not bear to play with the train set again—something he and Willie enjoyed playing together.

37 Baker, *Mary Todd Lincoln*, 214–15.

38 Epstein, *Portrait of a Marriage*, 259. Though with the knowledge of science and medicine at the time, Mary would have no way of knowing that Willie's scarlet fever, during the summer of 1860, probably weakened and compromised his immune system and made him more susceptible to the ravages of his next disease acquisition.

39 Clinton, "Mourning in America," 82.

disembodied spirit via a medium, and encouraged the First Lady to pursue the same endeavor with Willie's spirit.

Soon charlatans and spiritualists were allowed access to Mary in the Executive Mansion. They claimed to make connections with Willie as well as to predict Confederate battle plans and political treachery. After meeting with self-described clairvoyants, Mary would often advise the president with their "information."

Mary told her sister that Willie came to visit her every night and stood at the end of her bed, smiling at her, sometimes with Eddie and Mary's deceased brother Alec too. Mary hosted as many as eight séances, and apparently they proved more comforting and actionable to her than visits from Presbyterian clergymen. Spiritualists provided her with companionship and never encouraged her to resign herself to a Job-like status. They deceptively enabled Mary to feel in control and powerful. She was so enamored with them, she even put mediums on the government payroll in the Department of Agriculture, where they could pack seeds by day and practice the occult arts by night. She called on Willie less often as time went by, but she would carry a blend of religion and spiritualism for the rest of her life.[40]

Lincoln did not believe in the unsavory ways or theology of spiritualists, but tolerated them for Mary's sake. He appreciated the fact that General Dan Sickles sometimes accompanied Mary to séances to keep an eye on her. Lincoln had other friends scrutinize some of the charlatans which met with Mary. Eventually, he booted

---

[40] Epstein, *Portrait of a Marriage*, 381; Baker, *Mary Todd Lincoln*, 33, 218–22, 310, 322, 363. Later in life, Mary would test mediums by appearing as an anonymous widow and using a fictitious name. Her spiritualism combined with monomania—the partial, progressive, form of insanity that rendered her irrational in some behaviors but perfectly sane in others. When Mary told Emilie that Willie, Eddie, and their brother Alec, came to visit her at night, Emilie described Mary's eyes as "wide and shining and I had a feeling of awe as if I were in the presence of the supernatural" (Packard, *Lincolns in the White House*, 165). Emilie wrote that her sister's behavior frightened her and said these actions were largely due to the fear of Robert joining the army.

one well-known spiritualist from their summer residence at Soldiers' Home when tricks and mechanical devices—used to produce the alleged vocal manifestations of the deceased—were uncovered.[41]

To this point, achieving political power had been a lifelong goal for Mary—but not so much anymore. "The *world* has lost so much of its charm," she wrote to a friend during the election of 1864. "My position requires my presence, where my heart is *so far* from being." She feared that "the *deep waters*" of grief would overwhelm her.[42] She continued to cling to the notion that God had allowed Willie to die as a punishment for her sins. Only later, after many years passed, would she say that death "is only a blessed transition" to a place "where there are no more partings & *no more* tears shed."[43]

Mary's anguish remained for the rest of her days. Four years after her husband's assassination, she told a blind girl who had written to offer her sympathies that "life is all *darkness*," and the sun "is a mockery to me, in my great sorrow."[44] She spoke of her "heavy cross," "daily crucifixion," and "Gethsemane." She had been "baptized by Sorrow." Reflecting on the biblical account of the two sisters of Bethany—Mary (who sat obediently at Jesus's feet) and Martha (whom Jesus rebuked for being occupied with busy things)—the former First Lady asserted that "I feel that I am *very* Martha." She told a friend to pray that she "may personate instead the 'Mary of the Bible'—sitting at the feet of Jesus—resigning myself to his will."

While the First Lady struggled for years to find comfort in traditional, orthodox Christianity, her husband found comfort in the promises of Scripture and the pastors who delivered God's Word to him in a caring, loving manner. Dr. Francis Vinton, Rector of Trinity Church of New York, told Lincoln that long-term mourning was the way of heathens and not of Christians. Since "God is not the

41 Packard, *Lincolns in the White House*, 143–44; Keneally, *Lincoln*, 118–19.
42 Epstein, *Portrait of a Marriage*, 454.
43 Goodwin, *Team of Rivals*, 422.
44 All of the quotes in this paragraph come from Baker, *Mary Todd Lincoln*, 257.

God of the *dead* but the living,"[45] Dr. Vinton assured the president that Willie "is *alive* in Paradise." The "most comforting doctrine of the church," he said, were "founded upon the words of Christ himself."

After escaping his initial shock and skepticism at the preacher's comments, Lincoln approached Vinton, threw his arms around him, and sobbed in his breast. "*Alive? Alive?*" he repeated.

"My dear sir," Vinton asserted, "believe this, for it is God's most precious truth. Seek not your son among the dead; he is not there; he lives today in Paradise!" He quoted Jesus's words in Luke 20:38 (KJV) that God is "not the God of the dead, but of the living, *for all live unto him!*" God had called Willie "into his upper kingdom—a kingdom and an existence as real, more real, than your own." When Vinton told the president that he had another sermon on the topic, Lincoln begged him to send it to him, which Vinton did. Eventually, Lincoln made a personal copy of the sermon and returned the original to Vinton. Lincoln would reread the sermon for the rest of his life.

After the death of Willie, Lincoln approached the Bible with an even deeper appreciation than he had before. He established an early morning routine of Bible reading and prayer.[46] He had already become a more overtly religious man since being elected president, frequently asking for God's aid in letters and speeches. Looking back on Willie's death a few months later, Lincoln recognized that he had undergone what he called "a process of crystallization" in his religious beliefs.[47] Willie's death made him realize he had to look outside of his own mind and heart for help and strength.

The profound paradox is that Lincoln grew more confident in his own decision-making and leadership once his ultimate confidence

---

[45] The ensuring conversation between Dr. Vinton and Lincoln is recorded in Carpenter, *Six Months at the White House*, 138–39.

[46] Szasz and Szasz, *Lincoln and Religion*, 39; Owen, *The Man and His Faith*, 142.

[47] Donald, *Lincoln*, 337.

and peace came not from his own thinking or doing, but from a transcendent God. As one biographer notes, out of this terrible ordeal "a gigantic figure had at last emerged. The outer and the inner Lincoln had fused ... the result of a profound interior change."[48]

While he still did not officially join a church, Lincoln relied more than ever on the spiritual encouragement and sustenance of Holy Scripture. Like the Civil War, which continued to rage on indefinitely, Lincoln understood that life had plenty of hardship and could not be controlled. God's ways were not the ways of man. The Almighty had His own purposes.

The Truth

Even the most callous reader can certainly feel the anguish that the Lincolns endured at the death of their son. Indeed, there is nothing more painful in this world to a parent than the loss of a child. As many have said before, parents should not have to bury their own children. Yet we know that children too often die before their parents. Hardship and suffering are a part of this sin-filled world.

While we can certainly sympathize with Mary's extreme grief, she unfortunately turned to spiritualists to ease her suffering—something they never fully accomplished. The Bible warns us about spiritualists and clairvoyants: "Do not turn to mediums or necromancers; do not seek them out, and so make yourselves unclean by them: I am the Lord your God."[49] Indeed, if you are worshipping or putting your faith in someone or something else, you are not trusting or believing in God. If Christians "inquire of the mediums and the necromancers who chirp and mutter," they are

---

[48] Trueblood, *Lincoln: Lessons in Spiritual Leadership*, 33–35.

[49] Lev. 19:31.

not going to God and seek His wisdom but "inquiring of the dead on behalf of the living."[50]

Unfortunately, false prophets have always existed and still do. The Bible warns that "there will be false teachers among you, who will secretly bring in destructive heresies, even denying the Master who bought them, bringing upon themselves swift destruction."[51] God tells us not to believe every spirit, "but test the spirits to see whether they are from God, for many false prophets have gone out into the world.[52] While Mary Lincoln enjoyed the companionship and false promises of the spiritualists, they played her for a fool and preyed on her emotional vulnerabilities to make a buck or gain access to power and influence. Their deceptive ways never gave her the peace that surpasses all human understanding.[53] Only "the Lord is near to the brokenhearted and saves the crushed in spirit."[54]

The death of a loved one, let alone a child, is a horrific ordeal. You may never really get over it, only through it by the grace of God. Moreover, one pastor once said that when you lose a parent, you lose part of your past. When you lose a spouse, you lose part of your present. When you lose a child, you lose a big part of your future. The bottom line is the pain and earthly grief will never completely go away.

Yet the Bible teaches that you can find comfort in the words and promises of God, even at the loss of a loved one, especially if your loved one knew Jesus as Lord and Savior. Christians do "not grieve as others do who have no hope. For since we believe that Jesus died and rose again, even so, through Jesus, God will bring with him those who have fallen asleep." For when Jesus returns in all of His glory, "the dead in Christ will rise … and so we will always be with

---

[50] Isa. 8:19.

[51] 2 Pet. 2:1.

[52] 1 John 4:1.

[53] Phil. 4:7.

[54] Ps. 34:18.

the Lord."[55] As bittersweet as it may be for those left behind on earth, "precious in the sight of the Lord is the death of his saints."[56] They are in their heavenly home, while those who remain on earth patiently and confidently await their heavenly homecoming someday.

God's salvation promise does not mean that we will not miss or grieve for our lost loved ones, but it does mean that God will be with us in all things. God, "the Father of mercies and God of all comfort, who comforts us in all our affliction," will "comfort those who are in any affliction, with the comfort with which we ourselves are comforted by God. For as we share abundantly in Christ's sufferings, so through Christ we share abundantly in comfort too." A Christian's hope and assurance in Christ "is unshaken," for we know that Jesus shares in our sufferings and in our comforts.[57]

The Bible shares these comforting words: "For I consider that the sufferings of this present time are not worth comparing with the glory that is to be revealed to us. For the creation waits with eager longing for the revealing of the sons of God."[58] In heaven, "death shall be no more, neither shall there be mourning, nor crying, nor pain anymore, for the former things have passed away."[59] For those who know Jesus, they can shout: "O death, where is your victory? O death, where is your sting? The sting of death is sin, and the power of sin is the law. But thanks be to God, who gives us the victory through our Lord Jesus Christ."[60]

Parents who lose children too soon will not see their children again on earth, and that hurts. If their children knew Jesus, however, parents will have peace and comfort knowing that their beloved children are home with God and have an eternity to look forward

---

[55] 1 Thess. 4:13-14, 16–17.

[56] Ps. 116:15.

[57] 2 Cor. 1:3–5, 7.

[58] Rom. 8:18–19.

[59] Rev. 21:4.

[60] 1 Cor. 15:55–57.

to in the company of Jesus. That is a future worth living for and embracing.

Your Life

To the guests at the Executive Mansion party, the Lincolns looked like they were living the dream life. Yet we know they were worried about their son's deteriorating health even as they entertained the attendees. They wore masks in front of their guests. Why do people wear masks or try to cover up things? When have you worn a mask? Why did you do it?

Even something as tragic as the death of a child can be used for good by God. Many contemporaries believed that Willie's death changed Lincoln and brought him closer to God. Why do so many turn to Christian faith after the loss of a loved one?

In her grief, Mary could not peacefully accept God's plan for Willie. Can you blame her for feeling this way? Have you ever had anyone tell you to accept God's plan in the midst of your valley experience or suffering? How did these comments make you feel at that moment? Is there a right or wrong time to tell someone "that for those who love God all things work together for good, for those who are called according to his purpose" (Rom. 8:28) or that God has plans for them (Jer. 29:11)?

Lincoln had many strong Christians surrounding him during the ordeal of Willie's death. What kind of impact did their kindness and testimony have on him? How can you witness to others in times of duress and suffering?

10

Terrible Twilight

Better is the end of a thing than its beginning, and the patient in spirit is better than the proud in spirit.
—Ecclesiastes 7:8

The Lincoln Way

Effective leaders know the importance of finishing strong and leaving an uplifting legacy.

In a tragic but ironic way, Abraham Lincoln probably got off easier than his wife did. He died in his prime and at the apex of his prodigious achievements. She lived on, enduring more painful memories and losing yet another son before her passing. As the victorious commander in chief of the Union in the spring of 1865, Lincoln could have demanded almost anything from anyone. By the end of her life, in the summer of 1882, Mary could not garner even sympathy from anyone.

Contemporaries scorned and mocked the former First Lady during her twilight years. Subsequent biographers and historians have consistently vilified her pathetic end of life while exalting her husband. She never received the praise other, lesser-known widows of the time were accorded.[1]

---

[1] Canavan, *Lincoln's Final Hours*, 171. Sallie Pickett spent fifty years writing and lecturing about Confederate general George Pickett, rarely mentioning her husband's infamous and futile charge at Gettysburg. Elizabeth Custer wrote a children's book that used her husband, General George Custer, as

Mary endured the early deaths of her parents, three of her four sons, her husband, and numerous relatives during the war. She was estranged from family and friends during the Lincoln presidency. She was the target of relentless criticism from the press, disinterest from United States citizens after her husband's death, and disdain from Congress, which refused to give her a pension for years. Yet Mary negated any sympathy she might have received with her own erratic behavior and self-centeredness.[2]

In the months immediately following her husband's horrible death, Mary refused, often obnoxiously, to receive people who came to offer their condolences. She thereby cemented negative feelings toward her. Those who did see her were stunned and bewildered at the depths of her grief, displayed in uncontrollable wailing and terrible convulsions. On some occasions, she recounted the assassination in gory detail. She overstayed her welcome in the Executive Mansion for weeks after her husband's death. She sold some of her husband's clothing to shady characters. When she finally left, she took several dozen boxes and twenty trunks. Some journalists and government officials accused her of stealing spoons, forks, linen, crystal, china, and other silver. The residence, which had received over $100,000 of appropriations in the previous four years, appeared gutted. One Republican senator claimed that Mrs. Lincoln could run a big hotel with all the stuff she carried off.[3]

Mary's intense grieving soon turned into permanent sickness. She demonstrated symptoms of what we now call bipolar disorder: depression, delusions, hallucinations, narcissism, insomnia, mood swings, and extravagant spending. These early manifestations later

---

a model for manliness. Varina Davis, widow of Jefferson Davis, become a columnist for the *New York World* and, ironically, a good friend of Julia Grant.

[2] Emerson, "Madness of Mary Lincoln," 242.

[3] Packard, *Lincolns in the White House*, 251–53; Lachman, *The Last Lincolns*, 57; Burlingame, *Lincoln*, 2:827. There is little doubt that Mary took some things that did not belong to her, but other White House items were actually stolen by sightseers and dishonest staff members.

developed into serious psychotic issues. She became violent toward others and attempted suicide.[4]

Only two months after Lincoln's passing, Dr. Gurley noticed that while almost everyone back home in Illinois loved Mr. Lincoln, "hard things" were said of Mrs. Lincoln "by all classes of people." While Gurley and his wife were fond of Mary, "the ladies of Springfield" cynically and cruelly asserted that "Mr. Lincoln's death hurt her ambitions more than her affections."[5] Between this general opinion and the fact that Mary had fallen out of favor with her sisters over politics, her husband's polarizing policies, and her own ambition in the past, Mary had almost no one to associate with in Springfield.[6]

In the midst of her severe depression, grief, and mental anguish, there were flashes of Mary's orthodox faith. "In this great trial, it is difficult, to be taught resignation," she confided to a friend a few months after the assassination. The "only comfort, that remains to us," she explained, "is the blessed consolation, that our beloved ones, are rejoicing in their Heavenly home, free from all earthly trials & inn the holy presence of God & his Angels," and "are singing the praises of the Redeemer." She could not wait to lay her "own weary head, down to rest, by the side of my darling husband." She prayed that God would grant her "sufficient grace to await *his* time" for her own earthly passing. "Without my idolized husband," she lamented, "I do not wish to remain on earth."[7]

Mary recalled the last three weeks of her husband's life, when he knew the Civil War would finally end in a Union victory, and how the realization had bolstered his spirits. He had become "supremely cheerful," "playful," and "almost boyish in his mirth & reminded me, of his original nature, what I had always remembered of him, in

---

4 Emerson, "Madness of Mary Lincoln," 240–41.

5 Canavan, *Lincoln's Final Hours*, 172.

6 Burlingame, *Lincoln*, 2:826.

7 Turner and Turner, Mary Lincoln to Eliza Henry, August 31, 1865, *Mary Todd Lincoln*, 273–74.

our home—free from care, surrounded by those he loved so well & *by whom* he was so idolized." On the Friday of his assassination, she recollected their joyful carriage ride and how he told her that they both must "'be more cheerful in the future—between the war & loss of our darling Willie—we have both, been very miserable.' Every word, then uttered, is deeply engraved, on my poor broken heart."[8]

With her husband gone, Mary could not cheer herself up. A few weeks before the first Christmas without her husband, she spoke of her "overwhelming sorrow," which removed her from the world. Abe had been the one she leaned on "for support & loving tenderness," and now he had been "so sadly & cruelly removed." She missed her "idolized husband. Yet I, wretchedly, live on the comforting thought, that our Maker, in *this,* will be gracious, by allowing me, soon to rejoin him—Where no more tears shall be shed is a solace to me" she wrote to a friend. She truly appreciated "dear little Taddie" and his optimism that there were "'three of us on earth & *three* in Heaven.'" She also found comfort that Abe "always told me & his actions all proved, that he had never thought or cared for any one but myself—or I might have added had ever noticed any other lady." This "memory, is some solace, to me in my misery, & yet it reminds me, very sorrowfully, of all the devotion, I have lost."[9] A little over a year after her husband's death, she told William Herndon that Abe "was the kindest most tender and loving husband & father in the world."[10]

No matter where Mary resided, her erratic and self-centered behavior never allowed her to develop a nurturing support system. After returning from Washington, she felt so little sympathy in Springfield that she moved to Chicago, where she continued to grieve and lament her life in near isolation. She spent mornings

---

8 Turner and Turner, Mary Lincoln to Francis Bicknell Carpenter, November 15, 1865, *Mary Todd Lincoln*, 284–85.

9 Turner and Turner, Mary Lincoln to Elizabeth Blair Lee, December 11, 1865, *Mary Todd Lincoln*, 301–2.

10 Wilson, *Herndon's Informants*, 357.

reading through love letters she and Abe had written to one another long ago. "I miss my beloved husband more & more," she told one of her few remaining contacts. "How I am, to pass through life, without *him* who loved us so dearly, it is impossible to say." She would "patiently wait" for the hour "when 'God's love' shall place me by *his* side again—where there are *no more* partings & no more tears."[11]

Mary's solitude only grew over time, and she tried to live her life through tear-stained letters which revealed her misery, disillusionment, and humiliation.[12] "I am alone," she wrote a Washington acquaintance. "My Husband gone from me, the agony is insupportable. I am scarcely able to sit up ... My health is so miserable." If it were not for Tad and Robert, both of whom she believed depended on her, she said she would be fine with death. "I would pray our Heavenly Father, to remove me from a world, where I have been so bitter a sufferer," she petitioned. "To rejoin my Husband, who loved me so devotedly & whom I idolized, would be bliss indeed."[13] Far from being the ambitious and sophisticated First Lady who first came to the nation's capital and could converse charmingly in French, she unraveled and faded into a sickly, reclusive, and deeply depressed woman. Only the companionship of her two sons brought her any relief from her despondent state.[14]

There were other difficulties Mary faced, many of them of her own doing. She worried about money. She constantly solicited congressmen to secure a government pension for her. She also insisted that her husband's remaining presidential salary should be issued to her immediately. Two weeks before Christmas 1865, Congress gave her exactly $25,000—one year of Lincoln's salary—in honor of her husband's past service to the county. She used the money to buy an

---

11 Oates, *Lincoln*, 181.

12 Lachman, *The Last Lincolns*, 78.

13 Lachman, *The Last Lincolns*, 74.

14 Packard, *Lincolns in the White House*, 255.

expensive home in Chicago, which she later had to give up because she could not maintain it.

She eventually rented a hotel room, where she became increasingly reclusive and embittered. She was carrying a $20,000 debt. Creditors warned that they would go public and expose Mary's refusal to pay her bills. Attorneys sent letters threatening litigation. Her money woes led her to solicit funds using locks of her husband's hair for bids. She pretended to be a wealthy benefactor as she solicited other folks with financial means. Robert Lincoln called them "Mother's begging letters."[15]

Newspapers carried stories about Mary's Old Clothes Scandal—how she attempted to sell in New York the clothes she had accumulated during the presidential years. The stories hurt Robert Lincoln's growing law practice in Chicago. Mary lost even more sympathy when it became public that she would inherit $36,000 (over half a million dollars today) from her husband's estate. There seemed to be no need to sell her clothes or her husband's locks of hair. Soon the media claimed that insanity had overtaken Mary's life.[16]

In addition to her perceived financial woes, Mary had to endure the painful revelation of her husband's first love, Ann Rutledge. The story was told by William Herndon, who had no love lost for Mary, at a lecture at the Old Courthouse in Springfield. Mary claimed that her husband had never even spoken of Rutledge during their twenty-three years of marriage. Nevertheless, when the story broke, almost every major newspaper reported that Ann Rutledge had been the true love of Abraham Lincoln's life.[17]

To make matters worse, Herndon wrote other scathing and disparaging accounts of the former First Lady: He claimed that Lincoln only wed Mary because of his vulnerability and melancholy,

---

15 Lachman, *The Last Lincolns,* 94.

16 Lachman, *The Last Lincolns,* 81, 93–94, 118–19, 124.

17 Lachman, *The Last Lincolns,* 105–7.

that she secretly tried to auction off her wardrobe and was embarrassed when no one bought her clothes, and that she orchestrated the "ghoulish idea" of sending on a tour the stained dress she had been wearing the night Lincoln died.

Mary then felt betrayed by another exposé, this one written by her personal attendant, Elizabeth "Lizzy" Keckley. A "strikingly handsome light mulatto," Keckley had purchased her son's freedom, as well as her own, before being employed by the First Lady. When Lizzy started one of the first contraband relief societies for former slaves who flocked to Washington, Mary contributed generously to the cause. This may have been one reason Keckley's *Behind the Scenes, or, Thirty Years a Slave, and Four Years in the White House* attempted to portray Mary in a positive light.

But the general public only seemed to notice the reporting on Mary's conspicuous faults and imperfections—her obnoxious jealousy of any women who paid attention to her husband, her spending habits and debt, and her conspiratorial distrust of cabinet officers. The *Chicago Tribune* published a front-page story on Keckley's revelations, and newspapers all across the country soon followed suit. Mary felt betrayed by her former attendant, who shared many of Mary's personal letters in the book, and immediately terminated the friendship. Keckley, whom Mary coldly labeled "the colored historian" the only time she mentioned her again, later regretted the publication.[18]

The publication of *Behind the Scenes* broke Mary's faith in the American people for good. She and Tad went into exile, leaving the "ungrateful Republic" to "flee to a land of strangers."[19] They initially sought the alleged healing power of the spas in Frankfurt, Germany. Mary hoped for a cure for her gynecological problems, body aches, and debilitating migraines. In the winters, they lived

---

[18] Peterson, *Lincoln in American Memory*, 51; Lachman, *The Last Lincolns*, 131–33.

[19] Lachman, *The Last Lincolns,* 133.

in Nice, France. Together they toured Paris and London, and spent almost two months in Scotland.

When the Franco-Prussian War escalated, they left Frankfurt after two years of exile and took up residence in Leamington Spa, England, again hoping that the salty waters of the famous resort would cure Mary's health problems.[20]

Isolated even more than before, Mary continued to write to Congress, pleading for federal assistance. Eventually, in July 1870, Congress granted her a generous pension. Finally debt-free and with money to spare, Mary still could not stop worrying. "I am so broken hearted myself," she wrote a friend from Europe. "I cannot fully sympathize with—In *Gods Own Time* … 'Over the river,' our loved ones are watching & waiting for us—But yet the time of that reunion, appears so far distant. With sorrow, as a companion, the time passes, *but* slowly."[21]

Finding little healing in the spas, Mary and Tad returned to the United States in May 1871. Unfortunately, Tad caught a cold on the return trip across the Atlantic.[22] When they gathered for a family reunion a few weeks later in Chicago, where Robert was now a successful attorney, Tad's health deteriorated rapidly. Eventually forced to sit upright because his lungs had filled with mucus and

---

[20] Lachman, *The Last Lincolns,* 148, 155.

[21] Turner and Turner, Mary Lincoln to Rhoda White, January 30, 1870, *Mary Todd Lincoln*, 544–45.

[22] Lachman, *The Last Lincolns*, 159. When Tad and Mary returned from Europe in the spring of 1871, they ran into John Hay, who once served as Lincoln's personal secretary, in New York. At the time, Hay was writing editorials for the *New York Tribune.* During his White House days as Lincoln's personal secretary, Hay considered Tad an "absolute tyrant"—shrewd, lawless, and with a "very bad opinion of books and no opinion of discipline." Now Tad presented himself as a fine, gracious man "fixed" and sober after the terrible shock of his father's assassination. That Tad had demonstrated benevolence, kindness, and compassion by remaining at his mother's side through three years in exile impressed Hay immensely. Hay found the mature Tad a "cordial, frank, warm-hearted boy" and "greatly improved" by his time abroad.

bacterial fluid, he suffered and labored over each breathe. Fluid not only surrounded his lungs but also the entire left side of his body. Every cough felt like a knife plunging into his chest. Diagnosed with dropsy, or what would be labelled pleurisy today—a viral infection that probably had tuberculosis as its cause, Tad's heart eventually gave out on July 15, 1871, while Robert and Mary looked on helplessly. Having grown especially close to her eighteen-year-old-son, whose tenderness reminded her of her husband's, Mary had lost yet another (her fourth) nuclear family member in her tragedy-filled life.[23]

After Tad's passing, Mary wandered again to various spas and spiritualists, hoping to find an antidote to her pain.[24] In November 1873, she contracted a urinary tract infection. When a doctor called on her, he found Mary in a self-induced trance attempting to raise the dead. The spirit of a dead Indian, she claimed, had gotten into her head and produced bizarre hallucinations. Every so often the Indian lifted her scalp and then lowered it back into place. The doctor prescribed chloral hydrate—a sleep-inducing depressant prescribed today for stress or as a tranquilizer before surgery—for

---

[23] Lachman, *The Last Lincolns,* 161–67. Tad's coffin was eventually taken to Oak Ridge Cemetery in Springfield and placed in the same tomb with those of Willie, Eddie, and their father.

[24] Lachman, *The Last Lincolns,* 174–76. Among the spiritualists she sought out, Mary met numerous times with Caroline Howard in St. Charles, Illinois—one of the most famous spiritualists in the West. Believing Mrs. Howard to be a medium, Mary believed she could be put in direct communication with the spirits of her husband and sons. She also called on the legendary Fox sisters—Margaretta and Catherine, in upstate New York. They had a unique ability to adjust their kneecaps with a loud clack, and they insisted that these sounds were from a spirit called Mr. Splitfoot. Mary, nevertheless, believed the Fox sisters put her in contact with her husband's spirit. Mary also met with the biggest charlatan of all, William Mumler, in New York City. He had somehow learned to doctor photographs with images of dead relatives or ghosts in a time when photography remained a new art form.

her "nervous derangement and fever in her head."[25] Unfortunately, she soon became addicted. As the months passed, Mary responded to voices in the walls and floor and became possessed of a terrible fear and delusion of fire. She continued to squander prodigious amounts of money. A few months later in 1784, while wintering in Florida looking for curative elements in the plentiful sulfur springs there, she had an acute apparition of Robert lying on his deathbed. In her delusion, she traveled all the way to Chicago, to find him perfectly well.

Slowly but surely, her mental state worsened. She once mistook the elevator for a lavatory and refused to come out. When Robert and a hotel employee tried to get her back in her room, Mary screamed and accused her son of attempted murder.

Robert, whose business and wife kept him from his insufferable mother, consulted with doctors and some of his father's closest friend and advisors, who had known Mary for decades, seeking advice on what should be done. Reluctantly, based on their advice, Robert petitioned the Cook County Court to have Mary enrolled in a sanitarium. At that time, a finding of insanity required a jury trial under Illinois law. At the trial, her gynecologist, the hotel manager, housekeepers, and other hotel workers testified to Mary's insanity. On the witness stand, Robert stated that his mother "has been of unsound mind since the death of Father; has been irresponsible for the past ten years." He talked about her sad state of finances and added, "I do not regard it safe to allow her to remain longer unrestrained … She has no home, and does not visit my house because of a misunderstanding with my wife. She has been kind to me." Nevertheless, he had "no doubt my mother is insane." He had conferred with many of her associates, and they considered the former First Lady "eccentric and unmanageable."[26]

---

[25] Lachman, *The Last Lincolns*, 179.

[26] Lachman, *The Last Lincolns*, 199-200.

After three hours of testimony, the jury took just ten minutes to declare Mary insane and order her placed in an asylum. She was admitted to Bellevue Place in Batavia, Illinois. That night, she tried to kill herself with a lethal dose of camphor and laudanum. Fortunately, the druggist had substituted a harmless ingredient for her laudanum, and Mary survived. The next day, she rode with Robert as he transferred her to a private sanitarium on the west side of Chicago. Mary soon went into a deep depression and refused to get out of bed.[27]

Of course Mary felt betrayed by her oldest son. "It does not appear that God is good, to have placed me here. I endeavor to read my bible and offer up my petitions three times a day," she wrote an associate. "But my afflicted heart fails me and my voice often falters in prayer. I have worshipped my son and no unpleasant word ever passed between us, yet I cannot understand why I should been brought out here."[28]

Even as she suffered from deepening depression, Mary plotted her emancipation from the asylum. Robert had already been cast as a villain and denounced in sermons around the country for dumping his widowed mother in an asylum. Mary too targeted Robert, even threatening his life, while portraying herself as the innocent victim.[29]

Mary's cause was aided by feminists Myra and Judge James Bradwell, as well as her sister Elizabeth and brother-in-law Ninian Edwards. A new court ruled Mary sane in June 1876, four months

---

[27] Lachman, *The Last Lincolns,* 178–211; Emerson, "The Madness of Mary Lincoln," 243.

[28] Emerson, "Madness of Mary Lincoln," 237.

[29] Lachman, *The Last Lincolns,* 236. When Mary got a break from the insane asylum, she went to visit her sister Elizabeth Edwards in Springfield. Soon a message came from Aunt Lizzie's husband, Ninian Edwards wrote to Robert: "I'm sorry to say that your mother has for the last month been very much embittered against you and has on several occasions said that she had hired two men to take your life. On this morning we learned that she carries a pistol in her pocket."

after her initial commitment. The judgment found her capable "to manage and control her estate." Released into the Edwardses' care and no longer officially labeled a lunatic, Mary felt exonerated.[30]

After her release, Mary unleashed her fury at Robert. Just four days after the jury verdict, she demanded that he ship all her paintings, silver, jewelry, silks, clothes, and household items to her immediately. "I am now in constant receipt of letters, from my friends, denouncing you in the bitterest terms," she taunted Robert. "Two prominent clergy have written me ... They think it advisable to offer up prayers for you in Church on account of your wickedness against me and High Heaven." She also wanted him to return any letters she had sent him. Instead of signing the letter "Mother," she wrote the more formal "Mrs. A. Lincoln."[31] In a follow-up letter, she labeled him a "monster of mankind."[32] Only after receiving legal counsel did Mary relent in her verbal threats on Robert's reputation, property, and life.

Not wanting to face the whispers of being called a lunatic in her Springfield home, Mary went into exile yet again. She settled in the foothills of the Pyrenees near Pau, France, and did not relent in scorning her oldest son. "'My Gethsemane' is ever with me," she wrote a friend. Her "bad son" had "cruelly persecuted" his own mother. "That wretched young man, but *old* in sin, has a fearful account yet to render to his Maker! And God does not allow sin to go unpunished."[33]

Soon, a life of exile and travel no longer suited Mary. Now in her sixties, and at a time when few lived to be much older, Mary suffered from a plethora of medical conditions—diabetes, cataracts, rheumatism, high blood pressure, chronic back pain, and a "great

---

[30] Lachman, *The Last Lincolns,* 23, 244; Packard, *Lincolns in the White House,* 261.

[31] Lachman, *The Last Lincolns,* 245-46.

[32] Lachman, *The Last Lincolns,* 246.

[33] Lachman, *The Last Lincolns,* 258.

bloat"—an undiagnosed disorder that, for a time, caused her body to balloon. Delicate health was no match for a busy travel schedule.

In the fall of 1880, Mary returned to Springfield and moved back into her sister's home, bringing sixty-five trunks and crates of possessions with her. Elizabeth Edwards graciously stored her sister's belongings in two of their rooms. The estimated four tons of Mary's stuff caused one room's floor to buckle in the center. The two sisters bickered incessantly. Elizabeth's small-town frugality contrasted significantly with Mary's avarice and luxury. Compounding the tension in the Edwards household, Mary began to live like a hermit and hypochondriac. She had her curtains drawn and perpetually darkened her bedroom to protect her weak eyes. Mary insisted she was going blind due to her constant weeping.[34]

Mother and son at this point had not spoken to each other for more than five years. Robert initiated a reconciliation with his mother in May 1881. Bringing his twelve-year-old daughter Mamie to melt Mary's heart, Robert apologized and begged forgiveness. Between Elizabeth Edwards working on Mary's heart, Mary's pride in Robert's rise to the position of secretary of war under the Garfield administration, and the charm of her granddaughter, Mary accepted her son's apology.[35]

As soon as she and Robert reconciled, Mary took a trip east to Niagara Falls and New York City, looking for spas, medicines, or anything that could offer her diminishing body relief. Not finding any, she returned to Springfield in the spring of 1882. During her last few weeks of life, boils appeared all over her skin. The pus-filled blisters popped, creating much additional pain. Weighing only one hundred pounds, partially paralyzed, suffering from diabetes, and nearly blind (she could hardly blink because her eyelids were so

---

[34] Lachman, *The Last Lincolns,* 259, 271–72.

[35] Lachman, *The Last Lincolns,* 274.

painful), Mary Lincoln died at sixty-four years of age on July 16, 1882.[36]

Whenever people thought of the former First Lady, they could not help but think of her husband. Mary certainly contributed to this reality. After all, she told people that she only slept on one side of the bed because she did not want to disturb "the President's place" beside her.[37] Even at her funeral, at First Presbyterian Church in Springfield, the Reverend James Reed compared Mary and Abe's marriage to two pine trees with interlocking roots. When lightning struck down the taller tree, the shorter tree absorbed a deadly blow too. "Both trees had suffered from the same calamity," Reed commented, reflecting on Lincoln's assassination. "They had virtually been killed at the same time." When Abe died, Mary died.[38]

They set the former First Lady's casket in Oak Ridge Cemetery in Springfield, where an impressive obelisk marked the Lincoln family tomb. Her remains were placed beside those of her husband and three sons. Joining those whom she loved most in the world, Mary's mind and body could finally rest.

There would be no portrait of Mary Todd Lincoln hung in the White House until 1924. Every other First Lady had a portrait located somewhere, but Mary's was overlooked for decades. Her obstinate and abhorrent behavior during her twilight years directly contributed to this slight. She had tried to make the Executive Mansion her own palace; she was jealous of anyone who had wanted her husband's time or attention; she spent the people's money and the Lincolns' own on luxuries she did not need; she mourned too long after her husband's death; she pressed Congress for money she felt entitled to; she spoke of her husband's assassination constantly; she left her country often for Europe; she publicly feuded with her eldest and only surviving son; and she disobeyed every rule of

---

36 Packard, *Lincolns in the White House*, 263.

37 Oates, *Man Behind the Myths,* 181-87.

38 Lachman, *The Last Lincolns*, 279–80.

anonymity expected of Victorian ladies.[39] In the eyes of far too many Americans, instead of finishing life strong, Mary finished it almost all wrong.

Yet in so many ways, we can relate to the life of Mary Todd Lincoln as she grieved lost loved ones and sacrificed so much for her husband and country. While her husband's ability to deal with setbacks and tragedy seemed almost superhuman, Mary's frailty and limitations in coping with sacrifice, change, and tragedy make her, perhaps, even more human and real. Mary kept trying to find something that would take away her intense pain—physical, emotional, and spiritual. Spas, séances, soothsayers, shopping sprees, and financial security—none of these could touch her soul and give her relief. She never found peace. There is a lesson there for all of us.

The Truth

Even though Mary Lincoln had been born into a well-to-do family and became the First Lady of the United States, much of her life in this fallen world consisted of tragedy, loss, and suffering. Unfortunately, she turned to spiritualists and séances to dull her pain. The historical record is mixed on her precise religious faith in the last years of her life.

No matter the earthly hardships one endures, the Bible teaches that "she who is truly a widow, left all alone," should "set her hope on God" and continue to reach out to Him "in supplications and prayers night and day." A widow, like anyone, should not be "self-indulgent … while she lives."[40]

Of course, earthly temptations and trials will come in this life. The Bible insists "that the testing of your faith produces steadfastness" and more intimate reliance on God.[41] God promises

---

[39] Lachman, *The Last Lincolns*, 364–65; Baker, *Mary Todd Lincoln*, xiv.

[40] 1 Tim. 5:5–6.

[41] James 1:3.

to heal the brokenhearted and "bind up their wounds."[42] No matter your life circumstances, you are "to walk in a manner worthy of the Lord, fully pleasing to him, bearing fruit in every good work and increasing in the knowledge of God."[43]

This is easier said than done, to be sure, which is why God promises to strengthen you "with all power, according to his glorious might, for all endurance and patience with joy, giving thanks to the Father, who has qualified you to share in the inheritance of the saints in light."[44] You can be confident that God will be enough to enable you to overcome your current pain and suffering. After all, He delivered all of His followers "from the domain of darkness and transferred us to the kingdom of his beloved Son, in whom we have redemption, the forgiveness of sins."[45]

All by yourself, you will not be able to handle tragedy, hardship, pain, and suffering. God calls on you to "let all bitterness and wrath and anger and clamor and slander be put away from you, along with all malice. Be kind to one another, tenderhearted, forgiving one another, as God in Christ forgave you."[46] One of Lincoln's most famous statements in his second inaugural address called on the Union to have "malice toward none" and "charity for all."

Certainly, as caring and compassionate Christians, we feel for someone who suffers as greatly as Mary Lincoln did. We help them in their moments of great need. God's Word encourages us to "learn to do good; seek justice, correct oppression; bring justice to the fatherless, plead the widow's cause."[47]

In this fallen and sinful world, however, all of us will endure hardship and suffering. And even during these excruciating times, God calls on His followers to endure in the faith. "Therefore, since

---

[42] Ps. 147:3.

[43] Col. 1:10

[44] Col. 1:11

[45] Col. 1:13-14.

[46] Eph. 4:31–32.

[47] Isa. 1:17.

we are surrounded by so great a cloud of witnesses," the Bible exhorts, "let us also lay aside every weight, and sin which clings so closely, and let us run with endurance the race that is set before us."[48] God urges us to "press on toward the goal for the prize of the upward call of God in Christ Jesus."[49] Whenever the end of our earthy lives come, God wants us to be able to confidently say, "I have fought the good fight, I have finished the race, I have kept the faith."[50] Then we can find joy and comfort in God's words: "Well done, good and faithful servant."[51]

Your Life

The intensity of Mary's mourning turned off a lot of friends and associates who truly wanted to reach out to her. She rudely pushed many well-wishers away, even months after Abe's passing. One can certainly understand Mary's deep anguish. On the other hand, one can also understand the ungratefulness many might have felt who tried to console Mary. Have you ever been on either side of that equation—intensely grieving a loss or trying to console one who has? What lessons can we learn from how Mary Lincoln handled that situation?

If you had been a friend of Mary's, how would you have tried to share God's Word and the gospel of Jesus Christ with her so that she might know "the peace of God, which surpasses all understanding" (Phil. 4:7)? How might you approach someone as volatile as Mary in your own life?

---

48 Heb. 12:1.

49 Phil. 3:14.

50 2 Tim. 4:7.

51 Matt. 25:23.

The relationship between Mary and her eldest son, Robert, was certainly an emotional one. The nadir occurred when Robert made the decision to commit his mother to an insane asylum. Have you ever had to make a decision like that? What was the most difficult part of the decision? The Fourth Commandment says, "Honor your father and your mother, that your days may be long in the land that the Lord your God is giving you" (Exod. 20:12). Do you think Robert honored his mother? Why or why not? How does one "honor" one's father and mother when they are cruel or uncaring parents?

THE MAKING OF A LEADER

11

Poverty-Stricken

For you know that the testing of your faith
produces steadfastness.
—James 1:3

The Lincoln Way

Materialism or social class does not define a leader.

One of the more endearing features of the Abraham Lincoln life story is that a poverty-stricken boy emerged from the formidable frontier to become the United States' most powerful political figure and most venerated president. More than going from rags to riches, Lincoln would emerge from the backwoods and ascend to the front of Mount Rushmore. He came, seemingly, from nothing to become something, from a no one to the one everyone wants to emulate and co-opt. even today.

Indeed, for all its beauty and freedom, the frontier was a daunting and often inhospitable place. Whether we look at his time in Kentucky, Indiana, or Illinois, Lincoln's character-shaping years were hard. Hostile and ravaging Native Americans concerned the minds of frontier families daily. If one had a conflict with a neighbor, justice might be administered through fists, gunfights, thievery, or destruction of property. Excessive drinking did not help matters and often turned trivial differences of opinion into brutal violence. Frontier shooting matches, card games, horse racing, cock and dog fighting, drinking, and competition for the affection of single women regularly led to vicious brawls. Combatants kicked, punched, bit, and gouged eyes to prevail in a scrap. The next day men would often be seen with bruised faces, missing fingers, eyes, or ears. Women placed bets on the outcomes of fights. Even the more friendly contests men took part in were violent. In one popular game—Gander pulling—a contestant would grease the neck of a gander (adult male goose), tie its feet together, and suspend it on a high tree limb. While riding his horse at full speed, the contestant would move underneath the limb, reach up, grab the gander's head, hoping to snap it off. If successful, the rider got to keep the decapitated bird. With his intrinsic abhorrence of violence, there is little wonder why Lincoln never wanted to embrace the life his father had led on the frontier. To cloth and feed a family, members had to hunt constantly and live off the land. Bear and deer meat had to last through the winter. Chores were never ending. Simply maintaining your home or living quarters, never mind improving them, required constant vigilance and effort in the most humid of summer days and the most extreme and cold winter months. In the winter, a young Lincoln could only afford catnaps at night as he had to make sure that the fireplace would not go out. Rainstorms could wash crops away in a moment while a drought could slowly starve a family over a period of weeks. Forests had to be cleared and fields plowed. Wild animals—raccoons, squirrels, opossum, skunks, deer, bears, wolves, wildcats, and panthers—were so ubiquitous that community hunts were employed to not only acquire wild game for food and clothing but to protect their crops, livestock, and even human life.[1] Lincoln once wrote a poem indicating that out on "the frontier line: The panther's scream, filled night with fear and the bears prayed on the swine."[2]

---

[1] Kigel, *Becoming Lincoln*, 15, 41-–42; Donald, *Lincoln*, 25; Wheeler, *Faith and Courage*, 40; Burlingame, *Lincoln*, 1:58; Holzer and Garfinkle, *A Just and Generous Nation*, 17.

[2] Basler, Lincoln's The Bear Hunt, September 6, 1846, *CW*, 1:186.

With very few towns or schools, and only a few primitive churches, superstitions and ignorance flourished on the frontier. If one broke a mirror or carried an ax into a cabin, death would come to that person's family within a year. Bad luck would ensue if a dog crossed a hunter's path or if crops were planted on a Friday. If birds hoped or flew into a house, hardship would soon come. For a bountiful harvest, certain crops should only be planted under a full moon and others not. If a horse breathed on a child, whooping cough would soon infuse the child's body. To expedite the discovery of one's true love, young were told to swallow chicken hearts. If men could successfully carry a bag of eggs in one hand and a bag of salt in the other, while riding their horse or mule backwards for a mile without accident, they would receive good luck throughout the coming year. Lincoln himself subscribed to some of these superstitions. Once when a dog bit one of his children, he took his son to Terre Haute, Indiana, to find the "mad stone" that would supposedly drain away the poison and cure the lad.[3]

Disease was a constant fear in the backcountry. No one, including doctors, understood how diseases were contracted or spread. They did not know about germs, antiseptics, or even why people should bother to keep things clean. Most Americans took one or two baths a summer and perhaps none during the rest of the year. When the special occasion of a bath did occur, the entire family jumped in the tub one after another, from the oldest to the smallest child. The old saying to refrain from "throwing the baby out with the bath water" came about because too many babies drowned in bath water so filthy that no one recognized one had slipped under the surface.[4]

The average nineteenth-century man went through three wives. Women often died shortly after giving birth to a child, and no one knew why. Today we know that mothers often died from postpartum infections, which led to puerperal fever, because neither doctors nor

[3] Burlingame, *Lincoln*, 23–24.

[4] Wheeler, *Faith and Courage*, 7.

midwives knew enough to wash their hands between patients.[5] The Lincolns were obviously familiar with disease and death on the frontier. Abe's mother, Nancy Hanks, died an excruciating death from the milk-sickness disease when he was just nine years of age. A decade later his older sister, Sarah, would pass giving after giving birth to a child.

While the hinterland could be brutal, Lincoln's upbringing greatly benefitted him in the long term—physically, emotionally, mentally, and psychologically. Wooded terrains needed to be cleared. Game had to be hunted and prepared for winter storage. Lincoln hauled logs, built cabins, dug wells, fetched water from wells and carried the precious liquid for miles. Already as a little boy at the age of eight, Lincoln became a proficient axman—chopping trees down, clearing undergrowth, and rooting out stumps. He plowed fields, planted seeds, harvested crops, and butchered livestock.[6] The manual labor required of a farmer and frontiersman toughened him physically. His strength became legendary and gave him contemporary notoriety. Moreover, the mental toughness required to do such work steeled his fortitude and independence. In the future, Lincoln would be identified by the iconic image of a rail-splitter.

Lincoln once told an Illinois neighbor that he had observed "a good deal of the back side of this world."[7] Indeed, in addition to the challenges which faced all settlers on the frontier, the Lincolns lived in poverty except for a few years early in Abe's childhood. Kentucky neighbors regarded the Lincolns as "the very poorest of people." When they moved to Indiana in 1817, the family lost the few possessions they did have when their raft overturned. For the first year, they resided in a half-faced, three-sided cabin. The next year they upgraded to an 18 x 20 cabin, which housed up to thirteen people counting relatives and friends, for almost fourteen years.

---

5 Wheeler, *Faith and Courage,* 7.

6 Donald, *Lincoln*, 25.

7 Burlingame, *Lincoln*, 1:17.

When Lincoln eventually set up in Springfield, Illinois, as a young man, he described himself as a "strange, friendless, uneducated, penniless boy."[8] Years later, when he had been elected to the state legislature, he asked his friend Coleman Smoot for a sixty dollar loan. His opening gambit was "Smoot, did you vote for me?" Smoot replied that he had. "Well," replied Lincoln, "that makes you responsible." Lincoln then asked his friend for money to purchase suitable clothing to wear in the legislature.[9]

Until he built his law practice and earned a considerable income, Lincoln simply endured his poverty. His toes poked through his shoes and his elbows through his shirts. One friend refused to invite him to his wedding because Lincoln lacked the appropriate clothing. Even at the age of twenty, Lincoln could not buy a pair of shoes on credit.[10] Whether it be food, clothing, or shelter, he progressed through life with very few material things and comforts. When a reporter interviewed him during his presidential run in 1860, and asked about his early life, Lincoln told him it was "folly to attempt to make anything out of my early life. It can all be condensed into a single sentence … the short and simple annals of the poor."[11]

The poverty-stricken youth he experienced in the backwoods, however, profoundly shaped the development of Lincoln as a man and leader. Lincoln confronted and overcame his upbringing. He never let himself become a victim of his context or social status. Indeed, the hardscrabble life steeled him mentally and provided a psychological maturity unmatched by any other figure in American history.[12] Joshua Speed, one of Lincoln's closest friends, later reflected that "to have lived to see such a man rise from point to point, and from place to place, filling all the places to which he was called, with honor and distinction," and to eventually fill "the

---

[8] Basler, Lincoln to Martin Morris, March 26, 1843, *CW*, 1:320.

[9] Lehrman, *Lincoln "by littles,"* 82.

[10] Burlingame, *Lincoln*, 16.

[11] Wilson, *Herndon's Informants*, 57.

[12] Burlingame, *Lincoln*, 1:xii.

presidential chair in the most trying of times that any ruler ever had, seems more like fiction than fact." Only a "genius like his could have accomplished so much." Lincoln rose like a "young eagle" and "soared to the top!"[13]

Lincoln would not let his social class or life of poverty shackle or suppress his pursuit of happiness. Dennis Hanks, who lived with the Lincolns after Abe's mother died, noted that Lincoln "was ambitious & determined & when he attempted to Excel by man or boy his whole soul & his Energies were bent on doing it, and he in this generally, almost always accomplished his Ends."[14] Lincoln once told his law partner, William Herndon, that "the way for a young man to rise, is to improve himself every way he can." One could not fail "unless you allow your mind to be improperly directed."[15] To his indolent stepbrother, John D. Johnston, who wanted to sell his farm in Illinois and move to Missouri, Lincoln asserted that "if you intend to go to work, there is no better place than right where you are. If you do not intend to go to work, you can not get along anywhere. Squirming & crawling about from place to place can do no good." Lincoln insisted that his stepbrother should "face the truth … you are destitute because you have idled away all your time." Lincoln had no patience for pretenses or excuses—they were "all nonsense" and "deceived no body but yourself. *Go to work* is the only cure for your case."[16]

For all of his pull-up-your-own-bootstraps mentality, Lincoln certainly had a heart for those who suffered on the low end of the socioeconomic ladder. This was one reason he worked so hard, as a state legislator and national representative, to advocate for legislation for internal improvements. He did not want anyone to endure the poverty and isolation on the rural frontier that he had endured. He also promoted usury laws with low interest rates so that everyone

---

13 Wilson, *Herndon's Informants*, 590.

14 Wilson, *Herndon's Informants,* 42.

15 Basler, Lincoln to William Herndon, July 18, 1848, *CW,* 1:497.

16 Basler, Lincoln to John D. Johnston, November 4, 1851, *CW,* 2:111.

could borrow money to take risks and better their financial future. He supported public education so that people could realize a bigger world and escape economic hardship. Lincoln knew how poverty-stricken folk felt about their condition, because he had lived it and overcome it.

While his poverty-stricken years certainly inhibited asset accrual, perhaps they have been underestimated for what they *did* provide for Lincoln. When Abe finally left his family and started out on his own in 1830, he left with nothing but the clothes on his back and what he could carry. Materially, he had next to nothing to make his mark in the world. Mentally, however, he had almost everything needed to serve and lead effectively—a mindset and inner constitution of grit, resilience, perseverance, entrepreneurship, self-education, curiosity, conversation, and storytelling—all forged while making a life on the frontier.

Lincoln's rise from poor, daunting origins is the most enduring and alluring component of his life story. For students of the man, the Lincoln legacy teaches that one can rise from any station in life, pursue happiness, and achieve impact and significance. Indeed, the poverty-stricken boy, the young man in shabby shoes and clothes from the harsh frontier and backcountry, came into the world with so little. Yet he overcame and became so much. If he could do it, anyone can do it.

The Truth

Far too many people in our world today live in abject material poverty. Scripture is filled with passages calling on Christians to serve and help those in need—the poor, downtrodden, widowed, orphaned, diseased, or oppressed. "Whoever has a bountiful eye will be blessed," the Bible asserts, "for he shares his bread with the poor."[17]

---

[17] Prov. 22:9.

Scripture calls on you to "remember the words of the Lord Jesus," when He proclaimed "it is more blessed to give than to receive."[18] You are to help the poor willingly, not grudgingly. God loves "a cheerful giver,"[19] and "will bless you in all your work and in all that you undertake."[20]

The Bible is clear that "there will never cease to be poor in the land." Therefore, God commands that "you shall open wide your hand to your brother, to the needy and to the poor, in your land."[21] Jesus says that "everyone to whom much was given, of him much will be required."[22] Odds are that if you are reading this, you have been given much materially compared to the plight of many others around the world. Inspired by Christ's love for you—that He died on the cross for the sake of your sins—you can serve and love others in His name. God's Word proclaims that "if anyone has the world's goods and sees his brother in need, yet closes his heart against him, how does God's love abide in him?"[23] Helping those who suffer in poverty is certainly a God-pleasing endeavor and a response to Christ's love for you.

Scripture reveals, however, that being rich or poor in faith is of far more significance than being blessed or not with material wealth. Wealthy or poverty-stricken, "the Lord is the maker of them all."[24] The Bible asserts that "whoever mocks the poor insults his Maker."[25] When Jesus told his disciples, "Blessed are you who are poor, for yours is the kingdom of God," He reinforced that what God values is not what man values.[26] God looks at the heart of His

---

[18] Acts 20:35.
[19] 2 Cor. 9:7.
[20] Deut 15:10.
[21] Deut. 15:11.
[22] Luke 12:48.
[23] 1 John 3:17.
[24] Prov. 22:2.
[25] Prov. 17:5.
[26] Luke 6:20.

children, not their possessions.[27] Jesus came to minister and die for all people, not just the powerful and wealthy.

Jesus's concern for the poor, downtrodden, and undesirable shocked the religious and political leaders of His time and remains countercultural today. "Listen, my beloved brothers," Scripture teaches, "has not God chosen those who are poor in the world to be rich in faith and heirs of the kingdom, which he has promised to those who love him?"[28] The Bible promises that a "man who remains steadfast under trial ... will receive the crown of life, which God has promised to those who love him."[29]

Being without money or material resources remains a daunting challenge for many in our world today. On the other hand, being blessed with material wealth brings notoriety, popularity, and influence. While these things certainly have advantages from a secular perspective, none of them help one reach paradise. When the rich man asked Jesus what he needed to do to enter heaven, Jesus told him, "You lack one thing: go, sell all that you have and give to the poor, and you will have treasure in heaven; and come, follow me." The man went away "disheartened" and "sorrowful, for he had great possessions."[30] Jesus asked a lot of this wealthy man (as He does of you). Wealthy people might be able to hire the best attorneys, make deals, or buy their way out of trouble on this earth, but money has no impact on God. He does not need it.

While being poverty-stricken may make earthly living more difficult, having a poor or nonexistent relationship with Christ is deadly for all eternity. One can be materially poor, on the other hand, yet spiritually wealthy and overflowing with God's riches and joy. Perhaps you have seen people living in abject poverty who also live with gladness and delight. The Bible reassures us that we should "rejoice in our sufferings, knowing that suffering produces

---

[27] 1 Sam. 16:7.

[28] James 2:5.

[29] James 1:12.

[30] Mark 10:21–22.

endurance, and endurance produces character, and character produces hope, and hope does not put us to shame, because God's love has been poured into our hearts through the Holy Spirit."[31] God promises "that the sufferings of this present time are not worth comparing with the glory that is to be revealed" when you join Him in heaven.[32] "For you know the grace of our Lord Jesus Christ, that though he was rich, yet for your sake he became poor, so that you by his poverty might become rich."[33]

Your Life

Lincoln is a terrific example of someone who climbed out of poverty and did something significant with his life. Why do you think Lincoln was able to do this when so many others fail?

How did Lincoln's tough frontier upbringing prepare him for his future leadership positions as a lawyer and politician?

What can poverty-stricken or hard times do for you as a Christian?

How can you be sure that your faith walk is not poor but rich?

[31] Rom. 5:3–5.

[32] Rom. 8:18.

[33] 2 Cor. 8:9.

12

Self-Directed Learning

Make me to know your ways, O Lord; teach me your paths. Lead me in your truth and teach me, for you are the God of my salvation; for you I wait all the day long.
—Psalm 25:4–5

Lincoln's Way

Effective and compelling leaders possess an insatiable desire to learn.

From his earliest days, Abraham Lincoln possessed not just a voracious appetite to learn but a *need* to learn. Physically strong and gifted, especially for a productive life on the frontier, Lincoln nevertheless spent an inordinate amount of time cultivating his mind, largely outside of the arena of any kind of formal education.

Young Lincoln's formal learning experiences were few. While living at the Knob Creek Farm, Abe and his sister Sarah walked four miles a day to a log schoolhouse, which had a dirt floor and one door. They sat on benches with no backs. At the age of six, in two brief stints, Abe learned to read almost all of his lessons out loud—something he would continue to do all his life—at an "ABC" or "blab" school. His first teacher was Zachariah Riney, a pious Catholic respected for his character. His second teacher was Caleb Hazel, known for his size, which aided with classroom discipline.

They encouraged and nurtured young Abe's blossoming affinity for reading and writing.[1]

During his short stays in blab schools, Lincoln learned from Thomas Dilworth's *New Guide to the English Tongue.* The textbook started with one-syllable words:

> *No Man may put off the Law of God*
> *The Way of God is no ill Way.*
> *My Joy is in God all the Day.*
> *A bad man is a Foe to God.* [2]

An eighteenth-century English minister, Dilworth had taught moral education, vocabulary, and grammar. Moreover, he required his students to read and memorize Scripture, especially the book of Proverbs and the Psalms, so that they could learn rhyme and practice cadence.

After moving from Kentucky to Indiana, Lincoln did not attend formal school for a number of years. Eventually, by 1818 or 1819, new schools opened in the Little Pigeon Creek region, and Lincoln again participated in ABC "schools by littles," as he would later say.[3] At the age of eleven, he attended Andrew Crawford's blab school for three months. A respected citizen of Spencer County and commissioned justice of the peace, Crawford's subscription school relied on tuition, paid in cash and commodities. Crawford loaned young Abe a copy of Mason Weems's *Life of Washington*, a book that Lincoln reread. It had a profound impact on him.

There is some discrepancy in the historical record as to the precise time Lincoln attended school under James Swaney and Azel Dorsey. Whenever he attended the school taught by Swaney, that time was brief. Azel Dorsey, a local businessman, opened up his

---

1 Bartelt, *Lincoln's Indiana Youth*, 26; Donald, *Lincoln*, 23; Kigel, *Becoming Lincoln*, 69.

2 White, *Lincoln*, 20.

3 Basler, Autobiography written for John L. Scripps, June, 1860, *CW*, 4:62.

school four miles away, in Crawford's old cabin. Lincoln probably received the best quality of instruction from Dorsey, especially in the area of mathematics. Years later, Dorsey recalled Lincoln's excellent poetry skills and how he often wrote about animal cruelty. He also remembered "the diligence and eagerness" with which Lincoln pursued his studies, and how he came to school in his "buck skin cloths [and] a raccoon-skin cap," holding his arithmetic book.[4] Nevertheless, with the schoolhouse so far from home, Abe attended irregularly. By his mid-teens, Lincoln's formal schooling ended, the total not amounting to one full year of study.[5]

While these schoolteachers were more educated than most, they still lacked the fundamental skills and knowledge we now expect of instructors. Local communities did not expect much of them, as demonstrated by their compensation, which often consisted of venison, hams, corn, animal skins, and other produce.[6] As Lincoln later recalled, "There were some schools, so called; but no qualification was ever required of a teacher, beyond 'readin, writin, and cipherin' to the Rule of Three." If a "straggler" happened "to understand latin," and "happened to sojourn in the neighborhood, he was looked upon as a wizard." Sadly, Lincoln noted that "there was absolutely nothing to excite ambition for education," which was one reason he stopped attending. While his formal schooling ended, his life learning moved forward. "The little advance I now have upon this store of education," he wrote a friend, "I have picked up from time to time under the pressure of necessity."[7]

Despite the lack of qualified teachers, Lincoln did learn from his school experiences. The "blab" emphasis helped him hear and see words, which aided his comprehension and became a lifelong study habit. Moreover, Lincoln embraced a growth mindset and developed

---

4 Capps, "Making a New Home," 61.

5 Bartelt, *Lincoln's Indiana Youth*, 27–28; Donald, *Lincoln*, 29.

6 Sandburg, *Lincoln*, 13.

7 Basler, Lincoln to Jesse Fell, Enclosing Autobiography, December 20, 1859, *CW*, 3:511.

a curiosity and inner discipline to master what at first stumped him. When he came to a passage that struck him, he would write it down so he could find an answer to his question and then permanently embed his discovery in his memory. He possessed a mind that thrived on retention and retrieval of details, which is one reason he continued to say things aloud. Indeed, Lincoln constantly repeated things until he understood and could recall and repeat them with ease and confidence.[8]

Lincoln also learned to exercise his sense of humor through the written word. In his sum book, he wrote:

> Abraham Lincoln
> his hand and pen
> he will be good
> but God knows When.

And another entry:

> Abraham Lincoln is my name
> And with my pen I wrote the same
> I wrote in both haste and speed
> And left it here for fools to read.[9]

Lincoln loved to write. He "wrote sentences, on boards, and other places and then read them, looked at them, over and over, analyzed them, thoroughly understanding them," his law partner William Herndon later recorded. "He would translate them into his boyish language and *would* tell his schoolmates, friends, and mother what they meant … and tell his thoughts he *would;* and his schoolmates, friends, and mother *must* hear or he would 'bust wide open.'" Herndon anticipated that many teachers would encourage their students to "Imitate Mr. Lincoln and his methods." Imitating

[8] Winkle, *Young Eagle*, 75.

[9] Bartelt, *Lincoln's Indiana Youth*, 32.

Lincoln's mind, however, would be almost impossible since "it is itself and nothing can be like it. A rat cannot be an eagle."[10]

Much of what Lincoln learned during his few months of formal schooling involved the hidden curriculum, or the social and emotional learning that inevitably accompany school life. He witnessed a teacher slapping a classmate for mispronouncing the biblical names Shadrach, Meshach, and Abednego. He defended a boy who stuttered. One day his teacher, Mr. Crawford, told the class that he would not let them go home unless each of them could spell the word "defied." While almost everyone in the class tried and failed to spell the word correctly, Lincoln somehow managed to spell it correctly and waited for his classmates. He stood outside the classroom, but was visible through a window. One classmate noticed Lincoln pointing to his eye with a big smile on his face. "I instantly took the hint that I must change the letter y into an I," she recalled. "Hence I spelled the word," and the students were let out. She remained grateful for this simple gesture many years later.[11]

Lincoln's classmates, while noting his gangly physical appearance and that his pants were too short, thereby exposing his shin bones also noticed his extraordinary gifts—especially his impressive storytelling and ability to make rhymes. He literally and figuratively stood head and shoulders above the rest, and he knew it too. His limited formal education instilled a self-confidence that he had surpassed his peers intellectually.[12]

The confidence that he possessed singular dispositions propelled Lincoln in his self-directed learning. He did not need a formal education, a schoolhouse, or even a teacher to help him grow, learn, and lead. Grasping how his intellectualism distinguished him from his peers, Lincoln nurtured his mental powers with even greater intensity away from any formal educational setting. Using

---

[10] Hertz, *The Hidden Lincoln*, 84–86.

[11] Wilson, *Herndon's Informants*, 131.

[12] Donald, *Lincoln*, 32.

modern vernacular, he understood that he could make the biggest impact on the world, and for his own reputation, by playing to his strengths. Thus the learning loop reinforced itself. He disciplined himself to make even more time for reading, writing, thinking, storytelling, and speaking aloud his thoughts, and that exercise in turn differentiated him further from his peers. Confidence led to success. Success inspired more confidence. Curiosity led to further discoveries and more curiosity. These self-affirming results and intellectual fulfillment encouraged him to do even more reading, writing, thinking, storytelling, and speaking aloud of his thoughts and inspirations. In short, Lincoln's self-directed education prepared him to lead and set him apart from his peers.

Many of Lincoln's favorite books dealt with morality tales and the triumph of good over evil. They also depicted how ordinary people could do extraordinary things. In addition to Webster's and Dilworth's *Spelling Books,* both of which had stories in them, Abe read and reread Parson Weems's *Life of Washington*, Daniel Defoe's *Robinson Crusoe, Aesop's Fables,* and the two most popular books on the frontier—John Bunyan's *Pilgrim's Progress* and the Bible. A family copy of *Barclay's Dictionary* enlarged his inventory of words. He also enjoyed reading Starke Dupuy's *Hymns and Spiritual Songs* out loud.[13]

Lincoln not only enjoyed reading books but applied the lessons learned from them to his own life. In *Aesop's Fables*, for example, there were exhortations at the end of each fable, giving the moral of the story. In the tale of "The Lion and the Four Bulls," Lincoln read about a lion that could not attack four bulls standing together in a pasture. Once they separated, however, the bulls became easy prey. The moral of the fable was "a kingdom divided against itself cannot stand." These words would be revisited and used by Lincoln in a most profound way in regard to the slavery issue.[14]

---

13 Keneally, *Lincoln*, 7; White, *Lincoln*, 33–34.

14 White, *Lincoln*, 33.

Beyond inspiration, these stories provided an intellectual inventory Lincoln could call on to make a point or persuade people of his position. In other words, Lincoln read and wrote, not just for his enjoyment, but to equip himself for action and the fruition of desired outcomes.

As he would use words to sway and move others to action in various letters, correspondence, and speeches in the future, Lincoln learned to take pride in his penmanship at a young age. He loved to sketch letters and construct words and sentences in his copybook. He became the family scribbler and wrote letters for his parents and neighbors—an invaluable experience that allowed Lincoln to see the world through the eyes of other people.[15]

As a self-directed, discerning individual, Lincoln developed a capacity for empathy and seeing issues from a variety of perspectives. Before he ever confronted the injustice and horrors of slavery, for example, Lincoln took an individual stand against animal cruelty—a fairly common occurrence on the frontier. Often at logrolling events, men would round up chipmunks, rabbits, and snakes and put them in burning logs, watch them squirm, and die. Lincoln once wrote an essay in which he took issue with his stepbrother, John Johnston, for smashing the shell of a land turtle against a tree, leaving the suffering animal quivering and defenseless. When his mother urged him to kill a snake, Abe refused, arguing that the snake enjoyed living as much as any human did.[16] His stepsister, Matilda, remembered him saying that "an ant's life was to it, as sweet as ours to us."[17] Anecdotes abound about Lincoln rescuing birds, animals, wandering kittens, a pet dog that fell behind on an 1829 trek to Illinois, a squealing piglet being eaten by its mother, and a hog mired in the mud. He scolded

[15] Oates, *With Malice Toward None*, 11.

[16] Burlingame, *Lincoln*, 1:31.

[17] Wilson, *Herndon's Informants*, 109.

his neighborhood friends when they stacked hot coals on terrapins, which forced the defenseless animals out of their shells.[18]

A keen observer of more than animals and insects, Lincoln learned by watching, listening, and doing. He enjoyed any kind of speech that demonstrated passion and wisdom. He regularly walked thirty miles to a courthouse to hear lawyers speak and see how they argued. He listened to political and religious speakers roar and rant. He enjoyed absorbing information shared by inventors and entrepreneurs. He learned how to read people as thoroughly as he read books. He drank enough whiskey to learn that he did not care for the taste and that it was not healthy for his mind or body. He smoked enough tobacco to learn he did not care for it.[19] Lincoln immersed himself in the moment—in the book he read, lecture he listened to, the trail he hiked, or the setting he inhabited.

As he grew older, Lincoln's self-directed learning habits only deepened. In New Salem he joined a debating society, which met twice a month in tavern parlors and churches. There he participated in debates on how society should care for the poor, whether women should be educated, whether public monies should be used to build canals and roads, and whether slavery remained a moral right or wrong. In addition to providing the intellectual stimulation his brain craved, these societies provided Lincoln his first sustained opportunity to learn the art of public speaking, and fed his enthusiasm for a good philosophical or political debate.[20]

Self-directed learners are generally curious individuals. Often on Sundays in New Salem, Lincoln visited with Mentor Graham at Graham's schoolhouse. He would borrow a book or talk with the schoolmaster about things that puzzled him, especially life's

---

[18] Miller, *Lincoln's Virtues*, 27–28; Donald, *Lincoln*, 27; Manning, *Father Lincoln*, 84. Lincoln had a special love for cats his entire life. Mary Lincoln described cats as Lincoln's "hobby." He played with them for long periods of time. The Lincolns eventually owned a yellow Labrador that they named Fido.

[19] Sandburg, *Lincoln*, 15.

[20] White, *Lincoln*, 53.

big questions and religion. Graham helped Lincoln improve his grammar, knowing how important that skill would be for one interested in entering the political arena.

Since his postmaster job paid so little, Lincoln also wanted to follow in the footsteps of one of his heroes, George Washington, and become a surveyor. There was a high demand for surveyors in an era of land speculation. Graham not only let Lincoln borrow many of his county surveyor's books, but often stayed up until midnight checking his young protégé's calculations and teaching the finer points of the craft. Thirty years later, Graham claimed that, in his forty-five years of teaching, he never encountered another learner as diligent, studious, and curious as Lincoln.[21]

Lincoln's unquenchable desire to learn was truly one of the most extraordinary features of his personality, and formal schooling had very little to do with it. William Herndon, Lincoln's longtime law partner in Springfield, asserted that a long formal education process might have hurt Lincoln and inhibited his curiosity, creativity, and romantic, natural way. "Had he gone to college and half graduated, or wholly so, and before his style was crystallized, or had he been educated in our founded, flat, dull artistic style of expression, writing or speaking," Herndon explained, "he would have lost, and the world would have lost, his strong individuality in his speech, his style, manner, and method of utterance."[22]

As soon as he could read, Lincoln took his own initiative in learning. He studied alone with extraordinary self-discipline and perseverance. His self-education, however, seemed out of place in a frontier culture and farming community. This is one reason why Lincoln received little encouragement from his father. Many contemporaries agreed with his father and thought Abe was a loafer.

---

[21] Oates, *With Malice Toward None*, 28–29; Wheeler, *Faith and Courage*, 75;

[22] Guelzo, *Man of Ideas*, 14.

They believed frontier farmer boys ought to be splitting rails instead of splitting their time between fieldwork and book study.[23]

While Lincoln certainly had supporters, he never really had one special, supremely influential teacher in his early life. Reflecting as an adult, he never expressed significant gratitude to any mentors or examples from his youth—not his father, not really his mother or stepmother (aside from their religious influence), not a school, not a church, nor any adults in Pigeon Creek or New Salem.[24] This is not to say that Lincoln did not learn from others. Certainly there were many individuals who taught him about a profession or specific job.

More than any teacher, Lincoln's own curiosity spurred his learning. His questions led him to figure things out on his own. Indeed, Lincoln's mind operated like a mountain climber—self-direction eventually got him to the top of the mountain. Once on top, he could see a whole new range of mountains on the horizon. So he would set out to climb the next one.

On a triumphant tour of the Northeast after his Cooper Union speech in 1860, Lincoln told a pastor that his inner drive to learn and understand started young, when he was a "mere child." Lincoln explained that he got irritated, even angry, when anyone talked in a way he could not understand. "That always disturbed my temper," Lincoln said, "and has ever since."[25] It bothered Lincoln not to know something.

In addition to his quest for knowledge, Lincoln believed that a mind needed exercise in order to stretch and grow. He believed, as many of his contemporaries did, that mental faculties, like muscles, could be strengthened by rigorous exercise. This is one reason why he secured a copy of Euclid's *Elements*, which laid out the principles of geometry, and set out to learn the theorems and solve problems.

---

[23] Winkle, *Young Eagle*, 74.

[24] Miller, *Lincoln's Virtues*, 57.

[25] Lowry, *Lincoln Unbound*, 24.

His mind needed exercise and training. In 1860, he reported that he had studied and nearly mastered the six books of Euclid.[26]

Very early in his young adult life, while running for his first elective office in New Salem, Lincoln told the people that "upon the subject of education, not presuming to dictate any plan or system respecting it, I can only say that I view it as the most important subject which we as a people can be engaged in." He believed that "every man may receive at least, a moderate education," so that one could read history and truly "appreciate the value of our free institutions," as well as learn the "advantages and satisfaction to be derived from all being able to read the scriptures and other works, both of a religious and moral nature, for themselves." A good education encouraged "morality, sobriety, enterprise and industry" and would "have a tendency to accelerate the happy period."[27]

Lincoln loved to learn at his own pace, in his own way, and in his own time. Learning was the obligation of the learner and not anyone else. Therefore Lincoln rarely talked about community. He showed little interest in the promotion of communitarian attitudes or values. Indeed, he believed local communities and parochial thinking put a restraint on individualism, independence, reason, ambition, and talent.[28] He wanted nothing that would hinder one's self-directed life path.

This emphasis on the responsibility of the individual to learn is one reason Lincoln did not strongly advocate for formal education. Students could learn in different contexts via different delivery methods. Even with his own children, he appeared indifferent to their formal education. Today's early childhood proponents of play would love what he said about his son Tad: "Let him run. There's enough time for him to learn his letters and get pokey."[29] Lincoln knew from his own experience that one learned and made one's

---

26 Donald, *Lincoln Reconsidered*, 72.

27 Basler, Lincoln to the People of Sangamo County, March 9, 1832, *CW*, 1:8.

28 Guelzo, *Man of Ideas*, 65.

29 Lachman, *The Last Lincolns*, 35.

greatest impact in areas of life where purpose and passion meshed, where natural curiosity and motivation coalesced.

Lincoln loved to joke about his lack of formal education throughout his entire life. At the fifth Lincoln-Douglas debate, held in Galesburg on October 7, 1858, the speakers stood on a platform that adjoined one of Knox College's classroom buildings. To reach the platform, the speakers had to walk through the building and climb out a window. When Lincoln eventually and appeared on the stage, he quipped, "At last I have been through college."[30]

Lincoln never went through any formal educational process to learn about the Bible. Yet he remained motivated to read, study, and reflect on the sacred book more than any other—even daily during his presidency. His parents introduced him to the Bible, and his mother nurtured his love for God's Word by reading it to him at an early age. But Lincoln went through his own self-directed learning process in regard to Scripture. As a boy and young man, he scorned uneducated Bible preachers who declaimed in an overdramatic manner and seemed to know little about the Bible. He denied the inerrancy of the Bible and scoffed at Bible-believing Christians during his doubting days at New Salem. Yet he kept reading Scripture because of his natural curiosity, the appreciation he had for the stories and writing styles, and the morality lessons one could learn.

When life's tragedies struck, not only did many pastors, preachers, and parishioners show Lincoln and his family compassion and care, but he rediscovered the promises of Scripture and the peace and contentment that God's Word could provide frail, sinful human beings in a fallen world. Especially in the 1850s and 1860s, he made friendships with knowledgeable, intelligent ministers who could engage him in deep theological discussions and who were also fluent in Christian apologetics.

---

30 Leidner, *Lincoln's Gift*, 97.

Lincoln integrated Bible verses and stories—and the lessons he learned from them—in his regular correspondence. As president, he made it a priority to start each day reading and meditating on Scripture. He laced his public speeches, including the sermon-like second inaugural address, with Scripture references strategically placed for impact. Lincoln's reading and use of the Bible became a singular, self-directed, and lifelong journey of exploration, curiosity, and growth.

Lincoln might be the most exemplary self-directed learner in American history. His desire to learn and grow in formal and informal settings had no peer. He did so by deploying various writing styles, reading deeply and broadly, listening to and speaking with folks from numerous backgrounds and vocations, working in various occupations, and being a keen observer of human nature. While no one can be exactly like Lincoln, those who study his life can learn much from his habits, disposition, and mindset. After all, Lincoln's learning led to better leading.

The Truth

As much as we can try to improve ourselves through self-directed learning like Lincoln did, when it comes to salvation, no self-directed efforts will ever merit paradise or be good enough to gain us entrance into heaven. This truth can frustrate many. We want to be in control of our lives. Often we work as hard as we can to attain a goal. We want to pull up our own bootstraps to get to heaven, and we want to do it ourselves, thank you very much.

Then again, do we really want heaven to be riding on our efforts? What if our best is not perfect or even good enough? What if we swing and miss on even one of the Ten Commandments? What if we freeze or have a senior moment and do not put others before ourselves? What if we totally break down and find out we cannot make it through the day without help? What if we doubt that there is even a God and a heaven? The truth is, we cannot self-direct our own entrance into heaven.

There is good news, however, for those who know Christ. Indeed, for the Christian, salvation comes from one direction only—God to man. The Bible teaches that "by grace you have been saved through faith. And this is not your own doing; it is the gift of God, not a result of works, so that no one may boast."[31] Put another way, "when the goodness and loving kindness of God our Savior appeared, he saved us, not because of works done by us in righteousness, but according to his own mercy, by the washing of regeneration and renewal of the Holy Spirit, whom he poured out on us richly through Jesus Christ our Savior."[32]

While you may be able to expand your earthly knowledge by your own self-directed efforts, salvation is a one-way ticket made available only by God through the Word and sacrament. You cannot study, improve yourself, or pass some entrance exam to be admitted into paradise. Full-ride scholarships to heaven are only offered through the blood of Christ and by Him alone.

That salvation comes from Christ alone does not mean that God does not encourage a life of learning among His disciples—quite the contrary. Christian leaders should possess an insatiable appetite for learning more about Jesus and God's Word. Indeed, the Bible is written "for our instruction, that through endurance and through the encouragement of the Scriptures we might have hope."[33]

Many people in today's world do not know what they want to do with their lives or what they want to be "when they grow up." Moreover, many who do know what they want to do often fear that requirements may change, leaving them unqualified or inadequately skilled for the new essentials of their job. Self-directed learning can

---

[31] Eph. 2:8–9.

[32] Titus 3:4–6.

[33] Rom. 15:4.

be murky or tough when you do not know what you want to learn or should learn.

The good news is that Bible teaches "you in the way you should go." God's Word provides counsel even as He keeps His "eye upon you."[34] Through Scripture, you know that God encourages you to "do your best to present yourself to God as one approved, a worker who has no need to be ashamed, rightly handling the word of truth."[35]

In order to rightly handle the word of truth, God exhorts you to "let the word of Christ dwell in you richly, teaching and admonishing one another in all wisdom, singing psalms and hymns and spiritual songs, with thankfulness in your hearts to God."[36] You are to get in the Word and stay in the Word, no matter your schooling or vocation. If you desire wisdom and insight, God plainly says not to "turn away from the words of my mouth," for they "will guard you."[37]

The Bible is the best curriculum you will ever need to study. It is life-changing and life-saving. God's Word "is living and active, sharper than any two-edged sword, piercing to the division of soul and of spirit, of joints and of marrow, and discerning the thoughts and intentions of the heart."[38] By the power of "the Helper, the Holy Spirit … he will teach you all things and bring to your remembrance all that I have said to you."[39] Not only are you to hear and receive the Word of God, but it will inspire and motivate you to "practice these things"—to live as God's faithful disciples.[40]

Knowing all that Jesus did for you on the cross, you are now called and compelled to be a good steward of the gifts, talents, and

---

[34] Ps. 32:8.

[35] 2 Tim. 2:15.

[36] Col. 3:16.

[37] Prov. 4:5–6.

[38] Heb. 4:12.

[39] John 14:26.

[40] Phil. 4:9.

blessings that God has so generously provided you. In other words, He expects you to use your God-given abilities fruitfully, frequently, and faithfully, in whatever way the Holy Spirit guides you. God has given you much, and He does not want you to waste what He has given you. From the very beginning, God designed you for good work. God took the very first human being, Adam, and "put him in the garden of Eden to *work it* and keep it" (italics added).[41] Since you have received gifts from God, He expects you to use them "to serve one another, as good stewards of God's varied grace."[42]

Lifelong, self-directed learning is one critical way you can be a good steward of God's generous provision. Learners are leaders, and leaders are doers. Christian leaders love to learn more about God's Word and plans. As a Christian leader dedicated to learning more about God's Word, you can provide inspiration, action, and leadership to friends, family members, and associates alike. Jesus says, "Everyone to whom much was given, of him much will be required, and from him to whom they entrusted much, they will demand the more."[43] You are God's "workmanship, created in Christ Jesus for good works, which God prepared beforehand," that you "should walk in them."[44] God is directing and empowering your life, leadership, and learning. As you grow in wisdom and truth, take action, and lead, He wants you to remember to "walk by faith, not by sight."[45] Whenever you learn, wherever you go, and whatever you do, "trust in the Lord with all your heart, and do not lean on your own understanding," for "he will make straight your paths."[46]

By God's grace, be a good steward and a self-directed, lifelong learner of God's Word. He has grand plans for you. Furthermore, Jesus delights in seeing you use your God-given gifts and talents

---

[41] Gen. 2:15.

[42] 1 Pet. 4:10.

[43] Luke 12:48.

[44] Eph. 2:10.

[45] 2 Cor. 5:7.

[46] Prov. 3:5–6.

in His name. He is directing your life and encouraging you to learn more about Him through His Word. Whether you complete a project or come to the end of your days here on earth, you want to hear these comforting and joyous words from God: "Well done, good and faithful servant. You have been faithful over a little; I will set you over much. Enter into the joy of your master."[47]

Your Life

Mark Twain allegedly once said, "I never let my schooling interfere with my education." Considering what you just read about Lincoln's formal education, or lack thereof, do you think Lincoln would have agreed or disagreed with this statement? Why or why not? What is your personal take on Twain's statement?

How are you a self-directed learner? In what ways? Why do some seem to be more self-directed than others?

How does God's Word inspire you to be a self-directed learner and leader in His name? Explain.

[47] Matt. 25:21.

13

Leaders are Readers

My son, be attentive to my words; incline your ear
to my sayings. Let them not escape from your sight;
keep them within your heart. For they are life to those
who find them, and healing to all their flesh.
—Proverbs 4:20–22

The Lincoln Way

Reading can change and charge a leader.

Of all the enduring images of Lincoln, none should surpass one of him with a book in hand. Lincoln looked at books the way teens today stare at their screens—he could not be separated from them. From his earliest childhood days, "he read all the books he could lay his hands on," his stepmother remembered shortly after his death. When he came across a passage that struck him, "he would write it down on boards if he had no paper & keep it there till he did get paper. Then he would re-write it, look at it, repeat it." Young Abe would restate what he read "over and over again & again till it was so defined and fixed firmly and permanently in his memory."[1] Lincoln's stepsister noted that "Abe was not energetic except in one thing: He was active & persistent in learning" and "read everything he could." When their mom and dad left for church on Sunday mornings, she remembered Abe reading the Bible, handing out hymnals, and

[1] Wilson, *Herndon's Informants,* 106–9.

singing together.[2] Dennis Hanks, a cousin of Lincoln's mother, also observed firsthand Lincoln's hunger for books, observing how he read everything "he could lay his hands on."[3]

Eastman Johnson's iconic *Boyhood of Lincoln* portrait properly displays Lincoln's love and passion for reading and learning. (Library of Congress)

One day Lincoln left Mason Locke Weems's classic *Life of Washington* in an open window. A rainstorm came and did irreparable damage to the book. When he discovered his mistake, he took the book to the Indiana neighbor who had lent it to him and offered to pay for it. Instead, the owner had him "pull corn blades for two days."[4] Lincoln owned his first book.

Despite his limited schooling, Lincoln did receive enough formal training that he could teach himself how to read and write. He studied *Dilworth's Spelling Book, The Columbian Class Book,*

---

[2] Wilson, *Herndon's Informants,* 109–10.

[3] Wilson, *Herndon's Informants,* 41–42.

[4] Wilson, *Herndon's Informatns,* 660–62.

and *The Kentucky Preceptor* so diligently that he went on to become a spelling bee champion.[5] Books became his higher education experience, and he combed the countryside looking for them. His early favorites included *Aesop's Fables, Robinson Crusoe, The Pilgrims Progress, Lessons in Elocution, A History of the United States,* and Weems's *Life of Washington.*[6] One night, when Abe was reading aloud to Dennis Hanks and his stepmother from *The Arabian Nights* and *Aesop's Fables,* Hanks chided, "Abe, them yarns is all lies." Abe responded, "Mighty darn good lies, Denny," and continued with his reading.[7]

In addition to George Washington, Lincoln read biographies on preeminent historical statesmen such as Thomas Jefferson, Henry Clay, and Daniel Webster.[8] The Bible and Shakespeare were the two texts Lincoln read and quoted the most. Encouraged by his religious mother, he never lost the habit of Scripture reading. "It is a pleasure to be able to quote lines to fit any occasion," he told a boy in Springfield one day. And, of course, "the Bible is the richest source of pertinent quotations."[9] The Bible and Shakespeare inspired and informed his writing style.[10] Eventually, Lincoln would become America's

---

5 Donald, *Lincoln*, 30.

6 Wheeler, *Faith and Courage*, 53.

7 Leidner, *Lincoln's Gift*, 11.

8 Wilson, *Herndon's Informants*, 91.

9 Carwardine, "Lincoln's Religion," 226–227. Carwadine tells the story of an Illinois Presbyterian minister walking past a group of citizens who were gathered around Lincoln as he entertained them with stories. The minister called out as he passed, "Where the great ones are there will the people be." Quickly Lincoln replied, "Ho! Parson a little more Scriptural: 'Where the carcass is there will the eagles be gathered together.'"

10 Kaplan, "Great Invention," 26-27. As president, Lincoln became a regular theatergoer in Washington, DC, and rarely missed a Shakespeare production. Nevertheless he preferred his own readings of Shakespeare to those of professional actors and actresses. He had stamped what Shakespeare's lines were supposed to sound like in his own mind from his own readings.

"only poet-president."[11] More importantly, reading biographies of men who possessed an outstanding work ethic, an entrepreneurial spirit, impressive leadership skills, and the perseverance to overcome hardship instilled in Lincoln a mindset and mental capacity for resilience, which would become a hallmark of his leadership throughout family tragedies and the Civil War crisis.[12]

Throughout his childhood and adolescence, Lincoln read everything and everywhere—in the woods, at the end of each plow furrow as his horse rested,[13] on top of wood piles, and underneath shade trees. As he grew older and worked on other farms and plantations, neighbors recognized young Abe's insatiable appetite for books. "When he worked for us he read all our books," remembered one Indiana farmer. He would stay up late at night reading by the fire. "We had a broad wooden shovel on which Abe would work out his sums, wipe off and repeat till it got too black for more: then he would scrape and wash off and repeat again and again."[14] Said another neighbor, "What Lincoln read he read and re-read, read and studied thoroughly."[15] Yet another Indiana planter noted that "Lincoln read every book he could lay his hands on" and "mastered" them.[16] He loved reading newspapers too, and "if there was any wit or good stories he was certain to find them & to read to others."[17] Even at school, one observer noticed that Abe kept "his clothes clean longer than any of the others" because he enjoyed the solitude of reading rather than playing with other kids.[18] "The things I want

---

11 Goodwin, *Team of Rivals*, 51–52.

12 Guelzo, *Lincoln*, 361.

13 Oates, *With Malice Toward None*, 11.

14 Wilson, *Herndon's Informants*, 126.

15 Wilson, *Herndon's Informants*, 121.

16 Wilson, *Herndon's Informants*, 130.

17 Wilson, *Herndon's Informants*, 426-–27.

18 Wilson, *Herndon's Informants*, 241.

to know are in books," Abe once insisted, and "my best friend is the man who'll get me a book I ain't read."[19]

Even as a young man, Lincoln continued his habit of reading everywhere, whenever he could. Between serving customers while working as a store clerk in New Salem, Lincoln often had other store clerks quiz him on the books he read.[20] Every night after clerking he would study for three hours, concentrating on English grammar because he did not wish to appear like a backcountry bumpkin. As a twenty-three-year-old man, he walked six miles to borrow a copy of Samuel Kirkham's *English Grammar in Familiar Lectures* to improve his reading comprehension and writing.[21] Lincoln "mastered a book quickly," recalled a New Salem resident, "as one who was simply reading, so comprehensive was his mind."[22] When he became postmaster in New Salem in the spring of 1833, he read the newspapers before he delivered them. He became an astute observer of political speeches, issues, and social trends.[23] Numerous New Salem residents recalled how Abe would sit and read, barefoot, as he leaned against a tree. To change up his position, Lincoln would then lie on his back and rest his long legs on the tree trunk. As the sun moved, he constantly shifted his position to remain in the shade.[24]

If Lincoln did not know something, he would admit it and then seek the answer with great earnestness and determination.[25] John Stuart, the esteemed lawyer who helped mentor Lincoln during his early law practice days in Springfield, noted that "in the evening Lincoln would strip off his coat and lay down on his bed, read,

---

[19] Sandberg, *Lincoln*, 13.

[20] Keneally, *Lincoln*, 14; Kigel, *Becoming Lincoln*, 166.

[21] Burlingame, *Lincoln*, 1:63; Donald, *Lincoln*, 47-48; Miller, *Lincoln's Virtues*, 52.

[22] Wilson, *Herndon's Informants*, 17–18.

[23] Sandburg, *Lincoln*, 34.

[24] Donald, *Lincoln*, 55.

[25] Winkle, *Young Eagle*, 73.

reflect, and digest. After supper, he would strip, go to bed, get a candle, draw up a chair or table and read till late of night." Lincoln, he observed, "read hard works."[26]

Once he read and comprehended a work, the content stuck. His friends recognized early on that he had been blessed with a phenomenal memory—"the best," the most "marvelously retentive" they had ever seen. His mind seemed "a wonder," a friend told him, "impressions were easily made upon it and never effaced."[27] Joshua Speed said that Lincoln's mind "was a wonder to me, that impressions were easily made upon his mind and never effaced." Lincoln told him he was mistaken. "'I am slow to learn and slow to forget that which I have learned. My mind is like a piece of steel, very hard to scratch anything on it and almost impossible after you get it there to rub it out." Speed noted that "intense thought with him was the rule and not as with most of us the exception."[28]

Lincoln's insatiable appetite for reading equipped him to thrive in prominent vocations as a lawyer and politician. Instead of being mentored by an accomplished attorney, as was customary in those days, Lincoln taught himself the law entirely on his own.[29] In his office with William Herndon, the self-made lawyer would often sprawl and read out loud from newspapers or books. To another young man who wanted to become a lawyer, Lincoln advised, "Get the books, and read and study them till you understand them in their principal features." It did not matter if you read or studied with someone else or if you came from a large or small town. "The books, and your capacity for understanding them are just the same in all places." One's "own resolution to succeed" was the most important attribute in becoming a lawyer.[30]

---

[26] Wilson, *Herndon's Informants*, 519.

[27] Goodwin, *Leadership*, 5.

[28] Wilson, *Herndon's Informants*, 498–99.

[29] Oates, *Lincoln*, 51.

[30] Basler, Lincoln to Isham Reavis, November 5, 1855, *CW*, 2:327.

The more Lincoln read, the more it fed his ambitions. As a boy, he quickly learned that there was more to life than plowing fields and splitting rails. Books provided a refuge from the harshness of the backwoods and backcountry.[31] Elected to the House of Representatives in 1847, and residing in the nation's capital, Lincoln spent'his free time reading and became one of the Library of Congress's most active borrowers. His fellow congressmen found his hyper-bookish ways amusing. "He did not drink, or use tobacco, or bet, or swear," they noted, but he did enjoy "mousing among the books" at the library.[32] Lincoln could often be seen selecting books, wrapping them in a bandanna, placing a stick in the knot, and transporting them over his shoulder to his boardinghouse.

Both in Washington and in Springfield, Lincoln read national and local newspapers, including antislavery ones, voraciously. During the Civil War, Lincoln read approximately seventy letters a morning and continued checking out books on military art and science from the Library of Congress. Rereading Weems's *Life of Washington,* Lincoln told the New Jersey State Senate that he loved reading about all the hardships Washington's army had to overcome, and he hoped that the Union could prevail in the same way for the good of the country.[33]

Reading aloud remained one of Lincoln's most distinctive and instructive habits. As a lad, he read out loud to amuse his friends and make himself the center of attention. When he became president of the United States, he read to entertain visitors, but also for personal wellness and as a coping mechanism to deal with his depression.[34] He loved hearing the sounds of words and the way he could emphasize certain syllables for effect. "When I read aloud," he told William Herndon, "two senses catch the idea: first, I see what

---

[31] Oates, *With Malice Toward None*, 11; Kigel, *Becoming Lincoln*, 77.

[32] White, *Lincoln,* 155.

[33] White, *Lincoln,* 169; Burlingame, *Lincoln*, 1:685, 2:31; Holzer and Garfinkle, *A Just and Generous Nation*, 136.

[34] Wilson, *Lincoln's Sword*, 180.

I read; second, I hear it, and therefore I can remember it better."[35] William Stoddard, Lincoln's assistant secretary during his first term, noted that Lincoln read aloud everything that he wrote to someone or some group before presenting it in public. "I can always tell more about a thing after I've heard it read aloud, and know how it sounds," Lincoln insisted. When Stoddard told him that he did not want to critique a speech, the president responded, "Yes, you will. Everybody else will. It's just what I want you to do. Sit still now, and you'll make as much of an audience as I call for."[36]

Lincoln's love for reading, as well as his skill in reading comprehension, often put him in a position to help others. For friends, neighbors, and associates, Lincoln wrote deeds, contracts, agreements, and other essential documents at no charge. Perhaps this was why, shortly before he became president, he gave a public lecture on discoveries and inventions in which he claimed that printing was one of the greatest inventions in human history and ended "the dark ages." In the past, people "were utterly unconscious that their conditions, or their minds, were capable of improvement." Those who could read were viewed "as superior beings," and those who could not "supposed themselves to be naturally incapable of rising to equality."[37] With decades of practice, Lincoln developed a confidence that he could read up on any subject and grasp it just as well, if not better, than someone with more formal learning.[38] One lawyer lauded Lincoln's "remarkably inquiring mind" and his ability to master any subject. "His love of and capacity for analysis was wonderful," said his friend and associate. He analyzes "every proposition with startling clearness."[39]

---

[35] White, *Lincoln*, 168.

[36] Wilson, *Lincoln's Sword*, 180–82.

[37] Basler, Lincoln's Second Lecture on Discoveries and Inventions, February 11, 1859, *CW*, 3:362–63.

[38] Miller, *Lincoln's Virtues*, 47.

[39] Wilson, *Herndon's Informants*, 506.

Unfortunately, Lincoln's love for reading contributed to the demise of his religious beliefs and his perspective on the Bible during his early and middle years. After freeing himself from his father's world and everything Tom represented, including Hard Shell Baptist religion, Lincoln began reading works that questioned and refuted the revelation and inerrancy of Scripture—or that simply criticized Christianity and Christians. For example, he consumed Edward Gibbon's *Decline and Fall of the Roman Empire,* which blamed Christianity for the fall of Rome. The Scot, Robert Burns—a favorite poet of Lincoln's, denigrated Calvinists for their perceived arrogance in claiming that they had been chosen by God while rejoicing that their fellow human beings were predestined for punishment. Thomas Paine, in his *Age of Reason,* insisted that his own mind was his church and railed against organized religion. C. F. Volney's *The Ruins, or Meditation on the Revolution of Empires: And the Law of Nature,* asserted that the Bible contradicted itself, and referenced Christ's alleged illegitimacy. A deist and Enlightenment thinker, Volney criticized revealed religion and argued that all religion evolved from the worship of nature and the sun. No Ten Commandments were needed for society. The laws of nature were not only universal, just, and reasonable but reigned supreme.[40] In the early 1830s, Sir Charles Lyell's three-volume *Principles of Geology* claimed to produce evidence that the earth's geography resulted from the product of gradual builds-ups over long periods of time rather than a sudden creation from the Great Flood, as recorded in Genesis. Robert Chamber's *Vestiges of the Natural History of Creation* took Lyell's notion of a slow and steady development of earth's geology and applied them to living organisms.[41]

These works and others filled Lincoln's mind with doubts in regard to the authority of Scripture, the divinity of Christ, and many

---

[40] Mansfield, *Lincoln's Battle with God*, 35–36, 38–41; White, *Lincoln*, 54; Szasz and Szasz, *Lincoln and Religion*, 19.

[41] Guelzo, *Lincoln*, 108.

other tenets of orthodox Christianity. While his skepticism about divine revelation and a God-breathed Bible grew, he wavered in his Christian upbringing and beliefs. Lincoln's avid reading led him to his village atheist days in New Salem. For a time, he was a man of the world rather than the Word.

If Lincoln's reading led him to doubt, it would also bring him back to the faith. Even during his darkest spiritual moments and the period of time in his life when he openly questioned, even occasionally mocked, biblical precepts and the teachings of Christian clergy, he never stopped reading the Bible—the greatest book ever written, according to Lincoln. Rediscovering the truth, peace, and contentment one finds in the Bible, Lincoln became a daily Bible reader and made it one of his first priorities every morning.

To intellectually grow and rise in antebellum America, aspiring leaders knew they must learn from the minds of distinguished men—or, even better, the thoughts and Word of God. Few would become more familiar with God's Word than Lincoln. Reading not only informed and shaped the leader and the man, but filled his spiritual cup too.

The Truth

Christians are people of the Book—the Holy Word of God. Sixty-six books make up the Bible. These books were written down by men, inspired by God, to be read, heard, and received by all of humankind. They are God's words, and He speaks to His people through them. We would be wise to listen.

We might occasionally hear people say words are important or powerful. Indeed, they are. We might reflect on the fact that words matter and mean something. Therefore we should choose them wisely. We probably do not think as much, however, about the fact that God chose to speak to us through words—*His words.*

The wonderful truth is that in addition to the sacraments, God chose *words*—Scripture—to reveal Himself and bring people to faith through the power of the Holy Spirit. To receive God's Word, one must either *read it* or *hear it being read*. As the Bible states unequivocally, "So faith comes hearing, and hearing through the word of Christ."[42]

The power and life-saving importance of God's Word is why the rise of Christianity in the Western world helped usher in a movement for education and literacy. Schools were often founded principally so that students could learn to read the Bible. Even women, who had few rights centuries ago, were allowed to read and write in order to share the Bible with their children. Indeed, Christians know and celebrate the truth that "all Scripture is breathed out by God and profitable for teaching, for reproof, for correction, and for training in righteousness, that the man of God may be competent, equipped for every good work."[43] To be sure, "whatever was written in former days was written for our instruction, that through endurance and through the encouragement of the Scriptures we might have hope."[44]

Sometimes we fail to pause and take note of such a wonderful and powerful blessing in our lives—*that God took time to have His words and thoughts written down for us so that we might understand and better know Him*. We can read His Word and let it comfort us, nurture our faith, and encourage us to serve others in His name. Scripture guides and directs our lives too. As the Psalmist writes, "Your word is a lamp to my feet and a light to my path."[45]

There are lots of books to read in this world. Unfortunately, too many of them lead people away from Jesus Christ and the truth that will set them free. As the Bible states, "The time is coming when people will not endure sound teaching, but having itching ears they will accumulate for themselves teachers to suit their own passions,

---

[42] Rom. 10:17.

[43] 2 Tim. 3:16–17.

[44] Rom. 15:4.

[45] Ps. 119:105.

and will turn away from listening to the truth and wander off into myths."[46]

So make sure you read well. Lincoln became lost when he read worldly, pagan works. Make sure you take time to regularly receive and listen to God's Word in divine worship and personal Bible study. God's Word is truth, not fiction. His Word provides inspiration, hope, and eternal life, not some fantasy or fake news. Since you cannot give what you do not have, fuel yourself regularly and plentifully with words that really matter. Jesus said, "It is written, 'Man shall not live by bread alone, but by every word that comes from the mouth of God.'"[47] God has spoken. He tells you that you are forgiven, thanks be to Jesus. You can read all about it in one special, inerrant, and infallible book called the Bible. Christian leaders are Bible readers.

Your Life

The historical images of Lincoln most people know are those of a rail-splitter, emancipator, log cabin frontiersman, debater, orator, politician, and president. How does the knowledge that Lincoln loved books and reading change or influence your view of him?

Some have said that you are what you read. Some of the books Lincoln read in his younger days contributed to his skepticism about the Christian faith. What lessons do you take from this realization, specifically in regard to what you read, your relationships, and education?

---

[46] 2 Tim. 4:3–4.

[47] Matt. 4:4.

Lincoln constantly read out loud. What might be some benefits in reading God's Word out loud or hearing others do so?

Lincoln's precise religious beliefs have been the subject of debate for two centuries. Knowing that he was a voracious reader of the Bible, what hope exists in regard to Lincoln's relationship with God and his faith?

14

The Write Stuff

And the Lord answered me: "Write the vision; make it plain on tablets, so he may run who reads it."
—Habakkuk 2:2

The Lincoln Way

The written word can produce clarity and fuel one's convictions.

Even when he was a little boy, people recognized Lincoln's writing skills. When word got out that seven-year-old Abe could read and write, Indiana neighbors asked him to write letters to family and friends back in Kentucky.[1] One Indiana neighbor recalled how Abe came to his mother's house, wrote some letters for her, and made copies of the letters at the family's request. He also left other writings for families, like this one: "Good boys who to their books apply; will all be great Men by and by."[2]

As he grew into a young adult, Lincoln found his writing skills to be a blessing and differentiator among his peers. One the very first day he moved to New Salem, Lincoln confidently asked if he could be election clerk for the town simply because he could write. Citizens would enter the polling station and verbally articulate who they were voting for, and clerks would record their vote. Since almost every eligible citizen voted in those days, Lincoln got to know most of the

---

[1] Kigel, *Becoming Lincoln*, 69.

[2] Wilson, *Herndon's Informants*, 473.

New Salem residents on his first day in town.[3] Official documents like wills, deeds, and business contracts required someone who could put pen to paper and make it reality. Attorney fees were often too costly for farmers and backwoodsmen, so Lincoln was a welcome help to family, friends, and neighbors. When he moved to Springfield, he wrote hundreds of newspaper articles—mostly for political purposes—aptly displaying his wit, critical thinking, and understanding of the issues of the day.

Even before Lincoln became president, he had already earned a reputation for being a persuasive writer. Alexander Stephens, a congressman from Georgia and soon to be vice president of the Confederacy, pleaded with president-elect Lincoln not to antagonize the South before he officially became the chief executive of the land, and to do it with the written word. "Personally, I am not your enemy—far from it; and however widely we may differ politically, yet I trust we both have an earnest desire to preserve and maintain the Union," he wrote Lincoln in late December 1860. Worried about the fanaticism and passions on both sides, Stephens pleaded for Lincoln to "do what you can to save our common country." Quoting Proverbs 25:11, Stephens asserted that "a word fitly spoken by you now would be like 'apples of gold in pictures of silver.'"[4] Any pacifying words—spoken or written—from Lincoln, which would end up in the press, could hold off what appeared to be an imminent secession movement and constitutional crisis for the Union.

Lincoln is considered by many to be the greatest writer among all American presidents. His public letters, for example, significantly contributed to his stature as a leader and to public support for the Union cause.[5] Harriet Beecher Stowe, author of *Uncle Tom's Cabin* and of whom Lincoln said, "So you're the little woman who wrote

---

[3] Kigel, *Becoming Lincoln*, 148.

[4] Basler, Alexander Stephens to Lincoln, December 30, 1860, *CW*, 4:160–61.

[5] Wilson, *Lincoln's Sword*, 197.

the book that made this great war," loved Lincoln's writings and said they ought "to be inscribed in letters of gold."[6]

Philosopher, essayist, and poet Ralph Waldo Emerson admired Lincoln greatly for being a man of letters too. "He is the author of a multitude of good sayings," he said, "so disguised as pleasantries that it is certain they had no reputation at first but as jests; and only later, by the very acceptance and adoption they find in the mouths of millions, turn out to be the wisdom of the hour." Emerson asserted that "if this man had ruled in a period of less facility of printing, he would have become mythological in a very few years, like Aesop … by his fables and proverbs." The compelling nature of Lincoln's writings, "the weight and penetration of many passages in his letters, messages, and speeches … are destined hereafter to wide fame. What pregnant definitions; what unerring common sense; what foresight; and, on great occasion, what lofty, and more than national, what humane tone!"[7] Emerson, who died in 1882, proved prophetic in his analysis of the long-lasting impact and legacy of Lincoln's writings.

A man of innovation and the only president to have created his own patent, Lincoln believed that writing remained the most important invention in history. Without writing, the idea of "progress" would not have been conceivable.[8] While Lincoln knew that speech remained as "valuable as it ever has been," it had "not advanced the condition of the world much." He pointed to "the degraded condition of all those tribes of human creatures who have no considerable additional means of communicating thoughts" as evidence of the limitations of speech. Conversely, Lincoln argued that writing—"the art of communicating thoughts to the mind, through the eye—is the great invention of the world." The written word allowed people to analyze ideas and concepts, as well as "converse with the dead, the absent, and the unborn, at all distances of time and

---

6 Oates, *With Malice Toward None*, 389.

7 Peterson, *Lincoln in American Memory*, 109.

8 Kaplan, "Great Invention," 18.

of space; and great, not only in its direct benefits, but greatest help, to all other inventions." Moreover, Lincoln insisted that writing's "utility" distinguished the human race "from savages." Indeed, "the Bible, all history, all science, all government, all commerce, and nearly all social intercourse go with it." When humankind relied on "speech alone, the chances of invention, discovery, and improvement, were very limited." The invention of writing, however, allowed "any important observation" or discovery "at least a chance of being written down, and consequently, a better chance of never being forgotten; and of being seen, and reflected upon, by a much greater number of persons; and thereby the chances of a valuable hint being caught, proportionably augmented." After the introduction of writing into the world, "the observation of a single individual might lead to an important invention, years, and even centuries after he was dead. In one word, by means of writing, the seeds of invention were more permanently preserved, and more widely sown."[9] Simply put, Lincoln believed writing spurred innovation and invention, which led to human progress and a better quality of life.

Whether writing a personal letter or preparing for a speech, Lincoln took his words and word meanings seriously. He knew they would be reprinted in newspapers and repeated in taverns and government chambers across the country. He took time, for example, to distinguish between "secession" and "rebellion"—for each had critically different meanings. Secession implied a peaceful legal right, versus rebellion, which indicated perpetuation of a violent, unlawful act. Lincoln did not want the Confederacy to get away with sugarcoating rebellion.

According to his son Robert, the president "was a very deliberate writer, anything but rapid … He seemed to think nothing of the labor of writing personally and was accustomed to make many scraps of notes and memoranda." For almost every letter, "he first wrote

---

[9] Basler, Lincoln's Second Lecture on Discoveries and Inventions, February 11, 1859, *CW*, 3:360–62.

it himself, then corrected it, and then rewrote the corrected version himself."[10]

While Lincoln wrote with clarity, his words were not as eloquent as other famous writers of his time, such as Herman Melville, Nathaniel Hawthorne, Walt Whitman, Henry David Thoreau, and Emily Dickinson. Lincoln, however, perfected a prose that expressed a uniquely American way of comprehending and ordering reality. He connected in a mainstream, down-to-earth language so that almost any audience could understand and be persuaded by his thoughts and words.[11] His colloquial middling way of writing and speaking appealed to the common man in his time and keeps his words accessible to readers today. As one biographer explains, "We don't feel at all out of place when we wake up and ask Lincoln just what he would do."[12] His explanations still connect.

Lincoln generally wrote short sentences in a compact style, his ear finely attuned to how his words would sound to the reader. He read aloud what he wrote to enable him to "catch the idea by two senses"—by hearing and sight. The practice also allowed him to hear the sounds that gratified and entranced listeners. His prodigious aural awareness helped him shape words to ideas and sounds to sense.[13]

A man driven to improve all aspects of his life, Lincoln worked relentlessly to improve as a writer, even after he became an exceptional one. With persistence and practice, he became adept at *re*writing and *pre*writing. His personal papers contain many drafts and fragments that show him trying out ideas and arguments. Many eyewitnesses testified to his practice writing and editing. John Nicolay noted Lincoln's impressive ability to accumulate and distill knowledge as he developed and enhanced his own insights and thoughts. The president's habit of prewriting, for example, became a key feature to

---

10 Wilson, *Lincoln's Sword*, 5, 91–93.

11 Wilson, *Lincoln's Sword*, 144–45.

12 Guelzo, *Man of Ideas*, 5.

13 Wilson, *Herndon's Informants*, 499; Wilson, *Lincoln's Sword*, 30.

his success—a quality of mental alertness, of always looking ahead, of actively trying to anticipate the future and not be caught off guard. This quality worked well in tandem with Lincoln's patience and preparedness to take full advantage of opportunities that inevitably presented themselves. Writing sharpened Lincoln's mind, helped him focus on the future, and prepared him to take the initiative on big-picture objectives.[14]

A critical component of Lincoln's writing is that he knew how to bring a letter, statement, or speech to a compelling conclusion. Perhaps as an admirer of epic stories with stirring endings, as well as through his experience as an attorney who had given many closing arguments, Lincoln knew the power that a speaker or writer could exert over an audience by closing strong. In the Gettysburg Address, Lincoln closed with the famous words "that these dead shall not have died in vain—that this nation, under God, shall have a new birth of freedom—and that government of the people, by the people, for the people, shall not perish from the earth."[15]

In his second inaugural address, Lincoln concluded, "With malice toward none; with charity for all; with firmness in the right, as God gives us to see the right, let us strive on to finish the work we are in; to bind up the nation's wounds; to care for him who shall have borne the battle, and for his widow, and his orphan—to do all which may achieve and cherish a just, and a lasting peace, among ourselves, and with all nations."[16]

Another distinguishing feature of Lincoln's writing is his knowledge of Scripture. The King James Version of the Bible significantly influenced his writing style later in life.[17] Lincoln integrated Bible verses frequently and strategically. The way he used these passages demonstrated the breadth and depth of his biblical

---

14 Wilson, *Lincoln's Sword*, 30.

15 Basler, Lincoln's Address Delivered at the Dedication of the Cemetery at Gettysburg, November 19, 1863, *CW*, 7:23.

16 Basler, Lincoln's Second Inaugural Address, March 4, 1865, *CW*, 8:332–33.

17 McPherson, *Lincoln*, 3.

understanding; they were almost always deployed suitably for the particular situation or context. No president has infused his private or public correspondence with more Bible verses than did Lincoln. He not only admired Holy Scripture, but found comfort in the divine wisdom and teachings of God's revealed Word.

A few months before his inauguration as president, Lincoln noted the power and long-lasting impact of the words in the Declaration of Independence. Without the Declaration, the American people would not have secured a free government and prosperity. "No oppressed, people will fight, and endure, as our fathers did, without the promise of something better, than a mere change of masters," he wrote. Then, in typical fashion, Lincoln wove Scripture (the same Proverbs 25:11 passage Alexander Stephens had quoted to him a few months earlier) into his close on how the Constitution preserved the ideals in the Declaration:

> The assertion of that principle, at *that time*, was the word, "*fitly spoken*" which has proved an "apple of gold" to us. The *Union*, and the *Constitution*, are the *picture of silver*, subsequently framed around it. The picture was made, not to *conceal*, or *destroy* the apple; but to *adorn*, and *preserve* it. The *picture* was made *for* the apple—*not* the apple for the picture. So let us act, that neither *picture*, or *apple* shall ever be blurred, or bruised or broken. That we may so act, we must study, and understand the points of danger.[18]

A deep and clear thinker, Lincoln with his pen could put his thoughts on paper and stir a nation.

From the Declaration of Independence to the Constitution, to the many letters he wrote to numerous citizens and politicians, to

---

[18] Basler, Lincoln's Fragment on the Constitution and the Union, January, 1861, *CW*, 4:169.

the words of the Holy Bible, Lincoln understood the enduring power and inspiration of the written word. More than comprehending the impact of the written word, he wrote in a compelling and persuasive manner. His written words still move us today.

The Truth

Alexander Stephens and Abraham Lincoln knew their Bible. They understood that "a word fitly spoken is like apples of gold in a setting of silver."[19]

Christians know the power and critical importance of God's written Word—namely, Holy Scripture. God chose His written Word as a means of His grace. The Holy Spirit gives us faith through God's written Word, whether it be heard or read.[20] Indeed, "for whatever was written in former days was written for our instruction, that through endurance and through the encouragement of the Scriptures we might have hope."[21] The Bible explains that "the word of God is living and active, sharper than any two-edged sword, piercing to the division of soul and of spirit, of joints and of marrow, and discerning the thoughts and intentions of the heart."[22] All Scripture "is breathed out by God and profitable for teaching, for reproof, for correction, and for training in righteousness, that the man of God may be complete, equipped for every good work."[23]

While there are many classics of literature to learn from, only God's Word, through the power of the Holy Spirit, brings life-saving and life-changing faith. For "the grass withers, the flower fades, but the word of our God will stand forever."[24]

---

19 Prov. 25:11.

20 Rom. 10:17.

21 Rom. 15:4.

22 Heb. 4:12.

23 1 Tim. 3:16–17.

24 Isa. 40:8.

Because you know what God has done for you as revealed through Scripture, He calls on you to embrace the script He has written for your life. God has blessed you richly with many gifts and in many ways. He wants you to live fruitfully and faithfully according to His designs and purposes. As the Bible states, "Let not steadfast love and faithfulness forsake you; bind them around your neck; write them on the tablet of your heart. So you will find favor and good success in the sight of God and man."[25]

Of all of God's children, Christians should especially appreciate the critical importance of writing and the *written word.* Our Savior, Jesus, "is clothed in a robe dipped in blood, and the name by which he is called is The Word of God."[26] God speaks to you through His Word. Christians know that "in the beginning was the Word, and the Word was with God, and the Word was God ... And the Word became flesh and dwelt among us."[27]

So grab your Bible or engage your Bible app. Read the written words on the pages or screen. These words were inspired by God and written for *you.* Get in the Word. Stay in the Word. Let the Holy Spirit dwell richly in you and write on your heart a divine message of faith.

Your Life

Most people are one way or the other—they either like to write or they do not. How about you? Why or why not?

What writing style do you prefer to read? What are some of your favorite books or magazines? Why? What are some of your favorite Bible passages or books in the Bible? Why?

---

[25] Prov. 3:3–4.

[26] Rev. 19:13.

[27] John 1:1, 14.

Lincoln made the point, referring to the Declaration and Constitution in particular, that things which are written down are permanent or hard to alter. Why do you think God chose His Holy Word as a means of grace for your salvation?

15

A Constant Inspiration

For the word of God is living and active, sharper than any two-edged sword, piercing to the division of soul and of spirit, of joints and of marrow, and discerning the thoughts and intentions of the heart.
—Hebrews 4:12

The Lincoln Way

The Bible is the greatest and most influential book in history.

Hearing and receiving Scripture remained a constant throughout Lincoln's life. As a young child, he had the Bible read to him by his mother and learned to read and memorize it for himself. As he grew older, he spent the first two hours of every morning reading, perusing the Bible more than any other work. Even during his New Salem days, when he questioned Christianity, he never stopped reading and appreciating the Bible as a splendid collection of literature. When tragedy struck his household, he found solace in the words of Scripture. During the tumultuous times of the Civil War, when frustrations with generals and casualty reports encumbered his days, Lincoln read and meditated on the Bible regularly and faithfully every morning[1] and other times throughout the day too. His private

---

[1] Conway, *Lincoln's White House*, 87; White, *Lincoln*, 490. Captain David Derickson, who picked up Lincoln every morning at the Soldier's Home at 6:30 a.m., noted that he would often find Lincoln "reading the Bible or some

secretary John Nicolay declared that Lincoln "had great faith in it."[2] God's Word healed, nurtured, sustained, inspired, and powered him.

Lincoln read Scripture so faithfully and frequently that the words became embedded in his mind. According to reporter Noah Brooks, who knew the president well, Lincoln had memorized most of Isaiah, many of the Psalms, scores of Proverbs, and numerous New Testament passages, especially the most famous sayings of Jesus.[3] Lincoln, in fact, made more references to the Bible than any other president in American history.[4] Family members, neighbors, associates, and politicians observed or knew of Lincoln's Bible-reading habit. Stephen Douglas, his political opponent in the great 1858 Senate race, complained about Lincoln's "proneness for quoting Scripture."[5]

Not only did Lincoln quote Scripture often, but his knowledge of the Bible's content exceeded that of most clergymen of his day. He constantly referred to God, prayer, and Jesus in his speeches, state papers, and correspondence. His "phraseology," or the way he wrote and spoke about the Bible and God, certainly made him sound like a longtime orthodox Christian.[6] When Stephen Douglas claimed that God gave Adam and Eve choice, as in the choice between freedom and slavery, Lincoln responded by saying no—God commanded Adam and Eve *not* to eat the fruit of that *evil* tree.[7]

Lincoln constantly used the Bible to bolster a deeply held conviction or support a political point he wanted to make. Some of his most famous and influential sayings as president—such as "a house divided against itself cannot stand"—used Scripture to make a

---

work on the art of war." The Soldiers' Home was half hour ride outside of Washington, three miles north in shaded hills (three hundred secluded acres).

2 Smith, *Faith and the Presidency*, 98.

3 Szasz and Szasz, *Lincoln and Religion*, 16.

4 Donald, *Lincoln Reconsidered*, 67.

5 Smith, *Faith and the Presidency*, 98.

6 Jones, *Lincoln and the Preachers*, 135, 140.

7 Miller, *Lincoln's Virtues*, 285.

point. In describing the purpose of the Declaration of Independence, Lincoln quoted Jesus's words in Matthew 5:48 (KJV): "As your Father in Heaven is perfect, be ye also perfect." Christ, he said, "set that up as a standard," to strive for "the principle that all men are created equal," and Lincoln desired "to let it be as nearly reached as we can."[8] Lincoln saw the Declaration as a moral covenant, an American Decalogue or Ten Commandments, which enshrined the articles of the nation's political creed—rights that came from a transcendent Creator through the divine revelation of the Bible.[9]

During the Civil War, when Major General John C. Fremont declared martial law in Missouri without consultation or notification (condemning to death civilians caught with weapons behind Union lines, freeing of slaves, and seizing property of rebels), Lincoln eventually relieved him of his command. The president later explained that he respected Fremont and his abilities, but that sometimes the best person to finish the job was not the one who started it. Moses emancipated the Jews, for example, but did not take Israel to the Promised Land. Joshua had to finish the task.[10]

When Mary Lincoln's brother-in-law, Confederate General Benjamin Hardin Helm, died at the Battle of Chickamauga, Lincoln quoted Scripture to properly capture his sentiments. He had grown very close to Helm and his wife before the war. When war broke out, Lincoln had offered Helm a Kentucky paymaster job with the rank of major. Helm rejected the generous offer and joined the Confederate army. Lincoln told a friend that he felt like the biblical David when told of the death of his son Absalom: he would have gladly exchanged places if he could.[11]

With bad news or good news, the words of the Bible informed Lincoln's thinking, articulation, and correspondence. When William Tecumseh Sherman's army captured the city of Savannah,

---

8 Basler, Lincoln's Speech at Chicago, Illinois, July 10, 1858, *CW*, 2:501.

9 Deutsch and Fornieri, *Lincoln's American Dream*, 26.

10 Burlingame, *Lincoln*, 2:210.

11 Burlingame, *Lincoln*, 2:555.

a wonderful Christmas gift for the Union in 1864, Lincoln credited Sherman, referencing Isaiah 9:2, "in showing to the world that your army could be divided … and yet leaving enough to vanquish the old opposing force of the whole," which "brings those who sat in darkness, to see a great light."[12]

Refusing to get bogged down with numerous patronage commitments, Lincoln confided to Lyman Trumbull, a senator from Illinois, that he did not want to make promises he could not keep. "Remembering that Peter denied his Lord with an oath, after most solemnly protesting that he never would," Lincoln said. "I will not swear I will make no committals; but I do think I will not."[13]

In addition to using Bible passages to communicate serious and substantive business, Lincoln ably deployed Scripture references with a sense of humor. Before he took the stage against Stephen Douglas during one of the senate debates in 1858, he handed his overcoat to a bystander and said, "Here, you hold my clothes while I 'stone Stephen.'"[14]

When he had to deal with three cantankerous congressmen as president, he told a story about a school in which students had to take turns reading from the Bible. On one occasion, the class was reading the account of Nebuchadnezzar's golden image from the third chapter of Daniel. A little boy named Bud had to continually recite the names Shadrach, Meshach, and Abednego. Recounting Bud's ordeal, Lincoln said, "Little Bud stumbled on Shadrach, floundered on Meshach, and went all to pieces on Abednego." Instantly the teacher struck the side of Bud's head and "left him wailing and blubbering as the next boy in line took up the reading." The boy composed himself until his turn to read approached again. "Then," Lincoln noted, "like a thunderclap out of a clear sky, he sent up a wail which even alarmed the master," who gently inquired

---

[12] Basler, Lincoln to William Sherman, December 26, 1864, *CW*, 8:181–82.

[13] Basler, Lincoln to Lyman Trumbull, June 5, 1860, *CW*, 4:71.

[14] Szasz and Szasz, *Lincoln and Religion*, 15.

about Bud's outburst. Pointing with a shaking finger at the verse he would be required to read, Bud managed to quaver out an answer: "Look there, master," he cried, "there comes them same … three fellas again!"[15]

In almost every kind of situation, Lincoln invoked Scripture. He truly believed that "the good old maxims of the Bible" were "truly applicable to human affairs" in every context and vocation of life.[16] During his visit to Niagara Falls in the fall of 1848, for example, he reflected that "when Columbus first sought this continent, when Christ suffered on the cross, when Moses led Israel through the Red-Sea, nay, even, when Adam first came from the hand of his Maker, then as now, Niagara was roaring here."[17]

The Bible remained a special book to Lincoln for the entirety of life. He kissed it after both of his inaugurations.[18] Hearing that a Massachusetts soldier had been saved from a rifle ball by the Bible he carried over his heart, Lincoln sent the man another Bible.[19] Moreover, he constantly meditated on the words of Scripture and took biblical accounts and verses to heart.

Three days before his assassination, Lincoln commented to his wife, his personal bodyguard, and a senator about the number of times dreams were written about in the Bible and how often God communicated with men through dreams. Bodyguards outside of his bedroom often heard Lincoln moaning in his sleep, apparently from his dreams.[20] God appeared to be telling him his time on earth would soon be over.

---

15 Leidner, *Lincoln's Gift*, 8.

16 Basler, Lincoln's Speech at Cincinnati, Ohio, September 17, 1859, *CW*, 3:462.

17 Basler, Lincoln's Fragment on Niagara Falls, September 25-30, 1848, *CW*, 2:10.

18 Burlingame, *Lincoln*, 2:61, 769.

19 Mansfield, *Lincoln's Battle with God*, 130.

20 O'Reilly, *Killing Lincoln*, 110–11.

While there is no debate that Lincoln read the Bible deeply and often, historians and biographers continue to dispute if Lincoln actually believed in the words he read, particularly with regard to the divine aspect and true nature of Jesus. Lincoln's contemporaries and associates debated his acceptance of Holy Scripture too. Ninian Edwards, a senator and governor of Illinois and the brother-in-law of Mary Todd Lincoln, recalled Lincoln telling him that "he believed that the Bible &c was the Divine Revelation" of God.[21] For every Ninian Edwards testimony, however, there were those who remembered Lincoln, particularly in his younger days, questioning the divinity of Christ and inerrancy of Scripture.

The indisputable truth is that the Bible was a lifelong source of strength and sustenance for Lincoln, and he read it and relied on it more often as his earthly years passed. Observers noticed the Bible lying on his desk in the Executive Mansion. He kept another Bible on a table at the end of a sofa. He routinely pulled out a pocket New Testament when he wanted to look up a relevant verse in the moment. If he could not find the verse he sought, he went to his library and consulted Alexander Cruden's *A Complete Concordance to the Holy Scriptures of the Old and New Testament.*[22] No one can know beyond a doubt about another's religious beliefs, but if faith comes from hearing and receiving the Word of God, then the evidence is compelling that Lincoln received and enjoyed a redeeming faith.[23]

There is considerable historical evidence that Lincoln's reliance on God's Word grew and matured over time. Enduring a number of family tragedies as well as presiding over a country being torn apart by a bloody civil war certainly takes a toll on a man. Seeking comfort, wisdom, order, and peace, Lincoln found all of these in the calming words of Scripture.

---

[21] Wilson, *Herndon's Informants*, 466.

[22] Mansfield, *Lincoln's Battle with God*, 128.

[23] Rom. 10:17.

Though he had always been a precocious child and well advanced in maturity and intellect compared to his peers, President Lincoln certainly possessed a different worldview in his fifties compared to his days as a frontier boy. One clergyman who knew Lincoln during the presidential years reported that Lincoln "read the Bible frequently, loved it for its great truths, and profound teachings and he tried to be guided by its precepts." He went on to assert that Lincoln "believed in Christ, the Savior of sinners, and I think he was sincerely trying to bring his life into the principles of revealed religion."[24]

This sentiment matches what Lincoln, late in his life, told a Treasury Department official: "If we had a witness on the stand whose general story we knew was true, we would believe him when he asserted facts of which we had no other evidence." Thus, he had "decided a long time ago that it was less difficult to believe that the Bible was what it claimed to be than to disbelieve it."[25] Once a skeptic, Lincoln had come to believe the words of Scripture were the truth and divine.

A few months before his death, Lincoln called the Bible the "Book of God," the "Great Book," and "the best gift God has given to man. All the good the Saviour gave to the world was communicated through this book." Without the Bible, no one could "know right from wrong. All things most desirable for man's welfare, here and hereafter, are to be found portrayed in it."[26]

Almost a decade after Lincoln passed, Mary Lincoln wrote that her husband's heart "was naturally religious." He had been especially appreciative of "his noble Mother," who read the Bible to him at a very early age and hoped he would grow up and become a very "pious boy & man." Mrs. Lincoln repeatedly told those who asked her "what an acceptable book, *that* Great Book, was always

[24] Mansfield, *Lincoln's Battle with God,* 128.

[25] Mansfield, *Lincoln's Battle with God,* 128.

[26] Basler, Lincoln's Reply to Loyal Colored People of Baltimore upon Presentation of a Bible, September 7, 1864, *CW,* 7:542.

to him." In so many settings and moments, including their "family bereavements, it was *there*."[27] Indeed, in the center of Lincoln's life, the Bible always remained *there*—a constant source of inspiration, comfort, and peace that surpasses all human understanding.

The Truth

For Lincoln the Bible was the greatest gift God had ever given to mankind. Indeed, God's Word, through the power of the Holy Spirit, gives us faith. More than a gift, the Bible is a means of grace, our salvation!

The Bible, however, remains a controversial book. It is hotly contested and refuted by pagans and secularists who accuse it of being outdated, misogynist, homophobic, inaccurate, inconsistent, mistranslated, and too exclusive, just to name a few epithets. Of course, the reasons for this are many. In our fallen world, too many humans do not want to be under the authority of a higher power—or anyone, for that matter. They do not want to be told how to live, what makes something right or wrong, or why they should feel guilty in any way. People want to be their own gods and "seek their own interests, not those of Jesus Christ."[28] Like the ancient Israelites, humans do not want to serve or worship God. They want to do what is right or convenient in their own eyes.[29]

Make no mistake, however. The Bible is clear on how you should live and how you will get to heaven. Jesus says, "I am the way, and the truth, and the life. No one comes to the Father except through me.[30] Jesus is "the Word" that "became flesh and dwelt among us, and we have seen his glory, glory as of the only Son from the Father,

---

27 Turner and Turner, Mary Lincoln to John Todd Stuart, December 15, 1784, *Mary Todd Lincoln*, 603–4.

28 Phil. 2:21.

29 Judg. 17:6.

30 John 14:6.

full of grace and truth."[31] Therefore the ultimate message of the Bible is clear: there are no other paths, alternate lifestyles, other beliefs, or works that will get you into heaven. Only Jesus, through His death and resurrection, can save you and lift you to heaven.

The clarity and exclusivity rankles many in our world today and invites scorn, criticism, and demonization. Of course, Satan knows the power of God's Word too. There is a reason the Bible is disputed and scrutinized more than any other book in human history. Satan is constantly working on getting people to doubt the words of Scripture—God's Word—at any cost. In fact, the very first question recorded in the Bible is that of Satan tempting Eve in the garden of Eden: "*Did God actually say*, 'You shall not eat of any tree in the garden?'" (italics added).[32] From the very first days of humans, Satan attempted to get humankind to doubt the inerrancy and truth of God's Word. This attack goes on today.

Despite the unfounded criticisms, the Bible lives on and continues to change and save lives each and every day. We should not be surprised, for the Bible teaches that "the grass withers, the flower fades, but the word of our God will stand forever."[33]

So do you want to trust in humankind's fickle thoughts and suppositions—a fancy speaker who has ulterior motives rather than your spiritual well-being in mind, or some pagan author's idea of salvation? Or will you trust the Bible—where "every word of God proves true" and God "is a shield to those who take refuge in him"?[34]

As Lincoln did, be thankful for the Bible and "thank God constantly for … the word of God," which you accepted "not as the word of men but as what it really is, the word of God, which is at work in you believers."[35] Moreover, never forget to "let the word of Christ dwell in you richly, teaching and admonishing one another

---

31 John 1:14.

32 Gen. 3:1.

33 Isa. 40:8.

34 Prov. 30:5.

35 1 Thess. 2:13.

in all wisdom, singing psalms and hymns and spiritual songs, with thankfulness in your hearts to God."[36] Indeed, it is well for your soul to do so.

Your Life

Lincoln's knowledge of Scripture—how he integrated it in his conversations, speeches, and correspondence—impressed even clergymen in his day. What inspiration and motivation do you take from Lincoln's deep and thorough knowledge of the Bible? How can you model Lincoln's integration of Scripture to be a witness to others?

As he aged and experienced more challenges in life, Lincoln leaned on and read the Bible more frequently. Has your view or use of God's Word changed over time? If so, in what ways?

Lincoln had multiple Bibles visible in the Executive Mansion. In our digital, social media age, how might we make the Word of God known or visible to others?

What are your Bible reading habits?

[36] Col. 3:16.

16

Looking the Part

But the Lord said to Samuel, "Do not look on his appearance or on the height of his stature, because I have rejected him. For the Lord sees not as man sees: man looks on the outward appearance, but the Lord looks on the heart."
—1 Samuel 16:7

The Lincoln Way

Being underestimated can be a terrific leadership advantage.

Abraham Lincoln was an odd-looking man—at least that is what many contemporaries concluded. Almost everyone who crossed his path commented on his physical appearance. To put it bluntly, he stood out and not always in a good way. "Ungainly," "stooped," "lanky," "long-armed," "homely," "odd and gawky," "shapeless," "grotesque," "raw," "raw bone," "bony," and, of course, "tall" and "long" were words frequently used to describe Lincoln—and these were from individuals who liked him.[1] A staff member of Union General George Meade called the commander in chief "the ugliest man I ever put my eyes on," and said that he had an "expression of plebeian vulgarity on his face."[2]

His political opponents or enemies called Lincoln much worse. Before he became Lincoln's secretary of war and developed a close friendship with him, Edwin Stanton called Lincoln a long-armed

[1] Miller, *Lincoln's Virtues*, 4.

[2] Johnson, *Last Weeks of Lincoln*, 53.

monkey. References to baboons, monkeys, or gorillas were most common. When he was running for president, even members of his own party ridiculed his looks. At the Republican convention in Chicago, New York Republicans called him a "horrid-looking wretch … soot and scoundrelly in aspect; a cross between the nutmeg dealer, the horse-swapper, and the nightman."[3] One Georgia satirist versified:

> His cheekbones were high and his visage rough,
> Like a middling of bacon, all wrinkled and tough;
> His nose was long, and as ugly and big
> As the snout of a half-starved Illinois pig;
> He was long in the legs and long in the face,
> A Longfellow born of a long-legged race.[4]

During a time when most grown men reached five feet six or five feet seven, the backwoods boy passed the six-foot mark at the age of sixteen and soon reached six feet four inches, weighing over two hundred pounds. He had a massive head, narrow shoulders, a short trunk, and endless legs. Thin, rawboned, and swarthy, he often wore caps made from animal skins and pants that were six to twelve inches too short for his lengthy frame. His clothing never fit properly, and Lincoln looked like he rarely put any thought into what he wore or how he wore it. Young girls often made fun of his appearance. Eight or nine inches taller than most mature men, Lincoln looked gangly, sinewy, awkward, and like an alien from another time or place.[5] One New Salem resident said that he "was about as ruff a specimen of humanity that could be found."[6]

When Lincoln went to the Illinois state legislature, one witness said that he possessed longer arms than any person he had ever seen.

---

[3] Guelzo, *Lincoln,* 247.

[4] Guelzo, *Lincoln,* 247.

[5] Fox, *Lincoln's Body,* 7.

[6] McGovern, *Lincoln,* 19.

When Lincoln's arms were at his sides, his fingers touched a point lower on his leg by nearly three inches than a normal person's reach.[7] When Lincoln rode on horseback, his lanky frame engulfed the horse and his feet nearly touched the ground. Since he did not strap his pant legs down, onlookers saw his long underwear exposed. His black suit was often mud-splattered. Few American presidents have ever looked more comical.[8]

There were advantages to his height and build. Young Abe excelled at sports and anything that had to do with running, hopping, pitching quoits (similar to horseshoes), swimming, and shooting. His height helped him to leverage things and display his truly remarkable strength. He could hold a seven-pound ax in one hand, perpendicular to his body, for minutes without his arm or the tool flickering even a bit—a feat he performed in front of astonished staff when he became president. He could also take two axes by the ends of their handles and raise them over his head with his elbows locked. He supposedly picked up a six-hundred-pound chicken house on one occasion and easily carried it to the location a farmer wanted it. Frontier reports circulated that he could lift as much as one thousand pounds.[9]

Abe's physical size and strength distinguished him on the frontier,[10] but these attributes inhibited the more cerebral life path he wanted to pursue. While he certainly earned respect and won friends with his athletic prowess, his father took advantage of him, constantly putting him to work clearing fields, harvesting crops, and splitting rails. Tom also hired Abe out to other farming families in the community. Every hour Abe worked over fields and split rails meant one less hour he spent reading, writing, and sating his curious and brilliant mind.

---

[7] Keneally, *Lincoln*, 23.

[8] Burlingame, *Lincoln*, 2:491.

[9] Freehling, *Becoming Lincoln*, 37; Winkle, *Young Eagle*, 64; Wheeler, *Faith and Courage*, 57.

[10] Goodwin, *Team of Rivals*, 50.

Lincoln loved to deploy self-deprecating humor in regard to his physical appearance. He told the story of a man who jumped him and held a revolver to his face. Fearing that his life would be eliminated at any moment, he courageously inquired of the perpetrator, "What seems to be the matter?"

"Well," replied the stranger, "some years ago I swore an oath that if I ever came across a man uglier than myself I'd shoot him on the spot."

A feeling of relief overtook Lincoln. "Shoot me," he demanded of the stranger, "for if I am uglier than you, I don't want to live!"[11]

After contracting smallpox in November 1863, Lincoln was told that it was contagious. He quipped that ever since he had become president, people had been asking him to give them something. Now, finally, he had something he *could* give to them. Referring to the scars that smallpox often caused, he reassured his doctor: the disease could not "disfigure" him.[12]

Lincoln, of course, recognized the importance of looking the part. When elected to the Illinois legislature, Lincoln had little money. He asked his friend, Coleman Smoot, for a $60 loan so he could purchase a suit to be presentable in the chamber. Since Smoot voted for him, Lincoln humorously insisted, he had a responsibility to lend him the money.[13]

As Lincoln matured, he realized that he would have to overcome his awkward outward form with his intellect, mental toughness, and intrinsic moral attributes. To be respected by his fellow citizens mattered more to Lincoln than his physical appearance.[14] He wanted to win over people's hearts and minds, not just their eyes.

A man with great emotional intelligence and political astuteness, Lincoln soon realized that he could use his reputation as an unsightly, uncouth commoner and turn it into an advantage. His

---

[11] Leidner, *Lincoln's Gift*, 20.

[12] Burlingame, *Lincoln*, 2:578.

[13] Lehrman, *Lincoln "by littles,"* 82.

[14] Burlingame, *Lincoln,* 1:173.

physical appearance lowered expectations people had for him. As people conversed with him or listened to him speak, however, they quickly discovered that there was far more to Abraham Lincoln than first met the eye. Just as a book provides so much more rich content than a movie ever can, this same analogy applies to the inner and outer Lincoln. The more people got to know Lincoln, the more engrossing and appealing he became. On the stump or in a committee meeting, Lincoln's features would suddenly come alive.[15] He filled up the stage with his physicality, arms and hands gyrating in an awkward, humorous, but always originally Lincolnian manner. When he spoke, the sadness in his face disappeared, replaced by a winning smile. Listening to or conversing with Lincoln, people saw and heard his keen intelligence, genuine kindness, and rapier wit.[16] He was polite, kind, gentle, accessible, and clear in his words. Lincoln surprised people who developed preconceived notions of his character and intellect based on his odd physical appearance.

Lincoln's most popular monikers, "Honest Abe" and "Rail-splitter," were accentuated by his awkward appearance and simple dress. Authentic and comfortable in his own skin, Lincoln exhibited the confidence of a down-to-earth leader and a genuine representative of the people's interests.

During the famous Lincoln-Douglas debates of 1858, Lincoln's appearance made a big impact on people's perception of the fairly unknown lawyer. Forty-five-year-old Stephen Douglas traveled in a luxurious private railroad car, wood-paneled and brass-fitted, trimmed with banners and bunting. An attached flatcar bore a shiny brass cannon. When the Douglas entourage drew near its destination, two men who attended the cannon would herald the arrival of "the Little Giant"—all five feet four inches of him—with a thunderous boom and powder flash. On stage, Douglas wore a blue

15 Fox, *Lincoln's Body*, 3.

16 Goodwin, *Team of Rivals*, 6.

serge suit with silver buttons and a shirt of brilliant white linen—the picture of a prosperous statesman.

Lincoln, contrarily, rode in a common coach, and sometimes arrived in a Conestoga wagon, escorted by a few friends on horseback and on foot. On the platform, Lincoln wore a weather-beaten, wrinkled black frock coat, with sleeves that were inches too short and trousers that showed his ankles.[17] He looked and spoke like a well-meaning commoner, and he could connect with common folk like no ordinary man.

As Lincoln's political career progressed, he got more comfortable with his appearance. He did not seem to care that he did not dress like everyone else. He often wore a tall black hat, which only highlighted his abnormal height. Perhaps Lincoln wanted to stand out—to look like Lincoln—and for voters to see that he was, indeed, somebody different.[18]

Lincoln first grew his beard after being elected president. During the campaign, some Republicans worried that unflattering photographs of Honest Abe would cost the party votes and the election. Perhaps a few whiskers would improve his appearance. Lincoln certainly heard the gossip.

He also received a letter from eleven-year-old Grace Bedell a few weeks before the election. Her father had brought home a picture of Lincoln from a local fair. Since she wanted Lincoln to be president "very much," she hoped he would listen to her advice. "If you will let your whiskers grow," she wrote, "you would look a great deal better for your face is so thin." Besides, "all the ladies like whiskers and they would tease their husbands to vote for you and then you would be President."[19]

Lincoln responded to little Grace a few days later: "As to the whiskers, having never worn any, do you not think people call it a

---

[17] Epstein, *Portrait of a Marriage*, 211–12.

[18] Simon, "Jonesboro Debate," 60.

[19] Basler, Grace Bedell to Lincoln, October 15, 1860, *CW*, 4:129.

piece of silly affection if I were to begin it now? Your very sincere well-wisher. A. Lincoln."[20] In a few short weeks, Lincoln had a beard.

At Lincoln's inauguration, future president James Garfield commented that while Lincoln looked "distressingly homely," his genuineness and transparency moved people to love and trust him. Lincoln's candor, especially contrasted with former president Buchanan's weakness and "cowardly imbecility," provided the strong and authentic leader they desperately craved and needed.[21]

From a distance, Lincoln's physical appearance could be construed as odd, awkward, or even alien. Once people got to meet him up close, however, they saw the depth of emotion and character in his eyes, smile, and other facial features. One high society member remarked that "something about the man, the face, is unfathomable."[22] Congressman Henry Laurens Dawes of Massachusetts opined early in the administration, "There is something in his face which I cannot understand. He is great. We can safely trust the Union to him."[23]

In hospitals during the war, Lincoln and his wife Mary distributed flowers and jelly beans to the troops. In addition, Lincoln looked for any soldier of above-average height and ask him to stand up, to compare their heights back to back. While the president never found one taller than himself, he did get many a soldier to laugh at the goodwill gesture and manly fun.[24] Lincoln's physical charisma, love of male sociability, and ease in laughing at his looks were all important parts of his political life and appeal.[25]

Once Lincoln assumed the office of the presidency, his physical deterioration and fatigue revealed the hardships and pressures of the

---

[20] Basler, Lincoln to Grace Bedell, October 19, 1860, *CW*, 4:129.

[21] Burlingame, *Lincoln*, 2:11–12.

[22] Sandburg, *Lincoln*, 402.

[23] Sandburg, 402. Later Dawes would remember Lincoln's face as "a title-page of anxiety and distress."

[24] Canavan, *Lincoln's Final Hours*, 44.

[25] Fox, *Lincoln's Body*, 18.

job. By the middle of the war, Lincoln's hand trembled fitfully. He looked feeble, worn, and haggard.[26]

Harriet Beecher Stowe, author of *Uncle Tom's Cabin* and the woman Lincoln credited for writing the book "that made this great war," visited Lincoln in the Executive Mansion during the war. She noticed his weary and pain-filled face. Lincoln told her that however the war ended, he would not last long after it was over. Later he would tell her, when the war almost appeared over, "No, Mrs. Stowe, I shall never live to see peace. This war is killing me."[27] After a horseback ride with his friend Noah Brooks, Lincoln shared that he could never get "rest" as most others understood it. "I don't know about 'the rest' you call it. I suppose it is good for the body. But the tired part of me is *inside* and out of reach."[28]

Orville Browning, a frequent guest of Lincoln's at the Soldiers' Home during summer evenings, visited the Executive Mansion in mid-July 1862 and observed that the president "looked weary, care-worn and troubled." They shook hands and Browning asked Lincoln how he felt. "Tolerably well," the president replied. Concerned, Browning told Lincoln he feared for his health. Lincoln then took Browning's hand, "pressed it, and said in a very tender and touching tone—'Browning I must die sometime.'" Browning reported that Lincoln "looked very sad, and there was a cadence of sadness in his voice." The two friends parted, "both of us with tears in our eyes."[29]

By the end of the war, Lincoln's appearance had changed dramatically. At the beginning of his presidency, he appeared youthful, vigorous, healthy, full of life, and prepared for the challenges at hand. By March 1865, the *Chicago Tribune* noted his "gaunt, skeleton-like appearance."[30] He was exhausted and hollow-cheeked, his beard giving his face the appearance of a death mask.

---

[26] Epstein, *Portrait of a Marriage*, 389.

[27] Sandburg, *Lincoln,* 385, 672.

[28] Sandburg, *Lincoln*, 385, 672.

[29] White, *Lincoln*, 498.

[30] Burlingame, *Lincoln*, 2:778.

Aware of the constant newspaper reports depicting "the exhausted appearance of the President," Julia Grant, wife of General Ulysses S. Grant, invited Lincoln to City Point where the army was encamped in the spring of 1865.[31] General Grant made it official: "Can you not visit City Point for a day or two? I would like very much to see you and I think the rest would do you good."[32] Lincoln's inner being could not be hidden from the face and body language of the man.

Lincoln's personal secretary John Hay had been with him for four years and saw the deterioration of his boss firsthand. Hay noted the commander in chief could not find refuge from the pressures and worries of war, and aged considerably for a man in his fifties. "Under this frightful ordeal his demeanor and disposition changed," Hay recalled, "so gradually that it would be impossible to say when the change began; but he was in mind, body, and nerves a very different man" after enduring the trials and tribulations of Shiloh, Antietam, Gettysburg, Vicksburg, Cold Harbor, and so many other horrific battles.[33]

Lincoln's acute fatigue and ill health stood out even more shortly after he gave his second inaugural address. He slept and ate poorly. Instead of noticing his height, people now noticed his thinness. His clothes barely hung on to his gaunt frame. Only fifty-six years of age, he looked much older, with a heavily lined face, sunken cheeks, sad eyes, and careworn facial expressions. In addition to his hands being cold and clammy, his feet were too. Joshua Speed once observed the president putting his feet so close to the fire that they steamed. "Sometimes I think I am the tiredest man on earth," he told a close associate.[34]

Mary Lincoln did not think her husband would get through another four-year term. The stress, political infighting, relentless visitors, passing of their son Willie, and of course the hundreds of

---

[31] Goodwin, *Team of Rivals*, 707.

[32] Basler, Ulysses Grant to Lincoln, March 20, 1865, *CW*, 8:367.

[33] Johnson, *Last Weeks of Lincoln*, 53–54.

[34] Donald, *Lincoln*, 568; McGovern, *Lincoln*, 132.

thousands of war casualties—which were reported to him daily, along with visits and letters from grieving families—continued to take their toll on Lincoln's soul.

Lincoln's depression might have been exacerbated by his addiction to blue mass pills, which contained potentially lethal doses of mercury and did slow damage. One insidious effect of mercury is the neurobehavioral damage it causes, including depression or worsening of preexisting depression. No one knows how many pills Lincoln ingested, but the recommended daily dose of two blue mass pills put patients at serious risk of mercury poisoning.[35]

In addition, Lincoln's compromised immune system had to deal with the pervasive filth and germs of the times and in the Executive Mansion. Dung and manure were tracked into White House, which attracted flies and more disease. Numerous pets were in the Executive Mansion—dogs, cats, domesticated goats. A turkey presented to the family as a holiday dinner became instead, thanks to Tad's tears, a pet after receiving a reprieve from the president. Furthermore, Lincoln had a minor problem with presbyopia, which caused him to wear reading glasses from his forties. He bought his first pair at a jewelry store in Illinois. The glasses were probably three times the strength he needed, being six and a half diopters strong. This may explain the headaches that he complained about after reading for long periods.[36]

All of Lincoln's fatigue and ailments ceased to matter on April 14, 1865, the day of his assassination. Even in his waning moments, Lincoln's physical appearance left a legacy to the world and revealed the character of the man: His body stubbornly fought for hours after the bullet entered his brain: his long frame lay angled on the bed in

---

35 Shenk, *Lincoln's Melancholy*, 112–13. Blue mass pills were made of pure mercury with a bit of rosewater and honey added for flavor. They were supposed to temper melancholy by clearing black bile out of the body—a laxative and antidepressant all at once.

36 Packard, *Lincolns in the White House*, 155–56.

the Petersen home, and the stained pillow exhibited just how much he had sacrificed for the Union.

Today the image of Lincoln's face—his piercing eyes and beard especially—is one of the most well-known in the world. He stares with conviction on the five dollar bill. His tall frame and hat create an iconic silhouette of the Great Emancipator. The physical appearance of the man is as much a part of the Lincoln legacy as any document or speech. Like his leadership, it is an original.

Lincoln's physical appearance is the book cover on his biography, a branding which reveals his uncommon leadership ability and uniquely American story. His physical appearance played a key part in his political rise as well as his legacy. More importantly, Lincoln never resented his physical appearance or questioned why God made him so. Instead, he embraced his uniqueness and turned it into a leadership asset. His physical quirkiness and spiky peculiarities not only endeared him to the nation, but helped solidify the art of his leadership as someone truly singular and special.

The Truth

There is an old idiom that says one should not judge a book by its cover. Indeed, too many of Lincoln's contemporaries disdainfully judged him by his awkward, lanky, homely appearance. By doing so, they underestimated him, even wrongfully determining that his looks disqualified him from leadership positions.

Physical beauty can be a significant influencer. Numerous studies have illustrated the effect that beauty has on others. People with athletic bodies often exude confidence, or at least the appearance of confidence, and thereby influence those around them. A flirtatious hello from an attractive individual of the opposite sex often generates "warm fuzzies" and internal flattery. A person's physical appearance can definitely make an impact on others.

An attractive physical appearance is certainly a gift from God and can be used for His purposes. One can use an eye-pleasing appearance as a tool, platform, or opportunity to connect with others in sharing the faith.

More important than one's physical appearance, however, is one's inner beauty. All humans are beautiful because all are "fearfully and wonderfully made"[37] and created "in the image of God."[38] As the Bible teaches, "Man looks on the outward appearance, but the Lord looks on the heart."[39] When people first saw Lincoln, many were repulsed at his physical appearance. Yet, after they got to speak with him and observe his inner strength, sense of humor, and kindness firsthand, they saw a different, far more alluring man. Proverbs 15:13 aptly describes Lincoln: one who has "a glad heart makes a cheerful face."

God reminds you to not let your "adorning be external—the braiding of hair and the putting on of gold jewelry, or the clothing you wear—but let your adorning be the hidden person of the heart with the imperishable beauty of a gentle and quiet spirit, which in God's sight is very precious."[40] While "bodily training is of some value, godliness is of value in every way, as it holds promise for the present life and also for the life to come."[41] There are many things that catch your human eyes in this fallen world that are not good for you. "Charm is deceitful, and beauty is vain," Scripture says, "but a woman," as well as any man, "who fears the Lord is to be praised."[42]

Someday your body, however gorgeous, firm, and healthy it may be right now, will grow old, decay, and fail. Friends and associates saw how drastically Lincoln aged during the four short years he served as president. While your body and physical appearance will

---

37 Ps. 139:14.

38 Gen. 1:27.

39 1 Sam. 16:7.

40 1 Pet. 3:3–4.

41 1 Tim. 4:8.

42 Prov. 31:30.

most certainly deteriorate as your earthly life progresses, your inner beauty will never diminish with Jesus. With Christ, "though our outer self is wasting away, our inner self is being renewed day by day."[43]

Remember that just as there has been only one Abraham Lincoln in human history, there has only been one person ever created like you. There will never be another one who looks just like you. You are "his workmanship,"[44] and God knit you together in your mother's womb.[45] He knows everything about your inner and outer makeup, even the number of hairs on your head.[46]

Most importantly, God sent His precious and perfect Son to die for you—a horrific crucifixion, but a beautiful sacrifice for a wonderfully divine outcome. Thanks to God's plan of salvation, "our citizenship is in heaven, and from it we await a Savior, the Lord Jesus Christ, who will transform our lowly body to be like his glorious body, by the power that enables him even to subject all things to himself."[47] Thanks to Jesus, you and your eternal life never looked so good.

Your Life

Lincoln had some distinguishing physical characteristics. What are yours? How has your physical appearance been a factor in your life?

Contemporaries underestimated Lincoln because of his physical appearance. How have you used your physical appearance for God's glory?

---

[43] 2 Cor. 4:16.

[44] Eph. 2:10.

[45] Ps. 139:13.

[46] Matt. 10:30.

[47] Phil. 3:20–21.

Humans look at the outward appearance while God looks at the heart. According to the Scripture passages you just read, what makes someone beautiful on the inside? How beautiful do you consider yourself to be? Do you consider others to be?

17

Job Training

Count it all joy, my brothers, when you meet trials of various kinds, for you know that the testing of your faith produces steadfastness. And let steadfastness have its full effect, that you may be perfect and complete, lacking in nothing.
—James 1:2–4

The Lincoln Way

To become a leader, one must practice leadership.

One of the most well-rounded leaders in American history, Abraham Lincoln had many different life experiences and occupations to thank for that. These various work contexts profoundly shaped his character, ingrained a productive work ethic, and reinforced the virtues of persistence, grit, and resilience. Most of all, through successes and failures, these formative experiences provided a laboratory where he could practice and develop his interpersonal, communication, and leadership skills.

In his youth, Abe executed the responsibilities that most children of frontier families did. He worked as a field hand, planter, harvester, hunter, corn shucker, fisherman, barn raiser, fence mender, rail splitter, axman, and much more. A skilled axman due to his height and leverage, Abe could size up a tree at a glance. Frontier folks often thought three people were hacking a tree in the distance only to discover Abe chopping one all by himself. His labor rented out by his father, at the Little Pigeon Creek Farm in southern Indiana,

Lincoln drove teams of horses, cut down trees, cleared land, and split logs to build cabins, pigpens, and fences. Especially good at building fences, Abe made sure they were "horse high, bull strong, and pig tight." He could make four hundred ten feet by four inch fence rails per day. Splitting logs for fences and steamboats made him a popular hire on the frontier. Fences protected people and livestock from attacks, preserved gardens and food supplies, and set borders between neighbors. At the age of sixteen, Lincoln ferried boats and learned to build flatboats at the age of eighteen. Before he turned twenty, neighbors and businessmen hired him to take merchandise and produce down to New Orleans.[1]

All of these boyhood responsibilities prepared Abe for future occupations. After he left home, he would find employment and purpose as a carpenter, riverboat man, store clerk, soldier, merchant, postmaster, blacksmith, surveyor, lawyer, and politician during the next two decades of his life.[2]

When Thomas Lincoln moved the family yet again to a homestead in Macon County, Illinois, in the summer of 1831, twenty-two-year-old Abe struck out on his own. He eventually settled in New Salem, Illinois, a place where he could experiment, fail, and find a calling for the next six years of his life. Located along the Sangamon River, New Salem had a population of a few hundred, a grist-mill, fifteen log cabins, a tavern, a church, a blacksmith, a schoolmaster, a preacher, and a general store. Farmers came from miles around to have their grain mashed into flour at the mill and to purchase salt, sugar, coffee, hardware, and cloth, among other supplies. In New Salem, Lincoln's life of manual labor would transform into a life of mental labor.[3]

Denton Offutt, a local businessman, hired Abe and a few others to build a flatboat and load it with pork barrels, corn, and hogs,

---

1 White, *Lincoln*, 36–37; Kigel, *Becoming Lincoln*, 112–13.

2 Donald, *Lincoln*, 38.

3 Mansfield, *Lincoln's Battle with God*, 34; Winkle, *Young Eagle*, 44; Goodwin, *Leadership*, 10; Manning, *Father Lincoln*, 15.

which were to be shipped to New Orleans and sold at the market. On the return trip, however, the flatboat got stuck on a flooded mill dam in New Salem. Townspeople cheered as they watched Lincoln save Offutt's flatboat and cargo. Grateful for Lincoln's heroics, Offutt hired him to run his general store. Soon Lincoln was directing his employer's leased mills too.[4]

Offutt's general store had two main challenges. First, his store was the third one to open in the small town. With competition for consumers already great, a third store simply oversaturated the market, thereby hindering profits. Second, the erratic and unreliable behavior of Offutt would eventually lead the store into bankruptcy. In fact, a year after he hired Lincoln, Offutt disappeared from the town.[5]

Despite the poor management of Offutt, Lincoln's clerking days were crucial in his development as a leader. People noted his attention to detail, work ethic, and sense of responsibility. Patient, considerate, kind, and honest, Lincoln made a positive impression on the townspeople. Many locals regarded him as one of the best clerks they had ever seen. Along with taverns, general stores were places to go for camaraderie and to hear the latest news and political talk. The storekeeper, by default, often became like a master-of-ceremonies. Lincoln thrived playing host, moderator, and referee as customers conversed and disputed—disputes that were often referred to him for judgment. When a lull in work appeared, he could always read a book he had stashed behind the counter.[6]

Perhaps because he could foresee the demise of Offutt's store, Lincoln decided to pursue politics at the age of twenty-three, only

---

[4] McGovern, *Lincoln*, 18.

[5] Winkle, *Young Eagle*, 55; Freehling, *Becoming Lincoln*, 29. Among his many miscues, Offutt stocked his store full of goods too late in 1831 for sales. Moreover, with funds sparse, he built a store for the merchandise too far away from town customers. Furthermore, he purchased one thousand hogs and three thousand bushels of corn before building any place to hold them.

[6] Donald, *Lincoln*, 41; Goodwin, *Leadership*, 11; Kigel, *Becoming Lincoln*, 159.

six months after moving to New Salem. His run for the Illinois state legislature, in 1832, revealed an impressive self-confidence and belief in his superior intellectual capabilities, especially considering that he had no family connections. He had, however, already built a reputation for enterprise, honesty, good humor, and studiousness. The people of New Salem took a fancy to him and embraced his sociability and kindness. He helped travelers whose carriages got stuck in mud, volunteered to chop wood for widows, and frequently offered his assistance to anyone in need.

As a Whig, his signature political issues were the creation of a national bank, protective tariffs, an expanded system of public education, and government support for infrastructure improvements—developing roads, railroads, and navigable waterways. In his very first political campaign, Lincoln finished eighth out of a field of thirteen candidates, but took satisfaction in knowing that he received 277 of the 300 votes in the New Salem precinct.[7] While he failed to get elected, he learned from his experience. He would go on win elections for a seat in the Illinois General Assembly in 1834, 1836, 1838, 1840, and 1854. Even when Lincoln was the second-youngest member of the assembly, members touted his leadership in moving the state capital from Vandalia to Springfield in 1837, and selected him as the minority leader for the Whig caucus. The choice demonstrated how much respect Lincoln had earned from his colleagues and exhibited his emotional intelligence. With his thorough knowledge of human nature, Lincoln set himself on a path to become a master politician and Whig Party workhorse.[8]

In the middle of his first campaign for the Illinois state legislature, the Black Hawk War erupted in western Illinois and eventually southwestern Wisconsin. Sauk and Fox Indians, who had

---

[7] Goodwin, *Team of Rivals*, 87; Goodwin, *Leadership*, 10–11; Donald, *Lincoln*, 42, 46; Winkle, *Young Eagle*, 81.

[8] McGovern, *Lincoln*, 30; Goodwin, *Leadership*, 15.

been manipulated into moving west of the Mississippi River and had ceded vast tracts of land in northwestern Illinois, repudiated their treaty with the United States government and migrated east from Iowa Indian Territory. Hoping to reclaim land, Chief Black Hawk and his 450 warriors, along with approximately fifteen hundred women and children, moved east, only to be confronted by United States forces.[9] Knowing his income would soon be gone from the failing general store, Lincoln signed up as a militiaman for a chance to make some money.

While he never saw combat during the war (the only blood he saw came from mosquitos, he humorously shared years later[10]), the Illinois Company from Sangamon County elected him captain. Lincoln said this was "a success which gave me more pleasure" and "satisfaction" than almost anything else in his life.[11] As captain, Lincoln learned to manage volunteers during a war. One time he found his company marching straight for a fence and could not remember the proper commands to maneuver them through a narrow gate. Being quick on his feet, Lincoln halted his men and dismissed the company for two minutes. Subtly but shrewdly, he then ordered them to reform on the other side of the fence so they could continue marching.[12]

While Lincoln saw no combat, he did demonstrate courage during his four thirty-day enlistments. When an old Indian appeared in camp to surrender, many in his company wanted the man killed, fearing he was a spy. Lincoln stood bravely between his outraged men and the Indian. When some called Lincoln a coward for standing up for the Native American, Lincoln challenged any

---

[9] Donald, *Lincoln*, 44.

[10] Basler, Lincoln in Speech to the House of Representatives on the Presidential Question, July 27, 1848, *CW*, 1:510.

[11] Basler, Lincoln to Jesse Fell, Enclosing Biography, *CW*, December 20, 1859, 3:511; Lincoln, Autobiography Written for John Scripps, *CW*, June, 1860, 4:64.

[12] Donald, *Lincoln*, 45.

man to test him. A few remarked on his advantageous height and size. Lincoln told them they could choose their own weapon. "This soon put to silence quickly all Charges of the Cowardice of Lincoln," the witness later reported.[13]

The one confrontation aside, most of Lincoln's company liked and respected him. Military authorities placed Lincoln under arrest once because some of his men were too drunk to finish a march. He had to carry a wooden sword for two days as punishment, but consistently defended his regiment to top military brass. His public defense of his men and courage in confronting military authorities only increased his popularity with the men.[14]

Lincoln worked hard and dutifully drilled his men, but also demonstrated the good sense of allowing his volunteers to have some leisure and fun too. Many a night were filled with horse races, relays, and wrestling matches—which Lincoln participated in and dominated. One man reported that Lincoln "was never thrown in a wrestle … and loved the sport as well as any man could." Lincoln "was seldom ever beat Jumping."[15]

In addition to spending leisure time with them, Lincoln told his company stories that stimulated constant laughter and good humor among his men. While Lincoln knew how to have fun, he prepared his soldiers for any contingency. He also endured every hardship his colleagues did. He never complained and did not fear the dangers of battle. Leading by example, he never asked his men to do anything that he would not do. He had the full confidence of his men, and they strictly obeyed his orders.[16]

Lincoln's steady leadership during the Black Hawk War thoroughly impressed his compatriots and extended his reputation. The war enlisted a who's who of Illinois and national figures, many of whom would help advance Lincoln's entrepreneurial and

---

13 Wilson, *Herndon's Informants*, 18–19.

14 Kigel, *Becoming Lincoln*, 184.

15 Wilson, *Herndon's Informants*, 363.

16 Wilson, *Herndon's Informants*, 363; Keneally, *Lincoln*, 19.

political trajectories. Lincoln would later help Zach Taylor run for the presidency; Robert Anderson would be the commander of Fort Sumter during Lincoln's first Civil War crisis; Jefferson Davis would become his political opponent as president of the Confederacy. Local figures like John Stuart and Stephen Logan would be his future law partners; John Hardin, Joseph Gillespie, and Edward Baker would become future Whig supporters and candidates. John Calhoun and Thomas Neale would soon hire him as Sangamon County deputy surveyor. Orville Hickman Browning, a conservative Quincy lawyer, became one of his most influential and critical friends (and would one day escort the president-elect from Springfield to Washington, DC). Physician Jacob Early and capitalist Elijah Iles, two titans in Springfield, would become influential hometown supporters. The Black Hawk War became Lincoln's Harvard, Yale, or Princeton experience and fostered a network of key players who would help spur his rise. The military experience also considerably enhanced his confidence in his own abilities.[17]

After returning from the Black Hawk War, Lincoln invested in another store, forming a partnership with William Berry, the son of a local minister and one of the corporals in Lincoln's company. Given New Salem's stagnant population, a new store required excellent managerial oversight—which Berry and Lincoln failed to provide. Instead of sweating the details of sales, Berry played poker. According to Herndon, while Lincoln was "at one end of the store dispensing political information, Berry at the other end was disposing the firm's liquors, being the best customer for that article of merchandise himself."[18] The duo were unable to pay the Sangamon County Circuit Court's judgment against the partnership for overdue notes in December 1834. The sheriff confiscated Lincoln's personal possessions—including his horse, saddle, bridle,

[17] Freehling, *Becoming Lincoln*, 40–41; Donald, *Lincoln*, 45; Keneally, *Lincoln*, 19.

[18] Kigel, *Becoming Lincoln*, 203–5.

surveying compass, and other equipment essential for a single male's livelihood on the frontier. When Berry died in suddenly in 1835 (probably from alcoholism), Lincoln insisted on adding all of Berry's debts to his own, despite the fact that only half of the debt was his responsibility. Lincoln referred to this stifling financial challenge as the "national debt."[19] In one of those fateful moments in history so often underappreciated, Lincoln's friend, James Short, bid on his surveying equipment for $120 and immediately returned it to Lincoln.

While Lincoln can be rightly criticized for his poor judgment and poor business decisions, his reputation was actually enhanced by these ordeals. Fifteen years later, as a member of the United States Congress, Lincoln was still sending part of his salary to pay creditors in New Salem. Locals and creditors not only appreciated the payments, but the integrity of a man who would validate the moniker "Honest Abe."[20]

Eventually, Lincoln's business failures compelled him to gravitate from manual to mental occupations, reorienting him to pursue law and political office. To make ends meet and survive in the short term, however, Lincoln took as many part-time jobs as he could find in New Salem. He split rails, ran a mill, clerked a store for Sam Hill, harvested crops, tended a still, clerked at local elections, and served as a New Salem agent for Springfield's Whig newspaper, the *Sangamon Journal.*[21]

In 1833 Lincoln became postmaster of New Salem. The previous one had had a bad habit of neglecting women standing in line for their mail in favor of men who desired to purchase liquor.[22] During the three years he served as postmaster, Lincoln made a name for himself for reliability, social grace, and integrity. The postmaster usually delivered the mail twice a week and collected fees from the

---

[19] Donald, *Lincoln*, 49, 54–55.

[20] Kigel, *Becoming Lincoln*, 206; Winkle, *Young Eagle*, 101.

[21] Winkle, *Young Eagle*, 98, 111.

[22] Donald, *Lincoln*, 50.

receivers of the letters. One day when he realized that a customer had overpaid for postage, Lincoln walked back several miles to return the proper change.

Lincoln enjoyed the benefits of the job—the pay, free mail services, exemption from militia and jury duty, and time to read (for free) all the newspapers that came through the office. Bantering with and getting to know almost everyone in the neighborhood, however, became the most important long-term benefit for Lincoln as postmaster.[23] He carried letters in his stovepipe hat, which ascended eight inches above his head,[24] and residents were just as happy to visit with the gregarious, tale-spinning Lincoln as they were to receive a letter from his hands. He made friends and earned future votes everywhere he delivered mail. Blessed with great discernment and emotional intelligence, he carefully listened to common folk and learned about their hopes, dreams, and wishes.

In the late fall of 1833, Lincoln became a surveyor. Hired by the county surveyor John Calhoun, who had served with Lincoln in the Black Hawk War, the gangly Lincoln made quite a sight hauling instruments across the wooded frontier, with letters stuck in his hat for delivery to farms along the way.[25] Lincoln taught himself how to be a surveyor, voraciously reading practical survey books and blabbing for understanding. He bought himself the sixty-six-foot chains, staffs, compasses, and other supplies needed for the occupation.[26]

Pushing through briar patches, slogging through swamps, and cutting through hazardous underbrush in order to set markers and measure angles, surveyors had to possess a strong work ethic, courage, and fortitude. At the end of the day, Lincoln often returned with torn clothes, scratches, and scrapes.[27]

---

[23] Winkle, *Young Eagle*, 112–13.

[24] Freehling, *Becoming Lincoln*, 43.

[25] Keneally, *Lincoln*, 22.

[26] Freehling, *Becoming Lincoln*, 43–44; Sandburg, *Lincoln*, 36.

[27] Donald, *Lincoln*, 51.

Much like his postmaster's job, surveying forced Lincoln to travel all around Sangamon County, even as far as one hundred miles away from New Salem. He met people and made friends over an ever-greater region than his postmaster's travels had afforded him. He boarded with local families until he completed a job and met many political operatives. Wherever he went and whomever he met, Lincoln earned a reputation for candor, kindness, and hard work. His expanding network of contacts would help propel him to electoral success the next time he ran for the Illinois General Assembly.[28]

Lincoln won his election to the Illinois state legislature in 1834 with a hands-on approach. One time during the campaign, he went out to a field where thirty men were harvesting grain. One of them said he would not vote for any candidate who could not hold his own in the field. When Lincoln took hold of the cradle with perfect ease and led the harvesters on a full round of the field, he won them over.[29]

The prominence and reputation Lincoln developed as a captain during his New Salem years propelled his political rise and growing popularity. William Butler, a close friend and fellow Whig, insisted that Lincoln got elected "because he was a good fellow" and "genial, kind, sympathetic, open-hearted." Citizens appreciated that Lincoln answered their questions in a succinct, "common way and manner, and yet exactly suited to the time, place, and thing."[30] John Stuart added that Lincoln's reputation for honesty and integrity

---

[28] Winkle, *Young Eagle*, 113–14; Freehling, *Becoming Lincoln*, 43–44; Guelzo, *Lincoln*, 69. A story illustrating Lincoln's kindness as a surveyor came to light thirty years after he had laid out a property line. A dispute arose over the "skewed" boundary. A neighbor explained that Lincoln, if he had kept the line straight, would have cut three or four feet off one family's house. "It's all he's got in the world and he could never get another," the neighbor recalled Lincoln saying. "Reckon it won't hurt anything out here if I skew the line a little and miss him" (Wheeler, *Faith and Courage*, 76).

[29] Donald, *Lincoln*, 52.

[30] Winkle, *Young Eagle*, 115.

made him trustworthy. "He ran on the square," Stuart said, "and thereby acquired the respect and confidence of everybody."[31] Accessible, down-to-earth, and possessing exceptional listening, communication, and people skills, Lincoln's various occupations had prepared him well for the life of a retail politician.

As an industrious legislator, Lincoln jumped right into the job, serving on twelve special committees and as secretary of the Whig party. He honed his oratorical skills on the chamber floor and took on the role of legislative correspondent for the *Sangamon Journal*, writing hundreds of unsigned, often humorous anti-Democratic editorials. Reelected to the state legislature in 1836, he received more votes than any candidate. He soon became the leader of the Long Nine—nine lanky and mainly young Whig legislators from the Sangamon area. Despite his partisan beliefs, Lincoln found that humor went a long way in breaking down barriers between parties. Speaker James Semple, a Jacksonian Democrat, appointed Lincoln to multiple committees and called upon him regularly to speak to key motions.[32]

Lincoln and his fellow Whigs successfully moved the Illinois capital from Vandalia to Springfield in 1837. With little promise of any political or economic future in New Salem, Lincoln moved to Springfield himself. The six years he had resided in New Salem were pivotal for his life trajectory. He had recovered from failure and setbacks, excelled at several different occupations, and enhanced his skills and confidence. He arrived in Illinois as a farmer, like 80 percent of his peers. When he left to live in Springfield, he cast his lot with the 20 percent of his peers who pursued nonagricultural livelihoods. He moved upward from the manual callings of flatboatman and miller to the commercial occupations of store clerk and merchant, which was practiced by approximately 3 percent of his peers. When he became a lawyer, at the age of twenty-eight, he

[31] Winkle, *Young Eagle*, 115.

[32] Keneally, *Lincoln*, 25, 28; White, *Lincoln*, 63–64.

joined the 2 percent of his peers who similarly practiced a profession. Overall, 95 percent of Sangamon County's breadwinners made a living from manual occupations. Fewer than 5 percent performed mental labor, as he did. By the age of thirty, Lincoln had gained experience serving the federal government as postmaster, the state government as a legislator, the county government as a surveyor, and later, the town of Springfield, as a trustee.[33] His will to rise and make a name for himself sprouted during his days in New Salem. In Springfield, which would be his residence from 1837 to 1861, his ascent would come into full bloom.

Lincoln arrived in Springfield with seven dollars in his pocket, proceeds of the sale of his surveying equipment.[34] He quickly reestablished his reputation and built new relationships and income streams. Lincoln wrote to Mary Owens, a woman he would later court, that "this thing of living in Springfield is rather a dull business after all, at least it is so to me. I am quite as lonesome here as ever was anywhere in my life." Not surprisingly, coming from his village atheist days at New Salem, Lincoln mentioned that he had not "been to church yet, nor probably shall not be soon. I stay away because I am conscious I should not know how to behave myself."[35]

When not in legislative session, Lincoln pursued his desire to become a lawyer. The law had always appealed to Lincoln—the reason, rational thinking, orderly presentation, quick wit, intelligent arguments, and merit-based attributes of the profession. Success as an attorney relied upon talent and energy and not accidents of birth, inheritance, or physical endowments. In addition to needing another reliable source of income, Lincoln appreciated that the profession afforded an opportunity for public service and a platform to pursue his avocation—politics. A lawyer's life provided order and structure, which appealed to Lincoln's makeup.[36]

---

33 Winkle, *Young Eagle*, 121, 179.

34 McGovern, *Lincoln*, 25.

35 Basler, Lincoln to Mary Owens, May 7, 1837, *CW*, 1:78.

36 Holzer and Garfinkle, *A Just and Generous Nation*, 21.

Lincoln soon became a junior law partner under the tutelage of John T. Stuart (1837–1841) and then Stephen Logan (1841–1844), whom he met during his time serving in the Black Hawk War. He later became senior law partner to William Herndon (1844–1860). Typical legal work dealt with such things as damage done to crops by foraging livestock, property disputes, assault and battery, and an occasional murder case. In addition, Lincoln took all kinds of cases, including divorce, rape, wills, maritime law, patent challenges and infringements, rights of way, foreclosures, debts, trespasses, slanders—and both sides of the fugitive slave issue. Talented and willing to defend people of all classes with equal care and diligence, Lincoln became one of the most sought-after attorneys in Illinois.

Lincoln's meticulous nature served him well in regard to preparation and jury selection. Once a trial began, his masterful cross-examining skills shone, as well as his exemplary ability to sway a jury with a mixture of logic, force, and wit. He could break down the most complex case into its simplest parts. Relying on his memory, Lincoln rarely had to use his notes. He looked each member of a jury in the eye and conversed with them as if they were friends. He laid out his arguments in logical, easy-to-follow words. Jurists appreciated his workhorse rather than show horse approach. A storyteller at heart, Lincoln excelled at putting the little pieces of a case together to create a big picture. He could also make a strong closing argument.

Attorney Lincoln eventually appeared before the highest court in Illinois over three hundred times. He won most of his cases. Hardworking, fair, and honest, Lincoln's thoroughness and care made him one of the most successful practitioners of his craft, and he earned a reputation for being a lawyer's lawyer.[37]

---

[37] McPherson, *Lincoln*, 12; White, *Lincoln*, 178; Donald, *Lincoln*, 100, 151; Goodwin, *Leadership*, 107; Oates, *With Malice Toward None*, 97, 100–101, 104. Lincoln had his biases as a trial lawyer: He believed fat men were ideal jurors because they were jolly by nature and easily swayed. He rejected people with high foreheads (he thought they had already made up their minds) and

As an attorney for the vast Eighth Circuit—also known as the "Mud Circuit" as snowmelt and flooded streams muddied the roads in the spring—Lincoln did casework across eleven thousand square miles in central Illinois, from the Wabash to the Illinois River (roughly two-thirds width and one-third length of the state), for more than eleven years. The five-hundred-mile circuit ride took place twice a year, spring and fall, over a ten-week period. Put another way, Lincoln spent three months of every year traveling the circuit. These tours, of course, were a political boon for him. In fact, his strongest supporters in future elections were attorneys and clients he met on the circuit.[38]

In many ways, Lincoln the circuit rider exhibited the quintessential man. In an age before railroads, telegraphs, telephones, and daily newspapers, Lincoln loved traveling and boarding with lawyer friends, intellectual minds, and people of the plains. He was never fussy about where he stayed or what he ate, nearly everyone on the circuit had keys hanging on their homes offering their hospitality to traveling lawyers. He stayed at rustic inns, taverns, and the farmhouses of litigants, often sharing a bed with fellow lawyers or sleeping on the floor. Lawyers battled by day and socialized at night. Hotel accommodations were meager, and only two or three could stay in a room and usually had to sleep on the floor. Nevertheless, Lincoln loved the camaraderie, conversation, card playing, music-making, and opportunity to play practical jokes on his associates.

---

considered blond, blue-eyed males inherently nervous and apt to side with the prosecution in murder cases. One example of Lincoln's honesty and integrity as a lawyer occurred when his law partner, William Herndon, filed a motion that contradicted the facts. Lincoln told him, "Hadn't we better withdraw that plea? You know it's a sham, and a sham is very often but another name for a lie. Don't let it go on record" (Lehrman, *Lincoln "by littles,"* 59).

[38] Freehling, *Becoming Lincoln*, 72; Donald, *Lincoln*, 104–6; Wheeler, *Faith and Courage*, 109.

And people loved being around Lincoln to hear his tales, hearty guffaw, and ability to laugh at himself.[39]

Rural settlers loved the traveling court as it disrupted the drudgery of farming and added an entertainment luster to their town. Lawyers were the celebrities of frontier life. Far and near, people would come to listen and watch the dramatic court proceedings. Local belles came to see and be seen. Most cases involved disputed wills, divorce, illegitimacy proceedings, slander and libel suits, patent challenges, collection of debts, murder, and robbery.[40]

Beyond his telling of a good tale, Lincoln's associates relied on him to determine the best place to cross rivers. He had long legs and could scout river depths. Taking off his boots and socks and rolling up his trousers, he would lead the party across. After one severe rainstorm, Lincoln led a party of lawyers, including a portly judge, into water so deep that all of them had to strip buck naked and carry their clothes over their shoulders.[41]

The circuit provided Lincoln with opportunities for solitude and professional growth. Cases stimulated his mind and reinforced the importance of accuracy, precision, detail, thoroughness, argument, persuasion, and reason. The profession also allowed him to more carefully discern human nature.[42] Of course, he continued to expand his network of personal and professional friends.[43] "In my opinion I think Mr. Lincoln was happy—as happy as *he* could be,

---

[39] Wheeler, *Faith and Courage*, 110; White, *Lincoln*, 85; Manning, *Father Lincoln*, 18.

[40] Goodwin, *Team of Rivals*, 149.

[41] Wheeler, *Faith and Courage*, 112–13.

[42] Basler, Lincoln's Fragment: Notes for a Law Lecture, July 1, 1850, *CW*, 2:82. Despite the realization of man's frailty, Lincoln gave advice one time to future attorneys. Recognizing that many people felt "that lawyers are necessarily dishonest," no young man should choose the law and "yield to the popular belief" that "you cannot be an honest lawyer." If that be the case, one should "choose some other occupation, rather than one in the choosing of which you do, in advance, consent to be a knave."

[43] Oates, *With Malice Toward None*, 102, 105.

when on this Circuit—and happy no other place," Judge David Davis recalled. "This was his place of enjoyment."[44]

For two short years after arriving at Springfield, Lincoln served as trustee—an individual who levied taxes, decided which roads and sidewalks would be paved and repaired, invested in drainage renovations, and awarded liquor licenses.[45] Other than this, Lincoln's primary occupations during his Springfield years were as lawyer and legislator.

Reelected to the Illinois General Assembly for a fourth straight term in 1840, Lincoln proved once again his mettle as a grassroots politician. (He would be elected to the General Assembly once more in 1854, but almost immediately declare himself a candidate for US Senate). Experience taught him that every aspect of the political process mattered—distribution of ballots, checklists, rounding up of voters, and every detail of campaigning. Both the vision and the mundane essentials were critical to a fruitful campaign and productive governing.[46]

Unfortunately, the Panic of 1837 and ensuing economic collapse across the nation led to Lincoln and the Whigs falling out of favor with the people. For someone who had run on the critical importance of developing his state's infrastructure, the stoppage of work on railroads, canals, bridges, and roads hurt Lincoln's political standing. He simply could not fulfill his political promises. Crushing government debts, reduced revenues for the public coffer, and lower credit ratings crippled the Illinois state government and deterred new settlers from coming. Land values plummeted, thousands of residents lost their homes, and banks closed. Having risen to prominence in the Whig Party, Lincoln took much of the blame for the economic crisis. His dream of becoming Illinois's De Witt Clinton (the New York politician who successfully had the Erie Canal built) stymied,

---

44 Wilson, *Herndon's Informants*, 349.

45 Winkle, *Young Eagle*, 179.

46 White, *Lincoln*, 92; Goodwin, *Team of Rivals*, 89.

Lincoln announced that he would retire at the end of his legislative term in 1842.[47]

Lincoln, of course, was not done with elected office. He defeated Methodist clergyman Peter Cartwright in 1846, to represent his district in the federal House of Representatives. As Lincoln and his wife Mary prepared to leave Springfield on October 25, 1847, the *Illinois State Journal* wished Lincoln well: "Success to our talented member of Congress! He will find many men in Congress who possess twice the good looks, and not half the good sense, of our own representative."[48]

The two-year term Lincoln served in Congress was a frustrating one, since he did not support the Mexican War and most of his constituents did. Derisively known as "Spotty Lincoln" for his "spot resolutions," which called for the acknowledgment of the exact "spot of soil" where Mexicans killed Americans to start the war, Lincoln strongly implied that the spot actually resided on Mexican soil. Moreover, he voted several times for the Wilmot Proviso, declaring that slavery should be prohibited in any territory acquired from Mexico. Democrats predicted the Illinois congressman's demise with the epitaph "Died of Spotted Fever."[49] They were right. Lincoln served only one term in Congress.

Not until 1854 did Lincoln reengage with politics and political office. After his unsuccessful term in Congress, he rededicated himself to his law practice. Though he had been practicing for twelve years, Lincoln admitted that he did not feel like "an accomplished lawyer."[50] Politics had taken up too much of his attention and time, and his legal skills had atrophied. Lincoln returned to his law partner, William Herndon, with a renewed focus and determination. "No man," Herndon said, "had greater power of application" than

---

47 Goodwin, *Leadership*, 98.

48 White, *Lincoln*, 139.

49 McPherson, *Lincoln*, 13–14.

50 Basler, Lincoln Fragment on Notes for a Law Lecture, July 1, 1850, *CW*, 2:81.

Lincoln. Once he fixed his mind "on any subject, nothing could interfere with or disturb him."[51]

This Alexander Hesler photograph taken in 1857 depicts the lawyerly and energetic Lincoln who reentered politics after passage of the Kansas-Nebraska Act in 1854. (Library of Congress, LC-USZ62-36582)

The various occupations Lincoln partook of during the 1830s and 1840s forever shaped the man and the leader. Whether a flatboatman, store clerk, miller, militiaman, merchant, postmaster, surveyor, legislator, trustee, or lawyer, Lincoln learned many life lessons from his successes and failures. He saw that hard work could take him places far beyond the frontier, and he possessed a work ethic second to none. "Mr Lincoln was so unlike all other men I had ever known before or seen or known since that there is no one to whom I can Compare him," said his friend Joshua Speed. "In all his habits eating, sleeping, reading Conversation & study, he was If I may so express it regularly irregular." Speed went on to explain that Lincoln worked so hard, he had "no stated time for eating, no fixed time for going to bed or getting up. No course of reading was ever

[51] Goodwin, *Leadership*, 106–7.

chalked out."[52] Lincoln's prodigious work ethic would carry him all the way to the presidency.

Charles Dana, a journalist for the *New York Tribune*, also noted Lincoln's work ethic and "immense physical endurance. Night after night he would work late and hard without being wilted by it, and he always seemed ready for the next day's work as though he had done nothing the day before."[53] After the Emancipation Proclamation had been passed, Lincoln maintained to associates that "we are a good deal like whalers who have been long on a chase. At last we have got our harpoon fairly into the monster; but we must now look how we steer, or with one flop of his tail, he will yet send us all into eternity!"[54] Lincoln understood that nothing worthy or great could ever be secured without diligence and hard work.

Along with a robust work ethic, Lincoln's work history helped fortify his resilience, perseverance, and grit. Failures would never be fatal or final with him. Years of experiencing wins and losses in the courtroom and at the ballot box steeled his resolve and strengthened his mental toughness. He intuitively understood that failures often came before successes. Moreover, letdowns and losses forced him to find ways to cope with stress and disappointment. Reading, storytelling, laughter, joking, and hard work helped him recover from setbacks and move on to the next endeavor better than most others.[55]

During the low point in the Civil War, President Lincoln never flinched or lost his resolve. When others were calling for peace, he told Secretary of State Seward that he would "maintain this contest until successful, or till I die, or am conquered, or my term expires, or Congress or the country forsakes me."[56] Having overcome it so often in the past, failure did not intimidate or scare the wartime President.

---

[52] Wilson, *Herndon's Informants*, 498–99.

[53] Guelzo, *Lincoln*, 276.

[54] Carpenter, *Six Months in the White House*, 98.

[55] Guelzo, *Lincoln*, 361.

[56] Basler, Lincoln to William Seward, June 28, 1862, *CW*, 5:292.

In addition to developing his resiliency, Lincoln's various occupations helped him learn how to connect with people. Not only could he carry on a conversation with anyone from any background on almost any topic, but he grew in his discernment and emotional intelligence. A sensitive and caring individual, he could feel another's thoughts, dreams, and desires through keen observation and listening skills. His ability to read audiences just as thoroughly and deeply as he comprehended books allowed his empathy to resonate directly in the hearts and minds of people in all stations of life. His capacity to see things from multiple perspectives prepared him for times when he would have to make tough decisions. Diversity of thought was always a welcome companion for Lincoln. Moreover, he understood from real-life experience that a leader could never please everyone. A leader had to take action knowing that others might not be happy with the decision or its result.

The many different employments Lincoln took on during his young adult life provided both mountain top and valley experiences, which helped him discover and embrace his own convictions, character, and leadership style. Indeed, these various life experiences separated him from his peers and provided a profound advantage over his political opponents.[57] If leadership experiences and opportunities could be captured in a neighborhood park, then Lincoln had walked the trails, picnicked at the scenic spots, and played on the swing sets and merry-go-rounds. He knew the leadership park well.

Living such an uncommon life allowed Lincoln to connect with the common man—the everyman. As he honed his leadership skills and dispositions throughout the 1830s, 1840s, and 1850s, Lincoln became a well-rounded, well-adjusted, singular leader prepared for the most turbulent of times. His accomplishments would soon be deeply drawn upon as he took on the greatest leadership challenge in United States history.

---

57 Goodwin, *Team of Rivals*, 254–255.

The Truth

Perhaps you have said or heard people say—even elderly people—that they cannot wait to see what they do or become when they "grow up." Or perhaps you have read reports that indicate that people today will probably switch jobs anywhere from ten to twenty times during their working lives.

The truth is that God has been preparing, shaping, and equipping you for His purposes throughout all of your life experiences. Through every hardship, mistake, or sin, God provides life lessons that can lead you closer to Him. Through every joy, success, and blessing, too, God instructs you in His way and His good timing. "The steps of a man are established by the Lord, when he delights in his way," the Psalmist explains. "Though he fall, he shall not be cast headlong, for the Lord upholds his hand."[58] As you make your way through life, you certainly gain knowledge of the ways of the world. "Wisdom is with the aged," the Bible maintains, "and understanding in length of days."[59]

Throughout his life, Lincoln experienced many setbacks and failures. He went bankrupt, suffered from poverty, lost his job, experienced election defeat multiple times, endured depression, watched his children pass, and saw a country tear itself apart. Through it all, Lincoln learned how to prepare for and overcome the hard knocks of life with the help of God. He also learned new skills, met new people, experienced the joy of personal growth, won elections, and grew closer to his God. A good steward of God's gifts and talents, Lincoln made the most of every task. New experiences meant new learning opportunities—to fail or to succeed, but always to grow and learn.

The Bible says that "whatever you do, work heartily, as for the Lord and not for men, knowing that from the Lord you will receive

---

[58] Ps. 37:23–24.

[59] Job 12:12.

the inheritance as your reward. You are serving the Lord Christ."[60] Perhaps what you do now may not be your dream job or the one you feel destined for when you "grow up." Remember, however, that God says, "My thoughts are not your thoughts, neither are your ways my ways … For as the heavens are higher than the earth, so are my ways higher than your ways and my thoughts than your thoughts."[61] You do not know how God is using your current occupation to shape you for something else He has planned for you. When tough times inevitably creep or jump into your life, remember that the "God of all comfort" will hearten and uplift you during your affliction, which will teach you "to comfort those who are in any affliction, with the comfort with which we ourselves are comforted by God."[62]

One assurance you have is God's holy, inspired Word, which reminds all "those who love God" that "all things work together for good, for those who are called according to his purpose."[63] Indeed, God will make known to you "the path of life."[64]

One might assert that the presidency was the most important job Lincoln ever had. But is this contention true? Lincoln might never have become president if he had not been a postmaster, surveyor, or store clerk. So which occupation was the most important? All of his jobs made an impact on his personal and professional development. Indeed, there are many valuable vocations and occupations in this life which are blessings from God. As the Bible says,

> For as in one body we have many members, and the members do not all have the same function, so we, though many, are one body in Christ, and individually members one of another. Having gifts that differ according to the grace given to us, let us

60 Col. 3:23–24.
61 Isa. 55:8–9.
62 2 Cor. 1:3–4.
63 Rom. 8:28.
64 Ps. 16:11.

> use them: if prophecy, in proportion to our faith; if service, in our serving; the one who teaches, in his teaching; the one who exhorts, in his exhortation; the one who contributes, in generosity; the one who leads, with zeal; the one who does acts of mercy, with cheerfulness.[65]

One final thought: Occupations or jobs do not define a person's life. Many people, even Christians, forget that Jesus had an occupation during His earthly life. Even as a *perfect* carpenter (can you imagine!), that occupation was not what ultimately defined Him or set Him apart. Jesus's carpentry skills are not what we cherish about Him. We love Jesus because of who He is—our Savior, the Word that "became flesh and dwelt among us."[66] He lived His earthly life with purpose, conviction, and mission. He died to take away your sins and granted you underserved salvation. His job description is the only one that can never be replicated. We thank God and His Son Jesus for this. Amen!

Your Life

Perhaps you have not had as many different jobs as Lincoln did. Looking back at the occupations you have practiced over the years, what lessons did you learn from each that shaped you into the person you are today? How did God use those experiences for your benefit?

Lincoln experienced many failures, losses, and hard knocks throughout his life. Yet he persevered and used his setbacks to set up future endeavors. How have you used your failings, setbacks, and

[65] Rom. 12:4–8.
[66] John 1:14.

tragedies to grow and learn? How has your faith helped you cope with life's changes?

How do your occupations or vocations define or not define your life? If you had twenty seconds to tell people what your life is all about, what would you tell them?

18

Friends in Low and High Places

Therefore encourage one another and build one another up, just as you are doing.
—1 Thessalonians 5:11

The Lincoln Way

One's brain and leadership acumen are influenced by the books one reads and the people one meets.

Abraham Lincoln possessed singular gifts and talents that allowed him to rise from obscurity to become one of the greatest presidents in American history. Supremely gifted and independent in many ways, Lincoln might not have been even a footnote in history if he had not received help from others along the way.

There are too many people to mention here who intersected with Lincoln's life and rise to fame. If not for his parents, of course, Lincoln never would have been born. Besides bringing Abe into the world, his father and mother passed on life essentials that would benefit their son to the end of his days. For all his faults and failures, Thomas Lincoln gave the gift of gab and storytelling to his son. His biological mother, Nancy Hanks, nurtured and encouraged Abe's love of reading, including the Bible.

While one would assume the importance and impact of parents, Abe's older sister, Sarah, has often been left out or underappreciated in the story of Lincoln's rise. Abe grew up adoring her, perhaps because she seemed to enjoy spending time with him more than his parents did. A clever girl with a terrific sense of humor, she had the ability to put everyone around her at ease. Moreover, Sarah embraced her younger brother's unorthodox ways without judgment or derision.[1] Yet she also shaped his upbringing. One day she discovered Abe picking on some girls. She scolded him, "Abe, you ought to be ashamed of yourself. What do you expect will become of you?" Abe quickly responded, "Be President of the U.S."[2] Sarah had a way of bringing out the best in her little brother.

Abe might never have survived childhood without his older sister. When their mother died, their father went to Kentucky in search of a new wife, leaving nine-year-old Abe and eleven-year-old Sarah to fend for themselves for months on their Indiana farm. Strong, independent, and dependable, Sarah cooked, cleaned, and took care of her little brother and their mother's cousin, Dennis Hanks.

At the age of nineteen, Sarah married Aaron Grigsby. Even though she moved just a few miles away, Abe struggled without his doting sister. A year and half later, on January 20, 1828, Sarah died giving birth to her son, who died too. A witness noted that when Lincoln heard about her passing, "he sat down in the door of the smoke house and buried his face in his hands. The tears slowly trickled from between his bony fingers and his gaunt frame shook with sobs."[3] Sarah's death sent Lincoln into a consuming grief. Having lost his mother already, he felt abandoned once again.[4]

---

[1] Goodwin, *Team of Rivals*, 48–49; Lehrman, *Lincoln "by littles,"* 8.

[2] Wilson, *Herndon's Informants*, 126.

[3] Bartelt, *Lincoln's Indiana Youth*, 36–37.

[4] Clinton, "Family," 257; Felzenberg, *Leaders We Deserved*, 20. The deaths of his mother and sister during his formative years, along with his family's periodic moves, may have developed Lincoln's self-reliance and tendency not to confide his personal thoughts to others.

While Lincoln's father and mother certainly brought him into the world, and his sister helped him survive it at a critical junctures in his life, there were other people who altered his life trajectory. Many of these names have been lost to history. For example, when Lincoln moved to New Salem, residents almost immediately took a fancy to the strange-looking newcomer. They lent him books, a horse, or a saddle when he needed one. Lincoln reciprocated these small-town niceties by helping travelers escape the mud, chopping wood for widows, and lending a hand or ax to overworked farmers. He never lived alone, always boarding with someone during these formative years.[5]

After leaving New Salem, Lincoln meet Joshua Speed, who not only took Lincoln in when he moved to Springfield, but would become his lifelong best friend. One of the proprietors of a general store in Springfield, Illinois, Speed felt pity for Lincoln when the newcomer inquired about bed furnishings (which he could not afford). Speed offered his own room and large bed to share. "Where is your room?" Lincoln asked. Speed directed him to the second floor above the store. Lincoln took his saddlebags and proceeded up the stairs. In a few minutes, Lincoln came down with a chipper countenance, declaring, "Well Speed I'm moved."[6] Speed was an essential support to Lincoln during some of his most difficult personal and professional crises, particularly in his dealings with women and marriage.

As captain of an Illinois regiment during the Black Hawk War in the spring and summer of 1832, Lincoln developed more lifelong friendships with men who later helped him in his legal and political careers. One of Springfield's most successful lawyers, John T. Stuart, encouraged Lincoln to study law and loaned him legal books. He eventually offered Lincoln a partnership opportunity in his law firm

---

[5] Winkle, *Young Eagle*, 56–58. It is significant that Lincoln devoted one-quarter of the word count in his autobiography to the six formative years he spent in New Salem.

[6] White, *Lincoln*, 80.

and invited Lincoln to join the local chess club, which certainly expanded Lincoln's social network.[7] Without Stuart, Lincoln might never have gotten on track as a lawyer and citizen of significance in Springfield.

While Stuart helped Lincoln get started as a lawyer, Stephen T. Logan made Lincoln an elite one. Esteemed in Springfield as "the greatest natural lawyer of his day," Logan possessed an impartial courtroom demeanor and a meticulous work ethic. No one came to a courtroom more prepared. He taught Lincoln that one should know one's adversary's case—both the logic and passion of it—equally as well as one's own, so that there would be no surprises in court. Logan not only had command of the law, but trained Lincoln to become well-versed in theory and judicial precedent. Lincoln's previous partner, Stuart, had permitted Lincoln to take a careless, seat-of-the-pants approach, mostly because that is how Stuart operated. Stuart had succeeded by taking advantage of spontaneous moments and relying on his own wit and ability rather than study and preparation. With Logan, Lincoln saw firsthand the methodical, industrious, particular, painstaking, and precise focus necessary to become a leading lawyer. Logan had high expectations for his junior law partner and demanded that Lincoln study authorities, precedents, and work methodically on each given lawsuit. Logan's exemplary and meticulous approach to the law rubbed off on Lincoln. In time Lincoln would be renowned for these qualities.

Shortly after their collaboration began, the Logan and Lincoln partnership became known as the top law firm in the state. During his four years with Logan, Lincoln participated in thirty-nine state supreme court cases.[8] Without Logan's influence, Lincoln might never have become the methodical, focused, and strategic man and leader he was as president.

---

[7] Winkle, *Young Eagle*, 180.

[8] White, *Lincoln*, 95; Wheeler, *Faith and Courage*, 97–98.

Lincoln's third law partner, William Herndon, nine years his junior, took care of much of the clerical work required of a law firm during their association. Herndon not only researched most of their cases, which allowed Lincoln to pursue his political avocation, but brought much camaraderie to the office.

Judge David Davis took charge of Lincoln's presidential campaign. Once elected president, Lincoln appointed Davis to the United States Supreme Court in 1862. Davis would be the executor of Lincoln's will after the assassination.[9]

Orville Browning, Norman Judd, Leonard Swett, Governor Richard Yates, Gustave Koerner, Jesse Fell, Ward Hill Lamon (who became one of Lincoln's bodyguards during his presidency) and many others played critical roles in securing the presidential nomination for Lincoln.[10]

Lincoln never forgot his Illinois friends and supporters, particularly those in Springfield. Before he left for Washington, DC, to assume his presidential duties, Lincoln gave a farewell address to his hometown at the Great Western Railroad Station on a cold, rainy day in February. As he prepared his speech, perhaps Lincoln reflected on the many acts of kindness the people of Springfield had shown him—John Stuart's lending of his law books; William and Elizabeth Butler providing room and board when he could not pay for it; how Butler had sold Lincoln's horse for him to help pay off his New Salem debts; Anson Henry's kindness and other doctors' care who had nursed him through his illness in the winter of 1840-41; Simeon and Eliza Francis's compassion and counsel during his uneven courtship of Mary Todd; Whigs who campaigned for him; Widow Sprigg and her seven children, one daughter which took care of Willie and Tad; James Gourley, a backdoor neighbor and kindly gentleman who shared a milk cow with the Lincolns and would

[9] Freehling, *Becoming Lincoln*, 72, 75.

[10] Donald, *Lincoln*, 248; Epstein, *Portrait of a Marriage*, 251.

often would soothe Mrs. Lincoln's delicate nerves when Abe had gone and lightening flickered in the distance.[11]

Having shaken many hands with so many friends and supporters, he could barely bring himself to address the crowd. Trembling with suppressed emotion, he told them that "no one, not in my situation, can appreciate my feeling of sadness at this parting. To this place, and to the kindness of these people, I owe everything." He went on to note that he had lived in Springfield for a quarter of a century, and had grown from "a young to an old man. Here my children have been born, and one is buried. I now leave, not knowing when, or whether ever, I may return, with a task before me greater than that which rested upon Washington." Then Lincoln got religious: "Without the assistance of that Divine Being, who ever attended him, I cannot succeed. With that assistance I cannot fail. Trusting in Him, who can go with me, and remain with you and be every where for good, let us confidently hope that all will yet be well. To His care commending you, as I hope in your prayers you will commend me, I bid you an affectionate farewell."[12] Reacting to Lincoln's plea, many Springfield residents responded out loud and with tears in their eyes that they would pray for him.[13]

Before his train departed, Lincoln received a flag from an admirer with the words of the first chapter of Joshua embroidered on it: "Be strong and of good courage; be not afraid, neither be thou dismayed: for the Lord thy God is with thee whithersoever thou goest. There shall not any man be able to stand before thee all the days of thy life. As I was with Moses, so shall I be with thee."[14]

The assistance of others would not end when Lincoln reached the Executive Mansion. Without John Hay and John Nicolay, his two personal secretaries, Lincoln would have been overwhelmed

---

11 Epstein, *Portrait of a Marriage*, 278-–279.

12 Basler, Lincoln's Farewell Address at Springfield, Illinois, February 11, 1861, *CW*, 4:190.

13 Burlingame, *Lincoln*, 1:759.

14 Owen, *The Man & His Faith*, 118.

by visitors, overlapping schedules, bureaucratic procedures, and the daunting task of winning a civil war. Without the stout leadership, resilience, and ultimate battlefield triumphs of Union generals such as Ulysses S. Grant, William Tecumseh Sherman, David Farragut, and Phil Sheridan, Lincoln would not have been reelected in 1864 or have been a victorious commander in chief. If Elizabeth Keckley had not provided support for his grieving wife after Willie's passing, Lincoln would not have been able to give the necessary attention to the Union war effort. Ministers and pastors provided spiritual companionship, support, and comfort during family tragedies. Frederick Douglass, a former slave, become a friend and confidante, providing the president with a different perspective on race, manumission, and equality.

As gifted, confident, self-reliant, and singularly intellectual as Lincoln became, his rise would never have occurred without the support of family members, friends, and well-wishing associates who intervened at crucial times and in various vocations throughout his life. Lincoln made a name for himself and achieved grand things for his country. Yet he could never have accomplished these things without help. No one of significance really can.

The Truth

Like many exemplary leaders, Lincoln possessed singular attributes. God gifted him with capacities for critical thinking, reasoning, speaking, resilience, persistence, clarity, storytelling, and even chopping wood. As gifted, talented, and hard-working as he was, however, Lincoln needed the others whom God put in his life to help him endure and succeed.

The truth is everyone needs others to help them survive and thrive in this world too. If you were to reflect on your own life, chances are you would run out of time thinking of all of the people—family members, friends, and even complete strangers—who interacted with you in some critical, life-changing, or life-directing way. We all need others to live in this fallen world.

Perhaps this is one reason why God wired humankind to be social beings. The fact that your God is a Triune God—one God with three distinct beings—itself demonstrates how He values community and interaction. Made in His image, you were created to have relationship with Him and with His creation. As we are told in His Holy Word, when two or three are gathered in God's name, Jesus is present with them.[15]

Exemplary leaders know they need others to succeed. After all, the Bible says that "iron sharpens iron, and one man sharpens another."[16] Moreover, Christian leaders know that men and women of faith can nurture and lift up one another with God's blessing and divine support. We can "rejoice with those who rejoice, weep with those who weep."[17] Christ-centered friends not only provide one another "earnest counsel,"[18] but encourage each other's spiritual growth and faith walk with God.[19]

Your Heavenly Father gives you a clear exhortation to "love one another as I have loved you." In case anyone needs to be reminded what it means to love one another, the writer goes on to say that "greater love has no one than this, that someone lay down his life for his friends."[20]

Jesus is the best friend you could ever have. Just as the most gifted and developed leaders need help in reaching their desired outcomes, you need help in reaching heaven. You cannot get there on your own. You need Jesus. He's the one you need to know. Only He can take you to the Promised Land, thanks to His agape love and sacrifice on the cross of Calvary. Without Him, you can

---

15 Matt. 18:20.
16 Prov. 27:17.
17 Rom. 12:15.
18 Prov. 27:9.
19 Rom. 1:12.
20 John 15:12–14.

do nothing of long-lasting significance. With Jesus, all things are possible, including your eternal salvation.[21] The Bible says, "For by grace you have been saved through faith. And this is not your own doing; it is the gift of God, not a result of works, so that no one may boast."[22] As the great hymn says, what a friend we—and *you*—have in Jesus!

Your Life

Reflecting on your own life, who are some of the people who intervened or made a significant difference in your life? In what ways did they make an impact on your life trajectory?

Why do people think they can make it in life or get to heaven by going it alone? When are you most vulnerable to this way of thinking? Why?

While Jesus is much more than simply your best friend (He's your Savior!), how does thinking of Jesus as the perfect friend or the best friend you could ever have potentially enrich your relationship with Him?

---

21 Matt. 19:26.

22 Eph. 2:8–9.

19

Ambition

Whatever you do, work heartily, as for the Lord and not for men, knowing that from the Lord you will receive the inheritance as your reward. You are serving the Lord Christ.
—Colossians 3:23–24

The Lincoln Way

Ambition is like water for a leader—too little can dehydrate and weaken one, and too much can inebriate and devour one.

While Abraham Lincoln's ambition is rightfully acknowledged in the historical record, many contemporaries, after Lincoln had passed, made his ambition stand out more by underscoring his poverty and humble origins. John Nicolay and John Hay asserted that Lincoln had been born "in the midst of the most unpromising circumstances that ever witnessed the advent of a hero into this world."[1] Another contemporary said that no one should "object to Abraham Lincoln because of his lowly birth. The Saviour of Mankind was born in a manger and his lineage miraculous and otherwise of lowly birth."[2] Even today, the hagiographic claim is made that "Lincoln was born in a log cabin that he built with his own hands."[3]

---

[1] Miller, *Lincoln's Virtues*, 54.

[2] Wilson, *Herndon's Informants*, 48.

[3] Peterson, *Lincoln in American Memory*, 196.

Lincoln in fact was born on a mattress of corn husks in a nest of bear rugs in a one-room, windowless, dirt-floored log cabin on the banks of Nolin Creek, at Sinking Spring Farm, near Hodgenville, Kentucky, on Sunday, February 12, 1809.[4] Readers today are wise to note the part personal ambition played in his rise from this beginning. Looking back, Lincoln condensed his early life into a brief sentence—that he lived according to the "short and simple annals of the poor."[5]

Yet from his very earliest days, Lincoln displayed a unique ambition for something beyond the backwoods. He believed "that he was going to be something," remembered Sophie Hanks, his cousin.[6] As one historian says, Lincoln possessed "a vision of an alternative future."[7] Indeed, Lincoln once told a neighbor that he did not "intend to delve, grub, shuck corn, split rails and the like" for the rest of his life. "I'll study and get ready, and then the chance will come," he insisted.[8]

At twenty-three years of age, Lincoln wrote that "every man is said to have his peculiar ambition." He desired to be "truly esteemed" by his fellow men, "by rendering myself worthy of their esteem." He did not know if he would "succeed in gratifying this ambition," for he certainly acknowledged that he had been "born and have ever remained in the most humble walks of life. I have no wealthy or popular relations to recommend me."[9] Yet the same man who penned these words believed himself capable of good and grand things that would elicit the honor, respect, and admiration of his neighbors and countrymen.

---

[4] Keneally, *Lincoln*, 1.

[5] Wilson, *Herndon's Informants*, 57.

[6] Goodwin, *Leadership,* 9.

[7] Goodwin, *Leadership,* 9.

[8] Goodwin, *Leadership*, 9.

[9] Basler, Lincoln to the People of Sangamo County, March 9, 1832, *CW,* 1:8–9.

One of the fascinating realities of Lincoln is that, while contemporaries and subsequent historians lauded him for his appeal to the common man, he was anything but common. His friends considered him to be the most ambitious man they had ever met. He burned for achievement, success, and making his mark on the world.[10] "To all human appearance the early life of Abraham Lincoln was as unpromising for becoming a great man as you could imagine," recalled one Illinois attorney who had known Lincoln. "Indeed I would say it was forbidding, and proves to me that nature bestowed on him an irrepressible will and innate greatness of mind, to enable to break through all those barriers & iron gates and reach the portion he did in life."[11] William Herndon, his junior law partner for over two decades, described Lincoln's ambition as "a little engine that knew no rest."[12] Lincoln's lifelong friend Joshua Speed also recalled how Lincoln had told him that "he had done nothing to make any human being remember that he had lived—and that to connect his name with the events transpiring in his day & generation and so impress himself upon them," he would have to "link his name to something that would redound to the interest of his fellow man was what he desired to live for."[13] Lincoln told Speed he possessed an "irrepressible desire" to accomplish something while he lived.[14]

After being elected to the House of Representatives in 1847, Lincoln wrote Herndon, "As you are all so anxious for me to distinguish myself, I have concluded to do so, before long."[15] Herndon surely agreed. No one had to tell Lincoln to distinguish himself and make his mark. Everyone saw Lincoln's raw determination to succeed and make a name for himself.

---

10 Oates, *Lincoln*, 51.

11 Wilson, *Herndon's Informants*, 67–68.

12 Epstein, *Portrait of a Marriage*, 97.

13 Wilson, *Herndon's Informants*, 197.

14 Shenk, *Lincoln's Melancholy*, 65.

15 Basler, Lincoln to William Herndon, December 13, 1847, *CW*, 1:420.

When running for the Illinois senate in 1854, Lincoln worked relentlessly to trap his foe, Senator Stephen Douglas, by doing what no one had ever done before: he followed the senator everywhere in central Illinois, badgering him to debate. Lincoln would let Douglas talk, then tell people that he would answer Douglas later, after the locals ate dinner.[16] Lincoln deployed the same strategy in 1858, ultimately forcing Douglas into a series of debates that have reverberated in history. Lincoln would not be deterred in his pursuits and desired outcomes.

Lincoln exhibited significant ambition as a young boy. His "mind & the Ambition of the man soared above us," recalled one Indiana neighbor. "He naturally assumed the leadership of the boys. He read & thoroughly read his books whilst we played. Hence he was above us and became our guide and leader & in this position he never failed to be the leader."[17] Out on a desolate frontier, teetering on the brink of poverty and hardship, young Abe told his sister that he expected to be president of the United States someday.[18] He had big plans for his life from the very beginning.

When Lincoln first moved to Springfield, he spoke publicly and nostalgically about the ambition of the nation's Founding Fathers. Back then, Lincoln explained, the creation of a free and independent nation began as "an undecided experiment" even as it eventually turned out "to be a successful one."[19] They staked their fame and destiny on the "success of that experiment." The Founding Fathers believed in "the capability of a people to govern themselves" despite the odds that this republican experiment might fail. Empowered by their ambition, they risked their fortunes and reputations for the cause.

---

16 Freehling, *Becoming Lincoln*, 157.

17 Wilson, *Herndon's Informants*, 114.

18 Wilson, *Herndon's Informants*, 124.

19 Basler, Lincoln's Address before the Young Men's Lyceum of Springfield, Illinois, January 27, 1838, *CW*, 1:113–14. The quotes in this paragraph and the next come from this source.

While the ambition of the Founding Fathers exhibited a noble determination and aspiration, Lincoln warned that other "men of ambition and talents" would "continue to spring up amongst us. And, when they do, they will as naturally seek the gratification of their ruling passion, as others have so done before them." The country would need to be on guard for ambitious despots like Napoleon, Caesar, or Alexander. Dictators such as these burn for distinction, but might not honor the vision the Founding Fathers put forth of a government run by the people. An ambitious, toxic leader would need to be confronted and defeated by a united people who remained "attached to the government and laws, and generally intelligent, to successfully frustrate his designs." For Lincoln, ambition could tapped for good or evil. The people of the United States, of course, should be on guard against those possessing extreme self-centered ambition.

Lincoln could make the case for positive and negative ambition because he certainly struggled with his own ambitions. One reason his self-centered ambition never completely dominated his soul is simply because he experienced failure so often. He went into the Black Hawk war as a captain and returned as a private. He had to sell his surveyor's equipment to pay off debt. He lost his first campaign for the state legislature as well as the first campaign he ran for Congress. Four times he suffered defeat as a candidate for presidential elector. Politicians in his own party denied his expectation and desire to be appointed the commissioner of the General Land Office. He failed miserably as a businessman too. These setbacks stayed with Lincoln for the rest of his life. He told his law partner Herndon that he remained keenly aware of his failures and that they made him "miserable." [20] In his mid-forties he lamented, "With *me*, the race of ambition has been a failure—a flat failure."[21] If ambition

[20] Burlingame, *Lincoln*, 1:358.

[21] Basler, Lincoln's Fragment on Stephen A. Douglas, December, 1856, *CW*, 2:383.

led to frequent failure, then perhaps, upon reflection, self-indulgent ambition should be eschewed and suppressed.

As he grew older and his failures and successes accumulated, Lincoln's ambition morphed into aspiration. At one time in his life, his most ambitious desire had been to become president of the United States. Once elected president, however, his aspiration crowded out his ambition. Lincoln now wanted to win the war, save the Union, and eliminate slavery as a national scourge—even if that meant sticking with war decisions and policies that would put his second term in jeopardy.

Late in the Civil War, he addressed Union soldiers on the importance of their cause. "It is not merely for today," he implored, "but for all time to come that we should perpetuate for our children's children this great and free government, which we have enjoyed all our lives." The president told them that while he temporarily occupied "this big White House," anyone of their children "may look to come here as my father's child has." The struggle to secure the nation should be maintained, Lincoln said, "to secure such an inestimable jewel."[22] He desired that the nation remain a "nation of aspiration"—just like his own life. A Union filled with aspirational people remained one worth saving.[23]

One of the remarkable aspects of Lincoln's life is that he found a way to channel his ambition for the good of the Union. Lincoln's ambition had been checked and transformed into an aspirational mindset. Having been humiliated and humbled often, he remained humble while pursuing great and grand outcomes. He relied more on God and the promises of His Word. He became more comfortable with the outcomes God intended for his country.

Eventually, Lincoln distinguished himself by serving the many different interests of each region of the country, freeing the slaves,

---

[22] Basler, Lincoln's Speech to One Hundred Sixty-Sixth Ohio Regiment, August 22, 1864, *CW*, 7:512.

[23] Lowry, *Lincoln Unbound*, 3, 8.

and saving the Union. Throughout the war, he suppressed many of his personal desires and plans for the nation. While never completely abandoning his own ambitions, he realized and believed that the needs of others must come before his personal agenda. Along the way, and ironically, he made a name for himself, a name that lives on in posterity.

The Truth

Ambition is such a two-sided word—it can be a good quality to possess in certain circumstances, but it can often be a destructive and self-centered force in one's life too. More often than not, your sinful flesh tempts you to act on your own self-centered ambitions. Jesus reminds you, however, "What does it profit a man if he gains the whole world and loses or forfeits himself?"[24] Indeed, if your ambition causes you to exalt yourself, the Bible promises that you will be humbled.[25] Too often leaders in today's world act on "the desires of the flesh and the desires of the eyes" and take "pride in possessions." These, the Bible explains, are "not from the Father" but "from the world."[26] Instead, you are called to "look not only" to your "own interests, but also to the interest of others."

Scripture further implores that "whatever is true, whatever is honorable, whatever is just, whatever is pure, whatever is lovely, whatever is commendable, if there is any excellence, if there is anything worthy of praise, think about these things."[27] When you put others before yourself and focus on God-pleasing endeavors, your ambition is not really your ambition anymore. Your soul has been moved and inspired by the Holy Spirit. You are living for others and carrying out God's plan for your life. When God's plan comes

24 Luke 9:25.

25 Matt. 23:12.

26 1 John 2:16.

27 Phil. 2:4, 8.

before your desires, you know that, by God's grace, your ambition has been checked and channeled for God's purposes.

Christians can encourage one another to live out a Christocentric life and not one focused on one's self-interest and misaligned ambition. The Bible teaches, "Since we are surrounded by so great a cloud of witnesses, let us also lay aside every weight, and sin which clings so closely, and let us run with endurance the race that is set before us, looking to Jesus, the founder and perfecter of our faith, who for the joy that was set before him endured the cross, despising the shame, and is seated at the right hand of the throne of God."[28]

Christians live for Jesus first and others second. Their ambitions become eclipsed by the inspiration they receive from God's Word. When the Holy Spirit works on your heart, your ambitions disappear or change into God-pleasing endeavors. Responding to Christ's love and by the power of the Holy Spirit, a Christ-centered leader *wants* to do God's will. Jesus says it like this: "Whoever would be great among you must be your servant, and whoever would be first among you must be slave of all. For even the Son of Man came not to be served but to serve, and to give his life as a ransom for many."[29]

Make no mistake: the will to live for God and others before oneself is not easy. You, like all human beings, are a sinner with a sinful flesh. You are self-centered, and your selfish ambitions can overcome and consume you just like everyone else.

Jesus knows the allure of toxic, earthly ambition. When the devil took Him "to a very high mountain and showed him all the kingdoms of the world and their glory" and "said to him, 'All these I will give you, if you will fall down and worship me,'" any man's ambition would have been tempted by the offer. Jesus, however, refused to give into the temptation. He responded: "Be gone, Satan!

---

[28] Heb. 12:1–2.

[29] Mark 10:43–45.

For it is written, "'You shall worship the Lord your God and him only shall you serve.'"[30]

Thank God you can find purpose, joy, and fulfillment in pursuing God's plan for your life. Whether you attain the fame of a Lincoln or not, only time will tell. More importantly, you will experience the joy of the Lord and hear the heavenly acclaim that really matters: "Well done, good and faithful servant. You have been faithful over a little; I will set you over much. Enter into the joy of your master."[31]

Your Life

There is no doubt that Lincoln was an ambitious man. Would you consider yourself an ambitious person? Why or why not?

Lincoln wanted to leave a legacy with his fellow human beings and link his name to something for posterity. What legacy do you want to leave and for whom? Why?

How do you make sure your ambitions or desires remain God-pleasing and centered in God's plans for you?

---

[30] Matt. 4:9–10.

[31] Matt. 25:21.

20

Resilience

For this light momentary affliction is preparing for us an eternal weight of glory beyond all comparison, as we look not to the things that are seen but to the things that are unseen. For the things that are seen are transient, but the things that are unseen are eternal.
—2 Corinthians 4:17–18

Effective and compelling leaders are resilient.

The most defining characteristic of Lincoln's life is his resilience. Stories of resilience, one chapter after another, fill his biography. Examples of his persistence, courage, and ability to rise after setbacks are numerous. Family hardship, a dysfunctional relationship with an emotionally abusive father, his mother's death, his father's literal abandonment on the frontier, poverty and economic privation, the lack of a formal education, derelict and careless business partners, political miscalculations, lost elections, public criticism and vicious name-calling, melancholy and depression, incompetent military commanders, extreme political platforms and agendas, and handling the fallout from emancipation are just a few of the adversities Lincoln confronted and overcame.

Before one can demonstrate resiliency, one must first experience hardship and failure. Yet Lincoln survived and advanced through his failures. Moreover, even as he endured and prevailed over incredible difficulties, he never sacrificed his kind, compassionate, and fun-loving personality. He stayed true to himself and remained comfortable in his own skin. Furthermore, he learned from hardship and grew as a leader and spiritual man. His setbacks prepared him for setups in the next chapters of his life.

Many who study Lincoln today admire his devotion to country, cause, and God. His resilience helped him rise beyond modern labels or self-selected identities of sect, region, race, class, or party.[1] If George Washington is the Indispensable Man in American history, Lincoln is the Resilient One. There is no question that if the nation had not had a strong and dogged president during the Civil War, the country would have remained permanently fractured.[2]

Long before he became president, Lincoln exhibited resiliency in his various vocations. During his six years in New Salem, Lincoln drifted from one job to another and survived significant changes in his life. Moreover, when his general store partner took all the profits and then died suddenly, Lincoln took responsibility for both his share of the store's debts and that of his negligent partner—something that he did not have to do, legally or ethically. Nevertheless, Lincoln insisted on paying all creditors in full—a rare and unusual gesture in a time where many other debtors simply skipped town in the middle of the night like Denton Offutt—Lincoln's first employer in New Salem—did. This integrity and resolve to pay off his "national debt" not only impressed the locals of New Salem, but earned Lincoln the nickname "Honest Abe."[3]

Resilience is a characteristic that allows one's strength or influence to persevere over the long haul. Lincoln's suppleness developed over his lifetime and from various experiences. When his business ventures failed in New Salem in the 1830s, "Uncle Jimmy" Short bought Lincoln's surveying equipment at a foreclosure auction and returned it to Lincoln. Touched by this generosity, Lincoln not only paid Uncle Jimmy back after a few months, but also gave him a plum patronage job many years later when he became president.[4]

---

1 McDonald, "Spiritual Growth of a Public Man," 93.

2 Leekley, *Catton's Reflections on Civil War*, 31–32.

3 McPherson, *Lincoln*, 5; White, *Lincoln*, 65.

4 Freehling, *Becoming Lincoln*, 44.

Lincoln had not only overcome his setback, he had triumphed to the point of helping one who had aided him.

Disappointments, disasters, and defeats did not stop the lawyer from Springfield. One of the more underrated setbacks in Lincoln's life occurred when he did not receive a patronage position—commissioner of the General Land Office—after campaigning earnestly for Zachary Taylor in presidential campaign of 1848. When party leadership selected another Whig, who had opposed Taylor's presidency, for the position, Lincoln felt his wishes had been trampled "in the dust."[5] Thoroughly disgusted with the move, Lincoln abandoned politics. Yet five years later, after passage of the Kansas-Nebraska Act, he returned to the political scene.

Unfortunately, he failed to get elected as senator from Illinois in 1855, in another bitter disappointment. It was particularly hard to swallow because he had led all candidates through the first six ballots. Lincoln eventually felt compelled to threw his support to Lyman Trumbull, an anti-Nebraska Democrat (soon to be become Republican), who finally got elected on the tenth ballot.

As Lincoln's campaign team coped with the devastating loss, Lincoln endured an acute case of his "hypo." Joseph Gillespie, who had known Lincoln for decades, said he had never seen his friend so "cut and mortified" or "more dejected" in his life. Lincoln told him he "could bear defeat by his enemies with pretty good grace, but it was hard to be wounded in the house of his friends."[6]

While Mary Lincoln would never forgive Trumbull or his wife for their betrayal,[7] Lincoln showed remarkable class and resilience on the evening of the election by attending a reception held at Ninian and Elizabeth Edwards's home, which had originally been intended as a victory party. Lincoln surprised many people by showing up. Withholding his bitterness at the loss, he told Elizabeth that he was

---

5 Shenk, *Lincoln's Melancholy*, 106.

6 Shenk, *Lincoln's Melancholy*, 141–42.

7 Keneally, *Lincoln*, 61

"not too disappointed to congratulate my friend Trumbull." Lincoln not only shook Trumbull's hand, but won him over too. Trumbull, admiring Lincoln's behavior, later wrote him, "I shall continue to labor for the success of the Republican cause and the advancement at the next election to the place now occupied by Douglas of that *Friend*, who was instrumental in promoting my own."[8] Lincoln was hard to resist.

In 1856, Lincoln suffered yet another political setback when he lost his bid to be elected vice president, alongside John Fremont, on the 1856 Republican ticket. In 1858, he took on "the Little Giant"—Stephen A. Douglas—for the US Senate. In his first debate with Douglas in Ottawa, Lincoln stumbled against an attacking opponent. He rushed through his speech, failing to use much of the time allotted to him. His tone wavered, and he did not sound like himself. He resorted to clichés and even lapsed into legal speak, which was all but incomprehensible to his audience. Moreover, he did not answer Douglas's challenges or questions directly. He looked overmatched and passive.

Lincoln's advisors told him that he needed to be more aggressive. Motivated to bounce back, Lincoln upped his debate game and showed a gritty determination to exceed expectations throughout the rest of the debates. The Lincoln-Douglas debates became riveting political theater. Huge crowds massed for the opportunity to listen to both candidates. Newspaper reporters gave breathless accounts of the exchanges and arguments.

Nevertheless, after traveling more than 4,300 miles around the state for three exhilarating months and outpolling the Little Giant by 125,430 votes to 121,609, Lincoln lost yet another bid for office. (Republican votes were not evenly spread by district, and Douglas won 54–46 in the legislature on a seat-by-seat basis).[9]

---

[8] White, *Lincoln*, 209.

[9] Donald, *Lincoln*, 287; Keneally, *Lincoln*, 72–73. Even though he lost, Lincoln felt he was on the right side of history and considered the contests with Douglas the high point of his life.

Most, including Lincoln, believed his political career had ended. He told one reporter that he felt like a little boy who'd had his finger smashed—too big to cry and too hurt to laugh. Yet resilience remained in Lincoln's DNA, and he responded to the challenge. On the walk home from the telegraph office the night he learned of his defeat, he slipped on the road. He could not resist the metaphor in regard to his political situation. His loss had been "*a slip and not a fall*."[10] He told friends that he looked forward to another fight and predicted victory in the future. Douglas had won this round, but a long political struggle remained.[11] Determined that "the fight must go on," Lincoln ardently believed the "cause of civil liberty must not be surrendered at the end of one, or even, one hundred defeats."[12] Though he had lost, the slavery issue remained unsettled. "New splits and division will soon be upon our adversaries," he predicted, and "we shall have fun again."[13]

While many Americans were surprised at Lincoln's presidential election victory in 1860, the secession of Southern states was what surprised him. For all of Lincoln's emotional intelligence and discernment, he had seriously misjudged the likelihood of the border states adopting emancipation, even when coupled with a policy of colonization and the willingness of most blacks to leave the country of their birth. More profoundly, he underestimated racism in the North as an obstacle to ending slavery. Certainly aware of secessionist talk, Lincoln had mistakenly believed that a silent majority of Southerners remained patriotic and would come to their senses and avoid secession when the passions of the moment subsided.[14]

---

10 Donald, *Lincoln*, 288.

11 Burlingame, *Lincoln*, 1:549–50; Oates, *With Malice Toward None*, 226. Douglas later supported Lincoln in office. He also helped rally Democrats to the Union cause early in the war.

12 Basler, Lincoln to Henry Asbury, November 19, 1858, *CW*, 3:339.

13 Basler, Lincoln to Eleazar Paine, November 19, 1858, *CW*, 3:340.

14 Foner, "Lincoln and Colonization," 166; McPherson, *Lincoln*, 31.

Lincoln continued to underestimate Southern Unionism during the Civil War and made other mistakes. He thought the rebellion would collapse after brutal losses at Vicksburg and Gettysburg, to no avail. He gave too many critical commands to "political" generals or incompetent professionals. The Union army suffered greatly and unnecessarily due to too many generals who either had the "slows" or reckless abandon, and Lincoln was the commander in chief who ultimately selected them.[15]

As an inexperienced executive, Lincoln tried to do everything himself and did not delegate or communicate enough with cabinet officials and government subordinates. As commander in chief, Lincoln had a good strategic sense but also knew his limitations. Not being a professional military man, he hesitated to draft military orders and offered only suggestions—"my poor mite," he would say—rather than commands to his generals, when clarity might have helped.[16] Moreover, his handling of the cotton trade left much to be desired. Fraud and corruption took place in the sending of supplies to the South and bringing Confederate cotton to the North. Lincoln issued valuable trade permits to friends in the North, attempting to placate Massachusetts cotton manufacturers as well as merchants and politicos in New York.[17]

Yet Lincoln learned from all of these mistakes and overcame them with sheer determination, persistence, and grit. Realizing the Confederacy would not settle for peace unless they could keep their peculiar institution, Lincoln issued the Emancipation Proclamation, allowing freedmen and escaped slaves to serve in the Union army. He condoned the use of total war to defeat the Confederacy. Even after many battlefield tragedies, he insisted that he would "maintain this contest until successful, or till I die, or am conquered, or my term expires, or Congress or the country forsakes me."[18] Eventually,

---

[15] Burlingame, *Lincoln*, 2:594; Oates, *Lincoln*, 126–27.

[16] Donald, *Lincoln*, 439.

[17] Burlingame, *Lincoln*, 2:763.

[18] Basler, Lincoln to William Seward, June 28, 1862, *CW*, 5:292.

he found generals—Phil Sheridan, William Tecumseh Sherman, and Ulysses S. Grant in particular—who understood that defeating the Confederate armies was the prime objective of the war. Lincoln gradually exhibited a more decisive, methodical, forward-leaning disposition in confronting the severing of the Union. He ignored pressure to bow to economic and political considerations. Instead he focused relentlessly on the higher moral ground of saving a more perfect Union. Even as manpower and resources were needed on the warfront, Lincoln ensured that the construction of the Capitol Building continued, to illustrate his resolution that the Union would remain strong. Observing the growth of Lincoln's mental toughness up close, John Hay declared that "the Tycoon is in fine whack." The president "is managing this war, the draft, foreign relations, and planning a reconstruction of the Union, all at once. I never knew with what tyrannous authority he rules the cabinet, till now. The most important things he decries & there is no cavil." Lincoln, he asserted proudly, "will not be bullied—even by his friends."[19]

Too humble to brag about his own resilience and determination as president, Lincoln did note in his second State of the Union address, one month before the Emancipation Proclamation became law, that "the dogmas of the quiet past, are inadequate to the stormy present. The occasion is piled high with difficulty, and we must rise with the occasion." In reflecting on the tattered state of the Union, Lincoln's words also reflected his personal beliefs about persistence and overcoming adversity. He insisted that "as our case is new, so we must think anew, and act anew. We must disenthrall ourselves, and then we shall save our country." Taking the long view of things, as he often did, Lincoln continued, "Fellow-citizens, *we* cannot escape history. We of this Congress and this administration, will be remembered in spite of ourselves. No personal significance, or insignificance, can spare one or another of us." Having himself

[19] Oates, *With Malice Toward None*, 358.

passed through many ordeals and overcome hardships of all sorts, Lincoln invoked 1 Peter 4:12, asserting:

> [T]he fiery trial through which we pass, will light us down, in honor or dishonor, to the latest generation. We *say* we are for the Union. The world will not forget that we say this. We know how to save the Union. The world knows we do know how to save it. We—even *we here*—hold the power, and bear the responsibility. In *giving* freedom to the slave, we *assure* freedom to the *free*—honorable alike in what we give, and what we preserve. We shall nobly save, or meanly lose, the last best, hope of earth.[20]

After the Union disaster at Chancellorsville, in early May 1863, Lincoln's spirits dipped to a new low. Stunned by the horrific news, the commander in chief turned as pale as a ghost. With tears streaming down his face, Lincoln paced the room, exclaiming, "My God! My God! What will the country say! What will the country say!" According to Noah Brooks, who read Lincoln the dispatch, the president had never seemed "so broken, so dispirited."[21]

Chancellorsville shook him, and then the criticism poured in relentlessly. Lincoln admitted that it might be "a misfortune for the nation that he was elected president. But having been elected by the people, he meant to be president, and to perform his duty according to *his* best understanding, if he had to die for it."[22] Despite feeling like the loneliest man in the country at the nadir of the war, Lincoln pressed on.

While contemporary Americans acclaim Lincoln's presidency, he endured harsh criticism in real time. He was viewed as neither a

---

[20] Basler, Lincoln's Annual Message to Congress, December 1, 1862, *CW*, 5:537.

[21] Burlingame, *Lincoln*, 2:498.

[22] Donald, *Lincoln*, 435–436.

liberal nor a conservative statesman. Most contemporaries considered him an ineffective chief executive. More generous critics viewed him as honest and well-intentioned, but lacking in force and execution. Hostile critics saw him as weak, vacillating, and opportunistic. During an unprecedented and tragic civil war, his administration seemed directionless. Moreover, he seemed unable to cope with or put an end to a national crisis.[23]

Lincoln not only put an end to the crisis and saved the Union, however; he did it with persistence, grit, and resiliency. Despite a traumatic and impoverished youth, Lincoln demonstrated psychological maturity, moral clarity, and impeccable integrity in middle age. His relentless and irrepressible leadership inspired many of his contemporaries, and still inspires Americans and students of history today.[24]

Lincoln, of course, provides a model of one who turned life's setbacks into setups. While he certainly did not see his misfortunes as hidden stepping stones at the time, one paradox of Lincoln's political career is that his defeats were as advantageous as his victories. If he, for example, had been elected senator in 1855 for a six-year term, he never would have campaigned again for Stephen Douglas's senate seat in 1858 and lost. And if he had not lost his senate campaign in 1858, he would never have run for the presidency in 1860.[25]

Moreover, years of constant win-loss scenarios in law and politics conditioned him to roll with the inevitable valley and mountaintop moments. Combine these experiences with his love for reading, storytelling, and telling jokes, and one can see how Lincoln built up a formidable foundation for resiliency.[26]

Lincoln's diligence and persistence, of course, would not have been possible without preparation and a prodigious work ethic. As a venerated attorney, Lincoln advised and mentored young lawyers to

---

23 Donald, *Lincoln Reconsidered*, 121–22.

24 Burlingame, *Lincoln*, 2:834.

25 Epstein, *Portrait of a Marriage*, 183.

26 Guelzo, *Lincoln*, 361.

rest their cases more on solid preparation than on witness-badgering or emotional pleas before the jury. Certainly "extemporaneous speaking should be practised and cultivated," Lincoln admitted, as this speech "is the lawyer's avenue to the public…And yet there is not a more fatal error to young lawyers than relying too much on speech-making. If any one, upon his rare powers of speaking, shall claim an exemption from the drudgery of the law, his case is a failure in advance."[27] Good lawyers put in the necessary time and hard work to be prepared.

Lincoln's own law office looked extremely messy at first glance. He had a parcel of documents tied with a string and classified with the words "When you can't find it anywhere else, look into this."[28] Apple seeds and orange rinds littered the floor. Herndon, a news hound, contributed newspapers and broadsheets strewn all over the floor. Lincoln filed papers in his stovepipe hat, a habit he'd picked up during his time as a postmaster-surveyor in New Salem. He made frequent use of the sofa, though his long frame was too big for it. Yet he worked hard to make sure he had fully prepared for each case in hand. Hard work was an essential ingredient in Lincoln's resiliency portfolio.

He may have often been called "Old Abe," but as a fifty-one year old president, Lincoln was a generation younger than his predecessor, James Buchanan. Vigorous and athletic, he kept up a relentless pace that tired out companions twenty years younger. He took no vacations, and his energy seemed inexhaustible.[29] An industrious individual, "Mr Lincoln was so unlike all other men I had ever known before or seen or known since that there is no one to whom I can Compare him," recalled Joshua Speed. "In all his habits eating, sleeping, reading Conversation & study, he was … regularly irregular. That is he had no stated time for eating, no

---

27 Basler, Lincoln Fragment: Notes for a Law Lecture, July 1, 1850?, *CW*, 2:81.

28 Keneally, *Lincoln*, 47.

29 Donald, *Lincoln*, 259.

fixed time for going to bed or getting up. No course of reading was ever chalked out."[30] According to another contemporary, Lincoln possessed "immense physical endurance. Night after night he would work late and hard without being wilted by it, and he always seemed ready for the next day's work as though he had done nothing the day before."[31] His son, Robert, said that "his methods of office working were simply those of a very busy man who worked at all hours."[32]

When George Latham failed to get into Harvard University and sought consolation, Lincoln sympathized and expressed great "pain" at the rejection. Then he encouraged young Latham to try again and "allow no feeling of discouragement to seize, and prey upon you." Lincoln insisted that George could get into Harvard and eventually graduate from Harvard if he worked hard and persisted. "'Must' is the word," he asserted. "I know not how to aid you, save in the assurance of one of mature age, and much severe experience, that you can not fail, if you resolutely determine, that you will not." George had to get Harvard's president to "grant you an interview, and point out the readiest way to remove, or overcome, the obstacles which have thwarted you." Lincoln continued to encourage the young man insisting that "in your temporary failure there is no evidence that you may not yet be a better scholar, and a more successful man in the great struggle of life, than many others, who have entered college more easily."[33] Drawing on his own experiences, Lincoln contended that one rejection should not be enough to deter a motivated young man from pursuing his dreams.

In addition to his ability to turn setbacks into setups, the inspiration and encouragement he received from God's Word, and his extraordinary work ethic, Lincoln's courage and confidence helped shape his resiliency too. One contemporary attorney declared that Lincoln's boldness and courage were not merely a "physical

[30] Wilson, *Herndon's Informants*, 498–99.

[31] Guelzo, *Lincoln*, 276.

[32] Guelzo, *Lincoln*, 276.

[33] Basler, Lincoln to George C. Latham, July 22, 1860, *CW*, 4:87.

courage" in the face of death, nor a "higher form of courage that inspires noble action in times of public or private danger," nor a still higher form of courage "that invests the countenance of the hero with that strange and flashing light in the hour of battle amidst the shock and conflict of armies, leading on to deeds of valor that startle and dazzle the world." Lincoln possessed "that highest of all forms of courage, that is only ambitious to do good, that rising far above the selfish prejudices of men strikes out boldly and grandly for liberty and humanity, that lofty courage that is inspired of Heaven, that dares to do *right* whatever may be the opinion of the world and *fears* only to do wrong." The attorney felt confident that in "regard the history of Earths *great men,*" there would be "few, if any, more prominent characters" than Lincoln.[34]

While Lincoln had always possessed inner strength, his four years as president certainly increased his self-confidence. Herndon wrote that Lincoln had "unbounded confidence in himself" and "thought he could do anything that other men could or would try to do."[35] So confident was he in his own abilities, Lincoln rarely consulted with his cabinet members and seldom revealed his thoughts until he had made up his mind. He dominated his cabinet, which is quite extraordinary considering the talented group of politicians he had assembled.[36] When Lincoln made a decision, as he did in replacing War Secretary Cameron with Stanton, he did so methodically, deliberately, and firmly. In the winter of 1861–1862, the *New York World* praised Lincoln's masculinity, assertiveness, poise, and "moral robustness."[37] While the president could often be too slow and deliberate in making a decision, once he made one, he stuck to it. The country had had many presidents in the past who made decisions quickly, but none who stayed so resolute and determined to bring their decisions to fruition.

---

[34] Wilson, *Herndon's Informants*, 193.

[35] Guelzo, *Lincoln*, 76.

[36] Gienapp, "Lincoln and Presidential Leadership," 67, 69.

[37] Burlingame, *Lincoln*, 2:285.

Lincoln never lost faith in himself or his God. When Lincoln nominated the Honorable William Fessenden, of Maine, to succeed Salmon Chase as secretary of Treasury, Fessenden hesitated. "Fessenden, the Lord has not deserted me thus far, and He is not going to now," Lincoln persisted. "You must accept!"[38] Indeed, Lincoln took on the role of cheerleader. He sustained the confidence and spirit of his cabinet members, party leaders, and military officials throughout the war. He guided and exhorted his colleagues with good humor, energy, steady focus, and clarity of purpose. Moreover, he learned from his mistakes, transcended the jealousy of rivals, and grew in his understanding of how to connect with people, collectively as well as individually.[39]

The more people worked with Lincoln, the more they saw his remarkable abilities and respected them—particularly his mental steadfastness and resilience. Even as he wrestled with melancholy, hardship, and the horrific casualties of war, Lincoln remained a determined optimist. In his exchanges with friends and associates, he was the one who constantly encouraged and lifted their spirits.[40]

Lincoln always possessed "psychic radiance."[41] His good friend and political ally Joseph Gillespie noted the specialness of Lincoln's "magnetic influence" with the masses.[42] Secretary of State William Seward, a critic of Lincoln during the 1860 election, told his wife that Lincoln possessed "almost superhuman" magnanimity, and that "his confidence and sympathy increase every day."[43] Poet Walt Whitman saw the president often in 1864, when public criticism of his leadership as commander in chief reached an apex. Lincoln "has conscience & homely shrewdness," he insisted, which "conceals an enormous tenacity under his mild, gawky western manner. The

[38] Carpenter, *Six Months at the White House*, 201.

[39] Goodwin, *Team of Rivals*, 703.

[40] Shenk, *Lincoln's Melancholy*, 147.

[41] Burlingame, *Lincoln,* 1:361.

[42] Burlingame, *Lincoln*, 1:361.

[43] Goodwin, *Team of Rivals*, 364.

difficulties of his situation have been unprecedented in the history of statesmanship. That he has conserved the government so far is a miracle itself."[44]

William Herndon commented numerous times on Lincoln's confidence—a "full and complete confidence in himself, self-thoughtful, self-helping, and self-supporting, relying on no man."[45] Lincoln impressed people with what Herndon called "that peculiar nature," an ability and differentiator that revealed his contentment in being himself. Joshua Speed insisted that Lincoln's "perfect naturalness" made him special. His mannerisms and style could not be replicated. He reminded people of no one else. Comfortable in his own skin, Lincoln remained true to himself and had no pretentiousness about him. If he did not know something, he acknowledged it. He did not fear looking ignorant or being vulnerable with his shortcomings. He had to be true to himself. John W. Forney, an influential newspaper editor who saw the president often, asserted that Lincoln's "intense individuality" and confidence to stand on his own was one of the "hidden forces of his character."[46] Admiral David Dixon Porter, who knew Lincoln during the Civil War, noted the president's profound originality. Another associate recognized that Lincoln's modest demeanor should not overshadow his "strong individuality." Lincoln possessed a "reserved power," or quiet dignity, that would not allow people to take advantage of him.[47]

This quiet dignity and inner power sustained Lincoln throughout his life. Resilience acted as the red blood cells of his leadership anatomy and personal life. Forged by a lifetime of hardship overcome, Lincoln the Resilient became comfortable with his own peculiarities, vulnerabilities, mental toughness, and steely resolve. There may be

[44] Fox, *Lincoln's Body*, 136–37.

[45] Hertz, *The Hidden Lincoln*, 191.

[46] Burlingame, *Lincoln,* 1:360.

[47] Burlingame, *Lincoln,* 1:360.

no other leadership attribute more admirable or more valuable than resiliency, and Lincoln had it in spades.

The Truth

There has never been a more resilient being on earth than Jesus: Three days after His brutal crucifixion, He rose from the dead. This is resilience personified.

Not only does Jesus's earthly life demonstrate resiliency, but God's Word encourages His followers to be resilient, gritty Christians. Knowing that sin permeates our fallen world, God exhorts all of His children to "lay aside every weight, and sin which clings so closely, and … run with endurance the race that is set before us."[48] When the world beats you up or down, you are to "wait for the Lord" to renew your strength, to "run and not be weary," to "walk and not faint."[49] With Jesus in you and by your side, you can forget what "lies behind" and focus on "what lies ahead." You can "press on toward the goal for the prize of the upward call of God in Christ Jesus."[50] Indeed, with the Holy Spirit strengthening your faith journey every day, there are no better words that you could ever say at the end of your life than these: "I have fought the good fight, I have finished the race, I have kept the faith."[51]

God knows the human condition—your weakness, frailty, selfishness, insecurities, sinful nature, sinful thoughts, and sinful ways. He also understands that suffering, pain, and rejection come in this fallen world. That is why, when times get tough or you get knocked down, He reminds you to "fear not, for I am with you; be not dismayed, for I am your God; I will strengthen you, I will help

---

[48] Heb. 12:1.

[49] Isa. 40:31.

[50] Phil. 3:13-14.

[51] 2 Tim. 4:7.

you, I will uphold you with my righteous right hand."[52] When you are afraid, He encourages you to "be strong and courageous. Do not be frightened, and do not be dismayed, for the Lord your God is with you wherever you go."[53] When you are wronged by your enemies or feel like you are being persecuted, God assures you that you will rise again. When you find yourself in some dark place, the Lord will be a light and encouragement to you.[54] The Bible says, "The sufferings of this present time are not worth comparing with the glory that is to be revealed" to you and all the faithful on Judgment Day.[55] "I have said these things to you that in me you may have peace," Jesus proclaimed. "In the world you will have tribulation. But take heart; I have overcome the world."[56]

Resilient Christians do not grow weary of doing good, nor do they give up doing good.[57] In fact, Jesus implores you to use Him as a resiliency station—to plug into Him and recharge. "Come to me, all who labor and are heavy laden," He says, "and I will give you rest."[58] Rested and renewed by the Holy Spirit, you receive from God "treasure in jars of clay, to show that the surpassing power belongs to God" and not you. Receiving God's Word builds spiritual resiliency and grit. This is why you may be "afflicted in every way, but not crushed; perplexed, but not driven to despair; persecuted, but not forsaken; struck down, but not destroyed." By God's grace and the power of the Holy Spirit, "the life of Jesus"—and His resiliency—is manifested in your body.[59]

In our fallen world, there is no doubt that you will endure hardships, setbacks, and tragedies. The Bible never says that a

---

52 Isa. 41:10.

53 Josh. 1:9.

54 Mic. 7:8.

55 Rom. 8:18.

56 John 16:33.

57 Gal. 6:9; 2 Thess. 3:13.

58 Matt. 11:28.

59 2 Cor. 4:7–10.

Christian's life will be easier than the life of a pagan. "I know how to be brought low," says Paul to the Philippians, "and I know how to abound. In any and every circumstance, I have learned the secret of facing plenty and hunger, abundance and need." Paul's resiliency secret: "I can do all things through him who strengthens me."[60]

The Holy Spirit instilled resiliency and grit in Paul, and He does so in you too. Indeed, we are all called and equipped to "be strong in the Lord and in the strength of his might,"[61] to "rejoice in hope, be patient in tribulation, be constant in prayer."[62] God "will be the stability of your times, abundance of salvation, wisdom, and knowledge."[63]

Embrace the trials and tribulations of your life as a means of growing closer to your Savior. For "we know that for those who love God all things work together for good, for those who are called according to his purpose."[64] Hard as it might be, the Bible calls on His followers to "rejoice in our sufferings, knowing that suffering produces endurance, and endurance produces character, and character produces hope, and hope does not put us to shame, because God's love has been poured into our hearts through the Holy Spirit who has been given to us."[65]

Hardship and tragedy demonstrate that no one controls their own destiny when it comes to salvation. You will "walk through the valley of the shadow of death."[66] You might be living in that valley right now, or it may come soon. Yet, by God's grace, you will pass through it and overcome it—not on your own merit or will, but because He will be with you and lead you through it. Thanks to Jesus—your Savior—and the power of the Holy Spirit—the one

---

60 Phil. 4:12–13.

61 Eph. 6:10.

62 Rom. 12:12.

63 Isa. 33:6.

64 Rom. 8:28.

65 Rom. 5:3–5.

66 Ps. 23:4.

who gives you faith and builds your spiritual resiliency—goodness and mercy will follow you for the rest of your life, and you will "dwell in the house of the Lord forever."[67]

Your Life

Lincoln's resiliency is impressive. What stands out the most to you about his resiliency? Why do people admire resiliency in their leaders?

Reflecting on your own life, where have you demonstrated resiliency? Where did that resiliency come from?

When has there been a time in your life when you wish you had been more resilient? What hindered your resiliency?

How does God's Word and your relationship with Jesus build and enhance your resiliency in this life?

[67] Ps. 23:6.

21

Continuous Improvement and the Will to Rise

For nothing will be impossible with God.
—Luke 1:37

The Lincoln Way

Exemplary leaders are industrious stewards of their God-given gifts and talents.

Perhaps more than any other American, Lincoln's life demonstrates what is possible. As one historian aptly puts it, "When we examine his life, we wonder what we can do with our own."[1] Another says that Lincoln is "the greatest of truly self-made men."[2]

When Lincoln was running for president in 1860, the populace responded to him because of his character and biography. His self-made image struck a chord with people all around the country, but especially common folk. He knew their language, toils, and tribulations. Working people admired, as they would often say, the "whole man" of Lincoln.[3] They felt they had a friend who understood what it meant to struggle to improve one's lot in life or simply to make ends meet. Lincoln's life story inspired people—for he was *just*

---

[1] McGovern, *Lincoln*, 153.

[2] Lehrman, *Lincoln "by littles,"* iv.

[3] Burlingame, *Lincoln*, 1:680.

like them and they were *just like him*. If he could rise, they could too. If he could run for president, they could do the same.

There is a statue of Lincoln that sits outside of the House of Commons in Great Britain. The monument aptly depicts what so many people, then and now, cherish about the man—that he came from nowhere to make a significant impact almost everywhere.[4]

Lincoln's rise came about despite his lack of affluence, position, and heritage. He ascended because of his own hard work, skills, and dispositions. Other presidents could claim to have come from the crowd of the common man, but not exactly like Lincoln. A new kind of American hero, Lincoln showed how to rise from the class of one's birth.

Contemporaries recognized this reality too. Horace Greeley, editor of the *New York Tribune*, noted that "the masses thought of him as one with whom they had been splitting rails on a pleasant spring day or making a prosperous voyage down the Mississippi on an Illinois flat-boat, and found him a downright good fellow."[5]

Lincoln's ascendance from nowhere is truly inspiring and remarkable—even legendary. Despite his origins in frontier hardship, Lincoln rose to the highest office in the land—the presidency of the United States. Just as impressive, even as he endured and dealt with adversity, he remained true to himself—a genuinely decent human being, compassionate husband, and loving father. He took the world, not by storm, but by stealth.[6]

There are many reasons the man from nowhere went somewhere. Lincoln's natural curiosity was one of the hallmarks of his life and an important factor in his success. No subject of inquiry was off-limits to him. "What do you suppose makes that tree grow that way?" he might ask.[7] He often took his kids' toys apart to see how they were made, and then try to put them back together, much to his son Tad's

---

4 Wood, "Tragic Sensibility," 233.

5 Peterson, *Lincoln in American Memory*, 31.

6 Epstein, *Portrait of a Marriage*, 4.

7 Sandburg, *Lincoln*, 403.

consternation. Inquisitive about a variety of subjects, Lincoln read almost anything he could lay his hands on. Whether on the circuit or in the Executive Mansion, he quizzed drivers, blacksmiths, farmers, politicians, and everyday citizens on anything, constantly pumping them for information and insight. He loved going to the patent office or Navy Yard to see the latest innovations.[8] In his cabinet, he wanted to hear various viewpoints on the issues at hand. He constantly asked ministers and other religious individuals for their takes on religious faith. His natural curiosity begot learning, which begot more curiosity and inquisitive thought.

Lincoln's alchemy of curiosity, work ethic, and resilience shaped and fueled his drive for self-improvement. A man once asked him for advice on how to become a successful attorney. Lincoln said that "the mode is very simple, though laborious, and tedious. It is only to get the books, and read, and study them carefully ... Work, work, work, is the main thing."[9]

After Lincoln had become an established lawyer in Springfield, he told William Herndon that "the way for a young man to rise, is to improve himself in ever way he can, never suspect that any body wishes to hinder him." At this time, younger Whigs had been complaining that they were being left out or discriminated against in leading the Whig Party. Lincoln told them "that suspicion and jealousy never did help any man in any situation." Sure, "there may sometimes be ungenerous attempts to keep a young man down; and they will succeed too, if he allows his mind to be diverted from its true channel to brood over the attempted injury." Lincoln warned,

---

[8] Burlingame, *Lincoln*, 1:334; 2:292–93. Lincoln championed the introduction of breech-loading rifles, which allowed a soldier to avoid the cumbersome, time-consuming, and dangerous procedures necessary to reload single-shot muzzleloaders. He even tested the new rifles behind the White House and demonstrated that he was a good shot.

[9] Basler, Lincoln to John Brockman, September 25, 1860, *CW*, 4:121.

however, that this kind of self-pity had only "injured every person you have ever known to fall into it."[10]

If anyone ever had a reason to complain about being held back in life, it was Lincoln. Yet he never let his circumstances inhibit his will to rise and make a name for himself. He did not believe that people had to remain stagnant or trapped in their socioeconomic class. They could work, work, work, and do something about it.

Lincoln failed often in his life, but he never let failure be final. He learned through and from his mistakes. Those who knew Lincoln best frequently commented on his ability to reflect upon ideas, the environment, and the world around him.[11] While he certainly did not want to commit errors, Lincoln intuitively understood that one could not be afraid to make mistakes if one wanted to learn and grow. On the frontier, if a rail did not get split just right the first time, the opportunity presented itself in the very next moment to split a better one.

Lincoln wanted a country where other Americans could rise as he had done. Lincoln's America would be built for growth and continuous improvement. Indeed, Lincoln committed himself to governmental policies designed to enhance opportunity for all (those enslaved were glaring exceptions). This worldview compelled him, as a politician in Illinois and later as president, to advocate for infrastructure and internal improvements. He knew from his days on the frontier how transportation challenges—unnavigable rivers, broken bridges, poor roads, or "prairie gumbo" (mud)—stymied economic growth. Thus he promoted the building of canals and railroads in order to knit together the nation's markets. He encouraged industry and modernized banking. He deplored isolation, backwardness, and any obstacles that hindered the development of a cash economy which would encourage openness and change. He enthused about and publicly supported the development of steam

10 Basler, Lincoln to William Herndon, July 10, 1848, *CW*, 1:497.

11 Bartelt, *Lincoln's Indiana Youth*, 93–94.

power, iron, technological breakthroughs, and anything else that could benefit the commercial economy.[12] If he could rise, so too could the nation and everyone in it.

Lincoln's ability to be a good steward of his own God-given gifts and to make the most of what he had is one of his most impressive character strengths. In the same way, he wanted the United States to steward and use all that it had been blessed with as a nation for continuous development, advancement, and prosperity. Shortly before he became president, he used the discovery of gold as a metaphor for his vision of the country: "Gold-mines are not the only mines overlooked in the same way. There are more mines above the Earth's surface than below it." He continued, "All nature—the whole world, material, moral, and intellectual—is a mine; and, in Adam's day, it was a wholly unexplored mine. Now, it was the destined work of Adam's race to develop, by discoveries, inventions, and improvements, the hidden treasures of this mine."[13]

Being a good steward of what God had provided to the United States meant the promotion and encouragement of inventions and commerce. The only president to ever register his own patent, Lincoln considered patents a boon to humankind and one of the great innovations of history, along with printing and the discovery of America. Moreover, he upheld the importance of private property, which he insisted was an essential and positive good in the world. Lincoln never forgot that his father had been swindled out of land in Kentucky (the state of Virginia, which once owned these lands, had sold off more land than actually existed) based on flawed land titles and lawsuits, which led to a downward spiral of the family's standard of living.[14] Property ownership was a key component of the American Dream and the building of a more prosperous society.

---

12 Lowry, *Lincoln Unbound*, 4, 97.

13 Basler, Lincoln's Second Lecture on Discoveries and Inventions, February 11, 1859, *CW*, 3:358–59.

14 Lowry, *Lincoln Unbound*, 94.

As president, Lincoln advocated for and enacted many policies which promoted the expansion, growth, and continuous improvement of the American economy for the common man. While Lincoln's domestic policy accomplishments do not receive as much attention or acclaim as his achievements regarding emancipation and saving the Union, the impact of these decisions is still felt today. They reveal a president who believed in an encouraging, incentive-based, smart government—a fine balance between an active, intervening, liberal government and a laissez faire, conservative, hands-off approach to governance. Most of all, his policies reveal a chief executive committed to continuous improvement so that Americans could prosper. For example, in order to build necessary infrastructure while protecting America's nascent industry, Lincoln increased tariffs and passed multiple revenue acts that increased income tax on higher-earning Americans. (The Revenue Act of 1862 also required employers, for the first time in American history, to withhold taxes from their employees' pay.) Excise taxes on liquor, professional licenses, carriages, yachts, medicines, corporations, stamps, and other goods were also passed. The National Bank Act of 1863 (with amendments in 1864 and 1865) set up a system to regulate national banks, reduce the cost and uncertainty of doing business across state lines, and encourage the implementation of a national currency. This act also mandated that one-third of a new bank's notes had to be backed by federal bonds, thus assisting the war effort. When state banks balked at new regulation, a provision of the 1864 Act imposed a ten percent tax on state bank notes. State banks then had to choose to comply or go out of business. Overall, the tax system grew so large that the president and Congress created the Bureau of Internal Revenue Service (IRS) to administer it.[15]

---

15 McGovern, *Lincoln*, 119. By the end of the war, nearly one in ten American households (mostly in affluent states in the industrial Northeast) paid an income tax.

These government actions, policies, and concepts would evolve or be exploited in the decades to come. To be sure, Lincoln never intended for the government to intrude into the daily lives of the common man. He believed his actions and policies would provide the tools that Americans could use to build a prosperous life.

There were other critical legislative actions Lincoln and Congress executed during the Civil War, which enabled and empowered his economic vision of America and the opportunity for the common man to rise. Created in 1862, the Department of Agriculture provided services and scientific knowledge to farmers so that they could improve their productivity. With the passage of the Homestead Act (1862), Americans were granted title to 160 acres of western land as long as they settled on it and farmed it for five years. This legislation became a model for the American family farm for the next century and helped thousands of Americans who had started out in life at the bottom of the social ladder, as Lincoln had, to become self-supporting, independent citizens.[16]

A high priority of Lincoln's administration, the Pacific Railway Act (1862) authorized subsidies and millions of acres of right-of-way land grants to the Union Pacific and Central Pacific companies, which ultimately led to the completion of a transcontinental railroad—a boon to national commerce.[17]

The Morrill Land Grant College Act (1862) awarded each state thirty thousand acres in or near its borders for each federal senator and representative it had been allotted in 1860. Proceeds from the sale of these acres were to be used to establish an "agricultural and mechanical" college.[18] Most of the sixty-nine colleges that benefited from Morrill grants grew into great state universities now admired around the world for the quality of their research and for the outstanding professional training they make available to millions.

---

16 McGovern, *Lincoln*, 120.

17 Bain, "The Transcontinental Railroad," 111.

18 Felzenberg, *Leaders We Deserved*, 192–93.

The land-grant legislation laid a foundation for broad access to higher education in the United States and fueled the emergence of America as a leader in scientific discovery and technological innovation. These policy accomplishments reveal how Lincoln pioneered an economic blueprint that remains central to modern America today.

Today some liberal government activists who want to claim Lincoln as one of their own argue that Lincoln initiated or set the precedent of "big government"—a term referring to high rates of taxation, the redistribution of wealth, intrusive government policies, and large government bureaucracies that stifle economic growth. While Lincoln did demand an increase in governmental power, intervention, and revenue to prosecute the war and execute the functions of the Union in wartime, he understood that these policies were to be temporary, ceasing after the completion of the war. Indeed, this is exactly what occurred. The income tax implemented in 1861 and progressive income tax implemented in 1863 were gone by 1872. The huge budget deficit the nation had accrued by 1865 was followed by twenty-eight consecutive years of budget surpluses, which halved the federal deficit fifty years after the Civil War.

These are not the legacies of a president who wanted to expand the federal government or transform it into a welfare state. For Lincoln, the government's focus was to secure and protect the individual's natural rights, specifically those outlined in the Declaration of Independence—life, liberty, and the pursuit of happiness. In this way, Lincoln embraced a limited constitutional government.[19]

For Lincoln, self-improvement came from an intentional mindset. In the past, "the great mass of men … were utterly unconscious, that their conditions, or their minds were capable of improvement." Too many people for too long, he explained, "only looked upon the educated few as superior beings; but they supposed themselves to be naturally incapable of rising to equality." Contrarily, Lincoln claimed that, especially with the invention of

[19] Krannawitter, *Vindicating Lincoln*, 293–94, 310.

printing and improvements in literacy, the minds of men could now be emancipated "from this false and under estimate of itself." To think one could not rise in society constituted a "slavery of the mind," which must be unshackled so that "a habit of freedom of thought" could be established. The prosperity and advancement of civilization depended on it.[20]

Lincoln's belief that others could rise came to fruition and made a lasting impact on the soul of an entire nation because he had lived that life himself—a life defined by hard work and determination. "Mr Lincoln is a man of *heart*, aye as gentle as a woman's and as tender, but he has a will as strong as iron," William Herndon stated in 1860. "He therefore loves all mankind, hates slavery, every form of Despotism ... This is Lincoln," and "God will keep Lincoln right."[21] Lincoln's biography is a story of a man dedicated to continuous improvement and driven to rise.

A few days before his inauguration as the sixteenth president of the United States, Lincoln told a crowd gathered at Independence Hall in Philadelphia that the greatness of the Declaration of Independence was not merely that it officially separated the colonies from England, but that it gave "hope to the world for all future time." He insisted that the Declaration promised "that in due time the weights should be lifted from the shoulders of all men, and that all should have an equal chance."[22]

One cannot give what one does not have. Lincoln knew about making the most of his blessings and opportunities. Through failures and successes and by God's grace, he learned how to improve and pursue his happiness. Having risen indeed, he wanted the same for his countrymen. The Lincoln rags-to-riches story, or more accurately,

---

20 Basler, Lincoln's Second Lecture on Discoveries and Inventions, February 11, 1859, *CW*, 362–63

21 Wilson, *Herndon's Informants*, 561.

22 Basler, Lincoln's Speech in Independence Hall, Philadelphia, Pennsylvania, February 22, 1861, *CW*, 4:240.

continuous improvement legacy remains embedded in the American dream and American psyche yet today.

The Truth

Your very best will never be enough. There is no amount of effort, no self-help guru or mentor, nor any plan you can implement that will help you improve enough to earn salvation and enter paradise. There is *nothing* you can do to get to heaven.

All human beings "have sinned and fall short of the glory of God."[23] Make no mistake: the reality of our sinful nature is tough to grapple with in a society that publishes self-help books every hour, enlists talk-show hosts to pontificate that "everyone has good in them," and relentlessly advertises ways you can become a "better" person. Even loving, well-intentioned parents tell their children that they can accomplish anything or become anyone they want to be in this world, if they work hard enough and chase their dreams.

When it comes to your salvation, however, Jesus is the only one who can "improve" your lot in life. He's the only one who lived a perfect life on earth. Even though He did not have to, He went willingly to the cross on that first Good Friday and died for your sins as well as the sins of the world. He set you free from all of your sins and then rose again on that first Easter Sunday. Talk about a *will to rise*! Jesus conquered sin, death, and the power of the devil. The Bible says you were "crucified with Christ," and now Christ lives in you. The life you now live, you "live by faith in the Son of God," who loved you and gave Himself up for you.[24]

Jesus did everything for you on the cross. His sacrificial love for you is unconditional. He has given you the gift of salvation and life eternal in Him. In the meantime, He has definitely improved your lot in this life by providing "the peace of God, which surpasses

---

23 Rom. 3:23.

24 Gal. 2:20.

all understanding," and will guard your heart and mind "in Christ Jesus."[25]

Since God sent His Son to rescue you from your sins, you are now called to steward these gifts, talents, and opportunities and live a fruitful and God-pleasing life. You can work to improve the way you live and lead so that the good news can be shared. "God is able to make all grace abound to you, so that having all sufficiency in all things at all times, you may abound in every good work."[26] By God's grace and empowered by the Holy Spirit, you can be about continuous improvement in your family life, work, and social interactions. You can embrace God's Word: "I can do all things through him who strengthens me."[27] Indeed, Jesus has already significantly and eternally improved your life. You are "a new creation. The old has passed away; behold, the new has come."[28] Through Christ's blood and resurrection, the Holy Spirit calls you to "put off your old self, which belongs to your former manner of life and is corrupt through deceitful desires, and to be renewed in the spirit of your minds, and to put on the new self, created after the likeness of God in true righteousness and holiness."[29]

Be careful not to be deceived by the shiny ways and acclamation of our fallen world. Earthly successes and accomplishments do not equate to faithfulness. Humans look at stature and "the outward appearance, but the Lord looks on the heart."[30] A Christian dedicated to continuous improvement, who desires to be a good steward of all that God has given, knows that the only way to truly improve in life is to "grow in the grace and knowledge of our Lord and Savior Jesus Christ."[31] Christians understand that they

---

[25] Phil. 4:7.

[26] 2 Cor. 9:8.

[27] Phil. 4:13.

[28] 2 Cor. 5:17.

[29] Eph. 4:22–24.

[30] 1 Sam. 16:7.

[31] 2 Pet. 3:18.

cannot improve themselves on their own. "If we confess our sins, he is faithful and just to forgive us our sins and to cleanse us from all unrighteousness."[32] Jesus does the redemption work. Through the Holy Spirit, He changes your heart and mind and calls you to godly service in this life. Only when you are empowered by the Holy Spirit can you rise in this world and "walk in a manner worthy of the Lord, fully pleasing to him, bearing fruit in every good work and increasing in the knowledge of God.[33] Jesus is risen. He has risen indeed!

Your Life

What have you worked hard to improve in your life? How are you doing at it?

Is there anything wrong with reading books, listening to speakers, or seeing coaches or counselors to make changes and improvements in your life? What might be the danger or temptation in seeking and relying on these sources?

How is continuous improvement, work ethic, and a desire to rise or achieve okay in secular pursuits but counter to what God has done for you in regard to your salvation? Why is this hard to reconcile in our society or culture today?

---

[32] 1 John 1:9.

[33] Col. 1:10.

22

Communication Keys

And when he was alone, those around him with
the twelve asked him about the parables.
—Mark 4:10

The best leaders communicate and connect with people through stories, wit, and humor.

Abraham Lincoln loved to tell stories. He once recounted an anecdote attributed to Colonel Ethan Allen, who made a visit to England after the Revolutionary War. Allen found his hosts took great pleasure in ridiculing Americans and George Washington in particular. To further irritate their guest, the English hung a picture of General Washington in the toilet or "back house." After Allen relieved himself and returned to the party, some of the obnoxious English hosts asked if he had noticed where they had placed the portrait of Washington. Not missing a beat, Allen announced that they had indeed found a great spot to hang the picture because "there is nothing that will make an Englishman shit so quick as the sight of General Washington."[1]

On another occasion Lincoln told a story about a preacher proclaiming that there never lived a perfect man, except for Jesus, and that no record existed of any perfect woman. Indignant at what she had heard, a woman arose in the congregation and said that she knew of a perfect woman—her husband's first wife.[2]

---

[1] Donald, *Lincoln*, 39–40.

[2] Epstein, *Portrait of a Marriage*, 469–70.

Another of Lincoln's favorite stories involved a wandering Methodist preacher who was trying to sell a Bible to a recalcitrant backwoods wife. Polite at first, she resented the hard sell and told the relentless pastor that her family had a Bible. When he asked to see it, her children searched the house. Finally one of the children dug up a few torn pages of Scripture. The woman took the pages and held them up in triumph. The preacher argued that that was no Bible. The wife retorted that it was, adding, "But I had no idea we were nearly out."[3]

Having watched his father often tell a good yarn, Lincoln learned to tell stories too. He told stories to make people laugh, think, and remember. He told stories to relieve his own stress and, as he got involved in law and politics, to accentuate a point.

The historical record contains numerous accounts of Lincoln's storytelling. The common denominator is that long after the laughter ended, his stories provoked thought and discussion. As his reputation grew, Lincoln drew crowds from the countryside, eager to be entertained by a master storyteller.[4] Even as a boy, he "was kind, jocular, witty, wise, honest, just ... full of integrity, Energy, & acting," said one Indiana neighbor. When he appeared on the scene, "boys would gather & cluster around him to hear him talk. He made fun & cracked his jokes making all happy, but the jokes & fun were at no mans Expense. He wounded no mans feelings."[5] Dennis Hanks said that Lincoln "would Commence his pranks, tricks, jokes, stories, and sure Enough all would stop, gather around Abe & listen, sometimes Crying, and sometimes bursting their sides with laughter." Often standing on a tree stump, chair, or box, Lincoln would tell stories, "anecdotes & such like thing; he never failed here."[6]

---

[3] Jones, *Lincoln and the Preachers,* 146.

[4] Goodwin, *Leadership*, 108.

[5] Wilson, *Herndon's Informants*, 114.

[6] Wilson, *Herndon's Informants,* 42.

One reason Lincoln became such an effective storyteller was because he thought about stories and storytelling constantly. "His world wide reputation for telling anecdotes, and telling them so well, was in my judgment necessary to his very existence," Joshua Speed recalled. "Most men who have been great students such as he was in their hours of idleness have taken to the bottle, to cards or dice. He had no fondness for any of these. Hence he sought relaxation in anecdotes."[7]

As he grew older, storytelling made Lincoln a celebrity. One associate claimed Lincoln could "make a cat laugh."[8] Townspeople would sit on logs and listen to him tell a tale, even crude and off-color jokes. People saw how much Lincoln enjoyed telling a story. Cheerfulness and wit were two of the most striking things people commented on regarding his personality. One time Lincoln told a story about a young soldier going off to war. His sweetheart made her beau a sash to wear into battle, bearing the brave motto "Liberty or Death." The cautious soldier asked if it could be amended to read "Liberty or Badly Wounded."[9] The stories were funny by themselves, but people especially loved seeing an exuberant and animated Lincoln marinating in the moment.

Affirmed for his storytelling, Lincoln pursued more public speaking opportunities. He lived at a time when the public lecture had become a major source of education and entertainment. Opera houses were constructed, even in the smallest of towns, to host famous traveling lecturers such as Ralph Waldo Emerson. Lyceum groups were created to provide venues for aspiring local speakers. For someone as intellectual and well-read as Lincoln, the public lecture arena inevitably provided an opportunity to grow and flourish.[10]

When Lincoln moved to New Salem, he joined a literary and debating society. Seeing Lincoln with his hands thrust deep down in

---

[7] Wilson, *Herndon's Informants*, 499.

[8] Burlingame, *Lincoln*, 1:53–54.

[9] Miller, *Lincoln's Virtues*, 72–73.

[10] Wilson, *Lincoln's Sword*, 39–40.

his pantaloons, elders and citizens were prepared to laugh at this tall, awkward-looking young man. Then they heard him speak and were awed by his eloquence and poise.[11] As would be the case throughout his life, Lincoln spoke "in an almost conversationalist tone, but with such earnestness and such deep feeling upon the questions of the day that he struck the hearts of all his hearers."[12]

While eloquent and compelling in his public speaking, he also connected with the common person in an authentic, common-man manner. He "heared" instead of "heard," would "git" instead of "get," and told people what he "done" instead of what he "did." In almost all cases, except for the occasional crude joke, he spoke with a simple and earnest dignity.[13] "If you would win a man to your cause," Lincoln said, "first convince him that you are his sincere friend."[14]

Lincoln gave his first lyceum (public lecture) when he was twenty-eight years old, just eight months after he moved to Springfield. Members of the Young Men's Lyceum took turns lecturing to and debating with each other on the topics of the day.[15] Reinforced in a positive cycle of speech, affirmation, and expansion of his messages, Lincoln continued to grow as a public speaker. He almost always relied on a good story to bring his message home. More than any other attribute, his public speaking opened the vocational doors for him to become a successful lawyer and politician.

As good a storyteller as Lincoln could be and as much public speaking as he did, he had one shortcoming as a communicator: he did not generally perform well as an extemporaneous or impromptu speaker, and he knew it. Whether given in the courtroom or on the

---

11 Burlingame, *Lincoln*, 1:65; Winkle, *Young Eagle*, 74.

12 Peterson, *Lincoln in American Memory*, 114.

13 Conway, *Lincoln's White House*, 50.

14 Basler, Lincoln's Temperance Address, February 22, 1842, *CW*, 1:273.

15 Miller, *Lincoln's Virtues*, 130.

stump, Lincoln's speeches were carefully crafted and revised to suit the particular audience or context.[16]

Lincoln's words and stories were the power of his speaking, but his physical presentation also made him captivating to watch. His "voice was, when he first began speaking, shrill, squeaking, piping, unpleasant; his general look, his form, his pose, the color of his flesh, wrinkled and dry, his sensitiveness, and his momentary diffidence, everything seemed to be against him," his law partner William Herndon explained.[17] Once Lincoln got going, however, "he quite generously placed his hands behind him, the back pat of his left hand resting in the palm of his right hand." As he warmed up, he moved his hands to the front, "generally interlocking his fingers and running one thumb around the other … In still growing warmer, as he proceeded in his address, he used his hands—especially and generally his right hand—in his gestures." Lincoln also "used his head a great deal in speaking, throwing or jerking or moving it now here and now there, now in this position and now in that, in order to be more emphatic, to drive the idea home." He "was cool, careful, earnest, sincere, truthful, fair, self-possessed, not insulting, not dictatorial, was pleasing, good natured; had great strong naturalness of look, pose, and act; was clear in his ideas, simple in his words, strong, terse, and demonstrative." When Lincoln spoke, he tried "to convince individuals and masses; he used in his gestures his right hand, sometimes shooting out that long bony forefinger of his to dot an idea or to express a thought, resting his thumb on his middle finger." While Lincoln "did not gesticulate much … every organ of his body was in motion and acted with ease, elegance, and grace." As time went on, "his shrill, squeaking, piping voice became harmonious, melodious, musical, if you please, with face somewhat aglow." When he felt most inspirational or when he wanted to make

---

[16] Conroy, *Lincoln's White House*, 18; Miller, *Lincoln's Virtues*, 377.

[17] Hertz, *The Hidden Lincoln*, 191–92. The ensuring quotes in this paragraph all come from this source.

a grand statement, "he held both of his hands out above his head at an angel of about fifty degree, hands open or clenched according to his feelings and his ideas ... If he was defending the right, if he was defending liberty, eulogizing the Declaration of Independence, then he extended out his arms, palms of his hands upward somewhat at about the above degree, angle, as if appealing to some superior power for assistance and support ... It was at such moments that he seemed inspired, fresh from the hands of his Creator."

Lincoln's exceptional speechwriting amplified his exemplary oratory. His Gettysburg Address and second inaugural address, in particular, are studied today in speech classes around the world for their eloquence, staying power, and stream of thought.

A test of stamina that required the histrionic skills of an opera singer or a revival preacher, community speechmaking was a critical component of American society in the nineteenth century. Lincoln could deliver this kind of marathon performance and rarely, if ever, swooned. He possessed the unique ability to hear his own words and be his own best editor. Indeed, he would fight with editors over commas, at a time when grammatical rules were relatively loose. These commas signaled Lincoln's attention to the dramatic pause and flow of the spoken word.[18] Lincoln took his speechwriting and speechmaking seriously.

Horace White, a reporter for the *Chicago Tribune,* observed many of Lincoln's speeches. White noted Lincoln's melancholy and how Lincoln drew on this gloom and depth of character to connect with his audience. Indeed, Lincoln spoke to the hearts of his listeners "because it came from the heart," and this is what made Lincoln's oratory special. Many speakers could hit the right notes and win loud applause, but Lincoln's speeches changed people's hearts and minds. "Mr. Lincoln's eloquence was of a higher type," White asserted, "which produced conviction in others because of the conviction of the speaker himself. His listeners felt that he believed every word he

[18] Delbanco, "Lincoln's Sacramental Language," 202–3.

said." Like the great reformer Martin Luther, Lincoln "would go to the stake rather than abate one jot or tittle of it."[19]

Despite his melancholy, Lincoln possessed a bountiful sense of humor. Whether in the courtroom or on the circuit, many of his contemporaries not only thoroughly enjoyed his wit and sense of humor, but looked forward to spending time with him because of it. When he was preparing to share an anecdote at dinner, he would set down his utensils, put his elbows on the table, cup his face in his hands, and preface his remarks with a "that reminds me" statement. His friends loved his humor, and also his amiability, kindness, and unpretentious manners.[20] When a young, skilled attorney lost a case in a Bloomington, Illinois, courtroom, Lincoln asked him what had become of his case. With a dour spirit, the young lawyer lamented that it had gone to hell. Lincoln responded, "Oh well. Then you'll see it again."[21]

Lincoln's stories were humorous because he knew the people intimately and could provide a tale that fit the context. He loved to repeat the story of a traveling preacher who asked permission of Thomas Campbell, secretary of state for Illinois, to deliver a series of lectures in the hall of the Illinois House of Representatives on "the second coming of our Lord." Lincoln quoted Campbell's reply: "It's no use. If you will take my advice you will not waste your time in this city. It is my private opinion that if the Lord has been to Springfield once, he will not come a second time."[22]

Lincoln once defended a client who was charged with assault and battery. The man had been insulted and attacked by the plaintiff, and thrashed him in return. In front of the jury, Lincoln compared his client's situation to that of a man who, in going along the highway with a pitchfork on his shoulder, had been attacked by a fierce dog that ran out at him from a farmer's dooryard. In repelling the dog,

---

[19] Shenk, *Lincoln's Melancholy*, 132–33.

[20] Burlingame, *Lincoln*, 1:260.

[21] Leidner, *Lincoln's Gift*, 65.

[22] Szasz and Szasz, *Lincoln and Religion*, 15–16.

the man stuck the prongs into the brute and killed him. When the farmer asked the man why he killed the dog, the man responded that the dog had tried to bite him and he had to defend himself. Still not satisfied, the farmer wondered why the man did not repel the dog with the other end of the pitchfork—the handle—rather than the sharp tines. The man sarcastically retorted with a question of his own, wondering why the dog did not come after him with *his* other end.[23]

Illinois judge John M. Scott noted that Lincoln almost always had a story that precisely fit the occasion or context. On those rare occasions when he did not, he seemed able to cobble one together and make it pertinent to the exact circumstance. His singular talent for constructing and speaking in parables amazed those who heard the tales firsthand.[24]

During recess in court, he often told the story of a farmer's lad who rushed up to see his father. "The hired man and Sis," panted the youngster, are "in the hayloft—she's liftin' up her skirts and he's apullin' down his pants and fixin' to pee all over the hay."[25] The father chuckled that the son had his facts right but his conclusion wrong, something that lawyers had to work through in defending their clients or prosecuting the accused.

Lincoln loved to laugh and hear others laugh too. One evening he asked Illinois judge John Dean Caton to confirm the rumor that all three Supreme Court judges came from Oneida County, New York. When informed that it was true, Lincoln replied with a pun: he could never understand why this had been a "*One-i-dea court*."[26]

Contemporaries enjoyed observing his quick wit in action. At a trial in Chicago, Lincoln led the indictment of a young US Army officer for an assault on an older gentleman. He opened the case

---

[23] Burlingame, *Lincoln,* 1:318.

[24] Burlingame, *Lincoln*, 1:318.

[25] Freehling, *Becoming Lincoln,* 68.

[26] Burlingame, *Lincoln,* 1:328.

by saying, "This is an indictment against a soldier for assaulting an old man."

Conscious of his superior rank, the officer indignantly interrupted by saying, "Sir, I am no soldier, I am an officer!"

"I beg your pardon," said Lincoln, grinning innocently. "Then gentlemen of the jury, this is an indictment against an officer, who is no soldier, for assaulting an old man."[27]

Lincoln's mentor and a local justice of the peace, Bowling Green, had the nickname "Pot" for his girth. Lincoln thought of him as a second father, and Green had great respect for Lincoln and his mind. Green allowed his mentee to argue minor matters in his court, in large part, just for his own amusement. Lincoln made him laugh so hard "as to produce," one witness of the courtroom said, "a spasmatic shaking of the very fat sides of the old law functionary."[28]

When Ward Hill Lamon, Lincoln's best circuit friend, split has pants before a court appearance, too much of Lamon could be seen. Lamon's amused colleagues started a fund for new pants. Each subscribed an absurdly small sum for the large size required. Lincoln could not resist a parting jab and last laugh: "I can contribute nothing," he said, "to the end in view."[29]

Many stories Lincoln told revealed his self-deprecating humor and humility. Leaving Springfield on the way to Washington in the spring of 1849, Lincoln rode with a Kentuckian who was on his way home from Missouri. The Kentuckian kindly offered him a chew of tobacco, a cigar, and brandy, but Lincoln declined each, stating that he did not chew, smoke, or drink. When the Kentuckian had to continue on another stage, he warmly shook Lincoln's hand in farewell. "See here, stranger," he said good-humoredly, "you're a clever, but strange companion. I may never see you again, and I don't

---

[27] Leidner, *Lincoln's Gift*, 101.

[28] Lowry, *Lincoln Unbound*, 50–51.

[29] Freehling, *Becoming Lincoln*, 73.

want to offend you, but I want to say this: my experience has taught me that a man who has no vices ... [has] few virtues. Good-day."[30]

Upon hearing that he had received the Republican nomination for the presidency in 1860, Lincoln exclaimed to supporters gathered around him, "Boys you had better come and shake hands with me now that you have an opportunity—for you do not know what influence this nomination may have on me. I am human, you know."[31]

Artists loved to work with Lincoln because of his modesty. Thomas Jones, a sculptor for whom Lincoln sat during the winter after his election, raved about Lincoln's simplicity and unpretentiousness. He told friends that Lincoln loved to have fun, shared the best stories in the world, and told lots of them. Another artist explained that one had to meet Lincoln in person to really appreciate him. After spending just ten minutes with Lincoln, one would feel like one had known Father Abraham for years. His candor and charm simply put people at ease and made them feel good about themselves.[32] Lincoln had a gift for bringing out the best of those in his presence.

While Lincoln loved to hear others laugh, there is no doubt that he relied on humor as his "opiate" or, as Judge David Davis put it, as a vehicle to "whistle down sadness."[33] Lincoln once told a story about an Irish sailor who had been overtaken on the sea by a mighty storm. The sailor thought he ought to pray, but had not been an especially devout individual and did not know how. So he fell to his knees and said, "Oh Lord! You know as well as meself that it's seldom I bodder ye, but if ye will only hear me and save me this time, bedad it will be a long time before I bodder ye again."[34]

---

30 Miller, *Lincoln's Virtues*, 35.

31 Lehrman, *Lincoln "by littles,"* 20–21.

32 Burlingame, *Lincoln*, 1:659.

33 Oates, *With Malice Toward None*, 100; Peterson, *Lincoln in American Memory*, 99.

34 Shenk, *Lincoln's Melancholy*, 118.

Especially during the tumultuous Civil War, Lincoln laughed so that he did not have to weep. He saw laughter as the "joyous, universal evergreen of life."[35] Lincoln's ability to laugh during tough times—a hearty and distinguished chortle that sounded like "the 'neigh' of a wild horse on his native prairie"—remained "the President's life-preserver!" said Judge Isaac Arnold.[36]

Lincoln used humor as a means of establishing personal rapport with strangers in public. Better than any American politician before or since, he understood that humor and wit helped forge a partnership between speaker and listener, and helped the hearer truly understand the message. Levity broke down barriers and fostered intimacy.[37] Lincoln's facial expressions, gestures, Hoosier accent, and ability to mimic were essential in eliciting laughter from the audience.[38]

On their trip to Washington, DC, for the inauguration, the president-elect often appeared on the platform or in front of the railcar with Mary. Lincoln would tell the audiences that now they "could see the long and the short of it!"[39]

As president, Lincoln became the humorist in chief. He had to be—for the sake of his own sanity and to keep those around him distracted from the terrible war news. After he read bad reports, he told humorous stories to provide relief. He visited regiments, trying to raise their spirits.[40] Telling stories brought pleasure and temporary reprieve to Lincoln's mind and intellect. As one biographer explains, a reason Americans still admire Lincoln is that "Lincoln is the president who laughs with us."[41] His winsome personality and self-deprecating humor made him likable and pleasant—someone people wanted to listen to on any subject.

---

[35] Goodwin, *Team of Rivals*, 103.

[36] Carpenter, *Six Months at the White House*, 170.

[37] Delbanco, "Lincoln's Sacramental Language," 209.

[38] Leidner, *Lincoln's Gift*, xiv.

[39] Donald, *Lincoln*, 275.

[40] Goodwin, *Team of Rivals*, 375.

[41] White, *Lincoln*, 5.

Reporters called his tales "Lincoln stories," but Lincoln did not claim to be the original author. "I am only a retail dealer," he told one correspondent. Yet he admitted that humor provided therapy for him. "A funny story, if it has the element of genuine wit," he explained, "has the same effect on me that I suppose a good square drink of whiskey has on an old toper; it puts new life in me."[42] Humor helped Lincoln escape the unending grind of his office. Aside from carriage rides, storytelling was the only recreation he could participate in consistently. According to Secretary of State Seward, storytelling "was what saved him."[43]

On his office desk, Lincoln kept joke books filled with rustic humor, in which he found "the excitement and relief which another man would have found in a glass of wine," said the editor of the *New York Times*.[44] The president often opened cabinet meetings by reading a chapter or two from one of the popular humorists, like Josh Billings or Artemus Ward. This could upset members like Stanton, who felt the issues of the day demanded a more serious tone. Lincoln never flinched. When someone asked Lincoln if he ever swore, he responded, "Oh, I don't have to. You know I have Stanton in my Cabinet."[45]

Lincoln loved and *needed* to laugh and be witty, even for the most serious of issues. Referring to divisions over the Missouri Compromise, Lincoln said, "It used to amuse me to hear the slaveholders talk about wanting more territory, because they had not *room* enough for their slaves; and yet they complained of not having the slave-trade, because they wanted more slaves for their room."[46]

One time Secretary Stanton refused a Lincoln request and called the president a fool for sending such an order. Lincoln, feigning astonishment, inquired, "Did Stanton call me a fool?" With the

---

42 Oates, *With Malice Toward None,* 249.

43 Oates, *With Malice Toward None*, 152.

44 Conway, *Lincoln's White House*, 95.

45 Sandburg, *Lincoln*, 565.

46 Carpenter, *Six Months at the White House*, 275.

comment confirmed, he remarked, "Well, I guess I had better go over and see Stanton about this. Stanton is usually right."[47] When physically pressed by well-wishers walking through the Executive Mansion, he gave a characteristic pun, calling them members of "the Press."[48]

Early in the war, after Lincoln replaced Secretary of War Simon Cameron, a Senate delegation recommended a total overhaul of the cabinet. The president responded with a story about a farmer bedeviled by skunks in the henhouse. One night the farmer went out with his shotgun, saw seven skunks, but only shot one. When the farmer returned to his house, his wife asked why he had not shot all of them. The man replied, "The one skunk made such a stink that I let the other six go."[49]

One of the ingratiating features of Lincoln's personality is that he could enjoy someone else's good joke as much as others enjoyed his. One time a woman visited him in the Executive Mansion and said her husband had been arrested months before and sent to prison. He had not been tried and seemed stuck in limbo. She appealed to Lincoln to expedite her husband's trial. Lincoln responded that he was sorry, but nothing could be done, adding that cases were much like the different sacks of grain at a country grist-mill, all waiting their turn to be ground, and that it would be unfair for the miller to show any favoritism.

The woman left, but came back the next day. Lincoln asked if anything new had happened. She said no, but she had been thinking about what he said concerning the "grists." She was "afraid mine will get mouldy and spoil before its turn comes around, so I have come to ask, Mr. President, that it may be taken to some other 'mill' to be ground." Amused at the wit and shrewdness of the request, Lincoln

---

47 Leidner, *Lincoln's Gift*, 150.

48 Burlingame, *Lincoln*, 2:29.

49 Peterson, *Lincoln in American Memory*, 100–101.

immediately gave the woman an unconditional discharge for her husband.[50]

Entering the political arena, Lincoln knew the importance of intimacy and connecting with his audience. His gifts as a historian, storyteller, and teacher, combined with lucid, relentless, yet always accessible logic, significantly aided his political aspirations. He did not use ornate language, but irony and humor instead. He spoke the working man's language with homespun images to make his points clear and understandable. He could take the proslavery argument, for example, that a vote for the Wilmot Proviso threatened the stability of the entire Union, and reduce it to absurdity by analogy: "Because I may have refused to build an addition to my house, I thereby have decided to destroy the existing house!"[51] He made sense to the common folk, connected with them in a way that they could not only understand but embrace, and communicated with authority, clarity, and conviction.

Stephen Douglas, the senator from Illinois whom Lincoln would so famously debate, admitted that Lincoln was "full of wit, facts, dates—and the best stump speaker, with his droll ways and dry jokes."[52] Lincoln also excelled at creating phrases that would be reprinted in newspapers—the electorate's primary access to the ideas, arguments, and aspirations of politicians. He intentionally deployed words to shape public opinion. "With public sentiment, nothing can fail, without it nothing can succeed," he told an Illinois crowd during one of his debates with Douglas. "Consequently he who moulds public sentiment, goes deeper than he who enacts statutes or pronounces decisions. He makes statutes and decisions possible or impossible to be executed."[53]

---

[50] Carpenter, *Six Months at the White House*, 314–15.

[51] Goodwin, *Team of Rivals*, 166.

[52] Holzer and Garfinkle, *A Just and Generous Nation*, 35.

[53] Basler, Lincoln's First Debate with Stephen A. Douglas at Ottawa, Illinois, August 21, 1858, *CW*, 3:27.

Of all of Lincoln's public speaking gifts, Douglas most feared Lincoln's storytelling ability because he knew it resonated with the people. "Every one of his stories seems like a whack across my back," he contended. "Nothing else—not any of his arguments or any of his replies to my questions—disturbs me. But when he begins to tell a story, I feel that I am to be overmatched."[54] Lincoln never repeated a story but, as one reporter noted, he could deliver one after another like bullets flying out of a magazine gun, all pertinent to the context.[55] One lawyer and confidante observed that no one could entertain a crowd like Lincoln. "He had an unfailing budget of genuinely witty and humerous anecdotes with which he illustrated every topic which could arise. The application was always perfect and his manner of telling a story the least degree histrionick." Lincoln "never invented any of his stories but simply retailed them but how he could gather up such a boundless supply & have them ever ready at command was the wonder of all his accquaintences." The attorney noted the common theme of Lincoln's storytelling ability: "He used his stories as much for producing conviction in the minds of his hearers as for creating merriment. He had great natural clearness and simplicity of statement and this faculty he cultivated with marked assiduity."[56]

Many people could tell a rollicking tale on the frontier, but few, if any, could tell the right story at the right time to elicit the desired effect the way Lincoln did. He intentionally selected stories to teach, affirm, challenge, encourage, and convince. "I believe I have the popular reputation of being a story-teller," Lincoln once said, "but I do not deserve the name in a general sense; for it is not the story itself, but its purpose, or effect, that interests me." He avoided "long and useless discussion by others or a laborious explanation on my own part" by using a short story "that illustrates my point of view."

---

[54] Leidner, *Lincoln's Gift*, 93.

[55] Burlingame, *Lincoln*, 1:261.

[56] Wilson, *Herndon's Informants*, 508.

In addition, Lincoln asserted that "the sharpness of a refusal or the edge of a rebuke may be blunted by an appropriate story, so as to save wounded feelings and yet serve the purpose. No, I am not simply a story-teller, but story-telling as an emollient saves me much friction and distress."[57] As president, Lincoln used humor or told folks "a little story" to distract them from what they came to ask of him, especially if he knew he could not accommodate their request.[58]

Watching Lincoln perform in the Lincoln-Douglas debates, reformer and journalist Carl Schurz noted that Lincoln's "voice was not melodious; rather shrill and piercing, especially when it rose to its high treble in moments of great animation." Moreover, his physical appearance "was unhandsome, and the action of his unwieldy limbs awkward. He commanded none of the outwardly graces or oratory as they are commonly understood." Instead, Lincoln's "charm was of different kind. It flowed from the rare depth and genuineness of his convictions and his sympathetic feelings."[59]

A young newspaper editor, William Stoddard, maintained that Lincoln spoke to you "as if you were a hundred thousand people of an audience, and as if he believes that fifty thousand of you do not at all agree with him. He will convince the half of you, if he can, before he has done with it."[60] Francis Carpenter, who spent six months with Lincoln at the Executive Mansion, said that Lincoln "was the strongest man I ever saw, looking at him from the standpoint of his reason—the throne of his logic. He came down from that height with an irresistible and crushing force."[61]

At the Lincoln-Douglas debates and the Cooper Union speech just a few years later, especially, the New York intelligentsia were impressed by the sheer clarity, organization, and presentation of the research Lincoln disseminated seamlessly. After Lincoln's celebrated

57 Peterson, *Lincoln in American Memory*, 99–100.

58 Donald, *Lincoln Reconsidered*, 171.

59 White, *Lincoln*, 282.

60 White, *Lincoln*, 588.

61 Carpenter, *Six Months at the White House*, 354.

Cooper Union address, Reverend John P. Gulliver praised him for "the clearness of your statements ... the unanswerable style of your reasoning, and especially your illustrations, which were romance and pathos and fun and logic all welded together."[62]

Lincoln made a political living out of appearing overmatched, then rising to the occasion. Lew Wallace, supporter of Stephen Douglas, held that Lincoln's pleasant demeanor, sincerity, candor, confidence, forthrightness, simplicity, and authenticity all combined to make for a compelling and persuasive communicator. Watching and listening to Lincoln, Wallace scrapped his old belief that an effective speaker must be graceful and good looking.[63]

Indeed, the contrast between their low expectations at the onset and his surpassing performance at the climax truly surprised and riveted Lincoln's audiences. The debates he took part in, as well as the speeches he made in the 1850s, changed the national perception of him from that of a country hick to a national seer.[64] Of course, the lawyer in Lincoln helped him focus on preparing and organizing his speeches—and getting to the crux of the matter. Lincoln's thinking—his disciplined intelligence and penetrating insight—was one of his greatest legacies, though many still do not view Lincoln as an intellectual.[65]

As a compelling thinker and speaker, Lincoln knew the power of a well-placed and timely story to accentuate his points. One day someone asked him how he became so adept at "putting things" and inquired about his education. Lincoln retorted that it had nothing to do with his formal education, which had been minimal. Instead he explained that as "a mere child," he used to get irritated when he could not understand what people were talking about. He would go to his "little bedroom, after hearing the neighbors talk of an evening with my father, and spending no small part of the night walking up

---

62 Peterson, *Lincoln in American Memory*, 84–85.

63 Burlingame, *Lincoln*, 1:520.

64 Freehling, *Becoming Lincoln*, 234–35.

65 Miller, *Lincoln's Virtues*, 9, 14–16.

and down, and trying to make out what was the exact meaning of some of their ... dark sayings." Lincoln could not sleep when he got "on such a hunt after an idea." Yet, once he understood an idea or concept, he did not become satisfied until he "repeated it over and over," and "put it in language plain enough ... for any body ... to comprehend."[66] This became one of his lifelong endeavors—making words and concepts stick with people.

Lincoln's strategic deployment of words served him well as the nation's chief executive. Harriet Beecher Stowe maintained that Lincoln's eloquent public utterances were spoken as a loving father would talk to his children. Father Abraham radiated the Old Man archetype and embodied the Wise Father. People trusted him.[67] When Lincoln said that he "*wanted* God on his side, but he *must* have Kentucky," people understood his point that keeping the border states in the Union was essential for victory.[68] Yet when urged to send troops into Kentucky to defend the Unionists living there, he demurred and told the fable of a farmer who returned home and found that, while his two little children were asleep, a number of snakes had slithered into their bed. He could not strike the snakes without endangering his progeny. Thus, the farmer decided not to strike.[69] Union troops would not be sent to invade Kentucky.

When Lincoln's concern that Britain might declare war against United States during the Trent Affair met skepticism in his cabinet, he recalled a story about a ferocious bulldog in his hometown. While neighbors convinced themselves they had nothing to worry about, one wise man observed, "I know the bulldog will not bite. You know he will not bite, but does the bulldog know he will not bite?"[70]

As the election of 1864 approached, many wondered if Lincoln should not run again. Lincoln admitted that he might not be "the

---

66 Carpenter, *Six Months at the White House*, 328–29.

67 Burlingame, *Lincoln*, 2:833.

68 White, *Lincoln*, 449.

69 Burlingame, *Lincoln*, 2:155.

70 Goodwin, *Team of Rivals*, 398.

best man in the country; but I am reminded, in this connection, of a story of an old Dutch farmer, who remarked to a companion once that 'it was not best to swap horses when crossing streams.'"[71] As Herndon explained, Lincoln's "expressions were strong, gnarly, and original ... Lincoln was Lincoln and no one else; and he spoke and wrote in Lincolnisms." Lincoln believed "he could do anything that other men could or would try to do; he had unbounded confidence in himself, in his capacities and powers; he asked no man's advice and sought no man's opinion, as a general, quite universal rule."[72]

Visitors to the Executive Mansion were stunned by the sheer volume of his words. The president freely shared his opinions, ideas, and anecdotes concerning almost every subject in the world. The real surprise for many who first met Lincoln was his seemingly unpresidential habit of regaling guests with jokes and stories. When he told tales, his face lit up, and at the punch line, his high-pitched laughter rang through the capital. He often punctuated the crux of the story with slap on the thigh. He loved puns and Irish bulls, like the story of Patrick and his new boots: "I shall niver git em on," said the Irishman, "till I wear em a day or two, and stretch em a little."[73]

Though Lincoln is rightly remembered for groundbreaking speeches—the Gettysburg Address and second inaugural address especially—he gave very few public speeches as president. In Lincoln's time, the president simple presided over the executive branch and reported his actions and wishes to Congress. Presidents rarely made public addresses and tried to maintain a sublime indifference to public opinion and political pressures. Therefore Lincoln did not feel compelled to give public speeches. He held no press conferences. This particular societal expectation served Lincoln well, since he

---

[71] Basler, Lincoln's Reply to Delegation from the National Union League, June 9, 1864, *CW*, 7:384.

[72] Hertz, *The Hidden Lincoln*, 125–26.

[73] Donald, *Lincoln*, 259.

struggled with extemporaneous speaking and rarely made public appearances outside the Executive Mansion.[74]

Yet when he spoke to individuals such as cabinet officials, politicians, or newspaper editors, or when he offered public pronouncements, people not only listened to him but were persuaded by his sentiments. Leonard Swett, a lawyer who rode with Lincoln on the circuit and campaigned for him as president in 1860 and 1864, said that "the great secret of his power as an orator, in my judgment, lay in the clearness and perspicuity of his statements. When Lincoln had stated a case, it was always more than half argued and the point more than half won."[75]

For his whole life, Lincoln was in the persuasion business, and most acutely during the last twenty-five years. He had become the most talented man in the country to shape public opinion. He had trained himself to become the convincer in chief.[76] And Lincoln indeed molded public opinion on topics such as the border states, conscription, income tax, using freedman in the Union army, the Emancipation Proclamation, and the will to endure horrific casualties for the preservation of the Union.

George Templeton Strong, a critic of Lincoln, marveled at the country's change of opinion on the slavery questions since 1860. No one could have predicted that slavery would be abolished in border states, such as Maryland and Missouri, even after Fort Sumter had fallen; or that the North would embrace the eradication of slavery in the South. "I think this great and blessed revolution is due, in

---

[74] Donald, *Lincoln,* 441. Lincoln needed time to prepare his public speeches. He did not deliver them well off the cuff. At the funeral of Bolling Green, Mrs. Green asked him to say a few words. Lincoln remarked "that he did not know what to say, that he had not thought about the subject" (Wilson, *Herndon's Informants*, 263). He eventually made a few remarks in relation to his mentor's manners, customs, habits of life. Most thought his speech a failure.

[75] Wilson, *Herndon's Informants*, 166–67.

[76] Wilson, *Lincoln's Sword*, 147–48; Szasz and Szasz, *Lincoln and Religion*, 28.

no small degree, to A. Lincoln's sagacious policy. But I do wish A. Lincoln told fewer dirty stories."[77]

Lincoln's storytelling, wit, humor, homespun analogies, and critical thinking were keys to his rise to the presidency. The delegates to the Republican convention could not have known the many great qualities that would go on to make Lincoln a great president—the courage, the executive capacity to make necessary decisions, the will to stay the course through a terrible war, the rare generosity of spirit. They did know, however, that he possessed a superb mind and tongue. They knew he could articulate the Republican cause and platform like no other.[78]

As president, Lincoln continued to hone these communication skills to persuade, lead, and move the people to action for the good of the country. Ironically, by deploying a prodigious wit and endless storytelling, Lincoln would become one of the most iconic and original American stories in the republic's history.

One day a visitor came to the Executive Mansion, demanding a favor. After badgering the president up and down the halls, he had the nerve to tell Lincoln that he had put him in the White House. Lincoln had had enough, and finally turned to the man. "So you think you made me President?"

"Yes, Mr. President. Under Providence, I think I did," said the discourteous visitor.

"Well," Lincoln said as he left him, "It's a pretty mess you've gotten me into, but I forgive you."[79]

Lincoln had a way of getting his point across, as all great leaders do.

---

[77] Wilson, *Lincoln's Sword*, 244–45.

[78] Miller, *Lincoln's Virtues*, 399.

[79] Conway, *Lincoln's White House*, 130.

The Truth

The Greatest Story Ever Told is recorded in the Bible, and the main chapters are riveting: Creation, The Fall, The Promise of a Messiah; The Birth of Christ, The Ministry and Mission of Christ, The Passion, The Crucifixion, The Resurrection, and The Everlasting Life to Come. Not only is the Bible all about the purpose and life of Jesus, but Jesus Himself spoke and taught His disciples (and us) through stories and parables. As the Bible explains, "All these things Jesus said to the crowds in parables; indeed he said nothing to them without a parable" in order "to fulfill what was spoken by the prophet: 'I will open my mouth in parables; I will utter what has been hidden since the foundation of the world.'"[80] Humans have been wired to listen to stories since the creation.

Parables are the inspired and inerrant Word of God. When Jesus taught by parables, "he spoke the word to them, as they were able to hear it."[81] When the disciples asked Jesus why He spoke in parables, He told them that without the stories, people "do not see, and hearing they do not hear, nor do they understand."[82] Jesus wants His children not only to hear His Word but take it to heart.

As told by the Master Storyteller, Jesus's parables carry divine inspiration. They teach the love, mercy, and grace of God—how He redeemed you from your sins and gave you salvation. His stories let the Holy Spirit work on your heart and mind and give you faith. "Everyone then who hears these words of mine and does them will be like a wise man who built his house on the rock," Jesus tells us in storybook form. "And the rain fell, and the floods came, and the winds blew and beat on that house, but it did not fall, because it had been founded on the rock." Jesus, the Rock of our salvation, continues, "Everyone who hears these words of mine and does not

---

[80] Matt. 13:34–35.

[81] Mark 4:33.

[82] Matt. 13:10–13.

do them will be like a foolish man who built his house on the sand. And the rain fell, and the floods came, and the winds blew and beat against that house, and it fell, and great was the fall of it."[83]

In the parable of the Prodigal Son (Luke 15:11–32), God's inspired Word makes it clear that you are the lost son—the one who has sinned and left your father, and who deserves no mercy, grace, or second chance for salvation. Yet in the parable, the father not only looks at his wayward son with compassion and takes him back, but celebrates his return. "'For this my son was dead, and is alive again; he was lost, and is found.' And they began to celebrate."[84]

Lincoln felt abandoned, disheartened, and depressed frequently throughout his life. Perhaps you do too. Our sinful, human condition makes us all weak, frail, and vulnerable. Yet Christ-followers know that Jesus loves them and will be by their side—always. Jesus will walk with *you* through the valleys—even the valley of the shadow of death.[85]

Your Heavenly Father wants you to come home with Him someday. Jesus provides that bridge to heaven. As He put it, "I am the good shepherd. The good shepherd lays down his life for the sheep … and they will listen to my voice. So there will be one flock, one shepherd … This charge I have received from my Father."[86] What a story to know and share.

Your Life

What are the Bible stories or biblical accounts that are the most sticky for you or easiest to remember? Why?

---

[83] Matt. 7:24–27.

[84] Luke 15:24.

[85] Ps. 23:4.

[86] John 10:11–18.

Lincoln used wit and humor effectively in communicating with people. How can Christians use wit and humor to witness Christ or build a platform for the teaching of God's Word?

What is *your* faith story to tell? Are you telling it? Why or why not? How are you telling it, if you are?

23

Empathy

Above all, keep loving one another earnestly,
since love covers a multitude of sins.
—1 Peter 4:8

The Lincoln Way

Empathy helps leaders build meaningful relationships and trust.

One day an elderly lady came to visit President Lincoln in the Executive Mansion. Her son had been in the army but had been court-martialed for some offense. Mother and son anticipated a severe penalty. After patiently listening to the lady make the case for her son, Lincoln told Congressman Thaddeus Stevens that her boy should be pardoned. Stevens agreed, and Lincoln told the mother that her son would be exonerated and released.

The woman walked with Stevens as he escorted her out of the building. After walking for a short time, she turned to the congressman and said with excitement, "I knew it was a copperhead lie!"

"What do you refer to, madam?" asked Stevens.

"Why, they told me he was an ugly looking man," she replied. On the contrary, the president "is the most handsome man I ever saw in my life!"[1]

One of the great ironies of President Lincoln's life was that he presided over the deadliest of all American wars—the Civil War—which belied his empathetic, kind, and compassionate disposition.

---

1 Carpenter, *Six Months at the White House*, 192–93.

Those who conversed with him were drawn to his sensitivity and kindheartedness. One night when young Abe and a friend were walking home, he noticed a man lying dead drunk and nearly frozen in a mud hole. Abe picked up the man and carried him all the way to his cousin's house, where he built a fire to warm him up.

On another occasion, young Abe and his friends passed a pig caught in a stretch of boggy ground. They continued walking for a half a mile until Lincoln's conscience eventually got the best of him. He told his friends that he had to go back to help the pig. He could no longer endure thinking about the pig's struggle without trying to help it.[2]

Whether it was insects, animals, or humans, Lincoln's kindness knew no limits. When his stepbrother, John Johnston, caught a land terrapin and threw it viciously against a tree, crushing its shell and watching it writhe in pain, Lincoln furiously chided Johnston in a rage rarely seen in the boy or man. Abe frequently preached against and wrote about the cruelty to animals and insects alike. He had a heart for lost cats, mired-down hogs, birds which had fallen out of a nest, and for turtles which endured cruelty from jokesters who had put hot coals on their back. After blasting a turkey to bits at eight years of age, young Abe never hunted again. His sense of empathy infused him with benevolence for the tiniest of creatures. He even insisted that an ant's life is just as precious to the ant as a human life is to a human.[3]

Lincoln's intense sympathy extended beyond insects and animals to human beings. He had compassion for the displaced Indian who wandered into the camp; the woman whose drunken husband beat her; the farm boy who would be shot for falling asleep on sentry duty; the coffle of slaves—chained together like fish on a line—on

---

[2] Goodwin, *Leadership*, 8–9.

[3] Wilson, *Herndon's Informants*, 110, 112.

the boat in the Ohio. His empathy and compassion for people certainly contributed to his growing antipathy to slavery.[4]

During his New Salem days, Lincoln had to prove his worth, like many on the frontier, in a wrestling match with a local favorite, Jack Armstrong—leader of a group called the Clary Grove Boys. Bets were made and a date set. During the match, Armstrong applied an illegal hold, and Lincoln reproached him for it. Eventually, Abe's immense strength and leverage allowed him to overcome Armstrong. Instead of becoming bitter toward one another, Lincoln and Armstrong let bygones be bygones. Armstrong would welcome Lincoln into his home for a week or more at a time, and his wife Hannah fed and clothed Lincoln. In return, Abe chopped wood and helped with chores on the farm. Abe also bounced Armstrong's children on his knees as he sat before the fire.

Like many of Lincoln's earliest associates, Armstrong became a lifelong admirer. Twenty-six years after the legendary encounter, Jack Armstrong's son, Duff, was accused of murdering a man in a drunken brawl. With no other resources, Jack's widow, Hannah, turned to Lincoln, now a prominent lawyer in Springfield. Lincoln not only took the case, but waived his fee and waged a brilliant legal battle that resulted in a surprise acquittal for Duff Armstrong.[5] Lincoln's propensity for kindness, forgiveness, and empathy had a way of turning adversaries into supporters.

During a council of war during the tension-filled days of the Civil War, an officer named Oliver Otis Howard, a future founder of Howard University, forgot his junior place and volunteered an opinion. Secretary of State Seward disagreed with his comment and sharply reprimanded Howard, indicating that the young colonel should be seen and not heard. Howard's superiors agreed with the reprimand and stared him down after the altercation. When the moment passed and the generals were absorbed with the map spread

4 Miller, *Lincoln's Virtues*, 364–65.

5 Keneally, *Lincoln*, 15; Winkle, *Young Eagle*, 68.

on the table, Lincoln casually rose from his chair, slipped around to Howard, who had slinked off to the far side of the room, and put his arm around the young officer. Lincoln gave him an affectionate pat and a look of tender sympathy, then went back to his seat. Howard never forgot the gesture. "I loved Lincoln from that hour," he later reflected.[6]

"Mr. Lincoln had a deep, broad, living conscience," Francis Carpenter noted.[7] Anyone who knew or observed Lincoln for any amount of time saw his care, compassion, and kindness toward others. Before making time with a political leader, Lincoln once spent a half hour with a mute young woman who spoke with paper and pencil. "That girl had no favor to ask," he told a politician who had observed the situation, "but she will live happier all her life because she met the President."[8]

In the fall of 1862, Lincoln created the new position of judge advocate general of the Union army, whose primary function was to determine whether to extend clemency to soldiers whose pleas had been sent up the chain of command for Lincoln's review. No execution of a soldier could take place, however, without Lincoln's approval. In cases that could draw the death sentence in civilian life—rape, murder, treason, dealing in slaves—Lincoln generally withheld clemency and allowed the execution to be carried out, though he sometimes granted a temporary stay to permit a condemned man time to get his affairs in order. Through numerous acts of kindness and clemency, Lincoln secured the nickname Father Abraham from thousands of Union soldiers, in large part because of his insistence that men receive justice and mercy.[9]

Lincoln's empathetic and forgiving nature set him up for criticism, even from many of his supporters. As the Union army conquered and occupied more sections of the South, Lincoln

---

[6] Conway, *Lincoln's White House*, 354.

[7] Carpenter, *Six Months at the White House*, 354.

[8] Conway, *Lincoln's White House*, 133.

[9] Packard, *Lincolns in the White House*, 146, 149.

issued an amnesty proclamation in December 1863, much to the consternation of many Union politicians and their constituencies. The proclamation 1) allowed for a full pardon for and restoration of property to all engaged in the rebellion, with the exception of the highest Confederate officials and military leaders; 2) allowed for a new state government to be formed in any rebellious state in which ten percent of the eligible voters had taken an oath of allegiance to the United States; and 3) encouraged Southern states admitted under this proclamation to enact plans to deal with the freed slaves, so long as the freedom of the formerly enslaved people was not compromised. Despite Lincoln's belief that "when a man is sincerely *penitent* for his misdeeds, and gives satisfactory evidence of the same, he can safely be pardoned, and there is no exception to the rule," the war-torn, casualty-ridden Northern public did not want to show any compassion to the Confederate South.[10]

No matter what happened in the war, including the Fort Pillow Massacre (located on the Mississippi River in Tennessee where Union soldiers, most African-American, were massacred by Confederate General Nathan Bedford Forrest while attempting to surrender) and the suffering of Union prisoners in the notorious Andersonville prison, Lincoln would not respond with an eye for an eye. With regard to Confederate prisoners in Union custody, Lincoln said, "I can never, never starve men like that! Whatever others may say or do, I never can, and I never will, be accessory to such treatment of human beings!"[11] Lincoln's kindness, empathy, and compassion simply ran too deep and remained a part of his seemingly untouchable inner core, even during a bitter and ferocious civil war.

Lincoln's kindness and compassion extended to his generals as well as the soldiers of the Union army. After the disaster at Bull Run at the beginning of the war, Lincoln took the blame and exonerated General Winfield Scott, who had told Lincoln that he deserved

---

[10] Carpenter, *Six Months in the White House*, 197.

[11] Carpenter, *Six Months in the White House*, 197.

removal. Having served as commander under six different chief executives, Scott remarked, "I have never served a President who has been kinder to me than you have been."[12] When General George McClellan blamed the War Department for the disaster of the Peninsula campaign, citing lack of troops, people called for Stanton's resignation. Lincoln vigorously defended him.[13] When General George Meade failed to attack Lee after Gettysburg, a critical moment that might have ended the war, Lincoln's exasperation with poor generalship reached its peak. Even in his extreme frustration, however, he found his empathetic bearings and tried to understand the situation from Meade's perspective. "I have not fully made up my mind how I should behave when mini-balls were whistling, and those great oblong shells shrieking in my ear," he admitted to a congressman. "I might run away."[14]

Contemporaries who knew Lincoln best saw his compassion and empathy frequently on display. "He was certainly a poor hater," said one. "He never judged men by his like, or dislike for them … If a man had maligned him, or been guilty of personal ill-treatment and abuse … he would put him in his Cabinet just as soon as he would his friend."[15] Indeed, Lincoln's cabinet was filled by a team of rivals—men who had sought the presidency and had ridiculed and maligned him, and then lost to him in the election of 1860.[16] Yet Lincoln wanted the most qualified and capable

---

[12] Donald, *Lincoln*, 308.

[13] Goodwin, *Leadership*, 226.

[14] Goodwin, *Team of Rivals*, 536.

[15] Wilson, *Herndon's Informants*, 166.

[16] Burlingame, *Lincoln*, 1:720. Lincoln wanted to hire talented people for his cabinet no matter how they felt about him. When advised not to appoint Salmon Chase to a cabinet post because the Ohioan regarded himself as bigger deal than the president-elect, Lincoln responded that he would love to fill his cabinet with people who thought they were bigger than him. In fact, the president included every major competitor at the Chicago Convention in his cabinet—evidence of supreme self-confidence. Wheeler, *Faith and Courage*, 143. Lincoln's cabinet had a solid, representative balance of East and West,

cabinet for the country, despite political affiliation, rivalry, or past pettiness. Whether they had called him a "gorilla," as Stanton had, or questioned his fitness for office, as Seward had done, Lincoln could forgive and forget and make people feel essential to the cause.

During the early phase of the war, Simon Cameron resigned under pressure after allowing severe corruption to take place in the War Department (purchasing of malfunctioning weapons, diseased horses, and rotten food). Despite having no obligation, Lincoln worked hard to assuage Cameron's pain and humiliation. The president wrote a long public letter to Congress, explaining that the unfortunate contracts had been spawned by the emergency situation facing the government in the immediate aftermath of Fort Sumter. Lincoln insisted that he and his entire cabinet were equally at fault for whatever errors or mistakes were committed. Filled with gratitude and admiration, the disgraced and devastated Cameron never forgot Lincoln's kindness and generosity. He became one of Lincoln's most intimate friends. Most men in Lincoln's situation, Cameron wrote, "would have permitted an innocent man to suffer rather than incur responsibility."[17]

At first disdainful toward the candidate, Seward's admiration of Lincoln grew considerably as he served as secretary of state. Late in the war, when Seward had suffered a terrible carriage accident that almost took his life, Lincoln hauled his long frame into the same bed with his friend to comfort him in his recovery. He wanted Seward to

---

former Democrats and Whigs, hard-liners and conciliators. White, *Lincoln*, 397. The president's cabinet selections also sent a strong leadership message. He did not choose lesser yes men. He surrounded himself with some of the nation's most able men: three ex-Whigs—Seward, Bates, and Smith; four ex-Democrats—Chase, Cameron, Wells, and Blair. Some Republicans criticized him for the number of ex-Dems in his cabinet, but Lincoln countered that he, as a former Whig, made the cabinet perfectly balanced: four to four. Lincoln knew how to bring divergent voices together.

[17] Goodwin, *Team of Rivals,* 413.

know that the war was almost won.[18] After the president had passed, Seward declared, "Lincoln will take his place with Washington and Franklin, and Jefferson, and Adams, and Jackson, among the benefactors of the country and of the human race."[19] Seward expressed the same sentiment in stronger language to Reverend Dr. Bellows: "Mr. Lincoln is the best and wisest man I ever knew!"[20] Lincoln's empathetic touch had won over his once fierce political rival.

Secretary of War Edwin Stanton did not agree with Lincoln's inclination to issue pardons. Lincoln often discovered an empathetic excuse to spare a soldier's life; Stanton believed swift and sure punishment ensured military discipline and acted as powerful deterrent to possible offenders. Yet when Stanton gave Lincoln his opinion in a gruff, blunt manner, Lincoln never took it personally. He knew the pressures Stanton faced during the war.[21] Stanton learned to appreciate the sensitivity and emotional intelligence of his commander in chief and became one of his strongest supporters.

Even when Lincoln lost his cool, he returned to his empathetic and compassionate nature. One day an army colonel rode out to the Soldiers' Home, hopeful of securing Lincoln's aid in recovering the body of his wife, who had died in a steamboat accident. Lincoln listened but grew impatient as his relaxation time disappeared. "Am I to have not rest?" an exasperated president interjected. "Is there no hour or spot when or where I may escape this constant call? Why do you follow me out here with such business as this?" The disheartened colonel returned to his hotel in Washington. The following morning, Lincoln appeared at his door. "I was a brute last night," the president said, and offered to help the colonel in any way possible.[22]

---

18 Packard, *Lincolns in the White House*, 234.

19 McGovern, *Lincoln*, 114–15.

20 Carpenter, *Six Months in the White House*, 104.

21 McGovern, *Lincoln*, 114–15.

22 Goodwin, *Team of Rivals*, 512.

After Lincoln passed, Alexander Stephens, former vice president of the Confederacy, said that "every fountain" of Lincoln's "heart was overflowing with the 'milk of human kindness.'"[23] Stephens was in a position to know, for he and Lincoln had formed a unique friendship. They became good friends in Congress during Lincoln's only House term (1847–1849). Lincoln asked the Georgia businessman, in late November 1860, for a copy of his recent pro-Union speech. They met in the cabin of the *River Queen*, at Fort Monroe, for the first time in sixteen years, at the end of the Civil War. They greeted each other warmly and with a firm handshake. "Little" and "slim"—he weighed ninety pounds—and wrapped in layers of coats and shawls, Stephens began to unwrap himself. Lincoln laughed at the sight. "Never have I seen so small a nubbin come out of so much husk."[24] They reminisced.

The Hampton Roads Conference (February 1865) led nowhere, but Lincoln thanked the Confederate delegates for coming anyway. He asked Stephens if there was anything he could do for him. Stephens mentioned that his nephew, John A. Stephens, was being held prisoner on Johnson Island. Lincoln wrote down his name and, on his return to Washington, ordered Lieutenant Stephens be paroled. When he met the young Stephens in Washington, he gave him three things: a five-day pass to visit friends in Washington; a note to his uncle asking that the senior Stephens release a Union soldier of equal rank whose "physical condition most requires his release"; and an autographed picture of himself, across which Lincoln wrote, "Don't have many of these where you are from." Stephens later recalled, "I almost wept when I saw it." Unfortunately, by the time Stephens received the communication, Richmond had fallen and President Lincoln was dead.[25]

---

[23] Lehrman, *Lincoln "by littles,"* 111.

[24] Miller, *Lincoln's Virtues,* 429-30.

[25] Miller, *Lincoln's Virtues*, 429–30; Lehrman, *Lincoln "by littles,"* 189.

Lincoln's empathy and sympathy were certainly attributes of his core being, but they were also important elements in his political success. He could remember people's names, where he had met them, and what they had talked about, even if it was a decade ago. For Lincoln, knowing people intimately helped him think about life from other perspectives and not just his own.

Lincoln's empathy kept him cool under fire and understanding of the plights of others. Sometimes he got so upset at cabinet officials, politicians, or generals, he would write a scorching letter of condemnation. Often, after cooling down for a few days, he never sent the letter. Lincoln simply did not want to hurt anyone's feelings. When Stanton got upset, Lincoln told him to write it down and think about it for a day or two—then throw it in the wastebasket. That would make him feel better.[26]

Gifted at reading people, Lincoln understood when to be direct or subtle, cajoling or persuasive, tender or aggressive. He formed formidable friendships with men who had previously opposed him and went out of his way to repair injured feelings that could have escalated into permanent hostility if not addressed. Especially as commander in chief, he took responsibility for the failures of subordinates, shared credit with ease, and learned from his mistakes. His emotional intelligence and empathetic nature helped him forecast what his opponents were likely to do and discern the inward feelings, motivations, and intentions of others throughout his career.[27]

Since he could read people, Lincoln confidently believed he could persuade people of his positions, like a lawyer making a case to an undecided jury.[28] His social and emotional intelligence were two key leadership abilities that separated him from other men. For example, as president he handled the prodigious egos of his cabinet in a masterful way. He knew that Seward's feelings had been

---

26 Goodwin, *Leadership*, 225.

27 Carpenter, *Six Months at the White House*, 75; Goodwin, *Team of Rivals*, xvii, 104; Pinsker, "Lincoln and the Lessons of Party Leadership," 197.

28 McGovern, *Lincoln*, 133.

hurt and his ego crushed when he surprisingly lost the Republican nomination in 1860. Therefore, almost every day of his presidency, Lincoln crossed the street from the Executive Mansion and visited his secretary of state in his townhouse at Lafayette Park. Lincoln knew that Seward's ego needed massaging.

In the same manner, Secretary of War Stanton, whom Lincoln loved to call "Mars," lived with high stress as he directly oversaw the war effort. Lincoln tried to help Stanton relax by sitting with him in the telegraph office, even holding hands with him as they anxiously awaited battlefield bulletins.

Indeed, Lincoln spent special, dedicated time with all of his cabinet officials. He often stopped in to see Wells ("Neptune") down at the navy department and Secretary of Treasury Salmon Chase at his stately mansion. He frequently dined with Postmaster General Montgomery Blair and his entire family, and took long carriage rides with Attorney General Edward Bates. "Everyone likes a compliment," Lincoln asserted.[29] Thus he took a great amount of time and care to write notes to colleagues and associates, especially eager to express his thanks for their leadership and actions in a time of war.

Even when Lincoln had to make decisions that were contrary to the desires of his cabinet, he did it in an empathetic manner. When he removed one of Chase's nominees, Lincoln put his arm around Chase's shoulders and explained why he'd made the decision he did. The ambitious Chase, who wanted Lincoln's job and often scorned his authority, nevertheless acknowledged that "the President has always treated me with such personal kindness and has always manifested such fairness and integrity of purpose, that I have not found myself free to throw up my trust."[30]

Lincoln's relationship with Chase is another terrific example of Lincoln's empathy and ability to forgive. Much like the other

---

[29] Basler, Lincoln to Thurlow Weed, March 15, 1865, *CW*, 8:356.

[30] Goodwin, *Leadership*, 223–24.

members of the team of rivals, Chase wanted to be president and felt himself eminently more qualified than the rail-splitter from Illinois. Unlike the others, however, Chase continued to undermine Lincoln's presidency behind the scenes and tried to manipulate politicians into removing Lincoln from office. He set his sights on running for the Republican ticket in 1864. Lincoln knew that Chase's mind was "full of Presidential maggots"[31] and that seeking the presidency consumed the Treasury secretary. Therefore when Chase tried to hire too many Radical Republicans, Lincoln simply blocked his appointments. Chase responded by threatening to resign from the cabinet several times, a move that caused Lincoln problems with Radical Republicans and abolitionists in the North. Finally, in 1864, Lincoln surprised Chase by accepting one of his resignations. Lincoln had lured him into a trap and called his bluff. Stunned by Lincoln's action, Chase tried to get his presidential campaign off the ground, to no avail.

Nevertheless, a few months later, Lincoln showed great magnanimity in selecting Salmon Chase as Supreme Court justice. Lincoln explained that while Chase had acted and behaved inappropriately, if not nefariously, he still admired Chase's talents and did not want to crush him. He gave Chase a second chance to serve his country. Lincoln's secretary John Nicolay later said that no one but Lincoln would have shown that degree of magnanimity and forgiveness toward someone who had tried to undermine the president and his administration. Montgomery Blair speculated that Chase might have been the only person Lincoln actually hated. Thus, appointing Chase to the Supreme Court demonstrated the president's benevolence and capacity to forgive. [32] Lincoln's empathy for Chase revealed, once again, the president's greatness in an age of small men.

---

31 Burlingame, *Lincoln,* 2:612.

32 Burlingame, *Lincoln*, 2:612, 735–36.

Perhaps Lincoln's empathy appears most clearly in his compassion toward the Confederacy and its people—civilians, political leaders, and military. He once said that he made more life-and-death decisions than all of his predecessors put together. The president generously granted innumerable pardons to Confederate soldiers, whom many Northerners wanted imprisoned or hanged as traitors. Lincoln, however, commanded that all deserters returning within sixty days would be pardoned on condition of returning to their regiments and companies. Lincoln suggested to General Grant and other commanders that he had no problem if Confederate leaders quietly escaped to Canada or Cuba.

Illustrating his merciful and empathetic spirit, Lincoln told an anecdote about a man who had taken the pledge never to touch a drop of alcohol, but was invited by a friend to have a drink. Rather than risk being thought unfriendly, the man said he would have a glass of lemonade. His friend agreed to pour him a glass of lemonade, but added a shot of brandy, thinking it would make the beverage taste that much finer. The man replied that he would not object if a dram was added, provided it was done "unbeknown" to him.[33]

Later, in his second inaugural address, Lincoln implored his countrymen to move on "with malice toward none; with charity for all" and "to bind up the nation's wounds" and "care for him who shall have borne the battle, and for his widow, and his orphan."[34] Lincoln's capacity to feel people and connect with them on a personal level was truly an impressive gift.

Whatever amount of empathy God had blessed him with at birth, Lincoln's capacity for it grew with his life experiences and habits. The books he read and theater productions he viewed stimulated his mind and constantly compelled him reflect on the human condition and the peculiarities of individuals—how they

---

[33] Johnson, *Last Weeks of Lincoln*, 55, 124.

[34] Basler, Lincoln's Second Inaugural Address, March 4, 1865, *CW*, 8:332–33.

thought, what made them tick, and why they believed in the things or the ways they did.

As president, Lincoln spent a great deal of time ruminating at the Soldiers' Home, a complex secluded in three hundred acres of hills three miles north of Washington, DC. He usually found sanctuary there from June to October. In his reflection time, Lincoln often looked at issues from different perspectives and contemplated the deeper meanings of things. He wrote many drafts of the Emancipation Proclamation at the Soldiers' Home. Lincoln often joined soldiers around a campfire, happily sharing a plate of beans and cup of coffee. He earnestly listened to these soldiers, and they frequently voiced their feelings about injustices or grievances, such as substandard socks.[35] The president's desire to help them was palpable.

Furthermore, Lincoln vigilantly watched for economic, social, and political trends. He voraciously perused newspapers to gauge the pulse of the country. Constantly engaging people of all backgrounds, classes, and vocations, he could infer and capture the essence of their moods, hopes, dreams, and aspirations. Lincoln's gift of discernment certainly aided his decision-making and his empathetic approach to people.

Acting on his curiosity was yet another way Lincoln nurtured his empathy. He never tired of asking people questions—about their backgrounds, families, religions, vocations, aspirations, politics, principles, inventions, innovations, and everything else. As intelligent and well-read as he became, Lincoln never believed he had things figured out or that he could not learn something new. He constantly looked for ways to improve things or grow in his own understanding and knowledge. Curiosity and possibility fueled his desire to learn more and engage with people, who never failed to intrigue or enlighten him. Cabinet officials and military commanders were honored he asked them so often for feedback and

---

35 Packard, *Lincolns in the White House*, 150.

insight, but so were common folk, who were impressed that he cared what they thought and took the time to solicit their opinions.

Beyond being curious and asking questions, perhaps one of Lincoln's most significant gifts that helped cultivate his empathy was his desire to listen. Even as a lad, Lincoln demonstrated excellent listening skills. "When old folks were at our house," remembered his stepmother, Abe "was a silent & attentive observer, never speaking or asking questions till they were gone and then he must understand Every thing, even to the smallest thing, Minutely & Exactly." Young Lincoln "would then repeat it over to himself again & again, sometimes in one form and then in another" until it became "fixed in his mind." Often after hearing sermons at church, Abe would come home and "get on a stump or log and almost repeat it word for word" in front of his siblings, cousins, and neighbors. "The sight of such a thing amused all and did Especially tickle the children."[36] He carefully listened to his father's stories and those told by neighbors and strangers passing through the frontier lands of Kentucky and Indiana. Moreover, in every one of his professions, Lincoln listened to and learned about people.

Starting almost from his first day as president, Lincoln and the White House staff were overwhelmed with office and patronage seekers. Lincoln insisted on meeting with anyone who bothered to come visit him, including the common folk, who often spent days and weeks traveling to Washington, DC, just to speak with him for fifteen minutes. As the duly elected man of the people, Lincoln felt it an important part of his duty to listen to the concerns, dreams, and aspirations of all Americans. Certainly these "public opinion baths" had a political motivation attached to them, but Lincoln truly wanted to hear what people had to say.

Moreover, Lincoln met with church leaders of every major faith and denomination. He aimed for broad religious representation among army and hospital chaplains. Some critics missed the

---

[36] Wilson, *Herndon's Informants*, 106–9.

political importance of Lincoln's time-consuming meetings with "preachers" and "Grannies," but Lincoln saw immense value in building relationships and trust through these conversations.[37] Whether personal or political in motivation, Lincoln intentionally spent a big chunk of each day listening to people.

As a politician and party leader, Lincoln demonstrated the importance of listening to his allies and opponents. He worked hard to gather as much information as he could and to obtain it from as many sources as possible. He consumed multiple newspapers every day. His curious and aggressive attitude in accumulating knowledge and information aided him in navigating the realities of war. He regularly left the Executive Mansion and visited citizens and politicians in Washington, workers and innovators at the Navy Yard, or special guests at the Soldiers' Home just to hear and digest other perspectives.[38] Listening helped Lincoln learn, grow, and improve, which is why he listened so well.

Two days after the First Battle of Bull Run, early in the war, Lincoln visited some troops in the field. He encountered William T. Sherman, commander of a brigade that had taken three hundred casualties in the clash. Lincoln wanted to encourage the troops, but Sherman asked Lincoln to discourage any sort of cheering and merriment—for that was how the troops behaved before the Battle of Bull Run, which ended in disaster. Sherman wanted his men to be calm, tough, hard-fighting soldiers who went about their business with great efficiency and got results.

Taking the request to heart, Lincoln gave "one of the neatest, best, and most feeling addresses I ever listened to," according to Sherman. Referencing the setback at Bull Run, Lincoln told the troops to remain steady because brighter days were coming soon. When the soldiers began to cheer, Lincoln promptly curbed their outward enthusiasm, noting Sherman's concern. Lincoln concluded

---

37 Carwardine, "Lincoln's Religion," 244.

38 Pinsker, "Lincoln and the Lessons of Party Leadership," 193–94, 196.

his speech by explaining that, as commander in chief, he would personally work to provide the soldiers everything they needed to win the war. He even encouraged them to send their requests to him personally if they were not being given everything they desired. The Union general could not have been more pleased with Lincoln's speech.

As Sherman showed him more camps, Lincoln complimented him on the order, cleanliness, and discipline of his brigade. At Fort Corcoran, Lincoln repeated his remarks, including the pledge to listen to soldiers' complaints if they felt they had been wronged.

One officer felt confident enough to complain, asserting that Sherman had threatened to shoot him like a dog after planning a trip to New York without leave. Lincoln gazed at the officer and rejoined in a stage whisper, loud enough for those nearby to hear, "Well, if I were you, and he threatened to shoot, I would not trust him, for I believe he would do it."[39] The officer turned and walked off to the laughter of his fellow troops.

As the small party drove on, Sherman felt the need to explain himself. But Lincoln demurred, insisting that Sherman knew his business best. He did not want to micromanage his general. Sherman thanked the commander in chief for his confidence and told him that his comments would help maintain discipline in the regiment.[40] Lincoln had placed himself in his commander's shoes. His empathy reigned again.

The ability to see the complexities of an issue was a strength of Lincoln's leadership. He deliberately disciplined himself to look at matters from different perspectives. In August 1862, he invited his old friend Leonard Swett to the Executive Mansion and asked him for input on the emancipation issue. When Swett arrived, Lincoln pulled out letters and put them on a table in the cabinet room. He first read one from William Lloyd Garrison, the New England

---

[39] Donald, *Lincoln*, 308.

[40] Burlingame, *Lincoln*, 2:186–87.

abolitionist, and then one by Garrett Davis, state senator from the border state of Kentucky, followed by one or two more letters from people with divergent viewpoints. Lincoln then debated the emancipation issue in front of Swett, voicing the various perspectives and adding some of his own arguments.

Swett, who had traveled the Eighth Judicial Circuit with Lincoln in Illinois, had observed this pattern in countless courtrooms. Lincoln could "state the case of his adversary better and more forcibly than his opponent could state it himself," he recalled. On this occasion, Lincoln carried on for more than an hour with his one-man debate. Swett became impressed that Lincoln's "manner did not indicate that he wished to impress his views *upon* the hearer, but rather to weigh and examine them for his own enlightenment *in the presence* of the hearer." Swett, so trusted by Lincoln, felt privileged to be "a witness of the President's mental operations." When Lincoln finished, he did not ask for Swett's opinion on the matter. He simply thanked him for coming, wished him a pleasant trip home, and sent greetings to their mutual friends.[41] Sometimes Lincoln had only to listen to himself, for he knew the arguments on all sides better than most advocates.

While Lincoln pondered all sides of an issue, he did not hesitate to draw his own conclusions. Lincoln solicited advice from Seward so often, for example, that some considered the talkative New Yorker the "power behind the throne." Yet Seward knew better. "There is but one vote in the Cabinet," he asserted, "and that is cast by the President."[42]

A short time before 1864 election, Harriet Beecher Stowe commented that the world marveled that "a plain working man of the people, with no more culture, instruction or education than any such workingman may obtain for himself," had been "called on to conduct the passage of a great people through a crisis involving the destinies of the whole world." She particularly admired Lincoln's

[41] White, *Lincoln*, 509–10.

[42] Goodwin, *Team of Rivals*, 669.

tenacious and steadfast determination to see his war objectives through to the end. A keen observer of the president, she knew that he had been "surrounded by all sorts of conflicting claims, by traitors, by half-hearted, timid men, by Border State men and free State men, by radical Abolitionists and Conservatives." While Lincoln had prudently "listened to all, weighted the words of all, waited, observed, yielded now here and now there," he had "in the main kept one inflexible, honest purpose, and drawn the national ship through."[43]

This was how Lincoln the leader operated. He asked questions, listened, received feedback, and then made his own decision, carrying it out with resolve and discipline. In short, his empathy made him a better executive.

Lincoln's empathetic personality—his tenderhearted patience, affection, generosity, kindness, and humility—significantly aided his ability to connect with people. He treated everyone the same, no matter their rank, class, power, wealth, or prestige.

Citizens believed him to be the most unassuming attorney they had ever met. One day a bunch of attorneys on his Illinois circuit convened a meeting at a local tavern. In those times, table seating reflected the hierarchy of the court. Judge Davis presided, surrounded by lawyers, at the head of the table. On one occasion, Lincoln seated himself at the foot, among the common clientele. The landlord objected to this social injustice: "You're in the wrong place, Mr. Lincoln, come up here." Lincoln responded: "Have you anything better to eat up there, Joe? If not, I'll stay here."[44]

The tenderness Lincoln displayed, combined with his frequent melancholy, proved to be an asset in both personal and political relationships. To be grave and sensitive—to connect and acutely feel

---

43 Sandburg, *Lincoln*, 475.

44 Goodwin, *Leadership*, 108.

the emotions of others—endeared Lincoln to many.[45] People felt the seriousness, care, and compassion from Father Abraham.

Lincoln believed kindheartedness and benevolence could be positive and powerful catalysts for change in the world. To influence people, Lincoln said that a "kind, unassuming persuasion, should ever be adopted. It is an old and a true maxim, that a 'drop of honey catches more flies than a gallon of gall.' So with men." To win one over to a cause, "first convince him that you are his sincere friend. Therein is a drop of honey that catches his heart, which … is the great high road to his reason," and, once gained, "you will find but little trouble in convincing his judgment of the justice of your cause."[46]

Kindness, compassion, and empathy were character attributes foundational to Lincoln the man and the leader, and these qualities took him far. "He was the best friend I ever had excepting my own wife and my mother," recalled a congressman from Illinois. "I think Mr. Lincoln was the best man, the kindest, tenderest, noblest, loveliest, since Christ. He was better and purer than Washington; and in my mind he stands incomparable, grandly looming up."[47] Dr. Stone, Lincoln's family physician at the White House, who differed with the president politically, remarked that "it is the province of a physician to probe deeply the interior lives of men; and I affirm that Mr. Lincoln is the purest hearted man with whom I ever came in contact."[48]

Lincoln's empathy and empathetic nature helped endear him to almost all who knew him. Father Abraham would come, listen, laugh, tell a story, encourage, and persuade. He could read people, connect with them, and lead them to a better and more gratifying life. People might not know as much as he did about the law, politics, or economics, but they did believe that he cared for them.

---

45 Shenk, *Lincoln's Melancholy*, 30.

46 Basler, Lincoln's Temperance Address, February 22, 1842, *CW*, 1:271–79.

47 Hertz, *The Hidden Lincoln*, 37.

48 Carpenter, *Six Months in the White House*, 104.

The Truth

The Bible clearly and constantly reveals God's mercy, grace, love, and empathetic nature. Since God is all-knowing and all-powerful, He certainly knows how every one of His children, including you, feel at all times. He knows what it feels like to walk in your footsteps. After all, he made your feet, and the rest of your body, mind, and soul too. Of course, He had mercy on all sinners—so much so that He put His grace into action by sending His Son, Jesus, to die for the sins of the world, and yours too. Talk about empathy. God *knew* exactly what we would need to join Him in heaven someday—a Savior. His empathetic and agape love is profound and divine: "For God so loved the world, that he gave his only Son, that whoever believes in him should not perish but have eternal life."[49]

Inspired by God's empathetic nature, mercy, grace, and love, Christians are called to model it. The Bible says to "rejoice with those who rejoice, weep with those who weep."[50] Christians are to "bear one another's burdens."[51] Indeed, "if one member suffers, all suffer together; if one member is honored, all rejoice together."[52] "Be kind to one another," the Bible urges, "tenderhearted, forgiving one another, as God in Christ forgave you."[53] And since we are called to think about the feelings of others and be sensitive to their needs, Scripture exhorts that "no corrupting talk come out of your mouths, but only such as is good for building up, as fits the occasion, that it may give grace to those who hear."[54] Sons and daughters of the Heavenly Father "have unity of mind, sympathy, brotherly love, a tender heart, and a humble mind."[55]

---

[49] John 3:16.

[50] Rom. 12:15.

[51] Gal. 6:2.

[52] 1 Cor. 12:26.

[53] Eph. 4:32.

[54] Eph. 4:29.

[55] 1 Pet. 3:8.

There has never been a more humble and empathetic individual ever to walk the earth than Jesus Christ. In his thoughts, words, and deeds, Jesus is empathy personified. He calls on His followers "to love one another as I have loved you,"[56] to "love your neighbor as yourself,"[57] and "as you wish that others would do to you, do so to them."[58] Everywhere Jesus's earthly ministry took Him, He had compassion for people, touched them, healed them, and provided the truth that would set them free from their sins. Jesus made it clear that "people will know that you are my disciples, if you have love for one another."[59] Even as He endured a brutal crucifixion on the cross of Calvary to pay for sin, including yours, His empathy poured forth through His words: "Father, forgive them, for they know not what they do."[60] So empathetic is Jesus that He knows you and your feelings better than you know yourself.

When you love people, you spend time with them and are sensitive to their every hurt, pain, need, hope, aspiration, and dream. Most often, empathy is needed when people are broken or suffer in some way. This is where God's mercy, grace, and love can fill you and others with peace, hope, and joy. For we know that our Triune God is "the Father of mercies and God of all comfort, who comforts us in all our affliction, so that we may be able to comfort those who are in any affliction, with the comfort with which we ourselves are comforted by God."[61]

Christians, "as God's chosen ones, holy and beloved," are to put on:

> compassionate hearts, kindness, humility, meekness, and patience, bearing with one another and, if one

---

[56] John 15:12.
[57] Matt. 22:39.
[58] Luke 6:31.
[59] John 13:34–35.
[60] Luke 23:34.
[61] 2 Cor. 1:3–4.

> has a complaint against another, forgiving each other; as the Lord has forgiven you, so you also must forgive. Above all these put on love, which binds everything together in perfect harmony. And let the peace of Christ rule in your hearts, to which indeed you were called in one body. And be thankful. Let the word of Christ dwell in you richly, teaching and admonishing one another in all wisdom, singing psalms and hymns and spiritual songs, with thankfulness in your hearts to God. And whatever you do, in word or deed, do everything in the name of the Lord Jesus, giving thanks to God the Father through him.[62]

Your Life

Lincoln's empathy continued to grow as he grew older. How does one develop or increase one's empathy and compassion for others?

How did Lincoln dispel the myth that "nice guys and gals finish last"?

Lincoln had keen observation skills. He could read people and possessed a high emotional intelligence. He could discern people's motivations, dreams, and heartbreaks. He also listened well and loved to analyze issues and situations from multiple perspectives. How would you rank yourself in terms of your observation skills, emotional intelligence, and listening skills? Are you simply born with these gifts, or can you develop them? If you believe you can

---

[62] Col. 3:12–17.

improve these skills, what's your plan to develop in any of these areas?

How does God's Word inspire you and help you grow in your compassion and empathy for others?

24

Honesty and Integrity

One who is faithful in a very little is also faithful in much, and one who is dishonest in a very little is also dishonest in much.
—Luke 16:10

The Lincoln Way

Character is destiny for a leader.

The Greek philosopher Heraclitus declared over two millennia ago that "a man's character is his fate."[1] One of the reasons Lincoln remains such treasure to study for young and old today is that his character not only made him a successful leader and president, but is an inspiration for citizens and aspiring leaders. Of all his nicknames, "Honest Abe" is perhaps the most enduring. In the internet age, information may be plentiful but truth and honesty are frustratingly elusive and rare. While certainly not perfect—especially in the political realm, where truth was often hidden or shaded—Lincoln's reputation as a man of honesty and integrity catapulted him to the top of his various professions.

There are many stories that highlight Lincoln's honesty and integrity. Most are even true. In New Salem, local citizens selected him to be the judge of horse races and athletic contests. As a storekeeper, he once walked three miles to a patron's home to return six cents he had overcharged. On another occasion he sold a half pound of tea right before the store closed. After a rush to

[1] Felzenberg, *Leaders that We Deserved*, 11.

complete the transaction, he later realized he had used the wrong weight (half-pound instead of a pound on the scale) and accidentally shortchanged the customer by a half pound. He weighed the rest of the tea the lady had paid for and ran off to deliver it.

After Lincoln served his first term in the Illinois legislature, he returned $199.25 of a $200 campaign gift, having only spent seventy-five cents for a barrel of cider to treat some farm laborers.[2] When attempts to own and run profitable stores failed for him, Lincoln incurred huge personal debt—so big he labeled it his "national debt." Yet, while many other debtors of the time simply shrugged off their commercial obligations, often fleeing town, Lincoln remained in New Salem and promised to pay all his debts, which he eventually did. By paying off his national debt and overcoming his business setbacks, Lincoln built a reputation based on resilience, hard work, and scrupulous honesty. His neighbors noticed and approved. One could count on his word. "Honest Abe" he would remain for the rest of his life.[3]

Friends and family members noted Lincoln's integrity. Dennis Hanks asserted that Lincoln "was honest, faithful," and loved truth, "speaking it at all times & never flinching therefrom."[4] Sarah Bush Lincoln, Abe's stepmother, claimed that "he never told me a lie in his life—never Evaded—never Equivocated, never dodged—nor turned a Corner to avoid any chastisement or other responsibility."[5] Lincoln's wife, Mary, sometimes lamented her husband's integrity, wanting him to be more politically expedient. "Poor Mr. L is almost a monomaniac on the subject of honesty," she once wrote.[6]

Associates regularly remarked about his honesty. William Greene—who worked with Lincoln in Denton Offutt's store in

---

2 McGovern, *Lincoln*, 19; Kigel, *Becoming Lincoln*, 160; Lehrman, *Lincoln "by littles,"* 82; Burlingame, *Lincoln*, 1:60.

3 Winkle, *Young Eagle*, 99-–101.

4 Wilson, *Herndon's Informants*, 21.

5 Wilson, *Herndon's*, 106–9.

6 Lehrman, *Lincoln "by littles,"* 59.

New Salem, served with him in the Black Hawk War, and was later appointed by President Lincoln to be a revenue collector in his district—praised Lincoln as "a man of kindness, courtesy, sincerity & honor, having a mind of great force & depth." The people were especially fond of him because of "the simplicity of his good nature, his honesty, his integrity, his virtue, his moral & noble qualities and when he once had a man's or woman's love he never willingly let go its hold."[7] Fellow Illinois attorney, Jesse Fell, said that "if there were any traits of character that Stood out in bold relief, in the person of Mr Lincoln, it was that of Truth, and Candor. He was utterly incapable of incincerity, or of professing views of this or any other Subjects, he did not entertain."[8]

Mentor Graham, one of Lincoln's cherished mentors, explained that "he was strictly *honest truthful & industrious* & in addition to this he was one of the most *companionable* persons you will ever see in this world."[9] Lawyer and confidante Joseph Gillespie contended that "to sum up his character I should say that he had greater natural mental cabilre [sic] than any man I ever Knew. He was extremely just and fair-mined."[10] Herndon declared Lincoln was "full of honesty, integrity, sincerity," and that Lincoln possessed an "intense honesty."[11] Joshua Speed maintained that "the beauty of his character was its entire simplicity … True to nature true to himself, he was true to every body and every thing about and around him." When Lincoln "was ignorant on any subject no matter how simple it might make him appear he was always willing to acknowledge it. His whole aim in life was to be true to himself & being true to himself he could be false to no one."[12]

---

[7] Wilson, *Herndon's Informants,* 21.

[8] Wilson, *Herndon's Informants,* 578.

[9] Wilson, *Herndon's Informants,* 76.

[10] Wilson, *Herndon's Informants,* 507.

[11] Hertz, *The Hidden Lincoln*, 89.

[12] Wilson, *Herndon's Informants*, 498–99.

Even when partaking in disreputable and sinful behavior, Lincoln lived up to the moniker of Honest Abe. One day Lincoln asked Speed, a womanizer in his day, where he could find a prostitute. According to Speed, he sent Lincoln with a note to a woman in the industry. Lincoln and the girl stripped and were in bed before Lincoln remembered to ask for the price. When the girl informed him of the five-dollar charge, Lincoln quickly told her he could only afford three dollars. The girl insisted that she could trust him for the rest, but Lincoln declared he had other debts to meet, clothed himself, and cordially departed.[13]

Lawyers and politicians are often regarded as deficient in matters of honesty and integrity. Yet Lincoln actually made a name for himself in these two professions *because* of his character and honor. Judge Samuel Parks held that "the great feature in Mr Lincoln's character was his *integrity* in the longest sense of that term—his devotion to truth justice & freedom in every department of human life & under every temptation." Especially impressed that he was "*both a lawyer & a politician,*" Parks declared Lincoln "the most honest man I ever knew. He was not only morally honest but intellectually so, he could not reason falsely, if he attempted it he failed. In politics he never would try to mislead," and "at the bar when he thought he was wrong he was the weakest lawyer I ever saw."[14]

Lincoln did indeed have difficulty making a case if the client had no integrity or truly had committed a wrong. Judge David Davis, who presided over many of Lincoln's cases, noted that Lincoln was an elite circuit court lawyer when he believed his cause or client just. Conversely, Judge Stephen T. Logan maintained that Lincoln struggled when given "a bad case" or when he did not believe in his client.

Lincoln once represented a man in a civil suit and made a solid argument in his defense. After opposing counsel produced clear

[13] Keneally, *Lincoln*, 31.

[14] Wilson, *Herndon's Informants*, 238–39.

evidence refuting that defense, Lincoln absented himself. Judge Davis sent someone to fetch him from his hotel. Lincoln told the court official to tell the judge that he would not be returning to the courtroom. He could not continue to defend the guilty. When he received this news, Davis merely remarked, "Honest Abe."[15]

Honesty helped Lincoln get elected president. He avoided extremes and maintained an even keel. Moreover, he rarely pontificated about things he did not know or pander just to earn a vote. While other political contenders had to frequently adjust and reposition themselves, Lincoln stood out as a man of conviction who lucidly said what he believed and believed what he said.[16]

Even before his presidential bid, Lincoln felt confident when preparing to face Stephen A. Douglas in the Illinois campaign debates of 1858, because he believed Douglas's dishonesty would be exposed. "Douglas will tell a lie to ten thousand people one day, even though he knows he may have to deny it to five thousand the next," he explained.[17] When someone felt compelled to lie to win an argument, Lincoln's confidence increased because he took it as an indicator that his argument occupied the right side of history. When Lincoln won the Republican nomination for president at the convention in Chicago, some of his closest advisors specifically credited Lincoln's integrity for the margin of victory. Citizens and delegates simply believed he could not and would not be manipulated by corrupt or dishonest men.[18]

The corruption in the Pierce and Buchanan administrations had scandalized the nation and left Americans craving someone they could trust. After winning the presidency, Lincoln told a visitor that he won the election because the people embraced and believed in the "Honest Old Abe" slogan. Having a reputation for honesty counted just as much as being antislavery. Four years later, Honest Abe would

[15] Burlingame, *Lincoln*, 1:321.

[16] Goodwin, *Team of Rivals*, 255.

[17] Keneally, *Lincoln*, 68.

[18] Burlingame, *Lincoln*, 1:627.

be reelected in large part because of his character. People believed he had no ambition for power and that he had only the welfare of the people as his goal. Hardly any politician, newspaper reporter, or citizen ever criticized him for being self-seeking or selfish. The American people trusted him.[19]

Lincoln could deal with people who made mistakes, but he abhorred liars. One day a man came to the Executive Mansion to make a request, but Lincoln would not grant it. He had a sixth sense and did not trust the individual. When the man sulked, Lincoln pounced. "You can't look me in the face," Lincoln told him. "You have not looked me in the face since you sat there. Even now you are looking out that window and cannot look me in the eye." He flung the written request into the man's lap. "Take it back. There is something wrong about this. I will have nothing to do with it."[20] Lincoln would not be played.

When Lincoln discovered that some manufacturers were making fortunes selling the government shoddy goods during the war, he set about ending the corruption by replacing Simon Cameron, his secretary of war, with Edwin Stanton. Lincoln also refused to permit the army butcher to supply the Executive Mansion with the choicest cuts of steak when he slaughtered cattle on the grounds of the Washington Monument. Told that this was a matter of little importance, he replied, "My observation is that frequently the most insignificant matter is the foundation for the worst scandal."[21] Honesty and integrity were no small matters to Lincoln.

Harriet Beecher Stowe considered Lincoln the safest leader the country could have in wartime because of his earnest appreciation for constitutional limitations and deliberateness. "A reckless, bold, theorizing, dashing man of genius," she said, "might have wrecked

---

19 Burlingame, *Lincoln,* 1:628, 681, 727–728.

20 Conway, *Lincoln's White House*, 136.

21 Donald, *Lincoln*, 325.

our Constitution and ended us in a splendid military despotism."[22] Honest Abe begat a confident electorate.

Even Lincoln's critics conceded his integrity. Stephen Douglas later acknowledged Lincoln's honesty, communication skills, kind heart, and amiability despite the harsh words and name-calling he had once directed at him on the campaign trail. Douglas had grown to respect Lincoln and would not allow any Democrat to say anything disrespectful or unkind about his former political opponent.[23] General McClellan, who feuded with and disobeyed the commander in chief repeatedly during the war, and later ran against him in the 1864 election, admitted that the president was "honest and means well" in the same letter in which he called Lincoln a "gorilla."[24] Massachusetts senator Charles Sumner called Lincoln "honest but inexperienced." Treasury Secretary Chase labeled the president "irresolute but of honest intentions" in his diary. Future Confederate Alexander Stephens noted that Lincoln "always attracted the riveted attention of the House when he spoke; his manner of speech as well as thought was original. He had no model. He was a man of strong convictions" and "an earnest man."

Honest Abe appreciated truthfulness in others too. Even if candor might indicate disapproval of his leadership, he welcomed straight talk. One night early in the war at Fort Monroe, at the tip of the peninsula in Virginia, General Benjamin Butler made a bold decision by refusing to give up three fugitive slaves, who had arrived after escaping from a Confederate battery. Since the rebels were using slaves in the field to support their troops, the enslaved people were considered contraband of war, and the federal government no longer had to return them to their masters. As Butler was a conservative Democrat from Massachusetts, his decision pleasantly

---

[22] Oates, *With Malice Toward None*, 389.

[23] Burlingame, *Lincoln*, 1:639.

[24] Lehrman, *Lincoln "by littles,"* 61, 188. The quotes in the rest of this paragraph are taken from this source.

surprised Republican conservatives, who had previously objected to the general's high position.

Lincoln named Butler a brigadier general as a reward and show of confidence. Butler said, "I will accept the commission," but "there is one thing I must say to you, as we don't know each other: That as a Democrat I opposed your election, and did all I could for your opponent." Now, however, Butler would "loyally support your administration as long as I hold your commission; and when I find any act that I cannot support I shall bring the commission back at once, and return it to you."

"That is frank, that is fair," Lincoln responded. "But I want to add one thing: When you see me doing anything that for the good of the country ought not to be done, come and tell me so, and why you think so, and then perhaps you won't have any chance to resign your commission."[25]

Lincoln's class and integrity were on full display in his relationship with Edwin Stanton. Lincoln selected Stanton as secretary of war even after Stanton had snubbed him years earlier in the McCormick reaper trial in 1855. Calling Lincoln a "the original gorilla,"[26] Stanton never informed the Illinois attorney that his services would not be needed when the trial moved from Illinois to Cincinnati. Lincoln kept preparing for the case and showed up ready to execute his duties. For Stanton, Lincoln did not look the part of an attorney. Stanton's dream team of lawyers only saw a tall, bony, ungainly backwoodsman in ill-fitting clothing. Stanton could barely stammer out a salutation when they first met.

Lincoln wanted to enter the Cincinnati courtroom as "a gang," but Stanton told the others that Lincoln could enter with his own gang. Even though they stayed in the same hotel during the case, Stanton's team never dined or conferred with Lincoln. They never

---

25 Goodwin, *Team of Rivals*, 368–69.

26 Miller, *Lincoln's Virtues,* 415-17, 422. The next two paragraphs contain material cited from this source.

read his brief for the case. They provided no role for him in the courtroom and did not invite him to dine with the judge and the other attorneys from both sides as had been the custom. The other attorneys left town after the case without saying goodbye to Lincoln.

Despite being intentionally snubbed, Lincoln returned the thousand-dollar stipend he had received for the case, saying he did not deserve it because he had not made any argument or contributed much to the trial. Ultimately, Stanton's team re-sent the check to Lincoln because he had prepared an argument, and this time he kept it. Herndon reported that when Lincoln returned to Illinois, he was silent and hurt. Stanton had been cruel to him. Lincoln had overheard him say, "Where did that long-armed creature come from, and what can he expect to do in this case?"

When Lincoln needed to replace Simon Cameron with a new war secretary, George Harding, a Philadelphia patent attorney whom Lincoln had gotten to know in the reaper case, told Lincoln he did not have appoint Stanton, Stanton's behavior toward Lincoln years before had been outrageous. Lincoln said that personal matters should be laid aside. He wanted to do the best thing for the country.[27]

In addition to the snub he had given Lincoln in the Great Reaper Trial, Stanton criticized and ridiculed Lincoln during the presidential campaign. A fierce Buchanan Democrat, Stanton twice referred to Lincoln's "imbecility" in the early days of his presidency. Moreover, he insisted that he met Lincoln "at the bar, and found him a low, cunning clown."[28]

When Lincoln called on Stanton shortly before the removal of Cameron, he showed no grudge. The two men were friendly and cordial with one another, and the meeting went smoothly, with no reference made to the past. Once appointed, Stanton forged the closest working relationship with the president that Lincoln had

[27] Burlingame, *Lincoln*, 2:244.

[28] Miller, *Lincoln's Virtues*, 418, 421–22, 425–26. The next two paragraphs contain material cited from this source.

with any of his cabinet members. Moreover, as Stanton observed the president's work and leadership firsthand, he regretted his past actions.

Stanton's associates and political friends praised "remarkable passages in certain state papers" and assumed Chase, Stanton, or Seward wrote them. When one of Stanton's friends from the reaper case complimented Stanton's authorship, Stanton corrected him. He had not written a word of it; Lincoln had. Stanton confided to his old friend that "no men were ever so deceived as we at Cincinnati." From that point on, Stanton would not tolerate "any disparagement of Lincoln" from anyone.

Just as Lincoln's magnanimity won over a one-time critic, so too did his character and perseverance rescue the nation and leave a remarkable legacy of integrity. The meat and potatoes on his leadership platter, Lincoln's honesty and integrity fed the American people with hope and built a reservoir of trust. Honest Abe told it like it was and led with heartfelt conviction. One always knew where one stood with Honest Abe.

The Truth

Living a life of integrity means placing the highest value on truth. Christians should be the champions of truth because the Bible, God's Word, *is* truth,[29] and "every word of God proves true."[30] Moreover, Scripture teaches that "the Word became flesh and dwelt among us, and we have seen his glory, glory as of the only Son from the Father, full of grace and truth … For the law was given through Moses; grace and truth came through Jesus Christ."[31]

During His earthly ministry, Jesus said, "If you abide in my word, you are truly my disciples, and you will know the truth, and

---

[29] John 17:17.

[30] Prov. 30:5.

[31] John 1:14, 17.

the truth will set you free."[32] In case His followers missed the point, Jesus later stated clearly, "I am the way, and the truth, and the life. No one comes to the Father except through me."[33] As C. S. Lewis once famously noted in his book, *Mere Christianity*, every human being has to make the determination that Jesus was either a liar, a lunatic, or the Lord. If you believe Jesus lied, then He did not live with integrity. If you consider Him a lunatic, then He did not know what He was doing when He went to the cross to pay the price for your sins. But if He is Lord, then you must embrace the truth and honesty of His words.

The Bible calls you to listen and receive God's truth: "Teach me your way, O Lord, that I may walk in your truth; unite my heart to fear your name.[34] God's desires and commandments, however, are not easy to follow faithfully. You are not to "bear false witness against your neighbor,"[35] "lie to one another,"[36] or be a "false witness" who "breathes out lies."[37] Have you met anyone who has never lied or gossiped?

While "lying lips are an abomination to the Lord," those "who act faithfully are his delight."[38] The Bible says that one who "gives an honest answer kisses the lips."[39] Therefore "having put away falsehood, let each one of you speak the truth with his neighbor, for we are members one of another."[40]

Scripture clearly encourages you to live of life of integrity and honesty. "Better is a poor person who walks in his integrity than one

---

[32] John 8:31–32.

[33] John 14:6.

[34] Ps. 86:11.

[35] Exod. 20:16.

[36] Col. 3:9.

[37] Prov. 14:5.

[38] Prov. 12:22.

[39] Prov. 24:26.

[40] Eph. 4:25.

who is crooked in speech and is a fool."[41] Indeed, "whoever walks in integrity walks securely, but he who makes his ways crooked will be found out."[42] This is why God says it is better for "a poor man to walk with integrity than a rich man who is crooked in his ways."[43] You are to hold fast to "whatever is true, whatever is honorable, whatever is just, whatever is pure, whatever is lovely, whatever is commendable," and "if there is any excellence, if there is anything worthy of praise, think about these things."[44] Truly, you are called "to do justice, and to love kindness, and to walk humbly with your God."[45]

Like all people, however, no matter how hard you try to live a life of integrity and honesty, you will fall short. Even Honest Abe lied, sinned, and made mistakes. The Bible tells the truth that "if we say we have no sin, we deceive ourselves, and the truth is not in us."[46] If you or "anyone thinks he is religious and does not bridle his tongue but deceives his heart, this person's religion is worthless."[47] The truth is that even in your attempts to do the right thing, you will fail. Unfortunately, your good intentions are not powerful enough to overcome sin.[48]

Even in your imperfection and sin, however, God can use you for good. The secular world loves to criticize Christians for being hypocrites. The truth is all Christians are hypocrites. The Bible encourages you to "show yourself in all respects to be a model of good works, and in your teaching show integrity, dignity, and sound speech that cannot be condemned, so that an opponent may be put

---

41 Prov. 19:1.
42 Prov. 10:9.
43 Prov. 28:6.
44 Phil. 4:8.
45 Mic. 6:8.
46 1 John 1:8.
47 James 1:26.
48 James 4:17.

to shame, having nothing evil to say about us."[49] Yet you know that you fail to live up to this ideal. You are a sinner and hypocrite—just like everyone else in the world.

Do not dread your sin and failures; Jesus has already washed away your sins on the cross. To live a life of integrity as a Christian means that you can and should be honest about your sins and the need you have for a Savior. You are eternally grateful that Jesus came to rescue you from your sins and an eternal life in hell.

Do not underestimate the witness you can provide to your family, loved ones, neighbors, and the world in apologizing for your mistakes, acknowledging your sins, and asking for forgiveness. For when you speak "the truth in Christ," you are "not lying" and your conscience will bear "witness in the Holy Spirit."[50] In Christ you will possess "a good conscience, so that, when you are slandered, those who revile your good behavior in Christ may be put to shame."[51]

You have been loved and cleansed by Jesus. In Christ, you now possess "a pure heart and a good conscience and a sincere faith."[52] God now "works in you, both to will and to work for his good pleasure.[53] By the power of the Holy Spirit, you can "stand therefore, having fastened on the belt of truth, and having put on the breastplate of righteousness."[54] You can "do your best to present yourself to God as one approved, a worker who has no need to be ashamed, rightly handling the word of truth."[55]

In one of the most dramatic moments in history, Pontius Pilate confronted Jesus. "So you are a king?" he asked the Savior of the world.

---

[49] Titus 2:7–8.

[50] Rom. 9:1.

[51] 1 Pet. 3:16.

[52] 1 Tim. 1:5.

[53] Phil. 2:13.

[54] Eph. 6:14.

[55] 2 Tim. 2:15.

Jesus answered, "You say that I am a king. For this purpose I was born and for this purpose I have come into the world—to bear witness to the truth. Everyone who is of the truth listens to my voice."

Pilate said to him, "What is truth?" After he had said this, he went back outside to the Jews and told them, "I find no guilt in him."[56] Of course Pilate could not find any guilt in Jesus—He lived a perfect life and was the Incarnate Son of God.

God's Word is truth, and the Word became flesh to rescue you and all humanity from sin, death, and the power of the devil. Only a perfect human being and Savior could do that. By God's grace, live a life of integrity and remember that God has "no greater joy than to hear that my children are walking in the truth."[57]

Your Life

When is it most difficult to live and lead with honesty and integrity? Why?

When you sin, fall short, or make mistakes, how can you live with integrity?

As a Christian, in what ways do you champion truth and God's Word?

---

56 John 18:37–38.

57 3 John 1:4.

25

Humility

For by the grace given to me I say to everyone among you not to think of himself more highly than he ought to think, but to think with sober judgment, each according to the measure of faith that God has assigned.
—Romans 12:3

The Lincoln Way

The more humble the leader, the greater the attraction.

Lincoln presents a fascinating character study on the subject of humility. For in many ways, Lincoln *was not* humble. In his early days, he had disdain for backwoods, frontier preachers who could not much read or write. He mocked Christianity and passages from the Bible for being nonsensical. He looked down upon his uneducated father.

As a lawyer and politician, he made the case to juries and his constituents that his vision and reason were the most sound and best for the people. During the Civil War, while he certainly took advice from his cabinet, he made his own decisions. John Hay, Lincoln's personal secretary, observed how cabinet members such as Chase and Sumner criticized Lincoln for "his intellectual arrogance and unconscious assumption of superiority." Moreover, Hay noted that Lincoln once told him that he knew more about the issues than did newspaper writers and editors. Hay, who greatly admired his boss, justified Lincoln's behavior by opining that "no great man was ever modest."[1]

While Lincoln deferred to his generals, he lamented their poor decisions and miscues. The confidence he possessed in his own thoughts, words, and abilities only grew over time, especially as he won numerous court cases, befuddled political opponents, won a presidential election, and saved the Union. He knew he could move and persuade people. He knew how effective he could be.

On the other hand, Lincoln *did* carry himself with humility. Perhaps because he suffered so many setbacks and failures throughout his life, Lincoln never took himself too seriously or allowed his considerable self-confidence to grow too big for his britches. Bankruptcy, debt, lost court cases, defeats at the ballot box, and a wife who constantly pointed out his shortcomings had a way of humbling even the most talented and gifted of men.

Lincoln never voted for himself to be president. Instead, he cut off the top of the ballot sheet, which listed the presidential electors, so that he could vote only for the state candidates.[2] One attorney who knew him well noted that "Mr Lincoln in the ordinary walks of life did not appear the 'great man,' that he really was."[3]

As president, he remained self-effacing and modest. He referred to himself as "a mere instrument, an accidental instrument … of a great cause."[4] To the legislature of New York, he described himself as "the humblest of all individuals" ever "elevated to the Presidency." He had "confidence," however, in "the Almighty, the Maker of the Universe," who had helped "through all the other difficulties of our country" and would bring the American people through the current ordeal.[5] The Honorable Henry J. Raymond once said that

---

1 Wilson, *Herndon's Informants*, 332.

2 Donald, *Lincoln*, 255.

3 Wilson, *Herndon's Informants*, 193

4 Basler, Lincoln's Reply to Oliver Morton, February 11, 1861, *CW*, 4:226.

5 Basler, Lincoln's Address to the Legislature at Albany, New York, February, 18, 1861, *CW*, 4:226.

"nothing was more marked in Mr. Lincoln's personal demeanor than his utter unconsciousness of his position." Even with the "sudden transfer from the obscurity of private life in a country town to the dignities and duties of the Presidency," Lincoln never felt it incumbent upon himself "to assume something of the manner and tone befitting that position. Mr. Lincoln never seemed to be aware that his place or his business were essentially different from those in which he had always been engaged." Moreover, President Lincoln "brought to every question—the loftiest and most imposing—the same patient inquiry into details, the same eager longing to know and to do exactly what was just and right," as well as the same "plodding, laborious devotion, which characterized his management of a client's case at his law office in Springfield."[6]

In other words, Lincoln never let his electoral victory, or the realization that he had become the most important and powerful person in the country, get to his head. He remained grounded and true to his modest self.

In 1864, Joseph T. Wells, a Wisconsin judge, did not hold a high opinion of the president. After meeting him, however, he changed his mind. Lincoln's deep convictions, supreme intellect, candor, honesty, republican simplicity, "gushing sympathy" for those who fought for their country, and his selflessness truly impressed the judge. He considered Lincoln an instrument of God, called to lead his people through the current "red sea" of casualties to the Canaan, or Promised Land, of "peace and freedom."[7] Citizens saw Lincoln as God's instrument on earth because of his valiant sacrifice and humility. Of course, Lincoln himself often acknowledged that he served the country as an instrument of God.

The way Lincoln designated precious time to meet and converse with almost anyone who visited him in the Executive Mansion, no matter their social class or status, revealed his kindness, love of

---

6 Carpenter, *Six Months in the White House*, 117–18.

7 Burlingame, *Lincoln*, 2:527.

people, and humility. As a public official, Lincoln never forget that he served the people and not the other way around.

The more public acclaim and attention Lincoln received, the more he felt compelled to profess his humbleness and live humbly.[8] Moreover, he found comfort and contentment in Holy Scripture. He often read the book of Job as president, particularly in the tumultuous summer of 1863. Lincoln certainly saw the parallels: Job lost his family. He lost his child, many friends, and vast numbers of soldiers under his charge. Job lost his immense estate. He lost the country he had once known—for by 1863 there would be no more preserving the Union but rebuilding it. Lincoln learned to cry out to God in pain and despair, but then humbly and resolutely turn to the work at hand. "There was something touching," asserted the journalist Noah Brooks, "in his childlike and simple reliance upon Divine aid, especially when in such extremities as he sometimes fell into."[9] While in these treacherous circumstances, "he more earnestly than ever sought that strength which is promised when mortal help faileth." On another occasion, Brooks overheard Lincoln say, "I am very sure that if I do not go away from here a wiser man, I shall go away a better man, for having learned here what a very poor sort of man I am."

Enduring the horrific Civil War and losing his son Willie humbled and exhausted Lincoln, and it showed. Yet despite defeats, humiliations, and sufferings, Lincoln persevered. He *did* become an even better leader and man than when he first took the oath of office. The notion that humility is not thinking less of yourself, but thinking of yourself less certainly fits the life path of Lincoln. As his attention decreased in regard to his own self-interests, his attention increased in regard to the greater interests of the nation. This served

---

[8] Miroff, *Icons of Democracy*, 92, 94.

[9] Shenk, *Lincoln's Melancholy*, 197, 200. The remaining quotes in this paragraph are attributed to this source.

him well as president, and serves as a terrific reminder to all about what makes leaders great.

The Truth

Human beings can never be humble enough. We were originally designed for perfection and to live forever. After the Fall of Adam and Eve, however, sin entered the world. Ever since that day, instead of being humble and having a lower view of their importance, humans have desired to be just like God—all-powerful and all-knowing. Yet humans cannot be God or a god. We feel pain. We get hurt. Our bodies break down. We feel loss. We do horrible things. We act selfishly. We succumb to the power and whims of the devil. We sin. We die. We cannot get to heaven on our own.

The Bible is clear about our sinful condition and why we are to be humble. Yet Scripture also reminds us that Jesus humbled Himself, taking on the form of a man, and eventually died on the cross for our sins.

Thanks to Jesus, you know what awaits you in heaven. You remain humble because Jesus earned the victory for you on the cross. While you still struggle with your sinful nature—you "know how to be brought low," and you "know how to abound"—you also know that "in any and every circumstance" you "have learned the secret of facing plenty and hunger, abundance and need," thanks be to Jesus.[10] So if you must boast, you will boast of the things that show your weakness.[11] For "the Lord lifts up the humble" and "casts the wicked to the ground."[12] The Bible makes it clear that "everyone who exalts himself will be humbled, and he who humbles himself

[10] Phil. 4:12.

[11] 2 Cor. 11:30.

[12] Ps. 147:6.

will be exalted."[13] Indeed, "when pride comes, then comes disgrace, but with the humble is wisdom."[14]

Clearly, Scripture teaches that Christians are to live and serve with the humility of Christ. "He leads the humble in what is right, and teaches the humble his way."[15] God encourages all of His people to "have unity of mind, sympathy, brotherly love, a tender heart, and a humble mind."[16] Moreover, He calls on us to "live in harmony with one another. Do not be haughty, but associate with the lowly. Never be wise in your own sight."[17] A fool does what "is right in his own eyes, but a wise man listens to advice."[18] So do not be "rash with your mouth, nor let your heart be hasty to utter a word before God, for God is in heaven and you are on earth. Therefore let your words be few."[19] If someone you know, including yourself, "thinks that he is wise in this age, let him become a fool that he may become wise."[20]

The relationship between wisdom and humility has always been difficult to grasp but especially so in a time when earthly knowledge can be accessed around the globe with a tap on a screen. For many people, "the word of the cross is folly to those who are perishing, but to us who are being saved it is the power of God."[21] The Bible says that God "will destroy the wisdom of the wise." Indeed, too many people today think they know it all. They are not humble. God's Word, however, speaks truth: "Where is the one who is wise? Where is the scribe? Where is the debater of this age? Has not God made foolish the wisdom of the world? For since, in the wisdom of

---

13 Luke 14:11.

14 Prov. 11:2.

15 Ps. 25:9.

16 1 Pet. 3:8.

17 Rom. 12:16.

18 Prov. 12:15.

19 Eccles. 5:2.

20 1 Cor. 3:18.

21 1 Cor. 1:18–21. The ensuing quotes in this paragraph come from this passage.

God, the world did not know God through wisdom, it pleased God through the folly of what we preach to save those who believe."

Too many people in our world today do not consider the Bible to be wisdom or *the* truth. They say the book is old, outdated, bigoted, and far from acceptable. There are many truths. Everyone has their own truth and voice—and they should have the right to share it. They are absolutely sure there is no absolute truth. Instead of God's Word, they rely on their own words and knowledge. They grab self-help books or listen to daytime talk show hosts espouse their truths, and cling to those—at least until the next book or show. They puff themselves up with a bunch of mindless and soulless chatter. They are not humble before God. Instead, they defy Him. They ridicule Bible believers or those who claim the inerrancy of Scripture.

Scripture makes it clear, however, that God loves the preciousness and power of humility. After all, "God chose what is foolish in the world to shame the wise; God chose what is weak in the world to shame the strong; God chose what is low and despised in the world, even things that are not, to bring to nothing things that are, so that no human being might boast in the presence of God. And because of him you are in Christ Jesus, who became to us wisdom from God, righteousness and sanctification and redemption, so that, as it is written, 'Let the one who boasts, boast in the Lord.'"[22]

Jesus is our example and inspiration to live a humble life—the life of a servant. The Bible says that you should:

> Do nothing from selfish ambition or conceit, but in humility count others more significant than yourselves. Let each of you look not only to his own interests, but also to the interests of others. Have this mind among yourselves, which is yours in Christ Jesus, who, though he was in the form of God, did not count equality with God a thing to

[22] 1 Cor. 1:27–31.

> be grasped, but emptied himself, by taking the form of a servant, being born in the likeness of men. And being found in human form, he humbled himself by becoming obedient to the point of death, even death on a cross. Therefore God has highly exalted him and bestowed on him the name that is above every name, so that at the name of Jesus every knee should bow, in heaven and on earth and under the earth, and every tongue confess that Jesus Christ is Lord, to the glory of God the Father.[23]

Jesus washed feet. He touched those infected with disease. He spent time with the lonely, widowed, orphaned, lowly, downtrodden, and disenfranchised. He served others first. He died on the cross for your sins and the sins of the world. As John the Baptist said in regard to Jesus, "He must increase, but I must decrease."[24] This is humility. Amen.

Your Life

Do you consider yourself to be a humble person? Why or why not?

While Lincoln certainly exhibited humility, he struggled with it too. Most successful people carry a bit of ego with them. In fact, some antonyms of humility are boldness, confidence, arrogance, assertiveness, egoism, pride, and self-importance. How do you combat these temptations or characteristics of your personality? How can you humble yourself or stay humble?

---

[23] Phil. 2:3–11.

[24] John 3:30.

God humbled Himself by sending His Son in the form of a man (Jesus) to walk among us (known as the Incarnation in the Christian faith). Jesus humbled Himself for you on a cross because He loves you. When have you, in Christian love, humbled yourself for the sake of others?

26

Coping with Criticism and Ridicule

If you are insulted for the name of Christ, you are blessed, because the Spirit of glory and of God rests upon you … Yet if anyone suffers as a Christian, let him not be ashamed, but let him glorify God in that name.
—1 Peter 4:14, 16

The Lincoln Way

Exemplary leaders persevere and thrive despite criticism and persecution.

While viciously criticized and ridiculed in his own day, Lincoln is nonetheless consistently ranked by presidential historians and public surveys as the greatest United States president. There is an important lesson there to grasp: excellent leaders may not be recognized for their greatness until their accomplishments are reviewed in retrospect.

After his adolescent growth spurt, Lincoln's peers picked on him, mostly for his awkward, gangly physical appearance and social ineptitude. As his political star ascended later in life, the criticism and derision only increased. Haters called him an ape, a gorilla, a filthy storyteller, and innumerable other epithets.[1] When Lincoln received the Republican nomination for president in 1860, Northern Democrats labeled him "an obscure lawyer," a "weak and

[1] Sandburg, *Lincoln*, 594.

unfit man for so high a place," a "third-rate country lawyer," an "uneducated man—vulgar village politician," a "fourth rate lecturer, who cannot speak good grammar," and a man obsessed with negro slavery and who was "brim full" of negro blood himself. Democratic newspapers, like the *Cincinnati Enquirer,* ridiculed him and his supporters unmercifully. Republicans had elected "an ignoramus" for president."[2] The conduct of the Republican Party revealed "a remarkable indication of a small intellect, growing smaller." Lincoln's speeches were "illiterate compositions ... interlarded with coarse and clumsy jokes." Having "the leanest, lankest, most ungainly mass of legs, arms and hatchet-face ever strung upon a single frame," Lincoln had "most unwarrantably abused the privilege which all politicians have of being ugly."[3]

Critics dubbed him a "simple Susan,"[4] "an illiterate partisan,"[5] a "border-ruffian," a "slang-whanging stump speaker," a "half-witted usurper," a "mole-eyed" monster with a "soul ... of leather," a "turtle," and the "the ghoul at Washington." Even some of his fellow Republicans, who were supposed to be his political allies, showed no loyalty and characterized Lincoln as "unfit," a "political coward," a "dictator," "timid and ignorant," "pitiable," "too slow," a man of "no education," "shattered, dazed, utterly foolish." Diplomat and historian George Bancroft said Lincoln "is ignorant, self-willed, & is surrounded by men some of whom are almost as ignorant as himself." One Republican editor described him as "an awful, woeful ass," and a correspondent for *Chicago Tribune* said that former president Buchanan "seems to have been a granite pillar compared to the 'Good natured man' without any spinal column."

Political criticism of Lincoln picked up when he reentered the political scene after the passage of the Kansas-Nebraska Act of

---

[2] Burlingame, *Lincoln*, 1:630; 2:19, 475.

[3] Goodwin, *Team of Rivals,* 257-58.

[4] White, *Lincoln,* 376.

[5] Donald, *Lincoln Reconsidered,* 166-169. The quotations throughout this paragraph come from this source.

1854, and especially when he debated Stephen Douglas during the Illinois senate race in 1858. Douglas knew how to needle Lincoln. At the first debate in Ottawa, Douglas assured audiences that he had known Lincoln for twenty-five years and meant "nothing personally disrespectful or unkind to that gentleman."[6] An astute and savvy politician, Douglas offered flattering remarks about Lincoln's career, but not without adding sarcasm to each comment. He described Lincoln as a "flourishing grocery-keeper" and liquor salesman in New Salem. He offered mock praise for Lincoln's stint as a congressman who "distinguished himself by his opposition to the Mexican war, taking the side of the common enemy against his own country." Douglas attacked Lincoln on his "House Divided" speech. Even as the audience responded with "good," Douglas declared Lincoln's words were "revolutionary and destructive of the existence of this government."

Douglas also set up straw-man arguments. For example, he countered Lincoln's criticisms of Dred Scott by asking the audience if they were in favor of giving blacks the rights and privileges of citizenship, striking out the state's constitutional clause that kept enslaved people and free blacks out of the state, and allowing "the free negroes to flow in and cover your prairies with black settlements." Of course, the crowd shouted "no, no!" or "never" to such histrionics. "I do not question Mr. Lincoln's conscientious belief that the negro was made his equal, and hence is his brother," Douglas proclaimed sarcastically, "but for my own part, I do not regard the negro as my equal, and positively deny that he is my brother or any kin to me whatever."

Douglas loved to race-bait Lincoln and tell the audience that Frederick Douglass, an escaped slave and abolitionist, was one of Lincoln's most trusted advisors. "All I have to say of it is this, that if you, Black Republicans, think that the negro ought to be on social

---

6 White, *Lincoln,* 266, 271. The quotes in the next three paragraphs all come from this source.

equality with your wives and daughters, and ride in a carriage with your wife, while you drive the team, you have a perfect right to do so." He concluded, "Those of you who believe that the negro is your equal and ought to be on an equality with you socially, politically, and legally; have a right to entertain those opinions, and of course will vote for Mr. Lincoln."[7]

Douglas's barbs and political stunts were just a foretaste of the feast of criticism that would come during the Lincoln presidency. After South Carolina seceded from the Union, Lincoln lamented, "I am in the Garden of Gethsemane now, and my cup of bitterness is overflowing."[8]

Lincoln never received a honeymoon period after he took the oath of office. A local Democratic newspaper described the president as a "clever man" and a "well-disposed gentleman," but not qualified to confront the present crisis.[9] The writer feared that his triumphant entrance to the nation's capital would soon transform into a funeral procession for his reputation. Lincoln would have been better off not running for president and simply retaining the popularity he had achieved in the Lincoln-Douglas debates.

Critics battered the new president, accusing him of lethargy and inaction. More Southern states were threatening to secede from the Union, seemingly without any plan of response from the nation's chief executive. Both Republicans and Democrats pleaded for an Andrew Jackson-like executive even as Democrats referred to Lincoln as the "the Illinois Baboon."[10] A writer for the *New York Herald* doubted that Lincoln had the capacity to bring order out of the chaos. The president might have good intentions and a good heart, but the times demanded someone firm and resolute—like President Jackson.[11]

---

[7] White, *Lincoln*, 266, 271.

[8] Peterson, *Lincoln in American Memory*, 88.

[9] Burlingame, *Lincoln*, 2:17.

[10] Peterson, *Lincoln in American Memory*, 10.

[11] Wilson, *Lincoln's Sword*, 50.

The theme of Lincoln's complacency, inaction, and lack of command would dog him throughout the war. Critics rebuked him for his leniency with regard to presidential pardons, reprieves, and military courts-martial. Hearing the political jabs that he was no Jackson, Lincoln simply asserted that God had made him the way he was, and he could not change.[12] Further agitating and infuriating his critics, he often insisted that his "policy is to have no policy." The pragmatic Lincoln did not want to have preset and prescribed solutions to problems that were unpredictable and fluid by the nature of war. Treasury Secretary Salmon Chase, among others, condemned this as "an idiotic notion."[13]

Criticism almost always hurt, but especially when delivered by individuals of repute in Lincoln's inner circle. From the beginning of the war, the president's hand-picked cabinet officials did not hold back their disdain for the commander in chief. Before the 1860 election, William Seward had derogatorily referred to Lincoln as a "prairie statesman."[14] Attorney General Bates wrote in his last diary entry in 1861 that "the Prest. is an excellent man, and, in the main wise, but he *lacks will and purpose*, and, I greatly fear he, has not the power to command."[15]

There were many who felt as Bates did—that Lincoln was well-meaning and honest, but not up to the job. After the humiliating defeat at Bull Run in July 1861, many condemned the folly of administration, proclaiming that the president and his cabinet were unfit for duty. Stanton, not then in the cabinet, piled on and ascribed the catastrophe to the "imbecility" of the Lincoln administration.[16]

Lincoln responded by encouraging his critics to make war on the Confederates rather than each other. To get rid of cabinet members would not be prudent in the middle of a war. The Bull

---

[12] Burlingame, *Lincoln*, 2:493.

[13] Donald, *Lincoln Reconsidered*, 123.

[14] Burlingame, *Lincoln,* 1:581.

[15] Donald, *Lincoln*, 328.

[16] Donald, *Lincoln,* 333.

Run defeat, however, affected Lincoln significantly. The loss hit him hard enough by itself, but to have cabinet officials join in the criticism only added to his agony. Hell could not be worse, he said.

The resilient Lincoln, of course, pressed on. He assured the House speaker that Union soldiers would lick their wounds and learn from their mistakes. Eventually, they would march on Richmond and win the war. Years later, Walt Whitman paid tribute to Lincoln's buoyancy and grit at that key moment in history—"a crucifixion day" that did not defeat or overwhelm him. Instead, Lincoln worked relentlessly to bring the Union back from shocking defeat to ultimate victory.[17] Yet the criticism he received only increased as the war continued and the casualties mounted.

Cabinet officials grew to appreciate Lincoln's loyalty to them, as well as his brilliance as commander in chief, and their criticism of him waned, turning into admiration. But other people of prominence outside the administration continued to criticize the president vigorously. Disappointed in Lincoln's conciliatory inaugural address, his defense of the Fugitive Slave Law, and his lack of progress on freeing the slaves, Frederick Douglass repeatedly spoke out against the president's apparent hesitancy to do the moral and courageous thing—eradicating the institution of slavery. He claimed that Lincoln's administration was no different from the inept presidencies of Pierce and Buchanan.[18]

General George McClellan, a favorite of Congress and the Army of the Potomac, railed against Lincoln's leadership in the fall of 1861, hypocritically blasting the commander in chief for timidity, vacillation, and inefficiency. Congressmen like Henry Dawes maintained that times were so dark and gloomy, and confidence so low in the incompetent and corrupt administration, that some wondered if the Union would survive another sixty days.[19] Radical

---

[17] Burlingame, *Lincoln*, 1:581, 2:185–86; Donald, *Lincoln*, 328, 333; Goodwin, *Team of Rivals*, 374–75.

[18] Goodwin, *Team of Rivals*, 331.

[19] Burlingame, *Lincoln*, 2:215.

Republicans criticized the president for not pushing the war more vigorously, while "Copperheads," or those who made up the "peace party," disparaged the commander in chief for being a warmonger.[20]

Like Frederick Douglass, others attacked Lincoln for moving too slowly on slavery. Francis W. Bird, one of the original organizers of the Republican Party in Massachusetts, exclaimed that the "key of the slave's chain is now kept in the White House."[21] An Illinois man, enraged by Lincoln's course, predicted that "if a speedy change" did not happen, "some Brutus would arise and love his country more than he did the president."[22] Abolitionists protested that Lincoln should free the slaves immediately while border state politicians feared he moved too fast and too far in imposing federal will on the states. When Lincoln pushed colonization, critics charged him of "colorphobia."[23] Abolitionist William Lloyd Garrison denigrated the president's competence and insisted that he should have stuck with splitting rails instead of trying to run the government, especially during a crisis. Lydia Maria Child, an abolitionist and women's rights activist, mocked "King Log" for his "stagnant soul" and "wooden skull."[24] Wall Street attorney George Templeton Strong declared Old Abe "a first-rate second-rate man."[25] Others alleged he leaned too much on his subordinates, did not have firmness of character, possessed an average intellect, and seemed too gentle and conscientious for a job that required a savage mentality. They wanted more audacity from the president. A Wisconsin Republican sneered that a mule that brayed could perform better than Lincoln, who only "blabs."[26]

---

20 Trueblood, *Lincoln: Lessons in Spiritual Leadership*, 32.

21 Donald, *Lincoln,* 342.

22 Donald, *Lincoln*, 342.

23 Burlingame, *Lincoln,* 2:234.

24 Burlingame, *Lincoln*, 2:233.

25 Burlingame, *Lincoln,* 2:367.

26 Burlingame, *Lincoln,* 2:367.

The cascade of the Union's poor battle results and outright defeats only egged on critical reporters, editors, congressmen, and citizens. The Confederate invasion of Maryland in September 1862, coming so close after Lee's smashing victory at the Second Battle of Bull Run, brought more criticism of Lincoln's leadership. According to George Templeton Strong, the president was an "honest old codger" who was simply "unequal to his place."[27]

After a horrific defeat at Fredericksburg in December, 1862, Lincoln's popularity reached its nadir. A Cincinnati newspaper editor called him a "cowardly imbecile," while congressmen claimed that "nobody believes in him anymore."[28] One critic asserted that the nation needed the leadership of "a Bengal tiger" and not a "domestic cat" in the Executive Mansion.[29] Former friends turned on him, and these incidents were widely reported. Others argued that Lincoln's administration made Buchanan's administration look exemplary by comparison. Depicted as blundering, corrupt, ignorant, and stubborn as a mule, calls for Lincoln's removal increased. Rumors of an impending, violent revolution persisted and grew in the North unless Lincoln resigned.

The criticism cut Lincoln up for a while. He understood that radical senators wanted him out of office. Half-joking and half-serious, he responded that he sometimes wanted to gratify their desires. He had moments when he lost hope. He even wondered if God, in His infinite wisdom, had sided against the Union cause.[30]

After the disaster at Chancellorsville in early May 1863, Lincoln endured some of his darkest days of the war. The Union appeared to be losing. Critics questioned Lincoln's handling of civil rights issues. Abolitionists escalated their demands and hammered away at Lincoln's refusal to appoint abolitionist generals like Benjamin Butler and John Fremont. On the other side of the spectrum, after

---

[27] Donald, *Lincoln*, 373.

[28] Oates, *With Malice Toward None*, 327.

[29] Donald, *Lincoln*, 424–25.

[30] Burlingame, *Lincoln*, 2:449, 452.

the Emancipation Proclamation had become the law of the land and shortly after the Battle of Gettysburg in early July 1863, Samuel F. B. Morse, inventor of the telegraph, mocked Lincoln's intelligence and railed at his inability to confront what Morse considered to be the zealotry and fanaticism of the abolitionists.[31] No matter what action he took or what position he espoused, Lincoln could not escape the criticism cartel.

Even after Union victories, Lincoln received potent criticism. When Meade failed to pursue and destroy Lee's battered army after the Battle of Gettysburg, despite repeated and desperate pleas from Lincoln, the president broke down—the only time his son, Robert, ever saw his father cry.[32] A chance to end the war had escaped, and the criticism came pouring in accordingly.

With the casualties of the Civil War mounting and the Union advance stymied in Virginia and around Atlanta, Lincoln's reelection chances looked bleak in the summer of 1864. Politicians and newspaper editors railed against his leadership, as did other prominent individuals who had interested audiences. Women's rights leader Elizabeth Cady Stanton referred to the president as "Dishonest Abe" and deplored "the incapacity and rottenness" of his administration.[33] Moreover, she issued harsh statements regarding Lincoln's appearance and sense of humor. Her opinion was that Lincoln should be dumped from the Republican ticket because he

---

31 Burlingame, 2:560.

32 Burlingame, 2:513; Oates, *With Malice Toward None*, 353. After Union General Meade failed to pursue Lee's army after the Battle of Gettysburg, Navy Secretary Gideon Wells quipped that Meade had dug in and was "watching the enemy as fast as he can."

33 Burlingame, *Lincoln*, 2:685. To Stanton's credit, she later regretted having opposed Lincoln. Later in life she had come to see the wisdom of him playing the long game in regard to abolition—slowly but steadily shaping public opinion until the proper time had come for complete emancipation and freedom. She even admitted that Lincoln's reconstruction plan would have been better and wiser than the one pushed through by the Radicals she supported.

had proved his ineptitude. She favored the generals Butler or Fremont for president. Comparing the president to Nero, who fiddled while Rome burned, she pledged to leave the country and take residence in the Fiji Islands if Lincoln were reelected.

Another feminist called Lincoln "an Ass" and scoundrel for allowing slavery to continue to exist. Other abolitionists like William Goodell, Susan B. Anthony, George and Henry Cheever, and Wendell Phillips complained about Lincoln's slowness on abolition. One said that while God sent Egypt ten plagues, the Almighty massed all ten in the form of one Pharaoh-like person—namely Lincoln.[34]

Democrats, of course, showed no mercy toward Lincoln heading into the 1864 election. A Democratic congressman accused him of being nothing more than a smutty storyteller. Samuel F. B. Morse renewed his criticism, accusing the president of being illiterate, inhuman, evil, irreligious, bungling, vulgar, and unsophisticated. The Democratic Party, which vigorously defended slavery, charged Lincoln with having descended from black ancestry. A leading party newspaper fraudulently declared the president's insanity simply because he had African blood in his family tree. His mannerisms as well as his physical appearance—face, hands, and especially feet—were used as evidence of the African ancestry assertion. Lincoln's tomfoolery and abolitionist politics were also referenced.[35] Political opponents labeled him a "lover" of Negros and referred to him as "Abraham Africanus the First." In addition, they created Lincoln's Ten Commandments, the first of which was "Thou shalt have no other God but the negro."[36] One publication printed on New Year's Eve 1864, "The people of the North owe Mr. Lincoln nothing but eternal hatred and scorn." Under his leadership, "there are 500,000 new made graves; there are 500,000 orphans; there are 200,000

[34] Burlingame, *Lincoln*, 2:634.

[35] Burlingame, *Lincoln*, 2:696–97.

[36] Packard, *Lincoln's in the White House*, 205; Donald, *Lincoln*, 537.

widows" due to the horrific nature of the war. Moreover, "there is the Constitution broken; there are liberty and law—liberty in chains and in a dungeon, thieves in the Treasury, provost marshals in the seats of justice, butchers in the pulpit"—all thanks to Lincoln.[37]

Like every president of the United States, Lincoln endured criticism, scorn, and ridicule. Unlike most presidents, he withstood more of it and from many different constituencies. As mentally tough and resilient as he had become, the mockery and reproach he bore took its toll on his well-being. Halfway through his presidency, friends noticed that his hand trembled. He looked worn and haggard, and did not tell jokes as frequently as he once did. As much as he desired to be reelected, he told confidantes that he did not know if he could stay healthy enough to endure a presidential election or second term. Though he remained surrounded by bureaucrats, job applicants, and sightseers, he felt like the loneliest man in Washington. Since his political positions appeased or pleased no one completely, he was socially ostracized and had no close friends in Congress.[38]

As Lincoln started his second term, John Hay noted that "he was in mind, body and nerves a very different man from the one who had taken the oath in 1861." The president retained "the same kindly, genial, and cordial spirit he had been at first; but the boisterous laughter became less frequent year by year; the eye grew veiled by constant meditation on momentous subjects." Lincoln became much more reserved "and detachment from his surroundings increased."[39]

While the criticism affected him, Lincoln never got intimidated by it. He had his own way of handling it. As voracious a reader of newspapers and letters as Lincoln had been before he became president, he avoided reading them too often as commander in chief. Since he only had time to read some of the correspondence

---

[37] Trueblood, *Lincoln: Lessons in Spiritual Leadership*, 122.

[38] Donald, *Lincoln*, 426.

[39] Goodwin, *Team of Rivals*, 702.

sent to him, his secretaries made sure that he saw some positive letters. When the First Lady tried to share hostile commentary, the president would try to shut her down, maintaining that he did not need the extra stress.

One Sunday, Lincoln read an hour's worth of anti-administration editorials from Henry Ward Beecher's New York *Independent*. The renowned preacher snobbishly dismissed Lincoln's lowly birth, pedigree, and refinement. He also mocked the president's dearth of formal education. When finished reading, Lincoln indignantly threw them down and heatedly referenced 2 Kings 8:13. His critics were treating him worse than a dog even as he worked tirelessly to do the people's business.[40] Almost every time Lincoln attempted to read a newspaper, he could count on less than kind remarks about his personal life, policies, or leadership. Consuming a newspaper no longer stimulated him as it once had.

To counter the negative press, Lincoln took what he called "public-opinion baths."[41] While these meetings took an inordinate amount of time in his daily work schedule, Lincoln insisted that connecting with ordinary citizens from all walks of life was an essential priority of his presidency. He always wanted to know the pulse of the people he served.

During these public-opinion baths, Lincoln employed humor and wit, which was therapeutic for him. "I have endured a great deal of ridicule without much malice," he told an associate, "and have received a great deal of kindness, not quite free from ridicule. I am used to it."[42] Constantly Lincoln tried to get his own mind, and the minds of others, off of the negative news of the war. He once told a story of a storm that came upon a traveler on the frontier. The man tried to continue, but his horse gave out. While the lightning flashes were the only things that could help him find his way, they were

---

40 Burlingame, *Lincoln*, 2:288.

41 Keneally, *Lincoln*, 103.

42 Basler, Lincoln to James Hackett, November 2, 1863, *CW*, 6:559.

frightening too. One bolt landed close to the traveler and brought him to his knees. He was by no means a praying man, but he stayed on his knees anyway. "O Lord, if it is all the same to you, give us a little more light and a little less noise!"[43] Even in tough times, while enduring harsh criticism, Lincoln *knew* he had to laugh and make others laugh too.

Lincoln also possessed an inner resilience to appreciate the positive in his life. Late in the war, he met with General Sherman, General Grant, and Admiral Porter on the *River Queen*. After conversing freely and pleasantly for a while, Lincoln took Sherman aside privately. "Sherman, do you know why I took a shine to Grant and you?"

Slightly taken aback by the question, the general responded, "I don't know. You have been extremely kind to me, Mr. Lincoln, far more than I deserve."

"Well," the president said, "you have never found fault with me."[44]

Lincoln's relationship with God and God's Word steeled him for tough days in a fallen world and lifted his spirits. As he looked back at the arc of his life, he saw how God's plans always prevailed. He had endured a dismal youth, four failed terms as a state legislator, a sole frustrated term in the United States House of Representatives, two defeats for a United States Senate seat, a failed pursuit of the vice presidency, a wretched bankruptcy, a difficult marriage, and a murderous war. Lincoln had learned how to bounce back, and expected to recover from plunges in life.[45]

Lincoln also took criticism as a challenge and an opportunity to convert his critics. "He used to say to me when I talked to him about Chase & those who did him Evil—Do good to those who hate you and turn their ill will to friendship," his wife Mary

---

43 Carpenter, *Six Months at the White House*, 71.

44 Johnson, *Last Weeks of Lincoln*, 125.

45 Freehling, *Becoming Lincoln*, 1, 63.

remembered.[46] Indeed, once a critic and skeptic of Lincoln, Seward came to see greatness in the president. He especially appreciated Lincoln's executive skills and stamina, calling the commander in chief "the best of us" shortly after the Confederate attack on Fort Sumter. Later that year, Seward declared Lincoln the best man in the country to lead the nation through the crisis. The following year, he praised Lincoln's wisdom and pragmatism. In 1863, in front of dinner guests, he commended the president as the greatest and wisest man he had ever known, repeatedly comparing Lincoln and his task to Jesus and His mission.[47]

There is one other thing to note about Lincoln's ability to cope with criticism. Despite the cruel disparagement of his leadership and policy positions from all sides, he never ceased to move forward, ultimately doing what he thought was right. Of course he listened to differing viewpoints. He modified his pace when necessary to bring a task to completion. He even offered compromise solutions in order to keep the momentum moving toward his eventual goal. Yet, though he might be walking in the valley of scorn, he did not turn away or stop walking. His convictions and desire to make a mark propelled him forward to the looming mountaintop. Derision and mockery did not stop him from achieving his ends. In doing so, he proved his critics wrong with class and dignity we all can admire and praise.

The Truth

If Jesus—the only perfect individual in history—could be ridiculed, mocked, persecuted, and crucified for living His mission, rest assured you will receive criticism and even persecution in this life too. Scripture promises that "all who desire to live a godly life in

---

[46] Wilson, *Herndon's Informants*, 358.

[47] Burlingame, *Lincoln*, 2:129.

Christ Jesus will be persecuted."[48] In fact, if you are a Christian, get ready for the hate: "If the world hates you, know that it has hated me before it hated you," Jesus says. "If you were of the world, the world would love you as its own; but because you are not of the world, but I chose you out of the world, therefore the world hates you."[49]

Jesus promises, however, that you will be blessed even as you endure the hatred. "Blessed are you," He says, "when people hate you and when they exclude you and revile you and spurn your name as evil, on account of the Son of Man!"[50] He knows that "you will be hated by all for my name's sake. But the one who endures to the end will be saved."[51]

When you endure rebukes, remember that Jesus knows what you are going through. He has lived it. Nevertheless, be inspired by His love and strength—for He will not forsake you in the midst of your suffering and misery. The Bible calls on you to remember and "consider him who endured from sinners such hostility against himself, so that you may not grow weary or fainthearted."[52]

As tempting as it might be to strike back against those who malign and torment you, Scripture encourages you to turn the other cheek: "Love your enemies and pray for those who persecute you."[53] Even your critics will be "surprised when you do not join them in the same flood of debauchery" and an eye-for-an-eye mindset.[54] God will deal with your enemies in a just manner. Especially when you have been genuinely wronged, slandered, or libeled, remember that you should "never avenge yourselves, but leave it to the wrath of God, for it is written, 'Vengeance is mine, I will repay, says the Lord.'"[55]

---

[48] 1 Tim. 3:12.

[49] John 15:18–19.

[50] Luke 6:22.

[51] Matt. 10:22.

[52] Heb. 12:3.

[53] Matt. 5:39, 44.

[54] 1 Pet. 4:4.

[55] Rom. 12:9.

As much as you might first think of those who criticize or hurt you, do you dish out ridicule, condescension, or hate to others? The Bible warns against this hypocrisy. "Judge not, that you be not judged," we are told. "For with the judgment you pronounce you will be judged, and with the measure you use it will be measured to you." You might see "the speck that is in your brother's eye," but not "the log that is in your own eye."[56] "Do not speak evil against one another, brothers. The one who speaks against a brother or judges his brother, speaks evil against the law and judges the law." The Bible makes it clear that "there is only one lawgiver and judge, he who is able to save and to destroy. But who are you to judge your neighbor?"[57] Therefore you have no excuse to judge another person. "For in passing judgment on another you condemn yourself, because you, the judge, practice the very same things."[58]

Of course, this does not mean one cannot provide constructive criticism or receive it in order to be a better steward of God's gifts and talents. Scripture teaches that "the ear that listens to life-giving reproof will dwell among the wise."[59] After all, "iron sharpens iron, and one man sharpens another."[60]

Nevertheless, a Christian should "let no corrupting talk" come out of one's mouth, but only such as is good for building up, as fits the occasion, that it may give grace to those who hear."[61] Since every human is a sinner, those "who are spiritual should restore" one's neighbors in "a spirit of gentleness," and "keep watch on yourself, lest you too be tempted."[62] Everyone should "be quick to hear, slow to speak, slow to anger; for the anger of man does not produce the

---

[56] Matt. 7:1–5.
[57] James 4:11–12.
[58] Rom. 2:1.
[59] Prov. 15:31.
[60] Prov. 27:17.
[61] Eph. 4:29.
[62] Gal. 6:1.

righteousness of God.[63] One "must not be quarrelsome but kind to everyone, able to teach, patiently enduring evil," and correct one's opponents "with gentleness." After all, through the power of the Holy Spirit, "God may perhaps grant them repentance leading to a knowledge of the truth."[64]

The Bible is clear that you should not be rash "with your mouth, nor let your heart be hasty to utter a word before God, for God is in heaven and you are on earth." Instead God encourages you to "let your words be few. For a dream comes with much business, and a fool's voice with many words."[65]

While the Bible insists that you should be careful in judging another, He has every right to condemn or be critical of you. You are far from perfect. You fail to keep the Ten Commandments. You make mistakes, act selfishly, and sin—every day. You deserve to be banished to hell and eternally separated from God, just like every other human who has walked the planet.

Thanks be to Jesus's death on the cross, however, the record of your wrongs and misdeeds has been washed away. You have been justified or made right before God because of Jesus's death and resurrection. God cannot be critical of you anymore because His Son died for you. You are "in Christ" and "a new creation. The old has passed away; behold, the new has come."[66]

This assurance of eternal salvation, even as you live as both saint and sinner in an imperfect world, should inspire and strengthen you in your daily walk. For you "are afflicted in every way, but not crushed; perplexed, but not driven to despair; persecuted, but not forsaken; struck down, but not destroyed." You have been "given over to death for Jesus' sake, so that the life of Jesus also may be

---

[63] James 1:19–20.

[64] 2 Tim. 2:24–25.

[65] Eccles. 5:2–3.

[66] 2 Cor. 5:17.

manifested" in your "mortal flesh." So "death is at work in us, but life" is in Christ.[67]

So when the criticism or persecution comes, and when you cry for help, the Lord hears and will deliver you. God "is near to the brokenhearted and saves the crushed in spirit. Many are the afflictions of the righteous, but the Lord delivers him out of them all. He keeps all his bones; not one of them is broken."[68]

There is an old childhood saying that "sticks and stones may break my bones but names will never hurt me." You know the truth. Name calling, mockery, and any kind of verbal mistreatment hurt. When persecution comes your way, remember that "God will supply every need of yours according to his riches in glory in Christ Jesus."[69] The Bible says that "it is better to suffer for doing good, if that should be God's will, than for doing evil."[70] No matter what you might be enduring, remember the words of the Psalmist: "Even though I walk through the valley of the shadow of death, I will fear no evil, for you are with me; your rod and your staff, they comfort me."[71]

You should "not fear what you are about to suffer. Behold, the devil is about to throw some of you into prison, that you may be tested, and for ten days you will have tribulation." Yet, empowered by the Holy Spirit, you are to "be faithful unto death" so that God can give you "the crown of life."[72] For Jesus's sake, you can be "content with weaknesses, insults, hardships, persecutions, and calamities." For when you are "weak," then you are "strong" because you cling to Christ.[73]

---

[67] 2 Cor. 4:8–12.
[68] Ps. 34:17–20.
[69] Phil. 4:19.
[70] 1 Pet. 3:17.
[71] Ps. 23:4.
[72] Rev. 2:10.
[73] 2 Cor. 12:10.

So whether you are suffering from unfair and relentless criticism or persecution, or coming to the grips with your sinful nature, always remember God's precious words: "'My grace is sufficient for you, for my power is made perfect in weakness.' Therefore I will boast all the more gladly of my weaknesses, so that the power of Christ may rest upon me."[74]

Your Life

When criticism, mockery, ridicule, hate, or persecution come your way, how do you handle it? What has worked for you? What *does not* work for you?

How is constructive criticism a good thing for a Christian? What makes criticism constructive? How should a Christian accept constructive criticism?

How critical are you of others? Why? Reflecting on this criticism and the words of Scripture quoted in the last section, how do you plan to check or self-monitor your criticism of others?

What criticisms could God have of you? How does knowing Jesus change that reality?

[74] 2 Cor. 12:9.

27

Dealing with an Insubordinate

Whoever keeps his commandments abides in God, and God in him. And by this we know that he abides in us, by the Spirit whom he has given us.
—1 John 3:24

The Lincoln Way

Effective leaders anticipate insubordination and prepare ways to surmount it.

The remarkable leadership Lincoln provided the Union as commander in chief is one of his most substantial achievements. Lincoln had far less experience in war compared to his Confederate counterpart, President Jefferson Davis. He often joked about his military career in the Black Hawk War, claiming that he had gained extensive knowledge and experience from charging wild onions and participating in gory battles … with mosquitos. As in so many other aspects of his life, however, Lincoln learned quickly how to serve as commander in chief. He read works on military history and strategy, and carefully observed the successes and failures of the Union armies as well as those of the Confederacy. Despite setbacks and the inevitable fog of war, he became an exemplary wartime president.[1]

---

[1] McPherson, *Lincoln*, 19–20.

The Union would not have survived if Lincoln had not become an effective war president. Indeed, almost the entire duration of his presidency took place amid a war. On his very first day in the Executive Mansion, Lincoln received as his first official document a letter from Major Robert Anderson, informing him that the garrison at Fort Sumter must either be withdrawn or resupplied at the risk of war. His last day as president, the day Booth assassinated him, took place only five days after Robert E. Lee surrendered at Appomattox Court House.

Throughout the war, Lincoln spent more time in the telegraph office than anywhere except the Executive Mansion. He rarely left Washington except to visit the Army of the Potomac, which he did eleven times for a total of forty-two days. Starting with his first day in office, Lincoln understood that the survival of the United States depended on his performance as commander in chief. Fortunately for the Union, Lincoln's humility, curiosity, incessant questioning of commanders, ability to admit mistakes, and pragmatism helped him grow and eventually become the best strategic mind of the war.[2]

At the beginning of his presidency, the Union was severely underprepared for war. Union military leaders did not really know what their precise goals were or where to send armies. Accurate maps did not exist.[3] Seventy-five-year-old Winfield Scott, the general in chief, suffered from poor health, gout, and vertigo. He lacked the necessary energy to lead a war effort. He could not even mount a horse due to his obesity.[4]

---

[2] McPherson, *Lincoln*, 20; Marszalek, "Old Army," 43.

[3] Marszalek, "Old Army," 41. General Henry Halleck, commanding in the West in 1862, purchased maps in a bookstore for his usage. Not until 1863 did the military high command have a reliable map on the state of Virginia. In terms of an overall military strategy, Winfield Scott's so-called Anaconda Plan was not a mature operation proposal but rather a response to McClellan's proposal to cross the mountains from Ohio to capture Richmond.

[4] McGovern, *Lincoln*, 81.

Being inexperienced, Lincoln intuitively realized that he had to rely on those who did possess military experience. Yet George McClellan, Don Carlos Buell, Henry Halleck, John Pope, Ambrose Burnside, Joseph Hooker, and William Rosecrans all failed to measure up to his initial expectations. Five times during the war, Lincoln tried to get his field commanders to trap or destroy Confederate armies that were raiding northward, by cutting in south of them and blocking their retreat. Tragically, on all five occasions, his generals failed. Not until Ulysses Grant emerged from his triumphs out west would Lincoln find a commander he trusted to execute military campaigns properly.[5]

The failures and incompetence of Union generals were not only major setbacks to the cause, but cost human lives. The carnage haunted Lincoln. After twelve thousand Union casualties resulted from the Battle of Fredericksburg (the Confederates suffered only five thousand), Lincoln wondered if those living in Satan's domain suffered less than he did. Literally moaning and groaning in anguish, he walked the floor and wrung his hands. He wondered why God had burdened him for this time and task.[6]

While there have been other war presidents in American history, no war saw more American casualties and fatalities than the Civil War. While other wars were mostly fought in foreign lands, the Civil War took place on American soil. Lincoln could see the corpses rotting on battlegrounds just a few minutes away by carriage or train. Brothers fought against brothers, fathers against sons. Violent *and* personal, the Civil War took place in many American homes as much as on the battlefields. Six hundred and twenty-three thousand soldiers died in the Civil War, which is the equivalent of approximately 6.2 million deaths today in proportion to the population.[7]

---

[5] McPherson, *Lincoln*, 28, 34.

[6] Burlingame, *Lincoln*, 2:446.

[7] Wheeler, *Faith and Courage*, 195–96.

During the Civil War, more than ten thousand battles would be fought across sixteen states, plus New Mexico and Indian territories. Two-thirds of the soldiers who perished in the war died from disease, not combat. Moreover, thousands of soldiers went home without a leg, an arm, a face, testicles, eyes, or feet. Others suffered permanently damaged brains. More than a hundred and fifty prisons were established to hold prisoners of war, and most were filled to capacity. Some fifty thousand men died in these prisons from disease, exposure, and malnutrition. Half-crazed prisoners frequently beat or killed one another over near-starvation food rations.[8] The horrors of the war knew no bounds.

The backdrop of butchery and suffering is important to remember when considering the exasperating and, ultimately, defiant behavior General George McClellan exhibited toward his commander in chief. The sad truth is that the Lincoln-McClellan relationship could have been a fruitful and ultimately glorious partnership for the good of the Union, but McClellan did everything his power to ensure that this would not occur.

The men knew each other before the war. In the late 1850s, McClellan worked as the superintendent of the Illinois Central Railroad, which Lincoln occasionally counseled as an attorney. Having been raised in the upper strata of Philadelphia society, McClellan viewed Lincoln then much as he would during the Civil War—as a social, intellectual, and moral inferior who did not have the intelligence and discipline to understand sophisticated things like the military. McClellan supported Stephen A. Douglas, the champion of the Illinois Central, who had pushed the first land-grant railroad bill through Congress in 1850. During the Lincoln-Douglas debates in 1858, McClellan provided Douglas with his own, plush personal railcar and a platform car with a brass twelve-pounder that boomed the Little Giant's arrival and whistle stops. McClellan often accompanied Douglas to his celebrated debates

8 McGovern, *Lincoln*, 130.

with Lincoln, certainly imbibing the senator's disdain for Lincoln. McClellan also made sure that a train carrying Lincoln supporters, who were planning to vote (illegally) in another county in the 1858 senatorial election, broke down.[9] Well before Lincoln ever became president and commander in chief, McClellan had already been groomed to disdain the country lawyer from Springfield.

Once the Civil War commenced and it became clear that the war would be a protracted contest, Lincoln needed an all-star general to lead the Army of the Potomac. Almost every indicator at the time pointed to George McClellan as most qualified to lead the Union army to victory.

Acutely aware of his inexperience and quite busy with other affairs of state, Lincoln wanted to hire the best generals, support them, and stay out of their way—as long as they stayed focused on destroying Confederate armies and preserving the Union. Lincoln made clear that he supported his generals and did not want to micromanage them. This philosophy, however, would be severely put to the test by a headstrong general who did not believe in the same war aims as the president.

George McClellan possessed a fatal character flaw that would ultimately be his undoing—an unbridled hubris. As one nineteenth-century British radical said of another, McClellan appeared to be a "self-made man who worshipped his creator."[10] Self-absorbed and insensitive, McClellan had little regard for civilian authority. Moreover, he felt no need to keep the president informed, let alone seek his advice. While Lincoln was reluctant to interfere with military matters, when he did make a request or give an order, he expected the general to follow through. Mutual distrust inevitably developed between the two, keeping them from having any chance of a successful relationship.[11]

---

[9] Waugh, *Lincoln and McClellan,* 1–3, 36–37.

[10] Waugh, *Lincoln and McClellan,* 214.

[11] Donald, *Lincoln*, 338–339.

As in most cases involving an insubordinate employee, there were layers of complexity to the situation that made it difficult for Lincoln relieve McClellan from his duty when things went sour. First, there simply were not that many experienced commanders to choose from at the start of the war. McClellan at least had an impressive West Point résumé. Second, McClellan exhibited success in organizing volunteer Ohio troops. Lincoln not only noticed his achievement but elevated him over entire Department of Ohio, which included Ohio, Indiana, Illinois, western Pennsylvania, western Virginia, and Missouri. Third, as a major general, McClellan received undeserved credit for a few early skirmishes that secured West Virginia for the Union. Even though these victories came because of much superior numbers, McClellan would telegraph them as strategic triumphs.[12] Since the Union had few other victories early in the war, McClellan looked like the one commander who could get things done.

In July 1861, Lincoln invited McClellan to the Executive Mansion to get to know him better. He eventually appointed the thirty-four year-old McClellan to command the Army of the Potomac. Needing something positive to latch on to, Congress lionized the new general.

While in town and receiving acclaim, McClellan found time to visit photographer Matthew Brady's studio. He struck a pose with his right hand pressed into his coat, à la Napoleon. The photograph sold throughout the North. Newspaper writers and soldiers dubbed him "Young Napoleon." The August 1, 1861, edition of the *New York Tribune* ran an editorial entitled "Confidence Renewed" and praised McClellan's first days on duty as commander of the Army of the Potomac.[13]

---

[12] Waugh, *Lincoln and McClellan*, 30–33. McClellan's small victories in western Virginia did not deserve a lot of acclaim. One newspaper editor called him "'the little corporal' of unfought fields" (Waugh, "Lincoln and McClellan," 216). McClellan had nothing directly to do with any of the skirmishes in western Virginia, nor was he present on any battlefield.

[13] White, *Lincoln*, 441.

McClellan wrote to his wife Nelly almost daily, revealing his unbridled hubris already in full bloom. Everyone in power deferred to him. He had become the most formidable and influential leader in the country. If he had further success, he told her, he would become so popular that he could take over the country as a dictator if he wanted. Of course, because of his "admirable self-denial!" he would not do so.[14] Since "the people call upon me to save the country—I *must* save it & cannot respect anything that is in the way." Despite the numerous letters begging him to assume the presidency or to become a dictator, he would "cheerfully take the Dictatorship & agree to lay down my life when the country is saved."[15] He proudly pontificated, "Who would have thought when we were married, that I should so soon be called upon to save my country?" He had heard that the Confederates say "that there is only one man they feared & that was McClellan."[16]

The hyperpraise and acclaim McClellan received while in Washington fed an already oversized ego. Handsome and full of vigor, McClellan looked like a general and carried himself like a prince. He fit the Napoleonic profile of answering the call of destiny. Someone regarded him as "the only man ever born who can strut sitting down." He swaggered and had an attitude to match it.

McClellan admitted that he had a "naturally defiant disposition."[17] He disdained compromise and prided himself on being right. He believed himself to be the smartest person in any room, nitpicked every little point to show his intellectual superiority, and defended his sentiments accordingly. He abhorred criticism. "I don't care much for anybody's opinion," he once wrote his brother John, "as long as I am in the right." The sentiment bears repeating: he always assumed himself to be in the right. Once he came to a

---

[14] Burlingame, *Lincoln*, 2:191.

[15] Goodwin, *Team of Rivals*, 379.

[16] Waugh, *Lincoln and McClellan*, 30–33.

[17] Waugh, *Lincoln and McClellan*, 35. The quotes in the remainder of the paragraph come from this same source.

resolution on something, he rarely changed his mind. Certainly McClellan's record of military service revealed an impatience under another's command, constant criticism of superiors, haughtiness, and irritation with interference or advice. Despite this track record, almost everyone, including congressmen, wanted to shake the new general's hand.

McClellan did have several attributes that made him a distinguished and valuable commander, no matter his attitude. He could be charming, which allowed him to flatter others and win friends. Along with intelligence, education, and competence, McClellan possessed key ingredients of leadership that inspired admiration. He instilled confidence in his officers and soldiers, which was perhaps his most important leadership trait.[18] "I must ride every day," he wrote his wife, because "it is necessary for me to see as much as I can every day & more than that let the men see me & gain confidence in me."[19] No dummy, McClellan realized visiting and flattering his men every day would spur affection toward him as their commander. The soldiers of the Army of the Potomac learned to love him and called him "Little Mac." They cheered loudly whenever he rode by, and he would acknowledge their cheers, snatching off his cap and twirling it above his head. Often he stopped to chat casually with the troops. McClellan taught his men how to be soldiers and made them feel like soldiers. He looked like a soldier himself. He saw to it that they were kept busy and well fed, got proper uniforms and supplies, and had access to hospitals and doctors.[20] One officer praised McClellan's "personal magnetism" and characterized it as a "potent, if not irresistible force."[21] He had an angelic, protective love of his men, and an astounding ability to stir the love of his army. One biographer asserts that "no other commander ever aroused the same enthusiasm in the troops" as did

---

[18] Waugh, *Lincoln and McClellan*, 36.

[19] Waugh, *Lincoln and McClellan*, 44-45.

[20] Leekley, *Bruce Catton's Reflections on the Civil War*, 82.

[21] Waugh, *Lincoln and McClellan*, 216.

McClellan. "The soldiers fairly loved to look upon him; the sight of him brought cheers spontaneously from every lip; his voice was music to every ear."[22] Soldiers and officers adored him because he seemed to care about them and made them feel good about themselves, their duty, and their capabilities. These characteristics were real and made McClellan almost untouchable for any supervisor, even the commander in chief, to discipline or admonish.

There were other notable qualities for which McClellan deserves credit. He did commendable work, for example, in reorganizing the forces around Washington, DC. A skilled engineer, he developed a ring of fortifications to protect the nation's capital. He trained his men with a hands-on approach, keeping a close eye on them as they did close-order drills, target practice, and maneuvers. He formed patriotic volunteer regiments into a well-drilled system of brigades and divisions. Omnipresent on his magnificent horse, he allowed no detail of his soldiers' lives to escape his notice.

McClellan had no peer when it came to military organization, strategy, and tactics. A genius at the science of war, he whipped the Army of the Potomac into shape and prepared it for combat. Within a few short months after he took command, he succeeded in building the biggest, greatest, and most disciplined army in the world.[23]

The chief problem with McClellan, as Lincoln would discover shortly after promoting him, was that, while he had done a masterful job preparing the Army of the Potomac, he simply did not want to use it. Repeatedly he refused to take the initiative and bring the fight to the enemy. Like a runner who has trained for a competition for months but declines to race when the starting gun goes off, McClellan had instilled a confidence in his army to win the war, but did not possess the will to deploy it in battle. When his nation

---

[22] Waugh, *Lincoln and McClellan*, 216.

[23] Donald, *Lincoln*, 317–318; Waugh, "Lincoln and McClellan," 217; Keneally, *Lincoln*, 112.

needed a fighter, McClellan did not want to fight. He even had the audacity to call one retreat a "change of base." Lincoln and other high cabinet officials never understood this glaring deficiency in McClellan's acumen. The president eventually compared his outwardly impressive general to a rooster that, at a safe distance, proudly spread its feathers and crowed, but turned and ran when the cockfight began.[24]

There were indications in McClellan's past that he did not have the stomach to make the tough decisions required of a wartime general. True, he had finished second in his class of 1846 at West Point, served credibly in the Mexican War, led a prestigious commission to observe the Crimean War, invented a saddle that became standard cavalry issue, and became president of a railroad after quitting the service in 1857. Likewise, before 1861 he had never really experienced failure or taken any big risks. He remained cocky yet hesitant, resistant to bold moves. It solidified his fixed mindset. He never wanted to fail or be seen as a failure.

Moreover, McClellan's study of the Crimean War taught him that a general should not take any important operation or initiative without reliable reconnaissance and information. History also demonstrated that Young Napoleon loved to take credit due others, unfairly chastised subordinates, was indecisive at key points, failed to follow up on his victories, failed to keep his promises, arrived tardy and irresolute on the battlefield, showed a lack of initiative, and tended to whine unjustly about insufficient support.

Despite all of these character and performance flaws, McClellan's star had risen because he skillfully and deceptively promoted himself after writing vainglorious dispatches exaggerating his accomplishments after some small victories in western Virginia early in the war.[25]

---

24 Waugh, "Lincoln and McClellan," 221–22; Owen, *The Man and His Faith*, 17–18.

25 Burlingame, *Lincoln,* 2:191–192; Waugh, *Lincoln and McClellan*, 39.

In fairness to McClellan, no American general had ever commanded men on such a large scale. This reality presented a particular challenge to someone who had always been a consummate micromanager. Moreover, like many control freaks, McClellan had too much confidence in himself and not enough in others above or below him. Once he complained to his wife that he had not met a general "worth his salt—Thomas Morris is a timid old woman—Rosencranz a silly fussy goose—Newton Schleich knows nothing."[26] Nobody, of course, measured up to him.

Overconfident in his own knowledge and abilities, McClellan had a fixed mindset and could not adapt when the moment called for it. One soldier referred to him as "McClellan the Unready." This was ironic because his namesake, Napoleon Bonaparte—a commander renowned for adaptability, celerity, instinct for strategic advantage, and going for the jugular—was McClellan's hero. McClellan "habitually magnified obstacles into impossibilities," one critic wrote, "and deferred great deeds to a future that had no possibility."[27] In a war in which the commander in chief needed a general itching to take the offensive, McClellan defaulted to a defensive mindset. Cautious instead of bold, McClellan quickly became a major disappointment to Lincoln.

Since he believed himself to be superior in every way to the president, McClellan never took any time to bond or even build a cordial relationship with Lincoln. Unlike Grant and Sherman, who enjoyed spending time conversing with the president, McClellan's upper-class upbringing bred hubris, which would eventually become a fatal liability. An aristocratic snob, he truly believed Lincoln did not measure up to him in class, culture, intellect, and social savvy. Years after the war, McClellan was still insisting that Lincoln lacked a "very strong character, & as he was destitute of refinement—certainly in no sense a gentleman—he was easily wrought upon

---

[26] Waugh, *Lincoln and McClellan*, 38, 47.

[27] Waugh, *Lincoln and McClellan*, 216-217.

by coarse associates whose style of conversations agreed so well with his own."[28] One who did not take the time to notice the talents, dispositions, or brilliance in others, McClellan remained a nearsighted leader. Even when Lincoln went out of his way to build a relationship, McClellan blindly ignored his offerings. He had no time for inferiors, who were almost everyone else.[29]

Once in command of the Army of the Potomac, McClellan immediately disappointed political leaders in Washington with his lethargy and inaction. After pleading with McClellan to move on the Confederate forces throughout the summer of 1861, Lincoln finally coaxed his general to venture across the Potomac River and engage Confederate forces at Ball's Bluff. Thrown back with heavy losses, which included Lincoln's longtime friend and senator from Oregon, Colonel Edward D. Baker (the Lincolns had named their son, Eddie, after him), McClellan took no responsibility and blamed the loss on the leadership of Baker and Scott. Since McClellan's star still shone brightly at that time, his rant against that "perfect imbecile" and "*dotard*" Scott, carried the day.[30] Pressured by the Senate, Scott resigned his command.

McClellan told all who would listen "that officers & men all declare that they will fight under no one but 'our George,' as the scamps have taken it into their heads to call me."[31] With no one else apparently suitable to lead, Lincoln put McClellan in charge of the whole Union army. "I can do it all," McClellan assured the president.[32]

---

28 Keneally, *Lincoln*, 113.

29 Waugh, *Lincoln and McClellan*, 218.

30 Goodwin, *Team of Rivals*, 379.

31 Goodwin, *Team of Rivals*, 382. McClellan also called Scott a "traitor" and accused him of "eternal jealousy of all who acquire any distinction."

32 Donald, *Lincoln*, 319; Burlingame, *Lincoln*, 2:193–94. McClellan had wanted to get Scott out of his way since the beginning of his command of the Army of the Potomac. Ironically, he criticized Scott for being too defensive and hesitant to take the offensive.

Yet McClellan still treated Lincoln as an irritating nuisance. Two weeks after his promotion, McClellan returned home from a wedding. Lincoln, John Hay, and Seward were waiting for him in his parlor. After being notified by his porter of his guests, McClellan proceeded to go upstairs to rest. After a half hour, the servant again reminded the general of his guests. Eventually, the porter returned to the parlor to report that McClellan had gone to bed. While Hay bemoaned the rude and disrespectful behavior, Lincoln brushed off the snub.[33] He would not let personal slights lure him into a spat with his temperamental general. He had a war to win.

With Scott out of the way, McClellan still dithered. He had promised a relentless "On to Richmond" strategy, yet the army did not advance. Instead, McClellan had the army, now 168,000 troops strong, perform huge, impressive parades and reviews—for themselves. Lincoln gave his star general the benefit of the doubt and supported him.[34] Moreover, the president defended Little Mac when Radical Republicans threatened to take drastic action to force McClellan to move on the Confederate army. They created a joint committee on the conduct of the war and were set to have hearings. McClellan turned to Lincoln for help: "Don't let them hurry me, is all I ask."

"You shall have your own way in the matter I assure you," Lincoln promised.[35]

For the next three years of the war, a pattern emerged. McClellan refused to relentlessly pursue, engage, and defeat the Confederate army, much to the extreme frustration of his commander in chief. Instead he offered a plethora of excuses why he would not advance on Lee's army. Though he had superior forces—in troop numbers, artillery, rifles, materials, and provisions—McClellan made incessant requests for more supplies and more troops.

---

33 Burlingame, *Lincoln*, 2:196.

34 Waugh, *Lincoln and McClellan*, 57.

35 Waugh, *Lincoln and McClellan*, 58–59.

One reason why McClellan did not want to fight was he enjoyed his reputation as a pristine commander. The public had praised McClellan for those early, insignificant victories in western Virginia. He remained one of the few Union commanders who could boast of victories.[36] Yet he knew he had never faced a Confederate army with the caliber of generalship of a Lee or Jackson. A general cannot lose a battle if he does not fight one. McClellan did not want to risk a loss.

Another reason McClellan lacked the vigor to prosecute the war is that he did not believe in the Union cause the same way Lincoln did. A partisan Democrat, McClellan had little sympathy for the abolitionists, whom he believed had hijacked the Republican Party. Lincoln did not always approve of abolitionists' rhetoric and uncompromising ways either, but he believed them to be on the right side of history. The general confided that he possessed a prejudice for his own race, crudely comparing the odors of slaves with goats.[37] In the years ahead, when Lincoln pressed for emancipation and the arming and integrating of black Americans into the Union army, McClellan dragged his feet, not wanting to risk his beloved troops for enslaved people.

In order to prop himself up, McClellan felt it necessary to put others down, from General Winfield Scott to cabinet members to Lincoln. He used rhetoric and allusions to the commander in chief that would be unheard of today. McClellan frequently called Lincoln an "idiot," "the original gorilla," "baboon," an "old stick—and pretty poor timber at that," "giraffe," "coward," and other derogatory comments. Cabinet members were some of the "greatest geese" he had ever seen and worthless politicians. He labeled Seward the meanest of all and as incompetent as a puppy. Wells was a talkative and annoying old woman, and Bates was a harmless old man.[38]

---

36 Waugh, *Lincoln and McClellan,* 48.

37 Burlingame, *Lincoln*, 2:198.

38 Burlingame, *Lincoln,* 2:196-97.

McClellan continued to snub the president when Lincoln tried to visit him. Staffers denied the president access because the general was napping or eating breakfast. Sometimes Young Napoleon simply wanted to demonstrate who really owned the field. When the two did get together, Little Mac said little.

Despite McClellan's lack of respect and inappropriate behavior, the president wanted to support his general. When McClellan failed to show up for a meeting, Lincoln told others he would hold McClellan's horse if that is what it took to garner success on the battlefield.

While Lincoln used visits to conduct soft oversight and reconnaissance of his commander, McClellan resented Lincoln's appearances at army headquarters. He could not stand to listen to Lincoln's stories. One day, Admiral David Porter and McClellan were discussing the New Orleans campaign when they were interrupted by a servant announcing that Lincoln wished to see the general. McClellan told the servant to let the president wait, as he was busy. Stunned by McClellan's arrogance, Admiral Porter asked McClellan to relent, insisting that Lincoln would be interested in their discussion. Unfazed by Porter's position, McClellan reiterated that the president could wait. He did not need to know the general's business.[39] The utter disdain McClellan had for Lincoln remained palpable throughout the war.

Lincoln would have been willing to put up with McClellan's arrogance indefinitely if it had been accompanied by military victories. Alas, McClellan failed to produce progress, and so tension grew between the Lincoln administration and congressional leaders on the one hand, and McClellan on the other. After Union soldiers discovered that they had been fooled by "Quaker guns"—logs painted black to resemble cannons—at Munson's Hill in September

---

[39] Burlingame, *Lincoln*, 2:196–98; Krannawitter, *Vindicating Lincoln*, 40.

1861, McClellan still failed to pursue the fleeing Confederates, even though the Union army was three times larger.[40]

As 1862 commenced, Treasury officials told Lincoln that the country would soon go bankrupt. "The bottom is out the tub," Lincoln lamented. "What shall I do?"[41] Union armies needed to advance and win battles quickly or the war would end in two separate nations. If McClellan did not intend to put the army in motion, Lincoln told his commander that he would like to "borrow it."[42] When Lincoln went to visit McClellan and other commanders in mid-January, Little Mac remained aloof and hardly participated in the discussion. The reason became clear the very next day. McClellan had spent three hours sharing his plans with a *New York Herald* reporter.[43]

On January 27, 1862, Lincoln ordered all land and naval forces to begin moving against the enemy. Lincoln had tired of McClellan's dithering, and he reestablished the hierarchy between commander in chief and military commander. From that point on, when Lincoln wanted a chat with his general, McClellan would come to him. Lincoln also issued a directive to attack Confederate supply lines at Manassas, something he had told McClellan to do weeks earlier. Still wanting to show support, Lincoln acquiesced to McClellan's alternative plan, which ended up being a disaster.[44]

---

[40] Burlingame, *Lincoln*, 2:199.

[41] Waugh, *Lincoln and McClellan*, 61.

[42] Burlingame, *Lincoln,* 2:220.

[43] Burlingame, *Lincoln*, 2:220–21.

[44] Burlingame, *Lincoln*, 2:296–96. McClellan's plan involved going by water to attack Urbanna on the Rappahannock River and then drive to the Confederate capital. The Union boats, however, were too wide to move from the Chesapeake and Ohio Canal to secure pontoon bridges on the Potomac at Harper's Ferry. Lincoln erupted upon learning about the mistake. Banging his fist on the table, he could not understand why army leadership had failed to measure the waterway and boats before commencing with the operation.

After Lincoln's son Willie died in late February, McClellan did offer his "sincere & deep sympathy" to the president. "You have been a kind and true friend to me in the midst of the great cares & difficulties by which we have been surrounded during the past few months," he said. "Your confidence has upheld me when I should otherwise have felt weak. I wish now only to assure you & your family that I have felt the deepest sympathy in your affliction."[45] The condolences and charm offensive would not last.

McClellan, knowing the president grieved and was somewhat distracted, still did not make any advance on the enemy forces. Even as the nation mourned with the Lincolns, frustration grew with the quagmire. Mary Lincoln had once called Little Mac "a humbug" because "he talks so much and does so little."[46] When her husband wanted to believe the best of his general, Mary cut her beloved off, telling him that McClellan made enough of his own excuses. He did not need any from the commander in chief.

Stanton, who once considered McClellan a sincere friend, had also had enough of the general's intransigence. After less than two weeks as secretary of war, Stanton told a friend that "while men are striving nobly in the West, the champagne and oysters on the Potomac must be stopped."[47] McClellan had enough time to host sprawling dinners, the guests at which were prominent figures in Washington, but not enough time to hunt down the Confederate army.

Lincoln pressed any button he could in hopes of springing McClellan into action. Without consulting the general, the president issued War Orders 2 and 3, which created four army corps and deeply offended McClellan's sense of order and control.[48] Finally in March, McClellan ordered his 112,000 troops forward to Centreville and Manassas—only to discover that the Confederates had pulled out.

---

45 Waugh, *Lincoln and McClellan*, 72.

46 Oates, *With Malice Toward None*, 287.

47 Goodwin, *Team of Rivals*, 427.

48 Waugh, *Lincoln and McClellan*, 74.

Quaker cannons had intimidated McClellan yet again. If McClellan had moved in late February, as Lincoln ordered him to, General Johnston would have been routed.[49]

The lack of alacrity had become a pattern all too familiar and infuriating. For the first time, Young Napoleon received widespread criticism. Newspapers dubbed him the "Quaker general." The Committee on the Conduct of War demanded his resignation. Lincoln also received criticism for his judgment. Why did he keep an incompetent general in command? Lincoln responded to the committee and members of Congress by asking them who they proposed to replace McClellan. When one of the committee members replied, "Anybody," Lincoln quickly responded, "*Anybody* will do for you, but not for me. I must have *somebody*."[50]

By this time in the war, Lincoln's confidence in Little Mac had disappeared. He admitted McClellan's strength as an engineer, but not his "special talent for developing a '*stationary*' engine." Lincoln needed advancement and engagement. He needed victories in the field. When the hour of action approached, McClellan "became nervous and oppressed with the responsibility and hesitated to meet the crisis."[51]

On March 11, 1862, Lincoln removed McClellan from his position of general in chief of all Union armies. Then he ordered McClellan to advance, which McClellan grudgingly did. "I regret that the rascals are after me again," McClellan wrote his wife. "I had been foolish enough to hope that when I went into the field they would give me some rest, but it seems otherwise—perhaps I should have expected it." His superiority complex continued unchecked: "If

---

49 Burlingame, *Lincoln*, 2:304. Nathaniel Hawthorne noted that "the outcry opened against General McClellan, since the enemy's retreat from Manassas is really terrible, and almost universal; because it is found that we might have taken their fortifications with perfect ease six months ago, they being defended chiefly by wooden guns" (Waugh, *Lincoln and McClellan*, 76).

50 Goodwin, *Team of Rivals*, 428.

51 Goodwin, *Team of Rivals,* 431.

I can get out of this scrape you will never catch me in the power of such a set again."[52]

In April 1862, McClellan got out-generaled and outmaneuvered again. Confederate commander John Magruder marched and countermarched his seventeen thousand troops to fool Little Mac into thinking the Confederate force stood much larger than the Union's fifty-eight thousand men. The hypercautious Union general broke off his march to Richmond and besieged Yorktown instead.[53]

Meanwhile, Lincoln enjoyed some good news on the front out west. Union forces under Ulysses S. Grant and William Tecumseh Sherman had won a fierce contest at Shiloh, Tennessee. Lincoln implored McClellan to get moving and seize momentum for the entire Union war effort. Even in charge of a hundred thousand men, however, McClellan complained that he did not have enough troops. "Your despatches complaining that you are not properly sustained, while they do not offend me, do pain me very much," Lincoln wrote him. Frustrated that McClellan had just communicated that he had 108,000 troops a few days previous and now said he only had 85,000 at his disposal, Lincoln wanted to know where the other 23,000 troops went. "And, once more let me tell you, it is indispensable to you that you strike a blow." Lincoln insisted that "the country will not fail to note—is now noting—that the present hesitation to move upon an intrenched enemy, is but the story of Manassas repeated." Lincoln assured McClellan that he had "never written you, or spoken to you, in greater kindness of feeling than now, nor with a fuller purpose to sustain you, so far as in my most anxious judgment, I consistently can. *But you must act.*"[54]

A few weeks later, and still without having acted on Lincoln's exhortation, McClellan had the gall to ask for more artillery. An exasperated Lincoln responded, "Your call for Parrott guns from

---

52 Waugh, *Lincoln and McClellan*, 76.

53 Burlingame, *Lincoln*, 2:308.

54 Basler, Lincoln to George McClellan, April 9, 1862, *CW*, 5:184–85.

Washington alarms me—chiefly because it argues indefinite procrastination. Is anything to be done?"[55] Amid his extreme frustration, Lincoln did send an extra division from Washington to reinforce McClellan's army. Grateful for the president's "firm friendship and confidence," he promised military success soon.[56]

Publicly Lincoln continued to defend his general. In May 1862, he chided army officers at dinner for criticizing McClellan because it hurt *his* feelings.[57] Meanwhile Radical Republicans believed that McClellan's intentions were to postpone a decisive battle as long as he could, hoping that some compromise would be reached—the Union saved but the South still left with its slaves.[58] Criticism and suspicion mounted against Little Napoleon.

While Lincoln absorbed the criticism and protected his general, McClellan continued to treat Lincoln with disrespect. If the commander in chief wanted the Confederate line broken or armies smashed, he could come and do it himself, McClellan told others.[59]

When McClellan did fight, the results were indecisive or worse. In late May and early June 1862, the Army of the Potomac fought to a stalemate at the Battle of Fair Oaks (Seven Pines), just five miles from the Confederate capital in Richmond. The losses horrified McClellan, and he became even more conservative in his approach. Moreover, because he kept his men for a month in their encampments in the turpentine forests, many soldiers died from malaria, typhus, and dysentery.[60]

In late June, the Confederates routed McClellan at the Battle of Seven Days. McClellan froze, refusing to counterattack and capture Richmond when the opportunity beckoned. His excuse for the loss: the army remained too small and Lincoln had done nothing about

---

55 Basler, Lincoln to George McClellan, May 1, 1862, *CW*, 5:203.

56 Donald, *Lincoln*, 350.

57 Burlingame, *Lincoln*, 2:311.

58 Waugh, *Lincoln and McClellan*, 97.

59 Burlingame, *Lincoln*, 2:311.

60 Keneally, *Lincoln*, 120.

it despite McClellan's pleas. He railed directly at his commander in chief, charging that Lincoln had tried to sacrifice the Army of the Potomac. McClellan had to save it not only from the Confederates but the president. Filled with grief and frustration, Lincoln believed McClellan could have ended the war if he had counterattacked. Instead of feeling connection and partnership with his commanding general, Lincoln told Bishop Charles Gordon Ames of Illinois that he felt like the most lonesome man in American.[61]

McClellan's accusation that Lincoln had deliberately kept back reserves did not hold water. The president had actually stripped Washington to a bare-bones defense of twenty-six thousand troops.[62] McClellan, however, did not care about Lincoln or his predicament. Shortly after the Seven Days Battle, the general told his wife that Lincoln, even if he wanted to, would never relieve him of duty because "his cowardice alone prevents it. I can never regard him with other feelings than those of thorough contempt—for his mind, heart & mortality."[63]

By the summer of 1862, both men were being labeled cowards—McClellan for being afraid to fight and Lincoln for not having the guts to relieve his commander. At a time when the president and general needed to be in harmony to fight the war, they were as far apart as the North was from the South.

Abolitionists, especially, turned on the president. Wendell Phillips accused Lincoln of being twice as wretched an enemy to the Union as Jefferson Davis. Millions of dollars were being spent and thousands of lives extinguished because of the president's ignorance and timidity. Abolitionist Samuel J. May Jr. pugnaciously projected that if the Union lost the war, Lincoln "is the criminal" responsible for the failure.[64]

---

[61] Burlingame, *Lincoln*, 2:322, 324.

[62] Keneally, *Lincoln*, 121.

[63] Waugh, *Lincoln and McClellan*, 115.

[64] Burlingame, *Lincoln*, 2:325.

Abolitionists did not seem to understand the predicament Lincoln faced with his defiant general. The president actually worried that McClellan might surrender the Army of the Potomac in the late summer of 1862. In what became a preview of his 1864 presidential run, McClellan sent a letter to Lincoln advocating that the property rights of the Confederate states, including slaves, be preserved. According to Navy Secretary Gideon Wells, Lincoln regarded the painful letter as a veiled threat to march on Washington and overthrow the government. After Lincoln visited McClellan's headquarters, the general told his wife that the president did not seem capable of handling the magnitude of the moment. As the summer days passed, Lincoln continued to urge McClellan to advance upon the enemy at Richmond. When McClellan asked for more reinforcements, Lincoln got sarcastic. If he could magically send another 100,000 troops to McClellan, a telegraph would return from the General certain that the enemy's army had grown to 400,000 men, and that he must have more reinforcements before he could advance. Lincoln sarcastically explained that Little Mac had so skillfully maneuvered troops everywhere except to Richmond—the primary land-based objective—that their self-confidence increased. Unsurprisingly but no less infuriating, McClellan could not account for half of the soldiers sent to him.[65]

While Lincoln's frustration with McClellan grew, the president still tried to maintain order and a working relationship with his commander. As one senator called for McClellan to be shot, Lincoln defended and praised his general's bravery and abilities in front of a crowd of ten thousand people at the capital. McClellan simply wanted more men to serve in the army. The commander in chief even took the blame for not providing more troops to the General, something McClellan had been advocating for unceasingly.[66]

---

65 Burlingame, *Lincoln,* 2:328–331.

66 Burlingame, *Lincoln,* 2:331.

While Lincoln continued his public and private efforts to make the relationship work, McClellan pouted, fumed, and undermined his commander in chief. He became so jealous of the president, he started rumors that the only reason soldiers cheered when Lincoln arrived at camp was because they were ordered to cheer. Moreover, McClellan continued to ignore orders. In late August 1862, he failed to support General John Pope at the Second Battle of Bull Run. Lincoln believed, correctly, that McClellan wanted Pope defeated so that McClellan could look good by comparison.

Despite his anger and distress, Lincoln put McClellan in charge of the defense of the capital in early September, much to the consternation of his cabinet. Lincoln still believed in McClellan's superb organizational skills and defensive tactics, as well as his popularity with the troops. Besides, no other viable generals existed at that point in the war. Lincoln relieved Pope and restored McClellan to the command of the Army of the Potomac.[67]

Yet Lincoln struggled with his own decision to place the fate of the Union army in McClellan's control again. On the one hand, Lincoln told critics that McClellan had to be a good commander because so many military officers and soldiers believed him to be so. On the other hand, the data had come in on his general's primary weakness: for whatever reason, McClellan did not seize the moment or initiate action. He did not or could not produce meaningful results.

In his second go-around as commander of the Army of the Potomac, nothing changed. McClellan moved slowly, constantly appealed for reinforcements, and greatly overestimated the enemy's numbers. Even after striking a military goldmine and retrieving Confederate battle plans, Special Orders No. 191, at an abandoned campsite (dubbed the "Lost Orders"), McClellan failed to take immediate action. He could have scored a smashing victory if he had acted swiftly on the news that General Robert E. Lee had divided

[67] Burlingame, *Lincoln*, 2:328, 373–78; Donald, *Lincoln*, 371.

his army for his Northern invasion strategy. Instead, McClellan's lethargy allowed Lee time to regroup. Despite all the confidence Lincoln had shown in the general and all of the criticism he had taken on McClellan's behalf, Young Napoleon remained the same passive, disappointing commander he had shown himself to be for months.

On September 17, 1862, Confederate and Union forces clashed at the Battle of Antietam—the single deadliest day of the Civil War. The Army of the Potomac suffered twelve thousand casualties, while the Army of Northern Virginia endured fourteen thousand. On the field, the battle appeared to be a stalemate, but McClellan let Lee escape across the Potomac River. He had committed only two-thirds of his forces in the battle and could have pursued Lee's battered army with fresh troops the next day, but he stayed put. Lincoln bemoaned, once again, how Little Mac refused to do the competent and necessary things to win a battle.[68]

McClellan, however, boasted that he had achieved a great victory. Hearing him sing his own praises disheartened millions of Americans who wanted to destroy the Confederate army and end the war.

Lincoln visited McClellan in Sharpsburg after the battle. McClellan acknowledged that the president had treated him so kindly and affably that he truly believed Lincoln liked him. A kind man by default, Lincoln had an incentive to treat his general kindly. They needed to work together. Beyond the benevolence, however, Lincoln grilled McClellan with questions and candid criticism. Recognizing and praising the general's organizational abilities, as well as his service to his country, Lincoln candidly asserted that McClellan's timidity, lack of self-confidence, or something else he could not put his finger on kept Little Mac from achieving significant results. Before leaving McClellan's headquarters, the

---

68 Burlingame, *Lincoln,* 381.

president insisted that the army advance should get underway in two weeks.

Indignant at Lincoln's boldness, McClellan scornfully wrote to his wife, disparaging the president for not knowing what it took to lead an army and for being stupid.[69] As much as Lincoln tried, there would be no changing the heart and mind of Young Napoleon, who seemed to know it all.

While McClellan could not get his "victorious" army moving again, Confederate General Jeb Stuart led eighteen hundred cavalrymen around the Army of the Potomac and caused significant mischief, damaging military stores, machine shops, and railroad lines throughout Maryland and Pennsylvania. The raids also served to embarrass the president before the 1862 midterm elections. Lincoln wanted to fire McClellan but worried about the political damage it would cause to his Republican Party so close to the election.[70]

One evening, observing the Union encampment from a hill, Lincoln expressed his deep frustration with McClellan's refusal to advance on the enemy claiming a lack of shoes, clothes, and horses for his men. The president asked his friend Ozias M. Hatch what he saw. When Hatch responded that he observed a large portion of the Army of the Potomac, Lincoln corrected him: they were looking at McClellan's personal bodyguard.[71]

Lincoln's frustration finally turned to anger. "You remember my speaking to you of what I called your over-cautiousness," he wrote the general. "Are you not over-cautious when you assume that you can not do what the enemy is constantly doing? Should you not claim to be at least his equal in prowess, and act upon the claim?" Exasperated, Lincoln started giving military advice. "Again, one of the standard maxims of war, as you know, is 'to operate upon the enemy's communications as much as possible without exposing

---

[69] Burlingame, *Lincoln,* 2:426.

[70] Donald, *Lincoln*, 388; Burlingame, *Lincoln*, 2:428–29.

[71] Burlingame, *Lincoln*, 2:426–27.

your own.' You seem to act as if this applies against you, but can not apply in your favor." Lincoln insisted that McClellan should cut off and crush Lee's army. "You dread his going into Pennsylvania. But if he does so in full force, he gives up his communications to you absolutely, and you have nothing to do but to follow, and ruin him; if he does so with less than full force, fall upon, and beat what is left behind all the easier."[72]

McClellan mocked the commander in chief's thoughts. He told Lincoln he could not pursue Lee because his cavalry horses were worn out. Lincoln's temper snapped. "I have just read your dispatch about sore tongued and fatigued horses. Will you pardon me for asking what the horses of your army have done since the battle of Antietam that fatigue anything?"[73] He told Francis Blair Sr. that "he had tried long enough to bore with an auger too dull to take hold."[74]

Infuriated at Lincoln's terse letter, McClellan told his wife that he despised having to submit to men and leaders who were socially, intellectually, and morally inferior to him. He especially resented having to take orders from Lincoln—the "Gorilla."[75]

Lincoln could no longer afford to live with an insubordinate, do-nothing commander who moved at a tortoise's pace. After McClellan failed yet again to intercept the Confederate army on the way to Richmond, Lincoln fired the general the day after the midterm elections. McClellan could not or refused to overcome "the slows."[76] He did not seem to want to defeat the enemy and had lost the confidence of his subordinate generals.

Moreover, McClellan seemed to be preparing for a presidential run. He had wanted to denounce the Emancipation Proclamation in public, but his advisors persuaded him otherwise. He settled for an army order that called attention to the decree and reminded

---

72 Basler, Lincoln to George McClellan, October 13, 1862, *CW*, 5:460.

73 Basler Lincoln to George McClellan, October 24, 1862, *CW*, 5:474.

74 Donald, *Lincoln*, 389.

75 Burlingame, *Lincoln*, 2:429–431.

76 Oates, *With Malice Toward None*, 324.

his troops that political errors could be corrected at the polls. Furthermore, the negative election results compelled Lincoln to become more aggressive in the pursuit of victory.[77]

Relieved of duty, McClellan told his wife that "more than a hundred thousand soldiers are in great grief to-night."[78] Many soldiers did openly grieve when they heard of McClellan's firing. Others rejoiced. Said one soldier, "The papers lie; they lie horribly. They are trying hard to make McClellan a great man; whereas I sometimes fear he is a great donkey."[79]

Robert E. Lee also mourned the loss of McClellan, but for different reasons. He understood McClellan. Now he feared that Union high command would continue to make leadership changes "till they find some one whom I don't understand."[80]

In the short term, the sacking of McClellan hurt the Union war effort. Generals who succeeded McClellan knew he had been fired for being insubordinate and sedate in the pursuit of Lee's Army of Northern Virginia. In trying to please their commander in chief and a public tired of war, they overcompensated by being too aggressive and reckless, which led to Union disasters at places like Chancellorsville and Fredericksburg. Eventually, however, Lincoln found the right general to win the war in the East.

The contrast between McClellan and Ulysses S. Grant could not have been more stark. Lincoln never felt comfortable with McClellan nor respected by him. Visiting and conversing with McClellan was always a painful experience. Conversely, Lincoln and Grant respected one another and enjoyed each other's company. Lincoln loved Grant's straightforwardness, humility, informality, and unpretentiousness. That Grant preferred to wear a private's simple blouse instead of a general's gold braid and seemed totally unconcerned with his own appearance resonated with the former

---

77 Burlingame, *Lincoln*, 2:429–31; Oates, *With Malice Toward None*, 321.

78 Goodwin, *Team of Rivals*, 485.

79 Waugh, *Lincoln and McClellan*, 186.

80 Waugh, *Lincoln and McClellan*, 186.

rail-splitter.[81] Moreover, Lincoln trusted Grant and vice versa. They shared the same agenda and mission—the pursuit and defeat of Lee's army and the Confederacy. Grant fought without demanding reinforcements. He did not make excuses or complain. Lincoln admired his calm demeanor and persistence in achieving objectives. Grant possessed the "*grit* of a bulldog!"[82] Once he got his teeth in, nothing could shake him loose.

In a candid moment, the commander in chief stated that Grant was the first general he could count on in the war. All other generals he appointed had not taken ownership or responsibility for the battle plans the way Grant did. Unintentionally or intentionally, the other generals put accountability on the president and not themselves. In addition to being the commander in chief, Lincoln had felt the pressure of being the general of every campaign.

Grant led differently. He took the initiative without fearing the repercussions. He never asked Lincoln for something that the president could not deliver.[83] Grant's drive, initiative, and self-motivation were refreshing to Lincoln. One day Lincoln hugged and kissed a young reporter who arrived at the Executive Mansion with a message from Grant that said, "There is to be no turning back."[84]

On another occasion, Lincoln shared a story that summed up his feelings about Grant. There was an "automaton chess player, which many years ago astonished the world by its skill in that game. After a while the automaton was challenged by a celebrated player, who, to his great chagrin, suffered defeat twice against the machine. At the end of the second game, the player, significantly pointing his finger at the automaton, exclaimed in a very decided tone. '*There's a man in it!*'" That, the president explained, referring to Grant, remained "the secret" to the army's fortunes.[85]

---

81 Johnson, *Last Weeks of Lincoln*, 202.

82 Burlingame, *Lincoln*, 2:655.

83 Burlingame, *Lincoln*, 2:655.

84 Goodwin, *Team of Rivals*, 620.

85 Goodwin, *Team of Rivals*, 620.

Unlike McClellan, Grant showed loyalty, admiration, and affection for his superior. When Democrats and Radical Republicans asked him to run for president in 1864, he refused. "Nothing would induce me to think of being a presidential candidate," he said, "particularly so long as there is a possibility of having Mr. Lincoln reelected." When he heard of Grant's allegiance, Lincoln responded, "No man knows when that presidential grub gets to gnawing at him, just how deep it will get until he has tried it; and I didn't know but what there was one gnawing at Grant."[86]

As Grant prepared to launch an offensive in the East in the spring of 1864, Lincoln wrote to his new general, "I wish to express, in this way, my entire satisfaction with what you have done up to this time, so far as I understand it. The particulars of your plans I neither know, or seek to know. You are vigilant and self-reliant." The president did not want to place "any constraints or restrains upon you. If there is anything wanting which is within my power to give, do not fail to let me know it. And now with a brave Army, and a just cause, may God sustain you."[87]

Grant replied, "The confidence you express for the future, and satisfaction with the past, in my Military administration is acknowledged with pride. It will be my earnest endeavor that you, and the country, shall not be disappointed." Grant reassured the president that he "never had cause of complaint, have never expressed or implied a complaint, against the Administration … for throwing any embarrassment in the way of my vigorously prosecuting what appeared to me my duty." Indeed, he was "astonished at the readiness with which every thing asked for has been yielded without even an explanation being asked. Should my success be less than I desire, and expect, the least I can say is, the fault is not with you."[88] It had taken far too long, but the president finally had his general.

---

[86] McGovern, *Lincoln*, 102.

[87] Basler, Lincoln to Grant, April 30, 1864, *CW*, 7:324.

[88] Basler, Ulysses S. Grant to Lincoln, May 1, 1864, *CW*, 7:324–325.

Meanwhile when Lincoln heard that McClellan had accepted the Democratic nomination on August 29, 1864, in Chicago, he quipped that surely the general "must be intrenching."[89] More seriously, he figured that Little Mac probably had not made up his mind to accept or decline the nomination. As had been his hesitant and timid nature as a commander, somebody would need to make the decision for McClellan. Lincoln found McClellan to be the most indecisive man he had ever met.

With a Northern public tired of the war, and particularly of the rise in casualties under Grant, McClellan was the favorite to win the election. Moreover, Americans loved electing former generals for president: Washington, Jackson, Harrison, Taylor, and Pierce had all been elected because of their military bona fides. Furthermore, because McClellan was a Peace Democrat, or Copperhead, most Democrats thought he was the perfect candidate to defeat Lincoln—he could challenge the president's war policy without making his party look unpatriotic or putting his own patriotism in question.[90]

One problem facing the Democratic Party was that white supremacy permeated it. A Democratic president, most likely a racist proslavery president, was likely to try to save the Union with slavery intact.[91] Therefore, while many soldiers insisted they liked Little Mac, they did not like the company he was keeping. Democrats were calling the war a failure and seeking to negotiate with the enemy. As horrific as the war had been, most Northerners were not racists, nor did they want to surrender to the Confederates.

When the election of 1864 finally took place in November, McClellan lost the army vote by a significant margin. In fact, seven

---

89 Burlingame, *Lincoln*, 2:681.

90 Waugh, *Lincoln and McClellan*, 191–92. The epithet "Copperhead" came into existence in 1861 to evoke the image of serpents of conspiracy. They were "like copperheads and rattlesnakes in winter," the *Cincinnati Daily Commercial* described them, "cold in their stiff and silent coils," the "blind and venomous enemies of our government found in our midst."

91 Striner, "Lincoln and the Struggle to End Slavery," 174.

out of ten troops in Army of the Potomac voted for Lincoln; eight out of ten in the West. Of the 150,636 soldier votes, McClellan received 33,748 to Lincoln's 116,887.[92] If Union soldiers liked McClellan, they had learned to like Lincoln even more—and, more importantly, trusted and agreed with his political positions too.[93]

McClellan's brilliant rise to fame was mirrored by a rapid fall and fizzle. After losing the election (and undoubtedly embarrassed that he could not defeat the "gorilla"), he became bitter that the country had not shown him proper gratitude for saving it twice—securing the nation's capital after the chaos of First Manassas and again at Antietam. In 1865, the McClellans sailed for Europe and remained there for three years.

Breaking a vow never to run for office again, McClellan won the New Jersey governorship in 1878, and served one term without distinction. At the age of fifty-eight, he died suddenly from a heart attack on October 29, 1885. That a man of such vigor and talent could die so young without tapping his considerable potential seemed the real tragedy of McClellan's life.[94]

After the war, Grant generously suggested that McClellan had been given too much responsibility too soon. "McClellan is to me one of the mysteries of the war," he opined. "He had the way of inspiring you with the idea of immense capacity, if he would only have a chance." Appointed major general at the beginning of the war, "McClellan was a young man when this devolved upon him, and if he did not succeed, it was because the conditions of success were so trying." Grant thought that "if McClellan had gone into the war as Sherman, Thomas, or Meade, had fought his way along and up,

---

[92] Waugh, *Lincoln and McClellan*, 214.

[93] Burlingame, *Lincoln*, 2:328. Lincoln's frequent visits to soldiers in the field boosted their morale, and they learned to love him. A visit from Lincoln equaled a reinforcement of ten thousand men according to one general.

[94] Waugh, *Lincoln and McClellan*, 214.

I have no reason to suppose that he would not have won as high a distinction as any of us."[95]

The conflict between McClellan and Lincoln remains a fascinating case study of the relationship dynamics between a popular employee and boss. In hindsight, it's easy to suggest that Lincoln should have known better and dismissed McClellan much sooner than he did. From a personnel management standpoint, however, McClellan presented a very difficult case. He was competent, vigorous, and well-liked by soldiers and officers alike. Union high command needed a leader who would be respected and followed. However overrated or unremarkable his early victories were, they came at a critical time, when Union forces had few successes. Moreover, there were few qualified applicants for the job. Lincoln had little choice but to appoint McClellan and support him. Eventually, however, Lincoln realized that he not only had to fire McClellan but eradicate the hesitant, defeatist, and defiant attitude that had seeped into the Union army mindset and discourse.

When Lincoln fired McClellan, he took the greatest political risk of his life. "I knew that his dismissal would provoke popular indignation and shake the faith of the people in the final success of the war," the president told Noah Brooks.[96] Rumors and warnings abounded that McClellan and the Union army might march on Washington and take charge of the government. Yet Lincoln knew a change in leadership and vision must take place.

The study of the relationship between McClellan and Lincoln also shows how context can impact a leader's options. For much of the time McClellan commanded Union forces, Lincoln was between a rock and a hard place. He could relieve McClellan from duty, but then what? Moreover, the Civil War itself demonstrated how leaders cannot control events. If the Union military had only needed to fight a defensive war, McClellan would have been a much better fit, due to

---

95 Waugh, "Lincoln and McClellan: A Reappraisal," 224.

96 Guelzo, *Lincoln*, 310.

his understanding of logistics, defenses, and organization. Lincoln, however, needed a hunter—a general who could find Lee's army and destroy it without wasting time. Understanding context is crucial in leadership and achieving one's goals.

McClellan and Lincoln were never in alignment in regard to mission. Lincoln had no desire to micromanage his general and tried to let McClellan lead, but McClellan did not believe in the objectives of the Union war effort. With irreconcilable differences in desired outcomes, Lincoln had no choice but to relieve his commander. Having defied an all-time great president and disappointed an entire nation, McClellan eventually sealed his fate and legacy as one who ended up on the wrong side of history.

The Truth

Before you cast too many aspersions on McClellan and his insubordination, reflect upon your own life and your relationship with your superior—God. Do you show Him proper respect, loyalty, and honor? Do you follow His orders and commandments? Do you communicate with Him regularly in a respectful manner? Do you listen to Him and His vision for your life—both now and the everlasting? Do you truly honor Him and His authority? Are you using the gifts, talents, and potential He has blessed you with, or are you afraid to advance in serving Him? Are you afraid of being mocked, stymied, or ridiculed? Do you walk the talk in your relationship with God?

The Bible explains that people "profess to know God, but they deny him by their works." God says that these individuals "are detestable, disobedient, unfit for any good work."[97] Moreover, those "who are insubordinate, empty talkers and deceivers ... must be

---

[97] Titus 1:16.

silenced, since they are upsetting whole families by teaching for shameful gain what they ought not to teach."[98]

When you disobey God or His Holy Word, you are being insubordinate to Him. This is tragic, for Scripture says that "the unrighteous … the sexually immoral, nor idolaters, nor adulterers, nor men who practice homosexuality, nor thieves, nor the greedy, nor drunkards, nor revilers, nor swindlers will inherit the kingdom of God."[99] Indeed, the "works of the flesh are evident: sexual immorality, impurity, sensuality, idolatry, sorcery, enmity, strife, jealousy, fits of anger, rivalries, dissensions, divisions, envy, drunkenness, orgies, and things like these." God warns us that "those who do such things will not inherit the kingdom of God."[100] Are you on any of these lists?

Even if the culture or the Supreme Court justifies unholy behavior, God makes clear that His Word is truth. "Dishonorable passions," for example, such as women exchanging "natural relations for those that are contrary to nature" and men likewise giving up "natural relations with women" to be "consumed with passion for one another" can lead to "shameless acts" and "the due penalty for their error."[101] Instead of disobeying or rebelling against God's Word, we are to acknowledge "the love of God, that we keep his commandments," and understand that "his commandments are not burdensome" but for our own eternal good.[102]

As they did with McClellan, one's mouth and words can get one into trouble. Scripture reminds us that "if anyone thinks he is religious and does not bridle his tongue but deceives his heart, this person's religion is worthless."[103] The "tongue is a fire, a world of unrighteousness … staining the whole body, setting on fire the

---

[98] Titus 1:10–11.
[99] 1 Cor. 6:9–10.
[100] Gal. 5:19–21.
[101] Rom. 1:26–27.
[102] 1 John 5:3.
[103] 1 James 1:26.

entire course of life, and set on fire by hell."[104] Whether it be by word, thought, or deed, when you sin, you are being insubordinate and disobeying your Heavenly Father.

The good news is that Jesus came into the world to die for your sins and insubordination before God. He did not come to court-martial, imprison, or kill you for your defiance. Instead Jesus rebuilt the relationship between you and God. "For as by the one man's disobedience the many were made sinners, so by the one man's obedience the many will be made righteous."[105]

In response to God's love, you are called to follow His Word to the best of your ability. "If you love me," Jesus tells His followers, "you will keep my commandments."[106] Again, He says clearly, "Truly, truly, I say to you, if anyone keeps my word, he will never see death."[107] By receiving and following God's Word, you will be brought to His heavenly home for eternity when your work and time are up on earth.

Jesus lays out the challenge for you this day: "Blessed rather are those who hear the word of God and keep it!"[108] To anyone who believes in Him, He promises, "If you abide in my word, you are truly my disciples, and you will know the truth, and the truth will set you free."[109]

Your Life

Too often people are quick to judge a situation that they have not experienced for themselves. Have you ever been in a difficult working

---

104 James 3:6.
105 Rom. 5:19.
106 John 14:15.
107 John 8:51.
108 Luke 11:28.
109 John 8:31–32.

relationship, whether as the boss or employee? How did you handle it? What did you do to make things better?

In your own life, where have you seen insubordination or disobedience? When is it okay to disobey and when it is not okay?

How do you reconcile your insubordination and disobedience toward God?

28

Playing Politics

But Peter and the apostles answered, "We must obey God rather than men."
—Acts 5:29

The Lincoln Way

The ability to persuade is power.

Abraham Lincoln had many vocations in his fifty-six years of life, but none more prominent than that of politician. Lincoln would never have issued the Emancipation Proclamation or become the Great Emancipator if he had not excelled at playing politics. In survey after survey, historians rank Lincoln as the top president of the United States (usually followed by Washington and FDR). That a master politician like Lincoln could hold on to the moniker Honest Abe is quite an accomplishment in itself.

Contemporaries recognized Lincoln's political potency. "The truth is, that Mr. Lincoln was at once the ablest and most adroit politicians of modern times," one opined. "In all the history of the world I can recall no example of a great leader, having to do with a people in any degree free, who himself shaped and guided events to the same extent, unless it was Julius Caesar."[1] Another noted Lincoln's shrewdness. "He was always on the alert" and "did not try to club men into line." Lincoln did not have to use force because "it was a case by persuasion. People gave them his support because they

---

[1] Lehrman, *Lincoln "by littles,"* 163.

came to believe he was right, and he showed them this was so by his reason." Lincoln "was the best judge of public sentiment the country ever produced." He never acted "until he believed the country was ripe for action."[2]

One Congressman contended that "the political sagacity of no other man was ever equal to that which enabled him to gather around him in earnest support of his administration, rivalries, opposing purposes, conflicting theories, and implacable enmities, which would have rent asunder any other administration." The president "grew wiser and broader and stronger as difficulties thickened and perils multiplied, till the end found him the wonder in our history." As Lincoln overcame "obstacles and escaped entanglements, it grew upon me that he was wiser than the men around him, that the nation had no other man for the place to which he was assigned by the Great Disposer."[3]

Lincoln first ran for political office (Illinois legislature) while residing in New Salem in 1832. He won and lost many elections over the course of decades. He campaigned for others and knew the disappointment of having promises broken to him by those politicians. For more than thirty years, Lincoln was intimately involved in politics. Having interacted with so many people in various settings throughout his career, he learned how people thought, lived, dreamed, hoped, and persevered. He knew what they needed and how they would respond to ideas. He learned how to listen and talk to folks of all backgrounds. His emotional intelligence set him apart as one who could really *feel* what others were feeling, thinking, and hoping. As his confidence, capacity, and skills as a writer, speaker, and politician grew, he learned how to influence and persuade people.

Leonard Swett, a circuit-riding lawyer and friend of Lincoln who also campaigned for him in 1860 and 1864, said that people

---

2 Peterson, *Lincoln in American Memory*, 161.

3 Sandburg, *Lincoln*, 402.

who considered Lincoln a "frank, guileless, unsophisticated man" never made a "greater mistake." Indeed, "beneath a smooth surface of candor and an apparent declaration of all his thoughts and feelings," Lincoln "exercised the most exalted tact and the wisest discrimination. He handled and moved man *remotely* as we do pieces upon a chessboard." Yet, while Lincoln could influence and persuade people, he never did so in a manipulative or coercive fashion. Swett further noted that Lincoln "retained through life, all the friends he ever had, and he made the wrath of his enemies to praise him. This was not by cunning, or intrigue in the low acceptation of the term, but by far seeing, reason and discernment." As an effective politician, Lincoln "always told enough only, of his plans and purposes, to induce the belief that he had communicated all; yet he reserved enough, in fact, to have communicated nothing."[4]

Unless they have seen Steven Spielberg's historical drama *Lincoln* (2012), which depicts a politically shrewd and astute politician, most Americans know Lincoln in simple terms as a president, the Rail-Splitter, Honest Abe, and the Great Emancipator, or as a boy who came from humble log cabin origins and lived a rags-to-riches story. Few think of him as a media savvy, political player.

But Lincoln excelled at shaping public opinion. He exaggerated, for example, his humble beginnings to great effect, which helped him promote the notion that his life had been about personal triumph over adversity.[5] He used the media to promote his log cabin and rail-splitter images, which helped him get elected president. The rail-splitter image in particular harbored enormous popular appeal. This image could be packaged as a powerful advocate of free-soil ideology; as a folksy, unpretentious, storytelling campaigner; as the embodiment of the self-made man; as the representative of free labor; and as spokesperson for the West. Ironically, most Americans never

---

[4] Wilson, *Herndon's Informants*, 168.

[5] Winkle, *Young Eagle*, ix.

knew that Lincoln had little love for his pioneer origins and disliked physical labor on the frontier.[6]

Playing politics helped vault Lincoln to the presidency. He masterfully navigated, for example, the politically treacherous race issue, both in his home state and nationally in the presidential election of 1860. Frustrated by Lincoln's apparent inconsistencies on slavery and racial equality, many contemporaries tried to call him out on his alleged hypocrisy. In their fifth debate in Galesburg, Illinois, on October 7, 1858, Illinois senator Stephen Douglas complained that when campaigning in the northern part of the state, Lincoln "stood up for negro equality," while in the south he "discarded the doctrine and declared that there always must be a superior and inferior race."[7] In Chicago, Lincoln asked his audience to stop quibbling about "this race and that race and the other race being inferior, and unite as one people throughout this land, until we shall once more stand up declaring that all men are created equal." Douglas denounced Lincoln's "Chicago doctrine" as "a monstrous heresy" and condemned him for refusing to say such things in the most southern parts of the state.

For political expediency, and like many Northern politicians who lived in "free states" with racially biased electorates, Lincoln did sometimes offer contradictory views on the equality of blacks and whites. After losing the senatorial election of 1858, Lincoln suddenly and shrewdly dropped term "ultimate extinction" when talking about slavery in his run for the Republican presidential nomination in 1860. Even as he abhorred the peculiar institution, Lincoln knew he could not win the 1860 election as the Great Emancipator.[8]

Lincoln's political opponents almost always underestimated him. To them, Lincoln looked, talked, and thought like a country bumpkin. Very few took him seriously as a politician (Stephen

---

6 Donald, *Lincoln*, 245.

7 Oakes, *Lincoln and Race*, 109. The following quotes in this paragraph come from the same source.

8 Freehling, *Becoming Lincoln*, 221, 227.

Douglas remained an exception after debating him so often in 1858). Knowing that Seward was the front-runner, Lincoln's strategy to win the nomination was to deploy a combination of relentless determination and self-effacing humility. He gained the goodwill of tens of thousands of fellow Republicans by speaking on behalf of the Republican Party and cause rather than his own candidacy.[9] He wanted to be everyone's favorite second choice. Like a horse drafting closely behind the leader in a race, Lincoln waited for the right moment to pounce.

Lincoln took the Republican nomination for president in 1860 primarily through shrewd political moves at the convention in Chicago. First, he hired cunning, energetic operatives and campaign managers. Second, he had the Illinois delegation cast all its votes under the unit rule (the entire delegation going to the majority's candidate). This move hurt Salmon Chase (Ohio) and Simon Cameron (Pennsylvania), neither of whom could garner all the votes from their own states. Third, despite his insistence that they not make any promises to constituents, Lincoln's managers did anyway.

Cameron (Pennsylvania) was named secretary of war and Caleb Smith (Indiana) was named secretary of interior in Lincoln's future cabinet. Courting these men turned out to be a fruitful endeavor. Lincoln's nomination gained twenty-two of Indiana's delegate votes on the first ballot—a key in expanding Lincoln's appeal. The forty-eight votes from Pennsylvania's delegation on the second ballot provided significant momentum for Lincoln's nomination.

Fourth, the plan of gently persuading delegates to make Lincoln their second choice worked well to produce another momentum-building process. Fifth was another important political move: Lincoln's team helped postpone the voting from Thursday to Friday. The extra day allowed Lincoln's managers to print a large supply of extra tickets, forge official signatures, rouse Lincoln supporters, and pack the hall. When overconfident Seward supporters arrived the

---

[9] Goodwin, *Leadership*, 119.

next morning to take the seats they had occupied on other days, they found those seats already taken by Lincoln people. Furious, Seward supporters had to wait outside.[10]

When nomination day came, Lincoln and his supporters had left little to chance. They had played the inside politics game well. In what became known as the "Night of a Thousand Knives," Horace Greeley—the legendary newspaper tycoon—grew frustrated that Republican frontrunner William Seward and Thurlow "Boss" Weed would not offer him a party job. Greeley finally turned on Seward, knocking on the doors of delegates and telling them that Seward could not win the border states. Seizing the moment, Lincoln's close supporters capitalized on Illinois Central's new Chicago-to-Cairo train route (seven hundred miles long—longest in nation) and arranged a special, reduced rate on all Illinois trains connecting with Chicago. Jessie Fell and Ward Hill Lamon printed a large number of duplicate tickets for Friday's session, taking up Seward supporters' seats. Leaving almost nothing to chance, Lincoln craftily sandwiched the entire Pennsylvania delegation between the Illinois and Indiana delegations in order to make sure Pennsylvania did not change allegiance. Lincoln's team also hired men, many of them champion hog callers, to cheer and shout when Lincoln's nomination was called. Even with a convention hall packed with Lincoln enthusiasts who had used counterfeit tickets to elbow out Seward men from the galleries, Seward had a commanding lead, holding 173.5 of the 233 votes needed for nomination after the first ballot. Lincoln placed second with 102 votes. On the second ballot, Seward's count went up to 184.5, but Lincoln also went up, to 181. On the third ballot, Lincoln had 231.5 and Seward had 180. A delegate from Ohio then announced the transfer of four votes to Lincoln, and he thereby won the Republican nomination.[11] Lincoln demonstrated he could lead

---

10 Miller, *Lincoln's Virtues*, 396.

11 Holzer and Garfinkle, *A Just and Generous Nation*, 51; Wheeler, *Faith and Courage*, 137–38.

a campaign and do what it took to master the inside game in the most powerful political arena in the country. He soon became the sixteenth president of the United States.

As president, Lincoln continued to grow as a savvy and effective politician for many reasons. As the nation's first media president, he understood the power of stories, mass communications, and imagery—one reason he willingly sat so often to have himself photographed and painted.[12] Lincoln also used his humor to influence people. Often he would tell people "a little story" to distract them from what they came to ask of him. He also used stories to accentuate a point or persuade people. In addition to being a good listener, he understood the importance of time. He embraced pragmatic approaches to problems and was discerning and opportunistic throughout his adult life.[13]

A newspaper junkie, Lincoln intentionally invested time in courting and corresponding with powerful newspaper editors, even the ones who were frequently critical of him. During the Civil War, he learned how to craft and use "public letters" to reach a wide audience.[14] Newspapers, Herndon noted, were Lincoln's "food,"[15] and he enjoyed manipulating journalists. Shrewdly, he distributed inside information in proportion to the favorable press each newspaper was willing to give him.[16]

Lincoln listened vigilantly to the American people and made himself accessible in an unprecedented manner from the very first day of his presidency. Counseled that it would be polite to wear white gloves on Inauguration Day, he shook literally thousands of hardened hands in the receiving line, many of them unwashed. His

---

12 Peterson, *Lincoln in American Memory*, 386.

13 Donald, *Lincoln Reconsidered*, 171–72.

14 White, *Lincoln,* 6.

15 Guelzo, "Public Sentiment is Everything," 184.

16 White, *Lincoln*, 501–2.

once-white gloves were filthy enough at the end of the day that his wife picked them up with tongs and dropped them in the fire.[17]

Moreover, from nine o'clock in the morning till late at night, Lincoln's office in the Executive Mansion was open to the public. Petitioners were so numerous that one could not walk into the mansion or climb the stairs. They were an "ill-bred, ravenous crowd," according to one senator.[18] Lincoln's advisors constantly pleaded with him not to give so much time or access to people, but Lincoln refused. He not only felt it his duty as an elected official to remain accessible, but meetings with citizens provided a way to stay in touch with the pulse of the American people. This easy access to the president astonished the American people and government officials.

Two days after the inauguration, more than one thousand job hunters came to the People's House. The country's economic slump continued and many were desperate for work. A deluge of office seekers, or "vultures" as he called them, came to see him. They insisted that he owed them commissioner's jobs, cabinet positions, postmasterships, custom posts and almost any other government job that existed.[19] "Were it believed that vacant places could be had at the North Pole," Lincoln mused, the road to the Article Circle "would be lined with dead Virginians." Nevertheless, Lincoln tried to see everyone, which only encouraged more to visit as word of mouth spread to communities that the president took precious time to listen to common folk. And come they did—like a cloud of Egyptian locusts moving on crops to consume said Lincoln's personal secretary John Hay. Lincoln, however, could not help himself. "Thank God for not making me a woman," he once self-deprecated in mocking his own inability to say no.[20]

---

17 Conway, *Lincoln's White House*, 11.

18 Donald, *Lincoln*, 285.

19 Oates, *With Malice Toward None*, 195.

20 Conroy, *Lincoln's White House*, 21, 28.

One satirist noted that the swarming hordes at the Executive Mansion could not be driven off. Bars and bolts on doors, frowns of janitors, secretaries intentionally snubbing visitors could not stop guests from requesting an audience with the president. People came to talk to him about draft quotas, the number of days to be set aside for fasting, suggestions for post offices, to make a pitch about selling blankets to the army, to give religious advice and instruction. Everyone from anywhere came to see Lincoln, and they talked way too long. These interlopers were often crude and made lengthy speeches. Finally able to sit down with the president, they hung around too long and would not leave—the president or the Executive Mansion. Lincoln's aides and secretaries wondered how he might have been more productive with the nation's business if he spent less time with these attention seekers.[21]

After the inaugural surge of visitors, the president settled into a daily routine. After rising early in the morning, Lincoln typically had an egg, toast, and coffee for breakfast. He spent the next couple of hours reading newspapers, signing documents, writing letters, or studying subjects most pressing at the time. Then he headed over to the War Department telegraph room, next door to the Executive Mansion, to review the latest war updates. Next he went through mail with a secretary. By ten o'clock, he admitted visitors, giving precedence to cabinet members, senators, congressmen, and the general public respectively.[22]

Lincoln immediately recognized the opportunity to make the government his own, particularly through the power of patronage. He wanted to unite the Republican Party. Lincoln understood that President Taylor had mishandled benefaction, and that presidents Pierce and Buchanan had inadvertently divided the Democratic Party with their unwise and uneven hires. Thus, he spent a great deal of time focusing on replacing eleven hundred civil servants with

---

[21] Burlingame, *Lincoln*, 2:253.

[22] Burlingame, *Lincoln*, 2:252.

individuals who agreed with his positions. From sunup to sundown, people came looking for jobs, and Lincoln filled many of them with individuals who supported his war aims and economic philosophy. As many politicians do, Lincoln also rewarded people with jobs to make them new allies. Some supporters were upset that the president seemed to give more patronage to enemies than supporters. Lincoln, however, understood that there were too many pigs at the trough and not enough fodder to go around.[23]

For a duly elected president who had not received even 40 percent of the popular vote, Lincoln had no compunctions about reshaping the government through the power of patronage. Of the 1,520 presidential officeholders in the country's history up to that time, he removed 1,195 of them and appointed almost all Republicans to the posts.[24] As the war progressed, the number of civilian patronage jobs in the government quintupled, from 40,000 in the entire network of federal employment to nearly 195,000 by the war's end. Almost all of them became plums for Republican loyalists.[25]

The president's astute handling of patronage helped him immensely in the political arena. Even in selecting members of his cabinet, he took leaders from all factions of his own party, giving hope to all groups but dominance to none. Cabinet members were so suspicious of one another that they hardly had time to be jealous of the president. Patronage helped him win re-nomination and defeat McClellan in the 1864 presidential election too.[26] Getting the right people—individuals who subscribed to his policies and vision for the country—in positions of influence remained an important focal point of his presidency.

As part of his policy of making the Executive Mansion accessible, Lincoln held levees—semiformal receptions to which members of the public could come and share their concerns. Lincoln soon called

---

23 Burlingame, *Lincoln,* 2:69–71, 86.

24 Miller, *Lincoln's Virtues*, 101.

25 Guelzo, *Lincoln*, 278.

26 Donald, *Lincoln Reconsidered*, 174,

these receptions "public opinion baths," or "The Beggars' Opera." He once told a friend that he could only escape job applicants if he hanged himself on the South Lawn or moved his office to a smallpox hospital.[27] Government officials could not believe what they observed on a daily basis. "There never was a man so accessible to all sorts of proper and improper persons," said Seward.[28] "He said that as a Republican government all men & women & Children had a right to see the Presdt & State his grievances," said another official.[29]

Visitors asked the president for everything including his autograph. Lincoln loudly called them forward to get them to speak up or withdraw. Amy officers wanted promotions, foreign diplomats wanted to press their country's interests, inventors touted their creations, cabinet members solicited favors for friends, women came to appeal on behalf of their sons, husbands, or fathers, and businessmen came in quest of contracts. Generals and military officers came to make a case for their militia brigades to be inducted and recognized by the War Department. Mothers pleaded that their sons were underage or ill and should be let go from military service. Officers' wives came to flirt and hope to enhance their husbands' chances for a promotion. The daughter of late John C. Calhoun asked to visit her son in a prisoner-of-war camp. An enterprising ragman wanted to follow the Army of the Potomac and pickup castoff clothes. One wanted him to peddle ale to the troops. Another woman repeatedly came to ask Lincoln for a license to practice medicine. Landlords came to ask for help collecting rents. Firemen came requesting new equipment. Southerners solicited for financial restitution for property damaged during the war.[30] Many citizens treated and viewed Lincoln more like Santa Claus than president.

---

[27] Conway, *Lincoln's White House*, 135; Keneally, *Lincoln*, 103.

[28] Guelzo, *Lincoln*, 277.

[29] Guelzo, *Lincoln*, 277.

[30] Burlingame, *Lincoln*, 2:253, 255; Conway, *Lincoln's White House*, 129; Keneally, *Lincoln*, 107.

Most visitors to the Executive Mansion, however, came looking for government jobs. Long after Lincoln's presidency, civil service reform bills were passed, and life become easier for new administrations. In Lincoln's time, however, the administration had to find replacements for thousands of positions (postmasters, port collectors, marshals, superintendents, paymasters, doorkeepers, etc., each having deputies and assistants). Hounded nonstop by office seekers, the president incurred blisters on all four fingers of his large right hand because he greeted and shook so many hands. He explained that he sometimes felt like a hotel keeper trying to put out a fire in one wing of his establishment while renting rooms in another. People set up outside the White House at dawn and still clogged the halls of the Executive Mansion at midnight. The president felt shackled in his own office. Every time he stepped out into the hallways to go the family quarters, visitors besieged him with complaints and petitions. Sometimes the crowds and endless demands got too much. He could snap and call someone a "rascal," or explode at a persistent visitor: "Now go away! I can't attend to all these details. I could as easily bail out the Potomac with a teaspoon," he told one unrelenting visitor. When a caller asked to lend his name to his business, Lincoln sprang from his chair and asked the man if he took him to be a broker. When a disappointed job seeker dared to call the president unjust, he took him by the collar and physically threw him out. When a loyal woman said she had lost her slaves to the army and wanted refugees for wage laborers, Lincoln said he would rather throw up or take a rope and hang himself. Noah Brooks commented how people "exhausted his strength." He spoke of "the great flood gates" that opened on him every day, everyone wanting something, resenting time he wasted on others. From "the senator seeking a war with France down to a poor woman seeking a place in the Treasury Department they darted at me with thumb and finger, picked out their special piece of my vitality, and carried it off." They left him with a feeling of "flabbiness." With no private passageway between his family's private quarters and the office unit on the second floor of the Executive Mansion, crowds of office-seekers, petitioners, and visitors crushed the president when he attempted to get from one end of the residence to the other. To rectify this situation and gain a little privacy, he ordered the only structural addition made to the Executive Mansion during his administration—a partition built through the reception room, which allowed him to retreat unobserved from his office into his family's private rooms.[31]

The constant onslaught of unsolicited visitors certainly took a toll on the president. When he acquired a fever, a mild smallpox, after giving the Gettysburg Address, his doctor put him on bedrest. For three weeks he remained under quarantine in the Executive Mansion, seeing very few visitors and transacting little public business. "Now," he is supposed to have said, "I have something I can give everybody"[32]

As the day of his second inaugural approached, he told Senator Clark of New Hampshire that he was going to make very few changes in patronage offices except for good cause. "It seems as though the bare thought of going through again what I did that first year here, would *crush* me."[33] To another he said, "I will not remove a single man, except for delinquency. To remove a man is very easy, but when I go to fill his place, there are *twenty* applicants, and of these I must make *nineteen* enemies."[34]

Despite the exhaustion brought upon him by the Beggar's Opera, Lincoln never changed or limited the easy access people had to the president. He especially continued to make himself available for soldiers who came to see him.[35] His assistant attorney general,

---

31 Wheeler, *Faith and Courage*, 167–68; Donald, *Lincoln at Home*, 22, 25; Canavan, *Lincoln's Final Hours*, 14; Oates, *With Malice Toward None*, 246; Guelzo, *Lincoln*, 276; Conway, *Lincoln's White House*, 133–34.

32 Donald, *Lincoln*, 467.

33 Carpenter, *Six Months at the White House*, 293.

34 Carpenter, *Six Months at the White House*, 293.

35 Packard, *Lincolns in the White House*, 145.

Titian Coffey, recalled that in wartime Washington, Lincoln was "far more accessible than any secretary or clerk. many a chief of bureau or clerk." The president truly felt empathy for many of the people he met. "They don't want much," he told one associate. "They get but little, and I must see them." [36] He also learned from them.

Lincoln received many pardon requests. A forgiving man by default, he granted so many pardons that stories of his clemency became a major part of his contemporary reputation and subsequent legend. These acts of mercy and grace revealed the kindheartedness of the man. Moreover, sparing a life provided him a much-needed therapeutic moment and empowered him to do something positive in the midst of a horrific war.[37]

Americans felt and believed that their president truly represented them, and they showered him with gifts. Visitors to the Executive Mansion returned to their communities and told stories about the president in church and taverns and at barbecues. Those who could not travel to Washington could write to him—and they did. Lincoln received hundreds of letters from citizens every day, two or three dozen of which he took the time to read.[38]

Lincoln learned much about the people of the country and democracy in general from his public opinion baths. Often visitors inspired him and raised his morale, especially with tales of military heroism or hardship overcome. He listened intently to each visitor, as if he or she was the only person in the nation's capital. He constantly asked questions. Many went away surprised that they had given more than they had taken. He often asked, "What are people talking about?"[39]

His inquisitive and curious nature, as well as his listening skills, served him well as he championed republican government and the preservation of the Union. Lincoln continued to learn and appreciate

---

36 Miroff, *Icons of Democracy*, 106.

37 Miroff, *Icons of Democracy*, 106.

38 Donald, *Lincoln at Home*, 30–32.

39 Conway, *Lincoln's White House*, 138.

how democracy must be nurtured and shaped by constant vigilance and engagement in the political arena. Advocating for causes and persuading citizens required grit, resilience, and meticulous, diligent work within the political process.[40] "Public opinion in this country," he told a crowd a short time before he became president, "is everything.[41]

Lincoln relished making a case or argument to the American people—one reason why he thrived as a lawyer and politician. He loved to persuade people. He thrived on the campaign trail, and others noticed how it energized him. "His eyes were full and bright," wrote one observer, "and he was in the fullness of health and vigor."[42]

In order for the people to be persuaded by a message, they must trust the messenger. One reason Americans trusted Lincoln is that he carefully crafted a trustworthy, common man image. Indeed, Lincoln would pose for more than a hundred and twenty photographs in the last eighteen years of his life. He also sat for painters, sketch artists, and sculptors. He would become one of the most frequently photographed celebrities of the century.[43] For most Americans, a Lincoln portrait resided in their home—on the fireplace mantel, bedroom, or dining area. Father Abraham not only *felt* people but lived *with* them.

Lincoln's power of persuasion is certainly evident in the way he selected and influenced his cabinet. Assembling a team of rivals, Lincoln chose men whose political views ranged right and left on the critical issues of the day. He also made sure he brought Northerners and Southerners into the fold to not only have representation from

---

[40] Winkle, *Young Eagle*, 232.

[41] Basler, Lincoln's Speech at Columbus, Ohio, September 16, 1859, *CW*, 3:424.

[42] Manning, *Father Lincoln*, 91.

[43] Holzer, *Visualizing Lincoln*, 83--84. It did not hurt that Lincoln came of age at a time when the proliferation of photographs and print portraits were on the rise too.

the different regions of the country, but so he could learn from them and, in turn, influence them.

Once the cabinet had been assembled, the president masterfully controlled these renowned officials eventually winning most them over as no one could have foreseen or predicted. Lincoln turned his team of rivals into a team of advocates for his war, emancipation, and other critical domestic policies. Lincoln excelled in the politics of personal persuasion and made it a point to visit face-to-face with someone if he really felt the individual could be persuaded on some issue. He persuaded Congress and the people to embrace many of his domestic policies, which had just as profound a long-term impact on the country as did winning the Civil War. Lincoln's leadership fed and led a Republican ascendancy that lasted for the next fifty years (with the minor interruption of Grover Cleveland).[44]

As a talented politician, Lincoln did what he had to do to win the election of 1864—an election that seemed doomed by war fatigue and mounting casualties with no end in sight. Convinced that a Democratic victory would lead to a peace settlement with an intact Confederacy, Lincoln pulled out all the political stops.

He suspended habeas corpus in Kentucky from July through November, fearing that the region had become a breeding ground for the Confederate cause. He approved treason proceedings against the Copperheads in Indiana, Ohio, and Pennsylvania, even though there was no precedent to do so. He had Stanton dismiss army quartermasters who supported McClellan or other Democrats. He sanctioned the practice of mandatory deductions from officers' pay, making sure the funds were diverted to his party. He invited newspaper editors to the Executive Mansion, even offering one editor the position of United States' minister to France. While the editor declined, so did the writer's criticisms of Lincoln in the days leading up the election. Perhaps most importantly, the commander in chief encouraged field commanders to allow soldiers to leave their

[44] Guelzo, *Man of Ideas*, 10.

units and return home to vote in October. As the election results would bear out, winning a huge percentage of the soldiers' vote helped reelect Lincoln.[45]

In September 1864, Lincoln asked Postmaster Blair to resign from his position. It was a purely political move made to bolster Lincoln's reelection chances. The candidate of the third-party Radical Democracy Party, John C. Fremont, threatened to split the Republican vote in November. The Radical Democrats wanted to abolish slavery immediately, not wait for end of war. Fremont was popular enough that he might take away critical votes from Lincoln and allow George McClellan to win. He agreed to withdraw in exchange for Montgomery Blair's resignation. Lincoln made the political move without hesitation.[46]

Lincoln became the first president since Andrew Jackson to win reelection. Carefully exploiting his innocent image as a babe in the Washington wilderness, he took advantage of politicians who constantly underrated him and his effectiveness. Once the object of his scorn in his more youthful days, Lincoln met with church leaders of every major faith and various denominations. Some wondered why Lincoln spent so much time with "preachers" and "Grannies," but he knew that these folks were mavens who went back to their communities to talk and encourage others to vote.[47] Moreover, Lincoln used the power of patronage to move the party and win votes too. Government employees, for example, were ordered to support the Union ticket or lose their jobs.[48] Once reelected, the Lincoln presidency would ignite twenty-four uninterrupted years of Republican control of the White House.[49] Not too extreme on either side of the slavery issue, Lincoln dominated the political center

---

45 McGovern, *Lincoln*, 109.

46 Johnson, *Last Weeks of Lincoln*, 47.

47 Carwardine, "Lincoln's Religion," 244.

48 Oates, *With Malice Toward None*, 398.

49 Donald, *Lincoln Reconsidered*, 169--170.

and easily defeated the leftist candidate, George McClellan, for the highest office in the land.[50]

Lincoln's ability to persuade the American people, as well as other politicians, never waned throughout his presidency. His writings, public speeches and comments, one-on-one talks, and liberal use of patronage helped convince Congress to pass the Thirteenth Amendment—which abolished slavery in the United States—in January, 1865. To achieve successful passage of this momentous accomplishment, Lincoln had to cajole former Whigs, in the name of Henry Clay, to support the amendment in order to "bring the war to a speedy close." He also singled out "sinners" among Democrats, letting them know they had a better chance for the federal jobs they desired if they voted for the amendment. When the outcome of the vote remained in doubt, Lincoln participated in "certain negotiations" behind the scenes which helped bring wavering Republicans and opposition Democrats into line. The Thirteenth Amendment would pass the House 119-58 on January 31, 1865—just three more votes required than the 2/3 majority.[51] A lesser politician as president would not have been able to pass such a landmark piece of legislation.

The Lincoln legacy and legend often depict a man of humble origins who rose to the highest office of the land through hard work, determination, and conviction. While all of these attributes are true, they do not complete the picture. For Lincoln's greatest successes occurred in the political arena, and these accomplishments would not have transpired if Honest Abe had not known how to play politics. Lincoln excelled at playing politics—the inside game as well as the public side. If he had not known how to be political or navigate the political realities of his time, he would not have been an effective and accomplished leader.

---

50 Freehling, *Becoming Lincoln*, 321.

51 Oates, *With Malice Toward None*, 405.

One lesson to be learned in studying the life of Lincoln is that a dream or vision for an organization will never come to fruition unless one can successfully persuade people or win them over to the cause. From his experiences in dealing with a variety of people and his vigorous self-education, Lincoln implicitly understood how to deploy arguments, resources, and supporters in order to persuade people to endorse his policies. In short, Lincoln not only learned how to play politics, he thrived at it.

Americans can be grateful that Lincoln did become such a successful politician. For without the president's wily political maneuvers, there would have been no Emancipation Proclamation and no Union victory. Lincoln won key elections. He influenced Congressmen and citizens from all points on the political spectrum. He persuaded the American people of the righteousness of the Union cause. He got things done. He played the political game well so that he could lead and end the war well.

The Truth

The Bible does not tell you which political party to vote for in the next presidential election. On the other hand, Scripture does talk about government and politics, because we cannot escape them on this side of heaven.

In Romans 13 God calls on you, as a Christian, to:

> be subject to the governing authorities. For there is no authority except from God, and those that exist have been instituted by God. Therefore whoever resists the authorities resists what God has appointed, and those who resist will incur judgment. For rulers are not a terror to good conduct, but to bad. Would you have no fear of the one who is in authority? Then do what is good, and you will

> receive his approval, for he is God's servant for your good. But if you do wrong, be afraid, for he does not bear the sword in vain. For he is the servant of God, an avenger who carries out God's wrath on the wrongdoer. Therefore one must be in subjection, not only to avoid God's wrath but also for the sake of conscience. For because of this you also pay taxes, for the authorities are ministers of God, attending to this very thing. Pay to all what is owed to them: taxes to whom taxes are owed, revenue to whom revenue is owed, respect to whom respect is owed, honor to whom honor is owed.[52]

No matter the kind of government, you are to "be subject for the Lord's sake to every human institution, whether it be to the emperor as supreme, or to governors as sent by him to punish those who do evil and to praise those who do good." God's will for you is "that by doing good you should put to silence the ignorance of foolish people. Live as people who are free, not using your freedom as a cover-up for evil, but living as servants of God." Followers of Christ should "Honor everyone. Love the brotherhood. Fear God. Honor the emperor."[53]

Confronted by the Pharisees in Jerusalem—who were trying to get Him to say something against the law so they could imprison or kill Him—Jesus said that government or governance is to be treated as a gift from God. "'Tell us, then, what you think. Is it lawful to pay taxes to Caesar, or not?'" the Pharisees said. "But Jesus, aware of their malice, said, 'Why put me to the test, you hypocrites? Show me the coin for the tax.' And they brought him a denarius. And Jesus said to them, 'Whose likeness and inscription is this?' They said, 'Caesar's.'

52 Rom. 13:1–7.

53 1 Pet. 2:13–17.

Then he said to them, 'Therefore render to Caesar the things that are Caesar's, and to God the things that are God's.'"[54]

God's plans unfold through any man-made system of government. He does warn us, however, to "avoid foolish controversies, genealogies, dissensions, and quarrels about the law, for they are unprofitable and worthless."[55] The institution of government is a gift from God, but that does not mean that a political system is not corruptible. Anything that involves fallen, sinful human beings is already corrupt. Rulers may be given the power of the sword, but they are expected to be godly and God-pleasing. They are expected to obey God's Word. Unfortunately, politicians are sinful human beings, and they can lead others astray. "If a ruler listens to falsehood, all his officials will be wicked."[56] This is why the Bible tells you to "put not your trust in princes"—or your favorite political party or candidate—"in whom there is no salvation."[57]

Too many people today put their hope in flawed, frail, sinful human beings. They put their trust in cradle-to-grave government, wrongfully believing that government can solve all their problems. One reason the politics of our time has become so polarized is that for far too many people, government has become this generation's false god. Politics today is not just a clash over domestic and foreign policy, but a battle over worldviews and identity. Too many believe in man's ideas and solutions rather than God's Word and truth. Yet the Bible says "that when you received the word of God ... you accepted it not as the word of men but as what it really is, the word of God, which is at work in you believers."[58]

You should be concerned about and advocate against politicians who legislate policies contrary to God's Word. Evolution, abortion, infanticide, affirmation of alternative lifestyles, and redefining

---

[54] Matt. 22:17–21.

[55] Titus 3:9.

[56] Prov. 29:12.

[57] Ps. 146:3.

[58] 1 Thess. 2:13.

marriage are just a few of the cultural hot-button issues that are contrary to Scripture. On the other side of the coin, refusing to serve and care for widows, orphans, the underprivileged, the downtrodden, and the poor also differs from God's will. Scripture teaches, "Blessed is the nation whose God is the Lord, the people whom he has chosen as his heritage!"[59] The Bible does not encourage a theocracy, but a nation or tribe that recognizes God for who He is—Lord of all! Indeed, we may reside and vote in a certain country, but "our citizenship is in heaven, and from it we await a Savior, the Lord Jesus Christ."[60]

Government, of course, is a gift and instrument of God's love for us. A government and its representatives can defend us, provide numerous services, and help improve the lives of many. Politicians and political systems, however, are far from perfect and should not be treated as gods. Being a conservative or liberal, Republican or Democrat, may give you a momentary identity in the secular world, but you are something more than how you vote or lobby for a political issue. You are a citizen of God's creation. Therefore you, as well as your government, are to "seek the Lord and his strength; seek his presence continually!"[61]

Unfortunately, in this fallen world today, many are trying to persuade you that the Bible is outdated and ill-suited for our time. This argument is nothing new, and it is the plan of Satan to get you to think in this manner. At the beginning of time, Satan's first words to Eve in the garden of Eden were meant to cast doubt on God's Word. "*Did God actually say*, 'You shall not eat of any tree in the garden'?" (italics added).[62]

Indeed, we live in a political world—a world full of contrasting views, a world of persuasion. Satan is trying to persuade you that

---

59 Ps. 33:12.

60 Phil. 3:20.

61 1 Chron. 16:11.

62 Gen. 3:1.

you do not need Jesus. He wants to pull you away from God and kill you—forever and for all of eternity.

Thank goodness for the power of the Holy Spirit, the Helper who gives you faith. The Holy Spirit works on your heart and mind and persuades you or makes you understand that you are a beloved child of God. Jesus, through His death and resurrection, has washed away your sins.

The Bible encourages Christians to share this good news with others and to let the Holy Spirit do the work of conversion and "persuade others."[63] "We are from God. Whoever knows God listens to us; whoever is not from God does not listen to us. By this we know the Spirit of truth and the spirit of error."[64]

As you honor and share Jesus, the Bible calls on you to always be "prepared to make a defense to anyone who asks you for a reason for the hope that is in you; yet do it with gentleness and respect."[65] You never know when you will have a chance to witness or give a testimony to another. Moreover, there is nothing more persuasive than a person on fire for Jesus. As Paul, a persecutor and murderer of Christians before his conversion, said, "I am not ashamed of the gospel, for it is the power of God for salvation to everyone who believes, to the Jew first and also to the Greek."[66] How sweet it is to hear these powerful and persuasive words of Scripture: "Though your sins are like scarlet, they shall be as white as snow; though they are red like crimson, they shall become like wool."[67]

If you want a certain political candidate to win an election, you might make a financial donation on a campaign website, put signs in your yard and bumper stickers on your car, and go door-to-door in your neighborhood, handing out campaign literature. You take action.

---

[63] 2 Cor. 5:11.

[64] 1 John 4:6.

[65] 1 Pet. 3:15.

[66] Rom. 1:16.

[67] Isa. 1:18.

If you truly care for someone's soul, you want this person to *know* Jesus. You want that person to be persuaded by the power of the Holy Spirit, and to believe in Him as Lord and Savior, for "there is salvation in no one else, for there is no other name under heaven given among men by which we must be saved."[68] You want this individual to be in heaven with you someday—forever!

Thank goodness the Holy Spirit is the one who gives people faith. You do not have the burden of making someone believe or forcing them to come to Jesus. The Holy Spirit, through God's Word, gives faith and saves, not you. Yet God can work through you as His instrument and vessel. When you share God's Word with someone, He uses you as part of His persuasion package. And unlike too many politicians, God never breaks His promises.

Your Life

Most people consider the connotation of "playing politics" or being "political" in a negative light. Why do you think that is? When or how can being "political" be a good thing?

What specifically has worked for you in regard to persuading people?

When do you know you have crossed the line from persuasion to manipulation?

The world is full of different views, religions, and beliefs constantly clamoring for our attention. In regard to influence or persuasion, why is it important for you to receive God's Word regularly?

---

[68] Acts 4:12.

RELIGION AND RELATIONSHIPS

29

Doubting Lincoln

Now Thomas, one of the twelve, called the Twin, was not with them when Jesus came. So the other disciples told him, "We have seen the Lord." But he said to them, "Unless I see in his hands the mark of the nails, and place my finger into the mark of the nails, and place my hand into his side, I will never believe." Eight days later, his disciples were inside again, and Thomas was with them. Although the doors were locked, Jesus came and stood among them and said, "Peace be with you." Then he said to Thomas, "Put your finger here, and see my hands; and put out your hand, and place it in my side. Do not disbelieve, but believe." Thomas answered him, "My Lord and my God!" Jesus said to him, "Have you believed because you have seen me? Blessed are those who have not seen and yet have believed."

—John 20:24–29

The Lincoln Way

Every leader must confront and overcome their insecurities and doubts.

Much like the historical debate over George Washington's religious faith, the disputation over Lincoln's religious faith continues to rage.[1] Aside from his views on race and slavery, there is no other field of Lincoln study that has generated as much attention as his religion. Scholars and biographers, intrigued by "the anomaly of an unbaptized saint in the White House," have written more about Lincoln's faith than that of any other president. Moreover, his faith has been more vehemently disputed than any other president, primarily because so many of his closest contemporaries ardently disagreed about his precise religious beliefs.[2]

Since Lincoln kept most of his personal beliefs about religion private, with a few written exceptions, many have filled the void to claim him as one of their own. Baptists note that Lincoln's parents belonged to their church, and that young Abe helped with parish activities in the Little Pigeon Creek Baptist Church in Indiana. Episcopalians claim Lincoln because he attended Reverend Charles Dresser's services in Springfield while he courted Mary Todd. The Lincolns were married in an Episcopal ceremony, and they spent their early life together in the Episcopal church. Presbyterians state that the Lincolns purchased a pew in Dr. James Smith's Presbyterian church in Springfield, and they continued to hold that pew until their departure in 1861. After the Lincolns moved to Washington, they attended Second Presbyterian Church, which has long maintained the pew where Lincoln sat during services. Quakers point out that Lincoln's ancestors in Pennsylvania were most probably Quaker.[3] After the president's assassination, Rabbi Isaac Mayer Wise declared that Lincoln had told him he was Jewish. The

---

[1] For in-depth coverage of the historical debate on Washington's religious faith, see James Pingel's *Confidence and Character: The Religious Life of George Washington* (2014).

[2] Smith, *Faith and the Presidency*, 92, 104–5.

[3] Szasz and Szasz, *Lincoln and Religion*, 35. Quakers, led by Eliza Gurney, visited Lincoln in the White House on October 26, 1862. An American widow of a notable British Orthodox Quaker, Gurney spoke with the president for a few minutes, and then she and her three friends prayed silently in Lincoln's office. They did not offer specific advice for the war, a rare occurrence which

Society for Freethinkers insisted he belonged to their denomination. A Pietist church group stated that Lincoln planned to join after the war ended, reporting that he had been secretly baptized in their faith. In addition, Methodists, Unitarians, Universalists, Catholics, Spiritualists, Freemasons, Mormons,[4] and atheists have found or invented reasons to claim or acclaim Lincoln as one of their own.[5]

There is historical evidence for the Doubting Lincoln—the Lincoln who rejected the divinity of Christ, denied the inerrancy and divine revelation of Scripture, and disbelieved other traditional doctrinal teachings of the Christian faith. Some of Lincoln's cynicism may have stemmed from the unfortunate events and circumstances of his upbringing. His parents' deep, almost obsessive devotion to their Calvinist faith, the uneducated element of many of the first preachers Lincoln listened to and observed, and his father's dearth of loving affection all may have contributed to Lincoln's recusal from organized religion early in his life. Lincoln's gentle soul seemed to struggle to come to grips with a Calvinist God who harshly judged so many and saved so few. He may have also wondered how God could allow his beloved sister, Sarah, to die while allowing Aaron Grigsby—Sarah's husband, whom Lincoln despised—to live.

Lincoln appreciated. Quaker legend has it that her very first letter written to Lincoln was discovered in his coat pocket after his assassination.

[4] Szasz and Szasz, *Lincoln and Religion,* 36. Brigham Young worried that Lincoln and the Republicans would outlaw polygamy in the 1860 election—it was in their platform. Lincoln, however, shared this story with Mormon journalist, T.B.H. Stenhouse: "Stenhouse, when I was a boy on the farm in Illinois there was a great deal of timber on the farm which we had to clear. Occasionally we would come to a log which . . . was too hard to move, so we ploughed around it. That's what I intend to do with the Mormons. You go back and tell Brigham Young that if he will let me alone, I will let him alone." In April 1862, Lincoln asked Young to provide soldiers to protect the stage (mail) and telegraph line in southern Wyoming, and the Nauvoo Legion did as instructed. In December 1877, the Saints baptized Lincoln in proxy.

[5] Szasz and Szasz, *Lincoln and Religion*, 67; Carwardine, "Lincoln's Religion," 224.

Sometime in 1834, at the age of twenty-five or twenty-six, Lincoln wrote "Little Book on Infidelity," attacking the divinity of Christ, the inspiration and inerrancy of Scripture, and the logic of predestination. Before he could send his work to the New Salem newspaper, however, a friend took the manuscript from him and burned it in a fire.[6]

After examining pivotal moments in Lincoln's life, which certainly influenced his religious faith, debaters over Lincoln's religion usually descend into a battle of quotations and conflicting sources, some of which even contradict themselves. Journalist Noah Brooks reported to a friend that Lincoln had "a hope of blessed immortality through Jesus Christ."[7] William O. Stoddard, one of Lincoln's secretaries, countered, "I cannot at this moment recall any distinct assertions made by Mr. Lincoln, relating to the matter of his religious belief." Yet Stoddard also said, "I am convinced this day that, in the best and truest sense, Abraham Lincoln was a Christian." John Nicolay famously stated, "Mr. Lincoln did not, to my knowledge, in any way change his religious views, opinions, or beliefs, from the time he left Springfield to the day of his death." Yet Nicolay also reported that "benevolence and forgiveness were the very basis of his character. His nature was deeply religious … he had faith in the eternal justice and boundless mercy of Providence, and made the Golden Rule of Christ his practical creed." Another White House regular during the Civil War wrote, "I would scarcely call Mr. Lincoln a religious man—and yet I believe him to have been a sincere Christian." According to Edward D. Baker, who

---

[6] Keneally, *Lincoln*, 15–16; Szasz and Szasz, *Lincoln and Religion*, 21. A publication criticizing Christianity in the way that Lincoln had could have ruined him politically. Burning this tract may have saved Lincoln's political future. Lincoln may have written the "infidel book" amidst his suffering and grieving for the loss of Ann Rutledge, his first romantic love and rumored fiancée. Perhaps he believed he would never see her again.

[7] Mansfield, *Lincoln's Battle with God,* 171. The following quotes in this paragraph come from this source.

often debated Lincoln on religious issues and defended orthodox Christianity, Lincoln never blasphemed or mocked the Bible, but sincerely did not believe in the divine inspiration of Scripture.[8]

Much of the evidence for the Doubting Lincoln comes from William Herndon, Lincoln's third and final law partner. After Lincoln's death, Herndon spent a great deal of time and effort trying to prove that Lincoln's religious views were similar to his own—nonconventional, atheist, agnostic, or a mixture of Unitarian and Universalist (which Herndon eventually settled on later in his life). According to Herndon, Lincoln told him a thousand times that he did not believe in the Bible's divine revelation, as most Christians did. Often Lincoln challenged friends and associates on the authenticity of Scripture.[9] Herndon gave public lectures describing Lincoln as a nonbeliever or skeptic, prompted others to speak out in the same manner, and distributed his "research" to other writers, encouraging them to write books on Lincoln's religious skepticism.[10] Relentlessly pursuing evidence of Lincoln's disbelief, Herndon found some. The individuals Herndon interviewed later become known as Herndon's informants.

While there is no doubt that Herndon had an agenda in portraying an agnostic or doubting Lincoln, the historical record does show that Lincoln questioned many attributes and tenets of the traditional Christian faith. Especially during his twenties and thirties, Lincoln eagerly embraced the role of the village atheist—mocking preachers, disdaining "revealed religion" in writing, and carrying a Bible around only to ridicule it.[11] While living in New Salem, he once told a friend that the New Testament revealed Christ as an out-of-wedlock child and his mother an unchaste woman.[12]

---

[8] Burlingame, *Lincoln*, 1:239.

[9] Burlingame, *Lincoln,* 1:83.

[10] Szasz and Szasz, *Lincoln and Religion*, 67, 74.

[11] Mansfield, *Lincoln's Battle with God*, xx.

[12] Keneally, *Lincoln*, 15.

The Lincoln who lived in New Salem (1831–1837) and in Springfield early on could be sharp in his sarcasm. He mocked Jesus's "superhuman wisdom" in selecting Judas, who "turned out a traitor and a devil," as the treasurer of the disciples.[13] John Stuart informed Herndon that Lincoln "was an avowed and open Infidel," who sometimes "bordered on atheism … Lincoln went further against Christian beliefs, & doctrines, & principles than any man I ever heard: he shocked me … Lincoln always denied that Jesus was the son of God as understood and maintained by the Christian world."[14]

James Matheny, a lawyer and political operative in Illinois and best man in Lincoln's wedding, also labeled Lincoln an "infidel" and wrote that Lincoln ridiculed the Bible on "grounds of reason" as well as for its alleged contradictions. "Sometimes Lincoln bordered on absolute Atheism," he suggested. "He went far that way & often shocked me."[15] Matheny went on to report that when Lincoln first came to Springfield, he would "pick up the Bible, read a passage, and then comment on it, show its falsity, and its follies on the grounds of *reason*."[16] Matheny also indicated that "Lincoln played a sharp game here on the Religious world" later in his life—pretending to become a Christian in order to get elected president.[17]

---

[13] Basler, Lincoln's Speech on the Sub-Treasury, December 26, 1839, *CW*, 1:167.

[14] Wilson, *Herndon's Informants*, 576. Stuart and Lincoln parted ways politically in the late 1850s. Stuart would eventually become a Democrat, while Lincoln joined the nascent Republican Party. Stuart may have become jealous of Lincoln's political rise to power.

[15] Wilson, *Herndon's Informants*, 576.

[16] Wilson, *Herndon's Informants*, 472.

[17] Wilson, *Herndon's Informants*, 577. It should be noted that Matheny and Lincoln also had a falling out and uneven friendship due to politics. Matheny supported another politician rather than Lincoln to lead the coveted General Land Office in 1848. Moreover, Matheny did not join Lincoln's move from the Whig Party to the Republican Party in 1856. Lincoln did, nevertheless, support Matheny's run for Congress in 1858.

Jesse Fell, a liberal Christian and lawyer from Bloomington, Illinois, said that Lincoln did not believe in orthodox Christianity. His religious views were "practical" and best summed up with two propositions: "the Fatherhood of God and the Brotherhood of Man."[18] He also said that while Lincoln "held many opinions in common with the great mass of Christian believers, *he did not* believe in what are regarded as orthodox or evangelical views of Christianity," such as the depravity of man, the atonement, the infallibility and inspiration of Scripture, and miracles.[19]

"There is no god, and I hate him" is a common coping mechanism for many duplicitous atheists who believe that God has rejected them or left them to suffer unjustly. Perhaps Lincoln's tough upbringing made him angry at God and fueled his religious skepticism.[20]

Herndon claimed Lincoln "could not believe, as a rational man, a logical-minded one too, that the Bible was the *peculiar*, only, and *special* revelation of God, as the theological Christian world understands it."[21] Lincoln did not believe "in the Miraculous Conception of Jesus, as the theological Christian world understands the question, subject," although he did believe "in the absolute necessity of some form of Christianity." According to Herndon, Lincoln "loved the broad Christian philosophy, maxims, sayings, and moral of Christianity, not because any particular man said them, but because they were and are great, grand leading truths of human consciousness, the highest and loftiest inductions, deductions, if you please, of human reason or intuition of the human soul." If Lincoln had been a Christian, he would "*have boldly said so and so acted like a deeply sincere man and an honest one.*"

---

[18] Carwardine, "Lincoln's Religion," 228.

[19] Wilson, *Herndon's Informants*, 579.

[20] Mansfield, *Lincoln's Battle with God*, 44–45. Herndon would later say of Lincoln, "Did not God roll him through His furnace?"

[21] Hertz, *The Hidden Lincoln*, 43–45. The following quotes in this paragraph all come from this source.

Herndon repeatedly told others that Lincoln was "*an infidel,*" a Universalist, Unitarian, deist, or fatalist, but "he did not believe that Jesus was God nor the Son of God." After all, Lincoln had told him "a thousand times that he did not believe that the Bible, etc., were revelations from God, as the Christian world contends, etc."[22]

Making what sounds very much like a twenty-first century argument, Herndon asserted that Lincoln became "a firm believer in the theory of development [evolution]," or Darwinian evolution, as opposed to the creation account in Genesis. [23] Herndon had "all the works of Spencer, Darwin" and others who purported Darwinian evolution in his office, and Lincoln read many of them. "He soon grew into the belief of a universal law, evolution, and from this he has never deviated." Lincoln's "firm" belief in evolution led him to reject miracles outside of the universal laws of science. There could be "no such thing as a miraculous conception and it follows that Lincoln did not believe that Jesus was God, nor a special child of Him." There could be "no special inspiration, no special revelations, no miracles in his mind; he demanded facts, well-authenticated facts, as foundations of his belief; he had no faith in 'say soes,' no respect for that kind of authority in the religious world." While Lincoln did believe in "an overruling Providence, Maker, God" Who put morals "on the human soul," he did not believe, or come to believe, "in a personal God." Herndon rejected the claims that Lincoln's faith changed or grew over time, carefully suggesting that "Lincoln was a thoroughly religious man, not a Christian, a broard liberal-minded man," but still a "free religionist, an infidel, and so he died."

There is no question that Lincoln read and digested books critical of the divinity of Christ and the inerrancy and divine inspiration of Scripture, especially in the first half of his life. Thomas Paine's *Age of Reason*, for example, dismissed the Bible as "a book of lies,

---

22 Hertz, *The Hidden Lincoln,* 64–65.

23 Hertz, *The Hidden Lincoln,* 406–9. The following quotes in this paragraph all come from this source.

wickedness, and blasphemy for what can be more blasphemous than to ascribe the wickedness of man to the orders of the Almighty?"[24] Paine's work asserted the deist position that the Bible contained riddles, mysteries, and outright distortions by the human writers. Books like *Age of Reason* influenced Lincoln's worldview and turned him into the "Thomas Paine of New Salem."[25]

Conceding that the vast majority of Lincoln's contemporaries considered Lincoln a Christian, some biographers have focused on the testimony of friends from Lincoln's early adulthood to make the case for Lincoln as a "Calvinized" deist, Universalist, or fatalist.[26] The deist Lincoln believed in God, a God who gave order, shape, and predictability to the world, but nothing more than that.[27] Another associate reported that Lincoln believed "that if eternal punishment were man's doom than he should spend that little life in vigilant & ceaseless preparation, by never ending prayer."[28] Deists, however, generally did not believe in prayer, because the Creator God did not intervene in the daily lives of people or nations.

"Mr. Lincoln believed in God," and "that nations like individuals were punished for their Sins," said his New Salem friend, Isaac Cogdal, but "he did not believe in Hell, eternal punishment as Christians say." The Universalist Lincoln "did not believe in the orthodox theologies of the day … Lincoln thought that God predestined things and governed the universe by Law nothing going on by accident." God would not create a world for condemnation and punishment. Lincoln's mind "was skeptical in a good sense," Cogdal said.[29]

Joseph Gillespie, a state senator from Illinois, shared that "there was a slight tinge of fatalism in Mr. Lincoln's composition which

---

24 White, *Lincoln*, 54–55.

25 Mansfield, *Lincoln's Battle with God*, 44.

26 Guelzo, *Lincoln*, 447.

27 Guelzo, "Lincoln and Religion," 190.

28 Wilson, *Herndon's Informants*, 458.

29 Wilson, *Herndon's Informants*, 441.

would or might have led him to believe somewhat in destiny."[30] Gillespie claimed that Lincoln once told him that he could not avoid believing in predestination even though "he considered it a very unprofitable field of speculation because it was hard to reconcile that belief" with taking responsibility and action on matters of importance. Interestingly, however, Gillespie noted how Lincoln "trusted more in Divine power that in human instrumentality," especially as the Civil War progressed. "Mr. Lincoln had a strong faith that it was in the purposes of the Almighty to save this Country," and God had chosen him as his instrument to save the Union and emancipate the slaves in the same manner that God had used Moses to free the Israelites from Egyptian bondage. Not a "blind believer in fate or destiny," Lincoln nevertheless "considered the means foreordained as well as the end and therefore was extremely diligent in the use of the means."

Doubting Lincoln proponents argue that Lincoln appeared religious or "naturally religious" but did not subscribe to an orthodox Christian belief system. For example, Leonard Swett, a lawyer on the Illinois circuit with Lincoln and one who campaigned for Lincoln as president in 1860 and 1864, admitted that as Lincoln "became involved in matters of gravest importance … a feeling of reverence, and belief in God—his justice and overruling power—increased upon him." [31] Lincoln "was full of natural religion" and "believed in God as much as the most approved Church member," but did not like formal rituals or ceremonials. Even though Lincoln "failed to observe the Sabbath very scrupulously," ridiculed the Puritans, and swore occasionally, "his heart was full of natural and cultivated religion." Lincoln's religion focused on deeds, not creeds. He believed in "unyielding fidelity to the right and acknowledging God as the Supreme Ruler," and loving one's neighbor as oneself.

---

30 Wilson, *Herndon's Informants,* 506–8. The following quotes in this paragraph all come from this source.

31 Wilson, *Herndon's Informants,* 167–68. The following quotes in this paragraph all come from this source.

Lincoln's inconsistent church attendance and his unwillingness to become a member of a particular church denomination have long been talking points for Doubting Lincoln proponents. Compared to Mary, Lincoln did indeed attend church less frequently. She often worshipped while he worked in his law office or traveled the circuit. In Antebellum America, however, most Americans did not officially join a church. Many eschewed church membership because it involved an inquisitional probing of one's life. That did not mean that these individuals did not believe in God or considered themselves nonreligious. The Bible remained the most read and referenced book in the land. Moreover, in many cases, dancing and bawdy jokes—two activities Lincoln engaged in—excluded one from membership in a congregation.[32]

Since the historical record is clear that Lincoln read the Bible daily, incorporated Scripture into his writing and public pronouncements, and *thought* about religion more than any other president, most Doubting Lincoln advocates concede the religious nature and tendencies of the man.[33] They acknowledge that he believed that God intervened in and directed history, used people to accomplish his plans ("one of the plainest statements of the Bible," Lincoln said[34]), and saw himself as an agent of God on earth. "I am satisfied that when the Almighty wants me to do or not do a particular thing," Lincoln once told a government official, "he finds a way of letting me know."[35] Even Herndon admitted that his law partner "was a deeply and thoroughly religious man at all times and

[32] Deutsch and Fornieri, *Lincoln's American Dream*, 30; Wheeler, *Faith and Courage*, 108. According to Wheeler, in 1860, only 23 percent of Americans belonged to a particular church. Wheeler notes that today, ironically, we see the exact opposite of Lincoln's day—high church membership coupled with abysmal ignorance of what is in the Bible.

[33] Carwardine, "Lincoln's Religion," 223–24.

[34] Smith, *Faith and Presidency*, 101.

[35] Smith, *Faith and Presidency*, 101.

places and under all conditions," but "his religion was of the noblest and grandest and the broadest kind."[36]

While being religious or spiritual in nature is one thing, believing in the traditional doctrine of the Christian church is quite another. Thus, the case for the Doubting Lincoln is typically made using certain particulars. Lincoln attended church irregularly. He never officially joined a church body. He often, especially in his younger days, questioned and ridiculed the intelligence of Christian clergy. As much as he lauded and read the Bible, the young Lincoln openly scoffed at and questioned the inerrancy of Scripture. As much as he talked about Jesus and even referred to Him as "the Savior," there is no evidence that he ever called Jesus "my Savior" or expressed a personal need for Christ's atoning sacrifice on the cross.[37]

Sometimes Lincoln gave the impression that he lamented his own lack of faith. One story claims that two Pennsylvania women interviewed Lincoln in the White House. As they were leaving, they thanked him and said they hoped to meet him in heaven someday. "I don't know that I will ever get to heaven," Lincoln allegedly responded.[38]

Albert Taylor Bledsoe, who often debated religious issues with Lincoln in Springfield, indicated that Lincoln pondered and struggled with religious sentiment and life's big questions. Abe's gloomy worldview and outlook on eternity made Bledsoe pity him. When Samuel Hill's wife asked Lincoln if he believed in an afterlife, Lincoln explained that he did not. He painfully revealed his belief that when people die, that would be the last of them.[39]

The truth is that Lincoln did periodically struggle with doubt. He once told an elderly lady that "probably it is to be my lot to go on in a twilight, feeling and reasoning my way through life, as

---

36 Hertz, *The Hidden Lincoln*, 86.

37 Smith, *Faith and the Presidency*, 102.

38 Guelzo, *Lincoln*, 328.

39 Burlingame, *Lincoln*, 1:83–84.

questioning, doubting Thomas did."[40] Of course, Thomas would later claim, "My Lord and my God!"[41] Indeed, human frailty and depravity produces doubt and skepticism in all sinners. Believers can doubt, and doubters can believe.

The Truth

You can understand why so many in the world doubt the teachings of the Bible. How could the world be created from scratch in six days? Why would a so-called loving God decide to flood the entire planet? Why does an all-powerful God allow sin and evil to exist? How could one man—Moses—part the Red Sea or bring on the plagues in Egypt? How can water and God's Word save you? How does a virgin in ancient times get pregnant? How could a guy who endured a gruesome crucifixion and was put in a tomb for three days rise again? Who moved the stone at the tomb? You mean to tell me that a "holy ghost" enters my soul, heart, and mind and empowers me to have faith?

These and many other questions are often asked, not to seek answers, but to ridicule the Christian faith. Christians are mocked for being anti-science and believers of myths, legends, and impossible miracles. And if Christians are honest with themselves, there are many things we trust and take on faith, not by sight.[42]

Since we all have inherited a sinful nature from the Fall, all Christians struggle with doubt about the promises of Scripture. Just like Peter after falling into the Sea of Galilee, Jesus can rightfully say to us, "O you of little faith, why did you doubt?"[43] There is no question that doubting the divinity of Jesus and the promises of

---

[40] Guelzo, *Lincoln*, 155–56.

[41] John 20:28. Perhaps this was a "small sign" that Lincoln wanted to become certain in the Almighty (Meacham, American Gospel, 132).

[42] 2 Cor. 5:7.

[43] Matt. 14:31.

Scripture can lead to dangerous place. The Bible says that "the one who doubts is like a wave of the sea that is driven and tossed by the wind."[44]

What are your particular doubts when it comes to your faith? If you do not know, there is one who does—Satan the great deceiver. He zeroes in on your areas of weakness and preys upon you like a roaring lion.[45] Jesus warns that the devil "was a murderer from the beginning, and has nothing to do with the truth, because there is no truth in him. When he lies, he speaks out of his own character, for he is a liar and the father of lies."[46]

You need to remember that Satan wants you to doubt God and become a skeptic of everything God shares with you in His Word. The devil works nonstop to blind "the minds of the unbelievers, to keep them from seeing the light of the gospel of the glory of Christ, who is the image of God."[47] Even in the very beginning, in the garden of Eden, Satan tried to sow the seeds of doubt.[48]

You must understand that the battle for your heart and mind is not a simple little dispute. Christians do not "wrestle against flesh and blood, but against the rulers, against the authorities, against the cosmic powers over this present darkness, against the spiritual forces of evil in the heavenly places."[49] The valley of doubt is a very dangerous place to live.

Jesus predicted that those who sow doubt would wreak havoc in our time. In the book of Jude, He tells us that "'in the last time there will be scoffers, following their own ungodly passions.' It is these who cause divisions, worldly people, devoid of the Spirit," He warned. But then Jesus gives the antidote to the problem: He encourages Christians to build themselves "up in your most holy

---

44 James 1:6.

45 1 Pet. 5:8.

46 John 8:44.

47 2 Cor. 4:4.

48 Gen. 3:1.

49 Eph. 6:12.

faith" and to pray that the Holy Spirit keeps you "in the love of God, waiting for the mercy of our Lord Jesus Christ that leads to eternal life." Since we all doubt at times, we are to "have mercy on those who doubt; save others by snatching them out of the fire; to others show mercy with fear, hating even the garment stained by the flesh."[50] Indeed you are to model the father of the child who cried out and said, "I believe; help my unbelief!"[51]

Hold fast to the truths of Scripture. As the Bible teaches:

> Trust in the Lord with all your heart,
> and do not lean on your own understanding.
> In all your ways acknowledge him,
> and he will make straight your paths.
> Be not wise in your own eyes;
> fear the Lord, and turn away from evil.
> It will be healing to your flesh
> and refreshment to your bones.[52]

To be sure, you will be tempted to doubt God's promises and His Word. But this is what makes faith so special and powerful. As the Bible states, "Faith is the assurance of things hoped for, the conviction of things not seen."[53] Put another way, by the power of the Holy Spirit, it takes faith to have faith. Remember, if you are going to believe that Jesus Christ is your Lord and Savior—that He took on the sins of the world, died, and rose again—it will require a faith that can only come from the divine. You can take heart in God's Word: "With man it is impossible, but not with God. For all things are possible with God."[54]

---

[50] Jude 17–23.

[51] Mark 9:24.

[52] Prov. 3:5–8.

[53] Heb. 11:1.

[54] Mark 10:27.

Your Life

Many people claimed to know Lincoln's precise religious beliefs. Yet their takes on his religion, or lack thereof, were all over the religious spectrum. What lessons can you draw from this historical reality for your own personal life?

William Herndon did not want contemporaries or posterity to regard Lincoln as a traditional, orthodox Christian. Why do you think that was? Is this kind of agenda being carried out today? How so?

Particularly during his twenties and thirties, Lincoln distrusted organized religion, ridiculed aspects of Christianity, and put his skepticism on full display. What kinds of temptations and challenges are more prominent for people in their twenties and thirties in regard to the Christian faith? What can you do to help them stay in the faith?

How can you prepare for those who will mock the Christian faith and the Bible? On the other hand, how should we treat those who question the Christian faith?

What can you do to combat or confront your skepticism and doubts when it comes to God's promises?

30

Substandard Shepherds

Do your best to present yourself to God as one
approved, a worker who has no need to be ashamed,
rightly handling the word of truth.
—1 Timothy 2:15

The Lincoln Way

The quality and character of the messenger is just as important as the message.

Lincoln's life demonstrates the power and influence of clergymen on one's religious and spiritual development—for better and for worse. Frontier clergymen contributed significantly, if inadvertently, to the growth of his religious skepticism, particularly during the intellectually formative and early adult years of his life.

Few formal credentials were required for clergymen in the backwoods of Kentucky and Indiana in Lincoln's day. Preachers were often primitive, shallow, dogmatic, smug, noisy, and intellectually weak. The two Baptist ministers the young Lincoln knew best, William Downs and David Elkin, were not models of Christian decorum. Evidence indicates that Pastor Downs was disorderly, lazy, and slovenly. Pastor Elkin likewise appeared to be ignorant, impoverished, indolent, and unkempt. Elkin could barely read, recognizing only the letter *O* because it was round. Both imbibed too much alcohol.[1]

If not intellectual or steeped in years of theological training, backwoods preachers had to be able to hold a congregation's attention. While Parson Elkin could not read or write, Dennis Hanks (cousin of Nancy and who lived with Abe in Indiana) claimed Elkin was a "good, true man and the best preacher & finest orator" he had ever heard. Hanks could hear Elkin's words "distinctly & clearly one fourth of a mile" away.[2]

Frontier preachers who focused on entertaining, however, were too frequently all hat and no cattle, the sizzle without the steak. They often lacked compelling spiritual content and deep biblical knowledge. Lincoln's upbringing and early life took place during the Second Great Awakening, when religious revivals became almost a spectator sport. Preachers worked hard to keep their parishioners engaged and interested. In their attempt to win larger followings, their preaching became extreme and sensationalist. Religious doctrine became more fluid and evangelism excessively emotional. Revivalist preachers entertained their audiences, imbibed the adulation, and let their egos become inflated. Worship services often turned into traveling shows.[3]

The emotional evangelism of the time collided with Lincoln's strict religious upbringing in his parents' Separate Baptist church. Separate Baptists were radical predestinarians and adhered to a strict moral code. Profanity, intoxication, gossip, horse racing, and

---

1 Burlingame, *Lincoln*, 1:19–20; Jones, *Lincoln and the Preachers*, 17–18; Bartelt, *Lincoln's Indiana Youth*, 22; Szasz and Szasz, *Lincoln and Religion*, 7; Owen, *The Man and His Faith*, 6. One tradition is that no official funeral took place immediately after his mother's passing, which bothered young Abe greatly. Therefore, he wrote to Reverend Elkin, asking him to preside over his mother's funeral, which Elkin did, albeit almost one year after her passing.

2 Wilson, *Herndon's Informants*, 40.

3 Mansfield, *Lincoln's Battle with God*, 23; Jones, *Lincoln and the Preachers*, 135.

dancing were forbidden and condemned. They believed that God ordained every event, and therefore one did not need to sponsor missionaries, Sunday schools, or professional clergy. If God wanted the heathen to be converted, He would find a way to do it without human contribution.[4]

While they may have differed on doctrine, the leaders of the Separate Baptist church and the revivalist preachers of the Second Great Awakening had one thing in common—a reliance on zeal and emotion. Throughout his adult life, the calm, rational, cerebral Lincoln poked fun at the fervor of clergymen. During the Civil War, the emotional outbursts and volatile personality of his secretary of war, Edwin Stanton, frequently amused Lincoln. The president compared him to a preacher who "was in the habit of going off on such high flights at camp meetings that they had to put bricks in his pockets to keep him down."[5]

Baptist preachers often worked themselves up into a frenzy and cultivated an artificial preacher's voice. They denounced Methodists and Presbyterians and gave fire and brimstone sermons about the atrocities of hell with all the emotionalism they could muster, while also revealing their own intellectual inadequacies. Before the age of twenty-eight, Abe did not meet a preacher who believed the earth was round.[6]

As a boy returning home from worship, Lincoln repeated sermons almost verbatim to his friends, mimicking the gestures, mannerisms, and accents of the speakers. Climbing on a box or tree stump, he would play act to the great amusement of family and friends. When Lincoln mocked, however, his father would scold him and make him quit. One time when Lincoln mimicked a preacher's prayer, he included a petition that God might put stockings on chickens' feet to keep them warm during the winter.[7]

---

[4] Donald, *Lincoln*, 24; Guelzo, "Lincoln and Religion," 190.

[5] Leidner, *Lincoln's Gift*, 149.

[6] Burlingame, *Lincoln*, 1:40.

[7] Burlingame, *Lincoln*, 1:40.

Mockery remained a part of Lincoln's shtick throughout his life. He told a story of a Baptist preacher in Indiana who started out his sermon claiming that he would represent Christ. Then a blue lizard ran underneath his baggy pantaloons, and the preacher tried to continue his sermon. When the lizard made its way up to his waist line, the preacher kicked off his pants, but the critter had already made its way up the preacher's shirt. The preacher then took off his shirt. As the congregation looked on in bewilderment for a few moments, one old lady rose from the back of the church and shouted that if the preacher represented Jesus, she would be done reading the Bible. Another time he shared a tale of a preacher who spoke randomly about anything or anyone to grab the interest his parishioners—the sacrament of baptism, Noah, Daniel in the Lion's Den, Shadrach, Meshach, and Abednego. When he noticed members were not paying attention to him, he adjusted his speech and told those gathered that he thought they might like to know that a local squire had lost a little bay mare with a tail.[8] As president, he told a story of how a Methodist complained that a member of the Universalist denomination promised that all would be saved. "But my dear brother," said the Methodist, "let us hope for better things."[9]

One reason for Lincoln's derision was that many backcountry preachers could not teach Scripture with clarity and in a compelling manner despite their emotional fervor which persuaded and impressed so many others. When Lincoln later lived in Springfield, Illinois, he had a two-hour conversation with Reverend Benjamin Smith, president of the Ladies Seminary in Bloomington, Illinois, and who also preached half-time in Springfield. Lincoln admired Smith's preaching and invited him to his law office to explain "the whole system of religion as taught by your people." Smith obliged and later commented that he had "never preached to such

---

[8] Burlingame, *Lincoln,* 1:40–41.

[9] Szasz and Szasz, *Lincoln and Religion*, 17.

an appreciative audience since or before."[10] Lincoln told Smith that what he said made sense to his head and heart.

Then Lincoln proceeded to tell Smith a story of "a darkey" who wanted to join the church. In order to join, the man would have to explain the doctrine of predestination. When the man claimed that he understood predestination, the preacher said that he would have verify the man's understanding by asking him some questions. After the back and forth, the minister asked the man if he understood predestination. Lincoln said, "The darkey replied: 'Well brudder, when you fust asked me, I knew all about it, but since you done splained it all out, I knos noffin about it at all." Lincoln's point was that the more preachers "explained the less I understood them, and my mind got more and more muddled." Lincoln said that "preachers have preached and talked this 'miraculous conversion,'" as well as other "very absurd theories of religion, and given such contradictory explanations of the Bible, that I have honestly at times doubted the whole thing."

As would be the case throughout his life, Lincoln needed clergymen who could engage his brilliant mind and directly answer his skepticism by using a Christian apologetics approach. Emotionalism and theatrics did not impress him. Neither did simply knowing Scripture, especially since Lincoln knew the Bible more intimately than most preachers. Clear, cogent, and intellectually stimulating ministers who addressed his skepticism directly earned his trust, gratitude, and deepest respect.

Though young Lincoln grew up with a disdain for the inadequacies of many backwoods preachers, his Calvinist upbringing did make a profound, lifelong impact on him. In 1820, an eleven-year old Lincoln helped his father and other carpenters chop down trees and erect the meetinghouse of Little Pigeon Creek Baptist Church in Indiana. As sexton, Lincoln regularly swept the church

---

[10] Jones, *Lincoln and the Preachers,* 75. The quotes in this paragraph and the next come from this source.

and furnished it with candles. More important, Lincoln heard anti-slavery sermons there regularly. Most Separate Baptists were strongly opposed to slavery.[11] "I am naturally anti-slavery," Lincoln wrote in 1864. "If slavery is not wrong, nothing is wrong. I can not remember when I did not so think, and feel."[12] The seeds of the Great Emancipator were sown early in his life thanks to his parents' church and those deficient ministers he loved to ridicule.

Lincoln's Calvinist fatalism permeated his psyche for most of his adult life. He frequently noted to Mary and friends that "what is to be will be." Life and things "were fixed, doomed in one way or the other, from which there was no appeal," and "no efforts or prayers of ours can change, alter, modify, or reverse the decree." He agreed with and often quoted Shakespeare's *Hamlet*: "There's a divinity that shapes our ends, Rough-hew them how we will."[13]

Some of Lincoln's most impressive traits—compassion, tolerance, a willingness to overlook mistakes—emanated from his fatalism. Like thousands of Calvinists who believed in predestination, he worked tirelessly for a better world. Moreover, his fatalism compelled him to take a pragmatic approach to problems—a recognition that anything should be tried in order to find a solution to any problem.[14] Fate ensured that no matter what was tried, God had already precast the ending. Thus, anything could and should be attempted. If Lincoln could not go through something, he would try to go over, under, or around it.

As much as he mocked the clergymen and teachings of his parents' church, Lincoln did, in fact, hear the Word of God spoken and preached. Matilda Johnston, Abe's stepsister, recalled how "Abe would take down the bible, read a verse—give out a hymn—and

---

[11] Donald, *Lincoln*, 24; Oates, *With Malice Toward None*, 9; Jones, *Lincoln and the Preachers*, 18.

[12] Basler, Lincoln to Albert Hodges, April 4, 1864, *CW*, 7:281.

[13] Carwardine, "Lincoln's Religion," 228–29.

[14] Donald, *Lincoln*, 15.

we would sing" at home while his parents were away. [15] Sometimes Lincoln would teach and explain what Scripture meant.

Even during his wilderness years, when his skepticism of the Christian religion was at its peak, Lincoln retained a profound admiration and deep knowledge of Scripture. This love of Scripture first took root in a young Lincoln as he lived in strict religious home and listened to the voices of substandard shepherds of the Christian flock.

The Truth

Lincoln had high expectations of pastors and ministers. Especially early on in his life, preachers disappointed him with their beliefs, performances, and personal characters.

There is no doubt that those who teach the Christian faith—pastors, teachers, parents—are the subjects of high expectations from God. He desires "shepherds after my own heart, who will feed you with knowledge and understanding."[16] Those who "proclaim the gospel should get their living by the gospel."[17] If Christian leaders teach false doctrine or cause "one of these little ones who believe in me to sin," Jesus tells us, "it would be better for him to have a great millstone fastened around his neck and to be drowned in the depth of the sea."[18]

This is why God calls on Christian leaders to be discerning in regard to every worldly new-age concept or postmodern fad. We should "not believe every spirit, but test the spirits to see whether they are from God, for many false prophets have gone out into the world."[19] The Bible is clear that teachers hold a special place of

---

[15] Mansfield, *Lincoln's Battle with God*, 26.
[16] Jer. 3:15.
[17] 1 Cor. 9:14.
[18] Matt. 18:6.
[19] 1 John 4:1.

influence on the hearts and minds of those whom they serve. "Not many of you should become teachers," says Scripture, "for you know that we who teach will be judged with greater strictness."[20]

God's expectations of pastors, ministers, and preachers are particularly noteworthy and a good guide for all of us who desire to live and serve with integrity and Christian character. Pastors are called to "shepherd the flock of God … exercising oversight, not under compulsion, but willingly … not for shameful gain, but eagerly; not domineering over those" who are in their charge, "but being examples to the flock." All Christian leaders should clothe themselves "with humility toward one another, for 'God opposes the proud but gives grace to the humble.'"[21]

The emotionalism, disheveled appearance, and ineptitude displayed by many backwoods preachers bothered Lincoln. These men were hard to respect and learn from in worship settings. The Bible says that a pastor or minister should be "above reproach, the husband of one wife, and his children are believers and not open to the charge of debauchery or insubordination." Moreover, a spiritual leader should "not be arrogant or quick-tempered or a drunkard or violent or greedy for gain, but hospitable, a lover of good, self-controlled, upright, holy, and disciplined." Furthermore, a minister should be a learned about the Word of God. "He must hold firm to the trustworthy word as taught, so that he may be able to give instruction in sound doctrine and also to rebuke those who contradict it."[22] In another section of Scripture, God reveals many of the same sentiments for anyone who hopes to be a pastor and leader in the church:

> [The pastor] must be above reproach, the husband of one wife, sober-minded, self-controlled, respectable, hospitable, able to teach, not a drunkard, not

20 James 3:1.

21 1 Pet. 5:1–5.

22 Titus 1:6–9.

> violent but gentle, not quarrelsome, not a lover of money. He must manage his own household well, with all dignity keeping his children submissive, for if someone does not know how to manage his own household, how will he care for God's church? He must not be a recent convert, or he may become puffed up with conceit and fall into the condemnation of the devil. Moreover, he must be well thought of by outsiders, so that he may not fall into disgrace, into a snare of the devil.[23]

God certainly wants pastors and ministers well-versed in His Word.

While the Bible insists that you should "respect those who labor among you and are over you in the Lord and admonish you, and to esteem them very highly in love because of their work," the Bible is also clear that pastors, ministers, teachers, and other Christian leaders are to be worthy servants and teachers of the Word of God.[24] So honor and "remember your leaders, those who spoke to you the word of God. Consider the outcome of their way of life, and imitate their faith."[25] And "do your best to present yourself to God as one approved, a worker who has no need to be ashamed, rightly handling the word of truth."[26]

Your Life

Lincoln mocked and ridiculed many of the backwoods preachers he heard. How does this make you feel about the younger Lincoln?

---

[23] 1 Tim. 3:1–7.

[24] 1 Thess. 5:12–13.

[25] Heb. 13:7.

[26] 2 Tim. 2:15.

How are pastors and ministers ridiculed in society today? What can you do about that?

How do you speak to or handle a Christian leader who does not meet your expectations? What is the proper Christian response in these situations?

As special and important as they are, Christian leaders are sinners too. How can you lift up and support them in their vocation?

31

Conflict and Competition

I appeal to you, brothers, by the name of our Lord Jesus Christ, that all of you agree, and that there be no divisions among you, but that you be united in the same mind and the same judgment.
—1 Corinthians 1:10

The Lincoln Way

Kindness and pleasantness are great tools for leaders to possess.

In addition to the performances of substandard frontier preachers, the religious sectarianism and disharmony among denominations contributed to Lincoln's religious skepticism. Sophie Hanks, who lived with Lincoln family for many years in Indiana, once heard a young Lincoln explain that if he could take the best features of every church, he could construct a new church better than any of them. Later, when he lived in New Salem, Lincoln told a friend that he would go to church more often if he could simply hear a good sermon rather than preachers tearing down and denouncing the denominations of others.[1]

Though New Salem had no churches, Baptists held services in the local schoolhouse, while other denominations met regularly in homes. Lincoln occasionally attended Clary's Grove Baptist Church, which was founded in a citizen's home and was known for its punitive discipline of members.

---

[1] Burlingame, *Lincoln*, 1:84.

One Presbyterian minister, Reverend John M. Barry—the father of Lincoln's store partner, William F. Barry—actually denounced his son as a drunk and disowned his daughter for marrying at the age of fourteen. When his daughter's firstborn son died, Reverend Barry refused to attend the funeral and simply glared at the funeral procession as it passed by his farm. When William died of tuberculosis and hard drinking in 1835, his father preached a sermon on temperance rather than sharing a more grace-filled eulogy of his own son. Such unforgiving, unkind, hard-hearted ministers and congregational members turned Lincoln off from the Christian religion.[2] He wanted no part of such rigidity and unkindness.

Lincoln had a gift for speaking kindly to everyone. Not only did he find this personally appealing, but also smart and persuasive speech. "When the conduct of men is designed to be influenced, persuasion, kind, unassuming persuasion, should ever be adopted," he declared in a temperance address in February 1842. Lincoln believed in the old and "true maxim that a 'drop of honey catches more flies than a gallon of gall.'" To win someone "to your cause, first convince him that you are his sincere friend. Therein is a drop of honey that catches his heart, which, say what he will, is the great high road to his reason" and will eventually convince someone "of the justice of your cause, if indeed that cause really be a just one." If someone, however, dictates in such a way "as to be shunned and despised," he "will retreat within himself, close all the avenues to his head and heart."[3]

Lincoln found it disappointing that Baptists, Methodists, and Presbyterians were constantly quarreling with and ridiculing one another. Having grown up in a trauma-ridden and dysfunctional home, Lincoln wanted nothing to do with pugnacious preachers who seemed to crave acrimony rather than harmony. Religious disputes pushed Lincoln away from the Christian church and into

---

2 Burlingame, *Lincoln,* 1:75–76, 84.

3 Basler, Lincoln's Temperance Address, February 22, 1842, *CW,* 1:273.

conversations with freethinkers and others who disdained traditional church bodies and doctrine. Skeptics seemed more rational, calm, and willing to listen to one another. Lincoln began to read books that scorned traditional Christian orthodoxy.[4]

Lincoln's skepticism came to a head in the 1840s when he decided to run again for political office. Reverend Peter Cartwright and Lincoln were both running for the Seventh District seat of Illinois. A legendary Methodist circuit-riding preacher for the Democrats, Cartwright had lived in Illinois for forty-eight years, preached over eighteen thousand sermons, and baptized over fifteen thousand people. While he refused to meet Lincoln for public debate, Cartwright began a whisper campaign denouncing Lincoln as a skeptic and infidel, hoping to suppress the voter turnout of Christian Whigs.[5]

Angered, Lincoln first tried to rebut Cartwright's tactic on constitutional grounds, arguing that no religious tests were to be used as qualification for office.[6] Not getting the traction he wanted with this argument, Lincoln felt compelled to write a handbill directly denying the charges of infidelity. Admitting that he did

---

[4] Donald, *Lincoln*, 48–49; Mansfield, *Lincoln's Battle with God*, 125. Apparently Lincoln liked one aspect of backwoods preaching. In 1861, he declared that he did not like "to hear cut and dried sermons. No—when I hear a man preach, I like to see him act as if he were fighting bees!"

[5] Jones, *Lincoln and the Preachers*, 44. According to Carl Sandburg, during the 1846 election, Lincoln went to a revival meeting where Cartwright was to preach. Cartwright asked all who desired to give their hearts to God and go to heaven to stand. Then he asked all who did not wish to go to hell to stand. All stood up except Lincoln. "May I enquire of you, Mr. Lincoln, where you are going?" Lincoln responded: "I came here," he said, "as a respectful listener. I did not know I was to be singled out by Brother Cartwright; I believe in treating religious matters with due solemnity. I admit the questions propounded by Brother Cartwright are important. I did not feel called upon to answer as the rest did. Brother Cartwright asks me directly where I am going. I desire to reply with equal directness: 'I am going to Congress!'"

[6] Burlingame, *Lincoln*, 1:238; Szasz and Szasz, *Lincoln and Religion*, 22.

not have official membership in any Christian church, he countered that he had "never denied the truth of the Scriptures" and that he had "never spoken with intentional disrespect of religion in general, or of any denomination of Christians in particular." He went on to explain that he could not support any "open enemy of, and scoffer at, religion." Lincoln blamed those "whoever they may be, who falsely put such a charge in circulation against me."[7]

Many of Lincoln's friends at the time, however, had heard him deny the truth of Scripture, scoff at religion in general, and mock the Christian orthodoxies of his community. Showing his humanity and sinful nature, as well as the propensity of politicians in all ages, the campaign of 1846 exposed a dishonest Abe.[8]

During much of his twenties and thirties, Lincoln did not subscribe to the tenets and teachings of the orthodox Christian church. He told one associate that he doubted "the possibility of settling the religion of Jesus Christ in the models of man-made creeds and dogmas." He further explained that he had "mental reservations" in assenting "to long and complicated creeds and catechisms." For Lincoln, only a church that lived out Jesus's statement that everyone should "'love the Lord they God with all thy heart, and with all thy soul, and with all thy mind, and thy neighbour as thyself,'" would be one he could "gladly unite with" and join.[9] Almost two decades later in the White House, Lincoln would say almost the exact same thing to Connecticut Congressman H.C. Deming when asked why he had not formally joined a church. "I have found difficulty in giving my assent, without mental reservation, to the long, complicated statements of Christian doctrine which characterize their Articles of Belief and Confessions of Faith," he maintained. Lincoln insisted that any church which inscribed over its altar, "as its sole qualification for membership ... 'Thou shall love the Lord thy God with all thy

[7] Basler, Lincoln's Handbill Replying to Charges of Infidelity, July 31, 1846, *CW*, 1:382.

[8] Mansfield, *Lincoln's Battle with God*, 65.

[9] Mansfield, *Lincoln's Battle with God*, 106.

heart, and with all thy soul and with all thy mind, and thy neighbor as thyself,' that church I will join with all my heart and all my soul."[10]

Lincoln defeated Cartwright with approximately 56 percent of the vote, but their relationship did not end bitterly. When Cartwright's grandson was later indicted for murder, Lincoln helped him get acquitted. Cartwright strongly supported Lincoln in his presidential campaigns.[11] While they had battled over religion and politics, both men learned how to forgive and forget. They were no longer competitors. They were friends.

The Truth

Various Christian denominations exist because Scripture has been interpreted differently over time. For some, these denominational differences are significant, even critical. Since God's Word is truth, most people want to believe in the whole, pure truth, determined as they read and interpret Scripture.

To be sure, the Bible says that we are to "teach what accords with sound doctrine."[12] Sometimes factions or denominations bring clarity to what a church body believes, so that "those who are genuine among you may be recognized."[13] Moreover, many fear that followers will stray from the true teachings of the Bible and eventually adopt of a false religion unless they interpret Scripture properly.

God's joyous desire, of course, is for all of His children to be "of the same mind, having the same love, being in full accord and of one mind."[14] He does not desire "divisions among you, but that you be united in the same mind and the same judgment."[15] He

---

[10] Carpenter, *Six Months in the White House*, 208.

[11] Szasz and Szasz, *Lincoln and Religion*, 24.

[12] Titus 2:1.

[13] 1 Cor. 11:19.

[14] Phil. 2:2.

[15] 1 Cor. 1:10.

does not want quarreling among his people. Through His apostle Paul, God chided the Corinthians who said, "'I follow Paul,' or 'I follow Apollos,' or 'I follow Cephas,' or 'I follow Christ.' Is Christ divided? Was Paul crucified for you? Or were you baptized in the name of Paul?"[16] God's Word is clear that "there is one body and one Spirit—just as you were called to the one hope that belongs to your call—one Lord, one faith, one baptism."[17] Yet unfortunately on this side of heaven, there will remain divisions among Christians until the last days of earth.

While differences between Christian denominations are one thing, the teaching of false religion compared to the truth of God's Word is quite another. Heresy and false testimony are lethal—they can take someone away or break someone's relationship with God. This is why Paul, inspired by God, wrote, "I appeal to you, brothers, to watch out for those who cause divisions and create obstacles contrary to the doctrine that you have been taught; avoid them."[18]

When people do not speak the truth or share *the* truth, they are speaking lies to you. Honest Abe did not always behave or talk honestly. More important than any political lie, you do not want to abandon or disown your faith based on hearing a lie. The important thing to remember is that God detests and hates a "lying tongue."[19] The Bible explains that "better is a poor person who walks in his integrity than one who is crooked in speech and is a fool."[20] God's Word makes it clear that "lying lips are an abomination to the Lord, but those who act faithfully are his delight."[21]

Beware of false religions, lies, or pagan whims. Your eternal salvation is a stake. As Paul warned the Galatians:

---

[16] 1 Cor. 1:11–13.

[17] Eph. 4:4–5.

[18] Rom. 16:17.

[19] Prov. 6:17.

[20] Prov. 19:1.

[21] Prov. 12:22.

> I am astonished that you are so quickly deserting him who called you in the grace of Christ and are turning to a different gospel—not that there is another one, but there are some who trouble you and want to distort the gospel of Christ. But even if we or an angel from heaven should preach to you a gospel contrary to the one we preached to you, let him be accursed. As we have said before, so now I say again: If anyone is preaching to you a gospel contrary to the one you received, let him be accursed. For am I now seeking the approval of man, or of God? Or am I trying to please man? If I were still trying to please man, I would not be a servant of Christ.[22]

Paul's warning to the Galatians is a warning to you too.

Make sure you pray for discerning eyes, ears, and mind in regard to false religions and false prophets, for they will always be us until Jesus returns. Stay in the Word, not the ways of the world. Stay in "the word of truth, the gospel of your salvation." Your faith in Jesus is "sealed with the promised Holy Spirit" who guarantees your inheritance—your eternal salvation.[23]

Your Life

Mean-spirited and unkind pastors turned Abraham Lincoln off from the Christian faith. What might seekers or unchurched folks view today as examples of Christian unkindness, meanness, or callous behavior? What can you do about it?

---

[22] Gal. 1:6–10.

[23] Eph. 1:13–14.

For Lincoln, the bickering and ridicule that took place between different denominations remained a big turnoff. With this in mind, how can Christians today who believe strongly in the views of their particular denominations make sure they do not turn off the Abraham Lincolns of today?

Lincoln lied about his faith for political gain. When are you most tempted to lie about your faith? Why is that? What can you do to combat that temptation?

32

Power of One

And I will give you shepherds after my own heart, who will feed you with knowledge and understanding.
—Jeremiah 3:15

The Lincoln Way

One inspired individual can create significant change and make an eternal difference.

While Lincoln continued to encounter uneducated and belligerent clergy for the rest of his life, he also developed intimate friendships with many men of the cloth. The further he got away from his frontier roots, the more educated pastors he met who could engage him in an intelligent and winsome manner. For every "Honorable Jonathan Swellhead," "Reverend Dr. Blowhard," "Committee of the Synod of the Seek-No-Further Church,"[1] or preacher who defended slavery[2] or attacked his patronage of the theater, Lincoln found men of faith he learned to admire and respect.

---

[1] Conway, *Lincoln's White House*, 133. The *Albany Evening Journal* referred to these "White House bores" who traveled to the Executive Mansion to have their say with the president.

[2] White, *Lincoln*, 278–79. Frederick Ross, a Presbyterian minister from Huntsville, Alabama, provides one example of how Lincoln thought Christian preachers, who defended slavery, mishandled religion. Lincoln read Ross's *Slavery Ordained by God* (1857), which became an instant bestseller among pro-slavery advocates. Ross argued that slavery was a beneficent and ordering institution. In Lincoln's "Fragment on Pro-slavery Theology" (October 1,

Indeed, during the last three decades of Lincoln's life, the ministers who made a significant impact on him generally possessed many of these characteristics: they were kind, caring, approachable, knowledgeable of the world, wise in Scripture, emotionally intelligent, and erudite in Christian apologetics. These pastors helped redeem Lincoln's faith—in clergy, the Christian worldview, and his personal views of the Bible and Jesus Christ.

Kindhearted and intelligent ministers who possessed outstanding teaching skills always elicited Lincoln's respect. Even during his days of skepticism, Lincoln had no problem with preachers if they went

---

1858, *CW*, 3:204–5), he refuted Ross's position. "Suppose it is true, that the negro is inferior to the white, in the gifts of nature; is it not the exact reverse justice that the white should, for that reason, take from the negro, any part of the little which has been given him? 'Give to him that is needy' is the christian rule of charity; but 'Take from him that is needy' is the rule of slavery. The sum of pro-slavery theology seems to be this: 'Slavery is not universally right, nor yet universally wrong; it is better for some people to be slaves; and, in such cases, it is the Will of God that they be such.' Certainly there is no contending against the Will of God; but still there is some difficulty in ascertaining, and applying it, to particular cases. For instance we will suppose the Rev. Dr. Ross has a slave named Sambo, and the question is 'Is it the Will of God that Sambo shall remain a slave, or be set free?' The Almighty gives no audible answer to the question, and his revelation—the Bible—gives none—or, at most, none but such as admits of a squabble, as to it's meaning. No one thinks of asking Sambo's opinion on it. So, at last, it comes to this, that Dr. Ross is to decide the question. And while he consider[s] it, he sits in the shade, with gloves on his hands, and subsists on the bread that Sambo is earning in the burning sun. If he decides that God Wills Sambo to continue a slave, he thereby retains his own comfortable position; but if he decides that God will's Sambo to be free, he thereby has to walk out of the shade, throw off his gloves, and delve for his own bread. Will Dr. Ross be actuated by that perfect impartiality, which has ever been considered most favorable to correct decisions? But, slavery is good for some people!!! As a good thing, slavery is strikingly perculiar, in this, that it is the only good thing which no man ever seeks the good of, for himself. Nonsense! Wolves devouring lambs, not because it is good for their own greedy maws, but because it [is] good for the lambs!!!"

about their business "with some gentleness and moderation."[3] He admired and became a close friends with Pastor Josephus Hewitt of the First Christian Church in Springfield (1832–1838), an eloquent man who later became a practicing lawyer. After hearing one of his sermons in 1837, Lincoln called Reverend Peter Akers, a contemporary of Reverend Cartwright, "the most impressive preacher I have ever heard. It is wonderful that god has given such power to men." Lincoln concurred with Aker's interpretation of prophecy "and especially about the breaking down of civil and religious tyrannies."[4]

The preaching of Colonel James Jaquess, the pastor at First Methodist Church in Springfield, also made an impact on Lincoln. A "Son of Thunder" in the pulpit and well-versed in Greek, Latin, and mathematics, Jaquess possessed polished common sense. One day Lincoln sent a young boy to Jaquess to determine if he would be preaching on Sunday. Jacquess told the boy to "go back and tell Mr. Lincoln that if he will come to church he will see whether I am going to preach or not." The little boy responded, "Mr. Lincoln told me he would give me a quarter if I would find out whether you are going to preach."[5] Not wanting to keep the little boy from getting his quarter, Jaquess affirmed that he would be preaching.

Due to a full church and his late arrival, Lincoln had to sit on the altar during the entire service. Jaquess reported that Lincoln called on him a few days later to tell him how much Lincoln appreciated his sermon and that he wanted to talk further on the message delivered. According to Jaquess, he and his wife invited Lincoln into their home, where they "talked and prayed with him for hours." Jaquess said that if ever a person had been converted to Christianity, "Abraham Lincoln was converted that night in my house." Jaquess noted that even though Mary was a Presbyterian, Lincoln could

---

[3] Conway, *Lincoln's White House*, 138.

[4] Jones, *Lincoln and the Preachers*, 21–22.

[5] Jones, *Lincoln and the Preachers*, 23-25. The quotes and content in the following paragraph also come from this source.

never fully accept Calvinism. "He never joined my church," he continued, "but I will always believe that since that night, Abraham Lincoln lived and died a Christian gentleman." Jaquess would not be the first or last to claim to have had a hand in Lincoln's conversion or bourgeoning Christian faith.

As time passed, Lincoln found more frequent enjoyment and intellectual fulfillment in his daily interactions with local pastors. Dr. Francis A. McNeil, a physician and preacher, practiced in the 1830s and 1840s in Springfield. Together McNeil and Lincoln delivered the eulogy for Bowling Green, the New Salem justice of the peace, in 1842. Reverend Francis Springer, founder of the Lutheran Church in Springfield, who lived across the street from the Lincoln home, received twenty-five dollars from Lincoln to help start his church.

Highly educated at Brown University, Reverend Charles Dresser, professor of English and the Episcopal clergyman who married Abraham and Mary, sold his house to the Lincolns in 1844—the home that would later become the iconic Lincoln Home National Historic Site.

Charles Matheny, a zealous leader of the Methodist church in Springfield and proponent of temperance and educational advancement, became one of Lincoln's closest friends. In 1839, they served together on the board of trustees in Springfield. Stuart and Lincoln's law firm defended Matheny in a court case in 1838, and Lincoln supported Matheny's candidacy for county clerk in 1837 and 1839. In his official capacity, Matheny certified Lincoln's election to the Illinois legislature on three separate occasions.

The Reverend Charles Chiniquy, a one-time Catholic priest who turned Protestant and had a large following in Illinois, built an enduring friendship with Lincoln. He later visited President Lincoln in the Executive Mansion, warning about rumored assassination attempts.[6] Clergymen who excelled in their vocations and

[6] Jones, *Lincoln and the Preachers*, 25–27.

demonstrated that they lived *alongside* their parishioners *rather than above them* were trustworthy, authentic, and compelling to the earthy Lincoln.

Perhaps no minister had as significant an impact on Lincoln's faith development than Dr. James Smith of First Presbyterian Church in Springfield. Through his kindness, compassion, real-world knowledge, divine wisdom, faith applications, and logical, thoughtful, apologetic understanding Christianity, Smith helped Lincoln rediscover the attractive features of Christianity.

Smith and Lincoln had much in common. Both had mothers who died when they were young. Both were religious doubters in their early years and influenced by the skeptical works of Constantin Volney and Thomas Paine. Both were temperance advocates. Both enjoyed mocking the antics and eccentricities of preachers. At one time Smith considered himself a confirmed deist and loved attending camp meetings to heckle ministers. Only after listening to Reverend James Blackwell preach at a revival meeting in Indiana did Smith become a Christian. He became a revivalist and an ordained minister in 1825 at Cumberland Presbyterian Church in Kentucky. Cumberland Presbyterians favored free will over the strong predestination stand of traditional Presbyterians. He became pastor of First Presbyterian Church in Springfield in March 1849.

An exemplary speaker, lauded as Daniel Webster's equal, the scholarly Smith embraced a lawyerly, apologetic approach to Christianity that would make a significant impact on bookish Lincoln. During his early years of ministry, Smith founded a periodical, published a collection of hymns, and completed a history of the Cumberland Presbyterian Church. He also founded Cumberland College in Lebanon, Tennessee. He gave a series of popular lectures in the early 1840s bearing titles like "The Natures and Tendencies of Infidelity" and "The Evidences of Christianity." A well-known skeptic, C. G. Olmsted, challenged Dr. Smith on topics such as "Were the writers of the different books of the Bible inspired men? Did the facts which they detail occur? Was Jesus Christ miraculously begotten? Did he perform miracles? Did Jesus rise from the dead?" Over the course of eighteen evenings of debate, Smith crushed his opponent with his superior intellect, outsize personality, and skilled use of dramatic gestures (as well as occasional sarcasm and personal attacks on Olmstead).[7]

In 1843, Smith completed a book, written from an apologetic bent, that would have a profound impact on the faith development of Lincoln—*The Christian's Defence, Containing a Fair Statement, and Impartial Examination of the Leading Objections Urged by Infidels Against the Antiquity, Genuineness, Credibility and Inspiration of the Holy Scriptures; Enriched with Copious Extracts from Learned Authors.* Long on title and big on apologetics, Smith's work examined the evidence for Christianity and the claims of the Bible with a cool, rational analysis. While many theological readings of the day were dense, redundant, dogmatic, and controversial, Lincoln found Smith's book engaging and unique because it presented a two-way discussion about the evidence of Christianity. The viewpoint of the militant unbeliever as well as the devout believer were on display.

Smith made the case for the Bible as an attorney would before a grand jury. Instead of relying on emotionalism and sentiment, as frontier preachers had for much of Lincoln's life, Smith refuted skeptics' arguments by addressing their criticisms directly and with no fear of disputation. Smith made the case in a logical, sensible manner, which appealed to Lincoln's respect for order and reason. Smith believed that arguments must made without appeals to emotion and won on the merits of the evidence. Moreover, most skeptics of the time used racist arguments to refute the idea that all men might have a common ancestor like Adam. A progressive on this matter, Smith argued that the difference between the races was

[7] Mansfield, *Lincoln's Battle with God*, 78–80.

only "skin-deep," and that blacks and whites were essentially the same apart from the matter of color.[8]

While Lincoln visited Mary's family in Lexington, Kentucky, in October 1849, he picked up Smith's *A Christian Defence* and began to read with great interest. After returning to Springfield, he told fellow lawyer Thomas Lewis—an elder at Smith's First Presbyterian Church—that Smith's work had "led him to change his view of the Christian religion, and he would like to get that work and finish the reading of it, and also to make the acquaintance of Dr. Smith." Lewis brought Smith to Lincoln's office, where "Dr. Smith gave Mr. Lincoln a copy of his book, as I know, at his own request."[9]

Lincoln treasured the book. Robert Lincoln recalled seeing Smith's work often in his father's home—Lincoln seemed to reread it and refer back to it. Ninian W. Edwards, Lincoln's brother-in-law, recalled that Lincoln told him, "I have been reading a work of Dr. Smith on the evidences of Christianity, and have heard him preach and converse on the subject, and I am now convinced of the truth of the Christian religion."[10]

Two years after Lincoln's assassination, Smith shared for posterity that "Mr. Lincoln did avow his belief in the Divine Authority and Inspiration of the Scriptures."[11] Lincoln had called on him often and they enjoyed "pleasant Conversations in drives over the prairies." Trained as a lawyer and equipped with great emotional intelligence to see things from different points of view, Lincoln made "arguments on both sides" of the religion issue after "a most patient, impartial and Searching investigation." Lincoln told Smith that "'he examined the Arguments as a lawyer who is anxious to reach the truth investigates testimony.' The result was the announcement by himself that the

---

[8] White, *Lincoln*, 181; Mansfield, *Lincoln's Battle with God*, 81; Jones, *Lincoln and the Preachers*, 30–34.

[9] Mansfield, *Lincoln's Battle with God*, 80.

[10] Mansfield, *Lincoln's Battle with God*, 81.

[11] Wilson, *Herndon's Informants*, 547–50. The following quotes in this paragraph all come from this source.

argument in favor of the Divine Authority and inspiration of the Scripture was unanswerable." Smith obviously took some pride in claiming to have influenced someone of Lincoln's stature. Writing his book had been a "long and arduous mental labor," he asserted, but "if No other effect was ever produced by it, then the influence it exerted upon the mind of that man whose name thrills the heart of every patriotic American, I thank God that I was induced to undertake the work." Smith claimed that immediately after the Lincoln made his declaration of faith, "Mr. Lincoln placed himself and family under my pastoral Care, and when at home he was a regular attendant upon my ministry."

While conversations about religion and mutual admiration for one another's intellect helped their relationship grow, the friendship of the two men became further cemented, unfortunately, by tragedy. When Mary and Abe's son Eddie died on February 1, 1850, Lincoln reached out to Dr. Smith and asked him to lead the funeral as well as provide counsel and care for his grieving wife (Mary's pastor, the Reverend Charles Dresser, was out of town). Faithfully and regularly, Smith visited the Lincoln home, offering the comfort and care of God's Word. During these visits Lincoln learned more about Smith's early skepticism of the Christian faith. With Smith's help, Mary made it through the ordeal. She penned a verse to commemorate her son's death: "Bright is the home to him now given, for of such is the Kingdom of Heaven."[12]

Not long after Eddie's passing, the Lincolns began regularly attending First Presbyterian Church, sitting in the "amen corner," where pews were free and boisterous shout-outs of agreement with the sermon were commonplace. In time they rented a pew, and Mary, with Abe's permission, officially joined the church in 1852. Three years later the Lincolns had their son, Thomas, baptized at First Presbyterian Church—the only child of the Lincoln family to

---

12 Clinton, "Family," 264.

be baptized, and the only child to have come into the Lincoln family after they had known Dr. Smith.[13]

Eddie's death certainly compelled Lincoln to reexamine his life and worldview. For years, Lincoln's take on the Christian faith varied from an outright disdain to an uneasy interest in and admiration for Scripture. After Eddie's death, Lincoln's law partner John Todd Stuart recalled that "Dr. Smith and Mr. Lincoln had much discussion in relation to the truth of the Christian religion," and that "Dr. Smith had furnished Mr. Lincoln with books to read on the subject, and among others one had been written by himself, some time previous, on infidelity." Stuart insisted that "Dr. Smith claimed after this investigation Mr. Lincoln had changed his opinion, and became a believer in the truth of the Christian religion."[14]

The historiographical battle over Lincoln's precise religious beliefs started before he died. There were many contemporary testimonials and witnesses on both sides of the argument after the death of Eddie and Lincoln's new found relationship with Reverend Smith. James Matheny, a groomsmen in Lincoln's wedding in 1842, believed Lincoln remained a "confirmed infidel" until elected president in 1860. Only after he got to Washington, D.C. and associated with religious people, Matheny explained, did Lincoln become a Christian.[15] While Matheny had no doubt that Lincoln had "been an infidel in his former life ... and his association principally with rough and skeptical men," he did believe that Lincoln "was a very different man later in life; and that after associating with a different class of men, and investigating the subject, he was a firm believer in the Christian religion."[16]

---

13 White, *Lincoln*, 182; Mansfield, *Lincoln's Battle with God*, 80–81, 87–88.

14 Mansfield, *Lincoln's Battle with God*, 86.

15 Wilson, *Herndon's Informants*, 582—583.

16 Mansfield, *Lincoln's Battle with God*, 89—90. James Matheny represents the conundrum in analyzing primary sources and on the evolving faith beliefs of Lincoln. According to one interview conducted by William Herndon, (Wilson, *Herndon's Informants*, 472), Matheny says that when Lincoln first

While there is little doubt that in the first half of his adulthood, Lincoln had become a religious skeptic and doubter, there is also little doubt that his religious outlook changed and blossomed in the second half. With pastors like Dr. James Smith gently, kindly, and intelligently encouraging his religious growth, Lincoln moved from being a village atheist or enlightened infidel to a seasoned and mature Bible believer. He no longer labeled the Christian church a hoax or called the Bible a work of mythologists. Lincoln demonstrated his appreciation for the work of Christian ministers and congregations, the Bible's encouragement on human conduct, and the promise of an eternal life after death. Even his skeptical law partner, William Herndon, later admitted that Lincoln "believed in God," went to church regularly, and became a "deeply and thoroughly religious man."[17]

Of course, Lincoln still struggled with his beliefs. Certain churches and pastors would continue to frustrate and befuddle him, especially those who sanctioned the evils of slavery from the

---

came to Springfield, he would "pick up the Bible, read a passage, and them Comment on it, show its falsity, and its follies on the grounds of Reason, would then show its own self made & self uttered Contradictions and would in the End, finally ridicule it and as it were Scoff at it." According to another interview conducted by William Herndon, (Wilson, *Herndon's Informants*, 576), Matheny insisted that Lincoln "was an infidel," referred to Christ an illegitimate child, and "attacked the Bible & new Testament on two grounds"—alleged contradictions of Scripture and from "the grounds of reason....Sometimes Lincoln bordered on absolute Atheism: he went far that way & often shocked me." In yet another interview conducted by William Herndon, (Wilson, *Herndon's Informants*, 577), Matheny said that "from about 1854 to 1860," as Lincoln thought of running for President, he "played a sharp game here on the Religious world." Lincoln knew that he could not be known as an "old infidel" or atheist and, thus, presented himself as "a seeker after Salvation &c in the Lord and a changed man."

17 Mansfield, *Lincoln's Battle with God*, 89–90. Mansfield says that after his early Springfield years, Lincoln became "a religious pilgrim, and his spiritual journey is among the more fascinating and defining realities of his life."

pulpit. Lincoln also struggled, like many Christians, with self-doubt, the inscrutable ways of God, and the divinity of Jesus. Nevertheless, Lincoln's faith grew and matured after his younger days in Springfield, and especially as he met and conversed with individuals such as Dr. James Smith.

Lincoln stayed friends with Smith for the rest of his life. Despite the fact that Smith remained a Southern Democrat, though not a secessionist, President Lincoln appointed him consul to Dundee, Scotland. When Lincoln died, Dr. Smith received Lincoln's gold-headed cane.[18] Much more than a spiritual crutch, Smith helped rescue the religious Lincoln by redeeming the Christian faith in Lincoln's mind. Indeed, the Smith-Lincoln relationship exhibits the power and impact that one faithful witness can have on someone even as mentally tough, skeptical, and stubborn as Lincoln.

The Truth

If you really love or care for someone, you want them to know Jesus Christ as Lord and Savior. One of the hardest things to endure in life is to have a loved one who rejects Jesus or does not believe in the inerrancy of God's Word. Many Christians are married to or live with a beloved unbeliever. Perhaps you have family members or close friends who are beloved unbelievers.

As we have read, Lincoln had special people who were very intentional in sharing the faith and witnessing to him. Perhaps God has placed you in proximity to someone for "such a time as this"[19]—to minister, teach, or share the faith. After all, the Great Commission calls on all Christians to "go therefore and make disciples of all nations, baptizing them in the name of the Father and of the Son and of the Holy Spirit."[20]

---

[18] Jones, *Lincoln and the Preachers*, 30—34.

[19] Esther 4:14.

[20] Matt. 28:19.

God has blessed you with unique gifts and talents to be a Christian witness in your own unique and winsome way. Dr. Smith realized that he had to appeal to Lincoln's rational and lawyerly mind to make a case for the Bible and Christianity. Thus, he witnessed and taught the faith through the use of apologetics and by sharing his own personal faith struggles. Smith patiently listened to Lincoln's questions and doubts and worked persistently to establish a loving dialogue and trust with Lincoln.

All Christians should always pray for the gift of discernment so that they might determine the best approach in witnessing to others. Indeed, the Bible teaches that you should "walk in wisdom toward outsiders, making the best use of the time." A Christian's words should "always be gracious, seasoned with salt, so that you may know how you ought to answer each person."[21]

Of course, if you want to share the good news with someone who does not believe or does not yet know Christ, you need to be familiar with and grounded in God's Word. You cannot give what you do not possess. Scripture asserts that you should always be "prepared to make a defense to anyone who asks you for a reason for the hope that is in you; yet do it with gentleness and respect."[22] A defense, in this context, means the ability to make the case for the Bible, a Christian worldview, and the love of Christ. The Bible encourages you to "preach the word; be ready in season and out of season; reprove, rebuke, and exhort, with complete patience and teaching."[23]

Some people get nervous and overanxious when they think about witnessing or giving a testimony of faith. They want to share the faith with their loved one, but, like Moses in the Old Testament, they feel inadequate, worried about how they will be received, or unsure of what to say. Remember that Jesus understands your fear.

---

21 Col. 4:5–6.

22 1 Pet. 3:15.

23 2 Tim. 4:2.

You do not have to do the work of conversion; that is the work of the Holy Spirit. So if you are nervous about witnessing, pray about it. "Do not be anxious about how you should defend yourself or what you should say," Jesus says, "for the Holy Spirit will teach you in that very hour what you ought to say."[24]

Most importantly, do not forget your purpose or mission. You want your loved one to know Jesus and be saved. The Bible challenges you: "How are they to believe in him of whom they have never heard? And how are they to hear without someone preaching? And how are they to preach unless they are sent? As it is written, 'How beautiful are the feet of those who preach the good news!'"[25]

You are the one with the beautiful feet, put right where you are for a reason. Make the most of it. Share the joy you have in Christ. Let God use you to make an eternal difference in the life of another.

Your Life

The death of his son Eddie certainly made Abraham Lincoln contemplate the meaning of life and reflect on the afterlife. How does the death or earthly loss of loved ones impact your faith?

Education advocates often say they want what is best for students or children. What's best for children, and all of us, is Jesus Christ. Yet too many schools no longer have God's Word present in classrooms or schoolhouses. How can the power or influence of one make a difference in these kinds of settings?

[24] Luke 12:11–12.

[25] Rom. 10:14–15.

The title of this chapter refers to the power or influence that one person can have another. Who has been a Dr. Smith in your life? How have you been or can you be a Dr. Smith to others?

Our culture is filled with skeptics of the Christian faith, as Lincoln once was. What can we learn from Dr. Smith's approach to teaching and sharing the faith with the skeptics of our time?

33

Minister Moments

For I am not ashamed of the gospel, for it is the power
of God for salvation to everyone who believes.
—Romans 1:16

The Lincoln Way

Ministers can profoundly impact the faith development and spiritual growth of people, positively or negatively.

Throughout his life, Abraham Lincoln had many good and bad interactions with men of the cloth. During his presidency, along with so many other citizens and government officials, pastors constantly called on him unsolicited. Some preachers were rude and dogmatic. In September 1862, a group of Connecticut clergy demanded that Lincoln liberate the slaves. While agreeing with their sentiments, Lincoln did not execute their request, because of the precarious political realities and tenuous cohesion of the Union. Like the pope's bull against the comet, he explained, his decrees alone would not free the slaves, especially those held in Confederate states. Moreover, he could not remedy the slavery issue at the moment without fatally damaging the cause to save the Union. On another occasion when a visitor claimed to be the Son of God, Lincoln's secretary John Nicolay wisely sent the man away, wittily urging him to obtain a letter of recommendation from his father.[1] One minister who came to visit explained that he actually did not have much to say. He

[1] Szasz and Szasz, *Lincoln and Religion*, 30.

only wanted to pay his respects to the president. A relieved Lincoln thanked the man for not coming to preach at him.[2]

With men dying daily in furious battles or from disease in military camps, ministers were motivated to give Lincoln their strong, unvarnished opinions on the issues of the day. Even in congregations throughout the Union, the mere mention of prayer for the commander in chief resulted in expressions of contempt or the sudden exit of worshippers, doors slamming shut behind them.[3] The War Between the States, and those leading the fight, brought out the rawest emotions.

Perhaps in response to the criticism and unsolicited advice he received from some ministers, Lincoln had his own critiques of the clergy. Many of the United States Army chaplains, in his opinion, were out of touch and underqualified. He denounced some pastors, especially Northern Methodists, who acted as if they were the sole spokesmen and representatives of the American people. Moreover, he disapproved of clergymen who took too active a role in politics and lobbied more than they cared for their congregations. He generally preferred Episcopalians, compared to other denominations, because they tended to be neutral or indifferent to an individual's religion and politics.[4]

The back and forth between the president and religious leaders never ceased. After Lincoln issued the Emancipation Proclamation in late September 1862, the Reverend Dr. Byron Sunderland visited the president as the New Year approached. He told the president that he and many others were praying for Lincoln to do the right thing—to keep moving forward with complete emancipation. The right thing, Lincoln responded, is not always so obvious. Both Northerners and Southerners prayed that their cause would be sanctioned by God and victorious. He added that he wished that the war could be settled

---

[2] Burlingame, *Lincoln*, 2:255.

[3] Lachman, *The Last Lincolns*, 30.

[4] Szasz and Szasz, *Lincoln and Religion*, 31.

without carnage and loss of life, but for some divine reason, the violence and killing were continuing. Sometimes God's plans were hard to discern.[5]

On New Year's Eve 1862, three clergy visited Lincoln and urged him to carry out God's will by extending the Emancipation Proclamation to the whole country, not just Confederate-held territory. Lincoln insisted that he too opposed slavery, but could not discern God's views and feelings on the matter. After all, Lincoln wanted the war ended with the Union fully intact and slavery eradicated. Obviously his views were not God's plans or desires. Lincoln conceded that God might look at the peculiar institution differently than he did. He added that just because slaves would be declared free, that would not actually make them free—at least at first. If a court maintained that a calf had five legs because they counted the tail as a leg, that did not make the tail an actual leg, Lincoln explained. As he ushered the trio of ministers out of his office, he good-naturedly teased them, saying he enjoyed receiving a delegation from God. One of the visitors, Reverend William Goodell, expressed admiration for the president's candor and sincerity as well as his willingness to listen to their frank and earnest comments.[6]

By and large, Union clergy respected Lincoln for his moral courage and actions. In their sermons, tracts, and newspapers, Protestant ministers praised his honesty, determination, and dogged patriotism. As president, he set aside more days for national religious observances, including the first Thanksgiving, than any of his

---

[5] Burlingame, *Lincoln*, 2:468. A year earlier Lincoln had a similar chat with Orville H. Browning, a Republican senator from Illinois, one Sunday afternoon in the White House library. Browning said the North had to rid itself of slavery or God would not help the Union cause. Turning the argument on its head, the President offered the counter-argument: What if God favored the Confederate view of slavery and the rebel cause? The senator said Lincoln's reply demonstrated his deep thinking and reflection on God's will and His intervention in history.

[6] Burlingame, *Lincoln,* 2:468.

predecessors. Bishop Charles McIlvaine especially thanked Lincoln "for what has never come into a Proclamation from that high seat of authority before"—invoking the Holy Spirit to change the hearts of the insurgents in the July 1863 Proclamation of Thanksgiving.[7] They noticed and appreciated that many of his orders included respect and reverence for the Sabbath and worship. The importance "of the prescribed weekly rest" and "deference to the best sentiment of a Christian people, and due regard for divine will," Lincoln wrote in a typical order, "demand that Sunday labor in the Army and Navy be reduced to the measure of strict necessity."[8]

Through almost daily interactions with ministers, Lincoln demonstrated his deep familiarity with Scripture and a growing affection for pastors who truly ministered and nurtured his spiritual growth. He supported Christian missionaries, called for and funded military chaplains, requested more ministers for hospitals, supported the work of the Young Men's Christian Association (YMCA) among the troops, and approved a bill that placed, for the first time, the slogan "In God We Trust" on a coin of the United States.[9]

Lincoln's relationships with clergymen also compelled him to reflect on his own faith. Lincoln spent a lot of time with Reverend Owen Lovejoy during the war. After seeing the mangled corpse of his brother, Elijah, who had been brutally murdered by a proslavery mob in Alton, Illinois, in 1837, Reverend Lovejoy vowed to fight against slave power and eradicate the peculiar institution. In addition to their shared abhorrence of slavery, Lincoln and Lovejoy had other things in common. Both were Republican, loved a good story, possessed a similar sense of humor, and resided in Illinois (Lovejoy served at the Congregational Church in Princeton, Illinois, for seventeen years). By the time of the Civil War, now Congressman Lovejoy had become a close friend, confidant, and counselor to

[7] Carwardine, "Lincoln's Religion," 245–46.

[8] Basler, Lincoln's Order for Sabbath Observance, November 15, 1862, *CW*, 5:497.

[9] Mansfield, *Lincoln's Battle with God*, 128; Jones, *Lincoln and the Preachers*, 79.

the president. Lovejoy believed his friend had been sent by God to liberate the slaves. Lincoln considered Lovejoy "the best friend" he had in Congress. When Lovejoy became bedridden with a sickness that would eventually take his life, Lincoln visited him regularly.[10]

Episcopal bishop Henry B. Whipple also had an important influence on Lincoln. The deadliest massacre on United States soil, prior to 9/11, took place in Minnesota during the summer and fall of 1862. Known as the Sioux Uprising or Dakota War of 1862, the Sioux—angry at white encroachment on their territory, the government's failure to deliver promised supplies and money, and the rampant corruption of Indian agents and traders—launched savage attacks on white settlers, including women and children, along the frontier. They killed hundreds, captured over three hundred women and children, and drove over thirty thousand white settlers from their homes. Children were nailed alive to trees and houses; women were violated and then disemboweled.

After Lincoln dispatched General John Pope to restore order, the Sioux Rebellion ceased by early October. Out of 303 Sioux who were condemned, Lincoln authorized only thirty-seven to be executed. Even though Lincoln's own grandfather had been killed by Indians in Kentucky many decades earlier, and despite his uncle Mordecai's fierce hatred of Indians because of this episode, Lincoln offered clemency to the other Sioux, primarily because of Bishop Whipple's influence. Whipple agreed that the Sioux must be punished but did not want to respond so cruelly as to inspire a long-term Indian war or to incur the wrath of God. Lincoln respected Whipple's courage in taking an unpopular position motivated by his faith.[11]

---

[10] Jones, *Lincoln and the Preachers*, 63–64, 68–69.

[11] Burlingame, *Lincoln*, 2:483. Commissioner of Indian Affairs, William P. Dole, added that executing all the condemned men would be contrary to the spirit of the times and out of character for a Christian nation which believed in forgiveness and second chances. Miller, *Lincoln's Virtues*, 36. The murder of Lincoln's grandfather altered the course of his father's life—plunging him into poverty at only eight years of age.

In his annual message to Congress late in 1863, Lincoln noted that treaties and order had been restored in the region. He hoped that the government would give "constant attention" to the "well-being" of the Native American tribes, their "progress in the arts of civilization and, above all, to that moral training which, under the blessing of Divine Providence, will confer upon them the elevated and sanctifying influences, the hopes and consolation of the Christian faith."[12]

While his attendance at First Presbyterian Church in Springfield had been inconsistent, President Lincoln regularly attended worship services and Wednesday prayer meetings at the nearby New York Avenue Presbyterian Church in Washington, DC. He had asked friends and associates for a church led by a pastor who detached himself from politics—someone like Dr. Phineas Gurley. The entire Lincoln family felt at home in Gurley's congregation. Mary and Abe purchased a pew and gave generously to the church, while Willie and Tad faithfully attended Sunday school. Willie even participated in the Youth Ministry Society, which raised money to support missionaries in China.[13]

Educated, intelligent, theological, principled, humble, and gifted in oratory, Gurley possessed attributes and qualities Lincoln deeply admired. A graduate of Princeton and Union College (NY), former chaplain in the United States Senate, and shepherd of a healthy congregation in Ohio before he moved to the nation's capital, Gurley spoke energetically, forcefully, and "with an authoritative air of sincerity," Lincoln told his secretary John Jay. Moreover, his "preaching was confined with remarkable closeness to the great central doctrine of the cross."[14] Lincoln told another associate, "I

---

[12] Basler, Lincoln's Annual Message to Congress, December 8, 1863, *CW*, 7:47–48.

[13] Mansfield, *Lincoln's Battle with God*, 125, 212; Burlingame, *Lincoln*, 2:256; Szasz and Szasz, *Lincoln and Religion*, 43; White, *Lincoln*, 404.

[14] Guelzo, *Lincoln*, 321.

like Gurley. He don't preach politics. I get enough of that through the week."[15]

Gurley's messages focused on God's inscrutability and loving providence in the world—how man proposes and God disposes. With Lincoln in attendance on August 6, 1863, Gurley preached a sermon in response to Lincoln's recent call for a national day of public humiliation, prayer, and fasting. The sermon, "Man Projects and God Results," found its inspiration in Proverbs 16:9 (KJV): "A man's heart deviseth his way; but the Lord directeth his steps." Gurley's contention that God accomplishes "His fixed eternal purposes through the instrumentality of free, and accountable, and even *wicked* agents" resonated with the wartime commander in chief who endured reports of human casualties almost daily.[16]

When Willie Lincoln died, Gurley led the funeral service. The minister acknowledged that in addition to the "unprecedented weight" of the Civil War, Lincoln now had to endure "the burden of this domestic sorrow." For the grieving family, Gurley promised that God's grace would be sufficient for them, "and that in this hour of sore bereavement and trial they may have the presence and succor of Him Who said: 'Come unto Me all ye that labor and are heavy laden and I will give you rest.'" Like others who suffered loss, God would be "their truest refuge and strength and a very present help in trouble." Gurley highlighted many pleasant things about the "excellent qualities of mind and heart" that "greatly endeared" Willie to so many.[17] Substantive, heartfelt, compassionate, and theologically sound, Gurley's words made a significant difference in the life of the Lincolns.

Shortly after Willie's death, the Lincolns gave Reverend Dr. Gurley an ebony cane. "Rev. P.D. Gurley, D.D. from Mr. and Mrs. Abraham Lincoln 1862" had been inscribed on the gold head.

---

15 White, *Lincoln*, 626.

16 White, *Lincoln*, 404, 625–27.

17 Jones, *Lincoln and the Preachers*, 37–38.

Reverend Dr. James Smith and Reverend Dr. Phineas Gurley were the only two ministers who were honored by gifts of gold-headed canes from the Lincolns.[18]

Forged by the tragic death of Willie, Gurley and Lincoln thereafter developed an intimate friendship, and the minister became a frequent guest in the Executive Mansion. Lincoln faithfully attended Gurley's private prayer sessions on Wednesday evenings, and the president once told the pastor that he needed and depended on prayer during the tumultuous days of the Civil War. The skeptical, disdainful Lincoln appeared to have completely vanished by this time in his life. Talking *with* God now reigned over mocking or even talking *about* God.[19]

With Willie's passing, the rising death toll from war, and his own twilight on the horizon, Lincoln pondered the afterlife more frequently as he continued to read Scripture and receive Gurley's pastoral counseling. One morning a congregational member saw Gurley leaving the Executive Mansion. The parishioner wanted to know what Gurley had been doing. "Mr. Lincoln and I have been having a morning chat," Gurley responded.

"On the war, I supposed?"

"Far from it," Gurley asserted. "We have been talking about the state of the soul after death. That is a subject of which Mr. Lincoln never tires. I have had a great many conversations with him on the subject. This morning, however, I was a listener, as Mr. Lincoln did all the talking." Lincoln believed his son Willie was in heaven.[20]

Shortly after Lincoln was shot at Ford's Theatre and taken across the street to William Petersen's home, Dr. Gurley arrived at the horrific scene. After lying diagonally on a bed for nearly nine hours, Lincoln was dead; his labored breathing had finally stopped. Edwin

---

18 Jones, *Lincoln and the Preachers,* 39-–40.

19 Trueblood, *Lincoln: Lessons in Spiritual Leadership*, 85.

20 Mansfield, *Lincoln's Battle With God*, 144.

Stanton, Lincoln's secretary of war, asked Gurley to offer up a prayer, with the sobs of twenty-one people in the background.[21]

Though his friend had died, Gurley's relationship with the Lincoln family did not end. After Lincoln's passing, Gurley escorted Mary back to the Executive Mansion and encountered Tad. "Where is my Pa? Where is my Pa" Tad repeatedly cried. Gurley told the young lad that his fathered had died. "Oh what shall I do? What shall I do?" Tad wailed inconsolably. "My brother is dead. My father is dead. O what shall I do?" Tad's grief immediately expanded into fear. "What will become of me? O what shall I do?" he exclaimed. "O mother you will not die will you? O don't you die Ma. You won't die will you mother? If you die I shall be all alone. O don't die Ma." Hearing Tad's raw and considerable grief, the normally steadfast Dr. Gurley broke down too.[22]

Sixty clergymen, accompanied by over six hundred military and government officials, attended the president's funeral services in the East Room of the Executive Mansion on April 19, 1865.[23] Mary Lincoln did not attend, her grief too much to overcome.

Dr. Gurley gave the funeral sermon and memorial tribute, printed in full in the April 20, 1865, edition of the *New York Times.* He noted the cruel timing of the assassination—when the war had ended, when peace and hope were just breaking through. He praised Lincoln's character, tone, kindness, truthfulness, integrity, and spirit of life. He also explained how the president had leaned on God for consolation and strength and witnessed God's hand acting throughout history and in the war. Gurley said that he often saw Lincoln, firsthand, rely on God's guidance and mercy, which "were the best hope he had for himself and for his country." He had no doubt that God had raised up Lincoln for this moment in history and used him as an instrument of His plans.

---

21 Canavan, *Lincoln's Final Hours*, 118; Donald, *Lincoln*, 599.

22 Manning, *Father Lincoln*, 180.

23 Jones, *Lincoln and the Preachers*, 41.

Lincoln's steady confidence in God, and in the belief that truth and justice would unfold according to God's plans and ultimately prevail, strengthened and carried Lincoln during the darkest days, even when others doubted. Lincoln's optimism endured throughout the war because he believed that God had sided with the Union cause. Lincoln's "sublime and holy faith," explained Gurley, "became an anchor to his soul, both sure and steadfast." His faith in God "made him firm and strong" and "emboldened him in the pathway of duty, however rugged and perilous it might be." Lincoln believed that God remained on his side, no matter the setbacks, and this inspired and encouraged Lincoln's resiliency, steadiness, and unflinching desire to see the war through to a victorious end.

As great as Lincoln's accomplishments had been in freeing the slaves and saving the Union, Gurley felt that even more "sublime … more holy and influential, more beautiful, and strong, and sustaining, was his abiding confidence in God and in the final triumph of truth and righteousness through Him and for His sake. This was his noblest virtue, his grandest principle, the secret alike of his strength, his patience, and his success." Having associated with Lincoln often over the last four years, Gurley insisted that Lincoln's confidence and faith in God, and that good would prevail over evil, remained the strongest principle and legacy that Lincoln had left. Gurley repeatedly mentioned how Lincoln wanted his fellow Americans to "have faith in God." Lincoln may be dead, "but the God in whom he trusted lives."[24]

As Lincoln's casket traveled over seventeen hundred miles via a circuitous route back to Springfield, Gurley traveled with the funeral party. Several pastors participated in Lincoln's funeral service in Springfield. Reverend Albert Hale spoke the prayers. Reverend R. W. Miner read the first chapter of John's Gospel. Reverend A. C. Hubbard recited the words of Lincoln's second inaugural address.

---

24 Gurley, "White House Funeral Sermon for President Lincoln," http://www.abrahamlincolnonline.org/lincoln/speeches/gurley.htm

Bishop Matthew Simpson of the Methodist Church, one of Lincoln's closest friends and esteemed counselors, gave a moving funeral oration. After the hymn "Praise God from Whom All Blessings Flow," Dr. Gurley gave the benediction.[25]

Gurley later indicated that he believed Lincoln had become a traditional Christian and had even made plans to make that information public. Gurley asserted that Lincoln had been "sound not only on the truth of the Christian religion but on all its fundamental doctrines and teaching." Especially after the death of Willie and Lincoln's visit to the battlefield of Gettysburg, Gurley reported that Lincoln had told him that "he had lost confidence in everything but God, and that he now believed his heart was changed, and that he loved the Savior, and if he was not deceived in himself, it was intention soon to make a profession of religion."[26] Gurley's words led to speculation that Lincoln had planned to be baptized, but there

---

[25] Owen, *The Man and His Faith*, 221.

[26] Mansfield, *Lincoln's Battle with God*, 169–70, 187. Major General Daniel Edgar Sickles's testimony on Lincoln visiting him after he lost his leg, on the second day of the Battle of Gettysburg, corroborates Gurley's contention that Gettysburg had a profound impact on Lincoln's faith development. When Lincoln visited the injured general, Sickles asked Lincoln how he felt during the battle. Lincoln told Sickles that "in the pinch of your campaign up there, when everybody seemed panic-stricken, and nobody could tell what was going to happen, oppressed by the gravity of our affairs, I went into my room one day and locked the door and got down on my knees before Almighty God and prayed to him mightily for victory at Gettysburg. I told him this was his war and our cause, but that we couldn't stand another Fredericksburg or Chancellorsville. And I then and there made a solemn vow to Almighty God that if he would stand by our boys at Gettysburg, I would stand by him. And he did, and I will. And after that, I don't know how it was and I can't explain it, but soon a sweet comfort crept into my soul that things would go all right at Gettysburg, and this is why I had no fears about you." Sickles then asked about the looming battle at Vicksburg, and Lincoln responded that he had "been praying over Vicksburg also and believe our Heavenly Father is going to give us victory there too because we need it in order to bisect the Confederacy and have the Mississippi flow unvexed to the sea."

is no corroborating evidence to support the claim. Whatever Lincoln intended or truly believed, there is no doubt that the Dr. Gurley had a profound impact on the life and spiritual growth of the nation's sixteenth president.

Bishop Matthew Simpson, one of Lincoln's closest friends and unofficial advisors in the Executive Mansion, gave the funeral oration at Lincoln's burial service at Oak Ridge Cemetery in Springfield, Illinois, on May 4, 1865. Inspired by Simpson's address to the Missionary Society of the Methodist Church in 1863, Lincoln had joined the society and agreed to serve on its board of directors.[27] Labeled the "the Patrick Henry of American Methodism" due to his eloquence, Simpson shared Lincoln's loyalty to the Union and disdain for slavery. He visited the Executive Mansion often, and Lincoln cherished the minister's advice on politics, especially as the election of 1864 approached.[28] During his funeral sermon, Simpson shared that "Abraham Lincoln was a good man; he was known as an honest, temperate, forgiving man; a just man; a man of noble heart in every way."[29] Simpson admitted that "as to his religious experience I cannot speak definitely, because I was not privileged to know much of his private sentiments." He did know, however, that Lincoln "read the Bible frequently, loved it for its great truths, and he tried to be guided by its precepts. He believed in Christ the Saviour of Sinners, and I think he was sincere in trying to bring his life in harmony with the principles of revealed religion. Certainly if there ever was a man who illustrated some of the principles of pure religion, that man was our departed President."

Simpson stated, "As a ruler, I doubt if any President has ever shown such trust in God, or in public documents so frequently referred to divine aid." The president often remarked to friends and

---

27 Smith, *Faith and the Presidency*, 111.

28 Szasz and Szasz, *Lincoln and Religion*, 15–16.

29 Jones, *Lincoln and the Preachers*, 60. The quotes for the remainder of this paragraph and the next come from this source.

delegations "that his hope for our success rested in his conviction that God would bless our efforts because we were trying to do right."

Being on God's side became more important to Lincoln as the Civil War raged on. When a preacher commented that he hoped that God favored the Union, Lincoln responded, "I am not at all concerned about that, for I know that the Lord is always on the side of right. But it is my constant anxiety and prayer that I and this nation should be on the Lord's side."[30] The infidel of New Salem and skeptic of Springfield had come a long way in his spiritual journey and faith walk.

Many of Lincoln's closest friends and contemporaries were, indeed, struck by his faith development and growth in the late 1850s and during his presidency. John Wickizer, a fellow lawyer who knew the Lincolns well in the late 1850s, insisted that Lincoln "was *naturally* religious, but very liberal in his views." Nevertheless, "he believed in 'Jesus Christ, and him crucified.'"[31] Lincoln's close friend, Noah Brooks, asserted that "prayer and the reading of Scripture was his constant habit." Brooks claimed that Lincoln could quote whole chapters of Isaiah, the New Testament, and the Psalms. He reported that Lincoln could also recognize when someone misquoted the Bible and usually offered chapter and verse where the correct words could be found. Lincoln's ability to seamlessly work biblical phrases and concepts into his daily vocabulary, letters, and conversations with great ease was truly impressive even to well-versed religious leaders and clergy. Often times only well-trained ministers and pastors could understand his theological references or points.[32]

Perhaps the testimony of Lincoln's best friend, Joshua Speed, is most illustrative of Lincoln's deepening faith and spiritual growth. After Lincoln passed, Speed acknowledged that when he first met and knew Lincoln in Springfield, "he was skeptical as to the great

---

[30] Carpenter, *Six Months at the White House*, 299.
[31] Wilson, *Herndon's Informants*, 516.
[32] Mansfield, *Lincoln's Battle with God*, 153.

truths of the Christian religion." Years later, however, "after he was elected President, he sought to become a believer—and to make the Bible a preceptor to his faith and a guide for his conduct."[33]

While many of his friends and close associates noticed a spiritual change in Lincoln over the years, Lincoln's faithful and daily reading of Scripture, reinforced by caring, highly intelligent, and personable pastors who interacted with and ministered to him almost daily, made a significant impact on the president's faith life. Reverend Noyes Minor, a Baptist pastor and friend of Lincoln's during his Springfield days, visited Lincoln in the Executive Mansion in April, 1862. Minor made notes of his conversation with the president that day, recalling how Lincoln treasured "the prayers of God's people" during the pressures and hardships of the Civil War. Lincoln believed that God had placed him in his present position. Therefore he would continue "looking up to Him for wisdom and divine guidance" as he worked to fulfill his destiny. Years later Minor asserted that during his long and intimate acquaintance with Lincoln, and the many conversations he had with him from time to time, on numerous subjects, he "never heard a word fall from his lips that gave me the remotest idea that his mind was ever tinctured with infidel sentiments." Minor noticed quite the contrary: "The more intimate I became acquainted with him, the more deeply was I impressed with

---

[33] Wilson, *Herndon's Informants*, 156--158. In the same interview, Speed reported these words from Lincoln: ""Speed die when I may I want it said of me by those who know me best to say that I always plucked a thistle and planted a flower where I thought a flower would grow.'" Speed also shared a touching story about his mother and friend. "There are some traits of character for which Lincoln was peculiar above all I have ever known—He never forgot any thing especially any personal kindness. An instance of this. When he was in Ky in 1841 he was moody & hypochondriac. He was staying at the house of my Mother. She observed him and one morning when they were alone presented him with a Bible. Years rolled around & he was President. The old lady sent him word that she wanted his Photograph. He sent it with this sentence. 'To my very good friend Mrs Lucy G Speed who gave me an Oxford Bible twenty years ago. A Lincoln.'"

the conviction that he believed not only in the overriding Providence of God, but in the Divinity of the Sacred Scriptures, and had a profound reverence for everything true, and noble, and good … If Mr. Lincoln was not a Christian, he was acting like one."[34]

The death of his religious son, Willie, during the middle of a presidency filled with casualty and death told reports also caused Lincoln to listen and cling to the words of ministers more intently than at any other time in his life. After Willie had suffered and died, Dr. Francis Vinton, an eloquent preacher at Trinity Episcopal Church on Broadway in New York City, came to visit the Lincolns. A former West Point cadet and student at Harvard Law School, Dr. Vinton lovingly chided Lincoln for "showing so rebellious a disposition to the decrees of Providence and for mourning too somberly after Willie death." Dr. Vinton told Lincoln "that the indulgence of such feelings, though natural, was sinful" and "unworthy" of a faithful Christian. Lincoln "had duties to the living, greater than those of any man, as the chosen father, and leader of the people, and he was unfitting himself for his responsibilities by thus giving way to his grief." Dr. Vinton summarized and clarified his position in one sentence to his friend: "To mourn the departed as *lost* belong to heathenism—not to Christianity." Indeed, Dr. Vinton told Lincoln that his son *lived* in heaven. "Do you remember that passage in the Gospels," he reminded the president, which said that "'God is not the God of the *dead* but of the living, for *all* live unto him?'" When Lincoln questioned, as a weakened father might do, the certainty of Willie living in heaven, Dr. Vinton remained adamant: "No sir, believe me, it is a most comforting doctrine of the church, founded on the words of Christ himself."

Lincoln then got off the sofa, approached the clergyman, and threw his arms around him and sobbed in his breast. *"Alive? Alive?"* he president repeated.

[34] Mansfield, *Lincoln's Battle with God*, 107, 144—145.

"My dear sir," affirmed Dr. Vinton, "believe this, for it is God's most precious truth. Seek not your son among the dead; he is not there; he lives to-day in Paradise!" Dr. Vinton then shared Scripture passages that affirmed what he had just told Lincoln. God is "not the God of the dead," continued Dr. Vinton, "but of the living, *for all live unto him!*" Perhaps God had "called your son into his upper kingdom—a kingdom and an existence as real, more real, than your own." Perhaps Willie, "like Joseph, has gone, God's good providence, to be the salvation of *his* father's household." After He offered to send Lincoln a sermon on the topic. Lincoln asked him to send it immediately. Lincoln read and reread the sermon, and eventually made a copy for his own private use before returning the original. Though he certainly continued to mourn the death of his son, his cheerfulness began to return.[35] And, at about this same time, Lincoln firmly established an early morning hour of Bible reading and prayer.[36]

A little over four years after Lincoln had been assassinated, Mary Lincoln penned a letter to Reverend Dr. James Smith, who had played such a significant role in bringing Lincoln back to the Christian faith during the 1850s. Upset at William Herndon's research and claims of her husband's religious infidelity, Mrs. Lincoln wanted Dr. Smith to help set the record straight. Smith, "who knew him so well & held so many conversations, with him, as far back as twenty years since," should know that her husband, a man who "never took the name of his Maker in vain, who always read his Bible diligently, who never failed to rely on God's promises & looked up to him for protections, surely a man as this, could not have been a disbeliever, or any other but what he was, a true Christian gentlemen." Mrs. Lincoln explained that after their Eddie died in early February 1850, her "husband's heart was directed towards religion & as time passed on." When he became president and dealt with the stresses of office

---

[35] Carpenter, *Six Months at the White House*, 138–140.

[36] Owen, *The Man and His Faith*, 142.

and Civil War, "then indeed to my own knowledge, did his great heart go up daily, hourly, in prayer to God for his sustaining power." She added, "When too, the overwhelming sorrow came upon us, our beautiful bright, angelic boy, Willie, was called away from us, to his Heavenly Home, with God's chastising hand upon us, he turned his heart to Christ."[37]

While Lincoln's precise religious beliefs—particularly on Jesus's divinity and other orthodox tenets such as the forgiveness of sins and resurrection of Christ—remain an ongoing debate among biographers, there is clear historical evidence that ministers had a profound impact on Lincoln's outlook. As the years of his presidency unfolded, Lincoln frequently referenced his growing intimacy and confidence in God—often confiding his thoughts to clergymen. Lincoln's Heavenly Father, no deistic God nor detached and disinterested earthly father, cared for His children and guided them in their earthly journey. "That the Almighty does make use of human agencies, and directly intervenes in human affairs, is one of the plainest statements of the Bible," Lincoln proclaimed near the end of his life. "I have had so many evidences of His direction, so many instances when I have been controlled by some other power than my own will, that I cannot doubt that this power comes from above. I am satisfied that when the Almighty wants me to do or not do a particular thing, he finds a way of letting me know it." Confident that God's plans were to "restore the Union," the president believed that God "will do it in His own good time." In the meantime, "we should obey and not oppose his will."[38]

Despite his prodigious emotional intelligence, Lincoln learned that he could not lean on his own understanding of the world. Slavery, war, death—these were real-world problems that could not be understood or solved by human rationality alone. Lincoln found solace and contentment in the words of Scripture as well as the

---

[37] Mary Lincoln to James Smith, June 8, 1870, *Mary Todd Lincoln*, 567—568.

[38] Mansfield, *Lincoln's Battle with God*, 150.

biblical messages many clergymen shared with him daily. These intimate relationships made an impact on Lincoln's worldview and bolstered his leadership during the nation's gravest crisis.

The Truth

You are either moving closer to God or further away from Him. While Lincoln never formally declared his precise religious views or officially joined a church, we know that he read the Bible daily and attended church more regularly later in life. Since faith comes from hearing and receiving the Word of God,[39] and God's Word, through the power of the Holy Spirit, does not return to Him empty, but accomplishes God's will and purpose,[40] it is more than plausible that the Holy Spirit transformed Lincoln's heart and mind as it does so many others. The Word of God has that kind of influence and power.

The Bible is full of verses that reveal the life-changing and life-saving power of God's Word. We are eternally grateful that God chose to communicate to us poor, miserable sinners through His Word. Indeed, "we also thank God constantly for this, that when you received the word of God … you accepted it not as the word of men but as what it really is, the word of God, which is at work in you believers."[41]

Whether we are mature Christians, new Christians, or those who are not yet Christians, God's Word truly speaks to and resonates with the soul. "Like newborn infants, long for the pure spiritual milk, that by it you may grow up into salvation—if indeed you have tasted that the Lord is good."[42] When we hear or receive God's Word, we also receive a peace, joy, and contentment that we cannot

---

[39] Rom. 10:17.

[40] Isa. 55:11.

[41] 1 Thess. 2:13.

[42] 1 Pet. 2:2–3.

find from anywhere or anyone else. The prophet Jeremiah said it this way: "Your words were found, and I ate them, and your words became to me a joy and the delight of my heart, for I am called by your name, O Lord, God of hosts."[43] The Bible fills us "with the knowledge of his will in all spiritual wisdom and understanding, so as to walk in a manner worthy of the Lord, fully pleasing to him, bearing fruit in every good work and increasing in the knowledge of God."[44]

In a changing, postmodern world in which fads come and go and everyone claims to have their own fluid truth—which could change the very next day—the Bible is clear that "the grass withers, the flower fades, but the word of our God will stand forever."[45] Amid all the chaos, craziness, and busyness of life, there is great comfort knowing that "Jesus Christ is the same yesterday and today and forever."[46] He died for your sins, rose again, and is with you today, guiding, leading, and encouraging you in this life as you await the life that is to come. Jesus said, "It is written, 'Man shall not live by bread alone, but by every word that comes from the mouth of God.'"[47] God's Word gives you just what you need each and every day. As the Psalmist so eloquently says, "Your word is a lamp to my feet and a light to my path."[48]

Pastors, preachers, priests, and ministers are the keepers and teachers of God's Word. For Lincoln, an effective minister made a significant difference in his life and spiritual wellness. "Remember your leaders, those who spoke to you the word of God," Scripture asserts. "Consider the outcome of their way of life, and imitate their

---

43 Jer. 15:16.

44 1 Col. 1:9–10.

45 Isa. 40:8.

46 Heb. 13:8.

47 Matt. 4:4.

48 Ps. 119:105.

faith."[49] Faithful and dedicated pastors are wonderful blessings who should be supported and affirmed for their service.

Whether you are a pastor or parishioner, take time to care for people and minister to them as so many preachers and ministers did for Lincoln. Hear these important words from Scripture:

> Put on then, as God's chosen ones, holy and beloved, compassionate hearts, kindness, humility, meekness, and patience, bearing with one another and, if one has a complaint against another, forgiving each other; as the Lord has forgiven you, so you also must forgive. And above all these put on love, which binds everything together in perfect harmony. And let the peace of Christ rule in your hearts, to which indeed you were called in one body. And be thankful. Let the word of Christ dwell in you richly, teaching and admonishing one another in all wisdom, singing psalms and hymns and spiritual songs, with thankfulness in your hearts to God. And whatever you do, in word or deed, do everything in the name of the Lord Jesus, giving thanks to God the Father through him.[50]

Your Life

Many clergymen made a significant impact on Lincoln's outlook on life. How have pastors, ministers, or other religious leaders specifically influenced your life?

---

49 Heb. 13:7.
50 Col. 3:12–17.

What characteristics or attributes did the ministers whom Lincoln admired possess? How did these characteristics allow them to build a close relationship with him? What lessons can you learn from this?

How can you support church workers?

34

Declarations of Dependence

Trust in the Lord with all your heart, and do
not lean on your own understanding.
—Proverbs 3:5

The Lincoln Way

All human beings need and depend on someone or something.

When Eliza Gurney and a small contingent of Quakers from Philadelphia visited the president in the Executive Mansion in October 1862, Lincoln expected to receive unsolicited advice or criticism about his job performance. After all, most people came to the Executive Mansion to tell him something. Gurney and her three associates, however, simply offered their support and prayers. As the Quakers kneeled and prayed silently, Lincoln bowed his head. When they shared a vocal prayer, beseeching God to provide wisdom and guidance for their commander in chief, tears ran down the president's cheeks. Lincoln appreciated their kindness and gesture of goodwill so much, he allowed them to stay much longer than the normal fifteen-minute allotment. He thanked Gurney for the "interview" as well as her prayers and sympathies. He also told her that as the country endured the "fiery trial," he had embraced "being a humble instrument in the hands of our Heavenly Father … to work out his great purposes." He would seek God's aid for all of his works and acts as commander in chief. If he failed, it would be God's will that he failed. While he had never wanted the war in the first place, Lincoln believed that God had permitted "it for some wise purpose of his own, mysterious and unknown to us." Human beings had "limited understandings" and should not try to comprehend the ways of God, but be content and confident that "he who made the world still governs it."[1] At the end of the "religious meeting," he asked Gurney to write him, and they began a correspondence.[2]

Several months later, Lincoln wrote Eliza Gurney, telling her that he had not forgotten—and "probably never shall forget"—her visit. He appreciated that her purpose had been "to strengthen my reliance on God." He was "much indebted to the good Christian people of the country for their constant prayers and consolations"—and none more than her. "The purposes of the Almighty are perfect, and must prevail, though we erring mortals may fail to accurately perceive them in advance," he reassured her. "We hoped for a happy termination of this terrible war long before this, but God knows best, and has ruled otherwise." Lincoln insisted that "we shall yet acknowledge His wisdom and our own error therein." In the meantime, "we must work earnestly in the best light He gives us, trusting that so working still conduces to the great ends He ordains." Surely God "intends some great good to follow this mighty convulsion, which no mortal could make, and no mortal could stay." He thanked Eliza for her "earnest prayers to our Father in Heaven."[3]

As he grew older, Lincoln's dependence on God, as well as his confidence in God's inscrutable ways and plans, increased and deepened. Even before his presidency began, evidence of Lincoln's growing reliance on God surfaced in numerous public speeches and settings. After leaving Springfield and during his train-whistle stops on way to the inauguration at Washington, DC, Lincoln told his fellow countrymen that he trusted in "Christianity, civilization

---

[1] Basler, Lincoln's Reply to Eliza Gurney, October 26, 1862, *CW*, 5:478.
[2] Trueblood, *Lincoln: Lessons in Spiritual Leadership*, 49–51.
[3] Basler, Lincoln to Eliza Gurney, September 4, 1864, *CW*, 7:535.

and patriotism,"[4] and in "the good sense of the American people … under the Providence of God, who has never deserted us."[5] Hearing Southern politicians and citizens calling for secession, Lincoln knew that Americans were nervous. The president-elect reassured them that he trusted "in that Supreme Being who has never forsaken this favored land," and that with God's assistance and guidance, he could not fail.[6] Indeed, Lincoln believed he had been selected by God to uphold the Union and Constitution as a "humble instrument in the hands of the Almighty" during those tumultuous times.[7]

On February 24, 1861, across Lafayette Square from the White House, Lincoln worshipped at St. John's Episcopal Church, already renowned as "the church of the presidents."[8] Two days later, in a report to Congress, he expressed gratitude to his countrymen for their confidence in him despite the "national perils" that were growing by the day. Nevertheless, "with a firm reliance on the strength of our free government" and "above all an unshakeable faith in the Supreme Ruler of nations," he accepted the trust the American people had placed in him.[9]

As Inauguration Day approached, political pressure continued to mount on the president-elect. Seven Southern states—South Carolina, Mississippi, Florida, Alabama, Georgia, Louisiana, and Texas—had already seceded from the Union. On the morning of March 4, 1861, at Willard's Hotel, Lincoln practiced reading his inaugural address to his family. Then he asked them to leave the

---

4 Basler, Lincoln Speech at Lafayette, Indiana, February 11, 1861, *CW*, 4:192.

5 Basler, Lincoln Speech at Cincinnati, OH, February 12, 1861, *CW*, 4:199.

6 Basler, Lincoln Speech at Buffalo, New York, February 16, 1861, *CW*, 4:220–21.

7 Basler, Lincoln's Address to the New Jersey Senate at Trenton, New Jersey, February 21, 1861, *CW*, 4:236.

8 Mansfield, *Lincoln's Battle with God*, 114–15.

9 Basler, Lincoln's Reply to the Committee of Congress Reporting the Electoral Count, February 26, 1861, *CW*, 4:246.

room so he could be alone. Mary Lincoln later recalled that she could hear her husband praying aloud, asking for God's grace and confidence for his first official presidential act.[10]

Protected by a large military force marshaled to protect the president from assassins, Lincoln delivered his inaugural address later that day, imploring both Northerners and Southerners to refrain from hostile action. "Intelligence, patriotism, Christianity, and a firm reliance on Him, who has never yet forsaken this favored land," he reminded his countrymen, "are still competent to adjust, in the best way, all our present difficulty." The president would "not assail" the South. Southerners had "no oath registered in Heaven to destroy the government, where I shall have the most solemn one to 'preserve, protect and defend' it."[11]

After Confederate guns opened fire on Fort Sumter in Charleston harbor and the Civil War officially commenced on April 12, 1861, Lincoln faced the most daunting task to ever confront an American president. As he executed his constitutional duties to preserve, protect, and defend the Union, Lincoln articulated his growing reliance on God.

In 1862, he wrote one delegation that "he was deeply sensible of his need of Divine assistance" as "an instrument of God's hands of accomplishing a great work." While God's way of accomplishing "the end" might "be different from theirs," he would earnestly and firmly rely "upon the Divine arm … to do his duty in the place to which he had been called."[12] Thanking the East Baltimore Conference of the Methodist Episcopal Church— "a body of intelligent Christian people"—for their encouragement and prayers, he assured them that "an all-wise Providence" continued to help him execute his duties.[13]

---

[10] Mansfield, *Lincoln's Battle with God*, 117.

[11] Basler, Lincoln's First Inaugural Address, March 4, 1861, *CW*, 4:270–72.

[12] Basler, Lincoln's Remarks to a Delegation of Progressive Friends, June 20, 1862, *CW*, 5:279.

[13] Basler, Lincoln to I. A. Gere, A. A. Reese, and George D. Chenoweth, May 15, 1862, *CW*, 5:215–216.

"You know I am not of a very hopeful temperament," Lincoln told Noyes W. Minor, a Springfield minister, in April 1862. "I can take hold of a thing and hold on a good while. But trusting in God for help," and believing that the Union "cause is just and right, I firmly believe we shall conquer in the end."[14]

To rely upon the arm or hand of God to execute his duties meant that Lincoln believed in an active, intervening God in human affairs, not some deistic, clockmaker deity who created the world and then left it to its own execution and development. A few months after the costly battles at Shiloh and the Seven Days battles on the Virginia Peninsula, Lincoln said that "the will of God prevails" in the world. Both the North and the South claimed to "act in accordance with the will of God." Lincoln believed; however, "one must be wrong. God can not be for, and against the same thing at the same time." Perhaps another divine possibility existed. "In the present civil war it is quite possible," Lincoln surmised, "that God's purpose is something different from the purpose of either party." He asserted, "God wills this contest, and wills that it shall not end yet … He could have either saved or destroyed the Union without a human contest. Yet the contest began. And having begun He could give the final victory to either side any day. Yet the contest proceeds."[15]

Lincoln's profound spiritual document "Meditation of the Divine Will" demonstrates how far he had moved away from a skeptic's fatalistic worldview to a more mature confidence in the providence and sovereignty of his Maker. The God of Christianity might sometimes act inscrutably or mysteriously for divine purposes, but He watches over his people with care and love nonetheless.[16]

The president acknowledged the conundrum that individuals from various religious denominations approached him "with the most opposite opinions and advice … who are equally certain that

---

14 Lehrman, *Lincoln "by littles,"* 71.

15 Basler, Lincoln's Meditation of the Divine Will, September 2, 1862, *CW*, 5:403–404.

16 White, *Lincoln*, 624–25; Wheeler, *Faith and Courage*, 24.

they represent the Divine will." He earnestly desired "to know the will of Providence in this matter," and if he could learn what he was supposed to do, he would do it. "These are not, however, the days of miracles," he maintained, and therefore he did not "expect a direct revelation." Defaulting to his lawyerly thinking, Lincoln could only "study the plain physical facts of the case, ascertain what is possible and learn what appears to be wise and right. The subject is difficult, and good men do not agree."[17]

When Lincoln decided to officially release the Emancipation Proclamation on January 1, 1863, after much debate with his cabinet throughout the fall of 1862, he privately told some cabinet officials that he had "*made the promise to myself, and (hesitating a little)—to my Maker.*"[18] When Secretary of Treasury Salmon Chase, asked Lincoln if he heard him correctly, Lincoln replied, "I made a solemn vow before God, that if General Lee was driven back from Pennsylvania, I would crown the result by the declaration of freedom to the slaves."[19] Gideon Wells, secretary of the navy, who was also at the meeting, recorded in his diary that Lincoln "remarked that he had made a vow, a covenant, that if God gave us the victory in the approaching battle he would consider it an indication of Divine will, and that it was his duty to move forward in the cause of emancipation."[20] Lincoln believed that God had decided in favor of the slaves. Thus, the Emancipation Proclamation, Lincoln's most renowned and crowning achievement, came to fruition in no small part because of a covenant he made with God.

As casualties and military disasters mounted well into 1863, Lincoln struggled to find a Union general who could lead competently and defeat Robert E. Lee's Army of Northern Virginia. Yet as the pressure and criticism increased on the commander in chief, so

---

[17] Basler, Lincoln's Reply to Emancipation Memorial Presented by Chicago Christians of All Denominations, September 13, 1862, *CW*, 6:114–15.

[18] Mansfield, *Lincoln's Battle with God*, 165.

[19] Carpenter, *Six Months at the White House*, 90.

[20] Mansfield, *Lincoln's Battle with God*, 166.

did his desire to "strengthen our reliance on the Supreme Being."[21] Thankful and gratified that Christians remained loyal to him and the Union cause, he reiterated that "our great struggle" would depend on "Divine interposition and favor." He would continue to rely "upon the Almighty Power," and the "support which I receive from Christian men" to end the rebellion.[22]

Once a self-proclaimed skeptic, Lincoln now cherished the loyalty and encouragement provided by "religious bodies of the country."[23] During "a time of the greatest difficulty that this country ever saw," he acknowledged "that nothing in my power whatever … would succeed without the direct assistance of the Almighty." Admitting that he wished he "was more devout man than I am," he remained grateful that "amid the greatest difficulties of my Administration," when he "could not see any other resort," he continued to place his "whole reliance in God, knowing that all would go well, and that He would decide for the right." No matter how bleak or desperate things became, or if "driven to the last resort," Lincoln proclaimed that "God is still my only hope."

As the war headed into the high-casualty months of 1864, Lincoln admitted to an associate that he did not control events, "but confess plainly that events have controlled me." God remained in control. "If God now wills the removal of a great wrong, and wills also that we of the North as well as you of the South, shall pay fairly for our complicity in that wrong," he went on, "impartial history will find therein new cause to attest and revere the justice and goodness of God."[24]

---

21 Basler, Lincoln to Reverend Alexander Reed, February 22, 1863, *CW*, 6:114–15.

22 Basler, Lincoln's Reply to Members of the Presbyterian General Assembly, June 2, 1863, *CW*, 6:244–45.

23 Basler, Lincoln's Remarks to Baltimore Presbyterian Synod, October 24, 1863, *CW*, 6:536–37. The remaining quotes in this paragraph all come from this source.

24 Basler, Lincoln to Albert G. Hodges, April 4, 1864, *CW*, 7:282.

Lincoln's trust in God and His will did not mean that the president remained free from torment and distress. The ironic and tragic circumstances were not lost on Lincoln. "Doesn't it strike you as queer that I, who couldn't cut the head off of a chicken, and who was sick at the sight of blood, should be cast into the middle of a great war, with blood flowing all around me?" he once asked Representative Daniel Voorhees of Indiana.[25] Yet here he presided as commander in chief during a civil war. Only daily Bible study soothed his conflicted soul while also providing a larger context.

Enduring the brutal casualty reports after the battles of the Wilderness, Cold Harbor, Petersburg, Fort Pillow, and Atlanta, as well as Sherman's March to Sea, during the summer and fall months of 1864, Lincoln desperately desired "the return of peace and good-will to our now unhappy country." Christians, he said, should feel duty-bound to "countenance and encourage any negotiations," which would "restore peace and union under the Constitution we have sworn to support and defend."[26]

Reelected as president in November 1864, Lincoln confided to Noah Brooks that he would be small-minded and egotistical "blockhead" if he ignored God's Word and will as he headed into his second term. He trusted God over men.[27] Grateful for the approval and confidence of the American electorate, Lincoln told Congress that he would continue to rely "on the Almighty Ruler who has so graciously sustained us so far" even as he faced "onerous and perplexing duties and responsibilities."[28]

As much as Lincoln depended on God's will to prevail and unfold according to His divine timeline, the commander in chief petitioned the Almighty often. Lincoln's wife, friends, and political associates

---

[25] Donald, *Lincoln*, 514.

[26] Basler, Lincoln to William B. Campbell and Others, October 22, 1864, *CW*, 8:63.

[27] Burlingame, *Lincoln*, 2:727.

[28] Basler, Lincoln's Reply to Notification Committee, March 1, 1865, *CW*, 8:326.

knew that Lincoln prayed frequently—at church, in private sessions with Dr. Gurley on Wednesday evenings, and even facedown on the floor in the Executive Mansion. John Nicolay called him a "praying man"[29] who often asked others to pray for him. Lincoln told Noah Brooks he often went to his knees because he had nowhere else to go. When reminded repeatedly that many Christians across the country were praying for him, he responded gratefully and acknowledged that he needed their prayers. The trials and tribulations of war remained a grueling and relentless Gethsemane for Lincoln.[30]

As arduous and exhausting as the war had become, the Scriptures and prayer bolstered the president. "I am upheld and sustained by the good wishes and prayers of God's people," Lincoln wrote early in 1863. "No one is more deeply than myself aware that without His favor our highest wisdom is but as foolishness and that our most strenuous efforts would avail nothing in the shadow of His displeasure." He would carry out God's will and would not undertake anything without asking for "His blessing." One thing all good men agreed upon "is imploring the gracious favor of the God of Nations upon the struggles our people are making for the preservation of their precious birthright of civil and religious liberty."[31]

An active prayer life reveals a personal dependence on a personal God. A deist would never offer up prayers of gratitude or ask for a guiding hand.[32] As Lincoln's spiritual life continued to grow, the personal expanded into the political and public. In one National Fast Day proclamation, for example, Lincoln publicly acknowledged that Almighty God is active "in all the affairs of men and of nations." Nations and individuals must "own their dependence upon the overruling power of God, to confess their sins and transgressions,

---

[29] Smith, *Faith and the Presidency*, 102.

[30] Smith, *Faith and the Presidency*, 102; Peterson, *Lincoln in American Memory*, 225.

[31] Basler, Lincoln to Caleb Russell and Sallie Fenton, January 5, 1863, *CW*, 6:39-–40.

[32] Trueblood, *Lincoln: Lessons in Spiritual Leadership*, 94–95.

in humble sorry, yet with the assured hope that genuine repentance will lead to mercy and pardon." They should also "recognize the sublime truth, announced in the Holy Scriptures and proven by all history, that those nations only are blessed whose God is the Lord." Lincoln explained that the United States had "been preserved, these many years, in peace and prosperity," and had "grown in numbers, wealth and power, as no other nation" had ever grown. "But we have forgotten God" and His "gracious hand which preserved us in peace, and multiplied and enriched and strengthened us." Americans had become "intoxicated with unbroken success" and "too self-sufficient to feel the necessity of redeeming and preserving grace, too proud to pray to the God that made us!" Lincoln implored the country to "humble ourselves before the offended Power, to confess our national sins, and to pray for clemency and forgiveness." If Americans prayed and confessed their sins to God, then they could "rest humbly in the hope authorized by the Divine teachings" and restore "our now divided and suffering Country, to its former happy condition of unity and peace."[33] Hardly the words of an infidel or doubter, the orthodox theological points in the proclamation could not have been made in a more lucid and incisive fashion by a well-educated minister.

In his Proclamation of a Day of Prayer on July 7, 1864, Lincoln encouraged American citizens "to implore the compassion and forgiveness of the Almighty" in hopes of bringing the war to an expedient end. They were "to implore Him as the Supreme Ruler of the World, not to destroy us as a people," but "to implore Him to enlighten the mind of the Nation to know and do His will … to implore Him in his infinite goodness to soften the hears, enlighten the minds, and quicken the consciences of those in rebellion." The proclamation extolled citizens "to assemble in their preferred places of public worship on that day, and there and then to render to the

[33] Basler, Lincoln's Proclamation Appointing a National Fast Day, March 30, 1863, *CW*, 6:155–56.

Almighty and Merciful Ruler of the Universe, such homages and such confessions, and to offer to Him such supplications."[34] Lincoln and the Union were depending and calling on God to help their cause.

During his forty-nine months as president, Lincoln issued nine separate calls to public penitence, fasting, prayer, and thanksgiving—two in 1861, one in 1862, three in 1863, and three in 1864—exceeding the total of any other president before or since. He was preparing a tenth public declaration at the time of his assassination.[35] As president and individual, Lincoln spoke openly about his dependence on God, giving future presidents a comfortable precedent and platform to embrace and call on prayer, divine guidance, and God without fear of embarrassment or ridicule.[36]

In 1863, Lincoln and his administration established national Thanksgiving Day as an annual holiday on the last Thursday of November.[37] The phrase "one nation, under God" was first articulated in the Gettysburg Address and later included in the American salute to the flag. The phrase "in God we trust" was first

---

34 Basler, Lincoln's Proclamation of a Day of Prayer, July 7, 1864, *CW*, 7:431–32.

35 Trueblood, *Lincoln: Lessons in Spiritual Leadership*, 97; McDonald, "Spiritual Growth of a Public Man," 101; Wheeler, *Faith and Courage*, 20.

36 Wheeler, *Faith and Courage*, 10. Wheeler contends that Lincoln was "the first openly Christian American president."

37 In the fall of 1863, Sara Josepha Hale, the editor of *Lady's Book*, proposed that the president set up a national celebration of Thanksgiving, which had only been sporadically observed since colonial days, and never at a set time. After victories at Gettysburg and Vicksburg, Lincoln was convinced there was much to be thankful for and agreed to her proposal. The annual day of Thanksgiving had been set (Wheeler, *Faith and Courage*, 26). The Thanksgiving declaration said that Americans should give thanks to "our beneficent Father." The proclamation also commended to God's care "all those who have become widows, orphans, mourners, or sufferers," and called on God "to heal the wounds of the nation" and restore it to "peace, harmony, tranquility and Union" (Goodwin, *Team of Rivals*, 577).

placed on an American coin.[38] "I have been driven many times upon my knees by the overwhelming conviction that I had nowhere else to go," Lincoln once admitted to Noah Brooks. "My own wisdom and that of all about me seemed insufficient for that day."[39] A statue of Lincoln on bended knee is located in the National Cathedral in Washington.

Lincoln came to view the Civil War as a divine intervention in human history, an event directed by God. "Fondly do we hope—fervently do we pray—that this mighty scourge of war may speedily pass away," he said toward the end of his second inaugural address. "Yet, if God wills that it continue … so still it must be said 'the judgments of the Lord, are true and righteous altogether.'"[40]

Lincoln's capacity for growth is one of the most remarkable features of his accomplished life. The Civil War, his crucible, only accelerated his spiritual development. Lincoln surrounded himself with men of faith in the Executive Mansion, and friends and associates noticed his religious inclination growing as the war progressed.[41] Lincoln supported churches and ministries that taught of a divine, resurrected Jesus Christ, and extolled a Bible that proclaimed Jesus Christ as God. The president read the Bible faithfully and prayed often. He certainly endured failures, yet he still led and lived with

---

[38] McDonald, "Spiritual Growth of a Public Man," 101–2.

[39] Szasz and Szasz, *Lincoln and Religion*, 44.

[40] Basler, Lincoln's Second Inaugural Address, March 4, 1865, *CW*, 8:333.

[41] Smith, *Faith and the Presidency*, 109. In the Executive Mansion, Lincoln surrounded himself by men of faith and selected individuals of strong religious convictions. Edward D. Neil, pastor of a number of prominent congregations and chaplain to a Minnesota regiment during the Civil War, was Lincoln's correspondence secretary. Quaker Isaac Newton served as the first commissioner of the Department of Agriculture. William Seward, Secretary of State, was an Episcopalian and Edwin Stanton a Presbyterian. Seward was well known for his argument that a "higher law" than the Constitution, the Bible, condemned slavery. Stanton frequently consulted with religious leaders and asked them to pray that God would guide the Union army.

the hope of a Christian who knew the ultimate fulfillment came at the end of a believer's faith walk on earth.

Lincoln's closest friend, Joshua Speed, who once believed Lincoln to be a religious skeptic, saw the change too. Speed saw how the Bible inspired the president's personal faith and guided his conduct.[42] Lincoln no longer mocked or questioned the validity of Christianity like he once did. Near the end of his life, he told Speed that one is better off without money than without religion.[43] The president even praised God for providing churches, and their parishioners' prayers, during "our great trial."[44]

Lincoln attended worship more frequently and regularly at the Old School Presbyterian Church on Washington's New York Avenue than he had before he came to the nation's capital. He continued to rely upon and find solace in Scripture. Elizabeth Keckley, Mary Lincoln's seamstress and intimate, crept behind Lincoln one night to see him reading intently from the book of Job. He remarked that "from the beginning" he had seen that "the issues of our great struggle depended on the Divine interposition and favor. If we had that all would be well." He talked of being a "humble instrument in the hands of our Heavenly Father." Even more significant, he used the possessive pronoun—"responsibility to my God," "promise to my Maker"—in ways that suggested a more personal relationship with God.[45]

Francis Carpenter, a painter who worked at the Executive Mansion for six months in 1864, also observed Lincoln's growing devotion to the Christian faith. He told William Herndon that Lincoln may have indeed been a skeptic before he became president. "But during the last four years of his life," Carpenter said, the president "passed

---

42 Mansfield, *Lincoln's Battle with God*, 108; Guelzo, *Lincoln*, 158, 312.

43 Wilson, *Herndon's Informants*, 476. Speed did add that while Lincoln "was a growing man in Religion," he was not sure if he was growing in the Christian religion.

44 Basler, Lincoln's Response to Methodists, May 18, 1864, *CW*, 7:351.

45 Carwardine, "Lincoln's Religion," 230–31.

through what few men could have experienced without growth and change." Carpenter thought that Dr. Vinton's contention that Lincoln had gone through a "process of chrystalization" (spiritually) after the 1860 presidential election seemed "rational and truthful." Had Herndon stayed in touch with Lincoln during the presidency, he would have found the president's "religious sentiments more fixed" and "possibly more *Christian*" than deistic.[46]

Carpenter also asserted that the "tenderness and humility of his [Lincoln's] nature would not permit the exposure of his inmost convictions, except upon the rarest of occasions, and to his most intimate friends." While the president might not have shown the emotion of charismatic Christians, "no man had a more abiding sense of his dependence upon God, or faith in the Divine government, and in the power and ultimate triumph of Truth and Right in the world."[47]

Carpenter's daily and close proximity to the president for six months in 1864 gave him special access and an insider's viewpoint into the life of Lincoln. The Reverend Mr. Willets, of Brooklyn, once told Carpenter of a discussion between a Christian woman and Lincoln on what constituted a true religious experience. One should acknowledge his sinfulness and weakness and, therefore, admit the need for a personal Savior. After hearing this explanation and pausing for a few moments, Lincoln hoped what she said "is really the correct view of this great subject" because then he could "say with great sincerity, that I hope I am a Christian." He further explained that until Willie died, he did not fully embrace this view. Willie's death, however, "overwhelmed me," and revealed his weakness as he had never "felt it before." His son's death had changed him. Acknowledging his change and personal growth in response to the

---

[46] Wilson, *Herndon's Informants*, 521.

[47] Carpenter, *Six Months at the White House*, 204–5.

tragedy, he insisted that his intention "for some time, at a suitable opportunity" was "to make a public religious profession."[48]

Short of a public confession of faith, Lincoln did seem to be growing more outspoken about his dependence on God and more comfortable with the promises of Christianity. After her husband's death, Mary Lincoln told Herndon that while her husband never joined a church, "he was a religious man always," and thought more about the Christian faith after Willie's passing. "He felt religious more than ever about the time he went to Gettysburg," she insisted. "He was not a technical Christian," but he did "read the bible a good deal in 1864."[49] Lincoln reportedly told Willie's nurse, Rebecca Pomeroy, and others that at the time of his first inauguration, he did not love Jesus as his Savior. When he stood on the battlefield of Gettysburg, however, he consecrated himself to Christ. Noah Brooks insisted that Lincoln came to believe in the saving knowledge of Christ, His atonement, the cross, and the power of prayer.[50]

As the horrific battles and casualties of 1864 passed and 1865 began, Lincoln continued to make bold declarations of dependence on God. Perhaps he did not publicly share his religious sentiments before he became president, or even prior to the 1864 presidential election, for fear of being charged with hypocrisy or political expediency. There is no doubt, however, that the death and destruction of the Civil War ravaged the commander in chief. By war's end, approximately 620,000 soldiers would die—almost two-thirds from the Union. Total Civil War deaths far exceeded America's dead in World War II (by almost 25 percent). In addition, the death toll had been personal for the Lincoln family. They lost close friends, they worried over their son Robert's service in the army, and their family ties had been divided by the war. While Mary Lincoln's oldest brother and the husband of a half sister joined the

---

48 Carpenter, *Six Months at the White House*, 205—206.

49 Wilson, *Herndon's Informants*, 360.

50 Smith, *Faith and the Presidency*, 105; Peterson, *Lincoln in American Memory*, 225.

Union army, three of her half brothers and the husbands of three of her half sisters joined the Confederates.[51] Criticism of his politics and decisions as commander in chief were relentless—sometimes fair but most of the time ludicrous.

Lincoln not only survived this crucible of leadership, however, but matured in his faith and trust in God over the duration of his presidency. "Never before," said Horace Greeley, editor of the New York *Tribune,* "did one so constantly and visibly *grow* under the discipline of incessant cares, anxieties and trials." A good man in 1861, Lincoln "worked his continued and unabated growth in mental and moral stature" to the very last day of his life.[52]

After the Confederate capital of Richmond fell and Lee surrendered, the Civil War finally came to a close. The healing of the nation, however, had only just begun. Fortunately for the Confederacy, Lincoln remained a forgiving man. He objected to hard-liners pushing retrospective oaths on Confederate states and individuals. A retrospective oath insisted that the state or individual had never left the Union in the first place and therefore had done nothing wrong. Lincoln found these retrospective oaths contrary to "the Christian principle of forgiveness on terms of repentance."[53] He understood the relationship between sin and redemption better than most.[54] "I am a patient man—always willing to forgive on the Christian terms of repentance, and also to give ample time for repentance" he had claimed a few years earlier.[55] Lincoln wanted to show mercy to the defeated adversary, even as many called for revenge when the suffering of Union soldiers in Libby Prison (Richmond, Virginia) became publicly disclosed. To those who wanted to punish the Confederates for their atrocities, Lincoln twice quoted the biblical injunction to not judge others unless they

---

51 McDonald, "Spiritual Growth of a Public Man," 93, 96–97.

52 Trueblood, *Lessons in Spiritual Leadership,* 103.

53 Basler, Lincoln to Edwin Stanton, February 5, 1864, *CW,* 7:169.

54 Meacham, *American Gospel,* 120.

55 Basler, Lincoln to Reverdy Johnson, July 26, 1862, *CW,* 5:343.

were willing to be judged by God in the same manner (Matt. 7:1).[56] God should and would ultimately render justice.

One of the many secondary tragedies of the horrific assassination of Lincoln is that the South lost one of its best friends in the North. Southerners knew it too. Inspired by a merciful God, Lincoln stood for peace, mercy, and forgiveness.[57]

As Lincoln's dependence on God grew, so too did his executive decisiveness. Once an infidel, he had changed and believed himself to be an instrument of God. Life circumstances, his relationships and interactions with clergymen and other Christians, and his daily Bible reading shaped his faith and helped him become more accepting of conventional orthodoxy and Protestantism. He understood the fallibility of humankind, which is one reason he remained humble throughout his life. Perhaps his Calvinist upbringing, adolescent rebellion, infidel tendencies, and enlightened anticlericalism in young adulthood and his realization of his own selfish ambitions and selfishness all combined to make him feel unworthy of God's grace. Perhaps the trauma of losing his mother, Ann Rutledge, and his own children hardened Lincoln's heart toward God, who did not seem that interested in a former rail-splitter. Wherever Lincoln had once been, by the end of his presidency, he now fully trusted God and did not need to know why everything unfolded the way it did.[58]

The historical record will always contain contrary viewpoints about Lincoln's personal faith because he *did* have contrary worldviews at different times in his life. Newton Bateman, in 1860, said that Lincoln had once told him, "I know there is a God, and that he hates injustice and slavery … I know that liberty is right,

---

56 Burlingame, *Lincoln*, 2:797.

57 Peterson, *Lincoln in American Memory*, 46.

58 McDonald, "Spiritual Growth of a Public Man," 99; Mansfield, *Lincoln's Battle with God*, 187; Szasz and Szasz, *Lincoln and Religion*, 82-–83; Trueblood, *Lincoln: Lessons in Spiritual Leadership*, 144; Guelzo, *Lincoln*, 461-–463; Smith, *Faith and the Presidency*, 126.

for Christ teaches it, and Christ is God."[59] Noah Brooks told a Congregationalist clergyman, Isaac Langworthy, "that I have a firm belief in Mr. Lincoln's saving knowledge of Christ; he talked always of Christ, his cross, his atonement; he prayed regularly, cast all his cares on God and felt inexpressible relief thereby." No concrete evidence of these claims exists and he could exaggerate his intimacy with Lincoln. William Herndon, on the other hand, became so infuriated with these kinds of testimonials that he went on his own obsessive quest to prove Lincoln was an infidel. He argued that "if Mr. Lincoln was really a converted man to the faith of three Gods, Revelation, Inspiration, Miraculous Conception, and their necessity, etc.," he would never have earnestly or publicly admitted it fearing a "mob furor." Yet Herndon would be surprised, in doing his own research, by the variance of reporting on Lincoln's faith—the growth and change that occurred in him after he left Springfield, and how little people knew of other certain aspects of Lincoln's life, such as Ann Rutledge, the near insanity after her death, his possible illegitimacy, his trapped marriage with Mary, and so much more.[60]

Biographers who zealously exaggerate or distort Lincoln's faith, or lack thereof, at the beginning or end of his life miss the process and the growth the man undertook, and we are the poorer for it.[61] Lincoln's spiritual journey is worth analyzing and reflecting upon because it is a trek being lived out by so many people today. Unorthodox views do not necessarily mean one is an unbeliever. Many of Lincoln's early reservations about religion—emotionalism, hypocrisy, ignorance, corruption of fire-and-brimstone preachers, miracles, claims of the inerrancy and revelation of Scripture—are still stumbling blocks for seekers and Christians today.[62]

As a seeker, however, Lincoln constantly sought the truth. Charles Zane, an attorney who knew Lincoln, reported that when

---

59 Guelzo, *Lincoln*, 442.

60 Guelzo, *Lincoln*, 442–443.

61 Mansfield, *Lincoln's Battle with God*, 192.

62 Fornieri, "Lincoln's Theology of Labor," 208.

Lincoln "spoke or reasoned he had a Strong desire to arrive at the truth … He loved the truth and hence he always Stated the Subjects of discussion and his propositions as well as those of his opponent with great fairness and clearness."[63] Perhaps, as he faithfully and regularly read the Bible—God's truth—the Holy Spirit compelled Lincoln's heart and convinced his mind.

"We will visit the Holy Land," Lincoln told his wife Mary in the president's box at Ford's Theatre moments before he was assassinated. "We will visit the Holy Land and see those places hallowed by the footsteps of the Savior. There is no place I so much desire to see as Jerusalem."[64] Many biographers and scholars exclude this episode because of their hesitation over Lincoln's religion, or perhaps because of their own biases on matters of religion and faith. Yet Mary Lincoln reported these words to Noyes W. Miner, pastor of First Baptist Church in Springfield, Illinois, in 1882. Of course we also know from the historical record that Lincoln had spoken to Mary about visiting the Holy Land on their carriage ride earlier on that fateful Good Friday too.

Which testimonies should biographers, scholars, and Lincoln followers rely on? Perhaps one's worldview and presuppositions will dictate one's response to the question. As for Lincoln, the evidence and truth are clear: as his life progressed, he grew in his dependence on God and the sacred words of Scripture. For the most brilliant, independent, and often skeptical of minds, this is quite the revelation.

The Truth

During the Civil War, Lincoln endured incredible hardship and psychological trauma. Yet he found the inspiration and strength, through prayer and the reading of Scripture, to push on until

63 Wilson, *Herndon's Informants*, 488.

64 Mansfield, *Lincoln's Battle with God*, xvii–xix.

the Union had won the Civil War. God's Word sustained and strengthened him when he needed it most.

How about you? Where do you turn when times are tough? To whom do you go to get your bucket filled when running on empty?

The Bible makes it clear that only God, through the power of the Holy Spirit, can regenerate and renew your spirit and soul in a transcendent way. In our fallen world, our bodies and society will continue to decay and fall into disrepair. God promises to sustain you. Therefore, even when times are tough, "we do not lose heart. Though our outer self is wasting away, our inner self is being renewed day by day. For this light momentary affliction is preparing for us an eternal weight of glory beyond all comparison, as we look not to the things that are seen but to the things that are unseen. For the things that are seen are transient, but the things that are unseen are eternal."[65]

Indeed, you can cast "all your anxieties on him, because he cares for you."[66] Know that God "will fight for you" as He does for all believers.[67] In fact, one reason we read all of God's Word—the Old and New Testaments—is because the Bible is so rich and filled with stories of how God rescued and redeemed the downtrodden, depressed, discriminated against, and demoralized. "For whatever was written in former days was written for our instruction," the Bible says, "that through endurance and through the encouragement of the Scriptures we might have hope."[68]

A pastor once told his Bible study class that he prayed for suffering so that he might grow closer to God. To which one of his attendees responded that he wanted to get closer to God, but not have to suffer! Perhaps this anecdote represents your feelings.

While the Bible does not encourage one to pray for suffering, God's Word does make it clear that all believers will suffer in our

---

[65] 2 Cor. 4:16–18.

[66] 2 Pet. 5:7.

[67] Exod. 14:14.

[68] Rom. 15:4.

fallen world and that suffering can be used for His purposes and good. In this way "we rejoice in our sufferings, knowing that suffering produces endurance, and endurance produces character, and character produces hope, and hope does not put us to shame, because God's love has been poured into our hearts through the Holy Spirit who has been given to us."[69] Christ-followers are to "rejoice in hope, be patient in tribulation, be constant in prayer."[70]

Many people in the world live for the moment or look for constant pleasure. Yet the world is decaying, fallen, and corrupt because of sin. While there is nothing wrong with the temporary enjoyment of pleasurable things, a mature Christian understands that life on earth will be filled with hardship, turmoil, and pain. Flawed, sinful humans cannot escape this truth.

Many people turn to vices such as drugs, sex, vile entertainment, and false gods to soothe their pain or fill their emptiness. Only a close, personal relationship with Jesus Christ can kill the pain and hardship in one's life. Only Jesus can give one true peace and rejuvenation. The Bible says that "if anyone is in Christ, he is a new creation. The old has passed away; behold, the new has come."[71] Those who know and receive Jesus Christ as Lord and Savior and "walk in him" will be "built up in him and established in the faith, just as you were taught, abounding in thanksgiving."[72] By the power of the Holy Spirit, "it is God who works in you, both to will and to work for his good pleasure."[73]

If you want to grow closer to Jesus and live with a peace and contentment that surpasses all human understanding, you have to listen to Him (receive His Word) and talk to Him (pray). "Let the word of Christ dwell in you richly," the Bible says, "teaching

---

69 Rom. 5:3–5.

70 Rom. 12:12.

71 2 Cor. 5:17.

72 Col. 2:6–7.

73 Phil. 2:13.

and admonishing one another in all wisdom, singing psalms and hymns and spiritual songs, with thankfulness in your hearts to God."[74] Just like your favorite appliance or machine must be plugged into an outlet or recharged every night, so too do you need to be plugged into and renewed in God's Word. "I am the vine; you are the branches," Jesus says to you. "Whoever abides in me and I in him, he it is that bears much fruit, for apart from me you can do nothing."[75] No matter your trials or tribulation, with Jesus you can weather any storm or hardship and even confront your fears and challenges with confidence. "Be strong and courageous," the Bible asserts. "Do not fear or be in dread of them, for it is the Lord your God who goes with you. He will not leave you or forsake you."[76] Indeed, nothing is impossible with God.[77]

Your Life

The casualties of the Civil War, along with the death of his son Willie, turned Lincoln's presidential years into the crucible or most trying time of his life. What has been the crucible in your life so far? What did you learn from your experience?

One of the themes in this chapter is Lincoln's dependence on God throughout his presidency. Our sinful nature, however, often causes us to depend on things rather than God. When you struggle or drift in your life, what things are you tempted to rely on rather than God?

---

[74] Col. 3:16.
[75] John 15:5.
[76] Deut. 31:6.
[77] Matt. 19:26.

What Bible verses comfort you most during your times of hardship?

Another major theme of this chapter is the growth and maturation of Lincoln's faith in God. What about you? Are you growing closer to God or more distant? Why? What do you plan to do about it?

35

Sermon for the Ages

Many are the plans in the mind of a man, but it
is the purpose of the Lord that will stand.
—Proverbs 19:21

The Lincoln Way

Often in leadership, less is more.

The fifty-six-year-old president who took the stage to give his second inaugural address on Saturday, March 4, 1865, looked drained and exhausted. His face showed deep ruts, sunken eyes, a pale complexion, and complete exhaustion. Overworked, undernourished, and having endured relentless stress for over four years, he weighed thirty pounds less than he had when he gave his first inaugural address. Always long and lanky, Lincoln now looked skeletal. Dark, blotchy skin covered his protruding cheekbones. His wife did not think he would make it for another four years.[1] In forty-one days, she would be proven correct.

The Lincoln of the second inaugural had changed and grown into a much more spiritual individual compared to the Lincoln of the first inaugural. The president had learned to appreciate those who were religiously inclined or viewed world events from a Christian perspective.

In addition, the election returns of 1864 had affirmed Lincoln's leadership and made him feel more grateful toward Christians and

[1] Packard, *Lincolns in the White House*, 217, 221.

their religious convictions. Indeed, the 1864 campaign revealed the most complete fusing of a religious crusade and a political mobilization in America's electoral history. Christian pastors participated in ward meetings and consistently commented on campaign speeches, addresses to the troops, and newspaper editorials in their sermons. Ministers helped distribute campaign literature supporting Lincoln and the push for emancipation. Many churches became de facto Union-Republican clubs.

Having made the point of consulting with religious leaders and praising their contributions to the war effort, Lincoln could not help but be gratified by their support of him. The impressive mobilization of support by leaders of Protestant churches, who saw themselves as agents of God and Lincoln, significantly contributed to the president's reelection, and Lincoln knew it.[2] "God … bless all the churches—and blessed be God, Who, in this our great trial, giveth us the churches," he exclaimed to a group of Methodists on election day, November 8, 1864. "I am thankful to God for this approval of the people … I give thanks to the Almighty for this evidence of the people's resolution to stand by free government and the rights of humanity."[3] Lincoln's worldview and that of most Christians seemed to be one and the same.

The day of his second inaugural address started out wet and windy, continuing a rainy weather pattern Washington had experienced the previous few days. Streets were saturated with mud—over ten inches in some places. Then fortuitously or divinely, just before Lincoln spoke, the sun broke through the clouds.

---

[2] Carwardine, "Lincoln's Religion, 248; Donald, *Lincoln*, 544. Lincoln won 55.4 percent of the popular vote and carried all states except Kentucky, Delaware, and New Jersey (a 212 to 21 total in the Electoral College). Lincoln enjoyed significant evangelical support, and he appreciated and acknowledged it. During the campaign, Lincoln said, "I rely upon the religious sentiment of the country, which I am told is very largely for me."

[3] Basler, Lincoln's Response to a Serenade, November 8, 1864, *CW*, 8:96.

The second inaugural address is one of the most memorable speeches in American history and the shortest inaugural address ever given (just over seven hundred words) by an American president. Knowing that the horrific Civil War would soon end, Lincoln desired to prepare the American people for a generous reconstruction policy.[4] He also said much more.

The president opened by saying there "is less occasion for an extended address than there was at the first." The peculiar institution, of course, was "the cause of the war." Yet neither side expected the "magnitude" or "duration" of the war to be so extreme. "Each looked for an easier triumph," and "both read the same Bible, and pray to the same God; and each invokes His aid against the other." Both sides implored "God's assistance in wringing their bread from the sweat of other men's faces; but let us judge not that we be not judged. The prayers of both could not be answered; that of neither has been answered fully." Much as he had discovered in his personal faith journey, Lincoln wanted the American people to understand that "the Almighty has His own purposes." He said further, "Fondly we hope—fervently do we pray—that this mighty scourge of war may speedily pass away. Yet, if God wills that it continue, until all the wealth piled by the bond-man's two hundred and fifty years of unrequited toil shall be sunk … so still it must be said, 'the judgments of the Lord, are true and righteous altogether.'"[5]

Lincoln reminded the divided country that God's will remained inscrutable, for there were surely good Christians on both sides of the Mason-Dixon Line. He succinctly summarized the moral dilemma of slavery in American history and the four-year conflict slavery had motivated. Inspired by Scripture, Lincoln wanted post-war policy toward the South to embrace the biblical teaching that the sin, not the sinner, should be hated. Quoting Psalm 19:9 (KJV), "the judgements of the Lord are true and righteous altogether," the

---

[4] Burlingame, *Lincoln*, 2:767.

[5] Basler, Lincoln's Second Inaugural Address, March 4, 1865, *CW*, 8:332–33.

president explained that the struggle would be divinely ordained and just. Therefore, by looking back at American's original sin, Lincoln could look forward to the Union's restoration. The man who had once ridiculed frontier preachers had now become the pastor to the Union.[6]

The second inaugural address had the character of a sermon. Lincoln actively reflected on the religious meaning of the war. He mentioned God fourteen times, quoted the Bible four times, and invoked prayer three times. These intentional insertions created a significant precedent: the Bible had only been quoted one time, by John Quincy Adams, in the previous eighteen inaugural addresses.

Lincoln focused on God's purposes and quoted the fiery verse Matthew 18:7 (KJV): "Woe unto the world because of offences! For it must needs be that offences come; but woe to that man by whom the offence cometh!" Even as God's purposes could bring judgment and war, Lincoln remained confident in "the judgments of the Lord."[7] These three themes—that every nation was a moral being with duties; that God's purposes were wise and mysterious; and that the American Union, under God, must be an agent of moral and political transfiguration—permeate the address. For these reasons, the United States should repent for the sin of slavery.[8]

The final paragraph of the second inaugural address is perhaps the most well-known and beloved portion of the speech: "With malice toward none; with charity for all; with firmness in the right, as God gives us to see the right, let us strive on to finish the work we are in; to bind up the nation's wounds; to care for him who shall have borne the battle, and for his widow, and his orphan—to do all which may achieve and cherish a just, and a lasting peace, among ourselves, and with all nations."[9]

---

6 Anastaplo, *Lincoln*, 248; Meacham, *American Gospel*, 121; Lehrman, *Lincoln "by littles,'* 147, 150.

7 White, *Lincoln,* 664–65.

8 Carwardine, "Lincoln's Religion," 238–39.

9 Basler, Lincoln's Second Inaugural Address, March 4, 1865, *CW,* 8:332–33.

Charles Francis Adams Sr., son of John Quincy Adams, immediately recognized the specialness of the address, calling it the "historical keynote" of the Civil War. "Not a prince or minister in all Europe could have risen to such an equality with the occasion," Adams asserted. Once scorned as a "mere village lawyer," Lincoln seemed destined to become one of "the foolish things of the world" who confound the wise.[10]

Frederick Douglass loved the second inaugural address too. The former runaway slave and confidante of Lincoln quoted the speech, especially the atonement passage—in which Lincoln interpreted the Civil War as the sacrifice and propitiation exacted by God for the nation's sin of slavery—in every postwar speech he gave.[11]

Some thought the president's words were too political. Even Lincoln himself, while believing the speech to be "better than anything I have produced," acknowledged that it would not be "immediately popular" to many Americans. "Men are not flattered by being shown that there has been a difference of purpose between the Almighty and them," he wrote to Thurlow Weed, an influential Republican boss in New York. "To deny it, however, in this case, is to deny that there is a God governing the world. It is a truth which I thought needed to be told; and as whatever humiliation there is in it, falls directly on myself."[12]

Most people, however, loved Lincoln's "sermon," and this gratified him immensely. He was truly touched and emotional when one lady asked him for an autograph written with the pen he used to compose his address. He acknowledged the great comfort he felt knowing his sentiments and well-being were supported and lifted up in prayer by Christian women throughout the country.[13]

The second inaugural address is almost universally regarded as one of Lincoln's best and bravest speeches. *The London Spectator*, a

---

10 Peterson, *Lincoln in American Memory*, 12.

11 Schaub, "Learning to Love Lincoln," 95.

12 Basler, Lincoln to Thurlow Weed, March 15, 1865, *CW*, 8:356.

13 Burlingame, *Lincoln*, 2:770.

longtime Lincoln critic, called it "the noblest political document known to history."[14] Biographers and scholars recognize the speech as his supreme oratorical masterpiece.[15] The "national sermon,"[16] or "greatest American political sermon," fully demonstrates "the fruit of Lincoln's mind."[17] Former president Bill Clinton called the address "the greatest of them all."[18]

Among other attributes, the address is truly remarkable for its religious inspiration and spiritual depth. Lincoln had certainly exhibited his religious motivation in public pronouncements previously in his life. The nine separate proclamations—appointing days of national fasting, humiliation, prayer, and thanksgiving—were notable during his presidency. Moreover, he had sent many public letters to clergy and congregations, giving his insight and thoughts on "Almighty God," "our beneficent Father who dwelleth in the Heavens," "the Divine Majesty," "the Almighty and Merciful Ruler of the Universe," "Divine Providence," "the Supreme Being," "the Father of Mercies," and "the Great Disposer of events."[19] Yet, the Second Inaugural revealed just how much Lincoln had grown in his faith during his four years in the Executive Mansion.

In reflecting on the life of Lincoln, Billy Graham once noted that from March 1861 to March 1865, the Bible became "a very different book for [Lincoln]. The events of four years in the White House had driven him to God in prayer and into a search of the Scriptures and a spiritual pilgrimage such as no other president has ever known." Franklin contended that Lincoln's "second inaugural sounds like a sermon on the will of God in the life of a nation. Its citations of Scripture are so frequent that the second inaugural

---

14 McDonald, "Spiritual Growth of a Public Man," 102.

15 Burlingame, *Lincoln*, 2:765.

16 Deutsch and Fornieri, *Lincoln's American Dream*, 31.

17 Mansfield, *Lincoln's Battle with God*, xx, 187.

18 Clinton, *My Life*, 477.

19 Carwardine, "Lincoln's Religion," 239.

address must factually be regarded as the most official religious document in American history."[20]

The second inaugural address did appear to represent the apex of Lincoln's religious journey, at least his public display of it. Contemporaries like Carl Schurz called it a "sacred poem."[21] Noah Brooks referred to it "as truly a religious document as a state paper." Frederick Douglass labeled the speech a "sacred effort."

While the historiographical debate continues over Lincoln's personal beliefs on such topics as the divinity of Christ, forgiveness of sins, and resurrection of Jesus, biographers clearly recognize the speech as the most religiously outspoken and biblically motivated presidential address in history. One historian says that the most striking feature about the address is that Lincoln refused to take the moral high ground for the North and did not demonize the South. Instead, he recognized that both sides were at fault and full of sinners. The entire address reveals Lincoln's appeal to all Americans to come and sin no more. Lincoln had not only come to understand and embrace the frailty and limitations of human nature, but had reflected deeply upon it.[22]

Two hundred and sixty-six of the 702 words in the document were quoted verbatim from the Bible.[23] No modern-day president of the United States, even the most religious, would dare quote Scripture in 38 percent of his or her presidential address today. The second inaugural address is considered "a theological classic,[24] unusually drenched in a "Biblical outlook,"[25] and much more than a speech. "It was Lincoln pleading the case of God," writes one

---

[20] Owen, *The Man and His Faith*, ix.

[21] Szasz and Szasz, *Lincoln and Religion*, 53. All quotes in this paragraph come from this source.

[22] Krannawitter, *Vindicating Lincoln*, 252–53, 255.

[23] Peterson, *Lincoln in American Memory*, 226.

[24] Wheeler, *Faith and Courage*, 30; Trueblood, *Lincoln: Lessons in Spiritual Leadership*, 3.

[25] Miller, "Zenith of Stagecraft," 340.

historian. "It was Lincoln as Jeremiah or Isaiah or Daniel."[26] Deeply rooted in a biblical understanding of history and humanity, the speech is replete with "genuine Christian wisdom and gentleness," a "charter of Christian statesmanship and the most lofty expression of prophetic civil religion in the English language," the "most far-reaching" reflection on God by "a major figure in American public life," according to scholars.[27] Lincoln had revealed the personal "Living God" in this public declaration.[28] The speech is carved on the wall on the Lincoln Memorial.

The words of the second inaugural address are hardly those of a skeptic or infidel. They demonstrate Lincoln's appeal to the divine and his understanding of the limitations of reason and humanity. Four years of a horrific war and daily Bible reading will do that to a mortal. The first inaugural address appealed to reason, while the second inaugural address appealed to revelation.[29] Perhaps the political leader, who had to carefully balance the interests of all regions of the country as he assumed the presidency in 1861, no longer felt constrained from speaking truth in 1865.

After Lincoln's address, Salmon Chase administered the oath of office. Lincoln then bent down and kissed the Bible, which had been opened to Isaiah 5:27 (KJV): "None shall be weary nor stumble among them." The major inaugural social event occurred two days later in the Patent Office building. Before leaving the inaugural ball to prepare Mary's bedroom, Elizabeth Keckley congratulated the president. "Well, Madame Elizabeth," Lincoln replied, "I don't know whether I should feel thankful or not. The position brings with it many trials." He solemnly added, "We do not know what we are destined to pass through. But God will be with us all. I put my trust in God."[30]

---

26 Mansfield, *Lincoln's Battle with God*, 185.

27 Smith, *Faith and the Presidency*, 120.

28 Trueblood, *Lincoln: Lessons in Spiritual Leadership*, 160–61.

29 Krannawitter, *Vindicating Lincoln*, 250–251.

30 Packard, *Lincolns in the White House*, 226.

The Truth

In Lincoln's second inaugural address, he makes the point that people from the North and the South, the Union and the Confederacy, "read the same Bible and pray to the same God, and each invokes His aid against the other." Both sides used Scripture to justify their respective positions.

In our fallen and sinful world, flawed humans will misread, misapply, or cherry-pick the Bible to suit their own selfish purposes. Or they will claim the Bible says something that it does not. "God helps those who help themselves" is not in the Bible, but is often quoted as if it is.

Make no mistake: Christianity has many different denominations because there are people of God who interpret Scripture differently and feel strongly about their own interpretations. The concern for interpreting God's Word properly is understandable and even admirable. The Bible teaches that you are to "do your best to present yourself to God as one approved, a worker who has no need to be ashamed, rightly handling the word of truth."[31] Perhaps you already know the importance of Scripture, that it "is breathed out by God and profitable for teaching, for reproof, for correction, and for training in righteousness, that the man of God may be complete, equipped for every good work."[32] Faithful and obedient Christians are encouraged to "think over" God's Word, "for the Lord will give you understanding in everything."[33]

There is no doubt people will continue to argue over the correct interpretations of Scripture. Thankfully God is clear on the important matters of faith—Jesus's death and resurrection, the forgiveness of sins, and God's grace. We rejoice over the fact that people are reading God's Word! As the Bible explains, "The fear of

---

[31] 2 Tim. 2:15.

[32] 1 Tim. 3:16–17.

[33] 2 Tim. 2:7.

the Lord is the beginning of knowledge; fools despise wisdom and instruction."[34]

Let God's Word and the Holy Spirit speak directly to your heart and mind. Receive and read Scripture often enough that you know when someone is telling you God's truth or sharing something that is not from Scripture. God warns that if anyone changes, deletes, or adds anything to His Word, He will "add to him the plagues described in this book, and if anyone takes away from the words of the book of this prophecy, God will take away his share in the tree of life and in the holy city, which are described in this book."[35] Translation: God takes His Word seriously and has left it to humankind just as He intends it to be. And what a blessing God's Word is for you and all believers. Through God's Word, "the Helper, the Holy Spirit … he will teach you all things and bring to your remembrance all that I have said to you."[36]

Lincoln's kindness and forgiving nature are evident in his second inaugural address—"with malice toward none, with charity for all." He had a good understanding of human nature—that people are far from perfect. As the Bible says, "All have sinned and fall short of the glory of God."[37] He knew well the biblical account of Jesus defending the adulterous woman against the religious leaders who wanted her stoned to death for her sin. Jesus fittingly declared, "Let him who is without sin among you be the first to throw a stone at her."[38]

Knowing our own sinful nature, and how Jesus erased our sins when He died on the cross, Christians should be charitable and show forgiveness to those who sin against them. Christians should "be kind to one another, tenderhearted, forgiving one another, as

---

[34] Prov. 1:7.

[35] Rev. 22:18–19.

[36] John 14:26.

[37] Rom. 3:23.

[38] John 8:7.

God in Christ forgave you."[39] Jesus asserts, "If you forgive others their trespasses, your heavenly Father will also forgive you, but if you do not forgive others their trespasses, neither will your Father forgive your trespasses."[40] He admonishes His followers to "judge not, and you will not be judged; condemn not, and you will not be condemned; forgive, and you will be forgiven."[41]

No matter how wronged you have been or hurt you may be from someone else's sin or hate, you are to forgive as Christ forgave you. Of course, this is not easy to do. You need Jesus to help you during these ordeals. People can be cruel and vicious. They may intentionally seek to hurt you or your loved ones. The temptation to strike back, get revenge, or even defend yourself or your family proactively is understandable, especially considering our flawed human nature. No matter the circumstances, however, God calls on you to "love your enemies" and "do good to those who hate you."[42] God will take care of the justice of the situation. "Beloved," the Bible teaches, "never avenge yourselves, but leave it to the wrath of God, for it is written, 'Vengeance is mine, I will repay, says the Lord.'"[43]

As hard as it might be not to strike back at someone who has wronged you, remember that you disobey and hurt God every time you act selfishly, sin, hurt others, or do not forgive others. Yet He still died on the cross for your sins. He forgives you of your sins. Thus, you are called to forgive others as Christ has forgiven you, and forgive constantly.

The disciples, fully human, often struggled with the concept of forgiving others. One day Peter came to Jesus and asked Him, "Lord, how often will my brother sin against me, and I forgive him? As many as seven times?"

---

[39] Eph. 4:32.

[40] Matt. 6:14–15.

[41] Luke 6:37.

[42] Luke 6:27.

[43] Rom. 12:19.

Jesus responded, "I do not say to you seven times, but seventy-seven times."[44] In other words, you are to forgive others to infinity and beyond, because Jesus forgave every single one of your sins—too many to count!

God requires you "to do justice, and to love kindness, and to walk humbly with your God."[45] Forgiving others who wrong you is not only kind and noble but also demonstrates that you understand that God has forgiven *your* sins and saved *you* from an eternity in hell. Thanks be to Jesus, you can walk humbly with your God, forgiving others because you know *you* are forgiven.

Your Life

One of the profound parts of the second inaugural address is when Lincoln reminds listeners that Northerners and Southerners "read the same Bible, and pray to the same God; and each invokes His aid against the other." What are some modern situations in which Christians seem to be at odds with each other or have different interpretations of Scripture?

Lincoln's second inaugural address is short but powerful. As a Christian, when are times that saying less is actually a productive and fruitful thing to do?

If you had to write a speech to your family, friends, or loved ones about what is important to you, in seven hundred words or fewer, what would you write about? Try it sometime on your own and see what you produce.

---

44 Matt. 18:21–22.

45 Mic. 6:8.

VISION

36

By Any Means Necessary

For the law was given through Moses; grace
and truth came through Jesus Christ.
—John 1:17

The Lincoln Way

Leaders constantly discern if the means justify the ends.

In almost every survey of the question taken in the last fifty years, Lincoln is regarded as America's greatest president. Yet many Americans might be surprised to hear that more historians have described Lincoln as a dictator than any other president. Some have even referred to him as the "American Pol Pot."[1]

There were more infringements on individual liberties during the Civil War than at any other time in American history. Lincoln repeatedly suspended the writ of habeas corpus—a common law and, in the United States, constitutional principle that someone who is detained has the right to be brought before a court to challenge their detention. Suspending the writ meant that the military authorities could arrest people who appeared to be aiding the Confederacy or attempting to overthrow the government. Once arrested, these individuals could be detained indefinitely without judicial hearing or indictment—the arresting officer did not have to release them when a judge issued a writ of habeas corpus.

---

[1] Krannawitter, *Vindicating Lincoln*, 317; McGovern, *Lincoln*, 60.

According to records, 864 people were imprisoned and held without trial in the first nine months in the war. After February 1862, when such arrests came under the authority of the secretary of war, the number of cases greatly increased. The best estimates are that more than thirteen thousand citizens were arrested over the course of the war without the benefit of habeas corpus, most of whom were Southerners. The detained had committed or were suspected of committing desertion, spying, supplying aid to the enemy, intimidating Unionists, and other offenses. When they were brought before judges, the arrested were tried in military, not civilian courts.

While most of the individuals arrested were, in fact, spies, smugglers, blockade-runners, deserters, and the like, some were jailed for expressing their beliefs as protected by the First Amendment. Lincoln often suspended the writ of habeas corpus for Northerners when judges released civilians for obstructing the Enrollment Act.[2] His administration employed a new conscription law not merely to raise troops for the war effort but also to suppress dissent. If provosts encountered dissent while recruiting, they were advised to jail these dissenters, which they often did. Newspapers editors who criticized these actions were suppressed and occasionally jailed too.

Lincoln created federal military districts to detain and try suspected rebels; enlisted volunteers and diverted funds to equip them without congressional sanction; ordered a blockade; and emancipated the Confederacy's slaves by presidential proclamation.

Lincoln supported government censorship and took control of certain publications. In 1863, he approved, for a short duration, the suppression of the *Chicago Times* for "disloyal and incendiary sentiments"[3] after the paper had criticized emancipation. Moreover, the administration censored the military news originating

---

[2] Keneally, *Lincoln*, 104; Donald, *Lincoln*, 304; Burlingame, *Lincoln*, 2:532–33.

[3] McGovern, *Lincoln*, 61.

from Washington and regulated telegraph news through the War Department. Most notably, in May 1864, the president ordered the arrest of the editors and publishers of the *New York World* and *New York Journal of Commerce*—Democratic newspapers that had published a bogus presidential proclamation calling for the draft of four hundred thousand soldiers. (The editors were imprisoned but were promptly released, and the papers were back in business only two days later).

For the most part, however, Lincoln stayed away from suppressing the speech of everyday Americans. He received an incredible amount of criticism and personally offensive remarks in the media even before the 1860 presidential election. He had grown accustomed to vitriolic and personal attacks in the press. As president, he shut down speech only when he felt publishers were acting in a treasonous manner—like giving away impending military actions—or causing "palpable injury to the Military."[4]

There is no doubt that Lincoln took action outside the accepted constitutional norms of the time and behaved like a dictator when needed. Early in the war, secessionists in Maryland destroyed the railroad bridges linking Baltimore with the North, and cut the telegraph lines. Many Unionists feared that a potentially impending Confederate attack would be aided by thousands of secessionist sympathizers from Baltimore.[5] When Lincoln learned of the situation, he ordered General Winfield Scott to "adopt the most prompt, and efficient means to counteract, even, if necessary, to the bombardment of their cities—and in the extremest necessity, the suspension of the writ of habeas corpus."[6]

In Washington, DC—always considered a Southern city, and one that harbored plenty of spies and many Confederate sympathizers—Lincoln encouraged the army to arrest saboteurs,

---

[4] Guelzo, *Man of Ideas*, 199; Donald, *Lincoln*, 419, 502; McGovern, *Lincoln*, 61.

[5] Donald, *Lincoln*, 298.

[6] Basler, Lincoln to Winfield Scott, April 25, 1861, *CW*, 4:344.

such as those who burned down the bridge over the Susquehanna, and hold them under military jurisdiction. When the Maryland legislature threatened secession, Brigadier General Benjamin Butler of the Massachusetts militia put Annapolis under martial law. The Maryland legislature, seeing the decisive stand the Lincoln administration took, and recognizing that secession would mean immediate battle in the streets of their cities, voted against joining the Confederacy. Showing his iron fist, Lincoln made it clear to Governor Thomas Hicks and to the mayor of Baltimore that he expected their support for the safe passage of federal troops moving through Baltimore.[7]

In August 1863, Lincoln gave his blessing to General Thomas Ewing Jr., Union commander of the District of the Border, for issuing the notorious Order No. 11, which banished approximately twenty thousand residents (and freed their slaves) of four Missouri counties bordering Kansas. Lincoln's support of this measure was the most repressive action ever undertaken by the government against American citizens on the grounds of military necessity until the internment of Japanese Americans during World War II. The president defended the stern measure by telling an anecdote about an Irishman who once asked for a glass of soda water and encouraged the doctor to put a little brandy in it without his knowledge. Lincoln wanted the military action to be executed and thought it necessary for the preservation of the Union, but he did not want to be tied to a directive violating the constitutional rights of Americans.[8]

In addition to concerned congressmen who, by law, had constitutional oversight of the executive branch, there were others who challenged Lincoln's ruthless drive to win the war and stretch his constitutional powers. Having created military tribunals in 1862 to try civilians, engaged in efforts to undermine the war effort (after war the Supreme Court declared such trials unconstitutional in areas

---

[7] Keneally, *Lincoln*, 104.

[8] Burlingame, *Lincoln*, 2:540–41.

where the civil courts had been open), the Lincoln administration ran into trouble when one military tribunal arrested and convicted Copperhead Clement L. Vallandigham of Ohio for speaking against war, the draft, and emancipation.[9] Lincoln never ordered the arrest of Vallandigham and found out about it after the fact. He did take advantage of the situation, however, to write a public letter, published by many newspapers, noting how the rebels "hoped to keep on foot amongst us a most efficient corps of spies, informers, suppliers, and aides and abettors of their cause."[10] Lincoln laid out his position in clear language: "Must I shoot a simple-minded soldier boy who deserts, while I must not touch a hair of a wily agitator who induces him to desert?" he pugnaciously asked.[11] The Constitution gave him the power and required him, during times of rebellion or invasion, to stake strong measures to save the Union and defend public safety but not in peace times. "I can be persuaded that a particular drug is not good medicine for a sick man," he explained,

---

[9] Goodwin, *Team of Rivals*, 522–23. In deliberate defiance, Vallandigham incited a large crown to a frenzy with his passionate criticism of a failed war. He called on the people to "hurl King Lincoln from his throne." Soldiers arrested him in the middle of the night, after he had fired two or three shots, and a military tribunal sentenced him to prison for the remainder of the war. His application for a writ of habeas corpus was denied. When the *Chicago Times* exacerbated the incident with incendiary coverage, General Burnside, on his own authority, shut the paper down. Lincoln, searching for compromise, publicly supported Vallandigham's arrest but commuted the sentence to banishment within the Confederate lines. Lincoln shrewdly prevented Vallandigham's martyr status by commuting his sentence. Burlingame, *Lincoln,* 2:507. According to Order 38, if Vallandigham returned he could be kept in custody for the term specified in his sentence. He was turned over to puzzled Confederates in Tennessee. Eventually, Jeff Davis let him migrate to Canada, where he spoke out against the Union. Donald, *Lincoln,* 421. Unfortunately, even after Lincoln commuted Vallandigham on May 19, 1863, the political damage had been done. Ohio Democrats nominated Vallandigham for governor while he was still in exile.

[10] McPherson, *Lincoln,* 44.

[11] Basler, Lincoln to Erastus Coming and Others, June 12, 1863, *CW,* 6:266.

"because it can be shown to not be good food for a well one." Some might "lose the right of public discussion, the liberty of speech and the press, the law of evidence, trial by jury, and Habeas corpus," for a short time during the war, but not for an "indefinite peaceful future which I trust lies before them."

As casualties and deaths mounted, Lincoln wondered if he had been doing enough and using all means necessary to win the war. If he and Union military forces had moved faster, they could have captured John Breckenridge, Robert E. Lee, Joseph Johnston, John Magruder, William Preston, Simon Buckner, and Franklin Buchanan, all of whom occupied high places in the rebel military. They "were all within the power of the government since the rebellion began, and were nearly as well known to be traitors then as now. Unquestionably if we had seized and held them," Lincoln reflected, "the insurgent cause would be much weaker." Since none of them had committed any crime, however, "every one of them if arrested would have been discharged on Habeas Corpus ... I think the time not unlikely to come when I shall be blamed for having made too few arrests rather than too many."[12] Once he saw how desperate and long-lasting the war had become, Lincoln would not stop arresting those who interfered with the Union war machine or closed down military transportation routes. He would stand firm against "the fire in the rear."[13]

Lincoln justified these actions on the grounds that he had taken an oath to defend the Constitution and preserve the Union. Since a rebellion had broken out, he had the constitutional duty to determine what was necessary for the defense of public safety.[14] He

---

[12] Lincoln to Erastus Coming and Others, June 12, 1863, *CW*, 6:264–68.

[13] Oates, *With Malice Toward None*, 345.

[14] Neely, "Constitution and Civil Liberties Under Lincoln," 42–44. Chief Justice Robert Taney argued that only Congress had the right to suspend the writ, because the suspension clause is found in Article I of the Constitution and the English monarch had long been deprived of this power. Moreover, Justices John Marshall and Joseph Story had established the suspension power

understood that he walked a fine constitutional line in his reasoning and actions, and he tried to reassure critics that he understood the means appropriate for an emergency were not suitable for normal times.

Lincoln directly addressed the concerns that his wartime decisions were violating the constitutional rights of American citizens in an official address to Congress early in the war. He pointed out that if the entire country fell apart, there would be no need to worry about the Constitution. Nevertheless, the president reiterated that he did not believe "that any law was violated." For the Constitution states that "the writ of habeas corpus, shall not be suspended unless when, in cases of rebellion or invasion, the public safety may require it.'" Lincoln acknowledged that "the provision was plainly made for a dangerous emergency."[15]

He insisted, however, that decisions needed to be made with expediency and suppleness, especially when dealing with a national crises. Congress took too long to deal with emergencies, while the chief executive could make quick and prudent decisions. Clearly "it cannot be believed the framers of the instrument intended, that in every case, the danger should run its course, until Congress could be called together; the very assembling of which might be prevented, as was intended in this case, by the rebellion."[16] Later in the war, Lincoln echoed the same sentiment, asserting that he could suspend habeas corpus and hold men without cause "'when, in cases of Rebellion or Invasion the public Safety may require it.' This is precisely our present case—a case of Rebellion, wherein the public Safety does require the suspension."[17]

---

as congressional too. Nevertheless, Congress would eventually give Lincoln power to suspend writ on March 3, 1863.

[15] Basler, Lincoln's Message to Congress in Special Session, July 4, 1861, *CW*, 4:430-31.

[16] Basler, Lincoln's Message to Congress in Special Session, July 4, 1861, *CW*, 4:430–31.

[17] Basler, Lincoln to Erastus Corning and Others, June 12, 1863, *CW*, 6:264.

There were many other opportunities during the tumultuous days of the Civil War when Lincoln could have violated the constitutional rights of American citizens, but did not fall to the temptation. He did not, for example, interfere with midterm elections or state and local elections, even when he knew that the passage of the Emancipation Proclamation had turned much of Northern public opinion against him and in favor of the Democrats. Moreover, when his own reelection looked bleak in 1864, he never considered postponing or canceling the presidential election. A dictator would not allow free elections to throw him out of office.[18]

Lincoln proudly noted how the country maintained its commitment to freedom and liberty during the national crisis. "On this point the present rebellion brought our republic to a severe test; and a presidential election occurring in regular course during the rebellion added not a little to the strain," he noted. "But the election was a necessity. We can not have free government without elections; and if the rebellion could force us to forego, or postpone a national election, it might fairly claim to have already conquered and ruined us."[19]

Since the president's life ended so abruptly at the hands of an assassin shortly after the start of his second term, Lincoln never had a chance to reflect on his use or misuse of constitutional power after the war. Yet the historical record is clear: he had no regrets for doing whatever it took to win the war and preserve the Union, which had been severed in a national emergency. He understood that he had taken an oath to "preserve, protect, and defend the Constitution of the United States."[20] He never desired to "take an oath to get power, and break the oath in using the power." Lincoln demonstrated that he would defend the Constitution and the rule of law even

---

[18] Donald, *Lincoln Reconsidered*, 156–57.

[19] Basler, Lincoln's Response to a Serenade, November 10, 1864, *CW*, 8:100–101.

[20] Basler, Lincoln to Albert Hodges, April 4, 1864, *CW*, 7:282. The quotes in this paragraph and the next come from this source.

if he personally opposed certain policies or laws. For example, he personally found the institution of slavery morally repugnant. Since the peculiar institution was the law of the land, however, he could not do anything about it. His duty and oath were to "preserve the constitution to the best of my ability … by every indispensable means, that government—that nation—of which that constitution was the organic law."

Yet Lincoln fully understood the national crisis. What good would it be "to lose the nation, and yet preserve the constitution?" For Lincoln, the choice was clear: "By general law life and limb must be protected; yet often a limb must be amputated to save a life; but a life is never wisely given to save a limb." Therefore, Lincoln "felt that measures, otherwise unconstitutional, might become lawful, by becoming indispensable to the preservation of the constitution, through the preservation of the nation. Right or wrong, I assumed this ground, and now avow it." He admitted that "I could not feel that, to the best of my ability, I had even tried to preserve the constitution, if, to save slavery, or any minor matter, I should permit the wreck of government, country, and Constitution all together." For the wartime commander in chief, saving the Union came first, while living within the tight limitations of the Constitution came second.

The Truth

Christians often face moral dilemmas in regard to the means justifying the ends or vice versa. The Bible teaches that stealing, for example, is forbidden in the Eighth Commandment. But is it a sin to steal food for your family if they are starving? To take another human life is contrary to the Sixth Commandment, but is it a sin to fire a cruise missile behind enemy lines when given the order? Is it a sin to shoot an intruder who breaks into your house and threatens your family? Abortion clinics kill thousands of innocent babies daily, but does this justify a menacing phone call or verbal threat to a doctor who performs abortions? We are taught not to "bear false witness against our neighbor," yet we justify "white lies" when we tell others they look nice when they really do not. Is it okay to lie when we want to conceal a surprise birthday party for our spouse? Why should we honor our fathers or mothers when such parents have physically and verbally abused us or abandoned our families? The list of life scenarios is almost endless when we humans justify the means or the ends for our own purposes.

Christians often face dilemmas too in obeying a government that passes laws or promotes policies contrary to Scripture. The Bible, however, is clear that Christians are "to be subject to the governing authorities" because God instituted them and "whoever resists the authorities resists what God has appointed, and those who resist will incur judgment."[21] Scripture goes on to state, however, that "rulers are not a terror to good conduct, but to bad" conduct. A ruler or government leader is "God's servant for your good." If your leader is a godly one and "you do wrong, be afraid, for he does not bear the sword in vain. For he is the servant of God, an avenger who carries out God's wrath on the wrongdoer." Since you "pay taxes" to the authorities, who "are ministers of God … pay to all what is owed to them: taxes to whom taxes are owed, revenue to whom revenue is owed, respect to whom respect is owed, honor to whom honor is owed."[22] Christians are to "be subject for the Lord's sake to every human institution, whether it be to the emperor as supreme, or to governors as sent by him to punish those who do evil and to praise those who do good." The Bible explains "that by doing good you should put to silence the ignorance of foolish people." Therefore Christians are to "live as people who are free, not using your freedom

---

21 Ram. 13:1-2.

22 Rom. 13:3, 4, 5, 6, 7.

as a cover-up for evil, but living as servants of God. Honor everyone. Love the brotherhood. Fear God. Honor the emperor."[23]

The key assumption in the previous passages, however, is that government leaders are called to be men or women of God and therefore to understand what constitutes good and evil, right and wrong according to God's Word. Unfortunately, this is not often the case in today's world. Too many governments are corrupt and anti-Christian. Their leadership is devoid of Scripture and God's design for humanity. Their means are not Christ-centered, so their ends will not be God-pleasing. As Peter and the apostles noted so many years ago, "We must obey God rather than men."[24] This exhortation applies to Christian leaders inside and outside of government.

The great news for Christians is that their "end" has already been taken care of thanks be to the death and resurrection of Jesus Christ. Christians' earthly end will be the beginning of lives of eternal bliss in heaven. This is good news because our means are far from perfect and clean. "For all who rely on works of the law are under a curse; for it is written, 'Cursed be everyone who does not abide by all things written in the Book of the Law, and do them.'"[25] God makes it clear that "whoever knows the right thing to do and fails to do it, for him it is sin,"[26] and "everyone who makes a practice of sinning also practices lawlessness; sin is lawlessness."[27]

Before you think you or your behavior is not as bad as others, remember that "whoever keeps the whole law but fails in one point has become accountable for all of it."[28] We must remember that "by works of the law no human being will be justified in his sight, since through the law comes knowledge of sin."[29] Moreover, "the

---

[23] 1 Pet. 2:13–14, 15-17.

[24] Acts 5:29.

[25] Gal. 3:10.

[26] James 4:17.

[27] 1 John 3:4.

[28] James 2:10.

[29] Rom. 3:20.

mind that is set on the flesh is hostile to God, for it does not submit to God's law; indeed, it cannot."[30] In other words, our means or "righteous deeds are like a polluted garment. We all fade like a leaf, and our iniquities, like the wind, take us away."[31] To be sure, "we know that a person is not justified by works of the law but through faith in Jesus Christ, so we also have believed in Christ Jesus, in order to be justified by faith in Christ and not by works of the law, because by works of the law no one will be justified."[32]

Thankfully God's end for your earthly life—His plan of salvation—erases all of your filthy means. Jesus came, died on the cross for your sins, and rose again in order that you "might be justified by faith," not your works or means.[33] Sin no longer has dominion over you, "since you are not under law but under grace."[34]

Knowing that salvation has already been won and that heaven awaits because Christ "has set us free" from sin, you do not need to "submit again to a yoke of slavery" and your sinful ways.[35] Your "citizenship is in heaven," where Jesus waits for your homecoming. When you die and go to heaven, He will transform your "lowly body to be like his glorious body, by the power that enables him even to subject all things to himself."[36] His ends will trump your feeble means. Praise God!

Your Life

Contemporaries criticized Lincoln for violating the Constitution, or America's individual liberties, during the Civil War, and many

---

30 Rom. 8:7.
31 Isa. 64:6.
32 Gal. 2:16.
33 Gal. 3:24.
34 Rom. 6:14.
35 Gal. 5:1.
36 Phil. 3:20–21.

historians continue to criticize him today. In your opinion, did the ends justify the means in Lincoln's case? Why or why not?

When or in what life issues have you struggled with the ends justifying the means? Or the means justifying the ends?

According to the Bible, why should Christians rejoice that our means do not justify the ends in regard to the afterlife? How does this realization change (or should change) the way we live our daily lives?

37

Economic Growth Mindset

Honor the Lord with your wealth and with the firstfruits of all your produce; then your barns will be filled with plenty, and your vats will be bursting with wine.
—Proverbs 3:9-10

The Lincoln Way

With freedom and a hearty work ethic, one will have an opportunity to rise and prosper.

Lincoln is generally known as the American president who won the Civil War and freed the slaves. Yet most of his political career focused, not on slavery, but on economic growth and opportunity. Indeed, perhaps more than any other American president, Lincoln became a strong advocate of liberal capitalism and the free market system. His support for market economics was central to his conviction that every American (except those held in bondage) had the right to rise as he had in his own life.[1]

Lincoln's beliefs in the government's role in the economy and social mobility were nuanced and moderate. Today, politicians and economists on both sides of the political spectrum want to claim Lincoln's economic vision as their own. Many far-left liberals, for example, paint Lincoln not only as a precursor to Franklin Delano Roosevelt's New Deal, but as an active government interventionist who wanted to control the economic engine of the nation. Some

---

[1] Lehrman, *Lincoln "by littles,"* iii, 77; Guelzo, *Lincoln*, 18.

far-right conservatives, on the other hand, try to paint Lincoln's economic philosophy as one that promoted a completely laissez faire, hands-off government.

The truth is Lincoln believed in what today might be labeled "smart government"—if there is such a thing. He held that wise, limited government intervention could provide a tipping point in helping the economy grow and prosper. Being both pro-labor and pro-business, Lincoln advocated for government support in building nineteenth-century infrastructure—canals, railroads, banks, turnpikes—that would help grease the national market and spur opportunity, productivity, and social mobility.

Lincoln's deep reverence for the Declaration of Independence—particularly "that all men are created equal" and "are endowed by their Creator with certain unalienable Rights," namely "Life, Liberty and the pursuit of Happiness"—certainly encompassed the core values of his economic vision. As important as the Declaration, Constitution, and Union were in enabling the economy to flourish, however, Lincoln believed that "the principle of 'Liberty to all'—the principle that clears the *path* for all—gives *hope* to all—and, by consequence, *enterprize* and *industry* to all" was most important.[2] Liberty gave hope to every American (except slaves) that they had the opportunity to pursue their own happiness and rise in society.

One profound reason why Lincoln empathized with those held in check, much as he had felt as a boy growing up in his father's household, was that the suppressed were not allowed to pursue their own talents and dreams. Lincoln's championing of free labor helped shape his growth and convictions as the Great Emancipator. He ultimately viewed slavery as a form of theft—stealing the fruits of one person's labor and appropriating it for another.[3] Moreover, Lincoln defended the free labor system against critics who argued

[2] Basler, Lincoln's Fragment on the Constitution and the Union, January, 1861, *CW,* 4:169.

[3] Clinton, "Family," 257; Foner, "Emancipation of Lincoln," 148.

that slaves were better off than hired laborers. The notion that a poor, honest, industrious man could rise in social status, make his own living, and eventually hire someone else to work for him was the American ideal. To secure this ideal for the American people had been the purpose for which the government was created.[4] Whatever racial views Lincoln held, he certainly acknowledged that enslaved people were not living a life of liberty or pursuing their own happiness.

Lincoln's own life story certainly shaped his economic worldview. Shackled by a father who did not see value in his son's intellectual pursuits, Lincoln knew how it felt to have a lid placed on one's desire to rise in society. When his father rented young Abe's labor out to other farmers, Lincoln understood what it meant to be required to work for someone's else's economic benefit. He resented the requirements of law and custom that any wages he earned before he turned twenty-one be turned over to his father.

At the age of seventeen, Lincoln found a job working on a ferry on the Ohio River, where he took travelers to meet steamers or continue south into Kentucky. One day he rowed two businessmen out to catch on oncoming steamer. As they climbed aboard, they each threw a silver half-dollar into the bottom of Lincoln's boat. These businessmen had no idea how their cash payment rocked Lincoln's economic and social worldview. His father had never paid for things. Thomas Lincoln grew his own wheat, corn, and vegetables; tanned his own leather; and made clothing out of buckskin, cotton, and flax. When he bought coffee and sugar from a store, Thomas Lincoln bartered with hogs, venison hams, and coonskins. Riverboat ferrying introduced Abe to the cash economy—one in which scholarship, initiative, and entrepreneurship could replace monotonous manual labor and the constraints of a farmer's life. Many years later as president, Lincoln indicated that this ferryboat episode remained

---

4 Burlingame, *Lincoln*, 1:567.

"the most important incident in my life" because it had made the world seem "wider and fairer before me."[5]

When Lincoln set out on his own at the age of twenty-two, he still labored for neighbor farmers, but now he did it on his own account and for his own income. He split rails, chopped wood, and plowed fields. He also listened to his neighbors' concerns about the quality of life and state of the economy. He soon entered the world of politics and began campaigning for improvements on the Sangamon River.[6]

Lincoln was always enthralled by the idea of continuous improvement and innovation. In many ways, he became America's first technology advocate and first technology president. In fact, he remains the only president hold a patent—No. 6569, an improvement for lifting boats and vessels over shoals (May 22, 1849). As a lawyer, he made a living defending the new technology of the railroad and the impact it had on opening and expanding economic markets, as well as in changing the culture of America.[7] Tall and techy, Lincoln stood out from his peers in many ways.

He loved innovations and inventions. Machinery, steam engines, and gadgets fascinated him. As president, he accumulated models of proposed new weapons—a cuirass (breastplate and shield—front and back) of polished blue steel, far too heavy for a solder; a grenade that served as a presidential paperweight; and a brass cannon that he used to hold down land patents. An inventor himself, he regularly welcomed visitors who claimed to have fresh inventions ready for review. Occasionally he tried out their proposals in the backyard of

---

5 Keneally, *Lincoln*, 8.

6 Winkle, *Young Eagle*, 27. According to legend, as young Abe plowed a field near Decatur, he "heard cheering upon 'the square,' so turned his oxen into a corner, vaulted the fence, and went to see what was 'going on.'" He listened to a Democratic speaker and then jumped on a stump to deliver his first political speech, urging improvement of the Sangamon River.

7 Wheeler, "Lincoln and the Telegraph," 112; Lehrman, *Lincoln "by littles,"* 166.

the Executive Mansion. Most often he went to the Washington Naval Yard, where he could watch tests on new weapons and explosives. He took a special interest in the repeating rifle of a French inventor named Rafael.

Inventions inspired Lincoln's enthusiasm for many reasons, not the least of which was because they brought subsistence farmers such as he had been into the cash economy, the world of literacy and numeracy, and the milieu of continuous self-improvement. In Milwaukee, Wisconsin, at the Wisconsin State Agricultural Society, Lincoln attacked the idea that "all laborers are necessarily either *hired* laborers or *slaves*," a favorite argument of Stephen Douglas.[8] Reflecting on his own life story, he saw all men as ascendant in society, liberated by American republican classlessness.[9]

Lincoln saw the world as a place where God put man to make discoveries and innovate. In a lecture on discoveries and inventions, Lincoln maintain that "all creation is a mine, and every man, a miner." Whether it be physical, moral, or intellectual in nature, the world possessed "leads" that man could discover and "dig out his destiny." While other creatures labored in the world, man "is the only one who improves his workmanship … by Discoveries, and Inventions." Take mankind's "first important discovery," which came about after he discovered "that he was naked." The discovery of nakedness led mankind to invent the fig-leaf-apron. Lincoln noted that this became "the origin of clothing," and "the one thing for which nearly half of the toil and care of the human race has ever since been expended."[10] From the very beginning, God planted a desire for exploration, discovery, and invention in the human heart.

A student of Henry Clay's American system, Lincoln ardently advocated for government support for internal improvements, protective tariffs, and a banking system that would spur discoveries,

---

8 Keneally, *Lincoln*, 74–75.

9 Donald, *Lincoln*, 432.

10 Basler, Lincoln's First Lecture on Discoveries and Inventions, April 6, 1858, *CW*, 2:437–38.

innovation, investment, and economic growth. Like Clay, Lincoln wanted a developed, improved, and prosperous nation. He dreamed of becoming "the DeWitt Clinton of Illinois"—the prairie equivalent of the governor of New York renowned for developing the Erie Canal.[11]

Lincoln did not favor direct taxation of income, which was a prime reason he supported tariffs. "The tariff is the cheaper system, because the duties, being collected in large parcels at a few commercial points, will require comparatively few officers in their collection," Lincoln explained, "while by the direct tax system, the land must be literally covered with assessors and collectors, going forth like swarms of Egyptian locusts, devouring every blade of grass and other green thing." Lincoln preferred tariffs because "the whole revenue is paid by the consumers of foreign goods, and those chiefly, the luxuries, and not the necessaries of life." Under a tariff system "the man who contents himself to live upon the products of his own country, pays nothing at all." With a robust tariff system in place, "the burthen of revenue falls almost entirely on the wealthy and luxurious few, while the substantial and laboring many who live at home, and upon home products, go entirely free."[12]

Lincoln's vision of a prosperous and developing nation centered around good stewardship of the country's resources, which included a vigorous work ethic among its citizens. The government should be engaged, but not do too much or too little. "The legitimate object of government, is to do for a community of people, whatever they need to have done, but can not do, at all, or can not, so well do, for themselves—in their separate, and individual capacities," he said. "In all that the people can individually do as well for themselves, government ought not to interfere."[13]

---

[11] Miller, *Lincoln's Virtues*, 109.

[12] Basler, Lincoln Campaign Circular from Whig Committee, March 4, 1843, *CW*, 1:311–12.

[13] Basler, Lincoln's Fragment on Government, July 1, 1854, *CW*, 2:220–21.

At a time when minimalist federal and state governments had few resources at their disposal, Lincoln favored a more activist government—so long as it played its proper role in assisting the efforts of all Americans to improve their economic condition.[14] He believed education and internal improvements could get everyone out of poverty; he wanted to spare all people the rural isolation he so intimately knew.

Moreover, Lincoln promoted usury laws that eschewed high interest rates on borrowers. Lincoln knew firsthand that people could not escape poverty without access to loans at reasonable rates. Furthermore, he advocated for smart government intervention, which would incentivize or encourage economic development and eliminate obstacles and barriers to growth and expansion. Like a parent fastening training wheels or holding on to the seat of the bike as a child begins to learn how to ride, Lincoln believed prudent government could lubricate the free market system for success and nurture economic opportunities for individuals to rise and prosper.

As someone who had climbed the economic ladder and knew of the satisfaction of doing so, Lincoln dedicated himself to public policies that could help free men prosper. His zeal for economic mobility—combining capitalist rigor with bottom-up populism—became a lifelong pursuit and would eventually come to define the Republican Party. Lincoln was even willing to fight a war to achieve this pursuit.[15]

In some ways Lincoln could be labeled the most unprepared American president, especially because of his lack of political experience in the nation's capital. In terms of an economic philosophy and vision, however, he could not have been better prepared. Lincoln had spent his entire life talking about and promoting economic growth and how he could help America become a more

---

[14] Holzer and Garfinkle, *A Just and Generous Nation*, 76.

[15] Lowry, *Lincoln Unbound*, 90; Holzer and Garfinkle, *A Just and Generous Nation*, 2.

prosperous nation for all of its citizens.[16] An economic nationalist and student of Henry Clay's American System, Lincoln—the "Great Protectionist"—might not have been elected president in 1860 if he had not convinced the people of Pennsylvania that he would increase tariffs on steel and coal. Lincoln constantly wrote newspaper editors in the manufacturing states and burnished his tariff and internal improvement credentials. As president, he endorsed the Morrill Tariffs, passed late in the Buchanan administration, which significantly increased tariffs to protect nascent American manufacturing and business interests.[17]

Before he became president, Lincoln had come to have strong convictions and beliefs in regard to an economic vision and philosophy. As a prominent member of the Whig Party for most of his adult life, Lincoln adhered to a philosophy that glorified the individual but also supported a government that would eliminate the obstacles and restraints on that individual. Whigs stood for emancipation from agricultural life. They glorified social mobility and believed that wage labor guaranteed the ability to improve one's condition. Lincoln's longtime law partner William Herndon reported that when Lincoln ran for state legislature, his stump speech could be boiled down to these words: "My politics is short and sweet, like an old woman's dance. I am in favor of a national bank, a high and protective tariff, and the internal improvement system."[18]

Lincoln strongly advocated for industrial development and defended wage labor that people could eventually graduate to higher paying wages. He favored a tariff and new technologies. He gave favorable sentiment to agriculture. Moreover, he never attacked wealth and objected to every notion of class conflict. He considered property in all forms (except for slavery) sacrosanct. He worked with the biggest corporate entities of his age, the railroads,

16 Lehrman, "Economic Principles," 91.

17 Buchanon, "An Economic Nationalist," 92.

18 Guelzo, *Lincoln*, 59, 63, 65.

when corporations had already long been attacked and criticized as tools for the rich.[19] Later defenders of the industrial working class and the labor movement, such as Eugene Debs, William Jennings Bryan, and Samuel Gompers, often appealed to the image of Lincoln the Rail-Splitter in order to promote fairness and equality for all. For Lincoln, however, "labor" and "capital" meant something very different. Labor was the springboard to advancement, at least for whites. Lincoln truly believed that any man, over the course of a life's work, could progress from earning a wage to becoming an employer or owner in his own right.[20] Especially if the government helped limit or eliminate barriers, Americans could pursue their own happiness, succeed, and rise. That was what made the United States exceptional.

A few weeks before his inauguration, Lincoln told a crowd that the value of life "is to improve one's condition. Whatever is calculated to advance the condition of the honest, struggling laboring man, so far as my judgment will enable me to judge of a correct thing. I am for that thing."[21] Contrary to the mudsill theory (the belief that every society rested upon some bottom rung of permanently fixed labor to perform menial work or that the lower class always had to exist to support an upper class), Lincoln argued that a free society was dynamic and defined by an improvement of condition. Each human being, according to the principles laid out in the Declaration, should be guaranteed the right to rise.[22] Moreover, Lincoln believed that almost every man desired to improve his own condition and that God had planted this desire on each man's heart. Western lands, for example, were a gift from God so that men could go west and make better lives for themselves.[23] If energetic, smart, capitalistic

[19] Lowry, *Lincoln Unbound*, 193.

[20] Fox, *Lincoln's Body*, 176–77.

[21] Basler, Lincoln's Speech to Germans, February 12, 1861, *CW*, 4:203.

[22] Fornieri, "Lincoln's Theology of Labor," 209.

[23] Donald, *Lincoln*, 234–35.

government policy could help an ordinary man rise, Lincoln would advocate for it and implement it.

Indeed, as president, Lincoln advocated for and implemented government action that helped the country develop. He pushed through higher tariffs and the Pacific Railroad Act, which eventually led to the completion of the transcontinental railroad and the opening of markets. The Central Pacific began laying tracks eastward on January 8, 1863, with the intent of meeting the Union Pacific line running westward out of Omaha. Both companies were given huge land grants as incentives to get the job completed. In 1862, Lincoln established the new federal Department of Agriculture, hoping to stimulate the domestic economy. In 1862, the Homestead Act passed (Southerners never wanted it because they feared antislavery Northerners would benefit and settle the western lands), which gave settlers a grant of 160 acres after occupying the land for five years and paying a small settler's fee. The Morrill Land-Grant College Act provided for agricultural colleges designed to teach the children of farmers "scientific husbandry"—how to implement the newest techniques of crop and livestock management and how to connect the farmer to markets—a marked advancement from a subsistence economy. The Morrill Land-Grants would be subsidized by the sale of federal lands.

To fund Union costs for the Civil War, an aggressive marketing campaign pushed the sale of war bonds. Under the Legal Tender Act, Congress issued $150 million in paper money. The greenback, one of the last transitions from the old barter economy to a more modern commercial one, had arrived. The National Banking Act revived the national bank, which President Jackson had killed in 1833. The new act unified currency and created a national system of chartered banks, replacing an antiquated and inefficient system in which states and state banks created their own money. The president also felt compelled to advocate for a 3 percent income tax on all incomes over $800 per year, which eventually passed. (The legislation produced little income, but definitely introduced the beginning of the fiscal policies that would become the norm in the twentieth century.)[24]

Lincoln's activist and centrist economic philosophy, coupled with his legislative successes, were new to the annals of the American presidency. He became the first president to use the federal government as an agency to lift up and support the American people in their effort to rise, prosper, and sustain a middle class standard of living. Put another away, Lincoln's presidency firmly branded the defining feature that all Americans (at least those not enslaved) could rise and live a middle-class lifestyle. Ralph Waldo Emerson, in his eulogy on Lincoln in 1865, noted that "the middle-class country had got a middle-class President, at last."[25]

While he may be better known for his Emancipation Proclamation, Gettysburg Address, or second inaugural address, one of Lincoln's crowning achievements is the democratization and entrenchment of the American dream. As a politician and entrepreneur, Lincoln possessed a hunger for economic opportunity and industrial development. He advocated for property rights, defended and litigated for corporations and railroads, and constantly thought of different ways to fuel economic expansion and growth. As one historian explains, he "took an economic point of view descended from Alexander Hamilton—with all the elitist baggage that implies—and baptized it in the great, rolling Jordan River of American democracy." In Lincoln, "the banks and the log cabin met," and "the laboring man became the master of his own economic destiny."[26]

The image of Lincoln as the Great Commoner has often been used to paint him as some social democrat or populist of the left. The characterization is quite misleading. While Lincoln certainly believed that smart democracy existed as the best form

---

[24] Holzer and Garfinkle, *A Just and Generous Nation*, 4–5.

[25] Holzer and Garfinkle, *A Just and Generous Nation,* 4–5; 64–65.

[26] Lowry, *Lincoln Unbound*, 7, 116.

of government in which ordinary people could rise, the American people had to rise on their own efforts in the tradition of the "self-made man"—a phrase made popular by Lincoln's hero, Henry Clay. Lincoln favored equality of opportunity, not the equality of result. Government support for industry and agriculture—the development of canals and railroads, high tariffs to protect infant manufacturing, the conversion of federal lands into family farms—made sense to him. Providing economic support for ex-slaves, however, did not. They, like everyone, must embrace the slogan "root, hog, or die."[27]

Even though progressives from Teddy Roosevelt to Barack Obama have tried to claim Lincoln as one of their own, the evidence tells another tale. Lincoln believed in a dynamic capitalism that transformed the old ways of life. While he certainly favored an active government, he did not imagine bloated government that would clog the arteries of independence, freedom, entrepreneurism, and economic expansion. Lincoln wanted precise, measured government intervention that would enable the economy, much like a lubricant enables efficiency and durability in the moving parts of an engine. The debate in Lincoln's time centered on how pro-business government would be. With most of the action still relegated to the state level, Lincoln believed in an aspirational federal government and not a redistributive one.[28] For decades after his presidency, the Republican Party would continue Lincoln's legacy of offering federal stimuli for economic takeoff, winning fourteen of eighteen presidential elections from 1860 to 1928.[29]

The economic vision of Lincoln knew no bounds. "I say that there is room enough for us all to be free," he asserted more than a year before the 1860 presidential election. Slavery not only hurt the enslaved, "but it positively wrongs the mass of the white men that the negro should be enslaved; that the mass of white men are really

---

27 Lind, *What Lincoln Believed*, 17.

28 Lowry, *Lincoln Unbound*, 198, 230, 234.

29 Freehling, *Becoming Lincoln*, 312.

injured by the effect of slave labor in the vicinity of the fields of their own labor."[30] In addition to the cruelty of the peculiar institution, Lincoln detested slavery because it placed slaves in a fixed economic condition for life. Slaves would never be able to advance or partake of upward mobility.[31]

For Lincoln, slavery was the ultimate economic barrier to a fruitful and prosperous life. Even the ant "who has toiled and dragged a crumb to his nest, will furiously defend the fruit of his labor, against whatever robber assails him," he wrote in 1854 after reentering the political arena. Even the "most dumb and stupid slave that ever toiled for a master, does constantly know that he is wronged."[32]

Lincoln became exasperated at the Southern argument that slaves were better off than hired or free labor, citing his own life as the counterpoint. "I was a hired laborer," he explained. "The hired laborer of yesterday, labors on his own account to-day; and will hire others to labor for him to-morrow. Advancement—improvement in condition—is the order of things in a society of equals." Free labor inspired hope where "pure slavery has no hope," and "the power of hope upon human exertion, and happiness, is wonderful." Demonstrating his mastery of the incentives of a capitalist economy, Lincoln argued that a slave had to be whipped in order to produce seventy-five pounds of hemp. Yet if a slaveowner demanded one hundred pounds of hemp and the incentive that whatever was harvested above one hundred pounds would be the slave's to sell, the slave would produce one hundred and fifty pounds of hemp. "You have substituted hope, for the rod," Lincoln said. Thus, the slave system needed to be replaced by the "free system of labor."[33]

---

30 Basler, Lincoln's Speech at Cincinnati, Ohio, September 17, 1859, *CW*, 3:446.

31 Holzer and Garfinkle, *A Just and Generous Nation*, 91.

32 Basler, Lincoln Fragment on Slavery, April 1, 1854, *CW*, 2:222.

33 Basler, Lincoln's Fragment on Free Labor, September 17, 1859, *CW*, 3:462–63.

Repeatedly, Lincoln told audiences that he had been "a hired laborer, mauling rails, at work on a flat-boat—just what might happen to any poor man's son!" Just as he had risen in society, Lincoln wanted "every man to have the chance," including the "black man." Everyone could "better his condition," and could "look forward and hope to be a hired laborer this year and the next, work for himself afterward, and finally to hire men to work for him! That is the true system."[34]

More than any other national leader, Lincoln articulated enduring expressions of the American dream and the right to rise. The inspiration for his theology of labor sprang from his response to proslavery theology, as well as biblical revelation and the republican principles of liberty, equality, and consent.[35] After all, the equality of man, promised in the Declaration, came from the Creator. If "anything can be proved by natural theology," Lincoln said, "it is that slavery is morally wrong. God gave man a mouth to receive bread, hands to feed it, and his hand has a right to carry bread to his mouth without controversy."[36]

Many former slaveholders and Founding Fathers knew this to be true. Even Thomas Jefferson admitted that he trembled for his country because God is just.[37] For Lincoln, America had become a "great empire" and "the wonder and admiration of the whole world" because "every man can make himself." Yet Southerners still declared that slavery had a right to spread and "that their slaves are far better off than Northern freeman." Lincoln could not believe the mistaken view that many Southerners held in regard to Northern laborers. "They think that men are always to remain laborers here—but there is no such class," he asserted with great exasperation. "The

---

[34] Basler, Lincoln's Speech at New Haven, Connecticut, March 6, 1860, *CW*, 4:24.

[35] Fornieri, "Lincoln's Theology of Labor," 218.

[36] Basler, Lincoln's Speech at Hartford, Connecticut, March 5, 1860, *CW*, 4:3.

[37] Basler, Lincoln's Speech at Columbus, Ohio, September 16, 1859, *CW*, 3:410.

man who labored for another last year, this year labors for himself, and next year he will hire others to labor for him."[38]

One reason Lincoln fought so fiercely against secession was that he believed ordinary people should have a voice in the government and be allowed to advance as far as their talent, virtue, and industry would take them.[39] Two decades before he became president, he refuted Reverend Frederick Ross, a Presbyterian minister from Alabama, who had written a book entitled *Slavery Ordained by God*—an allusion to Romans 13:1. Slavery is a necessary evil, a positive good, and in "absolute harmony with the word of God," Ross argued. Lincoln countered with Genesis 3:19 (KJV)—"In the sweat of thy face shalt thou eat bread"—as a theological defense of free labor. Lincoln said, "It has so happened in all ages of the world, that some have laboured, and others have, without labour, enjoyed a large proportion of the fruits. This is wrong, and should not continue. To [secure] to each labourer the whole product of his labour, or as nearly as possible, is a most worthy object of any good government."[40] God did not condone taking someone else's labor or someone else's property.[41]

The fact that many theologians in the South and North misapplied the Bible and exploited it for proslavery arguments did not lead Lincoln to reject the authority of Scripture. He saw through the ruse. Proslavery advocates dishonestly twisted the words of Scripture, changing "In the sweat of thy face shalt thou eat bread" to "In the sweat of other mans faces shalt thou eat bread," Lincoln noted. His aim was "robbing no man of his goods." When "professedly holy men of the South, met in the semblance of prayer and devotion, and, in the name of Him who said 'As ye would all

---

[38] Basler, Lincoln's Speech at Kalamazoo, Michigan, August 27, 1856, *CW*, 2:364.

[39] Burlingame, *Lincoln*, 1:685.

[40] Basler, Lincoln's Fragments of a Tariff Discussion, December 1, 1847, *CW*, 1:411–12.

[41] Lowry, *Lincoln Unbound*, 5.

men should do unto you, do ye even so unto them,'" claimed that the Bible or Christianity supported the enslavement of "a whole race of men," they condemned "and insulted God and His church, far more than did Satan when he tempted the Saviour with the Kingdoms of the earth." Lincoln asserted that "the devils attempt was no more false, and far less hypocritical. But let me forbear, remembering it is also written 'Judge not, lest ye be judged.'"[42]

The Civil War does not receive enough attention for being a fight over what kind of economy the country would embrace after slavery. Yet long before Lincoln fought for political or social rights for African Americans, he insisted that they were entitled to the same economic rights—the pursuit of happiness—as all other Americans. His commitment to economic opportunity inspired and lit up his path to emancipation.[43] From the very beginning of his presidency, even in the midst of a war that produced far more casualties and deaths than most people had anticipated, Lincoln talked about "the People's contest" from an economic perspective. The Union stood for government "whose leading object is, to elevate the condition of men—to lift artificial weights from all shoulders—to clear the paths of laudable pursuit for all—to afford all, an unfettered start, and a fair chance, in the race of life." Partial or temporary departures from this vision, such the Slave Power of Confederacy, must be refuted and confronted.[44]

Lincoln never relented in striving to make the American dream a reality for more of his countrymen. Free labor, not slave labor, reinforced the biblical notion that God "makes every individual with one head and one pair of hands, it was probably intended that heads and hands should co-operate as friends; and that that particular head, should direct and control that particular pair of hands."

[42] Basler, Lincoln to George B. Ide, James R. Doolittle, and A. Hubbell, May 30, 1864, *CW*, 7:368.

[43] Holzer and Garfinkle, *A Just and Generous Nation*, 4, 6.

[44] Basler, Lincoln's Message to Congress in Special Session, July 4, 1861, *CW*, 4:438.

These "particular pair of hands should feed that particular mouth," and therefore "every head should be cultivated, and improved, by whatever will add to its capacity for performing its charge."[45] Everyone had the capacity to self-direct their learning, growth, and prosperity. Lincoln never wanted individuals to be stuck or find themselves in a fixed "condition for life." Instead, he continued to tell the story of "the prudent, penniless beginner in the world," who "labors for wages awhile, saves a surplus with which to buy tools or land for himself; then labors on his own account another while, and at length hires another new beginner to help him." To the end of his days, Lincoln insisted that "this is the just, and generous, and prosperous system, which opens the way to all—gives hope to all, and consequent energy, and progress, and improvement of condition to all."[46] His vision solidified and ingrained the American dream in America's consciousness. His words and life story provided the catechism and biography for that dream.

The Truth

Just as the Bible was misused and manipulated in the defense of slavery back in Lincoln's time, so too has the Bible been exploited to defend almost any kind of economic system known to mankind today. Nevertheless, in His mercy, grace, and love for us, God's Word provides some basic foundations of work, labor, and economic practice for His disciples.

The Bible makes it very clear, from the time of Adam and Eve, that work is a gift from God. We are to be industrious, productive, fruitful, diligent, and conscientious in our stewardship of the time, talent, and treasures He gives us. After all, God "took the man and

[45] Basler, Lincoln's Address before the Wisconsin State Agricultural Society, Milwaukee, Wisconsin, September 30, 1859, *CW*, 3:478–80.

[46] Basler, Lincoln's Annual Message to Congress, December 3, 1861, *CW*, 5:52–53.

put him in the Garden of Eden to work it and keep it."[47] He tells us that "if anyone is not willing to work, let him not eat."[48] And we also know that the "laborer deserves his wages,"[49] and that "he who plants and he who waters are one, and each will receive his wages according to his labor."[50] Wages earned or wealth accumulated is not the enemy or problem. Instead, God tells us that "the *love* of money is a root of all kinds of evils. It is through this craving that some have wandered away from the faith and pierced themselves with many pangs."[51]

God certainly knows man's sinful condition and the temptations that abound in the realm of material wealth. "He who loves money," He tells us, "will not be satisfied with money, nor he who loves wealth with his income; this also is vanity."[52] We are commanded not to steal, not to covet your neighbor's house; not covet your neighbor's wife, or any of your neighbor's possessions.[53] God knows the damage that our selfishness and greed can do to our souls. As Jesus says, "For what will it profit a man if he gains the whole world and forfeits his soul? Or what shall a man give in return for his soul?"[54]

However you live and make a living, God calls you to use the gifts, talents, resources, and blessings He has given you to serve others in His name. Indeed, "if anyone has the world's goods and sees his brother in need, yet closes his heart against him, how does God's love abide in him?"[55] As hard as you work, you are not to "love the world or the things in the world. If anyone loves the world, the love of the Father is not in him." So much "that is in the

[47] Gen. 2:15.

[48] 2 Thess. 3:10.

[49] 1 Tim. 5:18.

[50] 1 Cor. 3:8.

[51] 1 Tim. 6:10.

[52] Eccles. 5:10.

[53] Exod. 20:15, 17.

[54] Matt. 16:26.

[55] 1 John 3:17.

world—the desires of the flesh and the desires of the eyes and pride in possessions—is not from the Father but is from the world. And the world is passing away along with its desires, but whoever does the will of God abides forever."[56] This is a difficult challenge for sinful human beings because the material blessings God provides are often wonderful and necessary, but can also be alluring and corruptive. In this fallen world, often what is meant for good can be twisted or used for bad. This is why Jesus warns that "no one can serve two masters, for either he will hate the one and love the other, or he will be devoted to the one and despise the other. You cannot serve God and money."[57] According to Jesus, Christ-followers must "take care, and be on your guard against all covetousness, for one's life does not consist in the abundance of his possessions."[58]

If you keep your eyes fixed on Jesus and are inspired by His love and servant leadership example, then wealth can be employed to serve others and glorify the Savior. The Bible explains that "whoever is generous to the poor lends to the Lord, and he will repay him for his deed."[59] Stewardship is a powerful example of a faith motivating one to serve others in Jesus's name. This service is not about you or the material wealth you may possess, but how God will supply every need "according to his riches in glory in Christ Jesus."[60]

The Bible shows that God's love is focused on you, not some particular economic system. For while there are some Bible verses that appear to support a more socialist economic mindset—recording how believers sold their houses and other possessions in order to distribute the proceeds to those who had need—there are also verses that promote a more capitalist or individual approach to the economy.[61] The Bible teaches that you are to work hard and

---

[56] 1 John 2:15–17.

[57] Matt. 6:24.

[58] Luke 12:15.

[59] Prov. 19:17.

[60] Phil. 4:19.

[61] Acts 2:44–45, 4:34–37.

earnestly so that you do not have to be dependent on others,[62] produce abundance, refrain from falling into poverty,[63] and earn a living.[64]

If you make, accumulate, or inherit a lot of wealth, use it and steward it so that God might be glorified. For "whatever you do, work heartily, as for the Lord and not for men, knowing that from the Lord you will receive the inheritance as your reward. You are serving the Lord Christ.[65] Remember that it is God "who gives you power to get wealth."[66] In response to His generous mercy, grace, and love, consider that God delights in a "cheerful giver." [67] He does not seek believers who reluctantly serve Him or give out of compulsion or offer their wealth on a quid pro quo or transactional basis.

God does not need your wealth. He is God. He owns it all and created it all. Whatever you have is His anyway. Therefore, do not store up treasures on earth, "where moth and rust destroy and where thieves break in and steal." Instead, lay up your "treasures in heaven, where neither moth nor rust destroys and where thieves do not break in and steal. For where your treasure is, there your heart will be also."[68]

Your Life

Lincoln believed that the individual controlled his or her own economic destiny. He felt each person had the opportunity to rise. How about you? What do you believe about your own ability to control your standard of living?

---

62 1 Thess. 4:11–12.

63 Prov. 14:23; 21:5.

64 2 Thess. 3:12.

65 Col. 3:23–24.

66 Deut. 8:18.

67 2 Cor. 9:7.

68 Matt. 6:19–21.

Why do you think God calls work a blessing? When might work not be a blessing in this fallen world?

Examine and reflect on your own life. Do you consider yourself rich, poor, or something in between? Why?

How well do you use your gifts, talents, material possessions, and wealth to honor and glorify God?

38

The Great Pragmatist

For there is a time and a way for everything,
although man's trouble lies heavy on him.
—Ecclesiastes 8:6

The Lincoln Way

While every human being is enslaved by something, not everyone acknowledges or recognizes it.

Although Lincoln's moniker "the Great Emancipator" is perhaps the most widely known, it also remains one of the most debated in Lincoln studies. Questions and arguments about Lincoln's views on the slavery and race continue to be the subject of numerous books. Was Lincoln a racist or white supremacist? Was he always against the institution of slavery? If not, when did his position change and why? Did he truly believe blacks to be members of an inferior race, or did he only appear to endorse this argument due to the political realities of his day? How critical should we be of Lincoln's moderate positions today? Does he really deserve the title "the Great Emancipator"?

The case for a racist Lincoln is mostly aptly and succinctly summarized as follows: he spoke disingenuously of the equality of blacks and whites for decades; he believed blacks were inferior; he advanced policies to suppress blacks or ship them out of the country; he failed to endorse black suffrage or policies that would allow blacks to testify in courts or serve on juries; and he supported fugitive slave laws and the repressive Illinois black codes prohibiting free blacks from taking up residence in that state.[1]

For many, Lincoln seemed a bit slow on resolving the slavery issue, even after he was elected president. One great irony of Lincoln's presidency is how the party of abolition vilified their own party leader. They disparagingly noted his Southern roots, his marriage to a woman from a proslavery family, and his failure to sign on to the "Testimony Law" in 1858 (to permit black men to testify against white men). He was elected on a platform of not allowing slavery to extend to the new territories, not for advocating the eradication of the peculiar institution. He went to war with the Confederacy to save the Union, not to free the slaves. He focused too much on the economic problems of slavery rather than its moral injustices. He placated border states by promising that he would not interfere with slavery. Even the Emancipation Proclamation, a hallmark of his political career, only came about as a military necessity—and it only freed slaves behind Confederate lines, not throughout the country. In short, Lincoln did not deserve credit for being an emancipator, only a shrewd politician who did what he needed to do to get elected. Abolitionists railed against Lincoln throughout his presidency.

There is much truth to these arguments, but they often neglect the nineteenth-century context. No one could have gotten elected in Lincoln's day by saying blacks and whites were equal. Senator Stephen Douglas, from a "free" Northern state (Illinois), consistently scored political points and votes by labeling Lincoln a "Black Republican." Very few abolitionists during Lincoln's time thought blacks would ever partake of genuine equality. The seemingly contradictory beliefs that slavery should be eradicated and that blacks were innately inferior to whites was common, embraced by Lincoln and the majority of Northerners at the time of the Civil War. Social integration for blacks into white America seemed unlikely, undesirable, and even impossible to many Americans. Despite these realities, Lincoln

---

[1] Krannawitter, *Vindicating Lincoln*, 13, 34, 37.

believed chattel slavery should end. The real historical debate is whether Lincoln represented a man of his time or moved public opinion on the institution of slavery.[2]

Lincoln's views on slavery developed over time just as his views on religion did. His general disdain for slavery, coupled with his keen and prudent sense of political timing, meshed in a way that helped propel him to office. Lincoln almost always favored emancipation, but struggled over the means of it. Since the days of the American Revolution, slavery had been a constitutional matter left up to the states. The federal government's power was limited. Despite the limitations, Lincoln believed the federal government could help persuade the American people of the evils of slavery and hasten its eradication. The government could provide financial incentives. According to Lincoln, the cheapest way to get rid of slavery was for the government to buy the slaves and then set them free. Once he became president and absorbed in a gruesome civil war, urgency trumped gradual, incentivized emancipation in his mind, even as he proposed incentivized emancipation for the entirety of his presidency.[3]

To have been pragmatic on the issue of slavery does not mean that Lincoln did not care deeply and personally about the issue. "Whenever I hear any one, arguing for slavery," he told some soldiers late in the war, "I feel a strong impulse to see it tried on him personally."[4] For Lincoln, the slavery issue had always been personal. His parents were committed and faithful Hard Shell Baptists who abhorred slavery—one reason they moved from the slaveholding state of Kentucky to the free labor state of Indiana. Moreover, Abe consistently demonstrated a tenderhearted sympathy for any person or beast that experienced persecution, pain, or

---

[2] Guelzo, *Man of Ideas*, 87, 89–93; Krannawitter, *Vindicating Lincoln*, 31; Packard, *Lincolns in the White House*, 128–29.

[3] Guelzo, *Man of Ideas*, 128, 143.

[4] Basler, Lincoln's Speech to One Hundred Fortieth Indiana Regiment, March 17, 1865, *CW*, 8:361.

suffering. As a flatboat trader in his twenties—tasked to deliver grain, meat, sugar, and tobacco—young Lincoln witnessed the brutality of slavery up close as he sailed down the Mississippi River to New Orleans. Seeing blacks chained, malnourished, whipped, and scourged astonished and angered him. The images of slave auctions, in particular, horrified him and shaped his contempt for human bondage for the rest of his life.[5] Throughout Abe's youth, Thomas Lincoln expressed frustration about competing with Southern aristocrats and their slave labor, which kept wages down.

While the economic tension with slavery existed throughout his upbringing, Lincoln's interactions with black folk continued to shape his worldview. There is a story that, in the fall of 1831, Lincoln returned to New Salem after a hard day's work in the woods. He encountered a black Haitian, William de Fleurville, who had run out of funds on his way to Springfield. Discovering that de Fleurville cut hair for a living, Lincoln took him to the Rutledge Tavern in New Salem, Lincoln's boardinghouse, and told his fellow lodgers about Fleurville's plight. Lincoln's persistence drummed up enough haircutting and beard-trimming to make Bill the Barber solvent and send him happily on his way to Springfield the next morning. Soon de Fleurville opened a barbershop in Springfield, and after Lincoln moved there in 1837, he went to Billy's shop for the rest of his Springfield life. He later served as Billy's lawyer and friend. Billy sent Lincoln a sympathetic and encouraging letter on New Year's Day 1864, which expressed hope in a second Lincoln term.[6]

---

[5] Keneally, *Lincoln*, 10, 13. In the spring of 1828, Lincoln accompanied Allen Gentry on a flatboat to deliver goods at New Orleans. One night they docked near a plantation in Baton Rouge, Louisiana. While they were trading their cargo, a group of seven slaves armed with knives attacked them. Abe and Allen drove them off with clubs. How ironic and tragic it would have been if the Great Emancipator had been killed on the Mississippi by those he would later free.

[6] Miller, *Lincoln's Virtues*, 40–41.

After getting elected to the Illinois state legislature, Lincoln stayed at Ann Sprigg's boardinghouse—a location where antislavery Whig congressmen gathered and had earnest, moral discussions about abolition and slavery. Never before had Lincoln been surrounded by intelligent politicians who possessed deep convictions on the topic.[7]

In 1837, in his second house term, Lincoln and another member boldly denounced slavery and filed a protest against the anti-abolitionist resolutions that the Illinois legislature had adopted six weeks earlier by the lopsided vote of 77–6 in the House and 18–0 in the Senate. Southern state legislatures were upset by the American Anti-Slavery Society's pamphlets depicting slaveowners as cruel brutes. They also objected to the call to end slavery in the District of Columbia. The resolutions declared that Illinois legislators were firmly against the formation of any abolitionist societies or the abolitionist propaganda emanating from these societies. They also argued that the federal government protected slavery and that the people could not be deprived of this right without their consent. Lincoln wrote a protest against these resolutions and circulated it among his colleagues, of whom only one would sign it (and he had decided not to run for reelection).[8] Lincoln quickly learned that advocacy for abolition remained a losing proposition in politics.

As he entered the legal profession in the late 1830s, he approached the slavery issue with the reasoning of a lawyer, carefully considering all of the arguments. Possessing a deep respect for the law and legal procedure, Lincoln often rebuffed abolitionist pressure to make slavery illegal in the Southern states. He abhorred the institution, but he was a man of law and order. Slavery had to die a legal death.[9]

Lincoln thought slavery would fade out if only it could be prevented from expanding. Having recently been elected to the US House of Representatives, Lincoln opposed the Mexican War and

---

[7] White, *Lincoln*, 148.

[8] Burlingame, "Lincoln and Race," 59–60.

[9] Packard, *Lincolns in the White House*, 130.

voted over forty times in favor of the Wilmot Proviso, which sought to exclude slavery from any new territory acquired from Mexico. In 1849, he also framed a bill to abolish slavery in the District of Columbia. The House had been considering legislation to outlaw slave trading in the capital, but Lincoln's measure went further, abolishing slavery altogether.[10] Of course, neither initiative had a realistic chance to pass.

As he continued to participate in the politics of the day, Lincoln had to deal with the reality of public opinion. One cannot be a politician if not elected. If he had demanded, in the 1840s and 1850s, that blacks be allowed to vote, sit on juries, and marry white people, Lincoln never would have been elected.[11] He detested slavery but he also did not or could not support abolition as a remedy.[12] This was one reason his halfway point, or mental compromise position, was the idea of colonization, or sending freed blacks to settlements outside of the United States, in places such as Panama and Haiti. Lincoln wanted to free the slaves but did not think they would assimilate into American society. In Lincoln's mind, colonization seemed the practical, if not ideal, solution to the issue.

Lincoln realized he had to suppress his own strong feelings about the peculiar institution and take a pragmatic, incremental approach in confronting it. First, he would work to contain it and not allow it to expand to new territories. Second, he would find a way to phase it out in a long-term program, offering financial incentives to slaveowners and voluntary colonization to the freed blacks as two ways to speed the process of eradication and defuse growing sectional tension.[13] He wanted to avoid confrontation with the South. "Pharaoh's country was cursed with plagues, and his hosts were drowned in the Red Sea for striving to retain a captive people

---

[10] Winkle, *Young Eagle*, 258; Burlingame, "Lincoln and Race," 61.

[11] McGovern, *Lincoln*, 65; Foner, "Emancipation of Lincoln," 147; Krannawitter, *Vindicating Lincoln*, 38.

[12] Winkle, *Young Eagle*, 253, 258.

[13] Striner, "Lincoln and the Struggle to End Slavery," 164.

who had already served them more than four hundred years," he noted. "May like disasters never befall us!" Colonization provided a less confrontational approach. Slaves would be freed and restored "to their long-lost father-land, with bright prospects for the future." Best of all, the process would happen "gradually" so that "neither races nor individuals shall have suffered by the change, it will indeed be a glorious consummation."[14] Lincoln's belief in colonization, of course, never accounted for the desires, dreams, and hopes of enslaved people.

Having taken a break from local and national politics for a few years in the late 1840s and early 1850s, Lincoln was provoked by the Kansas-Nebraska Act to get back into the political arena in 1854. Displaying his political acuity and pragmatism, he insisted that "Southern slaveholders were neither better, nor worse than we of the North, and that we of the North were no better than they." He understood how "we should act and feel as they do; and if they were situated as we are, they should act and feel as we do." Nonetheless, Americans should tolerate and protect slavery where it already existed but not let it expand "over a territory already free, and uncontaminated with the institution."[15] Even slave state resident Thomas Jefferson, in crafting the Northwest Ordinance, demonstrated that slavery should never be introduced into a new territory.

Moreover, Lincoln made the point that slaves were not property like hogs or horses—even Southerners admitted this reality. He noted how many Americans in Northern and Southern states had freed their slaves because they had "in some way and at some time, felt satisfied that the creatures had mind, feeling, souls, family affections, hopes, joys, sorrows—something that made them more than hogs or horses." Appealing to past and present proponents of

---

[14] Basler, Lincoln's Eulogy on Henry Clay, July 6, 1852, *CW,* 2:132.

[15] Basler, Lincoln's Speech at Bloomington, Illinois, September 12, 1854, *CW,* 2:230–31.

slavery, Lincoln asked, "Shall the Slaveholders require us to be more heartless and mean than they, and treat those beings as property which they themselves have never been able to treat so?"[16]

Lincoln saw the Kansas-Nebraska Act as an even greater evil than the institution of slavery itself, for two main reasons. First, the legislation destroyed the compromises on the slavery issue that had kept the Union together over the preceding three decades. Second, using popular sovereignty to decide the slavery question in each state would not only inject chaos into the political process, but would also trample the principle of equality and equal natural rights, which preceded the Constitution and legitimized self-government in the Declaration of Independence. Political leaders were abandoning the principle of freedom for the principle of slavery. As a nice-sounding "pro-choice" policy, popular sovereignty let the whims of the populace decide if slavery was good or evil. Moral progress—as inspired by the words of life, liberty, the pursuit of happiness, and that all men were created equal—seemed to have been replaced by moral degeneracy.[17] For this reason, Lincoln injected himself back into the political arena, for he truly believed the Kansas-Nebraska Act, if left to run its logical course, would destroy the Union.

Lincoln admitted that "the doctrine of self government is right—absolutely and eternally right," but clarified that the real question was whether "a negro is not or is a man." If the negro is not a man, then his owner could do whatever "he pleases with him. But if the negro is a man, is it not to that extent, a total destruction of self-government, to say that he too shall not govern himself?" Lincoln honed in on his main point: "When the white man governs himself that is self-government; but when he ... governs another man, that is more than self-government—that is despotism." If one admitted, as Lincoln certainly intimated, that "the negro is a man, why then my ancient

[16] Basler, Lincoln's Speech at Springfield, Illinois, October 4, 1854, *CW*, 2:245–46.

[17] Krannawitter, *Vindicating Lincoln*, 62–63, 71, 122.

faith teaches me that 'all men are created equal;' and that there can be no moral right in connection with one man's making a slave of another." Insisting that the "republican robe" had been "soiled" and that the time had come to "repurify" America as inspired by the American Revolution, Lincoln exhorted his countrymen "turn slavery from its claims of 'moral right' back upon its existing legal rights, and its arguments of 'necessity.'" Lincoln believed Americans needed to "re-adopt the Declaration of Independence, and with it, the practices, and policy, which harmonize with it. Let north and south—let all Americans—let all lovers of liberty everywhere" save the Union and keep it "worthy of the saving" for future generations.[18]

The Kansas-Nebraska Act compelled Lincoln to focus more on defending the Constitution and promises in the Declaration instead of abolishing slavery where it currently existed. Unity had to be maintained because the politics of the day were taking the country in the wrong direction. However naive he may have been, Lincoln felt a middle way or pragmatic approach to the slavery crisis remained the best option—certainly better than civil war. He knew the emotional and economic ties that each side clung to on the issue. "Slavery is founded in the selfishness of man's nature—opposition to it, is his love of justice," he said. "These principles are an eternal antagonism; and when brought into collision so fiercely, as slavery extension brings them, shocks, and throes, and convulsions must ceaselessly follow."[19]

For the next six years after the passage of the Kansas-Nebraska Act, Lincoln gave an estimated 175 speeches with the central message of the necessity to exclude slavery from the territories as the first step toward the extinction of slavery. He believed that his approach followed what the Founding Fathers had hoped for, and

[18] Basler, Lincoln's Speech at Peoria, Illinois, October 16, 1854, *CW*, 2:265–66, 276.

[19] Basler, Lincoln's Speech at Peoria, October 16, 1854, *CW*, 2:271.

that this was why the words "slave" and "slavery" could not be found in Constitution (slaves were called "persons held to labor").[20]

While Lincoln firmly believed that preserving the Union was the top priority, rather than the complete eradication of the peculiar institution, his pragmatic approach pained him. "You know I dislike slavery," he wrote his good friend Joshua Speed. "I confess I hate to see the poor creatures hunted down, and caught, and carried back to their stripes, and unrewarded toils; but I bite my lip and keep quiet." Recalling how, in 1841, he and Speed had taken a steamboat from Louisville to St. Louis, where they saw "ten or a dozen slaves, shackled together with irons," Lincoln said, "That sight was a continual torment to me; and I see something like it every time I touch the Ohio, or any other slave-border." Suppressing the fight over slavery in order to preserve the Union made him "miserable." He told Speed that he ought to "appreciate how much the great body of the Northern people do crucify their feelings, in order to maintain their loyalty to the constitution and the Union." He concluded with one of his most well-known statements on justice and equality:

> I do oppose the extension of slavery, because my judgment and feelings so prompt me ... As a nation, we began by declaring that "all men are created equal." We now practically read it "all men are created equal, except negroes." When the Know-Nothings get control, it will read "all men are created equal, except negroes, and foreigners, and catholics." When it comes to this I should prefer emigrating to some country where they make no pretence of loving liberty—to Russia, for instance, where despotism can be taken pure, and without the base alloy of hypocracy.[21]

---

[20] McPherson, *Lincoln*, 16.

[21] Basler, Lincoln to Joshua Speed, August 24, 1855, *CW*, 2:320.

Lincoln could see how the institution of slavery not only divided the nation but threatened it. In his riveting "house divided" speech, one that served as a template for his upcoming debates with the senior senator from Illinois, Stephen Douglas, Lincoln drew on both the practical and the moral as he quoted from the Bible, Declaration of Independence, and Constitution.[22] Echoing the words of Jesus admonishing the Pharisees in Matthew 12:25, Mark 3:24, and Luke 11:17, Lincoln claimed that "a house divided against itself cannot stand." He continued:

> I believe this government cannot endure, permanently half *slave* and half *free*. I do not expect the Union to be *dissolved*—I do not expect the house to *fall*—but I do expect it will cease to be divided. It will become *all* one thing, or *all* the other. Either the *opponents* of slavery, will arrest the further spread of it, and place it where the public mind shall rest in the belief that it is in course of ultimate extinction; or its *advocates* will push it forward, till it shall become alike lawful in *all* the States, *old* as well as *new*—*North* as well as *South*.[23]

While Lincoln abhorred slavery, he did not advocate for racial equality. Not an abolitionist until late in the Civil War, Lincoln remained a Union man first and foremost. Moreover, one must be mindful how, in the modern vernacular, Senator Douglas used the "race card" and other outright racist tactics to foil and bury Lincoln with Illinois voters. During the Lincoln-Douglas debates, when the Little Giant charged Lincoln with being a "Black Republican," Lincoln felt the need to respond for his political survival. His rejoinders certainly would not please any social justice warriors or

---

[22] Keneally, *Lincoln*, 67.

[23] Basler, Lincoln's House Divided Speech, Springfield, Illinois, June 16, 1858, *CW*, 2:461–62.

civil rights activists living in the present day, even as he tried to advocate for abolition. "I do not hold that because the negro is our inferior that therefore he ought to be a slave," Lincoln contended in the first debate. "On the contrary, I hold that humanity and Christianity both require that the negro shall have and enjoy every right, every privilege, and every immunity consistent with the safety of the society in which he lives."[24]

In the fourth debate with Douglas, Lincoln explained that he had never "been in favor of bringing about in any way the social and political equality of the white and black races," and that he had never "been in favor of making voters or jurors of negroes, nor of qualifying them to hold office, nor to intermarry with white people." In addition, he insisted "that there is a physical difference between the white and black races which I believe will forever forbid the two races living together on terms of social and political equality." But though "the white man is to have the superior position," negroes should not be denied everything. "I do not understand that because I do not want a negro woman for a slave I must necessarily want her for a wife." Lincoln went further: "I will add to this that I have never seen to my knowledge a man, woman or child who was in favor of producing a perfect equality, social and political, between negroes and white men." Carefully covering his constitutional bases, Lincoln asserted that the only place "where an alteration of the social and political relations of the negro and the white man can be made" is "in the State Legislature—not in the Congress of the United States—and as I do not really apprehend the approach of any such thing myself."[25]

In his fifth debate with the Little Giant, Lincoln stated that although "under our constitution and political system the negro is not a citizen, cannot be a citizen, and ought not to be a citizen, it

---

[24] Basler, Lincoln's First Debate with Stephen A. Douglas, Ottawa, Illinois, August 21, 1858, *CW*, 3:10.

[25] Basler, Lincoln's Fourth Debate with Stephen A. Douglas at Charleston, Illinois, September 18, 1858, *CW*, 3:145–46.

does not follow by any means that he should be a slave." Though the negro belonged to "an inferior race," he "ought to possess every right, every privilege, every immunity which he can safely exercise consistent with the safety of the society in which he lives." Continuing his balancing act, Lincoln asserted that "humanity requires, and Christianity commands that you shall extend to every inferior being, and every dependent being, all the privileges, immunities and advantages which can be granted to them consistent with the safety of society."[26]

Critics of his pragmatic and nuanced approach to the slavery issue—which displeased both abolitionists and defenders of the peculiar institution—exasperated Lincoln. Writing to a friend, he lamented, "I do not perceive how I can express myself, more plainly, than I have done" throughout the debates—disclaiming "all intention to bring about social and political equality between the white and black races," while making it "equally plain that I think the negro is included in the word 'men' used in the Declaration of Independence." Even though the Declaration's assertion that "'all men are created equal' is the great fundamental principle upon which our free institutions rest," the country had allowed Negro slavery to exist since its inception. Therefore, the states retained the power to decide the slavery question "at their own pleasure; and that all others—individuals, free-states and national government—are constitutionally bound to leave them alone about it."[27] As much as Lincoln advocated for restricting the spread of slavery to the territories, political realities kept him from promoting racial equality as a public official.

While Lincoln carefully and shrewdly navigated the political arena on the slavery issue in order to win or remain competitive in elections, he clearly advocated for abolition on a personal level.

---

[26] Basler, Lincoln's Fifth Debate with Stephen A. Douglas at Galesburg, Illinois, October 7, 1858, *CW*, 3:216–17.

[27] Basler, Lincoln to James Brown, October 18, 1858, *CW*, 3:327.

Agitated by arguments "written to prove slavery a very good thing," he came right to the point, noting that "we never hear of the man who wishes to take the good of it, by being a slave himself." Moreover, if one defended the institution of slavery by contending that darker-skinned people were deserving of bondage, Lincoln warned that "you are to be slave to the first man you meet, with a fairer skin than your own." If "whites are intellectually the superiors of the blacks" and can enslave others by this rationale, then one should beware of "the first man you meet, with an intellect superior to your own." If one maintained that enslavement remained "a question of interest," then someone else can make it in his interest that "he has the right to enslave you."[28]

Clergy who defended slavery were particularly irksome. Lincoln attacked the Reverend Dr. Frederick A. Ross, who had published a defense of slavery in 1857, for his "pro-slavery theology." Ross's argument—that slavery is not universally right or wrong, and that it is a good thing and the will of God for some people to be slaves—drew Lincoln's indignation. He could not believe that a man of the cloth claimed that "slavery is good for some people!!! As a *good* thing, slavery is strikingly peculiar, in this, that it is the only good thing which no man ever seeks the good of, *for himself*." Lincoln declared Ross's argument complete "nonsense." Relying on biblical language to make his point, Lincoln explained that Ross's reasoning meant that wolves devour lambs, "not because it is good for their own greedy maws, but because it is good for the lambs!!!"[29]

Lincoln criticized people who were "trying to establish the rightfulness of Slavery by reference to the Bible ... that slavery existed in the Bible times by Divine ordinance." When someone attempts to "establish that Slavery was right by the Bible, it will occur that that Slavery was the Slavery of the white man—of men without reference

---

28 Basler, Lincoln's Fragment on Slavery, April 1, 1854, *CW*, 2:222.

29 Basler, Lincoln's Fragment on Pro-Slavery Theology, October 1, 1858, *CW*, 3:204–05.

to color."[30] A voracious reader of Scripture, Lincoln knew slavery existed in Scripture, but not the same form of slavery practiced in antebellum America. In the Bible, slavery existed because of voluntary considerations, military conquest, or economic hardship and not because of race or ethnicity. Moreover, the kidnapping, rape, and murder of slaves were not allowed or condoned in Scripture.[31]

Despite those who misread and misapplied Scripture, Lincoln's admiration for the Bible and Christianity certainly bolstered his own personal views on slavery. One religious correspondent reminded Lincoln, during his debates with Douglas, to hold the high ground "of the Christianity of the day." The debates were "no less ... than for the advancement of the kingdom of Heaven or the kingdom of Satan." Lincoln had the "truth" on his side, while the opponent had "the devil on his side."[32]

Lincoln believed that the Bible, particularly the book of Genesis, inspired the basis of the Declaration of Independence. Since God had created all men equal and in His image, then "the justice of the Creator" had to be extended equally "to all his creatures, to the whole great family of man." Anyone created by the Creator should not be degraded or suppressed by another.[33] The rights of life, liberty, and the pursuit of happiness were divinely ordained. Moreover, as Scripture revealed, all human beings were entitled to the fruits of their labor, and that labor was worthy of its hire.[34] He recalled that "the Savior, I suppose, did not expect that any human creature could be perfect as the Father in Heaven; but He said, 'As your Father in Heaven is perfect, be ye also perfect.'" Therefore, if God set this "as a standard, and he who did most towards reaching that standard, attained the highest degree of moral perfection,"

---

30 Basler, Lincoln's Speech at Cincinnati, OH, September 17, 1859, *CW*, 3:445.

31 Mansfield, *Lincoln's Battle with God*, 104.

32 Carwardine, "Lincoln's Religion," 235–36.

33 Carwardine, "Lincoln's Religion," 229.

34 Oakes, *Lincoln and Race*, 114.

then Americans should, in the same way and "in relation to the principle that all men are created equal, let it be as nearly reached as we can." Lincoln exhorted that "if we cannot give freedom to every creature, let us do nothing that will impose slavery upon any other creature."[35]

The Bible significantly influenced Lincoln's worldview and opposition to slavery. Scripture's precepts affirmed that all men were "created in the image of God" (Gen. 1:27). The Great Commandment encouraged all to "love one's neighbor as oneself" (Matt. 22:39). Christians were to follow the Golden Rule to "do unto others" as they would want done unto them (Matt. 7:12). Moreover, God's command that "in the sweat of thy face thou shalt eat bread" (Gen. 3:19) reinforced the notion that all should labor free.[36]

Even before he won the presidency, Lincoln's two main arguments against slavery were that the institution posed an economic and moral threat to the nation. Yet Lincoln did not feel the country had embraced the idea of abolition. He told a compelling parable that encapsulated the conundrum he felt regarding simmering sectional tensions. Jean-Francois Gravelet, known as the Great Blondin, famously walked a tightrope across Niagara Falls on June 30, 1859. As he began his crossing on a hemp rope two inches wide, 1,300 feet long, and 160 feet above the rushing water, people shouted out, "Lean a little more to the North" or "to the South."[37] Lincoln thought it would have been better for them to hold their breaths until Blondin reached the other side. He shared this parable to hush those who demanded haste toward abolition. Like Blondin, who faced an incredible stress just to make it across the falls, Lincoln had to inch ahead deliberately, methodically, and carefully. A rushed misstep could be fatal—for him and the Union.

---

[35] Basler, Lincoln's Speech at Chicago, Illinois, July 10, 1858, *CW*, 2:501.

[36] Deutsch and Fornieri, *Lincoln's American Dream*, 27.

[37] Freehling, *Becoming Lincoln*, 147.

While he found abolitionists too zealous, too emotional, and too anti-constitutional in their "by any means necessary" spirit on the issue of slavery (well-known abolitionist William Lloyd Garrison had publicly burned a copy of the Constitution in 1854),[38] he did appreciate how evangelical Protestantism positively and singularly helped bring emancipation to fruition. Nonetheless, Lincoln stayed in the moderate middle lane, explaining that he did not want to "attack it where it exists." As he told a group of listeners:

> If I saw a venomous snake crawling in the road, any man would say I might seize the nearest stick and kill it; but if I found that snake in bed with my children, that would be another question. I might hurt the children more than the snake, and it might bite them. Much more, if I found it in bed with my neighbor's children, and I had bound myself by a solemn compact not to meddle with his children under any circumstances, it would become me to let that particular mode of getting rid of the gentleman alone. But if there was a bed newly made up, to which the children were to be taken, and it was proposed to take a batch of young snakes and put them there with them, I take it no man would say there was any question how I ought to decide![39]

Clergymen who supported slavery continued to disappoint the president. Flabbergasted that twenty out of the twenty-three Springfield clergymen opposed his election in 1860, he could not

---

[38] Guelzo, *Man of Ideas*, 94, 96, 98, 230.

[39] Basler, Lincoln's Speech at New Haven, Connecticut, March 6, 1860, *CW*, 4:17–18.

fathom how ministers could vote for candidates who favored human bondage while he did not.[40]

Nonetheless, Lincoln's interactions and relationships with clergymen continued to play a critical role in his faith formation and admiration for Christianity. While traveling in the spring of 1860, Lincoln visited Plymouth Congregational Church in Brooklyn. After hearing Henry Ward Beecher preach, Lincoln remarked that Beecher's mind had to be one of the most "productive" in human history. Beecher later campaigned vigorously for Lincoln in the presidential election.[41]

When Lincoln became president at the age of fifty-two, he entered the Executive Mansion with no administrative experience.

---

[40] Burlingame, *Lincoln*, 1:657. One rumor of the time purported that Lincoln did not attend Mary's church because its minister, John Howe Brown, favored Stephen Douglas for president.

[41] Burlingame, *Lincoln*, 1:591. Henry Ward Beecher—known as "the Shakespeare of the Pulpit" for his eloquent oratory, unconventional manner, and courage to speak out on the red-hot theological and political issues of the day— vehemently opposed slavery. A son of Old Lyman Beecher, a born polemic, and brother of Harriet Beecher Stowe, who wrote *Uncle Tom's Cabin*, Beecher had become one of the best-known American preachers. His Plymouth Church often filled to capacity, disappointing folks who had to be turned away on worship days. In one of his last acts before the assassination, Lincoln appointed Beecher to make the oration at Fort Sumter as the Union army regained control and raised the American flag. Lincoln appreciated Beecher's speeches on behalf of the Union cause in England in 1863. When Lincoln died, Beecher gave a eulogy in Plymouth Church entitled, "The Effect of the Death of Lincoln." The eulogy focused on Deuteronomy 34:1-4—the account of God leading Moses to the top of Mount Pisgah, where Moses viewed the Promised Land, which he would not enter (Jones, *Lincoln and the Preachers*, 86–87, 92, 95, 97). Beecher eulogized that "Cities and States are his pallbearers, and the canon beats the hours with solemn progression. Dead—dead—dead—he yet speaketh….Four years ago, O Illinois, we took from your midst an untried man…we return him to you a mighty conqueror. Not thine anymore, but the Nation's; not ours, but the world's. Give him place, ye prairies" (Peterson, *Lincoln In American Memory,* 18).

He had never been governor or even mayor, and had only served one inconsequential term as congressman in 1840s. He had no foreign correspondents or acquaintance with any ruler of a foreign nation.[42] Yet Lincoln knew the power of his own words—his ability to persuade people. He knew his words would shape Northern opinion, particularly on the emancipation issue, but it would take time.[43] A legal and political friend for decades, Joseph Gillespie, noted that Lincoln "could be a radical … so far as *ends* were concerned while he was conservative as to the *means* to be employed to bring about the ends." Gillespie believed that Lincoln "had it in his mind for a long time to war upon slavery until its destruction was effected but he always indicated a preference for getting rid of slavery by purchase rather than the war power."[44] Pragmatic, moderate, methodical—Lincoln wanted to end slavery in a way that would not involve secession, disunion, or violence.

Once elected president, the Great Pragmatist did not deviate from his approach on the slavery issue. The Union had to be saved, even if that meant ignoring the ugliness and inhumanness of the peculiar institution. Abolitionists railed against Lincoln's unwillingness to shift the war's focus from Union to abolition. Their anger intensified when the commander in chief revoked General John Fremont's and General David Hunter's emancipation orders. For abolitionists, the president's "face was turned toward Zion, but he seemed to move with leaden feet."[45] Their calls culminated in Horace Greeley's famous "Prayer of Twenty Millions," which demanded immediate abolition.[46]

---

[42] Donald, *Lincoln at Home*, 20.

[43] Fox, *Lincoln's Body*, 296.

[44] Wilson, *Herndon's Informants*, 507.

[45] Sinha, "Lincoln and Black Abolitionists," 177-78.

[46] Sinha, "Lincoln and Black Abolitionists," 177–78; Oates, *With Malice Toward None*, 260. After Confederates had whipped a Union force in late August 1861, Fremont issued an edict placing Missouri under martial law and declaring the slaves freedmen. Burlingame, *Lincoln*, 2:347. Lincoln struck

Yet if Lincoln had allowed Fremont's decrees to stand, Kentucky would have left the Union and joined the Confederacy. Moreover, to appease the abolitionists after rebuking Hunter's decision, Lincoln extended diplomatic relations to Haiti and Liberia, approved a treaty with Great Britain enforcing the ban on the African slave trade, and forbade the military to return slaves who reached Union lines. He also sanctioned General Benjamin Butler's strategy of declaring slaves who entered his lines "contraband," a policy Winfield Scott referred to as "Butler's fugitive slave law." [47] In early 1862, the president approved the hanging of Nathaniel Gordon, the only American ever hanged for slave trading. Lincoln's pragmatic, centrist approach continued to displease both ends of the political spectrum. But his balanced, meticulous approach kept the Union together and did not give political fodder for border states to leave the Union.

During the winter of 1861–1862, Lincoln worked with government officials in Delaware to draft a bill for gradual emancipation in a state where the number of slaves was inconsequential. He presented two proposals, each of which promised federal funds to pay state citizens for the freeing of their slaves. One offered emancipation by 1867, the other by 1893. Lincoln preferred the second version, which would require the nation to pay Delaware $23,200 per year for thirty-one years. The bills were never introduced due to perceived opposition, but Lincoln continued to look for a way to keep the Union together while eradicating slavery.[48]

In July 1862, Congress passed the Second Confiscation Act, freeing all slaves of disloyal masters—not just those directly employed in the Confederate military like the First Confiscation

---

down General David Hunter's decree of emancipation by military commander in the spring of 1862. As head of the Department of the South, Hunter had given an order on May 9, 1862, to liberate slaves, citing military necessity, in the Sea Islands off the coasts of Georgia, Florida, and South Carolina. He pressed them into military service and gave them weapons.

[47] Burlingame, *Lincoln*, 2:351.

[48] Donald, *Lincoln*, 345.

Act did. The bill allowed for the confiscation of rebel property and authorized the enlistment of freedmen as soldiers. Facing great pressure to veto it from moderate and conservative Republicans, Lincoln eventually signed it, paving the way for the Emancipation Proclamation.[49] As long as a legislative or executive act did not risk the war effort, Lincoln faithfully moved forward in approving antislavery legislation.

In July 1862, Congress approved Senator Henry Wilson's amendment to the Militia Act, which authorized the president to allow "persons of African descent" into the army for any military service they were competent to perform. Still careful not to move too fast, Lincoln decided to employ blacks only in supporting roles, such as teamsters, cooks, and laborers on entrenchments—almost every capacity except for combat. To accept regiments of black soldiers, Lincoln explained, would mean the Union could lose up to forty thousand white solders and drive the border states out of the Union. Too many white commanders and soldiers believed blacks did not have the courage to fight, or did not want to fight side by side with black soldiers. Lincoln would wait for a sign or a "direct command of Providence" before adopting such a policy.[50]

As the war progressed, Union casualties mounted and the concern about keeping the border states in the Union faded. Lincoln grew more confident to act on his desire to emancipate the slaves. In addition to his approval of General Benjamin Butler's contraband policy and the two Confiscation Acts, Lincoln supported Attorney General Edward Bates in his opinion to rescind the *Dred Scott* decision, supported the abolition of slavery in the District of Columbia and federal territories, and proposed plans for gradual and compensated emancipation for the border states. Moreover, Lincoln continually met with abolitionists, the vast majority of whom came

[49] Burlingame, *Lincoln*, 2:357–360.

[50] Burlingame, *Lincoln*, 2:464–65; White, *Lincoln*, 542.

away impressed with him and his conviction to secure a more perfect Union—one that was rid of slavery.[51]

Yet Lincoln could never satisfy both sides of the slavery debate, as evidenced by a meeting he had with black people in the White House on August 14, 1862—the first time in American history a president had done so. Lincoln wanted their support for his colonization plan. "You and we are different races," he told the delegation of five. Because of white prejudice, Lincoln said, "even when you cease to be slaves, you are yet far removed from being placed on an equality with the white race … It is better for both, therefore, to be separated." To round out his argument, he offered a powerful indictment of slavery: "Your race are suffering in my judgment, the greatest wrong inflicted on any people."

With that said, Lincoln still fell short of condemning white supremacy. Racism remained intractable and a part of life; whether it "is right or wrong I need not discuss." Unintentionally or not, Lincoln seemed to blame blacks for the Civil War: "But for your race among us there could not be war." Removal and colonization appeared to be the best remedy for their circumstances. He touted Central America as an area of fine harbors and "rich coal mines," where even a small band of colonists might succeed. He urged the black delegation to encourage other blacks to "sacrifice something of your present comfort" by agreeing to emigrate. To refuse would be "extremely selfish."

A stenographer was present for this meeting, and Lincoln's comments soon appeared in the nation's newspapers, as he probably intended. While Edward M. Thomas, the delegation's spokesman, found Lincoln's remarks persuasive, the bulk of the antislavery public and abolitionists howled with outrage. A. P. Smith, a black resident of New Jersey, wrote the president, "Pray tell us, is our right to a home in this country less than your own, Mr. Lincoln? Are you an American? So are we. Are you a patriot? So are we." Blacks

[51] Sinha, "Lincoln and Black Abolitionists," 178–80.

were outraged to hear from the president that their presence was "the cause of all this bloodshed." Frederick Douglass, soon to be a key influence in Lincoln's life, denounced the president's message. The practice of slavery had led the nation to civil war, not black people. Moreover, Douglass resented Lincoln for patronizing blacks by deciding what was "best" for them. They needed to be free.[52]

Lincoln could not win on the slavery issue. Both abolitionists and defenders of the institution of slavery continued to criticize his pragmatic and deliberate approach to emancipation. In September of 1862, a Massachusetts editor sarcastically remarked that Lincoln worshipped a strange God—a God that apparently did not stand for universal freedom. The president should try reading the Bible because he might learn something from it.[53]

White abolitionists in particular criticized Lincoln for his slow pace in advancing emancipation. Answering Horace Greeley's criticism in the *New York Tribune*, Lincoln insisted again:

> [My] paramount object in this struggle is to save the Union, and is not either to save or to destroy slavery. If I could save the Union without freeing any slave I would do it, and if I could save it by freeing all the slaves I would do it; and if I could save it by freeing some and leaving others alone I would also do that. What I do about slavery, and the colored race, I do because I believe it helps to save the Union; and what I forbear, I forbear because I do not believe it would help to save the Union. I shall do less whenever I shall believe what I am doing hurts the

---

[52] Foner, "Lincoln and Colonization," 155–56. Fourteen years later, when Douglass delivered the speech at the unveiling of the Freedmen's Memorial, the 1862 meeting still upset him. He could not shake his frustration when Lincoln "strangely told us that we were the cause of war...and were to leave the land in which we were born."

[53] Burlingame, *Lincoln*, 2:406.

> cause, and I shall do more whenever I shall believe doing more will help the cause.[54]

In 1863 the president supported a colonization expedition to Caribbean with volunteer blacks and fully funded by Congress. The adventure turned into a debacle, and a ship soon returned the colonists to the United States. As late as the fall of 1864, he sent one-legged General Sickles on an expedition to Colombia to see if it might prove appropriate for the colonization of former slaves.[55] Lincoln eventually abandoned his colonization notion because he no longer felt it necessary to appease the border states later in the war. Moreover, the valiant service of black soldiers as well as his burgeoning relationships with articulate black spokesmen such as Frederick Douglass, Martin Delany, Sojourner Truth, Bishop Daniel A. Payne of the African Methodist Episcopal Church, and residents of the educated free black community of New Orleans also changed his views on slavery.[56]

Back and forth Lincoln went—from the righteous moral crusader who personally abhorred slavery to the status quo, steady-as-she-goes Union leader who made prudent and safe decisions that would not rock the establishment. Lincoln's zeal to promote colonization, for example, might seem puzzling to some. His position on colonization, however, matched his pragmatic overall approach. Lincoln favored colonization, among other reasons, because he could not imagine

[54] Basler, Lincoln to Horace Greeley, August 22, 1862, *CW*, 5:388–89.

[55] Krannawitter, *Vindicating Lincoln*, 34; Keneally, *Lincoln*, 163.

[56] Foner, "Lincoln and Colonization," 163-–164. Freehling, *Becoming Lincoln*, 320. Before the war ended some 450,000 Southern troops (including around 130,000 Southern blacks) served in the Union army compared to 900,000 in Confederate armies. The Great Emancipator's final armed forces also included some 50,000 Northern free blacks. His war had become the North plus the northern third of the South, including most of its blacks and whites, against only two-thirds of the white South, with many of its slaves fleeing toward invading armies.

America as a biracial society. The American people, right or wrong, just would not accept free blacks and whites living in proximity. However flawed his reasoning or moral judgment, he earnestly thought blacks would welcome the opportunity to live in a land where they could fully enjoy their natural rights.[57]

As the progression of the war continued to shape Lincoln's ability to lead with more certainty on the slavery issue, he had the fortunate experience of entering into a special relationship with Frederick Douglass, a former slave and outspoken abolitionist. Impressed that Lincoln had willingly taken the time to meet with other African Americans in the Executive Mansion, Douglass visited the president several times. They struck up a friendship that had a profound influence upon both men.

Douglass's first visit took place on August 10, 1863. He expected to be asked to leave or to wait for hours before Lincoln would see him. Only minutes passed, however, before he was invited into Lincoln's office. "I was never more quickly or more completely put at ease in the presence of a great man in that of Abraham Lincoln,"[58] Douglass later recalled. As Lincoln extended his hand in greeting, Douglass tried to introduce himself. "I know who you are, Mr. Douglass," Lincoln said. "Seward has told me all about you. Sit down. I am glad to see you." Lincoln's warmth instantly put him at ease. Douglass later maintained that he had "never seen a more transparent countenance." He could tell "at a glance the justice of the popular estimate of the president's qualities expressed in the prefix 'honest' to the name of Abraham Lincoln." Lincoln listened with great sympathy as Douglass complained how discrimination hindered the black soldier recruiting effort. Lincoln impressed him with "with an earnestness and fluency of which I had not suspected in him." Douglass reported that he did not feel the "slightest shadow of

---

[57] Foner, "Lincoln and Colonization," 146.

[58] Goodwin, *Team of Rivals*, 552–53. The quotes and content in the next three paragraphs all come from this source.

embarrassment" for the meeting. He also said Lincoln's reasoning—that the black troop heroics at Milliken's Bend, Port Hudson, and Fort Wagner were needed to persuade white Americans that the war would not be about white men dying for negroes. Douglass found the argument "reasonable" if not agreeable. Moreover, Lincoln told Douglass that he could not grant equal pay to blacks serving in the war; wage differentials remained a necessary concession in a Union that still had too many white supremacists. Lincoln promised, however, that one day these black soldiers would receive the same pay as white solders. This came true in June 1864, albeit with a caveat—Congress mandated equal pay, but made it retroactive only to the first of that year.

Before Douglass departed, Lincoln told him that he had read a recent account in which the fiery orator had blasted Lincoln for being "tardy, hesitating, and vacillating" in his policies toward slaves and freedmen. Lincoln admitted that he might be moving too deliberately, but he refused to concede vacillation. "I think it cannot be shown that when I have once taken a position, I have ever retreated from it."

Douglass would never forget his first meeting with Lincoln, during which he felt "as though I could … put my hand on his shoulder." Later Douglass frequently commented on the gracious reception he received in the Executive Mansion. "Perhaps you may like to know how the president of the United States received a black man at the White House," he would say. "I will tell you how he received me—just as you have seen one gentleman receive another." As the crowd erupted into "a great applause," he continued, "I tell you I felt big there!" He added that the president did much to assure him that slavery would not survive the war or remain attached to the Union, and yet the Union would survive and thrive after the war and slavery's eradication. Douglass felt honored and deeply respected by the president who addressed him as "Mr. Douglass."

On another occasion, when guards tried to stop Douglass from entering the Executive Mansion, Lincoln personally intervened and greeted Douglass warmly.[59] To Douglass, like others, Lincoln made it clear that he opposed slavery, but that that patience and a keen understanding of good timing in the political process were needed to abolish the horrible institution.

Douglass had expected to meet a "white man's president, entirely devoted to the welfare of white men." Lincoln surprised him by being "the first great man that I talked with in the United States freely who in no single instance reminded me of the difference between himself and myself, or the difference of color." Douglass surmised Lincoln may have respected him "because of the similarity with which I had fought my way up, we both starting at the lowest rung of the ladder." The tough upbringing and rise from seemingly nothing made Lincoln, in Douglass's eyes, "emphatically the black man's president."[60]

Other blacks felt respected by Lincoln too. Bishop Daniel A. Payne of the African Methodist Episcopal Church, who called on Lincoln urging him to sign the District of Columbia Emancipation

---

59 Burlingame, *Lincoln*, 2:522-524, 769-70. A wonderful anecdote that reveals the mutual respect and admiration each man had for one another took place after Lincoln's reelection in 1864. When Douglass tried to enter a post-inauguration reception at the White House, two policemen blocked his way. Word got back to Lincoln that Douglass had been rebuffed. As soon as Lincoln heard of the situation, he had Douglass admitted immediately. Douglass later recalled how Lincoln's face lit up when he saw him and how special he felt when Lincoln loudly called out to his "friend" and shook his hand. When Lincoln asked for his opinion on his second inaugural address, because there was no one's opinion he valued more, Douglass tried to defer, insisting that thousands of people were waiting to greet the president. Lincoln, however, would not have it. He wanted to hear his good friend Douglass's opinion of the speech. Finally, Douglass told the President that the speech was a wonderful "sacred effort." Lincoln, of course, felt pleased that Douglass liked it. According to Elizabeth Keckley, Douglass proudly shared the respectful and esteemed manner in which Lincoln and greeted him at a reception after the event.

60 Guelzo, *Lincoln*, 350.

Act in April 1862, compared his gracious reception by Lincoln with the cold and stiff formality of John Tyler, for whose servant Payne had preached a funeral sermon. Sojourner Truth claimed she had "never been treated with more kindness and cordiality than I was by the great and good man, Abraham Lincoln," who signed her autograph book "Four Aunty Sojourner Truth A. Lincoln." [61] On Lincoln's death, Mary Lincoln made sure some of his prized personal possessions went to African Americans such as Douglass, Henry Highland Garnet, and Elizabeth Keckley, Mary's dressmaker and confidante.

The practical impact of ex-slaves and free blacks visiting him in the Executive Mansion should not be underestimated. If Lincoln did harbor doubts about the inequality of the races, his interactions with individuals such as Frederick Douglass slowly but steadily changed his mind. The president welcomed blacks to use the Executive Mansion grounds for public celebrations, and received black delegations graciously. In August 1864, months after the Emancipation Proclamation became law, Lincoln received a black delegation from Baltimore. They presented him with a beautifully bound edition of the Bible. The engraving on the front cover showed him striking the chains from the slaves. As he presented the Bible, Reverend S. M. Chase declared, "Towards you, sir, our hearts will ever be warm with gratitude. We come to present you with this copy of the Holy Scriptures as a token of respect for your active participation in furtherance of the cause of emancipation of our race."[62] Lincoln greatly admired the Bible and appreciated the gesture. He shook hands with the entire delegation and said he had always believed that "all mankind should be free."[63]

[61] Sinha, "Lincoln and Black Abolitionists," 181–82.

[62] Basler, Lincoln's Reply to Loyal Colored People of Baltimore upon Presentation of a Bible, September 7, 1864, *CW*, 7:543.

[63] Basler, Lincoln's Reply to Loyal Colored People of Baltimore upon Presentation of a Bible, September 7, 1864, *CW*, 7:542. Lincoln's response to this black delegation late in the war elicited one of his most powerful and

The following month, Lincoln showed the Bible to Sojourner Truth, abolitionist preacher and famous rescuer of many of her fellow blacks in slavery. When she complimented him as "the best President" ever,[64] he knew that her kind words were in reference to his push for emancipation. He modestly maintained that several of his predecessors, including Washington, would have done the same thing if they had served at this moment in history. He could never have pushed for legislation like the Emancipation Proclamation, he explained, if Southern states had not seceded from the Union. Truth insisted that she had never been treated by anyone "with more kindness and cordiality" than Lincoln. Proud of her connection with the president, she had him sign her autograph book "with the same hand that signed the death-warrant of slavery." She felt she was in the "presence of a friend," and thanked God "from the bottom of her heart" that she had "always advocated his cause."[65]

Lincoln's growing confidence in pursuing emancipation correlated with his growing reliance on Scripture. In September 1862, he claimed that slavery remained on his mind day and night. Whatever "shall appear to be God's will, I will do."[66] Unlike eighteenth-century Enlightenment philosophers who wanted morality separated from religion, Lincoln did not believe humans could understand right and wrong apart from the Bible.[67] The more Lincoln read Scripture, the more ardently he pursued emancipation.

---

compelling statements on the Bible. "In regard to this Great Book, I have but to say, it is the best gift God has given to man," he told them. "All the good the Saviour gave to the world was communicated through this book." Without God's Word, he explained, "we could not know right from wrong. All things most desirable for man's welfare, here and hereafter, are to be found portrayed in it. To you I return my most sincere thanks for the very elegant copy of the great Book of God which you present."

[64] Burlingame, *Lincoln*, 2:685.

[65] Donald, *Lincoln*, 541.

[66] Burlingame, *Lincoln,* 2:405.

[67] Miller, *Lincoln's Virtues*, 84.

Eventually, he came to believe that God had allowed the Civil War to occur as an opportunity to end slavery, and that humankind would be foolish to stand in way of this just and divine cause.

While Lincoln never saw himself ardent abolitionist due to his pragmatic approach in saving the Union first and foremost, he did eventually embrace their positions—abolition in the nation's capital (with compensation for slaveowners), wartime emancipation, enlisting black soldiers, amending the Constitution to abolish slavery, allowing some African Americans to vote. Abolitionists had the luxury of working outside system of inner workings of the government, while Lincoln had to play insider politics to accomplish his ends.[68] On emancipation, Lincoln had tough time balancing his convictions with his Constitutional duties. He had taken an oath to defend the Constitution and protect the laws of the land even if he disagreed with some and agonized over his antislavery convictions.[69]

One clear reason that Lincoln struggled over the slow pace of emancipation was that he heard about and saw the courageous contributions of African Americans who served and gave their lives for the Union cause. Perhaps more than any other factor, their contributions in battle made the commander in chief amenable to the idea of black rights and citizenship. By the end of the war, approximately 200,000 African Americans had served in army and navy, representing about 9 percent of the total Union armed forces.[70] They had been willing to sacrifice their lives for a cause—without waiting but in seizing the moment.

In early 1862, Lincoln told his cabinet that they were not united on what to do about slavery question even as it had become the most important one since the war began. Deploying his pragmatic and patient approach, the president told members that he would "float" with the tide until they coalesced around, or drifted to, a more united

---

68 Foner, "Emancipation of Lincoln," 147-48.

69 McPherson, *Lincoln*, 29.

70 Sinha, "Lincoln and Black Abolitionists," 188–89; Burlingame, *Lincoln*, 2:467.

and just position on the slavery question. When a congressmen asked him about some kind of emancipation proclamation, just after the president had relieved General Fremont for his emancipatory acts early in the war, Lincoln assured him that they were "*drifting*" toward that end.[71] Lincoln drifted, however, in a river he chose to place himself in—one headed toward an emancipation falls. Lincoln did not believe that the fiery, scalding rhetoric of abolitionists would eliminate the scourge of slavery. Instead, like the frog in a boiling pot analogy, he deemed that a slow but steady simmering of constant pressure would eventually kill the peculiar institution.

Lincoln had a sixth sense in regard to timing. He knew just the right time to appease the border states, suppress the emancipatory actions of rogue generals, push the Emancipation Proclamation, insist on the enlistment of black soldiers into the Union army, and push for the Thirteenth Amendment, which abolished slavery forever. As Lincoln's pragmatism revealed itself, many Northerners saw in retrospect the genius of his patience and deliberate action. They came to see the president as God's instrument in the destruction of the institution of slavery. Indeed, others echoed Esther 4:14 (KJV), explaining that God raised up Lincoln "for such a time as this."[72]

Lincoln certainly believed in his own power of persuasion and his ability to shape public opinion. When some came to object to his decision to use black troops, he responded in a pragmatic and direct way that revealed his true sentiments on the contentious issue: "Well, gentlemen, if you would rather have your sons die for a black man than have a black man die for your sons, I suppose there is nothing more to be said."[73]

During the middle of the war, Lincoln told those who disparaged his slow pace toward emancipation that one could not cross a river until one had arrived at it.[74] Lincoln once told a story to illustrate

---

[71] Burlingame, *Lincoln*, 2:232.

[72] Burlingame, 2:617.

[73] Krannawitter, *Vindicating Lincoln*, 41.

[74] Burlingame, *Lincoln*, 2:334.

his pragmatic approach to the slavery issue. "A man watches his pear-tree day after day," he explained, "impatient for the ripening of the fruit. Let him attempt to *force* the process, and he may spoil both fruit and tree. But let him patiently *wait,* and the ripe pear at length falls into his lap!"[75]

In the last three years of his presidency, the pear of emancipation fell into Lincoln's very capable hands. Prepared for the moment, the Great Pragmatist did not falter in ending the scourge of slavery and becoming known forever in history as the Great Emancipator.

The Truth

There are plenty of authors and leadership gurus in the world who tell us *what* to do in life. There are many fewer, however, who articulate *when* or *when not* to do something in life. Perhaps because we frail, sinful human beings cannot wrap our brains around the notion of eternity—*living forever*—it is no surprise that we struggle with a sense of timing here in our fallen world on earth, a place where we know human beings will not live forever, and a place that can, in fact, pass away in the blink of an eye.

As much as humans struggle with the notion of eternity juxtaposed against the finite and unpredictability of time here on earth, we know that time and timing are important. You probably recognize or have event stated the cliché often, because it is so significant: *Timing is everything.*

Pastors and Christian leaders struggle with timing issues all the time. Talking to a couple living together out of wedlock, does a pastor give them a fire and brimstone condemnation for "living in sin" during their first counseling session? Or does he try to build a relationship with the vulnerable and unchurched couple first, so they come back for session two? Is it better to reach the unchurched by preaching fire and brimstone outside a professional sports stadium

[75] Goodwin, *Team of Rivals*, 502.

when thousands of fans are trying to enter expediently? Or is it better to build a relationship with someone at work during a quiet moment on break? Timing is critical.

Lincoln had to discern the proper time to push hard for the eradication of slavery. His timing rarely pleased everyone. There is a lesson in there for Christians. We must constantly pray and ask God for guidance in our timing too, whether it be advocating for a political position, re-engaging a relationship, or making a significant life change.

The Bible talks a lot about time and timing. Scripture says that "for everything there is a season, and a time for every matter under heaven."[76] Jesus was acutely aware of his sense timing during his public ministry on earth.[77]

The hard part for us sinful human beings is that we are impatient with God's plans and timing. We want what we want when we want it—and we want it now. The Bible tells us, however, that "the vision awaits its appointed time; it hastens to the end—it will not lie." Even if our life vision "seems slow" to come, we are to "wait for it; it will surely come; it will not delay."[78]

Perhaps you have burdens or big decisions to make and simply want God to tell you what you should do. Or maybe you have been putting in your time and working hard on some project, and the results you want are simply not coming to fruition. If this is the case, God encourages you to never "grow weary of doing good," for in due season you will reap if you do not give up.[79]

Scripture is clear that you are to "trust in the Lord with all your heart, and do not lean on your own understanding. In all your ways acknowledge him, and he will make straight your paths."[80] Again and again, the Bible tells you to "wait for the Lord; be strong, and

---

[76] Eccles. 3:1.

[77] John 7:6.

[78] Hab. 2:3.

[79] Gal. 6:9.

[80] Prov. 3:5–6.

let your heart take courage; wait for the Lord!"[81] Those "who wait for the Lord shall renew their strength; they shall mount up with wings like eagles; they shall run and not be weary; they shall walk and not faint."[82]

In order to wait for Lord, you must listen to Him through His Word. The Bible tells you that He has grand plans for you, "plans for welfare and not for evil, to give you a future and a hope."[83] Often God's plans or timing will not make sense to you, especially in the short term. During these moments, be patient as you continue to listen to and wait for your Heavenly Father. For He reminds you that "my thoughts are not your thoughts, neither are your ways my ways … For as the heavens are higher than the earth, so are my ways higher than your ways and my thoughts than your thoughts."[84] Take comfort in these words, especially knowing "that for those who love God all things work together for good, for those who are called according to his purpose."[85] Rejoice that your time is in God's hands.[86]

Timing is important to God and has been since He created the world. The Bible teaches that our Heavenly Father "made everything beautiful in its time," and "has put eternity into man's heart."[87] Knowing these truths, one of your daily prayers should be for godly wisdom and discernment on matters of timing. Ask Him to guide you not only on what to do but when to do it.

Eternity in heaven is yours, thanks to Jesus's death and resurrection for the forgiveness of your sins. Your time in heaven is already reserved and guaranteed by His mercy, grace, and love. God's plan of salvation, from the very beginning of time, had you

---

[81] Ps. 27:14.
[82] Isa. 40:31.
[83] Jer. 29:11.
[84] Isa. 55:8–9.
[85] Rom. 8:28.
[86] Ps. 31:15.
[87] Eccles. 3:11.

and the entire world in mind. As the Bible affirms, "For while we were still weak, at the right time Christ died for the ungodly."[88] Indeed, "when the fullness of time had come, God sent forth his Son, born of woman, born under the law, to redeem those who were under the law, so that we might receive adoption as sons."[89] God's plan of salvation, crafted at the very beginning of Genesis, is always timely and timeless for you. You may not be able to control your daily schedule, let alone the trials and tribulations that come during your daily walk on earth. Be assured, however, that God is in control over all things, including time and timeliness. "What is impossible with men is possible with God."[90]

While God grants you time here on earth, make sure you make the most of it. Be a good steward of all the gifts He has given you. Remember: Mordecai's words to Esther are God's words to you: you have been put here on earth "for such a time as this."[91]

Your Life

Lincoln's practical approach to emancipating the slaves had a lot to do with timing. When have you had to make tough decisions—to do or not do something—based on timing? How did you know when the timing was right for you to take action or not take action?

Many people criticized Lincoln for being too slow to emancipate the slaves or for not having strong enough antislavery convictions to take action. Others criticized him for moving too fast. When can moving too slowly make it appear that one does not have the courage to make a decision, the conviction to move forward, or the

[88] Rom. 5:6.

[89] Gal. 4:4–5.

[90] Luke 18:27.

[91] Esther 4:14.

work ethic to complete something that is difficult to achieve? Or vice versa—when does moving too fast on something make it appear that one is reckless, careless, or too emotional to make a sound decision?

How was God's timing perfect in sending Jesus to take on human flesh and to die for our sins on the cross of Calvary?

Why do you believe God has put you here on earth "for such a time as this"? How do you know if this is His plan for you and God-pleasing?

39

The Great Emancipator

So Jesus said to the Jews who had believed him, "If you abide in my word, you are truly my disciples, and you will know the truth, and the truth will set you free."
—John 8:31–32

The Lincoln Way

Actions often speak louder than words.

On April 14, 1876, in Lincoln Park, Washington, DC, on the eleventh anniversary of Lincoln's assassination, former slave and abolitionist Frederick Douglass delivered a celebratory dedication address of the Emancipation Memorial, also referred to as the Freedman's Monument. The bronze, twelve-foot sculpture depicts an upright Lincoln benevolently and protectively extending his left hand over a kneeling (or rising?) slave while he holds the Emancipation Proclamation in his right hand.

The monument immediately elicited controversy. Some thought it depicted blacks in a passive way, showing Lincoln as the superior, great white father setting his children free. Others criticized the statue for making it look like a freed slave was shining Lincoln's shoes.[1]

[1] Peterson, *Lincoln in American Memory*, 380; Sinha, "Lincoln and Black Abolitionists," 167. Some critics insist that Lincoln himself would not have liked the monument. When liberated slaves greeted him in Richmond on

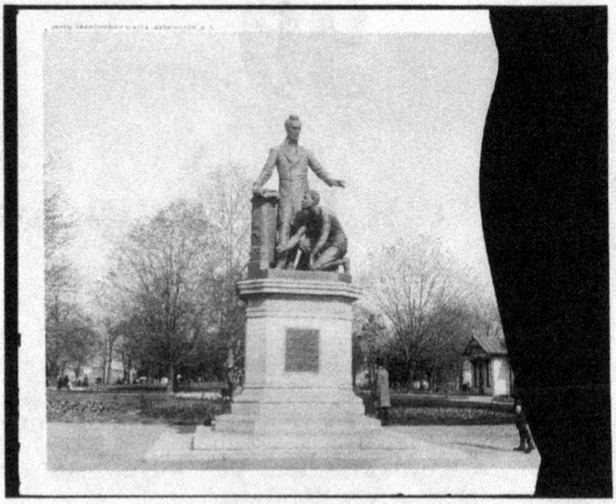

The Emancipation Memorial, or Freedman's Monument, depicted here in 1901, remains controversial today, though Frederick Douglass gave the dedication address, and funds for the monument were entirely raised by African Americans. (Library of Congress, LC-DIG-det-4a05594)

A closer look at the monument, however, illustrates the great care and attention to detail that went into the development of the project. Lincoln is hovering over a slave who is exercising his new-found freedom. The slave is clothed poorly but has a chiseled and muscular physique under his tattered textiles. The slave's clenched right wrist reveals determination and readiness. His left knee is still on the ground, but the right knee lifted—ready to spring into action. He is not a "crouching" or "kneeling" as some detractors claimed, but rising. His shackles are newly broken (still fixed to one wrist). The new freedman is looking away from the president without showing a sense of awe. This is an image of liberated slave, according to the *New York Tribune*. Lincoln is looking down on the freed slave with solemn attention, extending his left arm over the man's body as if to bless him. The former slave shows deference to the emancipator, as if waiting for him to wrap up his official duties so he can leap forward to freedom. In this way, the monument shows

April 4, 1865, he is known to have murmured in embarrassment, "You must kneel to God only."

both the grandeur of the completed work and the magnitude of the unfinished work of achieving social and political equality.

Douglass did not disparage the depiction of the freed slave. His very presence at the event demonstrated that he approved of the image. If he had found the monument offensive in any way, he never would have agreed to give a speech or appear at the dedication ceremony. The idea for the monument, after all, had been initiated by blacks, and the funds for the statue had been raised by African Americans, to the tune of $17,000.[2]

Douglass spoke of the "very favorable circumstances in which we meet today. They are high, inspiring, and uncommon."[3] After talking about how far the country had come on the slavery issue, he said that "we are here to express, as best we may … our grateful sense

---

[2] Kautz, "Democratic Statesmanship of Lincoln," 166; Fox, *Lincoln's Body*, 164–166. The idea for a monument began soon after Lincoln's death. Charlotte Scott, (Marietta, Ohio), when she heard of Lincoln's death, immediately told her employer, "The colored people have lost their best friend on earth … I will give five dollars of my wages toward erecting a monument in his memory." The biggest contributors were black soldiers of the Mississippi River region. Many wanted the monument built only with colored people's money. On July 4th, 1866, Henry Garnet, a Presbyterian minister and president of Colored People's National Lincoln Monument Association wrote a poem that included these lines:

> Our Lincoln Memorial of One shall speak,
> Like Moses faithful, and like Moses meek;
> Who led the people through a redder sea
> Than Israel passed, to light and liberty.
> Of him, who, humbly trusting in the Lord,
> Moved by the Holy Spirit, spoke thy word;
> And, as that word was plainly, firmly, spoken,
> The bonds-man's chains fell off, the tyrant's rod was broken (Peterson, *Lincoln in American Memory*, 57).

[3] Frederick Douglass, Oration in Memory of Abraham Lincoln, April 14, 1876, https://teachingamericanhistory.org/library/document/oration-in-memory-of-abraham-lincoln/. The Douglass speech quotes in the next several paragraphs come this same source.

of the vast, high, and preeminent services rendered to ourselves, to our race, to our country, and to the whole world by Abraham Lincoln." Today they would celebrate, as well as coming generations, and dedicate a monument to "the exalted character and great works of Abraham Lincoln, the first martyr president of the United States."

Douglass did not whitewash history. He spared no criticism of Lincoln the president or the man. Even at the celebration of a monument honoring the man, Douglass felt compelled to explain that Lincoln possessed the habits, thoughts, and prejudices of a white man. Lincoln "was preeminently the white man's President, entirely devoted to the welfare of white men." Noting Lincoln's calculated, pragmatic approach to the abolishment of slavery, Douglass said that the president frequently attempted "to deny, postpone, and sacrifice the rights of humanity in the colored people to promote the welfare of the white people of this country" during the first years of his presidency. Lincoln became president because he opposed the extension of slavery, not because he stood for complete abolition. White people were "the children of Abraham Lincoln," while black people were "at best only his step-children; children by adoption, children by forces of circumstances and necessity." Nevertheless, Douglass was grateful that while Lincoln "saved for you a country, he delivered us from a bondage."

Despite Lincoln's slowness to free the slaves, Douglass praised the deceased president for his devotion to the movement and for ultimately following through on the eradication of the peculiar institution. In the end, whether too fast or too slow in his advance toward emancipation, Lincoln deserved credit for being "at the head of a great movement" and "living and earnest sympathy with that movement" to abolish slavery forever in the United States. Even though "the Union was more to him than our freedom or our future, under his wise and beneficent rule we saw ourselves gradually lifted from the depths of slavery to the heights of liberty and manhood."

The Emancipation Proclamation, which the Lincoln statue held in his right hand, was a particularly notable document in the annals of history. "Can any colored man, or any white man friendly to the freedom of all men," Douglas asserted, "ever forget the night which followed the first day of January, 1863, when the world was to see if Abraham Lincoln would prove to be as good as his word?" Douglass would "never forget that memorable" moment which erased "all delay, and forgot all tardiness, forgot that the president had bribed the rebels to lay down their arms by a promise to withhold the bolt which would smite the slave-system with destruction." As long as slaves would become freed men, "we were thenceforward willing to allow the president all the latitude of time, phraseology, and every honorable device that statesmanship might require for the achievement of a great and beneficent measure of liberty and progress."

Douglass complimented Lincoln for his gentleness, transparency, strong convictions, and tolerance of other people's viewpoints. He also admitted that he understood better now the difficult challenge Lincoln had faced in not rushing to eliminate slavery at the beginning of the war. If Lincoln had favored abolition over Union, "he would have inevitably driven from him a powerful class of the American people and rendered resistance to rebellion impossible." Douglass said that from an abolitionist's viewpoint, the president "seemed tardy, cold, dull, and indifferent; but measuring him by the sentiment of his country, a sentiment he was bound as a statesman to consult, he was swift, zealous, radical, and determined." Douglass sympathized with the "fierce" criticism the president endured. In addition to receiving sharp and personal rebukes from his "friends," individuals from all sides of the political spectrum viciously attacked him—Abolitionists, slave-holders, peace proponents, war hawks. Lincoln "was assailed for not making the war an abolition war; and he was bitterly assailed for making the war an abolition war." Despite all the condemnation the president received, no man seem "better fitted for his mission than Abraham Lincoln."

Douglass ended his speech as he began it: "with congratulations" and in honor of "our friend and liberator." To show gratitude to

Lincoln on behalf of the freed people, "we may calmly point to the monument we have this day erected to the memory of Abraham Lincoln."

Despite Douglass's praise and celebratory words at the time of the dedication, W. E. B. Du Bois, founder of NAACP, was less enamored with Lincoln the Emancipator. While he praised Lincoln for his mental qualities, clear-sightedness, and capacity for growth, he agreed with Douglass's belief that Lincoln had not been wholeheartedly committed to black freedom and equality. He wanted to "demythicize" the Great Emancipator in order to improve African American self-confidence. "The picture of Lincoln looking out upon space with sad and loving eyes," he said, referring to the Freedman's Monument, "his right hand outstretched presenting the Emancipation Proclamation, his left hand resting tenderly upon the head of a newly freed and gratified slave kneeling at his feet, can no longer be satisfactory."[4]

Divergent viewpoints about the monument persist. That an aging washerwoman and former slave used her savings to initiate the project does not seem matter to many contemporary critics. Nor does it seem to matter that thousands of freed slaves, particularly African American veterans, contributed their pennies. Today some African Americans deem the monument offensive rather than moving. For some detractors, Lincoln is the Reluctant Emancipator or not an emancipator at all.[5]

The Emancipation Proclamation set in motion the series of events that eventually led to Lincoln becoming renowned as the Great Emancipator. At first blush, however, the Emancipation Proclamation appears to fit a Great Pragmatist moniker more appropriately, for the document did not free all slaves or outlaw slavery in the United States. Effective January 1, 1863, the document stated that "all persons held as slaves within any State or designated

---

[4] Peterson, *Lincoln in American Memory*, 174.

[5] Miller, *Lincoln's Virtues*, xiv.

part of a State, the people whereof shall then be in rebellion against the United States, shall be then, thenceforward, and forever free." In other words, only slaves in Confederate states were declared free.

Of course, the proclamation provided an incentive for slaves in the Confederacy to seek Union territory by noting that the "Executive Government of the United States, including the military and naval authority thereof, will recognize and maintain the freedom of such persons, and will do no act or acts to repress such persons, or any of them, in any efforts they may make for their actual freedom." Revealing the military advantages for freeing the slaves in the Confederacy, the document stated that these manumitted slaves "will be received into the armed service of the United States to garrison forts, positions, stations, and other places, and to man vessels of all sorts in said service." For Lincoln, emancipating the slaves in the Confederacy was an "act of justice, warranted by the Constitution," a "military necessity," and a moral obligation inspired by the "gracious favor of Almighty God."[6]

Critics of Lincoln the Emancipator contend that the Emancipation Proclamation became a reality only because of military and political necessity. There is truth to this argument, but it is also incomplete. The Union army and Northern public morale had certainly cratered by the summer of 1862. Lincoln, his cabinet, and other Union politicians recognized the need for a game changer. Secretary of State William Seward advised Lincoln to delay the announcement of the proclamation until after a Union military victory so that the Union would not look desperate, even if the situation remained dire. While not a clear victory, the Battle of Antietam, which prevented Lee's army from advancing into Northern territory, provided an opportunity to release the proclamation on September 22, 1862.

While certainly passed for pragmatic reasons, the Emancipation Proclamation did more than help Lincoln politically and militarily.

---

[6] Basler, Lincoln's Emancipation Proclamation, January 1, 1863, *CW*, 6:28–30.

In fact, the political ramifications were mixed. While many citizens of the North, particularly abolitionists, praised the document, many others balked at the notion of sending their sons into battle to free slaves rather than save the Union.

Nevertheless Lincoln believed the time had finally come for some kind of official pronouncement that slaves were being set free—even if only in Confederate-held territory. The Great Pragmatist had delivered and made emancipation a reality. The Emancipation Proclamation started a chain reaction that would lead in short order to the enlistment of black soldiers, fair pay for those soldiers, and passage of the Thirteenth Amendment, which would outlaw slavery for the entire nation. The Great Pragmatist had seen his long-term strategy come to fruition. Slavery had finally been outlawed in territory where it had existed for over four hundred and fifty years.

Neither the eradication of slavery nor a Union victory were assured in 1863. Much work needed to be accomplished on both fronts. Shortly after the Emancipation Proclamation took effect, Lincoln told a story that revealed his determination to uphold his declaration: "We are a good deal like whalers who have been long on a chase. At last we have got our harpoon fairly into the monster; but we must now look how we steer, or with one *flop* of his tail, he will yet send us all into eternity!"[7]

Now that the Emancipation Proclamation had laid down a gauntlet, Lincoln demonstrated his tenacity, grit, and persistence to stand firm on his landmark achievement. When peace offerings came from Copperheads (Northern Democrats) or Confederates to end the war, Lincoln rejected these overtures because they kept the Confederacy and slavery intact. "Still let us not be over-sanguine of a speedy final triumph," Lincoln said, fearing that a hasty peace might end the horrific war but retain slavery as a constitutionally sanctioned institution. "Let us be quite sober. Let us diligently apply

[7] Carpenter, *Six Months in the White House*, 98.

the means, never doubting that a just God, in his own good time, will give us the rightful result."[8]

As the war progressed, Lincoln continually revealed his desire to free the slaves. "At the beginning of the war, and for some time, the use of colored troops was not contemplated," he told one gathering. "Upon a clear conviction of duty I resolved to turn that element of strength to account; and I am responsible for it to the American people, to the christian world, to history, and on my final account to God."[9] Blacks and freed slaves would now serve in the Union army. The moral Lincoln had finally merged and emerged publicly with the pragmatic Lincoln.

By the time of the 1864 election, many black and white abolitionists—even ones whom had been critical of his slowness toward equality—had come around to support Lincoln. J. W. C. Pennington, a black Presbyterian minister, said that Lincoln should be considered the black man's president, since he had been the only American chief executive to give proper attention to colored people as citizens. Reelecting him would ensure that the good work and progress on black emancipation and freedom would be earnestly completed.[10]

When the commander in chief visited the Eighteenth Corps in Grant's army, in June 1864, near Petersburg, hundreds of excited black troops rushed to see him, hurrahing and cheering. A journalist reported the genuine spontaneity of joy, love, and affection that poured forth toward the man who had delivered them from bondage. They received the president with smiles and tears. As they swarmed the president, kissing his hands and reverently touching his dust-covered suit, Lincoln teared up, bowing right and left. The president became so emotional, he could barely articulate any words of gratitude or congratulation for their achievements. Almost

---

[8] Basler, Lincoln to James C. Conkling, August 26, 1863, *CW*, 6:409–10.

[9] Basler, Lincoln's Address at Sanitary Fair, Baltimore, Maryland, April 18, 1864, *CW*, 7:302.

[10] Burlingame, *Lincoln*, 2:643.

everyone present during these moving moments would never forget them.[11]

Lincoln hoped the Emancipation Proclamation would create change faster than it did. He lamented that slaves were not leaving Confederate territory as rapidly or in as great numbers as he had anticipated. Moreover, with his reelection prospects looking bleak in the summer of 1864, he worried that slaves would not get the news of the proclamation before the war's end.[12] If they remained behind enemy lines and a new president sued for peace with the Confederacy, those slaves would remain in bondage.

Frederick Douglass, meeting with Lincoln for the second time on August 19, 1864, newly appreciated the depth of the president's moral conviction against slavery. Lincoln boldly told Douglass that he hated slavery as much as the ex-slave did and wanted to see it completely eradicated from the nation. Douglass agreed to recruit a band of black scouts to carry the news of emancipation behind rebel lines and urge slaves to come within Union areas of control.

---

[11] Burlingame, *Lincoln,* 2:654.

[12] Oates, *With Malice Toward None,* 395. Lincoln's reelection truly looked unlikely in the summer of 1864. In June and July, Confederate Jubal Early raided the Shenandoah Valley—cutting telegraph lines, seizing Harper's Ferry, and menacing the cities of Baltimore and Washington—causing considerable fear in the region. In fact, Lincoln had to be pushed down to the ground for cover at Fort Stevens as bullets from Early's soldiers nearly struck him. Union general William Tecumseh Sherman's advance had stalled in Atlanta. Grant could not dislodge Lee from Petersburg. Newspaper reporter Horace Greeley begged Lincoln to negotiate for peace insisting that the people wanted the war to end. He echoed what many in the North believed—that "our bleeding, bankrupt, almost dying" country would not be able to take new conscriptions and one more year of carnage. One Republican legislator said, "I find everywhere a conviction that we need a change," and that "the war languishes under Mr. Lincoln and that he cannot and will not give us peace." A Republican from New York insisted that "there are no Lincoln men," and that folks did not "know which way to turn." Friends and foes alike were certain he could not be reelected. Even Lincoln admitted privately that he had a small chance to be reelected.

The abolitionist also asked the president to discharge his ailing son, Charles, from the army, which Lincoln did.

After the meeting, Douglass told General John Eaton that the president again treated him as a man and did not seem to care about the different colors of their skins. Douglass reiterated his satisfaction that Lincoln, under the circumstances, continued to do all that he could do for black people. Lincoln's mutual admiration for Douglass also continued to grow. Truly impressed by Douglass's life story and rise, and perhaps seeing similarities to his own life, Lincoln lauded the abolitionist as one of the most "meritorious" individuals in the nation.[13]

As Lincoln rejected peace offerings from Confederate emissaries, who were trying to rally the peace movement in the North and resist Lincoln's desire to save the Union and rid it of slavery at the same time, respect for the president grew among abolitionists who had been among the administration's earliest critics. Moreover, when the Democratic platform of peace, union, and restoration of states' rights (e.g., slavery) became conspicuous, many who had been disparaging toward Lincoln changed their tune. Frederick Douglass encouraged anyone who cared about slaves and the well-being of the nation to earnestly support the Lincoln-Johnson ticket.[14] The presidential election of 1864 presented a stark choice on slavery: Lincoln and the Republicans were for emancipation, while McClellan and the Democrats were for states' rights and the peculiar institution.

After Lincoln's resounding victory, the Great Emancipator moved forward on the passage of the Thirteenth Amendment, which would outlaw slavery throughout the entire country.[15] Certainly the

---

[13] Burlingame, *Lincoln*, 2:677–78.

[14] Burlingame, *Lincoln*, 2:683.

[15] Basler, Lincoln's Reply to Delegation from the National Union League, June 9, 1864, *CW*, 7:384. Lincoln won every state in the election with the exception of New Jersey, Delaware, and Kentucky. Military victories changed the political winds and helped Lincoln get reelected. Admiral David Farragut's capture of Mobile Bay in August, Sherman's decisive victory over Confederates

Great Pragmatist still lived: Lincoln believed passage would shorten the war. No evidence exists that Lincoln offered specific quid pro quo for votes as depicted in Steven Spielberg's biopic *Lincoln*, but it seems he did authorize his lieutenants to do so. Years later, rumors persisted that Democrats were offered substantial bribes to vote yea. Lincoln did pen a careful, lawyerly crafted message to thwart yet another Confederate peace conference attempt.[16]

The Great Emancipator ardently believed that all slaves and all Union citizens should be free. Owen Lovejoy once made this observation about Lincoln: "I tell you, Mr. Lincoln is at heart as strong as antislavery man as any of them, but he is compelled to feel his way." Lovejoy noted that "his mind acts slowly, but when he moves, it is forward. You will never find him receding from a position once taken. It is of no use talking, or getting up conventions against him."[17]

Proud that Illinois became first state to ratify the Thirteenth Amendment, Lincoln basked in the praise that proponents of the amendment sent his way.[18] Abolitionist William Lloyd Garrison applauded his commitment and "mighty work." He also praised God for sending Lincoln as an "instrument" of His hands and as a "chainbreaker" for the millions who had toiled in bondage for so long.[19] To commemorate passage, Lincoln, with the approval of the cabinet and congressional chaplains, had Henry Highland Garnet, a prominent black Presbyterian minister and emigration champion,

---

in Atlanta in early September, and General Phil Sheridan's triumphs in the Shenandoah Valley demonstrated competency from the commander in chief. With the war heading in the right direction, the American people could buy more easily into Lincoln's assertion that "it was not best to swap horses when crossing streams."

16 Burlingame, *Lincoln*, 2:745–46, 748.

17 Sandburg, *Lincoln*, 477.

18 McGovern, *Lincoln*, 129.

19 Burlingame, *Lincoln*, 2:750.

deliver a sermon in the House chamber on February 14, 1865.[20] Lincoln saw God's providence in the passage of the amendment; pointing across the Potomac toward the South, he said, "If the people over the river had behaved themselves, I could not have done what I have."[21]

Lincoln still tried every diplomatic angle he could to end the war and restore the Union without the institution of slavery. In February 1865, Lincoln reintroduced to his cabinet a resolution he had made earlier with the Confederates. The government would offer $400 million as compensation to slaveholders if the Confederacy would surrender by April 1, 1865.[22] By this time, however, Radical Republicans were in no mood to show the South any mercy for the sins of slavery and war.

After Union armed forces captured the Confederate capital of Richmond, Lincoln wanted to visit the city, though he was warned of possible assassination attempts. When he arrived on April 4, 1865, grateful freedmen mobbed him in the streets. When some tried to kneel before him, he became embarrassed. He asked them not to kneel for him but to God only. They should thank God for the liberty they now enjoyed.

Later at Capitol Square, Lincoln addressed a huge crowd of blacks, reminding them that liberty was their birthright and a gift from God. Though they had been denied freedom because of a sinful world and sinful men, the president challenged them to earn and safeguard their liberty. He called on them to obey God's commandments and show the world their gratitude to Him for their freedom and all good things.[23] Lincoln no longer needed to be the Great Pragmatist. He could lead now as the Great Emancipator.[24]

---

[20] Burlingame, *Lincoln,* 2:751.

[21] Oates, *With Malice Toward None*, 406.

[22] Burlingame, *Lincoln*, 2:759.

[23] Burlingame, *Lincoln*, 2:790–91.

[24] Striner, "Lincoln and the Struggle to End Slavery," 175. Striner maintains Lincoln masked his revolutionary impulse as much as he could

If Lincoln is remembered for anything today, the odds are that it is for the Emancipation Proclamation and the fact that he "freed the slaves." However he got there, he did more than just talk about emancipation—he actually did it. While his pragmatic approach certainly helped him free the slaves, accomplishing hard things required persistence and conviction. Lincoln not only truly believed slaves should be free, he also delivered. This is what makes him the *Great* Emancipator.[25]

---

in his presidential years. "He was a Machiavellian idealist—a reformer with exceptional 'street smarts.'" His secretary called him "the Tycoon" for a reason. The myth of Lincoln's "moderation" takes away from his brilliant moral strategy, which saved America. Burlingame argues that Lincoln was murdered not because he endorsed the Thirteenth Amendment or issued the Emancipation Proclamation, but because he had called for black voting rights. In this way, he argues, Lincoln should be considered as much a martyr to black civil rights as Martin Luther King Jr. (Burlingame, "Lincoln and Race," 73).

[25] McKenna, "On Abortion: A Lincolnian Position," 463–84. McKenna makes an interesting comparison of the slavery issue with the modern-day abortion issue. Much like slavery proponents in Lincoln's day, who rarely called slavery by its name, strong supporters of abortion today do not call abortion by name—they refer to abortion as a "reproductive health procedure," "reproductive health care," or a "termination of a pregnancy." Abortion clinics are "women's clinics," or "reproductive health clinics," and the right to obtain an abortion is about "reproductive freedom." In President Bill Clinton's 1993 health care plan, more than 1,342 pages long, the word "abortion" never appeared in the text even though the plan would have nationalized the funding of abortion through the "standard package" that everyone would be forced to buy. The concept of abortion appeared under the category of "services for pregnant women." The truth is abortion is a killing process. The only other institution treated so evasively in history like abortion was the institution of slavery. In the Constitution slaves were never called slaves but "persons," or "other persons," in contrast to "free persons." The slave trade was referred to as "the Migration or Importation of such Persons as any of the States now existing shall think proper to admit." Free states were required to return fugitive slaves to their masters in the slave states, but in that clause a slave was a "person held to Service or Labour" and a master was "the party to whom such Service or Labour may be due."

The Truth

Slavery is a horrific institution, no matter the time or place. Even today, almost two centuries since the eradication of slavery, the United States still bears the scars of an institution that held other humans in bondage.

There are many passages in Scripture that reference slavery. While slavery in colonial and antebellum America developed along racial lines, slavery in biblical times existed mostly as the spoils of war or as a means of entering into a voluntary arrangement to pay off one's debt. Indeed, a better translation of slave in the Bible is "bondservant." Bondservants were paid wages for their work until their debt was paid off in six or seven years. So when biblical writers, inspired by God, referred to slaves or bondservants, they were not endorsing any kind of institution of slavery such as America knew. They were speaking to people who were already bondservants/slaves. That God takes the time in His Word to directly speak to the lowest in society demonstrates how He values and loves all of His children.

President Andrew Jackson defended the "feelings and rights" of Southerners and "their institutions." Slavery, in the antebellum period, was usually spoken about in the language of rights. Illinois senator Stephen Douglas said this on the right to own slaves: "I am now speaking of rights under the Constitution, and not of moral or religious rights. I do not discuss the morals of the people of Missouri, but let them settle that matter for themselves. I hold that the people of the slaveholding States are civilized men as well as ourselves, that they bear consciences as well as we, and that they are accountable to God and their posterity and not to us. It is for them to decide therefore the moral and religious right of the slavery question for themselves within their own limits." Pro-abortion people say pro-life people are imposing their religious views on them today. By this same standard, Senator Douglas was pro-choice too. He argued that it should be up to individuals to determine whether they could own a slave or not. The morality of the institution of slavery was up to each individual. Susan B. Anthony and Elizabeth Cady Stanton were pro-life feminists. Abortion today, just like antebellum slavery almost two centuries ago, has become desensitized.

No one, no matter their social status, escapes the concern and love of God.

No matter one's station in life—master, bondservant, or anything in between—the Bible calls on you to be obedient and faithful to God so that others might know Him. Servants are told to be "subject to your masters with all respect, not only to the good and gentle but also to the unjust."[26] Those who "yoke as bondservants" should "regard their own masters as worthy of all honor, so that the name of God and the teaching may not be reviled."[27] As the writer of Colossians exhorts:

> Bondservants, obey in everything those who are your earthly masters, not by way of eye-service, as people-pleasers, but with sincerity of heart, fearing the Lord. Whatever you do, work heartily, as for the Lord and not for men, knowing that from the Lord you will receive the inheritance as your reward. You are serving the Lord Christ. For the wrongdoer will be paid back for the wrong he has done, and there is no partiality … Masters treat your bondservants justly and fairly, knowing that you also have a Master in heaven.[28]

In Ephesians, God tells bondservants:

> [O]bey your earthly masters with fear and trembling, with a sincere heart, as you would Christ, not by the way of eye-service, as people-pleasers, but as bondservants of Christ, doing the will of God from the heart rendering service with a good will as to the Lord and not to man, knowing

---

26 1 Pet. 2:18.

27 1 Tim. 6:1.

28 Col. 3:22–25; 4:1.

> that whatever good anyone does, this he will receive back from the Lord, whether he is a bondservant or is free. Masters, do the same to them, and stop your threatening, knowing that he who is both their Master and yours is in heaven, and that there is no partiality with him.[29]

In yet another book, Titus, we are told:

> Bondservants are to be submissive to their own masters in everything; they are to be well-pleasing, not argumentative, not pilfering, but showing all good faith, so that in everything they may adorn the doctrine of God our Savior. For the grace of God has appeared, bringing salvation for all people, training us to renounce ungodliness and worldly passions, and to live self-controlled, upright, and godly lives in the present age, waiting for our blessed hope, the appearing of the glory of our great God and Savior Jesus Christ, who gave himself for us to redeem us from all lawlessness and to purify for himself a people for his own possession who are zealous for good works.[30]

Unfortunately many of these verses have been misapplied or even used to justify the enslavement of people of African descent, even by Christians. Others, in an effort to distance themselves from the God, have conveniently and inappropriately claimed that the Bible endorses the institution of slavery. Nothing could be further from the truth. In fact, God lists slave traders as among the worst of sinners.[31]

---

[29] Eph. 6:5–9.

[30] Titus 2:9–14.

[31] 1 Tim. 1:10.

Abolitionists were primarily led by faithful Christians who believed in the dignity of all humans and all human life. They understood that God created all humans in His image and that all humans were of "one blood."[32]

Most importantly, the Bible clearly teaches that we humans are all slaves to sin and our human flesh. Much as bondservants were beholden to their masters, we are flawed and sinful people beholden to sin, death, and the power of the devil. Yet our spiritual freedom and eternal salvation have already been won. As wonderful as it is to be freed from human bondage, it is greater yet to be freed from our sins thanks to the blood of Jesus Christ. The Bible teaches that "for freedom Christ has set us free; stand firm therefore, and do not submit again to a yoke of slavery"[33]—the slavery of sin.

Everyone is a slave to someone or something. People who do not know Jesus as their personal Lord and Savior often do not realize that they are enslaved by sin. Christians know better. Thanks to Jesus, "we know that we can live as people who are free, not using your freedom as a cover-up for evil, but living as servants of God."[34] Indeed, the Christian does not feel enslaved to or by God, but wants to serve God because He first served us in sending His Son to die on the cross to forgive us of our sins.

Knowing what Christ has done for you is also why you can be clear, confident, and bold in your convictions. God wants your whole heart. He wants you to obey His commands and be faithful to His Word and truth.

Just as the United States could not endure half-slave and half-free, neither can the Christian endure in the faith by being only partially committed to God's Word. You cannot believe that part of God's Word is truth, and the rest of it is out of date. How would you know what part is truth or not? The halfhearted or convenient

---

[32] Acts 17:26 (KJV).

[33] Gal. 5:1.

[34] 1 Pet. 2:16.

Christian is not a God-pleasing one. "I know your works," God says, "you are neither cold nor hot. Would that you were either cold or hot! So, because you are lukewarm, and neither hot nor cold, I will spit you out of my mouth."[35] Jesus asserted, "Whoever is not with me is against me, and whoever does not gather with me scatters."[36]

Jesus cautioned that "every kingdom divided against itself is brought to desolation, and every city or house divided against itself will not stand."[37] Scripture also warns Christians not to be "unequally yoked with unbelievers. For what partnership has righteousness with lawlessness? Or what fellowship has light with darkness? Or what portion does a believer share with an unbeliever? What agreement has the temple of God with idols?" Christians are "the temple of the living God," and God will dwell among His people. Therefore Christians should not live with and behave like unbelievers. Instead, they should be "sons and daughters" of our Heavenly Father.[38]

When it comes to human bondage, most people now wholeheartedly condemn it, as they should. But sadly, too many only go halfway or halfheartedly into a personal relationship with Jesus. They believe they can exist half the time with a "Higher Power" and half the time without one. They might believe in God or gods but not the truth and inerrancy of Scripture. They might claim a faith in the "Big Guy in the Sky," but also expect that good works will get them to paradise. They may adhere to some aspects of Christianity, even unknowingly, but also embrace pantheistic, New Age, or other pagan teachings.

With Jesus, there is no halfway. The exclusivity of His statement is clear: "I am *the way*, and the truth, and the life. No one comes to the Father except through me" (italics added).[39] God's Word teaches that there is only one Savior and one way to heaven—through

---

[35] Rev. 3:15–16.

[36] Matt. 12:30.

[37] Matt. 12:25.

[38] 2 Cor. 6:14–18.

[39] John 14:6.

Jesus. There is no halfway point on this matter. Jesus is the Great Emancipator of our lives. For by Jesus's death and resurrection, "you have been set free from sin and have become slaves of God, the fruit you get leads to sanctification and its end, eternal life."[40] As Jesus says of those who know Him and His voice, you "know the truth, and the truth will set you free."[41]

Your Life

The Freedmen's Monument remains controversial today based on varied perceptions of the monument. What are some things that Christians do or say on a regular basis which are perceived or interpreted differently by other people? What can be done about these things?

Everyone is a slave to someone or something. What are some of the earthly masters that enslave communities and homes today?

How are you a slave to sin? How does being set free of your sin make all the difference in how you live your life?

---

[40] Rom. 6:22.

[41] John 8:32.

40

Word Power in the Gettysburg Address

Death and life are in the power of the tongue,
and those who love it will eat its fruits.
—Proverbs 18:21

The Lincoln Way

Powerful words inspire courageous leadership.

Of all the legacies Abraham Lincoln left his country, the Gettysburg Address might be the most renowned. More teachers and students have recited or read the Gettysburg Address than any other document in American history.[1] As a duchess of England correctly noted at the time, "The speech at the Gettysburg Cemetery must live."[2]

"Four score and seven years ago our fathers brought forth on this continent, a new nation, conceived in Liberty, and dedicated to the proposition that all men are created equal," Lincoln's address opens. "We are met on a great battle-field of that war"—a battle that most Civil War historians consider the turning point of the war—"to dedicate a portion of that field, as a final resting place for those who here gave their lives that that nation might live. It is altogether fitting

[1] McGovern, *Lincoln*, 91.

[2] Basler, Memorandum Concerning the Duchess of Argyll, Washington, March 22, 1865, *CW*, 8:372.

and proper that we should do this," he said. Noting that "the brave men, living and dead, who struggled here, have consecrated it, far above our poor power to add or detract," the president poignantly highlighted that actions matter far more than words. "The world will little note, nor long remember what we say here, but it can never forget what they did here. It is for us the living, rather, to be dedicated here to the unfinished work which they who fought here have thus far so nobly advanced."

Lincoln then advanced the story and significance of the sacrifices made at Gettysburg. "It is rather for us to be here dedicated to the great task remaining before us—that from these honored dead we take increased devotion to that cause for which they gave the last full measure of devotion." Americans "highly resolve that these dead shall not have died in vain—that this nation, under God, shall have a new birth of freedom—and that government of the people, by the people, for the people, shall not perish from the earth."[3]

In the hands of a masterful speechwriter and speechmaker, one had to assume that the words President Lincoln planned to share on that solemn Thursday afternoon, on November 19, 1863, would be memorable. Yet Lincoln almost did not attend the dedication of the Soldiers' National Cemetery, due to his son's illness. The Lincolns had already lost two sons, and Mary did not want her husband to leave her alone with a sickly Tad.[4] Moreover, Lincoln had not been selected as the keynote speaker. He was the warm-up act for Edward Everett, a classical scholar from Harvard; a former congressman, senator, and governor from Massachusetts; and a former secretary of state in the Fillmore administration. He was known as one of the great orators of the age. Everett spoke for two hours, while Lincoln spoke for two minutes. Many in the audience were just getting settled in to hear the president's remarks when he finished. So brief

3 Basler, Lincoln's Address Delivered at the Dedication of the Cemetery at Gettysburg, November 19, 1863, *CW*, 7:23.

4 Donald, *Lincoln*, 462.

were his comments, no one had time to interrupt with applause. Some were disappointed the president left the stage so quickly and said so few words.

There are advantages, however, that come with brevity. Since Lincoln's speech numbered only 272 words, newspapers were able to report the speech in its entirety, often on the front page. "Surprisingly fine as Mr. Everett's oration was in the Gettysburg consecration," wrote an editor for the *Springfield Republican,* "the rhetorical honors of the occasion were won by President Lincoln. His little speech is a perfect gem, deep in feeling, compact in thought and expression, and tasteful and elegant in every word and comma."[5] An editor of *Harper's Weekly* said that "the few words of the President were from the heart to the heart. They can not be read, even, without kindling emotion." Repeating Lincoln's famous words, the editor added, "'The world will little note nor long remember what we say here, but it can never forget what they did here.' It was as simple and felicitous and earnest a word as was ever spoken."

Even Edward Everett wrote Lincoln, shortly afterward to express his "great admiration" for the president's "eloquent simplicity & appropriateness at the consecration of the Cemetery." Everett wished he could have come "as near to the central idea of the occasion" in two hours as Lincoln did in two minutes. Reading Lincoln's speech in the newspaper the next day might have given Everett a new perspective on Lincoln's text, because he did not seem that impressed with the speech in the immediate aftermath.

Savvy about public opinion, Lincoln gave copies of the text to the Associated Press and wrote additional copies for souvenir albums and charity auctions. Lincoln knew newspapers that supported the Republican Party would reprint the speech.[6] As President Richard

---

[5] Wilson, *Lincoln's Sword*, 226, 229–230. The quotes and content in this paragraph and the next come from this source.

[6] Holzer and Garfinkle, *A Just and Generous Nation*, 140.

Nixon put it, reflecting on the Gettysburg Address, "a speech is measured not by its length but its depth."[7]

Brevity is especially powerful when attached to depth and beauty. Whether heard or read, Lincoln's Gettysburg Address is a tour de force of powerful words and phrases. Many Americans today may not even know the source of many of those phrases, but they are familiar with the words. From the opening sentence—"Four score and seven years ago our fathers brought forth on this continent, a new nation, conceived in Liberty, and dedicated to the proposition that all men are created equal"—to the last words of the speech—"that this nation, under God, shall have a new birth of freedom—that government of the people, by the people, for the people, shall not perish from the earth," Americans frequently quote the Gettysburg Address as if it were the primary document of the American spirit and experience. Like the hymn "Amazing Grace," the Gettysburg Address has become an unofficial national speech of wide application, often referenced in various settings and moments. Governor George Pataki of New York recited the address at Ground Zero on the first anniversary of the 9/11 attacks on the World Trade Center in Manhattan.[8] Americans not only like the sound of the phrases, but they believe in them. As historian Garry Wills writes, "All modern political prose descends from the Gettysburg Address."[9]

In addition to the beautiful prose, the Gettysburg Address is personal, familial, and image-rich. Words such as "birth," "death," "rebirth," "fathers," "sons," and "brave men" fill the text.[10] Moreover, Lincoln mentions "we" and "us" several times throughout the document. One reporter at the Philadelphia *Evening Bulletin* said that people would not be able to read Lincoln's speech without "moistening of the eye and a swelling of the heart."[11]

---

7 Nixon, *In the Arena*, 213.

8 Fox, *Lincoln's Body*, 278.

9 Keneally, *Lincoln*, 151.

10 Miroff, *Icons of Democracy*, 100.

11 Sandburg, *Lincoln*, 446.

Other newspapers declared the short address an "immortal" one that "glittered with gems."[12] Elegant in "every word and comma,"[13] the speech exhibited kindness, warmth, earnestness, beauty, and feeling. Ralph Waldo Emerson predicted, correctly as it turned out, that the impact of the address would not be surpassed in the future.[14]

A powerful aspect of the address is its religious language and imagery. The words "government of the people, by the people, and for the people" originates from a sermon given by Theodore Parker, who had defined democracy as "a government of all the people, by all the people, for all the people."[15] Although Lincoln never named the Bible or quoted directly from it, the address contains biblical inspiration, content, and cadence.[16] The famous word "fourscore" comes directly from Psalm 90. The controlling metaphor of the speech revolves around the birth, death, and rebirth of Jesus. Lincoln's reference to "our fathers" recalls not just Washington, Jefferson, and Adams, but also Jesus's heavenly and earthly fathers, Jehovah and Joseph. Likewise, the key phrases "brought forth," "conceived," and "dedicated" can be found, in that precise order, in the Book of Common Prayer's litany for the public baptism of infants. As Jesus had been conceived, brought forth, and dedicated to serve humankind, so too, Lincoln implied, had the United States been conceived, brought forth, and dedicated to the Jeffersonian ideal that "all men are created equal."[17] The national suffering would lead to a "new birth of freedom," which symbolically represented the redemption of the Union from the original sin of slavery.[18]

---

[12] Burlingame, *Lincoln,* 2:576.

[13] Donald, *Lincoln,* 465.

[14] Burlingame, *Lincoln*, 2:577.

[15] Donald, *Lincoln*, 461.

[16] While, *Lincoln*, 606.

[17] Szasz and Szasz, *Lincoln and Religion*, 50.

[18] Deutsch and Fornieri, *Lincoln's American Dream*, 32; Guelzo, *Lincoln*, 373. At that time, *our fathers,* like the biblical patriarchs, *brought forth on this continent, a new nations, conceived in Liberty* as though the republic were one

Lincoln did not write the Gettysburg Address on a napkin while riding in a train, as one myth has suggested. He took the time to write several drafts. In his first three drafts, he left out the word "God" from his most striking line: "that the nation shall have a new birth of freedom; and that government of the people, by the people, and for the people, shall not perish from the earth." Eventually, Lincoln, as the solemn occasion approached, inserted new words: "That this nation, *under God*, shall have a new birth of freedom" (italics added). As the war progressed, so did his reliance on and faith in God.[19]

The Gettysburg Address continues to be examined and cherished by historians and students of all ages today. The speech is a testament not only to the state of the Union and state of mind of commander in chief in the fall of 1863, but to the power and legacy of words—words that inspire and give hope.

The Truth

Words matter, and God's Word matters the most.

We all know the power and influence of words. Words can cut or can lift you out of a rut. They can ruin a reputation or regenerate a soul.

The Bible makes it clear that Christ-followers should be discerning with their words and careful how they use them. "Let no corrupting talk come out of your mouths," says God's Word, "but only such as is good for building up, as fits the occasion, that

---

with the woman of St. John's Revelation, who "brought forth a man child, who was to rule all nations" and "fled into the wilderness, where she had a place prepared of God." A *new birth of freedom* was a vivid form of evangelical transformation

[19] Mansfield, *Lincoln's Battle with God*, 175–76.

it may give grace to those who hear."[20] "Gracious words are like a honeycomb, sweetness to the soul and health to the body."[21]

As important and influential as human words can be, God's Word is lifesaving and life-changing. God appears to us in His Word and, in fact, He *is* the Word. "In the beginning was the Word, and the Word was with God, and the Word was God."[22] When our Heavenly Father sent His Son Jesus down to earth to redeem us from our sins, the Bible explains that "the Word became flesh and dwelt among us, and we have seen his glory, glory as of the only Son from the Father, full of grace and truth."[23] This Word that became Flesh—Jesus—right before He died on the cross exclaimed, "It is finished."[24] These powerful and loving words indicated that the sacrificial task of dying on the cross to save humankind from their sins had been completed by the only one who could do it.

Now that the Word that became Flesh has ascended into heaven, God has left you His Word—the Bible—to tell you what He has done for you through Christ. God's Word is what gives you faith. He promises that His Word "shall not return to me empty, but it shall accomplish that which I purpose, and shall succeed in the thing for which I sent it."[25] God's Word heals all believers and delivers them from hell and eternal destruction.[26] Therefore we are to "let the word of Christ dwell in you richly, teaching and admonishing one another in all wisdom, singing psalms and hymns and spiritual songs, with thankfulness in your hearts to God."[27]

So are you getting enough of God's Word in your daily diet? Jesus says, "It is written, 'Man shall not live by bread alone, but by

---

20 Eph. 4:29.
21 Prov. 16:24.
22 John 1:1.
23 John 1:14.
24 John 19:30.
25 Isa. 55:11.
26 Ps. 107:20.
27 Col. 3:16.

every word that comes from the mouth of God.'"[28] As the prophet Jeremiah says of the divine words of God, "Your words were found, and I ate them, and your words became to me a joy and the delight of my heart, for I am called by your name, O Lord, God of hosts."[29] In a world looking for truth in all the wrong places, "every word of God proves true," and provides "a shield to those who take refuge in him.[30]

You have probably said and heard a lot of words during your life, but none will be more important than those found in the Bible. As Jesus says, "Heaven and earth will pass away, but my words will not pass away.[31] How comforting it is to know that even as "the grass withers" and "the flower fades," the "word of our God will stand forever."[32]

Your Life

Words are powerful. What have been some words of wisdom spoken to you that have made a significant impact on your life? What are some words that you have shared with others and that have made a difference in their lives?

In today's world, we hear a lot about letting everyone find and share their own voice. How can Christians make sure people hear God's voice in a very noisy world?

Why do you think God chose to reveal Himself through His Word and the Word that became Flesh?

---

[28] Matt. 4:4.

[29] Jer. 15:16.

[30] Prov. 30:5.

[31] Matt. 24:35.

[32] Isa. 40:8.

THE CALLING

41

Assassination Preparation

You shall not murder.
—Exodus 20:13

The Lincoln Way

Leaders lead and cast a vision for the future, but live like tomorrow is not a given.

Death surrounded Lincoln. His grandfather had been killed by an Indian attack, forever haunting and stunting his father Tom's economic opportunities and emotional security. From his earliest days on the frontier, young Abe witnessed and knew of sudden deaths by drowning, animal encounter, Indian raids, farm accidents, and childbirth, as well as slower deaths caused by disease and old age. He had almost drowned at the age of seven, and was kicked in the head by a horse at the age of ten. He lost loved ones early and often—his mother, sister, and first love. He observed slaves being whipped and abused on plantations and on the auction block, and runaway slaves captured and punished severely. He lost two sons, enduring their valiant but futile battles with disease helplessly and without remedy. His close associates and friends were killed in battle. As president, he received casualty reports daily and visited battlefields and hospitals where he could hear, see, and smell the gore and brutality of war. His bodyguards, cabinet members, and friends constantly warned him about assassination threats on his own life. People wanted him dead.

Even before he became the Republican nominee for the presidency in 1860, Lincoln began receiving death threats. At first, they made him feel uncomfortable, but then he got used to them. He knew his life could be taken at any moment, he told Seward, but he could not afford to worry about it.[1]

"Just before Lincoln left for Washington," recalled one Springfield dentist, "I met him on the Street, and Knowing that he had received many threatening letters of assassination &c, I suggested to him the propriety of care, caution," and "told him he had better take a cook from his own true & tried female acquaintances." Lincoln appreciated the man's thoughtfulness and responded "earnestly" that he would "be cautious, but God's will be done. I am in His hands, & will be during my admr [administration], and what he does I must bow to, God rules, and we should submit."[2]

On election day in 1860, Lincoln experienced an instance of a morbid premonition he occasionally received. He saw two reflected images of his face in the mirror of his Springfield dresser. These images—one a separate, paler, and entirely distinct version of the other—remained no matter how he shifted his position. When he shared the dream with his wife, Mary claimed to understand it immediately. He would be elected to a second term but would not live to complete it. Noah Brooks would remind her of this dream when her husband got reelected in 1864.[3]

On his way to the nation's capital after being elected president, Lincoln received news that assassins planned to kill him as he passed through Baltimore on February 23, 1861. The killers planned to set fire to a bridge as Lincoln's train approached. When the train stopped, they would attack the cars and kill the president-elect. At the insistence of detective and spy Allan Pinkerton, Lincoln altered his travel plans. Wearing a brown Kossuth hat and an overcoat that

---

[1] Oates, *With Malice Toward None*, 416.

[2] Wilson, *Herndon's Informants*, 425–26.

[3] Baker, *Mary Todd Lincoln*, 237.

draped over his long arms, and accompanied by a heavily armed bodyguard, the president-elect arrived in nation's capital at six thirty in the morning. Mary and their sons arrived safely later, though their train had been intercepted in Baltimore by a pro-Southern mob that yelled insults about the "black ape."

Critics ridiculed Lincoln for sneaking into Washington, disguised allegedly as a highlander or even as a woman. Though it had been a prudent precaution, Lincoln came to regret the decision as an undignified "flight by night," telling friends he considered it one of the worst mistakes he ever made. The belief that he had let himself appear weak and fearful may have compelled him to avoid future actions that would paint him as a coward.[4]

Before South Carolina seceded from the Union, Lincoln received more death threats. Several anonymous letters, decorated with skulls and crossbones, had come addressed to Mrs. Lincoln, warning that if her husband took office, he would be assassinated. Just before Christmas 1860, Mary received a sketch of Lincoln with a noose around his neck, his feet chained, and his body tarred and feathered. Lincoln also had a grotesque black-faced doll sent to him.

On Inauguration Day, March 4, 1861, Lincoln received numerous death threats that told him to leave Mary at home, since he would be shot or kidnapped. Based on the frequency and specificity of these threats, and for first time in American history, planners constructed a wooden barricade that shielded those on the inaugural platform from the crowd. General Scott ordered green-coated sharpshooters to stand guard on housetops, while troops blocked off the side streets. Near the Capitol, two batteries of light artillery were deployed to protect the president-elect.[5]

Once Lincoln was in the Executive Mansion, death threats continued and murder attempts were foiled. Gift baskets filled with

---

[4] Burlingame, *Lincoln*, 2:32–34, 38–39.

[5] Baker, *Mary Todd Lincoln*, 164, 178; Conroy, *Lincoln's White House*, 5; Epstein, *Portrait of a Marriage*, 310.

poisoned fruit were sent to him, mostly from Southerners. Lincoln had the good sense to have them all tested. Starting in 1862, the commander in chief received military escorts beyond walls of the Executive Mansion. As threats became more specific and acute in 1864, the Washington Metropolitan Police assigned a select group of officers to protect Lincoln—though their priority orders were to protect the Executive Mansion from vandals. Secretary John Hay worried about Lincoln's exposure to the people.[6]

To escape Washington's heat and humidity, as well as the constant flow of visitors to the Executive Mansion, Lincoln often rode three and a half miles out of the capital to the Soldiers' Home, where he relaxed, took care of his correspondence, and reflected on his next actions in the war effort. Once while he was riding out in August 1862, a surprise gunshot rang out and startled the president's horse, aptly named Old Abe. Old Abe stampeded furiously all the way to the Soldiers' Home. Lincoln joked that two old Abes broke speed records that day. More seriously, while the president admitted that the bullet had just missed him, he denied that anyone had really tried to kill him. He assumed the gunshot had been an accident committed by some hunter.[7]

After the close call, a detail of cavalry was assigned to escort the president to and from the Soldiers' Home. Lincoln objected that the soldiers made such clatter with their sabers and spurs that he and Mary could hardly hear themselves talk. Eventually, a security presence of four officers was put on special duty at the Executive Mansion. These four men wore civilian clothes, carried concealed weapons, and were supposed to accompany the president on his walks and to the theater. At night one of them was on duty outside the Lincolns' private bedrooms.[8]

For most of his presidency, Lincoln took few security precautions. Whether taking long walks through the streets of Washington late at

---

6 O'Reilly, *Killing Lincoln*, 111–12.

7 Oates, *With Malice Toward None*, 416.

8 Donald, *Lincoln*, 538.

night or early in the morning, riding to the Soldiers' Home, attending the theater, or strolling through the densely shaded mansion grounds to the War Department, as he did almost every night, Lincoln dispensed with escort or security on most occasions. Ward Lamon, marshal of the District of Columbia, who felt responsible for his safety, often got angry and once threatened to resign when he heard the president had gone to the theater with only Charles Sumner and the Baron Gerolt, the elderly Prussian minister.[9] When asked in 1863 why he did not have Executive Mansion visitors screened, as military commanders did, Lincoln responded that people would then fancy him an emperor. That would only put the idea of assassination into the minds of more adversaries and inadvertently encourage the very scenario he intended to prevent.

That same year, Lincoln told Noah Brooks that he had come to the conclusion a long time ago that if an individual really wanted to kill him, that individual would find a way to get it done. Even if Lincoln surrounded himself with bodyguards around the clock, there would be no foolproof way to stop a determined killer.

On top of these realities, Lincoln simply could never bring himself to believe that there were people out there who wanted to kill him. He worried more about an accidental gun discharge by one of his bodyguards than an assassin's bullet.[10]

As the war progressed, the frequency of assassination threats and acts increased. On July 1, 1863, at the Soldiers' Home, an unknown assailant removed screws fastening the driver's seat to the body of the Lincolns' carriage. When the vehicle began to descend from a winding hill, the seat came loose, throwing the driver to the ground. Unable to restrain the runaway horses, Mary Lincoln tried to leap from the carriage. She landed on her back, hitting her head against a sharp stone. Though the wound was dressed that day, a dangerous infection set in that made her so gravely ill for weeks that Lincoln

---

[9] Donald, *Lincoln,* 547–48.

[10] Burlingame, *Lincoln*, 2:808.

summoned Robert from Harvard to assist in her recovery. Robert believed his mother never really recuperated from the effects of that fall, which exacerbated the debilitating headaches that she already endured. Rumors spread about the bolts being deliberately loosened in the hope that the tall and lanky president would fall to the ground and break his skull.[11]

One death threat arrived on January 4, 1864. "Your days are numbered," it read. "You have been weighed in the balance and found wanting. You shall be a dead man in six months from date December 31, 1863."[12] Letters that threatened kidnap or murder came regularly. When a woman abruptly burst into a cabinet meeting in early 1864, saying she wanted to get a look at Lincoln, he wittily replied that he had the better of the exchange. Cabinet members, however, had jumped from their seats at the intrusion and were not amused by her unimpeded access to the president.[13] One friendly resident alerted the president that there were "hordes of Secesh-sympathizers" around Washington who would not hesitate to shoot him on his rides to the Soldiers' House. She begged him to discontinue his trips out of the city.[14] Ward Lamon, in an effort to tighten security, began sleeping by the president's bedroom door.

A few newspapers encouraged the murder of Lincoln during the 1864 presidential campaign. The La Crosse, Wisconsin, *Democrat* hoped some bold killer would stab the president in the heart for the public good. The Albany *Atlas and Argus* paraphrased Patrick Henry's 1765 treason speech about Brutus murdering Caesar and Cromwell slaying Charles I. Speaking for the people, of course, the newspaper hoped Lincoln would profit by their example.[15]

Lincoln knew the threats were real and increasing. Whether it be from an assassin's bullet or the daily stresses of being commander

---

[11] Goodwin, *Team of Rivals*, 535; Keneally, *Lincoln*, 144.

[12] Conway, *Lincoln's White House*, 197.

[13] Conway, *Lincoln's White House,* 197.

[14] Donald, *Lincoln*, 548–49.

[15] Burlingame, *Lincoln*, 2:698, 808.

in chief, he told an associate in 1863 that his life would not outlast the rebellion. He made similar predictions to Harriet Beecher Stowe and his old friend Owen Lovejoy.[16] Reflecting on how he began receiving letters threatening his life soon after his nomination in Chicago, he told the painter, Francis B. Carpenter, in 1864, that the first few made him uncomfortable. After receiving written death threats weekly for years, however, they no longer bothered him much because had gotten used to them. He simply put them in a file marked "assassination letters."[17]

A few weeks before the 1864 election, a shot had been fired at the president on the grounds of the Soldiers' Home—though whether it was deliberate or accidental was never determined. The bullet swatted the president's stovepipe hat right off his head. Lincoln demanded that the incident be kept secret.[18] The night after his reelection, on November 8, 1864, Lincoln finally retired to his chamber to sleep. Unknown to the president, Ward Lamon came to Secretary Hay's room armed with pistols and bowie knives, borrowed some blankets, and lay down in the hall outside Lincoln's door. Lamon worried that somebody might try to murder the president now that he had been reelected. The next morning Lamon left before Lincoln awoke, leaving the blankets at Hay's door.[19]

As the second inaugural address loomed, rumors persisted that Lincoln would be assassinated while giving his speech. "I know I'm in danger," Lincoln confided to Seward, "but I'm not going to worry about it." Stanton ordered a company of Pennsylvania troops to camp on the Executive Mansion lawn for extra security.[20] After the fall of Richmond, Lincoln wanted to visit the city, much to the angst of Seward and Stanton. Seward told James Speed, Lincoln's attorney general, that "if there were to be assassinations, now was the time."

16 Burlingame, *Lincoln,* 2:799.

17 Burlingame, *Lincoln,* 2:807.

18 Packard, *Lincolns in the White House*, 204.

19 Oates, *With Malice Toward None*, 401.

20 Keneally, *Lincoln*, 164.

With the fall of Richmond, "the Southern people would feel as though the world had come to an end." At such times, desperate men might be prompted to take desperate actions, and the "President, being the most marked man on the Federal side, was the most liable to attack." Knowing that Speed would be visiting Lincoln soon, Seward begged him to "warn the President of the danger."[21]

When Lincoln visited the conquered Confederate capital of Richmond, on April 4, 1865, Union officers and political officials also worried about his safety. Given his height, Lincoln made an easy target for snipers. Elizabeth Keckley fretted about the president giving a speech on April 11 from the Executive Mansion and being illuminated "boldly in the darkness." He could be easily struck by a bullet and no one would be able to tell who fired the shot.[22]

The last photo of Abraham Lincoln, taken by Alexander Gardner, shows the physical and emotional toll the presidency took on him. (Library of Congress, LC-USZ62-12380)

[21] Goodwin, *Team of Rivals*, 718.

[22] Johnson, *Last Weeks of Lincoln*, 240.

While Lincoln almost always put on a courageous face and often downplayed threats on his life, they did affect him. On April 12, 1865, just two days before he would be murdered, he could not sleep due to the many warnings he had been receiving regarding assassination threats. Lincoln told Ward Lamon, his wife, and one or two others about a recent dream that continued to disturb him. In the dream, the president heard "subdued sobs,"[23] as though a number of people were crying. He got out of bed and went downstairs, where he heard "the same pitiful sobbing," but he could not see anyone. "I went from room to room; no living person was in sight." But he kept hearing the same "mournful sounds of distress" everywhere he went. He kept on looking, trying to find out what was taking place and why anyone should be sobbing and behaving so strangely. He finally found himself in the East Room, where he saw a catafalque (raised box) upon which was a corpse "wrapped in funeral vestments," its face covered. Soldiers were stationed around the catafalque, acting as guards. A crowd of people stood by, "weeping pitifully." Lincoln asked one of the soldiers, "Who is dead in the White House?"

"The president," the soldier replied. "He was killed by an assassin."

This was followed by a "large burst of grief" from the crowd, which woke Lincoln from his dream. Lincoln could not get this nightmare out of his mind. Mary Lincoln, frightened by her husband's retelling of the dream, chastised him for telling it. "Well," he said, "it's only a dream, Mary. Let us say no more about it and try to forget it."

But the dream had alarmed him. Ward Lamon noticed that Lincoln seemed to be "grave, gloomy, and at times visibly pale" because of the nightmare. He also remembered the president quoted from *Hamlet*, "to sleep, perchance to dream, ay, *there's the rub*!" emphasizing the last three words.

---

[23] Johnson, *Last Weeks of Lincoln*, 249–50. The quotes in the next few paragraphs come from this source.

Lincoln's death felt so sudden and dramatic because it came so soon after the Union victory.[24] Shot on April 14, just a few days after Lee surrendered to Grant at Appomattox Courthouse, Lincoln passed away the next morning in William Petersen's boarding house. The "Night of Madness" or "Night of Horrors" immediately lifted the martyred president to legendary fame, while John Wilkes Booth soon displaced Benedict Arnold as the ultimate American villain.[25] While many Christians considered theater attendance on a Good Friday to be a poor testimony, "Black Easter" transformed and transfigured the nation.[26]

The national search to bring justice to the assassin commenced almost immediately after Lincoln's last breath. Eighty-seven men drowned in swamps and rivers during the weeklong hunt.[27] Meanwhile, the nation mourned and commemorated the sixteenth president of the United States. The morning after his death, an extra-long pine box arrived. They wrapped Lincoln's nude corpse in an American flag and placed it in the box. The flag that covered him had thirty-five stars on it—one for each state. Illustrating his stubbornness and determination, Lincoln had refused to remove the stars for the states that had seceded from the Union.[28]

By Saturday morning, the entire Union was in mourning. The flags, triumphal arches, and bunting (a light cotton, woolen, or

---

24 Peterson, *Lincoln in American Memory*, 8.

25 Wheeler, *Faith and Courage*, xii.

26 Carwardine, "Lincoln's Religion," 248; Fox, *Lincoln's Body*, 35. Relocating Lincoln to a boarding house, after the medical and safety concerns, may also have been done to ensure that he would not die in a theater—a setting many Americans considered suspect at best with its gambling dens, dance halls, and gathering of vice—on Good Friday. Doctors might have been looking after his moral legacy just as much as his body which they knew would only survive for a little while longer. Lincoln had been chastised in the past for his love of theater (one historian counted forty-three theater visits during his four years as president).

27 O'Reilly, *Killing Lincoln*, 257.

28 Canavan, *Lincoln's Final Hours*, 123.

synthetic cloth used for making flags) that had gone up five days before, as the people celebrated their jubilation at the fall of the Confederacy, were taken down and replaced with black crepe. When the stores sold out of black fabric, old black dresses were cut up. Those who failed to drape their homes in black were accused of being traitors. Mobs threatened those who appeared to be Southern sympathizers. By Saturday night, any semblance of Lincolnian mercy or grace toward the South had practically disappeared.

Black Easter Sunday saw more people go to church than ever. Most churches were decorated in black, and pastors laid aside the sermons they had written earlier in the week to celebrate the Risen Christ, or blended them with reflections on the nation's tragedy. Their parishioners wanted to know how the assassination fit into God's purpose and plans, and the lessons that could be learned from it. Mary wondered if her husband's death atoned for the nation's sin of slavery.[29] People's souls hurt and their hearts ran on empty. They needed comfort for the moment and regeneration for the months ahead.

On April 18, 1865, twenty-five thousand people viewed Lincoln's embalmed body in the East Room. The next day, Dr. Phineas Gurley, pastor of the New York Avenue Presbyterian Church, preached the funeral sermon. He had been at Lincoln's side when the president died and would ride the funeral train to Springfield, Illinois, where he would conclude the burial service with a prayer. More than six hundred military and government officials attended the funeral. Mary Lincoln, too grieved to attend, remained sequestered in her upstairs bedroom.

Gurley tried to address the suddenness of the death and echoed a Lincoln sentiment during the war—that "the sovereignty of God"

[29] Wheeler, *Faith and Courage*, 240; Peterson, *Lincoln in American Memory*, 7–8.

is total, and that "His footsteps are not known." All one could do is "bow before His infinite majesty" and worship Him.[30]

Gurley testified to Lincoln's reliance on his faith to carry him through these tumultuous times, and said the American people must do the same. The murder took out the president "whom the people had learned to trust with a confiding and a loving confidence, and upon whom more than upon any other were centered, under God." Lincoln had been the best hope "for the true and speedy pacification of the country, the restoration of the Union, and the return of harmony and love." The timing of his loss—"taken just as the prospect of peace was brightly opening upon our torn and bleeding country"—was "a mysterious and a most afflicting visitation!" Nevertheless, God's "judgments are right … The death of the President, was overruled by Him whose judgments are unsearchable." The American people had to be patient, for God, "who has led us so well, and defended and prospered us so wonderfully during the last four years of toil, and struggle, and sorrow, will not forsake us now." He acknowledged that "weeping may endure for a night," but "joy will come in the morning. Blessed be God!"

Gurley put Lincoln's impact and influence on the American people in proper context. No man "since the days of Washington was ever so deeply and firmly embedded and enshrined in the very hearts of the people as Abraham Lincoln." The president merited the love and trust of the people because of his character, actions, tone, and spirit. Simple, sincere, plain, honest, truthful, just, benevolent, and kind, Lincoln possessed quick and clear perceptions, calm and accurate judgments, and clear and pure purposes. He always "aimed and endeavored to be right and to do right. His integrity was thorough, all-pervading, all-controlling, and incorruptible."

---

30 Gurley, "White House Funeral Sermon for President Lincoln," http://www.abrahamlincolnonline.org/lincoln/speeches/gurley.htm. The quotes from Gurley's funeral oration in the next several paragraphs come from this source.

Moreover, he had confronted the challenges of the Civil War with firmness and steadiness.

Of course Lincoln should be lauded for fighting for "the vast interests of Liberty and humanity" during the Civil War, but the president could not do that all on his own. Gurley had seen firsthand how the president personally relied on God. According to Gurley, Lincoln "recognized and received the truth that the 'kingdom is the Lord's, and He is the governor among the nations.'" Lincoln acknowledged that "God is in history" and felt that nowhere had "His hand and His mercy been so marvelously conspicuous as in the history of this nation." Lincoln knew and "prayed that that same hand would continue to guide us, and that same mercy continue to abound to us in the time of our greatest need."

Often Lincoln asked his friends and associates to pray for him, which they did, along with millions of others. God had heard those prayers and blessed the nation accordingly. Indeed, God had raised Lincoln up "for a great and glorious mission, furnished him for his work, and aided him in its accomplishment." While Lincoln's "strength of mind, and honesty of heart, and purity and pertinacity of purpose" were important attributes of his character, his "calm and abiding confidence in the overruling providence of God and in the ultimate triumph of truth and righteousness through the power and the blessing of God" was even more impressive.

Highlighting a signal strength in Lincoln's character and leadership, Gurley affirmed that Lincoln's "confidence strengthened him in all his hours of anxiety and toil, and inspired him with calm and cheering hope when others were inclining to despondency and gloom." He would never forget how an emotional president told a company of clergymen that his "hope of success in this great and terrible struggle rests on that immutable foundation, the justice and goodness of God." When things looked dark and dire, Lincoln believed that "all will be well in the end, because our cause is just, and God is on our side." Having been around the man often and seeing him in action up close, Gurley insisted that Lincoln's "sublime and holy faith" was "an anchor to his soul, both sure and steadfast" throughout his presidency. Lincoln felt emboldened in his "pathway of duty," and strengthened his resolve to fight "for the cause of God and humanity, and it held him in a steady, patient, and unswerving adherence to a policy of administration which he thought, and which we all now think, both God and humanity required him to adopt."

According to the Gurley, the American people loved Lincoln for many reasons—his "childlike simplicity," honesty, integrity, character, kind and forgiving disposition, industriousness, patience, persistence, devotion to duty, concern for the poor and suffering, charity, skill at handling differences among constituents in the Union, unifying abilities, wise policies, defense of the Declaration, and support for emancipation. All of these things and more were worthy of admiration and had left "the unmistakable impress of greatness." Even better and more "sublime," "influential," "beautiful," "strong," and "sustaining" than any of those things, however, was Lincoln's "abiding confidence in God and in the final triumph of truth and righteousness through Him and for His sake. This was his noblest virtue, his grandest principle, the secret alike of his strength, his patience, and his success." One of Lincoln's greatest legacies to his successors and all future Americans, Gurley maintained, was to "have faith in God." Lincoln's legacy for all "ages and to all rulers and peoples in every land" was to "cling to Liberty and right; battle for them; bleed for them; die for them, if need be; and have confidence in God." Gurley hoped that Lincoln's "voice" and "testimony" would sink into every American's heart "and into the heart of the nation."

Gurley closed his sermon by noting the truth that Lincoln "is dead; but the God in whom he trusted lives, and He can guide and strengthen his successor, as He guided and strengthened him." Americans should remember Lincoln's virtues, "his wise and patriotic counsels and labors," and "his calm and steady faith in God." No assassin could quench Lincoln's "inextinguishable life." Though the president had been slain, the country had been saved. Americans could be joy-filled because their "fallen Chief lived long enough to see the day dawn and the daystar of joy and peace arise upon the nation." Lincoln had indeed seen the dawning of a new nation.

Later that day, in a solemn military procession, they took Lincoln's body to the Capitol, where it would lie in state until the following evening. The Twenty-Second US Colored Infantry Regiment led the immense procession. Bringing up the rear were four thousand blacks who visibly mourned the loss of their champion and "best friend."[31] General Grant, who had grown close to Lincoln at the end of the war, wore a white sash across his breast, signifying his role as the head pallbearer, and was flanked by other top generals. Lincoln's eldest son, Robert, stood nearby in his captain's uniform, as did Tad, his face swollen with tears. Many of the Todds were present, but not Mary.

After the military service, Lloyd Lewis, a renowned chronicler of the time, remarked that now "Abraham Lincoln's trip to mythland begins." On Thursday, wounded soldiers were the first to enter Capitol Rotunda. Three thousand mourners per hour followed—twenty-five thousand in total on that day.[32]

On Friday, April 21, Lincoln's coffin was sent to Springfield, Illinois, for burial. The train traveled 1,654 miles in thirteen days, the longest train journey in history to that point, stopping in 180 cities before reaching Springfield. Special timetables were printed to inform citizens of the route. As the train passed at a stately twenty miles per hours, people gathered along the tracks, whether during torrential rainstorms or in the middle of the night, to get a look. Farmers left their fields just to get a brief glimpse of the moving train. A separate engine—decked with flags, flowers, and a framed photograph of the president over the cowcatcher—moved down the tracks ten minutes in front of the funeral train to alert citizens of its

---

[31] Burlingame, *Lincoln*, 2:820.

[32] Wheeler, *Faith and Courage*, 240–41.

approach. Out of a population of 31 million people, well over seven million Americans saw the train or the catafalque. The country had never experienced anything quite like it.[33]

The final public viewing and funeral took place on May 3 and 4. Amazingly, to a town of only fifteen thousand residents, approximately ninety thousand visitors came to pay their respects. In the rotunda of the Illinois House of Representatives, where Lincoln gave his Dred Scott speech in 1857 and his "house divided" speech in 1858, the lying in state began at ten o'clock in the morning and lasted twenty-four hours straight. Again, over twenty-five thousand mourners passed by Lincoln's body that day. Inscribed in a circle around the higher reaches of the rotunda were the words, "Sooner than surrender this principle, I would be assassinated on this spot."[34]

Many pastors took part in Lincoln's funeral service at Oak Ridge Cemetery. Reverend Albert Hale offered a prayer. Reverend R. W. Miner read a portion of the first chapter of John's gospel. Reverend A. C. Hubbard read the words of Lincoln's second inaugural address. Bishop Matthew Simpson of the Methodist Church, one of Lincoln's closest friends and esteemed counselors, gave a moving funeral oration. Those in attendance sang the hymn "Praise God from Whom All Blessings Flow." Dr. Gurley, who had given the funeral sermon in Washington, closed the service with a benediction.[35]

Simpson's eulogy, like Gurley's a few weeks earlier, illuminated the man and his motivation for leading. Labeling Lincoln "no ordinary man," Simpson spoke of how "the hand of God" had shaped and prepared Lincoln through all of his various life experiences to be president. His upbringing on the frontier, with its "physical education … prepared him for enduring herculean labors." From his "boyhood and the labors of his manhood, God was giving him an iron frame." Lincoln identified with "the heart of the great people"

---

[33] Wheeler, *Faith and Courage*, xi; Canavan, *Lincoln's Final Hours*, 136.

[34] Fox, *Lincoln's Body*, 117–18.

[35] Own, *The Man and His Faith*, 221.

and could understand "their feelings because he was one of them, and connected with them in their movements and life." Even though he received only a simple, formal education, his prodigious reading habits shaped his character and style. The hard work and various struggles he endured on the frontier "joined him indissolubly to the working masses." Lincoln "knew what it was to fell the tall trees of the forest and to stem the current of the broad Mississippi … He learned lessons of self-reliance which sustained him in seasons of adversity."

Lincoln's God-given "genius" allowed him to serve in government and law and prepared him to be a statesman. According to Simpson, Lincoln's greatest "mental characteristic" was his "quick and ready perception of facts." He possessed an incredible "memory, unusually tenacious and retentive; and on a logical turn of mind, which followed sternly and unwaveringly every link in the chain of thought on every subject which he was called to investigate." There had never been "a man who could follow step by step, with more logical power, the points which he desired to illustrate. He gained this power by the close study of geometry, and by a determination to perceive the truth in all its relations and simplicity, and when found, to utter it."

As exemplary as Lincoln's mental powers were, Simpson contended that the president's "moral power gave him pre-eminence … They saw in him a man whom they believed would do what is right, regardless of all consequences." This "moral feeling" was what "gave him the greatest hold on the people, and made his utterances almost oracular."

Simpson said, "Lincoln was a good man. He was known as an honest, temperate, forgiving man; a just man; a man of noble heart in every way." As far as Lincoln's "religious experience," Simpson explained that he could not "speak definitely," because he had not been "privileged to know much of his private sentiments."

> This I know, however, he read the Bible frequently; loved it for its great truths and its profound

teachings; and he tried to be guided by its precepts. He believed in Christ the Saviour of sinners; and I think he was sincere in trying to bring his life into harmony with the principles of revealed religion. Certainly if there ever was a man who illustrated some of the principles of pure religion, that man was our departed president. Look over all his speeches; listen to his utterances. He never spoke unkindly of any man. Even the rebels received no word of anger from him; and his last day illustrated in a remarkable manner his forgiving disposition. A dispatch was received that afternoon that Thompson and Tucker were trying to make their escape through Maine, and it was proposed to arrest them. Mr. Lincoln, however, preferred rather to let them quietly escape. He was seeking to save the very men who had been plotting his destruction. This morning we read a proclamation offering $25,000 for the arrest of these men as aiders and abettors of his assassination; so that, in his expiring acts, he was saying, "Father, forgive them, they know not what they do."

As a ruler I doubt if any president has ever shown such trust in God, or in public documents so frequently referred to Divine aid. Often did he remark to friends and to delegations that his hope for our success rested in his conviction that God would bless our efforts, because we were trying to do right. To the address of a large religious body he replied, "Thanks be unto God, who, in our national trials, giveth us the Churches." To a minister who said he hoped the Lord was on our side, he replied that it gave him no concern whether the Lord was on our side or not "For," he added, "I know the Lord is always on the side of right;" and with deep

> feeling added, "But God is my witness that it is my constant anxiety and prayer that both myself and this nation should be on the Lord's side."

In closing, Simpson said that while the nation mourned now, in the years ahead, "mothers shall teach thy name to their lisping children. The youth of our land shall emulate thy virtues. Statesmen shall study thy record and learn lessons of wisdom."[36] Indeed, Lincoln's biography provides many life lessons for those to learn from and embrace.

As soon as the funeral service ended, a military guard took up position outside the tomb to guard against souvenir hunters. Soldiers guarded the aboveground tomb just as they had for Jesus.[37]

Eulogies on Springfield's favorite son dominated the countryside for the next few months. One memorialist said the "one purpose of that strange manner of summoning him to the skies was to … engrave his traits all the deeper into the memories of coming generations."[38] Phillip Brooks in his sermon added a profound benediction: "May God make us worthy of the memory of Abraham Lincoln."[39] Flags remained at half-staff around the nation, and people continued to wear silk mourning badges. One badge in particular was highly visible almost everywhere in Washington during those grief-stricken days: "With malice toward none; with charity for all."[40] Lincoln would have approved.

Not until 1874 did Lincoln's vault at Oak Ridge Cemetery become a national monument. After reviewing thirty-seven proposals, the Springfield association selected a sky-high granite obelisk (initially 85 feet, later raised to 117 feet) and an eleven-feet-tall

---

[36] Simpson, Funeral Address Delivered at the Burial of President Lincoln, May 4, 1865, http://lincoln.digitalscholarship.emory.edu/simpson.001/.

[37] Fox, *Lincoln's Body*, 155.

[38] Peterson, *Lincoln in American Memory*, 35.

[39] Peterson, *Lincoln in American Memory*, 35.

[40] White, *Lincoln*, 676.

bronze Lincoln. Depicted in a "citizen's dress," Lincoln's right hand is resting on Roman fasces with an American flag draped over it. He is grasping the pen he used to sign the Emancipation Proclamation. His left hand grips a scroll of the document. The four Civil War bronzes positioned around the obelisk—battle scenes of the cavalry, infantry, artillery, and navy, with all of the soldiers depicted as white men—emphasize Lincoln's wartime command, not his role in ending slavery.[41]

The day after Lincoln passed, the military guard left William Petersen's boardinghouse. With the guard gone, people came and took anything from the home that could serve as a keepsake: soiled bandages, carpet strips, spoons, and splinters of furniture. Seeing how their house had become a national shrine overnight, fifteen year-old Fred Petersen, son of William, cut pieces of plain white paper into squares. He dated and signed each one and dipped them in the blood left on an oil cloth in the front hall—probably Major Rathbone's, who had been injured in the attack. As the gravity and historic tragedy continued to sink in, people clamored for Fred Petersen's grim souvenirs. He made $1.12 in fewer than ten minutes. Soon he would be charging fifty cents for admission to the room where Lincoln passed. Made into a museum in the 1930s, the Petersen House, as it is referred to today, is a part of Ford's Theatre and run by the National Park Service. The federal government never allowed John Ford to reopen Ford's Theatre after Lincoln's assassination. Federal officials paid him one hundred thousand dollars for it, and soon a contractor converted it into a three-story government office building.[42] Today the theater remains a top tourist destination as a museum, live theater, and learning station.

---

[41] Fox, *Lincoln's Body*, 155.

[42] Canavan, *Lincoln's Final Hours*, 121, 127, 130, 157, 161. After admitting Lincoln's body into his home, William Peterson disappeared for seven hours. When he returned home, he became upset when he saw the heaps of medical refuse and stinking piles of soiled bandages in his narrow hallway. Not quite realizing what had taken place or the ordeal that many had observed for hours

Lincoln's sudden death catapulted him to unending heights of fame. Russian novelist Leo Tolstoy provided a tribute in 1909, admiring Lincoln's moral power and character. Lincoln was in politics, he said, what Beethoven was in music, Dante in poetry, Raphael in painting, and Jesus in the philosophy of life. For Tolstoy, no one matched Lincoln. He was greater than Alexander, Frederick the Great, Caesar, Napoleon, Gladstone, and even the inestimable George Washington. Lincoln "was a Christ in miniature, a saint of humanity, whose name will live thousands of years in the legends of future generations."[43]

There are some who believe the impressive Lincoln Memorial in Washington, DC, which depicts a regal marble man sitting high on his throne-like chair, does a disservice to the real Lincoln—one who Americans considered a man of the people. The real Lincoln referred to the White House as "the shop," wore small, wire-rimmed spectacles when reading or writing, said his "ear bones" ached to hear a good joke, and constantly deployed self-deprecating humor to bring joy to others.[44] On the other hand, the prodigious monument is stalwart and seemingly immovable, just like Lincoln's convictions. Political cartoonists love using the iconic Lincoln Memorial to commemorate special moments. After a half century, the most memorable cartoon commemorating the assassination of JFK remains Bill Mauldin's depiction of a grieving Lincoln Memorial, Lincoln holding his head in his hands. When Americans elected Barack Obama president of

---

as the president clung to his life, Peterson stormed into the death room and rudely grabbed the stained top pillow out from under the dead president's head. Raising the thick window blinds, he tossed the stained pillow out onto the fieldstone courtyard two stories below. He loudly complained that they had turned his house into a mess—full of mud, unwashed basins, and other unsanitary evidence. Before Lincoln's body would be buried, Petersen would try to bill the federal government for every single thing he had provided for the president's makeshift hospital, including, falsely, for his own time.

43 Burlingame, *Lincoln,* 2:834.

44 Oates, *Lincoln*, 151.

the United States, one cartoon depicted the statue crying from joy; another had Lincoln beaming; while others portrayed the statue waving its arms in delight. A cartoonist in Australia showed Obama standing on the arm of the statue, with the caption, "Ready, Willing and Abe."[45]

Often mothers know best. "I did not want Abe to run for Presdt, did not want him Elected—was afraid Somehow or other—felt in my heart that Something would happen him," Lincoln's stepmother reflected a few months after the assassination. "When he came down to see me after he was Elected Presdt I still felt that Something told me that Something would befall Abe and that I should see him no more." She went on: "Abe & his father are in Heaven I have not doubt, and I want to go there—go where they are—God bless Abm."[46]

The Truth

For those who are Christ-followers, earthly death is not the end but the beginning of eternal life. The Bible teaches that "the wages of sin is death, but the free gift of God is eternal life in Christ Jesus our Lord."[47] While heaven will have streets of gold, this is not what will make it a special place.[48] Heaven is the home of all fallen saints, "a new heaven and a new earth," the "dwelling place" where "God is with man." In heaven, God "will wipe away every tear from their eyes, and death shall be no more, neither shall there be mourning, nor crying, nor pain anymore, for the former things have passed away." Heaven remains God's home and domain, where He makes "all things new."[49]

---

45 Szasz and Szasz, *Lincoln and Religion*, 62–63.

46 Wilson, *Herndon's Informants*, 106–9.

47 Rom. 6:23.

48 Rev. 21:21.

49 Rev. 21:1, 3, 4, 5.

As great as heaven will be for the believer, most people do not want to go there anytime soon. There is an old saying that "everyone wants to go to heaven, but nobody wants to die." Our sinful flesh and sinful nature lead us away from God and not toward Him. This is one reason why many people obsess over death too much—they fear death and do not want to die. On the other hand, there are those who think of death and the afterlife too little—they live only for the moment.

Christians, however, can live with confidence and joy, both in the present and in regard to the future. As the Bible teaches, "If we live, we live to the Lord, and if we die, we die to the Lord. So then, whether we live or whether we die, we are the Lord's."[50] Indeed, "precious in the sight of the Lord is the death of his saints."[51]

There is no doubt that death is bitter for those left to mourn the loss of a loved one. "The last enemy to be destroyed is death."[52] But Jesus conquered sin and death when He died on the cross for our sins. "I am the resurrection and the life," He tells all who hear Him. "Whoever believes in me, though he die, yet shall he live, and everyone who lives and believes in me shall never die."[53]

Abraham Lincoln saw death all around him—on the frontier, throughout a tumultuous Civil War, and in his household. He had premonitions about his own death. The truth is that we all face certain death here on earth. We just do not know when or how—and this is a good thing. Life is tough enough to live on a day-to-day basis without worrying about the when, where, and how of death.

No matter our hardships on earth, heaven promises to be a perfect place—paradise—because Jesus will be there right beside His Heavenly Father. The Bible assures Christ-followers "that the sufferings of this present time are not worth comparing with the

---

50 Rom. 14:8.

51 Ps. 116:15.

52 1 Cor. 15:26.

53 John 11:25–26.

glory that is to be revealed to us."[54] Therefore when "the righteous man is taken away from calamity; he enters into peace; they rest in their beds who walk in their uprightness."[55] "Blessed is the man who remains steadfast under trial, for when he has stood the test he will receive the crown of life, which God has promised to those who love him."[56]

When you are struggling in life, face challenges, or feel "heavy laden," Jesus exhorts you to come to Him for rest.[57] "Let not your hearts be troubled," He reassures you. "Believe in God; believe also in me. In my Father's house are many rooms. If it were not so, would I have told you that I go to prepare a place for you?"[58] Jesus has prepared a place in heaven for *you* and paid for it with the blood He shed on the cross for *you*. "I will come again and will take you to myself, that where I am you may be also," He promises. "And you know the way to where I am going."[59]

Whether you suffer a sudden, violent death or a slow, undignified one, you will not be alone or hopeless. Thanks to Jesus, death is not to be feared. The Christian knows that earthly death is not the end, but only the beginning of life. A follower of Jesus can confidently say, "'O death, where is your victory? O death, where is your sting?'" As the Bible makes clear: "The sting of death is sin, and the power of sin is the law. But thanks be to God, who gives us the victory through our Lord Jesus Christ."[60] Thanks to Jesus, Christians win in life and in death.

---

[54] Rom. 8:18.

[55] Isa. 57:1–2.

[56] James 1:12.

[57] Matt. 11:28.

[58] John 14:1-2.

[59] John 14:1–4.

[60] 1 Cor. 15:55–57.

Your Life

How often do you think about your death or the earthly passing of your loved ones? What triggers your thoughts on the topic? How do you cope with these thoughts?

Christians know that Jesus conquered sin, death, and the power of the devil by His death on the cross and resurrection on that first Easter Sunday. A life of eternity in heaven awaits those who believe in Jesus Christ as Lord and Savior. How does knowing this truth make a difference in the way you live in this fallen world?

The length of your days on earth is not guaranteed. This can be scary to some and liberating to others. How does this reality impact how you live your life? How does this truth motivate you to share what you believe with your loved ones?

42

Remembering Lincoln's Leadership

Remember your leaders, those who spoke to you the word of God. Consider the outcome of their way of life, and imitate their faith.
—Hebrews 13:7

Presidential Remembrances on the Lincoln Way

Legacies last.

Much like student athletes remember and cherish heartfelt words spoken of them by a favorite coach at an end-of-season banquet, twentieth- and twenty-first-century American presidents have long remembered and embraced the leadership aspects and words of Abraham Lincoln. President George W. Bush read seventeen Lincoln biographies while serving as president. "I've got his painting right there," he said one day in the Oval Office. "I have sat here and thought about what it was like to be the president when brother was fighting brother and cousin killing cousin. He clearly saw what needed to happen about keeping his country united."[1]

Since Lincoln's assassination, almost every American president has embraced Lincoln's legacy and aimed to place himself on the right side history—namely Lincoln's side. While there are innumerable things to remember and laud about the nation's sixteenth president,

[1] Gibbs and Duffy, *Presidents Club*, 525.

the mental real estate that Lincoln occupies in the minds of former chief executives of United States is instructive.

President Theodore Roosevelt commissioned the Lincoln penny in 1909—the centennial of Lincoln's birth.[2] The high energy "speak softly but carry a big stick" Republican and former Rough Rider admired Lincoln's "bodily vigor," intellectual growth, and personal fearlessness. According to Roosevelt, Lincoln lived "the strenuous life" and died for the Union and those held in bondage. Roosevelt believed Lincoln's refusal to demonize his enemies, as well as his effort to see things from his critics' perspectives, did not make him a weak appeaser, but a tougher, more formidable fighter. Principles, not personalities, mattered most to him—and he would fight for those principles with tenacity, relentlessness, and vision.[3]

As a little boy, Roosevelt watched Lincoln's funeral processional from his family's home in New York City. As an adult, he wore a lock of Lincoln's hair in his ring. While serving in the White House, he frequently told reporters that he kept a portrait of Lincoln behind his presidential desk. "When I am confronted with a great problem," he explained, "I look up to that picture, and I do as I believe Lincoln would have done."[4]

For President William Howard Taft, Lincoln was an "inspiration for heroism" more than any other man in history. "One cannot read Abraham Lincoln without loving him," he said.[5] At the dedication of the Lincoln Memorial, on May 30, 1922, Taft (then a justice of the United States Supreme Court) commented on Lincoln's compassion for all people: "We feel a closer touch with him than with living men. The influence he still wields ... has a Christ-like

---

[2] Szasz and Szasz, *Lincoln and Religion*, 64. With over 500 billion Lincoln pennies produced since 1909, the Lincoln penny remains the most viewed and popular coin in world history.

[3] Fox, *Lincoln's Body*, 182.

[4] Holzer and Garfinkle, *A Just and Generous Nation*, 181. Roosevelt acquired the lock from John Hay, his secretary of state and Lincoln's private secretary.

[5] Peterson, *Lincoln in American Memory*, 186.

character." Lincoln's legacy "has spread to the four quarters of the globe. The oppressed and lowly of all peoples, as liberty and free government spread, pronounce his name with awe, and cherish his assured personal sympathy as a source of hope."[6]

President Woodrow Wilson admired "the particular sweetness that Lincoln possessed" and lamented the brutal death of a leader in his prime. There "was more promise in him when he died than when he was born," Wilson maintained. "No man can think of the life of Lincoln without feeling that the man was cut off almost at his beginning." That Lincoln could "withdraw himself" so that he "himself could see the stage" was a big-picture leadership skill that Wilson greatly esteemed.[7]

President Warren Harding also spoke at the Lincoln Memorial dedication, praising Lincoln's political skill in threading the needle between opposing worldviews while not losing sight of the long-term goal. That Lincoln wanted the expansion of slavery halted, but did not push to abolish it in all parts of the country at the beginning of his presidency, revealed his keen political instincts and emotional intelligence. Lincoln could handle this crisis "because of the inherent righteousness of his cause and the sublimity of his own faith." While George Washington "inspired belief in the Republic in its heroic beginning, Lincoln proved its quality in the heroic preservation."[8]

Lincoln remained eminently quotable for later American presidents, especially when trying to establish their own policies. During his inaugural address at the height of the Great Depression, Franklin Delano Roosevelt paraphrased one of Lincoln's most popular statements when he said that "this nation cannot endure if it is half 'boom' and half 'broke.'"[9] In a fireside chat in the fall of 1934, FDR defended his progressive policies as something Lincoln would do: "I believe with Abraham Lincoln," he asserted, "that

---

[6] Manning, *Father Lincoln*, xi.

[7] Fox, *Lincoln's Body*, 202–03.

[8] Manning, *Father Lincoln*, xii.

[9] Friedel, *Rendezvous with Destiny*, 85.

'The legitimate object of Government is to do for a community of people whatever they need to have done but cannot do at all or cannot do well for themselves in their separate and individual capacities.'"[10] FDR hailed Lincoln for promoting a government that embraced its broad purpose of lifting up life, liberty, and the pursuit of happiness.[11] From the Fourth of July platform at Gettysburg in 1938, FDR addressed the question, "What Would Lincoln Do?" He answered his own question: America would "live by the wisdom and humanity of the heart of Abraham Lincoln."[12]

When President Harry Truman struggled to rein in General Douglas MacArthur, he studied Lincoln's actions with regard to his own intransigent general, George McClellan. Truman recalled a story Lincoln told of when his horse kicked up and almost threw him to the ground. Lincoln apparently said to the horse, "If you are going to get on, I will get off." While Truman later reflected that he could not match Lincoln's patience with his rogue general, he did try to emulate Lincoln's focus on the common folk.[13] Lincoln clearly understood and could relate to people because he possessed "a good head and a great brain and a kind heart." He "was the best kind of ordinary man"—one that served the people.[14] For Truman, there was no higher compliment to give a person or leader.

President Dwight Eisenhower actually bought a farm in Gettysburg, painted a portrait of the sixteenth president, and gave prints of it to the White House staff for Christmas.[15] Ike believed Lincoln's personal leadership qualities of dedication, selflessness,

---

[10] Holzer and Garfinkle, *A Just and Generous Nation*, 198.

[11] Landis and Milkis, *Presidential Greatness*, 157–58.

[12] Peterson, *Lincoln in American Memory*, 321.

[13] McCullough, *Truman*, 512, 695. Servants frequently told Truman how ghosts of Lincoln appeared in the White House over the years. Truman came to believe the "white jail," as he called the White House, had indeed become haunted.

[14] Meacham, *Soul of America*, 271.

[15] Gibbs and Duffy, *Presidents Club*, 525.

modesty, and humility made him special and worth emulating. In addition to keeping Lincoln's *Collected Works* in his office and worshipping in Lincoln's pew at the New York Avenue Presbyterian Church, Ike quoted Lincoln repeatedly. The words of Lincoln he repeated the most were these: "The legitimate object of government, is to do for a community of people, whatever they need to have done, but can not do, at all, or can not, so well do, for themselves—in their separate, and individual capacities. In all that the people can individually do for themselves, government ought not to interfere."[16]

Well aware of Lincoln's ability to inspire, President John F. Kennedy abandoned the idea of having the renowned poet Robert Frost read a poem at his inauguration. As much as he liked the idea, he worried about setting up a similar situation with Lincoln and Edward Everett at Gettysburg. As Frost was a "master of words," the poet might overshadow Kennedy's inaugural address much as Lincoln's short speech dominated American memory compared to Everett's two-hour-long oration. Instead, JFK asked his staff to study the Gettysburg Address. They reported back to him that brevity and the use of as few multisyllable words as possible were the keys to the speech's success.[17]

Much is made by historians of the similarities between the assassinations of Lincoln and JFK. JFK was elected exactly a century after Lincoln, and every president elected at twenty-year intervals since 1840 had died before leaving office. Both had vice presidents with the same last name—Johnson. Both would be shot on Friday—Lincoln in a theater named after Ford, and Kennedy in a Lincoln

---

16 Peterson, *Lincoln in American Memory*, 324–25.

17 Dallek, *An Unfinished Life*, 323–24, 470. During the height of the Cold War showdown between Nikita Khrushchev and JFK, when nuclear war seemed all too likely between the world's two superpowers, JFK's secretary found a note written in Kennedy's hand while clearing the president's desk of papers. It recalled Lincoln's reassurance to himself on the eve of the Civil War: "I know that there is a God and I see a storm coming. If he has a place for me I am ready."

convertible made by Ford. Both had lost consciousness at the instant they were shot.[18]

JFK often eerily speculated about his own possible assassination. He once asked a historian if Lincoln's reputation would have been diminished if he had not been shot at Ford's Theatre. The historian said that Lincoln's reputation almost assuredly would have plummeted because of the formidable and daunting challenge of reconstruction.[19]

Hours after her husband was gunned down in Dallas on November 23, 1963, a state department official asked what he could do for First Lady Jackie Kennedy. "Find out how Lincoln was buried," she replied. [20] Before dawn on the next day, she had the department's report in hand.

Newly sworn-in President Lyndon Johnson quickly pressed civil rights legislation. After "100 years of talking" about Lincoln's cause, he told a joint session of Congress on November 27, 1963, the time had come to enact the "dream of equal rights for all Americans, whatever their race or color."[21]

A framed picture of Lincoln, given to him by his grandmother on his thirteenth birthday, remained one of President Richard Nixon's most prized possessions throughout his life. But though Nixon believed Lincoln to be "the most revered of all American Presidents," he asserted that the Great Emancipator "would have failed in the TV age" with his "high-pitched voice and homely features."[22] Nixon, who looked lackluster in one of the first presidential debates on television in 1960 against JFK, added a contrarian and cynical view of Lincoln:

> His long, rambling anecdotes, while very effective in speeches to live audiences, would not have played

---

[18] Fox, *Lincoln's Body*, 266–67.

[19] Sabato, *The Kennedy Half-Century*, 132.

[20] Fox, *Lincoln's Body*, 264.

[21] Fox, *Lincoln's Body*, 268.

[22] Nixon, *In the Arena*, 219.

> well in a medium the candidates can win by using one-liners fed to him by his speechwriters. In an age of sound-bites, the three-minute Gettysburg Address would have been two and a half minutes too long. One of today's ambitious young correspondents would probably have summed it up this way: "The President himself admitted to this subdued Pennsylvania crowd what his men have been saying privately: that no one will long remember what was said here."[23]

After the Kent State shootings on May 9, 1970, Nixon took an early morning drive to the Lincoln Memorial, where he spoke directly to student protestors encamped there. He later copied the monument's inscription in his diary: "In this temple, as in the hearts of the people for whom he saved the Union, the memory of Abraham Lincoln is enshrined forever."[24] Engrossed in a Southeast Asian war he wanted to withdraw from—but only as an honorable victor—Nixon appreciated the political navigation and will of Lincoln to do anything to preserve the Union. War could not be "won on the cheap," Nixon later acknowledged. "If Abraham Lincoln had been worried about the budget in 1861," the Union never would have won. Instead, "Lincoln spent what he needed to win the Civil War" and ran up a significant deficit.[25]

President Ronald Reagan often joked about attending his "first Republican convention" at which he heard "Abraham Lincoln giving a speech that sent shivers down my spine."[26] Over the years, presidents often heard from maids, butlers, and guests who swore they had seen Lincoln's ghost in the White House. When Maureen Reagan, after a night in the Lincoln Bedroom, said as much to her

---

23 Nixon, *In the Arena*, 219.

24 Gibbs and Duffy, *Presidents Club*, 525.

25 Nixon, *In the Arena*, 134.

26 Noonan, *When Character Was King*, 237.

father, he told her, the next time Lincoln appeared, to send him down the hall because Reagan had "a few questions I'd like to ask him."[27]

Reagan extolled Lincoln's willingness to fight and speak for his vision—a vision that "first believes all men are created equal by a loving God who has blessed us with freedom."[28] He also drew inspiration from Lincoln's allegiance to deep, core convictions and his impassioned defense of God-given rights. During his speech to the National Religious Broadcasters, in January 1984, Reagan spoke against abortion and compared the cause to Lincoln's fight for emancipation. "Abraham Lincoln recognized that we could not survive as a free land when some could decide whether others should be free or slaves," he maintained. "Well, today another question begs to be asked: How can we survive as a free nation when some decide that others are not fit to live and should be done away with?" No challenge, Reagan believed, "is more important to the character of America than restoring the right to life of all human beings. Without that right, no other rights have meaning."[29]

President George H. W. Bush invoked Lincoln's words when he reversed his infamous no-new-taxes pledge. "I'm doing like Lincoln did, 'think anew'" he claimed, quoting from Lincoln's annual message to Congress on December 1, 1862, which called for restoration of the Union and the freeing of slaves.[30]

Even though he met JFK at the White House as a high school student, President Bill Clinton claims his favorite two presidents are FDR and Lincoln. He once noted, while running for a Senate seat, that "deep down I probably felt as Abraham Lincoln did when he wrote as a young man, 'I will study and get ready, and perhaps my chance will come.'"[31]

---

[27] Peterson, *Lincoln in American Memory*, 324.

[28] Kengor, *God and Reagan*, 229.

[29] Kengor, *God and Reagan*, 177–78.

[30] Williams, "Lincoln—Our Ever-Present Contemporary," 145.

[31] Clinton, *My Life*, 62.

Like Nixon, Clinton wondered how Lincoln would have fared in the modern era. Noting Lincoln's debilitating bouts of depression and melancholy, and how "he was unable to leave his house for a whole month," Clinton opined that if Lincoln had run for office "under modern conditions, we might have been deprived of our greatest President."[32] According to Clinton, Lincoln overcame his mental health issues because he became so "absorbed in the work and the mission and the suffering of others that it lifted the burden off of him."[33]

As George W. Bush endured his share of vicious, ad hominem attacks during his presidency, he remembered that Lincoln had been "compared to a baboon." Like Lincoln, Bush "found solace in reading the Bible, which Abraham Lincoln called 'the best gift God has given to man.'" Bush admired Lincoln's "moral clarity and resolve." In fact, in the Treaty Room of the White House hung one of Bush's favorite oil paintings—*The Peacemakers.* The painting depicts Lincoln aboard the *River Queen* steamer, consulting with General Ulysses Grant, General William Sherman, and Rear Admiral David Porter in the final month of the Civil War. "Before 9/11, I saw the scene as a fascinating moment in history," Bush recorded in his memoir. "After the attack, it took on a deeper meaning. The painting reminded me of Lincoln's clarity of purpose: He waged war for a necessary and noble cause."[34]

In addition to Lincoln's impressive diplomacy skills—"If you would win a man to your cause, first you convince him that you are his friend"—Bush most empathized and connected with Lincoln in regard to comforting those who lost loved ones in the line of military duty. Bush found great inspiration in the letter Lincoln wrote to Lydia Bixby, a Massachusetts woman who lost five sons in the Civil War:

---

32 Clinton, *My Life*, 333, 405.

33 Gibbs and Duffy, *Presidents Club*, 525.

34 Bush, *Decision Points*, 121, 140, 183.

> Dear Madam, – I have been shown in the files of the War Department a statement of the Adjutant General of Massachusetts, that you are the mother of five sons who have died gloriously on the field of battle. I feel how weak and fruitless must be any words of mine which should attempt to beguile you from the grief of a loss so overwhelming. But I cannot refrain from tendering to you the consolation that may be found in the thanks of the Republic they died to save. I pray that our Heavenly Father may assuage the anguish of your bereavement, and leave you only the cherished memory of the loved and lost, and the solemn pride that must be yours, to have laid so costly a sacrifice upon the altar of Freedom. Yours, very sincerely and respectfully, A. LINCOLN[35]

Like Lincoln, George W. Bush relied on his religious faith as he endured changes in generalship and casualties of war. Lincoln "watched his son Willie die in the White House and his wife, Mary Todd, sink into depression," Bush reflected. "Yet thanks to his faith in God and deep belief that he was waging war for a just cause, Lincoln persisted."[36]

From one Illinois lawyer and senator to another, President Barack Obama compared his own humble beginnings and life story to Lincoln's. A man "with a funny name," with "a father from Kenya and a mother from Kansas," could only be trumped by "a child born in the backwoods of Kentucky with less than a year of formal education."[37] Obama announced his presidential bid on February 10, 2007, outside of Lincoln's Old State Capitol, and took Lincoln's theme of division—a house divided against itself cannot

---

[35] Bush, *Decision Points,* 195, 203.

[36] Bush, *Decision Points,* 368.

[37] Fox, *Lincoln's Body,* 302.

stand—insisting that Americans could build "a more perfect union." Obama invoked Lincoln in terms of being a first-term senator from Illinois, "without money and family connections," and someone who loved "the power of words." Moreover, they each had a tall, gangly body. On January 20, 2009, Obama took the oath of office with his hand resting on the Bible Lincoln had used. After Obama's inaugural address, assorted members of Congress convened for a banquet of delicacies from the 1860s.[38]

Beyond the commonalities of their backgrounds and political ascendance, when President Obama appointed his Democratic primary rival, Hillary Clinton, to be his secretary of state, Obama's action paralleled Lincoln's move to offer his main competitor, William Seward, the same cabinet position. The Team of Rivals concept remained alive and well.[39]

Obama acclaimed Lincoln's self-study and "his capacity to overcome personal loss and his increased determination in the face of responsibilities"—crucial in shaping the American character and the American dream.[40] While he also praised Lincoln for keeping "his moral compass pointed and true," Obama did admit he could not "swallow whole the view of Lincoln as the Great Emancipator" and his "limited views on race." Nevertheless, Obama asserted that Lincoln's imperfections made him much more compelling. Lincoln's ability to improve, personally and professionally, reminded Obama of "the enduring belief that we can constantly remake ourselves to fit our larger dreams."[41]

While all presidents received their share of public scrutiny, perhaps no two presidents received more vitriolic criticism from media and contemporaries than did Lincoln and President Donald Trump. Like other presidents before him, Trump enjoys being associated in any way with Lincoln. The fact that Trump has

---

38 Fox, *Lincoln's Body*, 304–05, 307.

39 Fox, *Lincoln's Body*, xi–xii.

40 Szasz and Szasz, *Lincoln and Religion*, 60.

41 Morel, *Lincoln and Liberty*, xi.

given several television interviews at the Lincoln Memorial simply reinforces the notion of how all presidents, Republican or Democrat, found it helpful and beneficial to bask in the historical presence of the nation's sixteenth president.

Faith. Conviction. Courage. Clarity. Purpose. Resilience. Staying resolute for the long term. Overcoming loss and adversity. The will to rise and succeed. Compassion. Kindness. Empathy. These were the words and attributes most often referenced by America's later presidents in regard to Lincoln. They remain the traits, habits, and ideals of Lincoln's leadership legacy that still inspire leaders all around the world today. Future American presidents and citizens would do well to remember them.

The Truth

The Triune God is a God of history and legacy. One of the reasons He chose to reveal Himself through His Holy Word is because He wants us to remember all that He has done for us and how much He loves us.

God constantly implored the children of Israel to remember Him and all that He had done for them. Yet they continued to forget and reject him. The Bible says that "there arose another generation after them who did not know the Lord or the work that he had done for Israel." They did "evil in the sight of the Lord" and "abandoned the Lord, the God of their fathers, who had brought them out of the land of Egypt." Revealing the sinful nature of humankind, "they went after other gods, from among the gods of the peoples who were around them, and bowed down to them. And they provoked the Lord to anger … And they were in terrible distress."[42]

Like the children of Israel, we are sinful and often forget God. When times are good and prosperous, many neglect to thank Him for all that He has blessed them with or all that He has protected

[42] Judg. 2:9–15.

them from in a sinful world. Satan slowly and subtly convinces people that *their own* hard work is the reason that they have been blessed with material wealth or comfort. Or perhaps when times are tough, people turn to drugs, sex, false gods, self-help guides—anything or anyone but God. Or maybe we forget about worshipping God on Sunday or our worship day because a beautiful day at the lake cabin beckons, a charitable 5K run seems more alluring, or shopping or football gazing or sleep must take priority.

In His infinite wisdom, and knowing humankind's sinful nature and frailty, God promises to help you remember all that He accomplished through the death and resurrection of His Son, Jesus Christ, through the power of the Holy Spirit. As the Bible teaches, "the Helper, the Holy Spirit, whom the Father will send in my name, he will teach you all things and bring to your remembrance all that I have said to you."[43]

The Bible teaches that God does not want you to forget Him and what Jesus did for *you* on the cross. Moreover, He promises to never forget you. Recall the Good Friday scene on Mount Calvary, where Jesus had been put on a cross to pay the price for your sins:

> When one of the criminals who were hanged railed at him, saying, "Are you not the Christ? Save yourself and us!" But the other rebuked him, saying, "Do you not fear God, since you are under the same sentence of condemnation? And we indeed justly, for we are receiving the due reward of our deeds; but this man has done nothing wrong." And he said, "Jesus, remember me when you come into your kingdom." And he said to him, "Truly, I say to you, today you will be with me in paradise."[44]

---

[43] John 14:26.

[44] Luke 23:39–43.

God's plan of salvation is all about mercy, grace, and love. Thanks be to Jesus, *the only thing God will ever forget about you is your sins.* As He says in the Bible, "I am he who blots out your transgressions for my own sake, and I will not remember your sins."[45]

Find great comfort in the fact that Jesus came to die for you, rose for you, and will never forget you. Unlike many people who put a history book on a shelf, never to be opened or read again, Jesus will never put you on a shelf and leave you by yourself. He watches over you everywhere, every day, and always. His legacy—what He wants you to remember and embrace—is that He died for you and covets an everlasting relationship with you here on earth and for all eternity. That's not only great history, but good news for today and tomorrow.

Your Life

Why is it important to understand that the Christian faith is grounded in history?

What do you want people to remember about you? What are you doing to make this legacy a reality? How can you live your legacy now?

Exodus 20:8 says, "Remember the Sabbath day, to keep it holy." What does this mean? How else do you or will you remember God?

---

[45] Isa. 43:25.

43

Witnessing and Ministering to the Lincolns of Today

And Jesus said to them, "Go into all the world and proclaim the gospel to the whole creation."
—Mark 16:15

A historian once said that biography "offers an easy education in American history, rendering the past more human, more vivid, more intimate, more accessible, more connected to ourselves." Reading a biography "reminds us that presidents are not supermen. They are human beings too, worrying about decisions, attending to wives and children, juggling balls in the air, and putting on their pants one leg at a time."[1] As Ralph Waldo Emerson proclaimed, "There is properly no history; only biography."[2]

To learn from the past is only profitable if it stirs one to examine one's own life, change one's mindset, plan an action, or create positive change for the future. Studying the life of Lincoln is a pleasurable endeavor all by itself. He is, after all, a fascinating character of history and perhaps our nation's greatest president. A plethora of Lincoln biographies exist that can bring the reader immense literary and historical satisfaction.

This book, however, has attempted something beyond a Lincoln biography. In addition to examining the life of Lincoln in a thematic way, this work asks the reader to reflect his or her own life through

[1] McGovern, *Lincoln,* xvi.

[2] McGovern, *Lincoln*, xvi.

the lens of Lincoln's life and, more importantly, the lens of God's Word. *The Lincoln Way, The Truth, and Your Life* is a "threefold cord" that is not quickly broken.[3] By examining these three facets in conjunction with one another, the Christian leadership lessons one can learn, as well as the timelessness of God's wisdom recorded in the Bible, leap from the pages and into one's heart and mind.

The life of Lincoln provides an excellent blueprint for the contemporary Christian church to use in its evangelism efforts in the twenty-first century. To reach the growing population of unchurched, nones, and agnostics in our world today, not to mention the more hostile atheists, Bible-based Christians must not only be aware of and knowledgeable about the trends and mores of society, but they must understand the challenges and distractions that crowd out the voice of God in people's daily lives. When Lincoln's life is examined, one can see how poverty, fatherhood, family, education, lifelong learning, literacy, communication, false teachings, books, marriage, friendship, parenting, politics, reason, rationalism, self-improvement, vocation, ambition, physical appearance, dispositions, pragmatism, pastors, personal connection, slavery, service, freedom, sacrifice, and notions of the afterlife all had an impact on his faith walk and faith development.

The issues that made an impact on Lincoln's faith life are the same for many people today. If Christians now grasp the many different trials, life phases, and obstacles that presented themselves to Abraham Lincoln in his time, they will be better equipped to meet and serve the needs of the "Lincolns" in today's world. Indeed, if we truly care about our fellow human beings, we must use all suitable means that God has provided to reach those who do not yet know Jesus or the love of God in whatever valley they currently occupy.

This is no easy ministry task. Jesus said, "Everyone to whom much was given, of him much will be required, and from him to

---

[3] Eccles. 4:12.

whom they entrusted much, they will demand the more."[4] Knowing the life of Lincoln—particularly the struggles and challenges he faced in his faith walk—inspires a mindset, blueprint, or menu for faithful, Bible-believing Christians to use in their vocations as they witness, share, and teach the faith to Lincoln-like humans today.

Ministering to Those Suffering in Poverty and Economic Hardship

Too many people live in poverty today. The problem is only going to get worse as our world decays. In the United States, the gap between the have and have-nots widens each year. The middle class continues to shrink, and more students are put on federally assisted lunch programs than ever before. The breakdown and brokenness of the family continues to place more people into the vicious cycle of poverty with little hope for the future. This reality fits the biblical worldview that the further away humankind gets from the Fall, the more cursed and corrupt the world will become.[5]

In describing poverty, words like "scarcity," "deprivation," "need," "want," hardship," "shortage," "deficiency," "absence," "lack," "want," and "meagerness" come to the forefront. While not among the poorest of the poor, particularly in his earliest years, Lincoln experienced almost all of these descriptors. In addition to the material poverty he suffered, he felt deprived of fatherly love as well as vocational and educational encouragement.

While Lincoln lived in poverty for much of his early life, the actual scarcity of material things was not what generally bothered him. Other than during his courtship of Mary Todd, rarely does history record Lincoln complaining of or being concerned with his lack of wealth. More acutely than any material shortcoming, the condescending perceptions of others held of him and his

---

4 Luke 12:48.

5 Rom. 8:22.

backwoods family, as well as the prospect that he could never escape his hardscrabble, frontier lifestyle, were the deprivations that he felt most acutely.

Lincoln wanted to be respected. He wanted to rise. He wanted to make an impact. He wanted others to see him as a man of significance. And, yes, ambitiously or selfishly, *he wanted to make a name for himself.* Anything that got in the way of these aspirations—an unsupportive father, a lack of formal education, isolation on the frontier, the lack of financial security to support a wife and family—suppressed his dreams and kept him in a state of intellectual and emotional distress.

That Lincoln did rise, did live with purpose, did make an impact, and certainly did make a name for himself demonstrate that one can indeed rise and escape poverty. On both the material and emotional fronts, Lincoln overcame the poverty of his early years to live a rich and fruitful life.

These two features of poverty—the absence of material wealth and the presence of hopeless inability to pursue one's happiness—are important for Christians to recognize in people and communities today. Before Lincoln could make a name for himself and make an impact on the country, he had to cope with and eventually overcome the material and mental challenges of poverty.

Often Christians recognize material poverty, but overlook the inner poverty that cripples and tortures the soul. As much as Lincoln surely wanted more material goods and a better standard of living, he also wanted to feel that he had value to offer to others—that he had a purpose and could make a difference and a name for himself in his community, state, and nation.

Here's a question for you to reflect upon: How are you personally doing in meeting the needs of those who suffer from poverty—the material kind and the inner soul kind?

Here's another question for you to ponder: When people drive by churches on a Sunday morning, what do you think they see? Do they see parking lots filled with expensive SUVs, souped-up pickup trucks, and luxury cars? Do they notice people dressed in their finest designer suits and dresses? Do they observe an immaculate and expensive church building? Do they see the church sitting on fifteen acres of pristine, manicured landscape?

Of course, not all parking lots, church members, and church buildings appear this way. The question is, would people living in poverty feel welcome even approaching your church doors on a Sunday morning if they do not have a car or a new pair of dress shoes? Like a fancy grocery store, would people feel like they had to acquire a membership card before they could even come for a visit?

Please understand that there is nothing wrong with driving an SUV or wearing a designer suit to church. There is also nothing wrong with a church looking like a beautiful cathedral. Moreover, many churches do not match the description listed above—their sanctuaries are located in abandoned movie theaters, bankrupt outlet mall buildings, or house basements. Perhaps the church was constructed as a simple, small, humble building over a hundred years ago. Here's the point: Are you cognizant of how your church members and building appear to people who live outside of your typical social tribe or socioeconomic circle?

Educational research shows that K–12 students learn best from an outstanding teacher, and even more when an outstanding teacher *looks like them*. Congregations made up of primarily working- and middle-class members tend to attract more working- and middle-class families. If your church membership has an upscale, professional membership, then it will tend to attract more upper-income professionals. This is not something to eschew, but it is worth recognizing and being aware of if you care to witness and bring new members into your church community.

Regardless of the membership of their churches, most Christians are loving, caring people. They want anyone and everyone to feel welcome at their church so that all can learn about Jesus. They do not judge the faith walks of others based on their socioeconomic status. The challenge is that many living in poverty do not perceive that most Christians would welcome them into their congregations. Well-intentioned Christians need to remember that the "club membership" perception of their churches is real among folks living in poverty. This awareness is the first step in implementing an outreach plan to those living in poverty.

A few years ago, a member of my working-class congregation suddenly lost his manufacturing job. In the sixteen years I had known him, he had always been employed and had never missed Sunday worship service except for sickness. As soon as he became unemployed, however, he started missing divine worship. Embarrassed and down on his luck, he simply did not want to be seen. In his mind, *he did not look like or feel like the rest of us.*

Are you aware that people living in poverty often do not feel like they can or *should* go to the neighborhood church because they do not look like the rest of the congregation? If you have not thought about this before, this is a good time to start. If you truly want others to know Christ and God's Word, be sensitive to this mental poverty barrier. Go out of your way to be especially welcoming and encouraging to those who do not quite look like the rest of the congregation. Approach them in your own special way. God made you unique and put you right where you are "for such a time as this"[6]—perhaps even to help someone suffering from the physical and mental deprivations of poverty. Remind these individuals that Jesus died for *all* people, not only the picturesque Christian. Remind your fellow parishioners to be mindful of the mental struggle and guilt that so many suffering from poverty cope with daily. These mental deprivations and trials are probably infecting more parishioners or potential parishioners than you know.

Of course, the Christian church can and should address the needs of those suffering from poverty. Churches historically have been on the front lines in providing food, shelter, clothing, personal grooming essentials, and other physical needs for the downtrodden

---

6 Esther 4:4.

and economically disadvantaged. The history of the world is filled with examples of Christian charity and love. Pagan Roman emperors who tortured and executed Christians were stunned at the courage and love the early Christians showed by helping the poor, widowed, orphaned, sick, and diseased. Not only is caring for others encouraged and commanded by Scripture, but doing so gives Christians a solid platform to share and teach the love of Christ and God's Word. As demonstrated repeatedly throughout the gospels, Jesus often took care of the physical needs of people before He ministered to their spiritual needs. But Jesus did always address both the physical and the spiritual with each individual.

We must not forget the poverty lesson that Lincoln's life illuminates for us: Many people living in poverty feel trapped. They do not think that they will ever be able to pursue their own happiness or live a life of purpose. They suppress their dreams and aspirations or even give up on hope completely. This is the most horrific and wretched consequence of poverty.

This is not to suggest that people living in poverty never live with joy, purpose, or impact. Far from it. Perhaps you have had the experience of going on a mission trip where you intended to bring joy, hope, and material goods to people suffering in poverty, only to be lifted up by *their* joy, *their* love for Jesus, and *their* true appreciation for even the most basic possessions. They ministered to you instead of the other way around!

Nevertheless, poverty can crush a soul and suffocate one's desire to live a fruitful life. So when you meet and engage with people living in poverty or suffering from economic hardship—when you invite them to your church—you should be prepared for the mental and emotional anguish they have been enduring on a daily basis. They are wounded and suffering. They will need special care and love to heal and make them whole again.

To reach the poverty-stricken Abraham Lincolns today, Christians must be aware of the mental, social, and emotional scars that exist in the lives of so many suffering from poverty, *as well as* the material deprivations. Both needs must and can be met by the church at large and by individual Christians like you. Of course, you must rely on the Holy Spirit to equip and guide you in this endeavor and give you the right words to reach these folks. You must do more than *tell* them you love them; you must *show* them your love.

Beyond addressing their physical needs, make sure you minister to the people's emotional and spiritual well-being. There is bread and then there is the Bread of Life. Poverty-stricken folks, and all of us, need both.

By God's grace and the power of the Holy Spirit, open up your wallet and calendar and help those suffering in poverty. Use your platform to witness and share what they really need for spiritual sustenance. Walk beside those in poverty, being careful not to make them feel inferior in any way. Jesus died for them too. Most certainly, though, remind them about "the grace of our Lord Jesus Christ, that though he was rich, yet for your sake he became poor, so that you by his poverty might become rich."[7] Pray with them these words of Scripture: "May the God of hope fill you with all joy and peace in believing, so that by the power of the Holy Spirit you may abound in hope."[8]

Ministering to Those with an Absentee or Unloving Father

Too many people today have grown up without a father, or without a loving father. They may in fact have grown up with an abusive father. Unfortunately, those who have been abandoned or maltreated by an earthly father often find it difficult to believe in a loving Heavenly Father—one who loves them so much, He mercifully and lovingly sacrificed His one and only Son for them. What kind of father does that?

[7] 2 Cor. 8:9.

[8] Rom. 15:13.

Sadly, our culture does not want to talk about the critical crisis of fatherhood. Numerous studies in the United States have demonstrated how the single-parent family—the vast majority of which do not have fathers—is one of the leading indicators and gateways into the vicious cycle of poverty, not to mention spiritual and religious degeneration. The numbers are alarming in all racial and ethnic groups including whites, but is especially high in the black and Latino populations.

Absentee or abusive fathers are killing the family unit and hollowing out the stability and moral foundations of the United States, but very few major media outlets dare even to talk about the issue. The safer bet is to talk about some new social program that costs billions of dollars and will not work, to deal with the symptoms of the problem rather than the root cause. Those who venture to address the crisis of fatherhood or posit any social scrutiny of the impact and consequences of negligent or dysfunctional fathers—those who choose to have sex, impregnate women, and then leave or shirk their domestic responsibilities—are met with scorn and derisive charges of culturalism, racism, or religious bigotry. How dare you even ask the question!

To add fuel to the fire, Hollywood and the media often depict fathers as dysfunctional, inept, narrow-minded, unsophisticated, unintelligent, misogynist, unfaithful, absent-minded, fanatical, self-centered, cowardly, wimpy—anything but a positive Christian role model. Not only does our world truly have a shortage of strong, God-fearing, loving fathers, but the depictions of positive, God-fearing fathers are severely lacking.

An example of a dysfunctional father is none other than Thomas Lincoln. Thomas left his household for almost a year as he searched for a new wife. He literally left Abe and his sister Sarah to fend for themselves when they were very young. While Thomas would return and be physically present in the household again, he emotionally abandoned his son and never provided young Abe the unconditional love and fatherly nurturing he needed.

This is not to say that Abe did not learn from his father. Indeed, he modeled his work ethic on Thomas's and learned to tell a tale as good as, if not better than his dad's. Lincoln, however, also learned what *not* to do from his father. While Thomas never deviated from his vocations as a farmer and carpenter, Abe tried many different trades and never stopped dreaming of working with his mind instead of his hands. While Thomas enjoyed fishing, hunting, and the great outdoors in general, young Abe gravitated toward reading, writing, and ciphering. While Thomas never bothered to venture into his son's world of books, literature, and other educated interests, the adult Abe would drop anything to play with his sons. While Thomas disdained how his son's reading habits curtailed his rail-splitting and chores on the farm, Abe let his children pick and choose their interests, encouraging them to live out their own aspirations. While Thomas hardly ever showed his son affection, President Lincoln rolled around on the floors of the White House, wrestling and hugging his boys almost daily. While Thomas resigned himself to his existing social status, purpose, and quality of life, Lincoln relentlessly pursued his aspirations all the way to the highest office in the land. His will to rise and shake up the status quo became historic and legendary.

Whatever Lincoln's problems with his father, at least he had a father who was physically present in the home—at least most of the time. Sons and daughters can learn a lot from fathers, but only when those fathers are present on a daily basis.

Loving and caring fathers provide order, stability, encouragement, example, conviction, creativity, innovation, joy, thrills, and confidence for their children. Moreover, a Christian father models the love of our Heavenly Father, which has a long-lasting impact on the spiritual growth of his children. Numerous studies show that children are more likely to remain in the church if their father is an active participant in church. Children watch more acutely what their fathers *do* rather than what they *say*.

Actions speak louder than words when it comes to the Christian life. If Dad says God is important, but then goes fishing, golfing, or hunting every Sunday morning, the kids notice. If Dad insists that God comes first, but never puts money in the offering plate, even as he spends on cars, boats, homes, alcohol, food, and hobbies, a message is clearly sent and received by son and daughter.

Disinterest and disappointment were the primary messages Abe received from his father. Lincoln did not feel loved by his father, but abandoned, ignored, and disregarded. The only interest Thomas Lincoln seemed to have in his son revolved around chores and the extra income Abe could bring the family by working on other farms. Thomas built a transactional relationship with his son—*he only cared about what Abe could do for him and not who Abe was.*

Fathers are powerful shapers of their children's identities. Fathers who live with purpose in life pass on the importance of living with purpose to their children. They love, protect, and provide for their children because they love them. In this way, fathers nurture their children's confidence, security, and identity. With Dad around, everything will be okay.

Unfortunately, too many people in our world today never grow up with a father's love, protection, and security. They have adopted or are compelled to internalize the notion that they have to *do* something to be loved, appreciated, or considered special. This is one reason research shows that children who grow up without a strong, loving father are more likely to suffer from anxiety, depression, drugs addiction, and early sexual encounters. Instead of realizing that they are special children of a loving Heavenly Father who already sent His Son to die for them, kids who are denied loving fathers often feel they must do something to prove their worth.

This drive to succeed or receive affirmation can be a motivating factor in one's life. Many presidents of the United States, for example, achieved their powerful office without loving fathers in their lives. Their drive to *do* something to prove their worth fueled their rise. Lincoln's life is a testament to that narrative.

Yet for far too many who grew up without a father, or who were abused by their fathers, they were never given the time to establish and embrace a healthy sense of identity. They have not learned and accepted the notion that they are special because *who they are* and not *what they do.*

This identity crisis is alive and well in our pluralistic times, as the postmodern culture drifts further away from a biblical foundation. Many people are searching for or missing a father figure's assurance that they are part of a family and of the body of Christ—special and loved for who they are, and for *whose* they are, not for what they do. Searching for a tribe, these people identify themselves by pagan or secular categories such as ethnicity, race, sexual orientation, gender, job, wealth, property, popularity, friends, political party—anything that gives them a sense of belonging.

Our current state of politics is a prime example of the power and pull of misplaced identity. One of the reasons America's political rancor continues to escalate is because politics is not predominantly about issues or policies anymore, but identity and worldview. Even if people agree with a certain policy put forward by the other side, they will not or cannot admit it because this would be a betrayal of their self-selected identity. Once they have found a tribe, they do not want to leave it, no matter if another idea or policy seems to make good sense.

Into this fatherless, identity-confused world is where caring Christians must go and get busy. Too many people know that something is not right in their lives—they have a lack of security and peace. Too many people are not Christians and do not know of the love of their Heavenly Father. They do not know that they are "children of God … And the reason why the world does not know us is that it did not know him."[9]

To these folks, Christians must introduce, with clarity, our Heavenly Father—the God who knew them before they were

---

[9] 1 John 3:1.

born,[10] the God who knows the number of hairs on their heads,[11] and the God who loves them so much that He sacrificed His Son to have a relationship with them. Each of them is first and foremost a child of God, a son or daughter of a Heavenly Father who loves them and gives them mercy, grace, peace, and salvation. An intimate relationship with a strong, loving Heavenly Father begets strong, loving sons and daughters. As Scripture asserts, "But now, O Lord, you are our Father; we are the clay, and you are our potter; we are all the work of your hand."[12]

Perhaps you did not have a good relationship with your earthly father, or even have any relationship at all. You do not have to make the same mistakes your father did. You can start a new trend in your family like Lincoln did. You can be a God-fearing father or mother who knows and loves a merciful and gracious Heavenly Father.

There is an old saying that "Father knows best." The truth is that your Heavenly Father knows best and wants the best for you—a loving relationship with Him. He shapes your life and holds you in His loving hands. And He wants strong, Christian fathers (and mothers) to raise and nurture their children by modeling and showing His love for all. Inspired by our Heavenly Father, let us make every effort to lift up fathers and fatherhood, mothers and motherhood. Our nation, and our children's eternal salvation, depend on it.

Ministering to Families in Their Trials and Tribulations

There is no doubt that family tragedy brought Lincoln closer to God. He and his wife, Mary, lost their two of their sons—Eddie and Willie—when the boys were very young. No parents should

---

10 Jer. 1:5.

11 Luke 12:7.

12 Isa. 64:8.

ever have to bury their own child, but the Lincolns did it twice (and Mary saw a third son, Tad, die after Lincoln's assassination). After each boy passed, the Lincolns were caringly and lovingly supported by Christians and clergy who ministered to them in their time of immense suffering. Many of these caretakers continued to check on the Lincolns regularly long after the boys had passed. The Lincolns, particularly Abe, were greatly touched by their ongoing devotion.

Certainly pastors hope that people will attend church regularly in all times of their lives, good and bad. Yet we know from experience that many turn to pastors and churches only when things go bad. Christians must be ready for these ministry moments when they come. Sometimes simply showing up and being there for people during their time of greatest need is the most significant gateway moment to an agnostic or unbeliever's heart.

One of the keys to ministering to someone is to "be there" long after the emotional immediacy of the hardship moment has passed. Lincoln had pastors who continued to call on him regularly for months after the deaths of his boys. They showed a genuine interest in his mental, emotional, and spiritual well-being long after the funeral services.

Too many people in our world go weeks, even months, without experiencing a genuine act of kindness. When they do experience kindness and attention, those acts truly touch their hearts and open them up to hearing God's Word, much like the Parable of the Sower, in which seeds fall on good soil rather than rocky soil.[13] Many faithful sing, "They will know we are Christians by our love, by our love, yes they'll know we are Christians by our love." Agape love—that sacrificial love exhibited by Jesus for you on the cross—is a committed love that lasts for a lifetime and beyond.

Sometimes faithful church-attending Christians get frustrated at Christmas-Easter attenders or those who only seem to come to God or church when they are in crisis. While we certainly want

[13] Matt. 13:1–23.

people in church on a regular basis, let us not forget that the ultimate purpose of evangelism efforts are to bring people to Christ. However or whenever they come to God, we celebrate this occurrence.

Therefore when a crisis arises, when a traumatic event rocks a family, you can show people—God's sons and daughters—mercy, grace, compassion, and love, just as God did for us when He sent Jesus to redeem us from our sins. Christians "bear one another's burdens,"[14] because God is "the Father of mercies and God of all comfort, who comforts us in all our affliction, so that we may be able to comfort those who are in any affliction, with the comfort with which we ourselves are comforted by God. For as we share abundantly in Christ's sufferings, so through Christ we share abundantly in comfort too."[15] Be ready, willing, and able to minister to and serve those who suffer, those who are in need of comfort, and those who need the voice and inspiration of Jesus in their lives.

Real Christian leaders emerge in a crisis. Jesus always calmed the storms wherever he went. He empowers you to do the same in your family, neighborhood, church, workplace, and community. So be a first responder to those who endure a sudden setback or tragedy. Then continue to be a spiritual caregiver for the long haul. Your kindness, compassion, and service will not go unnoticed. When you live and show Jesus's love in service to others, they are more inclined to inquire about what makes you tick or discover *why* you live and serve as you do. When you gain their trust and attention, then you have a wonderful opportunity to share His Word and love with people, even as they endure, cope, and recover from trials and tragedies.

Ministering to Those in Educational Settings

We are living in biblically illiterate times. The days are long gone when we could assume that the general populace retains even

[14] Gal. 6:2.

[15] 2 Cor. 1:3–5.

rudimentary biblical knowledge or common language in regard to Christian beliefs. For far too many Americans, David and Goliath might as well be a touring rock band, Noah's ark a waterpark, the rainbow a symbol of pride in alternative lifestyles, and the Bible a book that slaveowners used to justify human bondage. Most Americans cannot name more than one or two of the Ten Commandments (and disagree with the ones they can name or criticize them for being "outdated"). Well-known biblical stories like the Flood, Exodus, the Tower of Babel, Jonah and the whale, and Peter walking on water, as well as hallmark biblical figures such as Adam, Eve, Abraham, Isaac, Jacob, Moses, Elijah, Esther, Ruth, Rahab, Daniel, Joseph, and so many others are simply not known or familiar to many people compared to a generation ago.

Moreover, if people even know that a book called the Bible exists, they wrongly associate pat statements like "God helps those who help themselves" or "there is good in everyone" or "everyone has their own truth" with passages inspired by God. Unfortunately, the only images that many people have of Christians or Christianity revolve around politics, biased news reporting, religion-bashing movies, and celebrities who mix New Age mantras with prosperity gospel tenets. Sometimes it is hard to tell what is worse—what people do not know about Christianity and the Bible or what they think they know about Christianity and the Bible.

Thus, especially in this postmodern, post-Christian world, the Christian church must remain dedicated and focused on *the teaching of the faith.* Like a child who must be taught and then reminded repeatedly to "look both ways" when crossing a busy intersection, Christians must be relentless in *teaching* people about the faith in every aspect of the church life. Indeed, just as first-century Christians had to teach *the Way* and *lead the way,* contemporary Christians *must teach people to reach people.*

This commitment to teaching the faith must be apologetic and comprehensive in nature, and assume that the listener knows little about the Christian faith. If you are a member in a liturgical church, do visitors or even your members know what the liturgy is or why it is used? Do people know that hymns capture theological concepts and Bible verses? Do they know what the purpose is of eating a wafer and drinking wine for Holy Communion? Do people know why the pastor is garbed in white? What does the Bible say about alternative lifestyles? What do "the Law" and "Gospel" mean, anyway? How do we know the Bible is true? Where in the Bible does it talk about abortion and the origins of the universe? Does the Bible say anything about science? Why do Christians sing hymns? Do Christians have to confess their sins? What if you forget to confess? What is absolution? Aren't church people supposed to be nice and honest? If God is supposedly about love, why do so many Christians have a problem with gay marriage?

In the age of the internet and social media, people not only feel they have a voice to contribute, but they have the means to ask questions and make judgments about anything at any time. If they have a question, they post it on social media or ask Google for an answer. Peers and "Alexa" are teaching and selling stuff to people all the time. Therefore the Christian church must be relentless in teaching and reteaching everything about the faith.

Abraham Lincoln remains an excellent case study for Christians to reflect on in their evangelism efforts today. We can see how his education—what he learned from others all along his life path as well as through his self-directed learning—made an impact on his life and worldview development.

While Lincoln grew up in a religious household, he disowned the faith during his young adult years, even mocking and attacking the Bible with vigor, particularly in his New Salem days. Unlike many skeptics today, at least Lincoln read the Bible and knew it well. He could pugnaciously debate or ridicule the backwoods, undereducated preachers and rock-ribbed Christians of his day because he knew and could quote the Bible better than they could. He became a kind of new atheist or ardent agnostic during his thirties and forties. This is one challenge the Christian Church faces today, particularly in the age of the internet: we need to be prepared to debate or engage the intellectual and agnostic Lincolns of the world.

Research demonstrates that the more advanced degrees someone acquires, the more likely they are to doubt the inerrancy, infallibility, and revelation of Scripture. Human nature has a tendency to allow earthly knowledge or man-made precepts to crowd out divine wisdom and the belief in divine revelation in a finite and limited human brain. This is often why "uneducated" Christians are mocked by the academic elites and the intelligentsia of our day. Christians are dumb—they do not believe in reason, science, changing mores, alternative lifestyles, and so-called "advances" in society. The skeptical Lincoln made the same arguments in his day. He mocked Christians for believing in unscientific miracles, a book written by God and revealed to humans, and reliance on emotion rather than reason.

While this intellectual challenge is nothing new to Christianity, today's Christian church faces a much less friendly ecosystem in which to make the case for divine revelation, miracles, the incarnation, and the resurrection. Christianity used to be innocent until proven guilty. The Bible was accepted as truth or, at the very least, noble and inspiring literature. In today's culture, Christianity is guilty and must prove its truth or value. The Bible is disdained or disparaged for alleged inaccuracies and old and irrelevant moral codes.

For intellectual skeptics or agnostics, the Christian church must deploy an apologetic approach to teach the faith. Pastors who deployed this approach with Lincoln won an audience and ongoing dialogue with him. He needed to be matched on a higher-thinking level. An overemotional country preacher who had no coherent rationale or could not articulate a reasonable argument for a biblical precept did not impress or interest Lincoln. The Christian church today must encourage their pool of intellectual ambassadors and missionaries to engage educated elites, administrators, professors, and intelligentsia who are skeptical of churches, religion, sacred books, and any metanarrative or divine authority that appears to be stuck in a time warp.

Today's Christian church must intentionally engage with those who arm themselves with arguments retrieved from armchair theologians or publications on the internet, and those who misapply Scripture to justify their liberal and false-doctrine positions on hot-button cultural issues like abortion, creation, evolution, marriage, women in the pulpit, LGBTQ+ lifestyles, and so on. The skeptical Lincoln, at least, thought deeply about issues of religion, but many skeptics and agnostics today do not think and read like Lincoln. Contemporary Christians not only need to be in the Word and familiar with it, they also need to be prepared for arguments contrary to Scripture that come from the pagan cultures in which we now reside.

Christians should examine and reflect on the reasons why Lincoln fell away from the "sound teaching" of the Christian faith during the middle of his life. They need to be self-aware of their "itching ears" and "teachers" who will manipulate their passions, leading them "away from listening to the truth" and "off into myths."[16]

Perhaps because he felt suppressed by his father in regard to his vocational aspirations, Lincoln did not want the Hard Shell Baptist church and teachings of his parents. This lesson from the life of Lincoln leads to another quick self-check for faithful Christians: Do your kids want to stay members of a church like yours? Why or why not?

Lincoln respected educated men who demonstrated reason, objectivity, thoughtfulness, logic, order, and truth. These were pragmatic attributes that helped get things done out on the rugged frontier. Emotion did not help the woods get cleared, the fences built, the rows plowed, the cabin constructed, or a new tool or invention designed and brought to fruition. One reason Lincoln

[16] 2 Tim. 4:3–4.

did not look favorably upon uneducated backwoods ministers is because too many relied on pure emotionalism rather than any reasoned interpretation of Scripture for their theological teachings. Not an elitist prude, Lincoln had no problem with someone who did not have a formal education. After all, he did not have one. What bothered him were those who used emotion to cover up or distract others from their lack of education, formal or informal.

Ironically, while Lincoln disdained the emotionalism of uneducated preachers and saw their emotionalism as an indicator or cover for their empty arguments and ignorance, too many students on college campuses fall prey to the emotional arguments of the LGBTQ+ movement. If two people love each other, the argument goes, why shouldn't they be able to be happy or marry even if they are the same sex? After all, "love is love is love." Why would any caring person be against this? A rational and logical Lincoln might respond to this emotionalism and ask: does the same emotional appeal apply to the love between a man and his dog? Can they get married? What if three adults love each other? Should they be denied marriage? Why would you want to stop them if "love is love"?

Another lesson for all Christians to digest from the life of Lincoln is the profound impact of words on a mind and soul. Put another way, you become what you consume. The words Lincoln read throughout his life had a profound impact on his worldview and the state of his faith. This reality begs the question for you and your loved ones: What are you or your loved ones consuming in traditional print and online? Are you reading or listening to secular screeds that move you away from God, or are you reading the Bible, Christian devotional material, and other spiritually healthy works that bring you closer to God? Again, just like your body receives healthy nourishment or suffers from unhealthy food intake, your heart, mind, and soul must be fed with spiritually healthy sustenance to thrive.

In his young adult life, Lincoln spent a lot of time reading works that espoused evolutionary and materialistic tendencies. He attacked the purported inerrancy and revelation of Scripture, and cast doubt on its truth. The minds and writings of skeptics made a significant impact on Lincoln's worldview and specifically how he viewed institutional religion. Their arguments against the orthodox teachings of the Bible were sharp, focused, seemingly well-reasoned, rational, scientific, and worldly. In other words, skeptical words fueled Lincoln's already nascent skepticism and convinced him of the Bible's inadequacies and outright deceptions. Lincoln's reading moved him away from God and sowed the seeds of doubt in regard to God's Holy Word.

Many Christian parents today send their eighteen-year-old Christian son or daughter off to a secular university, only to have him or her return at the end of that first year doubting the religious teachings and upbringing they once held dear. The truth is that books and well-respected teachers and intelligentsia of his day influenced Lincoln to move away from God, eschew his Christian faith, and ridicule the Bible. This is still happening today, but perhaps with greater frequency and acceptance. Unfortunately, too many schools are teaching young, vulnerable Christians to reject the teachings of Christian church, the inerrancy and inspiration of Scripture, and Jesus's claim to exclusivity in the Bible, or suffer the consequences of ridicule, persecution, and social ostracism.

Since books, writers, and educators are powerful influences and forces of change, Christians need to take a stand and be more intentional in the education world. They must not only be immersed and embedded in educational settings everywhere, but they must be prepared to teach and defend biblical and Christian doctrine. They cannot cede the educational landscape to hostile, secular, government-run institutions that house children for eight to ten hours per day. Christians are called to "train up a child in the way he should go; even when he is old he will not depart from it."[17] Too many Christians shut down when they hear the assertion of

[17] Prov. 22:6.

the "separation of church and state," forgetting that secularism and paganism are religions too (if not identified as such by public school boards).

Of course, in public schools especially, Christians cannot and should not teach or share God's Word in a coercive manner. Nevertheless, if the typical young person spends one-third of their day sleeping and one-third in school or an educational setting (the other third is filled up with the rest of their life), this is too much time to simply cede to secularists or pagans who may or may not hold your child's spiritual and eternal best interests as a priority.

For the sake of full disclosure, I am strong proponent of Christian schooling. Why would you, as a Christian parent, not want one-third of your child's first eighteen or twenty-two years—the most malleable and impressionable years—to be nurtured in schools that reinforce the teaching of Scripture and the life-changing and life-saving grace found in Jesus Christ? I get a kick out of education reformers who say, "Our kids deserve the best." Of course they do. So let us stop denying our kids the very best and teach them what they need the most—namely God's Word and Jesus Christ. Education fads come and go, but the "word of the Lord remains forever."[18] If you can send your kids to a Christian school, do it. If you or your church can build or support a Christian school, do it. If you can pray for, volunteer at, or financially support a Christian school, by all means do it.

Realizing, however, that Christian schools cannot be everywhere and that tuition and other funding of Christian schools remains a challenge, most people reading this book will only have access to public schooling or homeschooling (certainly a viable option for the Christian parent). One important move Christians should make, especially in our pluralistic society, is to encourage their public school districts to teach about *all* major world religions, including Christianity. Whether one is a religious person or not, religious

[18] 1 Pet. 1:25.

beliefs and worldviews certainly impact geopolitics, economies, trade, and social mores for countries at large. Therefore teaching the major tenets of all world religions, including Christianity, helps student learn more about their global world.

The key insight to embrace is that, while most public schools are already teaching aspects of Buddhism, Hinduism, and Islam in world history, geography, or world studies classes, they are not often not teaching Christianity, because the ACLU and other politically correct organizations love to jump all over any perceived breach of the Establishment Clause. If a school district, however, chooses to teach the fundamentals of all world religions, including Christianity, or offer specific world religion classes as electives, this is probably more exposure to the Bible or foundational teachings of Christianity than is currently being taught. As a Christian parent, you will at least have a window of opportunity to talk to your child about the Christian faith and how it compares to other world religions. So why not play for equal footing? Ask school districts to offer world religion or theology classes as electives in the curriculum. No religious course should be required or mandated in a public school, but students will have opportunity to learn more if they are interested.

A second way Christian parents can advocate for teaching or sharing the faith in public schools is to encourage the use of the Bible as a seminal piece of literature. Exhort your children to use the Bible as a source integrated throughout their research projects and papers. Christian students should quote from the Bible as they would from works by Shakespeare, Nietzsche, Darwin, Mother Teresa, Einstein, Freud, Sun Tzu, Gandhi, and so on. Use a parable, Bible story, or quotation from Jesus to accentuate a point in a communications, history, English, or sociology class. Most public school officials will not stop a student from making a reference to the Quran or Vedas. So encourage your child to quote the Reverend Dr. Martin Luther King Jr. using a biblical reference. Again, the main point is to get your child reading God's Word and knowing how to use it and integrate it into all subject areas—dare I say, all aspects of life.

Of course, you will probably run into a teacher who violates the Constitution and Bill of Rights and tells your child that he or she cannot use the Bible as one of their ten references (okay, can it be the eleventh?) or refer to a biblical story in a speech. When this happens, politely ask the teacher to put his or her rationale in writing. This will rattle the teacher a bit, and that is proper. Let the teacher really think about what he or she is doing and why.

To be completely transparent, your child may suffer a grade reduction. You can have a good discussion with your child at that time about the suffering servant or what to expect as a Christian in this postmodern age. If you choose to take up the matter with a principal or the teacher's supervisor, you can ask why your child's constitutional rights are being trampled. Is the Bible not a legitimate piece of history and literature? Why is only this one book outlawed or not permitted to be used as a source? Why aren't other sacred texts banned? Teach your son or daughter how to advocate for themselves and know the meaning of the Free Exercise Clause. Help prepare your kid for the challenges he or she will face in an ever-growing secular world. Do it gently and kindly, but stand your ground firmly. God's Word is always worth defending.

The good news is that while secular books and thinkers moved Lincoln away from God and the Christian faith in his New Salem and early Springfield days, Christian apologetic writers, caring ministers, and the reading of God's Word helped to influence him and bring him back to the faith. Apologetic writers, in particular, had a profound effect on the mind of Lincoln. A relentlessly curious man with a lawyer's mind for logic and reason, Lincoln read literature by talented Christian theologians who could make sound arguments even better than those who had sowed the seeds of doubt in Lincoln's mind early in his life. He meticulously scrutinized the arguments made against the teachings of the Bible and those that supported biblical teachings as truth. Based on his analysis as well as his life experiences, he found the writings of Christian apologetics to be more reasoned, rational, and reflective of real life.

Moreover, even during his wilderness days, Lincoln never stopped reading the Bible—the book he called God's greatest gift to man. He loved the Bible on multiple levels—as a piece of literature, for the rhymes and rhythms of the various styles of writing, as a book of history, for the parables and stories it told, for the morals it taught, and, of course, as a source of inspiration and peace, especially in his times of trial. Almost everyone who knew him for a long period of time said he became much more religious toward the end of his life. While no one can know for sure, the fact that Lincoln read the Bible as often and deeply as he did certainly allows for the strong probability that the Holy Spirit touched his heart and mind and brought him to faith, especially when considering the other historical evidence.

The point for Christians today is to *reach* people, we must *teach* people. People and books influenced Lincoln—his mindset and worldview. These writers and speakers never stopped teaching him. Of course, Lincoln loved to learn. His incessant curiosity and relentless drive for self-improvement were touchstones of his life. What he shared in common with everyone was a desire to make sense of his place in the world, to have purpose, and to make an impact. For someone who had very little formal education, Lincoln possessed a prodigious amount of wisdom—wisdom that came from Holy Scripture and those who taught it.

Ministering to Those Engaged in the Cultural Issues of the Day

No matter how good your bait, you will not catch fish if there are no fish in the pond. Conversely, you might have a subpar lure but still catch plenty of fish in a pond full of hungry fish. The point is if you want to catch fish, you have to go to a pond filled with fish.

Christians need to go where their neighbors are and participate in the issues or civic areas that people care about. As a lawyer and politician, Lincoln followed the action and engaged people on the issues that stirred their emotions and interests. Back in Lincoln's day, the cultural and economic hot-button issues revolved around economic development, internal improvements, land and railroad disputes, the tariff, and, of course, slavery. As a politician, he put himself out there on the front lines, and he received plenty of criticism for his convictions (or alleged lack thereof). He lost elections and endured numerous death threats as president. Yet Lincoln continued to engage the issues that were important to the people of his day. Of course, that is what politicians and political representatives are supposed to do, but the point is that Lincoln put himself out there and he often took a drubbing (and worse) for his convictions and public voice.

Thank goodness that Christians today do not have to contend with the horrific institution of slavery, though human trafficking remains an abhorrent and growing problem. Many political issues, especially for Christians, revolve around social and cultural issues such as abortion, religious freedom, free speech, poverty, racism, the breakdown of the family, the LGBTQ+ movement, marriage rights, privacy rights, and management of health care.

Whatever the issues of the day, one lesson from life of Lincoln that we can apply to our own lives is the reminder that Christians must be engaged and participate in our communities and public debates, because *this is where the people are.* Wherever the people are and whatever the issues of the time—that is where Christians must go. Whenever a platform presents itself, Christians have an opportunity to participate as members of the body of Christ and minister to folks as they share and teach the Word of God.

Of course, we must minister and witness in a winsome way. A Christian's motivation comes from the love of Christ and a desire to serve to all of God's people as Jesus first served us. We do not want to enter the public square displaying a "know-it-all" mentality of self-righteousness or a coercive spirit, especially on matters of adiaphora. We simply want to serve people, contribute to our communities in a positive manner, and use the platforms provided to share God's Word and the love of Christ. *If we truly care for and love people, we want to share God's Word and His love for them.*

Going where the people are to do ministry is not an argument for "getting political" or for voting for a particular political party, though we need Christian men and women to serve in elected and government positions too. The point is that sometimes there is a temptation for well-intentioned Christians to stay out of politics or the public sphere—to ignore the culture wars, social issues, debates, and movements that are shaping and making an impact on our churches, communities, and homes, because they are too messy, controversial, confrontational, or quite frankly nasty. Yet this is where we need to be—right in the thick of things, where the people are. Jesus did not hesitate to go to where the people were—from small towns to crossroads cities to the epicenter of activity in Jerusalem. While He occasionally went away to be alone with His Heavenly Father, the vast majority of the time, Jesus went where the people worked and lived. He ministered to *people.* Christians must do the same.

Ministering to Those Who Serve Caesar

Another lesson learned from the life of Lincoln is that our politicians, or those who serve in public leadership positions on the front lines of these very contentious cultural issues and societal debates, need to be affirmed and supported by Christians. Otherwise we simply risk the day when a Christian worldview will not be articulated or deployed in making political decisions. Christians must be mindful that those who serve in public leadership positions need to be nurtured, refueled, and recharged in the Word of God just like everyone else. In a time when those who hold traditional Christian values and beliefs—such as that life begins at conception, marriage is between one man and one woman, and God created the world in six days—are being labeled as radical, hateful, anti-science, and much worse, Christians must recognize that Christian politicians need support and affirmation too.

The scary reality is that the number of secular politicians, activists, and journalists who claim that traditional Christians are not qualified to hold positions in government grows each year. If Christians leave these charges unanswered, if they do not respond to the attacks, distortions, lies, and outright assaults on the Bible and against those Christian leaders who are taking the arrows for defending biblical truth claims, then Christians run the risk of living in a country dominated by pagan values and policies.

To serve in government in our pluralistic society and culture is a difficult vocation. Christian politicians often have to choose between a rock and hard place on policy issues. Lincoln faced this reality on the slavery issue. A few months before he became president, he noted the difficulty of trying to take the moral high ground. If he would take the position that slavery is wrong in all cases, he would be aiding the breakup of the Union. If he allowed slavery to exist everywhere in the nation, he would anger abolitionists and tacitly perpetuating a horrific institution. If he allowed slavery to stay where it already existed but not let it expand, he would anger people from all regions of the country. He shared this hypothetical story to capture his predicament:

> For instance, out in the street, or in the field, or on the prairie I find a rattlesnake. I take a stake and kill him. Everybody would applaud the act and say I did right. But suppose the snake was in a bed where children were sleeping. Would I do right to strike him there? I might hurt the children; or I might not kill, but only arouse and exasperate the snake, and he might bite the children. Thus, by meddling with him here, I would do more hurt than good. Slavery is like this. We dare not strike at it

> where it is. The manner in which our constitution is framed constrains us from making war upon it where it already exists. The question that we now have to deal with is, "Shall we be acting right to take this snake and carry it to a bed where there are children?" The Republican party insists upon keeping it out of the bed.[19]

The Bible shows that God has never and will never forsake His children, no matter which political party is in power and not even if pagan leaders persecute brothers and sisters of the faith. Christians are called to be "salt" and "light" everywhere in the world—in our homes, communities, churches, schools, and places of work, and on social media—so that people "may see your good works and give glory to your Father who is in heaven."[20] God has designed a better way to live, and He calls on His followers not only to live that way, but to show the way.

So pray for our Christian servant leaders in all vocations. Affirm, support, and defend them. Encourage them to get in the Word and stay in the Word. When they sin and make mistakes, remind them of God's grace and forgiveness. Satan and the secular world are targeting them, and there is nothing more thrilling to the devil than to take down Christian leaders who are prominent in the public eye.

After a fall from grace, repentance and forgiveness can be highlighted, helping to give a full testimony as to what the Christian faith is all about. Even in failure, a public Christian leader can witness and give a reason for the hope we have in Christ. When you go where the people are, you can always remind them how we are all similar—sinful and in need of a Savior.

---

[19] Basler, Lincoln's Speech at Hartford, Connecticut, March 5, 1860, *CW*, 4:5.

[20] Matt. 5:13–15.

Ministering to Those Who Have Been Blessed and Gifted in Special Ways

In education and equity advocate circles today, much activism is rightfully dedicated to the achievement gap or serving the underserved and underprivileged. Like many well-intentioned endeavors, however, there are unintended consequences that arise when focus is concentrated in one area of life. In education circles, gifted and talented students are often neglected because their needs do not seem as dire as the needs of those who cannot read or write.

By almost every recorded contemporary account, Abraham Lincoln possessed and displayed remarkable intellectual abilities at all stages of his life. His voracious desire to read anything anywhere made an indelible impression on strangers, neighbors, and friends alike. His ability to deliver anecdotes to accentuate key points in a speech or letter truly set him apart as a communicator. Moreover, his combination of emotional intelligence, resilience, ambition, grit, persistence, and determination truly revealed an endearing man and an exceptional leader.

Contemporaries, however, often ridiculed him for his singularity. To many, Lincoln seemed weird, freakish, different, and awkward—an outlier, to be sure. He did not look the part or conform to the norms of what others expected in a respectable citizen or leader. Some belittled his talents and skills, not wanting to admit that perhaps beyond being "different," Lincoln just might be something special.

Someone once said that if you want an Einstein on your team, you have to be willing to put up with the hairdo. Perhaps we fail to recognize the truly unique gifts and talents that God has given to many people in our midst. Perhaps they, like Esther, have been put in your church, organization, team, workplace, or neighborhood for such a time as this, and simply need to be encouraged to use their special gifts and talents in the service of the church.[21]

You can be a Barnabas, a son or daughter of encouragement to those in your sphere of influence.[22] Since God created everyone uniquely, encourage your spouse, coworkers, and friends to use their special God-given gifts for service in His kingdom. Help them recognize their gifts, talents, and blessings and the God-pleasing ways they can steward and use them for the spreading of the good news.

As many gifts and blessings as Lincoln received from God, he needed people around him to notice them and encourage him to use them in the pursuit of his various vocations, particularly in law and politics. Of course, Christians should encourage all people in the stewardship and use of their gifts and talents. The Bible says we are to "encourage one another and build one another up."[23] Be especially mindful and sensitive not to overlook the individual whom others might think of as "weird," "different," "abnormal," or "freakish"—anyone who seems not to fit a preconceived notion of a leader or a specific vocation. This individual just might be who God placed in your midst for such a time as this.

God breaks the mold every time he creates a human being, including you. Jesus died for everyone, including you. *You are special*, and so is the person next to you. Encourage others to serve and lead *in their special way* and never look back.

Ministering to Those Who Want to Rise and Improve Their Lives

For many, the most impressive feature of Lincoln's life is his rise from poverty on the frontier to the most powerful office in the land.

---

[21] Esther 4:14.

[22] Acts 4:36.

[23] 1 Thess. 5:11.

The Lincoln biography exhibits the American Dream at its most alluring and magnificent.

Congruent and correlated with Lincoln's desire to rise and make a mark in the world was his incessant desire to improve himself—not only his quality of life but his speech, his writing, his ability to persuade, his overall knowledge, and the quality of his thought. Lincoln practiced his speeches out loud and debated concepts with others as well as in his own mind. He interacted with people from all backgrounds, vocations, and political stripes. He loved people and he loved to learn. Even more, Lincoln loved to convince people of his policies, thoughts, and opinions through jokes, stories, anecdotes, sharp reasoning, and convincing rationale. A good listener, Lincoln could also be persuaded by a solid argument. This all fit in with one of the strongest themes of Lincoln's life: he was committed to continuous improvement—certainly in his own life and also for the communities and nation he served.

Most people who read about the life of Lincoln admire his tenacity and commitment to self-improvement as well as his ambition to rise and build a better life for himself and others. Today, numerous books, gurus, commercials, workshops, and products are sold to the American people as ways to live a better life. The self-help industry is huge and lucrative. There are, after all, many incentives to improve.

Self-improvement or the desire to excel in one's vocations is a God-pleasing endeavor. The Bible calls on Christians to be a good stewards of the many gifts and blessings He has given us. Jesus says that "everyone to whom much was given, of him much will be required, and from him to whom they entrusted much, they will demand the more."[24] A follower of Christ *should* want to achieve, succeed, thrive, and "work heartily," not for men, but for God.[25]

The temptation comes when continuous self-improvement gets equated or conflated with works righteousness in regard to one's

[24] Luke 12:48.

[25] Col. 3:23.

salvation. For example, an individual might posit that if they can work hard to become a more articulate trial lawyer, then they can also work hard to get closer to God. Or if an individual improves their writing skills and commits fewer writing errors, they may be tempted to think they can commit fewer sins (or none). Or perhaps, just as an individual's hard work and entrepreneurism can catapult them to a higher socioeconomic class, perhaps they can get closer to God or entrance into heaven by working hard at good works and service projects.

In regard to salvation, of course, no human can improve himself or herself. We are all born sinful and fall short of God's standards in thoughts, words, and deeds. Only the people who did not sin and were perfect on earth will be admitted to heaven. No one can work hard enough or improve enough to achieve perfection and pass through the gates of paradise on merit. We all need a mediator, a substitute, a replacement—we need a Savior.

That *your* efforts, work ethic, skills, talents, intelligence, emotional intelligence, creativity, entrepreneurship, innovation, and drive cannot improve your standing before God or get you admitted into heaven is a difficult concept to embrace. These things usually make a big difference in accomplishing earthly goals or achieving earthly prizes. Christians know that only Jesus's death and resurrection makes His followers "right" or perfect before God. Our sins have been washed away by the blood of our Savior, Jesus Christ. While there is nothing we can do to improve our sinful flesh and sinfulness before God, Jesus can intercede, improve our state of being, and make us acceptable for our Heavenly Father. And that is exactly He did that on the cross at Mount Calvary nearly two thousand years ago.

Not everyone, of course, is Christian. And even Christians fall prey to the works righteousness lie. Humans want to play God and think that they can control their own destinies, especially when it comes to the afterlife (if they believe in an afterlife). This temptation is especially notable in a world that often does, in fact, reward improvement, hard work, and pursuing one's dreams. Most people reading this book will agree with the sentiments that hard work leads to good things and that one should improve their skills for the betterment of their lives or careers.

The challenge remains that though this earthly life rewards those, like Lincoln, who work hard to improve, the salvation of a soul does not work that way. Only Jesus can redeem humans from their sins. These opposing realities often get confused by the average person not well-schooled in a Christian worldview.

Christians often work and live next to Lincolns who want to rise and improve their lives. They work hard in order to achieve these goals. They work hard to make more money. They desire to improve their skills, talents, mindsets—anything that will help them in their careers, family lives, and friendships. As Christians called to be good stewards of the gifts God gives us, we can applaud and encourage our neighbors who want to improve their quality of life and prosper.

To minister to folks who strive to rise, Christians need to mindful of the potential temptation and confusion that can occur in regard to one's salvation. Yes, in earthly matters one can work to improve and achieve. But no human can do anything to attain salvation on their own. Jesus did it all for humanity on the cross.

While both are desirable, there is a big difference between success and faith. A father once took his young son along on a house visit to minister and share the love of Christ with a wealthy family living a gated community. As father and son drove up the long driveway of the residence, they could not help but notice that this was no ordinary house. It was a palatial mansion, meticulously manicured and with multiple luxury cars and yachts gathered on the property. Before they exited their car, the son asked his father, "So, Dad, tell me again how bad and empty their life is?"

Christians should be careful not to judge a book too quickly by its cover, whether in earthly matters or spiritual ones. People can be hard workers and still not escape poverty or advance up the socioeconomic ladder. People who have inherited great wealth can be generous, caring givers. Regular churchgoers can get their doctrine wrong. We also know that hard work and self-improvement do not guarantee anything on this earth. A boy can train ten hours a day for years and still not earn a college scholarship in basketball. A girl can take voice lessons and practice for years and still not get a part on Broadway. Self-improvement and hard work, though often rewarded, are often not rewarded. The old statement that one can pull oneself up by one's own bootstraps is, in fact, a hotly contested idea in academia and politics today. Perhaps the reality that human efforts are often futile is just one more way God shows us our mortality and frailty and need for a perfect, infallible, reliable Savior.

One way Christians can witness and minister to modern-day Lincolns is to remind them that their salvation is not dependent on their efforts, reputation, material wealth, popularity, program outcomes, quarterly reports, commissions, or job titles. What a relief! Tell your colleague or friend that "by grace you have been saved through faith. And this is not your own doing; it is the gift of God, not a result of works, so that no one may boast."[26] Moreover, when inevitable failure comes and life kicks them down, when they find themselves feeling alone or empty despite any secular measurement of success, you can be at the ready to remind them how much Jesus loves them and that He alone assures and provides their salvation.

The ways of our fallen, sinful world are *not* the ways of a merciful, grace-filled, loving God who sent His one and only Son to die for them and redeem them from their sins. To all those who know Jesus as Lord and Savior and by God's grace, they will one day rise and live a beautiful and perfect life at the feet of the Lamb in heaven. "Behold, the dwelling place of God is with man. He will dwell with them, and they will be his people, and God himself will be with them as their God," says Scripture. "He will wipe away every tear from their eyes, and death shall be no more, neither shall there

[26] Eph. 2:8–9.

be mourning, nor crying, nor pain anymore, for the former things have passed away."[27] That's a rise and quality of life second to none.

Ministering to Those Who Doubt or Question the Faith

How would you have ministered and witnessed Christ to Abraham Lincoln? The answer depends on several factors—the quality of the relationship you had with him; when you knew him; your own particular strengths, insights, and witnessing toolbox; and much more. Considering all of these factors, the Lincoln persona provides a wonderful case study for Christians as they attempt to share God's Word and the love of Christ in our world today. Put another way, in their efforts to "always being prepared to make a defense to anyone who asks you for a reason for the hope that is in you," Christians must be prepared to witness, share, and teach the faith to the Lincolns in our world today.[28]

Raised in a devout Christian family, Lincoln fell away from the faith and became an outspoken skeptic. Then life experiences showed him the ways of the fallen world. He and his family experienced tragedies and deaths. He interacted with pastors, ministers, and other men and women of faith. The result was that Lincoln stopped mocking and questioning the teachings of Scripture. As he continued to read and study the Bible daily while enduring many trials, he changed and began to place his hope, confidence, and dependence in God.

Yet historians still debate Lincoln's precise religious views. Most admit that he read the Bible faithfully and that he believed in God. Some nevertheless question whether he ever came to believe in the orthodoxies of the Christian faith—the divine nature of Christ, the infallibility and inerrancy of Scripture, the atonement,

---

27 Rev. 21:3–4.

28 1 Pet. 3:15.

the forgiveness of sins, the two natures of Christ, the miracles of Scripture, and more. The historiographical dispute over Lincoln's religious beliefs echoes the historiographical debate over George Washington's religious faith and whether the Father of Our Country embraced deism or traditional Christianity.[29]

As public and well-known as Lincoln became in his own lifetime, and as famous as he remains today, one of the great paradoxes of his life is just how mysterious and hidden he remained in regard to his personal faith. His wife once divulged that he was a man of "deep feeling" but "not a demonstrative man." She noted that "what he felt most deeply" about, "he expressed, the least."[30]

Certainly Lincoln struggled to believe in the truths of Scripture during his younger years. Susceptible to the secular and pagan teachings and writings of his day, Lincoln questioned the certitude and divine aspects of the Bible and Christian faith. Intelligent, well-read, and possessing a brilliant analytical mind, Lincoln preferred the supposed rationalism and reason of science to the emotionalism or inspiration of divine revelation. In many ways, Lincoln presaged the postmodern, twenty-first-century argument that science and materialism matter more than anything else. In a show-me world and with a rational mind that wanted proof over sentiment, Lincoln illustrates the type of challenge Christians face in ministering to many people today—particularly folks who would be considered educated (at least in worldly, secular ways), spiritual but not religious, communal but not institutional, skeptical but not immoral, and pragmatic but not divinely inspirational.

Lincoln knew the Bible better than most. He could quote it better than most pastors, and included biblical references frequently in his writing. The reality is that there is a big difference between knowing *about* Jesus and *knowing* Jesus as Lord and Savior. This is the argument many biographers and historians try to make in regard

---

[29] See Pingel, *Confidence and Character.*

[30] Shenk, *Lincoln's Melancholy*, 216.

to Lincoln's faith—he may have *read* the Bible a lot but that does not mean he *believed* in it the way most traditional Christians do. There is a big difference between the two!

Despite the fact that he never officially joined a specific church body (a fairly common occurrence in Lincoln's day), my belief, after analyzing the historical evidence, is that the Holy Spirit worked faith in Lincoln's heart and he became a Christian, if not a member of a particular congregation. Deists do not pray to God or ask for His intervention because the deist God does not act in human history. Lincoln prayed for God's intervention constantly, especially during his presidency. Moreover, toward the end of his life, Lincoln spent more time with faithful Christians and ministers who fed his spiritual curiosities and filled his spiritual cup. Their testimonies, reasoning, rationales, and apologetic approaches made an impact on his worldview. The longer Lincoln lived, the more a biblical worldview made sense to him, and the more he found comfort in the words of Scripture and a merciful Savior.

Furthermore, and perhaps most importantly, Lincoln never stopped reading the Bible. His Bible reading increased at the end of his life, according to numerous witnesses and Lincoln's own words. The Bible says that "faith comes from hearing, and hearing through the word of Christ."[31] While one of the great unknowns in the Christian faith is why the Holy Spirit converts some but not others, Lincoln unquestionably craved God's Word as his daily bread. He needed to hear and digest God's Word daily. The Bible lifted his spirits, comforted him, and found its way into his speeches, correspondence, thinking, and worldview. Lincoln treasured his Bible.

For Christians today who want to teach and share the faith with others, there are a few lessons to learn from the life of Lincoln. First, do not give up on those who are skeptical or ridicule the faith. In the Bible, Saul persecuted Christians for years before he became a

[31] Rom. 10:17.

convert to the faith. The Holy Spirit can penetrate even the harshest critics of Christ. So keep witnessing, sharing, and teaching God's Word.

Second, use apologetic approaches to engage in conversations with people who are skeptical or critical of the faith. Start where they are so that they stay curious and engaged with you. Ask them questions about their worldview, the source of what they believe, and why they believe it. Often skeptics, who claim to respect reason, find their beliefs and opinions lacking when they are forced to apply rationalism to their own worldview. "So where did all the stuff in the primordial soup come from that started the cosmos?" Christians are often criticized for believing things on "faith." Yet critics of Christianity often fail to see how their own worldviews are based on faith too, albeit a faith of a different kind.

So be ready to ask questions without scorn, simply to understand and to have people analyze their own beliefs. "Are you *absolutely* sure that there is no *absolute* truth?" Once they share their views, then point out their fallacies and weaknesses. After all, your interlocutor's eternal well-being depends on knowing the truth. Remember to share the truth in a kind and gentle way, as encouraged in the Bible.[32]

Eventually, you must share and tell the truth—God's Word. The ultimate goal is not to win an argument. Make sure you do not frame or think of your conversation in terms of a win-loss scenario. Instead, share the Bible. Let God's Word work on the hearts and minds of your friends and loved ones. Keep putting it before them in winsome ways over time. Be persistent *and* patient with your associates, just as many pastors and women and men of faith were with Lincoln.

People go through different phases of life and their own faith walk. Be prepared to listen to people, meet them where they are, and pray that God gives you the right words to speak and share. God puts people in the right spots and at the right times to give testimony and

[32] 1 Pet. 3:15.

witness to Lincoln. God, in His infinite wisdom and perfect timing, has done the same with you.

There is much to like and admire about Abraham Lincoln. As great a president and leader as he might have been, however, he was a flawed sinner like you and all human beings. Yet though he was a fallible man, we can learn a lot from his life. Christianity, of course, is a religion grounded in history, especially featuring the biography of our Savior, Jesus Christ. As the Bible teaches, "Whatever was written in former days was written for our instruction, that through endurance and through the encouragement of the Scriptures we might have hope."[33] The Bible reveals historical events that really happened—and thank goodness they did.

Jesus really did come to earth in the form of a man. He really did get placed in a manger as a newborn. He really did die on a cross. He really did rise from the dead and leave the tomb empty. These historical facts are signature events of the Christian faith.

You are not living in the time of the gospel writers or the days of Lincoln, but you are living your own history in the chapters of life God has laid out before you. One day your life here on earth will end, but not for eternity. For all who know Christ as Lord and Savior, heaven will be their home. Jesus said, "I am the way, and the truth, and the life. No one comes to the Father except through me."[34]

By God's grace, your way and life testimony can make an eternal difference in the lives of others. You are, after all, an instrument of God's divine hand and grace in this world, well equipped to serve and honor God in many different vocations. You may never earn a moniker like "Honest Abe," "Father Abraham," or the "Great Emancipator." Nonetheless, you are a special child of God—a God who sent His one and only Son to die for *you.* You are just as special to Him as Lincoln. While someone may not write a book about you, you will leave your own legacy. What will it be?

---

[33] Rom. 15:4.

[34] John 14:6.

Bibliography

Anastaplo, George. *Abraham Lincoln: A Constitutional Biography.* Lanham, MD: Rowman & Littlefield, 1999.

Bain, David. "The Transcontinental Railroad." In *Abraham Lincoln: Great American Historians on Our Sixteenth President,* edited by Brian Lamb and Susan Swain, 109–111. New York: PublicAffairs, 2008.

Baker, Jean. *Mary Todd Lincoln: A Biography.* New York: W. W. Norton & Company, 1987.

Bartelt, William. *"There I grew up": Remembering Abraham Lincoln's Indiana Youth.* Indianapolis, IN: Indiana Historical Society Press, 2008.

Basler, Roy, ed. *The Collected Works of Abraham Lincoln.* 8 vols., New Brunswick, NJ: Rutgers University Press, 1953. In *The Abraham Lincoln Association,* https://quod.lib.umich.edu/l/lincoln/.

Blight, David. "The Theft of Lincoln in Scholarship, Politics, and Public Money." In *Our Lincoln: New Perspectives on Lincoln and His World,* edited by Eric Foner, 269–282. New York: Norton, 2008.

Boritt, Gabor, ed. *The Lincoln Enigma: The Changing Faces of an American Icon.* New York: Oxford University Press, 2001.

Buchanan, Patrick. "An Economic Nationalist." In *Abraham Lincoln: Great American Historians on Our Sixteenth President,* edited by Brian Lamb and Susan Swain, 92. New York: PublicAffairs, 2008.

Burlingame, Michael. *Abraham Lincoln: A Life.* 2 vols. Baltimore: Johns Hopkins University, 2008.

———. "Lincoln and Race." In *Lincoln & Liberty: Wisdom for the Ages,* edited by Lucas Morel, 9–77. Lexington, KY: University Press of Kentucky, 2014.

Bush, George W. *Decision Points*. New York: Crown Publishers, 2010.

Brue, Sandra. "Through the Cumberland Gap." In *Abraham Lincoln: A Living Legacy*, edited by Diana L. Bailey, 11–34. Virginia Beach, VA: Donning Company, 2010.

Canavan, Kathryn. *Lincoln's Final Hours: Conspiracy, Terror, and the Assassination of America's Greatest President*. Lexington, KY: University Press of Kentucky, 2015.

Capps, Mike. "Making a New Home." In *Abraham Lincoln: A Living Legacy*, edited by Diana L. Bailey, 39–73. Virginia Beach, VA: Donning Company Publishers, 2010.

Carnegie, Dale. *Lincoln the Unknown*. Garden City, NY: Dale Carnegie and Associates, 1932.

Carpenter, Francis. *Six Months at the White House with Abraham Lincoln: The Story of a Picture*. Washington, DC: White House Historical Association, 2008. First published 1866 by Hurd and Houghton (New York).

Carwardine, Richard. "Lincoln's Religion." In *Our Lincoln: New Perspectives on Lincoln and His World*, edited by Eric Foner, 223–248. New York: Norton, 2008.

Clinton, Bill. *My Life*. New York, Vintage Books, 2005.

Clinton, Catherine. "Abraham Lincoln: The Family That Made Him, the Family He Made." In *Our Lincoln: New Perspectives on Lincoln and His World*, edited by Eric Foner, 249–266. New York: Norton, 2008.

———. "Mourning in America: Death Comes to the Civil War White Houses." In *Exploring Lincoln: Great Historians Reappraise Our Greatest President*, edited by Harold Holzer, Craig Symonds, and Frank Williams, 66–87. New York: Fordham University Press, 2015.

Conroy, James. *Lincoln's White House: The People's House in Wartime*. Lanham, MD: Rowman & Littlefield, 2017.

Current, Richard. "Lincoln After 175 Years: The Myth of the Jealous Son." In *Lincoln's American Dream: Clashing Political

Perspectives, edited by Kenneth Deutsch and Joseph Fornieri, 141–147. Washington, DC: Potomac Books, 2005.

Dallek, Robert. *An Unfinished Life: John F. Kennedy, 1917–1963*. Boston: Little, Brown, 2003.

Delbanco, Andrew. "Lincoln's Sacramental Language." In *Our Lincoln: New Perspectives on Lincoln and His World*, edited by Eric Foner, 199–222. New York: Norton, 2008.

Deutsch, Kenneth, and Joseph Fornieri, eds. *Lincoln's American Dream: Clashing Political Perspectives*. Washington, DC: Potomac Books, 2005.

Donald, David. *Lincoln*. New York: Simon & Schuster, 1995.

———. *Lincoln at Home: Two Glimpses of Abraham Lincoln's Family Life*. New York: Simon & Schuster, 1999.

———. *Lincoln Reconsidered: Essays on the Civil War Era*. 3rd ed. New York: Vintage Books, 2001.

———. "Those Around Him." In *Abraham Lincoln: Great American Historians on Our Sixteenth President*, edited by Brian Lamb and Susan Swain, 32–42. New York: PublicAffairs, 2008.

Douglass, Frederick, "Oration in Memory of Abraham Lincoln," April 14, 1876, *Teaching American History*, Accessed July 10, 2019, https://teachingamericanhistory.org/library/document/oration-in-memory-of-abraham-lincoln/.

Emerson, Jason. "The Madness of Mary Lincoln: A New Examination Based on the Discovery of Her Lost Insanity Letters." In *Exploring Lincoln: Great Historians Reappraise Our Greatest President*, edited by Harold Holzer, Craig Symonds, and Frank Williams, 237–244. New York: Fordham University Press, 2015.

Epstein, Daniel Mark. *The Lincolns: Portrait of a Marriage*. New York: Ballantine Books, 2009.

Fehrenbacher, Don, ed. *Abraham Lincoln: Speeches and Writings, 1832-1865*. 2 Vols.

New York: Library of America, 1989.

Felzenberg, Alvin. *The Leaders We Deserved (And a Few We Didn't): Rethinking the Presidential Rating Game*. New York: Basic Books, 2008.

Foner, Eric. "The Emancipation of Abraham Lincoln." In *Exploring Lincoln: Great Historians Reappraise Our Greatest President*, edited by Harold Holzer, Craig Symonds, and Frank Williams, 146–162. New York: Fordham University Press, 2015.

———, ed. *Our Lincoln: New Perspectives on Lincoln and His World*. New York: Norton, 2008.

———. "Lincoln and Colonization." In *Our Lincoln: New Perspectives on Lincoln and His World*, edited by Eric Foner, 135–166. New York: Norton, 2008.

Fornieri, Joseph. "Lincoln's Theology of Labor." In *Lincoln & Liberty: Wisdom for the Ages*, edited by Lucas Morel, 207–221. Lexington, KY: University Press of Kentucky, 2014.

Fox, Richard W. *Lincoln's Body: A Cultural History*. New York: W. W. Norton, 2015.

Freehling, William. *Becoming Lincoln*. Charlottesville, VA: University of Virginia Press, 2018.

Freidel, Frank. *Franklin D. Roosevelt: A Rendezvous with Destiny*. Boston: Little, Brown, 1990.

Gibbs, Nancy, and Michael Duffy. *The Presidents Club: Inside the World's Most Exclusive Fraternity*. New York: Simon & Schuster, 2012.

Gienapp, William. "Abraham Lincoln and Presidential Leadership, In *"We Cannot Escape History": Lincoln and the Last Best Hope of Earth*, edited by James McPherson, 63–85. Urbana, IL: University of Illinois Press, 1995.

Goodwin, Doris Kearns. *Leadership in Turbulent Times*. New York: Simon & Shuster, 2018.

———. *Team of Rivals: The Political Genius of Abraham Lincoln*. New York: Simon & Shuster, 2005.

Guelzo, Allen. *Abraham Lincoln as a Man of Ideas*. Carbondale, IL: Southern Illinois University, 2009.

———. *Abraham Lincoln: Redeemer President*. Paperback ed. Grand Rapids, MI: William B. Eerdmans, 2003.

———. "Lincoln and Religion." In *Abraham Lincoln: Great American Historians on Our Sixteenth President*, edited by Brian Lamb and Susan Swain, 189–192. New York: PublicAffairs, 2008.

———. "'Public Sentiment is Everything': Abraham Lincoln and the Power of Public Opinion." In *Lincoln & Liberty: Wisdom for the Ages*, edited by Lucas Morel, 171–191. Lexington, KY: University Press of Kentucky, 2014.

Guinness, Os, ed. *Character Counts: Leadership Qualities in Washington, Wilberforce, Lincoln, and Solzhenitsyn*. Grand Rapids, MI: Baker Books, 1999.

Gurley, Phineas, "White House Funeral Sermon for President Lincoln," *Abraham Lincoln Online*, accessed July 4, 2018, http://www.abrahamlincolnonline.org/lincoln/speeches/gurley.htm.

Hertz, Emanuel, ed. *The Hidden Lincoln: From the Letters and Papers of William H. Herndon*. New York: Viking Press, 1938.

Hodes, Martha. *Mourning Lincoln*. New Haven, CT: Yale University Press, 2015.

Holzer, Harold. "Visualizing Lincoln: Abraham Lincoln as Student, Subject, and Patron of Visual Arts." In *Our Lincoln: New Perspectives on Lincoln and His World*, edited by Eric Foner, 80–106. New York: Norton, 2008.

Holzer, Harold, and Norton Garfinkle. *A Just and Generous Nation: Abraham Lincoln and the Fight for American Opportunity*. New York: Basic Books, 2015.

Holzer, Harold, Craig Symonds, and Frank Williams, eds. *Exploring Lincoln: Great Historians Reappraise Our Greatest President*. New York: Fordham University Press, 2015.

Johnson, David. *The Last Weeks of Abraham Lincoln*. Amherst, NY: Prometheus Books, 2018.

Jones, Edgar DeWitt. *Lincoln and the Preachers*. New York: Harper & Brothers, 1948.

Kaplan, Fred. "The Great Invention of the World: Lincoln and Literature." In *Lincoln & Liberty: Wisdom for the Ages*, edited by Lucas Morel, 17–35. Lexington, KY: University Press of Kentucky, 2014.

Kautz, Steven. "The Democratic Statesmanship of Abraham Lincoln." In *Lincoln & Liberty: Wisdom for the Ages*, edited by Lucas Morel, 145–170. Lexington, KY: University Press of Kentucky, 2014.

Keneally, Thomas. *Abraham Lincoln*. New York: Penguin Books, 2003.

Kengor, Paul. *God and Ronald Reagan: A Spiritual Life*. New York: HarperCollins, 2004.

Kigel, Richard. *Becoming Abraham Lincoln: The Coming of Age of Our Greatest President*. New York: Skyhorse Publishing, 2017.

Krannawitter, Thomas. *Vindicating Lincoln: Defending the Politics of Our Greatest President*. Lanham, MD: Rowman & Littlefield, 2008.

Lachman, Charles. *The Last Lincolns: The Rise & Fall of a Great American Family*. New York: Union Square Press, 2008.

Lamb, Brian, and Susan Swain, eds. *Abraham Lincoln: Great American Historians on Our Sixteenth President*. New York: PublicAffairs, 2008.

Landy, Marc, and Sidney Milkis. *Presidential Greatness*. Lawrence, KS: University Press of Kansas, 2000.

Leekley, John, ed. *Bruce Catton Reflections on the Civil War*. New York: Berkley Books, 1981.

Lehrman, Lewis. "Economic Principles." In *Abraham Lincoln: Great American Historians on Our Sixteenth President*, edited by Brian Lamb and Susan Swain, 91. New York: PublicAffairs, 2008.

———. *Lincoln "by littles."* New York: Lehrman Institute, 2013.

Leidner, Gordon. *Lincoln's Gift: How Humor Shaped Lincoln's Life & Legacy*. Naperville, IL: Cumberland House, 2015.

Levin, Jack. *Malice Toward None: Abraham Lincoln's Second Inaugural Address*. New York: Threshold Editions, 2014.

Lincoln, Abraham. *Speeches and Writings, 1832–1865*. Edited by Don Fehrenbacher. 2 vols. New York: Library of America, 1989.

Lind, Michael. *What Lincoln Believed: The Values and Convictions of America's Greatest President*. New York: Doubleday, 2004.

Lowry, Rich. *Lincoln Unbound: How an Ambitious Young Railsplitter Saved the American Dream—and How We Can Do It Again*. New York: HarperCollins, 2013.

Manning, Alan. *Father Lincoln: The Untold Story of Abraham Lincoln and His Boys—Robert, Eddy, Willie, and Tad*. Guilford, CT: Lyons Press, 2016.

Mansfield, Stephen. *Lincoln's Battle with God: A President's Struggle with Faith and What It Meant for America*. Nashville, TN: Thomas Nelson, 2012.

Marszalek, John. "The Old Army and the Seeds of Change." In *Exploring Lincoln: Great Historians Reappraise Our Greatest President*, edited by Harold Holzer, Craig Symonds, and Frank Williams, 36–48. New York: Fordham University Press, 2015.

McCullough, David. *Truman*. New York: Simon & Shuster, 1992.

McDonald, Alonzo. "The Spiritual Growth of a Public Man." In *Character Counts: Leadership Qualities in Washington, Wilberforce, Lincoln, and Solzhenitsyn*, edited by Os Guiness, 93–103. Grand Rapids, MI: Baker Books, 1999.

McGovern, George. *Abraham Lincoln*. New York: Henry Holt, 2009.

McKenna, George. "On Abortion: A Lincolnian Position." In *Lincoln's American Dream: Clashing Political Perspectives*, 463–484. Washington, DC: Potomac Books, 2005.

McPherson, James. *Abraham Lincoln*. New York: Oxford University Press, 2009.

———. "A. Lincoln, Commander in Chief." In *Our Lincoln: New Perspectives on Lincoln and is World*, edited by Eric Foner, 19–36. New York: Norton, 2008.

———, ed. *"We Cannot Escape History": Lincoln and the Last Best Hope of Earth*. Urbana, IL: University of Illinois Press, 1995.

Meacham, Jon. *The Soul of America: The Battle for Our Better Angels.* New York: Random House, 2018.

———. *American Gospel: God, the Founding Fathers, and the Making of a Nation.* New York: Random House, 2006.

Merry, Robert. *Where They Stand: The American Presidents in the Eyes of Voters and Historians.* New York: Simon & Schuster, 2012.

Miller, William. "Lincoln's Second Inaugural: The Zenith of Statecraft." In *Lincoln's American Dream: Clashing Political Perspectives,* edited by Kenneth Deutsch and Joseph Fonieri, 333–350. Washington, DC: Potomac Books, 2005.

———. *Lincoln's Virtues: An Ethical Biography.* New York: Vintage Books, 2002.

Miroff, Bruce. *Icons of Democracy: American Leaders as Heroes, Aristocrats, Dissenters, & Democrats.* New York: Basic Books, 1993.

Morel, Lucas, ed. *Lincoln & Liberty: Wisdom for the Ages.* Lexington, KY: University Press of Kentucky, 2014.

Mr. Lincoln's White House. *Employees and Staff: Rebecca R. Pomroy (1817-1884).* The Lehrman Institute. http://www.mrlincolnswhitehouse.org/residents-visitors/employees-and-staff/employees-staff-rebecca-r-pomroy-1817-1884/

Mukunda, Gautum. *Indispensable: When Leaders Really Matter.* Boston: Harvard Business Review Press, 2012.

Nixon, Richard. *In the Arena: A Memoir of Victory, Defeat and Renewal.* New York: Simon and Schuster, 1990.

Noonan, Peggy. *When Character Was King: A Story of Ronald Reagan.* New York: Viking, 2001.

Neely, Mark, Jr. "Early Years." In *Abraham Lincoln: Great American Historians on Our Sixteenth President*, edited by Brian Lamb and Susan Swain, 3–9. New York: PublicAffairs, 2008.

———. "The Constitution and Civil Liberties Under Lincoln." In *Our Lincoln: New Perspectives on Lincoln and His World*, edited by Eric Foner, 37–61. New York: Norton, 2008.

Oakes, James. "Natural Rights, Citizenship Rights, States' Rights, and Black Rights: Another Look at Lincoln and Race." In *Our Lincoln: New Perspectives on Lincoln and His World*, edited by Eric Foner, 109–134. New York: Norton, 2008.

Oates, Stephen. *Abraham Lincoln: The Man Behind the Myths*. New York: Harper & Row, 1984.

———. *With Malice Toward None: A Life of Abraham Lincoln*, HarperPerennial ed. New York: HarperPerennial, 1994.

O'Reilly, Bill and Martin Dugard. *Killing Lincoln: The Shocking Assassination that Changed America Forever*. New York: Henry Holt, 2011.

Owen, G. Frederick. *Abraham Lincoln: The Man & His Faith*. Wheaton, IL: Tyndale House Publishers, 1976.

Owens, Mackubin. "Abraham Lincoln as War President: Practical Wisdom at War." In *Lincoln & Liberty: Wisdom for the Ages*, edited by Lucas Morel, 225–275. Lexington, KY: University Press of Kentucky, 2014.

Packard, Jerrold. *The Lincolns in the White House: Four Years that Shattered a Family*. New York: St. Martin's Press, 2005.

Peterson, Merrill. *Lincoln in American Memory*. New York: Oxford University Press, 1994.

Pingel, James. *Confidence and Character: The Religious Life of George Washington*. Eugene, OR: Wipf and Stock, 2014.

Pinsker, Matthew. "Lincoln and the Lessons of Party Leadership." In *Lincoln & Liberty: Wisdom for the Ages*, edited by Lucas Morel, 191–205. Lexington, KY: University Press of Kentucky, 2014.

Remini, Robert. *Henry Clay: Statesman for the Union*. New York: W. W. Norton, 1991.

Sabato, Larry. *The Kennedy Half Century: The Presidency, Assassination, and Lasting Legacy of John F. Kennedy*. New York: Bloomsbury, 2013.

Sandburg, Carl. *Abraham Lincoln: The Prairie Years and The War Years One-Volume Edition*. Norwalk, CT: Easton Press, 1954.

Schaub, Diana. "Learning to Love Lincoln: Frederick Douglass's Journey from Grievance to Gratitude." In *Lincoln & Liberty: Wisdom for the Ages*, edited by Lucas Morel, 79–102. Lexington, KY: University Press of Kentucky, 2014.

Shenk, Joshua. *Lincoln's Melancholy: How Depression Challenged a President and Fueled His Greatness.* First Mariner Books Edition. Boston: Mariner Books, 2006.

Simon, John. "The Jonesboro Debate." In *Abraham Lincoln: Great American Historians on Our Sixteenth President*, edited by Brian Lamb and Susan Swain, 60–62. New York: PublicAffairs, 2008.

Simpson, Matthew. "Funeral Address Delivered at the Burial of President Lincoln, Simpson, Rev. Matthew, May 4, 1865." *The Martyred President Sermons Given on the Occasion of the Assassination of Abraham Lincoln.* Accesses July 22, 2019, http://lincoln.digitalscholarship.emory.edu/simpson.001/.

Sinha, Manisha. "Allies for Emancipation?: Lincoln and Black Abolitionists." In *Our Lincoln: New Perspectives on Lincoln and His World*, edited by Eric Foner, 167–196. New York: Norton, 2008.

Smith, Gary. *Faith and the Presidency: From George Washington to George W. Bush.* New York: Oxford University Press, 2006.

Steers, Edward, Jr. "The Assassination." In *Abraham Lincoln: Great American Historians on Our Sixteenth President*, edited by Brian Lamb and Susan Swain, 171–181. New York: PublicAffairs, 2008.

Striner, Richard. "Lincoln and the Struggle to End Slavery." In *Exploring Lincoln: Great Historians Reappraise Our Greatest President*, edited by Harold Holzer, Craig Symonds, and Frank Williams, 163-175. New York: Fordham University Press, 2015.

Szasz, Ferenc, and Margaret Szasz. *Lincoln and Religion*. Carbondale, IL: Southern Illinois University Press, 2014.

Taranto, James, and Leonard Leo, eds. *Presidential Leadership: Rating the Best and the Worst in the White House.* New York: Free Press, 2004.

Townsend, Timothy. "Almost Home." In *Abraham Lincoln: A Living Legacy*, edited by Diana L. Bailey, 79–151. Virginia Beach, VA: Donning Company, 2010.

Trueblood, Elton. *Abraham Lincoln: Lessons in Spiritual Leadership*. New York: HarperCollins, 1973.

———. "Theologian of American Anguish." In *Character Counts: Leadership Qualities in Washington, Wilberforce, Lincoln, and Solzhenitsyn*, edited by Os Guinness, 105–132. Grand Rapids, MI: Baker Books, 1999.

Turner, Justin, and Linda Levitt Turner. *Mary Todd Lincoln: Her Life and Letters*. New York: Alfred A. Knopf, 1972.

Waugh, John. "Lincoln and McClellan: A Reappraisal." In *Exploring Lincoln: Great Historians Reappraise Our Greatest President*, edited by Harold Holzer, Craig Symonds, and Frank Williams, 214–227. New York: Fordham University Press, 2015.

———. *Lincoln and McClellan: The Troubled Partnership Between a President and His General*. New York: Palgrave MacMillan, 2010.

Wheeler, Joe. *Abraham Lincoln, a Man of Faith and Courage: Stories of Our Most Admired President*. New York: Howard Books, 2008.

Wheeler, Tom. "Lincoln and the Telegraph." In *Abraham Lincoln: Great American Historians on Our Sixteenth President*, edited by Brian Lamb and Susan Swain, 112–120. New York: PublicAffairs, 2008.

White, Ronald, Jr. *A. Lincoln: A Biography*. New York: Random House, 2009.

Wilentz, Sean. "Abraham Lincoln and Jacksonian Democracy." In *Our Lincoln: New Perspectives on Lincoln and His World*, edited by Eric Foner, 62–79. New York: Norton, 2008.

Williams, Frank. "Abraham Lincoln—Our Ever-Present Contemporary," In *"We Cannot Escape History": Lincoln and the Last Best Hope of Earth*, edited by James McPherson, 139–157. Urbana, IL: University of Illinois Press, 1995.

Wilson, Douglas. "Herndon's Lincoln." In *Abraham Lincoln: Great American Historians on Our Sixteenth President*, edited by Brian Lamb and Susan Swain, 20–29. New York: PublicAffairs, 2008.

———. *Lincoln's Sword: The Presidency and the Power of Words.* New York: Alfred A. Knopf, 2006.

Wilson, Douglas, and Rodney Davis, eds. *Herndon's Informants: Letters, Interviews, and Statements about Abraham Lincoln.* Urbana, IL: University of Illinois Press, 1998.

Winik, Jay. "Abraham Lincoln." In *Presidential Leadership: Rating the Best and the Worst in the White House*, edited by James Taranto and Leonard Leo, 80–87. New York: Free Press, 2004.

Winkle, Kenneth. *The Young Eagle: The Rise of Abraham Lincoln.* Dallas, TX: Taylor Trade Publishing, 2001.

Wood, Gordon. "Tragic Sensibility." In *Abraham Lincoln: Great American Historians on Our Sixteenth President*, edited by Brian Lamb and Susan Swain, 233–235. New York: PublicAffairs, 2008.

About the Author

Dr. Jim Pingel currently serves as the School of Education Dean for Concordia University (Mequon and Ann Arbor). As an active member of ALSS (Association of Lutheran Secondary Schools), he advises and does consulting work for many Christian schools across the country.

Recent publications include *Prep Talks: Tales of Challenges and Opportunities in Christian Education* (2019); *Conversations on the Future of Christian Education* (2018); *One Team One Spirit: Inspiration for the Christian Coach* (2017); "Christian School Leaders and the MIT (Most Important Thing)" and "Tip of the Spear: Turning the Mission On for Off-Campus Employees" in *The Pedagogy of Faith: Essays on Lutheran Education* (2016); and *Confidence and Character: The Religious Life of George Washington* (2014).

Pingel previously served as executive director at Sheboygan Area Lutheran High School (Sheboygan, WI, 2004–2013) and as teacher, coach, dean of students, and executive director at Mayer Lutheran High School (Mayer, MN, 1994–2004).

He and his wife, Michelle, are blessed with two children, Joshua and Josie. In his leisure time, Pingel enjoys reading, traveling, and cheering on the Green Bay Packers.

CPSIA information can be obtained
at www.ICGtesting.com
Printed in the USA
LVHW020726090721
692197LV00001B/1

9 781489 730046